HANDBOOKS

# BUENOS AIRES

WAYNE BERNHARDSON

# Contents

► **Discover Buenos Aires** ...... **4**
Planning Your Trip ............. 6
Explore Buenos Aires ........... 10
 • The Best of Buenos Aires ...... 10
 • The Argentine Epic .......... 11
 • A Taste of Tango ............ 13
 • The Post-Business Weekend ... 14
 • Art and Architecture Tour ..... 15

► **Sights** ....................... **17**
Monserrat .................... 19
Microcentro .................. 26
Puerto Madero ................ 31
San Telmo ................... 33
La Boca ..................... 37
Balvanera ................... 39
Retiro ....................... 42
Recoleta and Barrio Norte ...... 45
Palermo ..................... 49
Outer Barrios ................ 58

► **Restaurants** ................ **65**
Monserrat .................... 67
Microcentro .................. 69
Puerto Madero ................ 72
San Telmo ................... 72
La Boca ..................... 75
Balvanera ................... 76
Retiro ....................... 78

Recoleta and Barrio Norte ...... 80
Palermo ...................... 81
Outer Barrios ................. 92

► **Nightlife** ................... **93**
Cafés ....................... 95
Bars and Clubs ............... 96
Live Music ................... 101
Jazz ........................ 103
Tango and *Tanguerías* ......... 104
*Milongas* .................... 107
Flamenco ................... 110
Gay and Lesbian ............. 111

► **Arts and Leisure** .......... **113**
The Arts .................... 115
Holidays, Festivals, and Events ... 130
Sports and Recreation ........ 135

► **Shops** ...................... **142**
Shopping Centers ............. 143
Street Fairs .................. 145
Antiques .................... 146
Books ...................... 148
Clothing and Accessories ...... 150
Crafts and Souvenirs ......... 154
Household Goods and Furniture . 156
Music and Video ............. 157
Wine ....................... 158

# Discover Buenos Aires

Cosmopolitan Buenos Aires has long enjoyed a reputation as the "Paris of the South," but Argentina's capital, the first Latin American metropolis to exceed a million inhabitants, is really a New World immigrant city that's nearer to being the "New York of the South."

Despite their cosmopolitanism, many *porteños* ("residents of the port") identify most strongly with their own barrios in what was, before massive 19th-century immigration, the Gran Aldea (Great Village). Like New Yorkers, they can be brash, and their characteristic accent sets them apart from the provinces. Like New York, Buenos Aires never sleeps – its cinemas, theaters, bars, and discos stay open until daybreak.

Every barrio has its own personality. The densely built Microcentro boasts the major shopping, theater, and financial districts. Immediately south, Monserrat's Plaza de Mayo has been the site of spectacle and debacle in Argentina's tumultuous history. Monserrat gives way to San Telmo's cobbled colonial streets, with its tango bars and famous Plaza Dorrego market. Farther south, La Boca is a working-class barrio also known for its artists and the Caminito, its colorful curving pedestrian mall.

Northern neighborhoods like Retiro and Recoleta are elegant and even opulent – the most affluent Argentines elect eternity at the exclusive Cementerio de la Recoleta. Beyond Recoleta, Palermo's parks were the dominion of 19th-century despot Juan Manuel de Rosas, but the bar-

► **Accommodations**............ **160**
  Monserrat.....................164
  Microcentro ...................167
  Puerto Madero.................171
  San Telmo.....................172
  Balvanera.....................175
  Retiro........................176
  Recoleta and Barrio Norte ......180
  Palermo.......................184

► **Excursions from**
  **Buenos Aires**................ **188**
  Tigre.........................191
  Vicinity of Tigre...............194
  Luján ........................198
  San Antonio de Areco..........202
  Lobos and Vicinity .............210
  La Plata......................213
  Montevideo, Uruguay...........221
  The Montevideo Wine Country...239
  Colonia del Sacramento.........244
  Carmelo......................255
  Punta del Este and Maldonado...258
  Vicinity of Punta del Este
    and Maldonado ..............266

► **Background**................. **269**
  The Land.....................269
  Flora and Fauna...............270
  Agriculture and
    Settlement Landscapes.......272

Environmental Issues...........273
History........................275
Government and Politics........280
Economy......................284
People and Culture.............287
The Arts ......................290
Religion.......................302

► **Essentials** ................... **303**
  Getting There..................303
  Getting Around ...............312
  Visas and Officialdom ..........318
  Food..........................322
  Conduct and Customs ..........327
  Tips for Travelers .............328
  Health and Safety .............331
  Money .......................337
  Tourist Information............341
  Communications and Media .....342
  Weights and Measures.........346

► **Resources** ................... **347**
  Glossary .....................347
  Spanish Phrasebook...........350
  Suggested Reading............354
  Internet Resources............357

► **Index**....................... **361**

► **Maps**....................... **385**

rio has become a middle- to upper-middle-class area with the finest dining and wildest nightlife. North of Palermo, woodsy Belgrano was briefly Argentina's capital.

Beyond the city limits, the Paraná river delta is a maze of meandering channels through wildlife-rich gallery forest; to the west, the gaucho homeland of the flat green pampas stretches beyond the horizon. Just across the river, Uruguay boasts the World Heritage Site of Colonia, the distinctive capital city of Montevideo, and the flashy beach resort of Punta del Este.

For much of the 20th century, Buenos Aires suffered a steady decline, punctuated by spectacular growth spurts and even more spectacular economic and political calamities. Yet somehow, like its melancholy music and dance – the tango – it's managed to retain a certain stability by way of an identity mystique that sets it apart from both Europe and North America.

# Planning Your Trip

## ▶ WHERE TO GO

### Monserrat

The nerve center of Buenos Aires's oldest barrio is the Plaza de Mayo, site of the Casa Rosada presidential palace and the Catedral Metropolitana (the barrio is also known as Catedral al Sur, South of the Cathedral). Except for vestiges of the Cabildo, colonial buildings are long gone from the plaza, but others survive nearby. The original grid extends in all directions except where modern thoroughfares, such as the east–west Avenida de Mayo and the broad north–south Avenida 9 de Julio, have obliterated narrow colonial streets.

### Microcentro

The Microcentro (also known as Catedral al Norte) is part of a larger barrio known formally as San Nicolás, which encompasses the traditional financial, commercial, and entertainment districts. One highlight is the pedestrian Calle Florida, whose historic Galerías Pacífico has become a stylish shopping mall. The cultural bellwether is the landmark Teatro Colón, while Avenida Corrientes is the axis of a rejuvenating theater district.

### Puerto Madero

Redeveloped Puerto Madero is a barrio of chic recycled warehouses and high-rise luxury flats with an air of exclusivity. Yet it's also the city's largest open space, drawing locals and visitors to its scenic yacht basin, riverside esplanades, and ecological reserve—a onetime landfill that went wild with volunteer flora and fauna. Yet there's a palpable sense of history in the former granaries and

the Obelisco, where Avenida 9 de Julio and Avenida Corrientes cross

rectangular basins, and especially in its ambitious immigration museum.

### San Telmo

With its narrow colonial streets, antiques shops, and street fairs, San Telmo is a favorite among Argentines and foreigners alike. It's also a pedestrian-friendly area—especially on Sunday, when Plaza Dorrego's Feria de San Pedro Telmo closes most of Calle Defensa to motor vehicles. San Telmo was once a prestigious address; today, it's a bohemian blend of the colonial barrio, peopled with artists and musicians, plus a scattering of old-money families and many *conventillos* (tenements) abandoned by old money. It's also a key entertainment district.

## La Boca

The working-class barrio of La Boca has never been prosperous, but it has a colorful immigrant history and an extravagantly colorful vernacular architecture along its Caminito pedestrian mall. It also has a palpable sense of community, symbolized by solidarity with the local soccer team and the presence of institutions like the Catalinas Sur theater company. Thanks largely to the late painter Benito Quinquela Martín, it's also an artists' colony with museums and galleries.

## Balvanera

Balvanera subsumes several smaller neighborhoods with scattered points of interest: The vaguely defined area commonly known as Congreso (home to Argentina's imposing legislature) overlaps the barrios of Monserrat and San Nicolás, while Once (the conspicuously Jewish garment district) and the Abasto (which gave the city tango legend Carlos Gardel) have their own distinct identities. The recycled Mercado del Abasto, a onetime wholesale produce market that's now a shopping mall, has helped revive the neighborhood.

## Retiro

Marking a transition to the northern and northwestern upper-middle-class residential barrios, the elegant area surrounding Plaza San Martín was once home to extravagant mansions that now hold federal government offices, foreign embassies, and luxury hotels. There are also key art museums and galleries here. Parts of Retiro, beyond the train and bus stations to the northeast, are desperate slums.

## Recoleta and Barrio Norte

Recoleta is one barrio that retains an almost undiminished air of elegance, especially in and around its legendary necropolis, the Cementerio de la Recoleta. In one of the city's most visited barrios, the line between vigorous excess and serene but opulent eternity is a thin one. In everyday usage, Recoleta means the area in and around the cemetery. Formally, it's a sprawling barrio that also encompasses parts of residential Barrio Norte, an informal designation that's widely accepted by both its residents and those of other neighborhoods.

the neoclassical Palacio del Congreso Nacional in Balvanera

## Palermo

Diverse, rapidly changing Palermo is the city's largest barrio; its wooded parks draw picnickers and recreationists, but the barrio is also ground zero for an explosion of gourmet restaurants, bars, and design and fashion shops. Palermo subdivides into several smaller units: the embassy row of Palermo Chico along Avenida del Libertador; the vibrant residential and nightlife zone of Palermo Viejo across Avenida Santa Fe, which further subdivides into Palermo SoHo and Palermo Hollywood; and Las Cañitas, on the Belgrano border.

## Outer Barrios

Outlying barrios offer museums, parks, *ferias* (street fairs), and other attractions. Among them are the southerly working-class barrios of Barracas, Parque Patricios, and Nueva Pompeya; middle-class Caballito, in what was once the city's periphery but is now its precise geographical center; and the far western Mataderos, where the countryside still has its urban outpost. Northerly Belgrano's leafy streets shelter an assortment of museums, while nearby Núñez and Saavedra have scattered points of interest.

# ▶ WHEN TO GO

Buenos Aires's urban appeal is largely independent of the seasons, but some visitors—and many Argentines for that matter—prefer to avoid the hot, sticky summer; business travelers should avoid January and February if possible, since many potential contacts will be on vacation. Activities like the theater and special events, most notably the increasingly popular Festival del Tango, resume in March as *porteños* return from summer holidays. The spring months of September, October, and November may be the most comfortable, but the relatively mild winter sees some stretches of warm, brilliant weather.

For most of this book's suggested excursions, weather will not be a factor either. The summer months of January and February, though, can be uncomfortably crowded at Uruguayan beach resorts like Punta del Este.

# ▶ BEFORE YOU GO

Unlike some Latin mega-cities, Buenos Aires has a broad-based, modern travel and transportation infrastructure, with contemporary accommodations, restaurants, and other services eager for overseas visitors. The devaluation-fueled demand of the last few years, though, has put pressure on the best accommodations and, unless you're flexible with respect to hotel needs, reservations are advisable and perhaps essential.

Likewise, for visitors traveling elsewhere in Argentina, peak-season demand has tested airline capacity in particular, and even long-distance bus tickets may be hard to come by at peak times, such as Christmas and Easter. If time is limited, advance planning may be crucial. Another factor to consider, for those interested in museums and galleries, is that many close in the summer months of January and February.

## Passports and Visas

U.S. and Canadian citizens, as well as most Europeans traveling to Argentina, need passports but not advance visas. Passports are also necessary for checking into hotels, cashing travelers checks, and even for credit card transactions. Argentina routinely grants foreign visitors 90-day entry permits in the form of a tourist card.

The Los Incas station is the terminus of the Subte's Línea B.

## Vaccinations and Health Insurance

Theoretically, Argentina demands no proof of vaccinations. However, a recent yellow fever outbreak in the area where the Brazil, Paraguayan, and Argentine borders converge makes vaccination desirable for anyone visiting Iguazú Falls or other humid subtropical areas.

Traveling to Argentina or elsewhere without adequate medical insurance is risky. Before leaving home, purchase a policy that includes evacuation in case of serious emergency.

## Getting There

Most visitors arrive in Argentina by air, via the international airport of Buenos Aires, Aeropuerto Internacional Ministro Pistarini (EZE), commonly called Ezeiza. Some will arrive overland from neighboring countries and others by ship.

Long-distance bus services from Bolivia, Brazil, Chile, Paraguay, and Uruguay are generally comfortable. Ferry services from Uruguay are even more comfortable. There are no international rail services, and long-distance trains within Argentina are generally poor.

Argentina has an extensive network of domestic airports and a handful of airlines centered on Buenos Aires, but while it's possible to fly to neighboring Uruguay for the excursions covered in this book, ferries are usually more convenient.

For excursions in the surrounding Buenos Aires province, buses along the principal highways are frequent, spacious, and comfortable—sometimes even luxurious. Fares are reasonable by international standards.

Renting a car is possible, but not advisable in Buenos Aires because public transportation (including buses, commuter trains, and taxis) is cheap, frequent, and efficient.

## What to Take

A good rule of thumb is to bring appropriately seasonal clothing for comparable Northern Hemisphere latitudes. The climate is mild in spring and autumn, hot and humid in summer, and cool but not cold in winter—though humidity and winter winds can make it feel colder than absolute temperatures might suggest (2007 saw the first snow in nearly a century). For summer, light cottons are the rule, while a sweater and perhaps a light jacket suffice for the shoulder seasons. For winter, a warm but not polar-strength jacket are advisable. It can rain heavily any time of year, making a compact umbrella a good idea.

Much depends, of course, on what sort of activities you prefer—for opera-goers formal clothing is obligatory. Likewise, business travelers will dress as they would in New York or London, with suits and ties for men and similarly appropriate clothing for women. Younger porteños out on the town dress as they would in any large city, taking a casual yet stylish approach.

# Explore Buenos Aires

## ▶ THE BEST OF BUENOS AIRES

In a city with so many highlights, it's truly hard to choose the best, but most visitors should agree with at least some of the following. These suggestions assume a Saturday-morning arrival in Buenos Aires, but they can be mixed and matched at your convenience.

### Day 1

After settling into your hotel, visit ground zero: the Plaza de Mayo, with its historic sites, including the Casa Rosada presidential palace, the colonial Museo del Cabildo, and the Catedral Metropolitana. Take a breather for coffee or a light lunch at Café Tortoni before visiting the underrated Museo de la Ciudad and the Manzana de las Luces.

Since it was a long flight, you may enjoy a nap before considering the theater (for an eye-opening perspective on Argentine history, consider Teatro Catalinas Sur, in the working-class barrio of La Boca), and go slumming for steaks at nearby El Obrero afterwards.

### Day 2

Enjoy a leisurely Sunday brunch at Recoleta's La Biela, also a nightlife hotspot, then make the short walk to the Cementerio de la Recoleta, where former La Biela clients are spending eternity. After a stroll among its historic crypts, grab a cross-town taxi to Plaza Dorrego's Feria de San Pedro Telmo, the capital's one can't-miss market, for antiques and street performers, including mimes and highly skilled *tangueros*.

After lunch overlooking Plaza Dorrego, or a few blocks away at the ageless Bar El Federal, take a bus or cab to the brightly painted houses along La Boca's Caminito pedestrian mall, a tourist trap that retains elements of integrity in a working-class barrio.

Any time after about 9 P.M., you can enjoy Buenos Aires's best beef at Cabaña Las Lilas, on the Puerto Madero waterfront. While this may be early for *porteños,* Puerto Madero restaurants are more accustomed to serving as early as 7 P.M., and you may be able to catch a floor show at one of the flashier *tanguerías,* which also serve dinner, but the food can't match Las Lilas.

### Day 3

Many museums and other attractions close on Mondays, so this makes a good day for excursions to the "gaucho capital" of San Antonio de Areco (also suitable for an overnight) or the riverside suburb of Tigre, which has the new, handsome Museo de Arte. Alternatively, via Tigre, it's possible to visit the Paraná delta destination of Isla Martín García, for both its history and the lush natural environment.

On your return, enjoy a drink at a fashionable Barrio Norte bar like Milión or Gran

The Catedral Metropolitana is Buenos Aires's main ecclesiastical landmark.

# THE ARGENTINE EPIC

Ever since Pedro de Mendoza stepped onto the Río de la Plata's *barrancas* in the 16th century, Buenos Aires was destined to be a larger-than-life place, even as it languished during colonial times. Some of the uprisings that led to the Latin American independence movement started here, on the periphery, and their imprint is still palpable. The tumultuous 19th century, dominated by caudillos like Juan Manuel de Rosas, and the chaotic 20th-century legacy of Juan and Evita Perón and their successors, are no less apparent.

At the central **Plaza de Mayo,** Perón and Evita played to their partisans from the balcony of the **Casa Rosada.** Naval planes strafed the nearby Economy Ministry in a 1955 coup that drove Perón from power, and the Madres de la Plaza de Mayo began their eloquently silent marches against the Dirty War dictatorship of 1976-1983.

Not so far away, across Paseo Colón, the university **Facultad de Ingeniería** (once the Fundación Eva Perón) and the **CGT labor union headquarters** were loci of Peronist power. In 1952, weeping working-class Argentines lined Avenida de Mayo from the Casa Rosada as Evita's casket proceeded to the **Congreso Nacional.**

Buenos Aires has an earlier history in the remains of the nearby colonial **Cabildo** (town council) and the narrow streets of Monserrat and San Telmo. Here, south of the Plaza de Mayo, the **Manzana de las Luces** was the colonial city's "block of enlightenment." The **Museo de la Ciudad** and the restored drainage tunnels at **El Zanjón** reveal everyday aspects of *porteño* life.

Also part of Argentine history are the individual stories of the millions of European immigrants who arrived at Puerto Madero's **Hotel de Inmigrantes** from the late 19th century. The port's fashionably recycled *diques* (boat basins), storehouses, and granaries, with their inert cranes still standing, recall the era when Argentina boomed with wheat, wool, and beef exports.

To see where many of those immigrants ended up and how they still live, travel to

Freshly painted, the Casa Rosada presidential palace has been the scene of spectacle and debacle in Argentine politics.

the brightly painted houses along La Boca's **Caminito.** The people here idolized the Peróns and filled the La Bombonera soccer stadium for working-class hero Diego Maradona.

In Francophile Recoleta, visitors can see how the affluent and influential sector of *porteño* society lives and dies – at the **Cementerio de la Recoleta,** many tombs are worth more than most city apartments. Though not an elite figure, Evita Perón is buried here, and her grave is a constant pilgrimage site. Get an even better grasp of Evita worship at nearby Palermo's **Museo Eva Perón.**

Across Avenida del Libertador in **Parque Tres de Febrero,** the **Jardín Japonés** and **Rosedal** are islands of calm, but it all belonged to 19th-century dictator Juan Manuel de Rosas, who claimed the gauchos as his allies but exploited them ruthlessly. Later landowners co-opted the gaucho instead, as is evident in the nearby **Museo de Motivos Argentinos José Hernández.**

To understand Buenos Aires and its hinterland, venture beyond the city limits. The gaucho tradition lives on in the pampas town of **San Antonio de Areco,** a potential UNESCO World Heritage Site that's home to a high density of gifted silversmiths. It's a doable day trip but better as an overnight, preferably at one of the area's historic *estancias* (ranches).

Tigre's Museo de Arte recalls the city's early 20th-century glory days.

Bar Danzón, which also have fine restaurant menus. Many other restaurants are closed Mondays, so consider a traditional *fugazza* (pizza with mozzarella, ham, and sweet onions) at Pizzería Güerrín, on Avenida Corrientes. For dessert, walk a few blocks west to Cadore, one of Buenos Aires's best ice creameries.

## Day 4

This high-culture day includes visits to the legendary Teatro Colón, the Southern Hemisphere's first great opera house, and the modern Latin American art collection at Palermo's state-of-the-art Museo de Arte Latinomericano de Buenos Aires (MALBA). For a view of recent Argentine history through partisan eyes, visit the not-so-distant Museo Eva Perón before taking a breather at Parque Tres de Febrero, the city's largest open space. Its Jardín Japonés (Japanese Garden) and Rosedal (Rose Garden) are islands of calm in a city of noise.

After sunset, take a leisurely walk from Plazoleta Cortázar (also known as Plaza Serrano) through the "gourmet ghetto" of Palermo Viejo before deciding on any of dozens of creative restaurants for dinner—one of the best is Palermo Hollywood's Olsen, across Avenida Juan B. Justo, with its improbable Scandinavian/Patagonian menu, creative vodka-based drinks, and Nordic garden.

## Day 5

More than just an opportunity for another stamp in your passport, Uruguay's UNESCO World Heritage Site of Colonia del Sacramento is only an hour from Buenos Aires by high-speed catamaran. There are plenty of good sightseeing, dining, and shopping options here, and it's worth considering an overnight. If so, consider returning to Argentina via Montevideo, touring its colonial core and visiting the nearby Bodega Bouza winery for lunch before catching the catamaran back from the Uruguayan capital.

## Day 6

If you're not on the way back from Uruguay, escape the tourist ghettos to visit outer barrios such as Belgrano or Caballito, both readily accessible by Subte, or the scattered sights of Barracas and Parque Patricios, better visited on a guided excursion because of more complicated logistics. In Belgrano, visit the Museo de Arte Español Enrique

# A TASTE OF TANGO

There's a tango tsunami, and its epicenter is still Buenos Aires. *Porteño* professionals and tango teachers may be going far afield to Europe, North America, and Japan, but thousands of foreigners are coming to Buenos Aires to watch the dancers, listen to the music, study with the finest instructors, and do their best to emulate them. There's a tension between the *milonga*'s "authenticity" and the flashiness of "for export" floor shows, but both offer something to discriminating visitors.

On Avenida de Mayo, **Café Tortoni** recalls the early 20th-century era when tango became a global phenomenon. In the same building, the **Academia Nacional del Tango** has an upstairs museum, but for a living museum, visit the **Confitería Ideal** – the site of afternoon *milongas* and tango lessons – whose aging facilities evoke tango's underlying nostalgia.

South of the Plaza de Mayo, the narrow colonial streets of San Telmo were part of the *arrabales* (outskirts) where the tango supposedly arose out of Afro-Argentine dance and music, transformed by the input of later European immigrants. Sunday dancers pass the hat on **Plaza Dorrego,** while others stride through La Boca's sidewalk cafés daily. Shows and concerts at the Tortoni's **Sala Alfonsina Storni** or San Telmo's **Torquato Tasso** showcase professional performers.

Argentina's elite repose at Recoleta, but tangophiles take the Subte to Estación Federico Lacroze and the **Cementerio de la Chacarita** to visit the grave of Carlos Gardel and other tango legends, including musicians Aníbal Troilo and Osvaldo Pugliese. Gardel, though, grew up in what is now the **Museo Casa Carlos Gardel** near the recycled **Mercado de Abasto,** reached

Juan Carlos Copes, one of the master tango dancers at Esquina Carlos Gardel

via the Subte's Estación Carlos Gardel. Venues like the **Esquina Carlos Gardel** draw disparagement from purists, but their musicians, singers, and dancers still manage to communicate history and emotion.

Tango lovers should shop for CDs at **Zivals** or other music stores, and browse through men's and women's fashions at **Tango Moda** in the landmark **Palacio Barolo.** Built as a metaphor for Dante's *Divine Comedy*, the building's upper floors must be close to heaven for aspiring *milongueros*.

Larreta and try Central Andean cuisine at Contigo Perú, and in Caballito don't miss the Museo Argentino de Ciencias Naturales Bernardino Rivadavia. Take a nap in order to enjoy a late-night *milonga* (the participatory alternative to the "for export" tango floor show) at Salón Canning in Parakultural.

## Day 7

Spend your last day shopping at Galerías Pacífico, Patio Bullrich, or the countless designer shops of Palermo Viejo, which offers a wealth of lunchtime options, such as Zadvarie Doc, before an evening flight from Ezeiza.

# ► THE POST-BUSINESS WEEKEND

At the end of the business week, there may be time to relax and enjoy the capital's cultural and entertainment offerings before resuming work or continuing the trip on Monday. Some of these are typical tourist activities, while others are less routine, but all of them are worthwhile.

## Day 1

As Friday's labors end, unwind with coffee or a cocktail at the landmark Café Tortoni, where tourists and locals alike crowd its marble tables; consider a tango music or dance show, or other live entertainment, at the Tortoni's Sala Alfonsina Storni. Any time after about 9 P.M., you can enjoy Buenos Aires's most succulent steaks at Puerto Madero's Cabaña Las Lilas, whose beef comes from its own Luján *estancia*.

## Day 2

For a change of pace, consider any of several possible excursions: the "gaucho capital" of San Antonio de Areco or a *día de campo* (day in the country) at a nearby *estancia*, the fascinating historic and natural environment of the Paraná Delta's Isla Martín García, or Uruguay's UNESCO World Heritage Site of Colonia del Sacramento. On returning to the city, have a drink on the terrace at Barrio Norte's hip Milión or martinis at the "neo-Andean" Mosoq; if not dining here, follow the drinks with spicy sushi at the Japanese-Peruvian Libélula, near the botanical gardens.

For a further antidote to the conventional business world, spend the night partying at Palermo's Niceto Club.

## Day 3

For a leisurely Sunday brunch, try the restaurant at Palermo Hollywood's Hotel Home Buenos Aires. Then do the tourist sights: Plaza Dorrego's Feria de San Pedro Telmo, the capital's one can't-miss market, for its antiques, mimes, and *tangueros,* and the brightly painted houses along La Boca's Caminito, a pedestrian mall with an iconic charm that transcends the presence of the hordes of tourists that overrun the street on weekends. Have lunch overlooking Plaza Dorrego, a few blocks away at the ageless

Puente Viejo, San Antonio de Areco

Bar El Federal, San Telmo

Bar El Federal, where there's refreshing hard cider on tap.

Following lunch, stroll through the world-famous Cementerio de la Recoleta, where the rich and famous flaunt their status in death as in life; many were clients of the nearby La Biela, an ideal stop for coffee and dessert. Alternatively, visit the more egalitarian Cementerio de la Chacarita, the final resting place for many arts and entertainment figures, including tango legend Carlos Gardel.

After sunset, take a leisurely walk through Palermo Viejo's "gourmet ghetto." Try the neo-Peruvian Zadvarie Doc or the Sardinian Sa Giara for dinner.

# ▶ ART AND ARCHITECTURE TOUR

Buenos Aires has a vital art scene, and the galleries, museums, and public art to prove it. It may have been late to establish its identity—one critic argues the colonial period lasted into the 20th century—but Argentine painters and sculptors have made an impact on the global art market.

Its Francophile mansions, with their conspicuous mansards, have given Buenos Aires its misleading "Paris of the South" nickname; in reality the city is far more diverse. Many Spanish colonial or colonial-style buildings still survive, and vernacular styles range from "sausage houses" with narrow frontages on deep lots to the gaudily painted metal-clad structures of La Boca. Many contemporary buildings are less distinguished, but a handful truly stand out.

## Day 1

After settling into your accommodations, orient yourself by visiting the Plaza de Mayo, with its historic sites, including the Casa Rosada presidential palace, the colonial Museo del Cabildo, and the neoclassical Catedral Metropolitana. Take a breather for coffee or a light lunch at the landmark Café Tortoni before visiting the underrated Museo de la Ciudad and the Manzana de las Luces. For an underground perspective on the colonial city, take a guided tour of the restored tunnels at San Telmo's El Zanjón; alternatively, visit the nearby Museo de Arte Moderno.

Late afternoon is a good time to stroll the Puerto Madero waterfront and appreciate how builders have recycled former granaries and mills into upmarket lofts, restaurants, and accommodations such as Faena Hotel & Universe; the Hilton Buenos Aires and architect Santiago Calatrava's Puente de la Mujer, a pedestrian bridge that swings open to allow yachts to pass, are modern design infusions.

While exploring Puerto Madero, consider testing Buenos Aires's best beef at Cabaña Las Lilas—the only truly worthwhile restaurant in the neighborhood—which has outdoor seating looking onto the yacht basin. Dining early would leave time for a flashy tango floor show or a more authentic alternative, such as live music or song at San Telmo's Torquato Tasso.

## Day 2

Take a leisurely breakfast or brunch in the shade of the *gomero* at Recoleta's La Biela, then cross the plaza to the Cementerio de la Recoleta, where Argentina's elite have built crypts to match their mansions. After strolling among its extravagant tombs, cross Avenida del Libertador to the Museo Nacional de Bellas Artes, the traditional repository of Argentina's best art. Recrossing the avenue, walk the surrounding Recoleta streets, where the "Paris of the South" comes closest to reality. Head toward Retiro, where galleries like Ruth Benzacar display the latest in Argentine art; en route, lift your eyes to the Edificio Kavanagh, the deco landmark apartment building that was Buenos Aires's first skyscraper.

After lunch, depending on the day, backtrack to Palermo's Museo de Arte Latinoamericano de Buenos Aires (MALBA), as distinguished for its contemporary design as for its regional art collections. If it's Tuesday, when the museum is closed, try the other extreme and take a bus or cab to the exuberantly colorful tenements along La Boca's Caminito pedestrian mall. The contemporary Fundación Proa and the Museo de Bellas Artes de La Boca Benito Quinquela

Martín, housing the works of a late barrio painter, both lend La Boca an artistic edge.

## Day 3

For an unconventional excursion, ride the Subte to Belgrano, stopping en route at stations like Facultad de Medicina and Plaza Italia to view their elaborate wall and floor murals. Detraining at Juramento station, walk past landmarks like the museum/house of Hispanophile novelist Enrique Larreta, the Museo De Arte Español Enrique Larreta with its elaborate gardens, and the dome of the Iglesia Nuestra Señora de la Inmaculada Concepción. The real gem, though, is the Museo Casa de Yrurtia, boasting the works of a sculptor whose monumental works challenged the equestrian-statue paradigm of *porteño* public art.

On the way back, detrain at Plaza Italia for a stroll through landscape architect Carlos Thays's Jardín Botánico, whose layout set a standard for public parks not just in Buenos Aires but throughout the country. Nearby Palermo SoHo boasts dozens of stylishly recycled "sausage houses" that have become restaurants, bars, and shops (many focusing on art, design, and fashion).

Jardín Botánico, designed by landscape architect Carlos Thays

# SIGHTS

For sightseers, Buenos Aires is a paradise of diversity. Like New York City, it's a city of barrios—48 of them, officially—but even that designation can be misleading. Many barrios split into even smaller neighborhoods with distinct identities and others, such as Barrio Norte (more a real estate term or a state of mind for its mostly upper-class residents), overlap official boundaries.

Gran Buenos Aires (Greater Buenos Aires) is a sprawling megalopolis that takes in large parts of surrounding Buenos Aires province. Even without those suburbs, it's a large, densely populated city, but its barrios give it a cozier feel, even in the downtown financial district.

Formally known as the Ciudad Autónoma de Buenos Aires (Autonomous City of Buenos Aires), the Capital Federal (Federal Capital) of Buenos Aires lies within the boundaries formed by the Río de la Plata, its tributary the Riachuelo, and the ring roads of Avenida General Paz and Avenida 27 de Febrero.

For much of the 20th century, the Plaza de Mayo and surrounding Monserrat were the nerve center of Argentine politics, the site of spectacle for the Peróns and their successors. The colonial quarter of San Telmo is the home of the tango, while the working-class La Boca neighborhood fuses its passion for soccer with a conspicuous commitment to the arts.

Downtown Buenos Aires, the Microcentro, is the traditional business, shopping, and theater district, with many museums and landmark buildings. To the north, the mansions of Retiro and chic Recoleta are home to the *porteño* elite and some of the best and newest

# HIGHLIGHTS

LOOK FOR **(C** TO FIND RECOMMENDED SIGHTS.

**(C Best Chance to See History in the Making:** Buenos Aires's **Plaza de Mayo** is ground zero for Argentine public life (page 25).

**(C Best Cultural Bulwark:** Through a century of political turmoil, the **Teatro Colón,** South America's most important performing-arts venue, has retained its style and dignity. It's currently closed for restoration work, but still worth seeing (page 30).

**(C Best Nature-Oriented Activity:** The lush woodlands and marshy wetlands of Puerto Madero's **Reserva Ecológica Costanera Sur** are ideal for bird-watchers: *Real* pink flamingos, black-necked swans, coots, and countless other species make a walk through this oasis of calm a unique experience in an often cacophonous city (page 32).

**(C Best Street Market:** Sunday is the day that vendors and spirited street performers clog San Telmo's **Plaza Dorrego** and surrounding streets (page 36).

**(C Top Post-Mortem Status Symbol:** The barrio of Recoleta is the capital's prestige address, but for the dead, a tomb at its **Cementerio de la Recoleta** is even more exclusive (page 46).

**(C Best Contribution to the Arts:** For decades, even during dictatorships, Argentina has had a thriving modern art scene, but businessman Eduardo Constantini's **Museo de Arte Latinoamericano de Buenos Aires (MALBA)** has given it a new focal point (page 53).

**(C Most Elusive Museum:** Promoted by

© WAYNE BERNHARDSON

**Cementerio de la Recoleta**

Eva Perón's partisans, the **Museo Eva Perón** is as notable for what it omits as for what it includes (page 54).

**(C Best Landscaping:** Once it was dictator Juan Manuel de Rosas's private estate, but French landscape architect Charles Thays made Palermo's sprawling **Parque Tres de Febrero** a place for the people (page 55).

**(C Most Underrated Museum:** In the decidedly untouristed barrio of Caballito, the improving **Museo Argentino de Ciencias Naturales Bernardino Rivadavia** has never attained the grandeur to which its original plans aspired, but the exhibits within this still handsome building shed light on the impressive Argentine dinosaur discoveries of recent decades (page 62).

**(C Most Famous Gravesites:** Having failed to qualify for Cementerio de la Recoleta, many of Argentina's most illustrious and/or notorious figures repose at the capital's more egalitarian **Cementerio de la Chacarita** (page 63).

museums. For wide-open spaces, *porteños* visit the parks of Palermo, an area with its own share of museums and monuments.

On weekends, the municipal tourist office offers free theme-oriented walking tours of many neighborhoods; some, but not all, have English-speaking guides. For each week's offerings, check the Friday "getOut!" section of the *Buenos Aires Herald* or the entertainment section of *Clarín.* In case of rain, tours are canceled.

# Monserrat

Map 1

Buenos Aires's oldest barrio takes its name from the Catalonian Nuestra Señora de Monserrat, a sacred image hidden in the mountains near Barcelona to guard it from Muslim invaders. Found after a century of weathering, the darkened Madonna resonated with Buenos Aires's black slave population, who feted her every September 8. Monserrat was also known as Barrio del Tambor for the drums Afro-Argentines played during Carnaval.

Monserrat encompasses substantial parts of the Congreso neighborhood, which also overlaps the barrios of San Nicolás and Balvanera. Monserrat's precise southern border with San Telmo is a more subtle transition—some businesses technically within Monserrat's limits vocally proclaim themselves part of tourist-friendly San Telmo.

Most major Argentine institutions surround the Plaza de Mayo, which has undergone significant transformations since its colonial origins to reach its present status as the city's civic heart. Its name derives from the date of the May Revolution of 1810, but its fame comes from the massive and spectacular demonstrations that have taken place here in support and protest of the Peróns, the Falklands/Malvinas War, and other political causes.

While the barrio has many prominent sights, it contains other lesser but still revealing points of interest. At the Plaza de Mayo's northeast corner, designed by renowned architect Alejandro Bustillo, the **Banco de la Nación** (1939) occupies the original site of the Teatro Colón opera house; if the economy were as solid as this state-run bank's neoclassical construction, Argentina would still be a global economic power.

Immediately south of the plaza, the marble facade of the **Ministerio de Economía** (Economy Ministry) still bears marks from the navy planes that strafed it and other public buildings in the 1955 Revolución Libertadora that sent Juan Domingo Perón into exile. Across Avenida Paseo Colón, generations

of military coup-mongers plotted against constitutional governments in the **Edificio Libertador** before belatedly realizing they were no more capable of governing than the civilians they overthrew.

## CASA ROSADA (CASA DE GOBIERNO NACIONAL)

Hipólito Yrigoyen 219, tel. 011/4344-3804, www.museo.gov.ar

**HOURS:** Mon.-Fri. 10 A.M.-6 P.M., Sun. 2-6 P.M.; free guided tours Mon.-Fri. 11 A.M. and 4 P.M., Sun. 4 P.M.

**COST:** Free

For better or worse, the presidential palace, which faces the Plaza de Mayo, has been the site of political spectacle. It's the place where Juan and Evita Perón summoned the cheering masses who later jeered the ruthless military dictatorship after the 1982 Falklands War; as recently as December 2001, it witnessed the shooting of demonstrators by federal police under the De la Rúa administration. Culturally speaking, one of its lowest points must have been pop singer Madonna's balcony appearance in director Alan Parker's film version of the stage musical *Evita* (an event that enraged die-hard Peronists).

The Casa Rosada owes its distinctive pink hue to President Domingo F. Sarmiento, who proposed the blend of Federalist red and Unitarist white to symbolize reconciliation between the two violently opposed factions of 19th-century Argentine politics. It was not originally a single building; in 1884, Italian architect Francesco Tamburini (who later worked on the Teatro Colón) merged the original Casa de Gobierno with the Correo Central (Central Post Office) to create the present slightly asymmetrical structure. On the east side, facing Parque Colón, pedestrians can view the excavated ruins of the colonial **Fuerte Viejo** (old fortress) and early customs headquarters (buried beneath landfill during 1890s port improvements).

In the basement, entered from the south

side on Hipólito Yrigoyen, its museum contains memorabilia from Argentine presidents, a 17,000-volume library, an archive, and newspaper and magazine collections; unfortunately, its charter prohibits inclusion of recent, more controversial items. Visitors can stroll among the colonial catacombs, which are also visible from the pedestrian mall outside.

Guided tours of the Casa Rosada itself normally take place Monday–Friday at noon and 4 P.M., but as of press time they were on hold because of restoration work. For up-to-date information, phone the museum.

## CATEDRAL METROPOLITANA

Av. Rivadavia and San Martín, tel. 011/4331-2845
**HOURS:** Mon.-Fri. 8 A.M.-7 P.M., Sat.-Sun. 9 A.M.-7:30 P.M.

At Plaza de Mayo's northwest corner, the capital's cathedral occupies the site of the original colonial church designated by Juan de Garay in 1580. It opened in 1836 in its present form; on the pediment above its Hellenic columns, Joseph Dubourdieu's symbolic bas-

reliefs (1862) equate the biblical reconciliation of Joseph and his brothers with the results of the battle of Pavón, in which Bartolomé Mitre's Buenos Aires forces defeated Santa Fe province caudillo Justo José Urquiza.

Even more significant for Argentines, a separate chapel contains the **Mausoleo del General José de San Martín,** the burial site of the country's independence hero. Disillusioned with the country's post-independence turmoil, San Martín suffered self-exile in France until his death in 1850; his remains returned to Argentina in 1880, after President Nicolás Avellaneda ordered construction of this elaborate tomb, marked by an eternal flame outside the cathedral's easternmost entrance.

## IGLESIA Y CONVENTO DE SANTO DOMINGO

Av. Belgrano and Defensa, tel. 011/4331-1668
**HOURS:** Mon.-Fri. 9:30 A.M.-1:30 P.M. and 3-7 P.M., Sat. and Sun. masses only

In 1601, shortly after the Dominican order

The tomb of General José de San Martín, repatriated after his death in France, occupies a corner of the Catedral Metropolitana.

The mausoleum of General Manuel Belgrano, designer of the Argentine flag, sits outside the Iglesia y Convento de Santo Domingo.

arrived in Buenos Aires, it acquired a large block of land stretching from present-day Avenida Belgrano and Defensa to the riverfront, which it used for vegetable gardens, livestock corrals, and a primitive chapel and convent. In 1751, the Dominicans finally laid the cornerstone for the present church and convent, but the second of its twin towers went uncompleted until 1858. Its altars and artwork date from the 17th and 19th centuries.

Santo Domingo (also known as the Iglesia de Nuestra Señora del Rosario) witnessed some of Argentine history's most dramatic events. It still contains banners captured by Viceroy Santiago de Liniers from the Highlanders Regiment No. 71 during the initial British invasion (1806), and its facade and left-side tower show combat damage from the following year's British occupation. After the independence wars, General Manuel Belgrano donated flags of the defeated Royalists to the collection.

On the east side, near the church entrance, an eternal flame burns near sculptor Héctor Ximenes's **Mausoleo de Belgrano** (1903), the burial site of Argentina's second-greatest hero, General Manuel Belgrano; by most accounts, Belgrano was an indifferent soldier, but he did design the Argentine flag.

Following independence, President Bernardino Rivadavia secularized the church, turning the main building into a natural history museum and one of its towers into an astronomical observatory. In 1955, during the overthrow of Juan Perón, anti-clerical Peronists set it afire.

## MANZANA DE LAS LUCES

Perú 272, tel. 011/4331-5934, www.manzanadelasluces.gov.ar
**HOURS:** Tours Mon. 1 P.M. and 3 P.M., Tues.-Fri. 3 P.M., Sat.-Sun. 3, 4:30, and 6 P.M.
**COST:** Tours Tues.-Sat. US$1.60, tours free Mon.
Ever since the mid-17th century, when the Jesuit order established itself on the block bounded by the present-day streets of Bolívar, Moreno, Perú, and Alsina, Monserrat has been a hub of the capital's intellectual life. While the Jesuits were perhaps the most intellectual of all monastic

# UNDERGROUND CULTURE

In his short story "Text in a Notebook," Julio Cortázar imagines a society of pallid people who never leave the Subte system – "their existence and their circulation like leukocytes." Filmmaker Gustavo Mosquera went even farther in his 1996 movie Moebius, which depicts a Subte train and its passengers in an endless loop beneath the city.

In reality, there is an underground culture in the city's subways, but nothing quite so enigmatic as Cortázar and Mosquera concocted. Beginning in the 1930s, builders embellished Subte stations with tiled ceramic murals; more recently, the private operator Metrovías has begun to restore some of these faded glories and, at the same, commission new ones and even construct mini-museums with rotating or permanent art and history exhibits at newer stations.

The Subte provides a means to see both classic and contemporary Argentine art on the move. Visitors can use the following details to orient themselves to this artistic legacy.

## LÍNEA A

Buenos Aires's oldest subway line, originally the Compañía de Tranvías Anglo Argentina (Anglo-Argentine Tramway Company) or Línea Anglo (Anglo Line) is its least decorated, though its classic wooden cars are works of art in their own right. Nevertheless, the vidrieras (display cases) at Perú and Congreso stations often hold items of historical interest. The walls of the passageways linking Línea A and Línea C contain Hermenegildo Sábat's three-part Músicos de Buenos Aires (2000) and also cartoonist Horacio Altuna's Gente de Buenos Aires (People of Buenos Aires, 2002).

## LÍNEA B

While it has some of the system's newest and most comfortable cars, Línea B is also short on decoration. The Abasto district's remodeled Carlos Gardel station, though, features a ceramic mural of an orquesta típica (typical orchestra) on its northern platform. More con-

temporary works include Carlos Páez Vilaró's Homenaje a Buenos Aires (Homage to Buenos Aires) and Mi Querida Buenos Aires (My Dear Buenos Aires, after a popular tango) and Andrés Compagnucci's Gardel por Tres (Gardel Times Three) and Abasto, depicting the old but since rehabilitated market building.

In late 2003, Metrovías re-inaugurated Uruguay station with a cinema-themed display that includes film posters and even its own Hollywood-style Walk of Fame, with aging stars (such as Alfredo Alcón and Mirtha Legrand) and newcomers (such as Gastón Pauls and Cecilia Dopazo).

## LÍNEA C

Imported Spanish tiles adorn the so-called Línea de los Españoles (Spanish Line) opened in 1934 with Iberian scenes, but more recent additions provide some balance. The most venerable pieces are a series of ceramic Paisajes de España, depicting landscapes from Lérida, Segovia, Sevilla, and other locales at Avenida de Mayo, Independencia, Lavalle, and Moreno stations. Martín Noël and Manuel Escasany were among the Argentine artists involved in the project.

The line is also notable for its Moorish masonry and elegant friezes, such as the ceramic coats of arms at San Juan station, the decorative dragon at Moreno station, and the Arabic script, also at Moreno, of the aphorism "There is no greater victor than God."

More recent works are more self-consciously nationalistic, such as Rodolfo Medina's La Gesta Sanmartiniana (1969), a series of eight narrative murals in polychrome cement on the achievements of national icon General José de San Martín. Appropriately enough, it covers the walls of the general's namesake station, which also includes a recent mural by Luis Benedit.

Since 1998, reproductions of three of gauchesco caricaturist Florencio Molina Campos's paintings have lined the western platform of Constitución station: El de Laj Once y Sais, depicting gauchos awaiting a train; Pa'

*Nuevos Horizontes,* showing a gaucho family on a horsecart loaded with personal belongings, bound for a new *estancia* (ranch); and *Beyaquiando Juerte,* a gaucho breaking a new mount. Molina Campos titled these pieces in the gaucho dialect.

Renovated Retiro station includes three murals by painter Fernando Allievi, also dating from 1998: *Historia de Sábado* (Saturday Story), a family on a city outing; *Las Primeras Luces* (First Light), a bedraggled shoeshine boy and his dog at daybreak; and the surrealistic *Las Máscaras* (The Masks).

## LÍNEA D

In contrast to Línea C's Iberian-themed murals, most of Línea D's are more strictly nationalist, dealing with Argentine landscapes, legends, traditions, and native customs interpreted by artists like Léonie Matthis de Villar, Rodolfo Franco, and Alfredo Guido. The line opened in 1937, so this change of focus may reflect events of the Spanish Civil War and the military regime then ruling Argentina. The thematic exception is Palermo station, whose ceramic vestibule mural resembles those of Línea C's *Paisajes de España.*

On Catedral station's north platform, *Buenos Aires 1936* reflects the modern city's construction, with its subways and skyscrapers. In the same station, the ceramic *Buenos Aires en 1830* recalls early republican times.

Ceramic murals at Facultad de Medicina station offer insight into provincial cities with *Rosario 1836, Santa Fe 1836,* and *Rosario 1938.* Agüero station's *Camino a Córdoba del Tucumán* suggests the rigors of 19th-century travel between provincial capitals.

Bulnes station's *Las Leyendas del País de la Selva* (Legends of the Forests) has a folkloric focus, while *Arqueología Diaguita* portrays northwestern Argentina's archaeological heritage. Scalabrini Ortiz station's *Evocaciones de Salta* depicts the far northwestern province.

Among this line's best works is Plaza Italia's *La Descarga de los Convoyes,* a series of port scenes based on sketches by Benito Quinquela Martín, which cover the platforms themselves.

The spacious, well-lighted new stations on the Línea D extension – José Hernández, Juramento, and Congreso de Tucumán – all feature custom-made display cases with rotating exhibits of historical and cultural artifacts and artwork, such as sculptures. José Hernández features several 1997 reproductions of Raúl Soldi murals originally created elsewhere in the city: *La Música* (Music), *El Ensayo* (The Rehearsal), *Los Amantes* (The Lovers), and *En el Jardín* (In the Garden). Juramento displays a reproduction of Cándido López's 19th-century *Batalla de Curupaytí.*

## LÍNEA E

Opened in 1944, Línea E reflects even more nationalistic times, coinciding with the rise of Juan and Evita Perón. San José is the only station to celebrate the country's scenic treasures, *Las Cataratas del Iguazú* (Iguazú Falls) and *Los Lagos del Sur* (The Southern Lake District).

Entre Ríos station, though, glorifies *La Conquista del Desierto,* General Julio Argentino Roca's 19th-century genocide against the Patagonian Mapuche and their allies, and the *Fundación de Pueblos en la Pampa,* the founding of the towns that displaced the indigenes.

Jujuy station represents its namesake province and people in *Jujuy, Sus Riquezas Naturales* (Jujuy's Natural Riches) and *Los Gauchos Norteños* (The Northern Gauchos). General Urquiza station celebrates the dictator Rosas's defeat in a reproduction of Cándido López's *La Batalla de Caseros* and *La Entrada Triunfal del General Urquiza en Buenos Aires* (General Urquiza's Triumphant Entry into Buenos Aires).

Boedo station, by contrast, contains more everyday scenes like *Boedo a Mediados del Siglo XIX,* showing the barrio's mid-19th-century economic activities. It also contains the ceramic lunette *Niños Jugando* (Children at Play). Medalla Milagrosa station contains surrealistic 2001 murals by Santiago García Sáenz.

orders, they were also the most commercial, and architect Juan Bautista Ronoli designed the five buildings of the **Procuraduría** (two of which survive, fronting on Alsina) to warehouse products from their widespread missions.

The Jesuit structures, which also housed missionized indigenous people from the provinces, contained a number of defensive tunnels; the tunnels were rediscovered in 1912 and are now open to the public. After the Jesuits' 1767 expulsion from the Americas, the buildings served as the Protomedicato, which regulated the city's doctors. Following independence, they housed at various times the Biblioteca Pública (Public Library, 1812); the Cámara Legislativa (Provincial Legislature, 1821); the Universidad de Buenos Aires (1821); the Academia de Medicina (Medical Academy, 1822); the Sociedad Literaria (Literary Society, 1822); the Banco de la Provincia de Buenos Aires (Buenos Aires Provincial Bank, 1822); the Museo Público de Buenos Aires (Public Museum, 1823); the Congreso Nacional (1824); the Museo de Historia Natural (1854); the Departamento de Ciencias Exactas (Department of Hard Sciences, 1865); the Facultad de Ciencias Exactas, Físicas, y Naturales (Faculty of Hard, Physical, and Natural Sciences, 1881); and others. After 1974, the Comisión Nacional de la Manzana de Las Luces attempted to salvage the historical buildings for cultural purposes, opening the tunnels to the public and restoring part of the "Universidad" lettering along the facade on the Perú side.

In 1722, a new **Iglesia San Ignacio** replaced its deteriorating namesake, which was begun in 1661 and finished in 1675. After the Jesuits' expulsion in 1767, the new building briefly served as the cathedral while the permanent cathedral underwent repairs; following an invitation from dictator Juan Manuel de Rosas, the Jesuits returned in 1836. In 1955, at Juan Perón's instigation, mobs trashed the building, which has recently undergone an exterior restoration.

The church has one common wall with the **Colegio Nacional de Buenos Aires** (1908), the country's most prestigious and competitive secondary school, taught by top university faculty. Another notable feature is the re-created

**Sala de Representantes,** the province's first legislature.

## MUSEO DE LA CIUDAD
Defensa 219, tel. 011/4343-2123,
www.museos.buenosaires.gov.ar/ciudad
**HOURS:** Daily 11 A.M.-7 P.M., closed Feb.
**COST:** US$1; free Wed.

In the same building as the remarkable Farmacia La Estrella, the city museum specializes in themes dealing with the city proper and elements of everyday life, including architecture, furniture, floor tiles, and postcards; the pharmacy's exterior windows have been turned into display cases. Though most of its displays are upstairs, above the pharmacy, there is also a ground-level exhibition room on the Defensa side. It features rotating programs on topics such as tango legend Julio Sosa (second only to Carlos Gardel among tango singers) and doors salvaged from buildings long ago demolished. Actress Niní Marshall once resided here.

## PALACIO BAROLO
Av. de Mayo 1370, tel. 011/4383-1063,
www.pbarolo.com.ar
**HOURS:** Tours Mon. and Thurs. 2-7 P.M.
**COST:** US$15

Topped by a high-powered rotating semaphore ostensibly visible from Montevideo's Palacio Salvo (also the work of architect Mario Palanti), the Barolo is a landmark homage to Dante Alighieri and the *Divine Comedy*. Palanti, who enjoyed the patronage of wealthy textile merchant Luis Barolo, designed the building to replicate Dante's cosmology of Hell (the lower floors), Purgatory (the middle floors), and Heaven (the upper floors). For what it's worth, the ground floor is now home to the Secretaría de Inteligencia del Estado (SIDE, Argentina's counterpart to the FBI).

At the time of its completion, in 1923, the Barolo was Latin America's tallest building; a few months after its dedication, when Argentine heavyweight Luis Angel Firpo fought Jack Dempsey at New York's Polo Grounds, a green light from the tower erroneously announced a Firpo victory and briefly caused joyous pandemonium. Twelve years later, Retiro's Edificio Kavanagh surpassed the Barolo's height standard. Australian director Russell Mulcahy shot parts of the ill-fated 1986 sequel to *Highlander* in the building.

Miqueas Thäringen (tel. 15/5027-9035, miqueast@yahoo.com.ar) handles tours of the building, whose ground floor is open to the public during normal business hours.

### ◖ PLAZA DE MAYO

Bordered by Av. Rivadavia, San Martín, Hipólito Yrigoyen, and Balcarce

In 1580, Juan de Garay reestablished Pedro de Mendoza's failed settlement on what is now the Plaza de Mayo. Garay platted the rectangular Plaza del Fuerte (Fortress Plaza), which became the Plaza del Mercado (Market Plaza) and then the Plaza de la Victoria (Victory Plaza), after the defeat of British invaders in 1806 and 1807. Colloquially known as the Plaza de Protestas for its frequent, large, and contentious political demonstrations, the Plaza de Mayo has often held center stage in Argentine history. Juan and Eva Perón used it for spectacle, convoking hundreds of thousands of the fervent *descamisados* (shirtless ones) who comprised their underclass disciples.

Internationally, though, the plaza became notable for some of its smallest gatherings ever. During the late 1970s, a handful of Argentine mothers marched silently every Thursday afternoon to demand the return of their adult children kidnapped by the armed forces and paramilitary gangs. Most of the *desaparecidos* (disappeared) died at the hands of their captors but, in the absence of a complete accounting, the Madres de la Plaza de Mayo continue to parade every Thursday at 3:30 P.M. around the **Pirámide de Mayo,** the plaza's small central obelisk. Nobel Prize winner V. S. Naipaul chronicled the mothers' bravery while making caustic comments on Argentine society in his long essay *The Return of Eva Perón.*

Buenos Aires's city hall overlooks Plaza de Mayo from Diagonal Sur.

Ironically, emotional throngs cheered the 1976–1983 dictatorship here following Argentina's April 1982 occupation of the British-ruled Falkland Islands, which Argentina still claims as the Malvinas. As the war went badly, though, crowds turned on General Leopoldo Galtieri's de facto regime and the military collapse brought a quick return to constitutional government.

Following Argentina's 2001 economic meltdown, the Plaza de Mayo witnessed major protests and a police riot that killed several demonstrators; this led to the resignation of President Fernando De la Rúa, an indecisive leader who was undercut by the opposition Peronists. Later, the protestors were family members and activists seeking a culprit—or scapegoat—for the tragic December 2004 fire that killed nearly 200 people at a rock concert in the neighborhood of Once.

# Microcentro    Map 2

One of the Microcentro's foci is the pedestrian **Calle Florida,** which runs north from Rivadavia and crosses Avenida Córdoba into Retiro. Florida first became a *peatonal* (pedestrian walk) in the early 20th century, but for just a few hours each day. When it was completely closed to automobile traffic, it became the city's smartest shopping area, sporting stores like the former Harrod's (1913), a subsidiary of the famous London retailer that became legally separate in the 1960s and closed in the late 1990s.

As a shopping district, Florida is less fashionable than it once was, with one major exception: the restored **Galerías Pacífico,** an architectural and historical landmark that occupies most of a city block.

East–west **Avenida Corrientes,** the traditional center of *porteño* nightlife, has taken a back seat to trendier areas like Puerto Madero and Palermo; several cinemas have closed and, while some traditional cafés and restaurants have survived beneath gaudy illuminated signs, others seem to be hanging on by a thread. This may change, though, as authorities have widened the sidewalks by 1.5 meters on each side of the avenue between Avenida 9 de Julio and Callao to make the traditional theater district more pedestrian friendly.

At the same time, though, the cinema district along the Lavalle pedestrian mall, which crosses Florida one block north of Corrientes, has experienced an unfortunate diversification. While movie multiplexes have taken up some of the slack, other cinemas have become bingo parlors, evangelical churches blaring amplified hymns, and raucous video arcades.

Named for Argentina's independence day, the broad **Avenida 9 de Julio** divides the Microcentro from the rest of the barrio—literally so, as only a world-class sprinter could safely cross its 16 lanes of seemingly suicidal drivers fudging the green lights. Fortunately for pedestrians, there are several traffic islands, as well as subterranean passageways, to help reduce exposure to high-speed traffic.

## ARCHIVO Y MUSEO HISTÓRICO DEL BANCO DE LA PROVINCIA DE BUENOS AIRES DR. ARTURO JAURETCHE

Sarmiento 362, tel. 011/4331-1775 or 011/4331-7943, www.bapro.com.ar/museo
**HOURS:** Mon.-Fri. 10 A.M.-6 P.M.; guided tours by appointment
**COST:** Free

Before Argentina existed as a true country (until the 1880s federalization of Buenos Aires, it was really a loose confederation of provinces, some governed by ruthless warlords), the provincial bank was its main financial institution. It held that status until 1891 and issued the first Argentine and Uruguayan banknotes.

The museum provides an even longer-term perspective, covering Argentine economic and monetary history since viceregal times. Its displays include banknotes, coins, and medallions

Evita Perón announced her departure from politics from the Ministerio de Obras Públicas on Avenida 9 de Julio.

© WAYNE BERNHARDSON

# MICROCENTRO'S HISTORICAL LANDMARKS

Like Monserrat, the Microcentro has some subtle landmarks of great significance in the country's history. Dating from 1910, for instance, the headquarters of the **Sociedad Rural Argentina** (Florida 460) houses an organization that has voiced the interests of large-scale landowners – many Argentines would say "the oligarchy" – since 1866.

Immediately southeast, dating from 1926, the **Edificio Menéndez-Behety** (Roque Sáenz Peña 543) was the command center for multinational wool merchants who, in Patagonia and Tierra del Fuego, were more powerful than the Argentine and Chilean governments under which they operated.

At the intersection of Avenida 9 de Julio and Corrientes, rising above the oval Plaza de la República, the 67.5-meter **Obelisco** (Obelisk, 1936) is a city symbol erected for the 400th anniversary of Pedro de Mendoza's initial encampment along the Río de la Plata. There are 206 steps to the top, but the structure is rarely open.

From the Obelisco, the diagonal Roque Sáenz Peña is now a pedestrian mall ending at **Plaza Lavalle,** which stretches north three woodsy blocks along Talcahuano and Libertad between Lavalle and Avenida Córdoba.

Occupying an entire block fronting on Talcahuano, the **Palacio de Justicia** (commonly known as Tribunales or Law Courts, 1904) has lent its colloquial name to the neighborhood. Every Monday, at 9:53 A.M., the capital's Jewish community gathers to observe a moment of silence to protest judicial inaction on the bombing of the Asociación Mutualista Israelita Argentina (AMIA), which took place July 18, 1994.

Across the plaza from the Tribunales, dating from 1907, the kaleidoscopic confines of the **Conventillo de las Artes** (Libertad 543) were once law offices but now house a motley assortment of artists and writers. In its present state, the Conventillo contrasts dramatically with Italian-born architect Carlo Morra's sober neoclassical **Escuela Presidente Roca** (Libertad 581), a 1902 building three doors north, distinguished by massive granite columns quarried at Tandil. (Morra designed some 25 Argentine schools in similar styles.) It's an even more dramatic contrast with the stately **Teatro Colón** (Libertad 621).

that offer insights on topics that include early economic geography, the financial mechanisms and consequences of independence (including controversial loans from Britain's Baring Brothers house), counterfeiting, and the 1980s wild hyperinflation.

The first of its kind in the country, the Museo Jauretche has operated since 1904, but its current facilities are the best it's ever had.

## LA CITY
Calle San Martín btwn. Avs. Rivadavia and Corrientes

Calle San Martín is the main axis of the financial district, colloquially known as La City. Directly west of the post office, dating from 1916, architect Alejandro Christopherson's **Bolsa de Comercio de Buenos Aires** (Stock Exchange, 25 de Mayo 375) is one of the key institutions. Other oligarchs include the financial and commercial house of **Bunge y Born** (25 de Mayo 501).

Argentina's central bank, the Italianate **Banco Central de la República Argentina** (San Martín 265), has an identical facade at Reconquista 266. One block south, the hanging concrete slab at the former **Banco de Londres** (Reconquista de Londres), Clorindo Testa's brutalist banking monument, may make visitors from earthquake country nervous.

At La City's end of Calle Florida, to express their *bronca* after the events of late 2001 and early 2002, angry bank depositors painted, scrawled, and scratched graffiti on the corrugated aluminum that covered the windows of financial institutions. Even sturdy, secure buildings, such as the elegant Spanish Renaissance **Standard Bank** (ex-Banco de Boston, 1924), at the intersection with the diagonal Roque Sáenz Peña, suffered deface-ment from *corralito* protestors.

## CORREO CENTRAL
Corrientes bordered by Av. Leandro N. Alem, Bouchard, and Sarmiento

At the foot of Corrientes, occupying an entire block, the Correo Central (central post office, 1928) is a Beaux-Arts landmark whose original architect, Norberto Maillart, based his design on New York City's General Post Office. After Maillart's departure, the Ministerio de Obras Públicas (Public Works Ministry) changed the plans to incorporate a Francophile mansard.

## GALERÍAS PACÍFICO
Florida and Av. Córdoba, www.galeriaspacifico.com.ar
**HOURS:** Mon.-Sat. 10 A.M.-9 P.M., Sun. noon-9 P.M.; 30-minute guided tours Mon.-Sat. 11:30 A.M. and 4:30 P.M., Sun. 1 and 4:30 P.M.

As Calle Florida became an elegant shopping district in the late 19th century, Francisco Seeber and Emilio Bunge were the main shareholders in the proposed Bon Marché Argentino, in-spired by Milan's Galleria Vittorio Emmanuelle II. Unfortunately for Seeber and Bunge, their French investors backed out during the early 1890s global recession. Seeber resurrected the project by 1894 as the Galería Florida, housing a variety of shops and other businesses.

At one time or another, the distinctive build-ing, divided into four discrete sectors by perpen-dicular galleries with a central cupola and a glass ceiling, held the Museo de Bellas Artes (Fine Arts Museum) and the Academia Nacional de Bellas Artes (National Fine Arts Academy), art-ists' studios, and even government offices. One of its era's tallest and broadest buildings, with a double basement and four upper stories, it cov-ered an entire city block bounded by Florida, Avenida Córdoba, San Martín, and Viamonte.

In 1908, though, the British-run Ferrocarril de Buenos Aires al Pacífico, which operated the railroad that ran from the capital to the west-ern city of Mendoza, acquired the sector front-ing on Córdoba for its business offices; within

Galerías Pacífico is a recycled railroad office building transformed into an upscale shopping center.

two years, it controlled the rest of the building. In 1948, when Juan Perón nationalized the railroads to create Ferrocarriles Argentinos, it passed into state control.

During a 1945 remodel, Argentine artists gave the cupola its most dramatic feature: some 450 square meters of murals, including Lino Spilimbergo's *El Dominio de las Fuerzas Naturales* (The Dominion of Natural Forces), Demetrio Urruchúa's *La Fraternidad* (Brotherhood), Juan Carlos Castagnino's *La Vida Doméstica* (Life at Home), Manuel Colmeiro's *La Pareja Humana* (The Human Couple), and Antonio Berni's *El Amor* (Love). Linked to famous Mexican muralist David Alfaro Siqueiros through Spilimbergo, all belonged to the socially conscious Nuevo Realismo (New Realism) movement; the murals have twice been restored, in 1968 under Berni's direction and then again by an Argentine-Mexican group in 1991.

For most of the 1980s, though, the Galerías languished through economic disorder until, in 1992, the murals became a highlight of the building's transformation into one of the capital's most fashionable shopping centers—finally achieving its original purpose. The tastefully modernized Galerías is well worth a visit even for anti-consumerists. On the basement level, it has a high-quality food court and, in addition, the city's best public toilets.

### MUSEO JUDÍO DE BUENOS AIRES DR. SALVADOR KIBRICK

Libertad 769, tel. 011/4123-0832
**HOURS:** Tues.-Thurs. 3-5:30 P.M.
**COST:** US$5

Alongside Plaza Lavalle's imposing synagogue, and named for its founder, the Jewish museum contains a small but impressive collection of medieval Judaica, along with documents, photographs, and recordings dealing with the Jewish presence in Argentina. There is also a gallery of Jewish-Argentine and Jewish-themed art.

Buenos Aires's Jewish community became prominent after 1862, with the founding of its first synagogue. The major impetus toward immigration came with the German-born Baron Maurice Hirsch's project to resettle persecuted Russian Jews in the Argentine countryside in the 1890s, and his achievements get major coverage here.

Guided tours of the Museo Judío, in Spanish, English, and Hebrew, include a visit to the adjacent synagogue, reached by an interior door. Identification is obligatory; knock loudly. Male visitors to the temple, even non-Jews, must wear a yarmulke (which is provided).

### MUSEO MITRE

San Martín 366, tel. 011/4394-8240,
www.museomitre.gov.ar
**HOURS:** Tues.-Sun. 10 A.M.-6:30 P.M.
**COST:** US$0.65

Bartolomé Mitre (1821–1906), Argentina's first president under its 1853 constitution, spent a good part of his 1862–1868 term fighting Paraguayan dictator Francisco Solano López in the War of the Triple Alliance, which pitted a seemingly overmatched Paraguay against Argentina, Brazil, and Uruguay. Also a serious historian and pioneer journalist, Mitre founded the daily paper *La Nación*, a *porteño* institution for well over a century.

Mitre rented the building that now houses the museum, a late 18th-century structure with several patios, before receiving it as a gift from the city upon completing his term. He lived there the rest of his life with his family; to what was originally a single-story building, he added an upper floor with a bedroom, bathroom, and private office. A side door led to *La Nación*'s offices.

Museum exhibits cover Mitre's military and civilian careers, and there's an 80,000-volume research library that includes original documents from such figures as independence heroes José de San Martín and Manuel Belgrano.

### MUSEO NUMISMÁTICO DR. JOSÉ E. URIBURU

Reconquista 266, tel. 011/4348-3882
**HOURS:** Mon.-Fri. 10 A.M.-3 P.M.
**COST:** Free

If the Banco Central could manage the

country's monetary policy as well as it's organized this museum, which tells the story of Argentine currency from colonial times to the chaotic present, Argentina might not experience dire economic straits so often. Its most unusual exhibit consists of coins minted in Buenos Aires and postage stamps printed for Romanian engineer and adventurer Julio Popper, who attempted to establish his own empire on the island of Tierra del Fuego in the 1880s. A historical display of provincial bonds is a reminder that "funny money" has a long history in Argentina.

Federal police guarding the gate demand identification from those ascending to the upstairs museum.

### ◖ TEATRO COLÓN

Libertad 621, tel. 011/4378-7100, www.teatrocolon.org.ar
**HOURS:** Tours Mon.-Sat. 9, 10:30, and 11 A.M., noon, and 1, 2:30, 3, and 4 P.M.
**COST:** US$2.50 non-resident adult, US$0.70 child up to age 17

Arguably the continent's most important performing-arts center, the ornate Colón (1908) has reached its centenary after undergoing a major restoration. The weak peso, a legacy of the 2002 economic crisis, makes paying for top-tier international opera, ballet, and symphonic performers difficult, but it still manages to present top-flight local talent in those and other performance media.

Argentine lyric theater dates from the early 19th century, immediately after the May Revolution of 1810, and its first European artists arrived in the 1820s. In 1825, Rossini's *Barber of Seville* was the first opera ever staged in the country, but artistic development stagnated under the Rosas dictatorship.

The original Teatro Colón, facing the Plaza de Mayo, seated almost 2,500 people and opened with Verdi's *La Traviata* in 1857. As the original theater became the Banco Nacional (later the still-existent Banco de la Nación), the city chose one of the country's first railway station sites, on Plaza Lavalle's west side, for the new facility. Architect Francesco Tamburini was responsible for the original

Italian Renaissance design, but his countryman Víctor Meano took charge of the project upon Tamburini's death.

Occupying a lot of more than 8,000 square meters, boasting nearly 38,000 meters of floor space on seven levels, the new Colón opened with Verdi's *Aida*. Seating 2,478 patrons with standing room for another 700, it's one of the country's most lavish buildings with its **Gran Hall,** outfitted with Verona and Carrara marble; a **Salón de los Bustos** studded with busts of famous figures like Beethoven, Bizet, Mozart, Rossini, Verdi, and Wagner; and a **Salón Dorado** (Golden Salon) modeled on palaces like Paris's Versailles and Vienna's Schoenbrunn. In 1961, Raúl Soldi replaced Marcel Jambon's earlier cupola murals with paintings of singers, dancers, and actors; Soldi's canvases cover 318 square meters of wall space.

The main theater follows lines of French and Italian classics with world-class acoustics; its stage is 35.25 meters wide, 34.5 meters deep, and 48 meters high. A rotating disc simplifies scene changes. The orchestra accommodates up to 120 musicians. The seating ranges from comfortably upholstered rows to luxury boxes (including a presidential box with its own Casa Rosada phone line, and a separate exit to Tucumán). Presidential command performances take place on winter's patriotic holidays of May 25 and July 9.

Since the Colón's opening, its performers have been a who's who of classical music: composers Richard Strauss, Igor Stravinsky, Camille Saint-Saëns, Manuel de Falla, and Aaron Copland; conductors Otto Klemperer, Wilhelm Furtwängler, Herbert von Karajan, Arturo Toscanini, and Zubin Mehta; singers Enrico Caruso, Lily Pons, Ezio Pinza, María Callas, José Carreras, Frederika von Stade, Kiri Te Kanawa, Plácido Domingo, and Luciano Pavarotti; dancers Anna Pavlova, Vaslav Nijinsky, Rudolf Nureyev, Margot Fonteyn, and Mikhail Barishnikov; and choreographer George Balanchine.

Foreign dance companies on the Colón's stage have included the Ballet de Montecarlo,

London's Festival Ballet, the Opera Privée de París, the Ballet de la Opera de París, and the Ballet de la Opera de Berlín; orchestras have included the New York Philharmonic, the London Philharmonic, and the Washington Philharmonic. Soloists have included Arthur Rubinstein, Pablo Casals, Yehudi Menuhim, Mstislav Rostropovich, Isaac Stern, Itzhak Perlman, Yo-Yo Ma, Andrés Segovia, and Anne Sofie Mutter. At times, though, the administration has let its hair down to accommodate performers like activist folksinger Mercedes Sosa, the *porteño* rhythm-and-blues unit Memphis La Blusera, and rock guitarist-songwriter Luis Alberto Spinetta.

In a season that runs mostly from May to November, the Colón presents some 200 events each year. About half are opera; the remainder comprise about 65 orchestra concerts and 35 ballet performances. The building fills an entire block bounded by Tucumán, Viamonte, and Cerrito (Avenida 9 de Julio); the ticket office (tel. 011/4378-7344, boleteria_colon@buenosaires.gov.ar) is open Monday–Friday 9 A.M.–5 P.M. Although the main entrance is on Libertad, tours enter from the Viamonte side.

For tour reservations, always available in Spanish and English and sometimes available in French, German, and Portuguese, contact the Colón (Viamonte 1168, tel. 011/4378-7132, visitas@teatrocolon.org.ar). Tours last 50 minutes and take you behind the scenes for glimpses of sculptors, seamsters, set-builders, wigmakers, and the like.

Because of restoration and remodeling work for Argentina's bicentennial, however, the Colón is closed to the public until 2010. That means it could reopen before the next edition of this book, but it's by no means certain.

# Puerto Madero · Map 2

Born in controversy and corruption in the 19th century and designated a separate barrio in 1991, modern Puerto Madero is an attempt to reclaim the riverfront, which languished off-limits during the military dictatorship of 1976–1983. Comparable to Baltimore's Inner Harbor and London's Docklands, it partly represents the political and economic excesses of the 1990s Carlos Menem presidency, when speculative privatization was rampant in Argentina.

At the same time, according to journalist Andrew Graham-Yooll, it also marks the beginning of a time when Argentines began to value their material past. Developers have recycled several handsome brick warehouses around its four large *diques* (basins, one of which has become a yacht harbor) into stylish lofts, offices, restaurants, bars, and cinemas, and other investors have followed their example. One measure of its success is that director Fabián Bielinsky used the pedestrian promenade for a uniquely entertaining chase scene in his con-man film *Nueve Reinas* (Nine Queens).

Historically, the Puerto Madero area is where immigrants arrived, and the developing **Museo de la Inmigración,** north of the Buquebus ferry port, is an essential stop for appreciating the scale and significance of the European invasion.

Built on landfill east of the river's *barrancas,* what is now Puerto Madero expanded during the dictatorship as the military dumped debris from its massive public works projects east and southeast of the *diques.* Ironically enough, as plants and animals colonized this expanse of rubble and rubbish, it became the **Reserva Ecológica Costanera Sur,** now a popular destination for Sunday outings.

Dique No. 3 holds a 450-berth yacht harbor, but the most eye-catching feature along the basins is Spanish architect Santiago Calatrava's **Puente de la Mujer,** a modernistic pedestrian bridge whose harp-like suspension section rotates to allow vessels to pass between

© WAYNE BERNHARDSON

In Puerto Madero, handsome brick *depósitos* (warehouses) have been recycled to house restaurants, apartments, and offices.

Dique No. 3 and Dique No. 2. Several original cranes remain in place along the west side of the basins, where British engineers designed the handsome but practical redbrick *depósitos* (warehouses), now recycled into some of the barrio's bars, restaurants, and entertainment venues, as well as apartments and offices.

Trending northwest to southeast, the **Avenida de los Italianos** features a broad esplanade that overlooks the Reserva Ecológica and is a favorite destination for weekend strollers, joggers, and cyclists. The city's **Centro de Museos** (Av. de los Italianos 851, tel. 011/4516-0944, Tues.–Fri. 2–6 P.M., Sat.–Sun. noon–6 P.M.) has some exceptional special exhibitions.

### MUSEO DE LA INMIGRACIÓN

Av. Antártida 1355, tel. 011/4317-0285, www.mininterior.gov.ar/migraciones/museo/index.html
**HOURS:** Mon.-Fri. 10 A.M.-5 P.M., Sat.-Sun. 11 A.M.-6 P.M., closed holidays
**COST:** Free

Toward the barrio's north end, the Hotel de Inmigrantes was Argentina's Ellis Island for European immigrants. From 1911 until 1953, arrivals from the Old World could spend five nights here before heading into the great Argentine unknown. By all accounts, it was an exemplary facility.

Reopened to the public as the country's immigration museum, it's still a work in progress, but the displays of sample family histories and panels showing the evolution of Argentine immigration and the treatment of new arrivals are an auspicious beginning. At present, the only areas open to the public are the reception and the dining room, where visitors can search a computer database for information on the 3.7 million immigrants from 60 countries who have arrived by boat since 1882. The upstairs accommodations—actually large dormitories—are due to undergo restoration. Progress, though, has been slow.

### ◖ RESERVA ECOLÓGICA COSTANERA SUR

Av. Tristán Achával Rodríguez 1550, tel. 011/4893-1597
**HOURS:** Tues.-Sun. 8 A.M.-7 P.M.; guided tours Sat.-Sun. and holidays 10:30 A.M. and 4 P.M., 2.5-hour moonlight tours 9 P.M. on designated Fri., by reservation only on previous Mon.

Plans to create a satellite city on landfill east of Puerto Madero were part of the military dictatorship's Proceso, but the Falklands fiasco short-circuited their projects to transform the city and the country. While matters were on hold, volunteer trees, shrubs, and grasses colonized the area and, ironically, turned it into a lush wildlife habitat that's become a major recreational destination for *porteños*.

A few years after the return to representative government, lobbying from the Fundación Vida Silvestre, the Fundación Amigos de la Tierra, and the Asociación Ornitológica del Plata persuaded city government to declare the area a nature reserve. It now offers hiking and bicycle trails and ample habitat for migratory wildfowl, such as black-necked swans, coots, and flamingos; permanent residents, such as black-crowned night herons

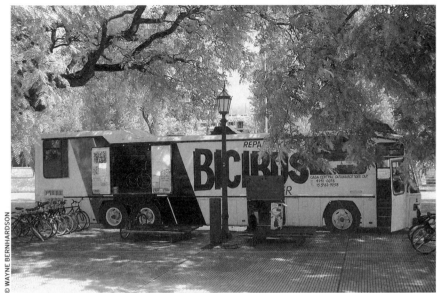

© WAYNE BERNHARDSON

Bicibús, a mobile bike rental company, spends weekends and holidays outside Puerto Madero's Reserva Ecológica Costanera Sur.

and parakeets; and reptiles like river turtles. It has also become a fairly discreet cruising area for the capital's gay men.

There is an entrance at the foot of Avenida Belgrano, as well as a convenient entrance at the north end of Avenida de los Italianos, where the mobile bike rental shop Bicibús (tel. 011/4941-0078 or 15/5163-9258) rents bicycles from 8 A.M. to 7 P.M. on weekends and holidays only. It's possible to ride around the reserve in a little over an hour, but that's pushing it; when it's been raining and the terrain gets muddy, bicycles are prohibited to reduce erosion.

# San Telmo

Map 3

Once an elite residential area, San Telmo faded in the 1870s after a devastating yellow fever epidemic drove moneyed families to higher ground in Palermo and Belgrano. Like La Boca, to the south, it became an area where impoverished immigrant families could find a foothold in its *conventillos,* abandoned mansions where large groups crowded into small spaces—often single rooms. Today, it's a mixed neighborhood where *conventillos* still exist, but young professionals have also recycled crumbling apartment buildings and even industrial sites into stylish lofts.

San Telmo is the barrio most closely identified with tango—at least the tango of high-priced floor shows and professional dancers. Otherwise, its nightlife is less impressive than that of other areas, such as Palermo, in part because some *porteños* perceive picturesque San Telmo as crime-ridden. Nevertheless, improvements are taking place, with increasing numbers of sidewalk cafés, wine bars, and restaurants popping up.

San Telmo's heart, though, is **Plaza Dorrego** (Defensa and Humberto Primo), site of the hectic weekend flea market; it's a more leisurely place during the week, when shaded tables replace the crowded stalls and it's easier to enjoy lunch. Antiques shops line both sides of Defensa, north and south from the plaza.

Although the Spanish Laws of the Indies dictated city plans with rectangular blocks of equal size, in practice things were not quite so regular here. North–south **Calle Balcarce,** for instance, doglegs several times between Chile and Estados Unidos, crossing the cobblestone alleyways of **Pasaje San Lorenzo** and **Pasaje Giuffra.**

Befitting its artists' colony reputation, San Telmo is home to a large and growing number of murals, usually collective efforts. At Independencia and Balcarce, the restored mural *Tango* covers the walls behind the **Plazoleta Leonel Rivera.** Six blocks south, at the corner of Avenida Juan de Garay and Avenida Paseo Colón, the stylized *Educación y Esclavitud* (Education and Slavery) tackles Argentina's authoritarian political heritage.

### CLUB ATLÉTICO
Paseo Colón under Autopista 25 de Mayo (freeway to Ezeiza)

One of the more unsettling sights, the so-called Club Atlético is a grisly archaeological dig, whose basement cells belonged to a building used as a torture center during the military dictatorship of 1976–1983 before being demolished to build the *autopista.*

### DANSK KIRKE
Carlos Calvo 257

Buenos Aires has many immigrant communities, but one of the unlikeliest must be the Scandinavians who have left their mark here. The Danish architects Rönnow and Bisgaard designed the distinctive redbrick neo-Gothic Dansk Kirke (Danish Lutheran Church), dating from 1931; its interior is known for its chandeliers. Five blocks southeast, dating from 1944, the comparable **Svenska**

**Kyrkan** (Swedish Lutheran Church, Azopardo 1428) looks as if it were airlifted intact from Stockholm. The interior of both churches are not open to the public.

### IGLESIA APOSTÓLICA ORTODOXA RUSA
Av. Brasil 315

Across from Parque Lezama, architect Alejandro Christopherson designed the turquoise-colored onion domes and stained-glass windows of the 1904 Iglesia Apostólica Ortodoxa Rusa (Russian Orthodox Apostolic Church), built with materials imported from St. Petersburg. The interior of the church is open to the public, but the hours are erratic.

### MUSEO HISTÓRICO NACIONAL
Defensa 1600, tel. 011/4300-7540
**HOURS:** Daily 11 A.M.–5 P.M.; summer Mon.-Fri. 3-5 P.M.; guided tours Sat.-Sun. 3:30 P.M.
**COST:** US$0.65

From the permanent exhibits at Parque Lezama's national history museum, it's hard to tell that Argentina lived through the 20th century, let alone survived into to the 21st. Mostly chronological, it offers a token account of pre-Columbian Argentina and a brief description of the founding of Spanish cities; its most vivid exhibits are meticulous 19th-century illustrations of Buenos Aires and the surrounding pampas by Royal Navy purser Emeric Essex Vidal.

It then follows a perfunctory narrative of independence and the 19th-century caudillos (provincial warlords), plus a substantial if stereotypical nod to the gaucho. The nadir is a chauvinistic version of the late 19th-century "Conquista del Desierto" (Conquest of the Desert), which expanded the country's territory on the Patagonian frontier at the expense of the indigenous population.

One entire salon extols the maturation of independence icon José de San Martín, but a superficial narrative of the conservative 19th-century republic—consisting mostly of presidential portraits—ends abruptly with the deposed Hipólito Yrigoyen, victim of the country's first modern military coup in 1930.

© WAYNE BERNHARDSON

The Museo Histórico Nacional is a Parque Lezama landmark.

There's nothing whatsoever on Juan Domingo Perón, his equally charismatic wife Evita, the 1970s' Dirty War, the 1980s' democratic restoration, or the 1990s' abortive boom.

Despite its shortcomings as a museum, the building itself is a well-kept landmark whose subterranean gallery hosts special exhibits, and on occasion there are weekend concerts.

As of press time, though, the museum was closed for reorganization after the highly publicized theft of a watch belonging to independence hero Manuel Belgrano. Both hours and other information may change when it reopens.

### PARQUE LEZAMA

Bordered by Av. Brasil, Av. Paseo Colón, Av. M. García, and Av. Regimiento de Patricios

The rumored (if improbable) site of Pedro de Mendoza's founding of the city, famed landscape architect Carlos Thays's Parque Lezama is an irregular quadrilateral on the banks above the old river course, which has long been covered by landfill. Shaded by mature palms and other exotic trees and studded with monuments, it's the place where aging *porteños* play chess, working-class families have weekend picnics, and a Sunday crafts fair stretches north along Calle Defensa to Avenida San Juan. The park appears better maintained than in recent years, despite its countless feral cats—a dilemma it shares with many other city parks.

On the capital's southern edge in colonial times, the property came into the hands of Carlos Ridgley Horne and then Gregorio Lezama, whose widow sold it to the city in 1884. Horne built the Italianate mansion (1846), which is now the **Museo Histórico Nacional,** the national history museum; at the park's northwest entrance, Juan Carlos Oliva Navarro sculpted the *Monumento a Don Pedro Mendoza* (1937) to mark the 400th anniversary of Buenos Aires's founding—a year too late.

### PLAZA CORONEL OLAZÁBAL

Av. Paseo Colón and Av. Independencia

To the east, where Avenida Paseo Colón narrows toward La Boca at the elliptical Plaza

© WAYNE BERNHARDSON

At Parque Lezama, Don Pedro Mendoza gets credit for the founding of Buenos Aires.

Coronel Olazábal, Rogelio Yrurtia's monumental *Canto al Trabajo* (Ode to Labor) may be the city's finest public sculpture. Unfortunately, a metal fence intended to dissuade vandalism blunts the impact of this tribute to hard-working pioneers, a welcome antidote to pompously heroic monuments elsewhere in the city.

On the plaza's east side, the Universidad de Buenos Aires's neoclassic **Facultad de Ingeniería** (Av. Paseo Colón 850, tel. 011/4343-0891, www.fi.uba.ar) originally housed the Fundación Eva Perón, established by Evita herself to aid the poor—and her own political ambitions. Immediately behind it, infamous for corruption, the controversial historical monument **Confederación General de Trabajo** (CGT, General Labor Confederation, Azopardo 802, tel. 011/4383-6853, www.cgtra.org.ar) is a traditional source of Peronist power.

### ◖ PLAZA DORREGO

Defensa and Humberto Primo

Six days a week, Plaza Dorrego is a shaded, nearly silent square where *porteños* sip *cortados*

and nibble lunches from nearby cafés. On weekends, though, when municipal authorities close Calle Defensa between Avenida San Juan and Avenida Independencia, it swarms with Argentine and foreign visitors who stroll among dozens of antiques stalls at the **Feria de San Telmo** (formally Feria de San Pedro Telmo), the most famous and colorful of the capital's many street fairs. Items range from antique soda siphons and brightly painted *filete* plaques displaying *piropos* (aphorisms) to oversized early radios and countless other items.

The plaza and surrounding side streets fill with street performers, like the ponytailed Pedro Benavente, known as El Indio, a smooth *tanguero* (dancer) who with various female partners entrances locals and tourists alike—even though his boom box provides the music. Up and down Defensa there are also live tango musicians and other dancers, not to mention puppet theaters, hurdy-gurdy men with parrots, and a glut of *estatuas vivas* (living statues or costumed mimes), some of whom are strikingly original and others of whom are trite. The author's favorite performers, though, are the trio who (for a small donation) will jabber in *cocoliche,* the Italian-Spanish pidgin that has influenced the Argentine language since the late 19th century.

The Feria de San Telmo takes place every Sunday, starting around 9–10 A.M., and continues into late afternoon. Even with all the antiques and crafts stands, there's room to enjoy lunch and the show from the sidewalk cafés surrounding the plaza and balconies overlooking it.

### EL ZANJÓN DE GRANADOS

Defensa 755, tel. 011/4361-3002, www.elzanjon.com.ar
**HOURS:** Tours Mon.-Fri. 11 A.M.-2 P.M., Sat.-Sun. 2-6 P.M.
**COST:** Tours US$10 Mon.-Fri., US$4 Sat.-Sun.

In 1986, when businessman Jorge Eckstein bought the Italianate building with the idea of recycling it for a music and events center, he had no idea that workers would stumble upon a labyrinth of tunnels that encased the Tercero del Sur, a Río de la Plata tributary, in late colonial times. Calling in urban archaeologist Jorge Schávelzon to supervise salvage and restoration, Eckstein worked around the remaining structures, including cisterns, wells, and even some houses, unobtrusively reinforcing them with concrete and other materials when necessary.

Visitors to El Zanjón can now tour these tunnels, which were filled with rubble during the 1870s yellow fever scare, and view the numerous colonial and republican artifacts, including tools and ceramics, that Schávelzon salvaged and organized. Despite its relatively recent exterior, the building itself has three impressive colonial patios and sits atop one of the city's oldest land grants, from city founder Juan de Garay himself. The tunnels run beneath neighboring buildings and, pending mutual agreement, the restoration may be extended.

Expertly led weekday tours of El Zanjón, in Spanish or English, are expensive by current standards, but this is a private initiative and an almost unique sight. Weekend tours are shorter because of high demand.

To make it even more appealing, tours include a visit to the famous **Casa Mínima** (San Lorenzo 380), an unoccupied "sausage house" that was ostensibly a slaveholder's gift to his former chattel (there is no documentary evidence to prove, or disprove, this legend). The narrow house entrance opens onto a slightly wider patio where the former kitchen sits, while a wall-hugging staircase leads to an even narrower bedroom, which has a street-side balcony directly above the exterior doorway.

## La Boca
Map 3

On the west bank of the twisting Riachuelo, which separates the capital from Buenos Aires province, the working-class barrio of La Boca owes its origins to mid-19th century French Basque and Genovese immigrants who worked in packing plants and warehouses during the beef-export boom. Perhaps more than any other neighborhood, it remains a community symbolized by fervent—most would say fanatical—identification with the Boca Juniors soccer team (the team's nickname "Xeneizes," by the way, comes from the Genovese dialect).

La Boca is, in a literal sense, the city's most colorful neighborhood, thanks partly to the brightly painted houses with corrugated zinc siding that line the pedestrian Caminito and other streets. Initially, these bright colors came from marine paints salvaged from ships in the harbor. The colors are inviting, but the poorly insulated buildings can be stiflingly hot in summer and frigid in winter.

La Boca owes another part of its color to Benito Quinquela Martín, a barrio resident who sympathetically portrayed its hard-working inhabitants in his oils and made the barrio an artists' colony in addition to a thriving

working-class neighborhood. Its gateway is Avenida Almirante Brown, at the southeast corner of Parque Lezama, where the *Mural Escenográfico Parque Lezama,* a three-dimensional mural erected by the barrio's Catalinas del Sur theater group, depicts community life through colorful caricatures. From the foot of the avenue, where it intersects Avenida Pedro de Mendoza at the Riachuelo, the remaining massive girders of the former **Puente Nicolás Avellaneda** (1940), towering above the river, are a civil-engineering landmark; the current namesake bridge parallel to the girders is an unremarkable concrete construction leading into the capital's major industrial suburb.

On either side of the Caminito, along Avenida Pedro de Mendoza, several landmarks lend character to the neighborhood. Immediately east, high-relief sculptures stand out above the display window of the ship chandler A. R. Constantino. Across the avenue, at permanent anchor, the former ferry **Nicolás Mihanovich,** which linked Buenos Aires to Uruguay, now houses a cultural center and crafts market.

© WAYNE BERNHARDSON

Ragged *conventillos* (tenements) are still common in La Boca, but they stand out for their colorful paint jobs and other decorations.

For residents, though, the key landmark is the **Estadio Alberto J. Armando,** better known by its nickname **La Bombonera** (at Brandsen and Del Valle Iberlucea); murals of barrio life cover the walls along the Brandsen side of the stadium.

*Porteños* may still claim that the barrio is dangerous, but anyone with basic street smarts should be able to visit without incident. There is, however, far more graffiti on the walls than in past years and more dog droppings on the sidewalks—perhaps signs of a declining sense of community. Some locals blame the police, who they say view the job not as a vocation but rather as a last-chance option. For this reason, some visitors prefer guided tours, which often start at the Caminito.

### CAMINITO

Caminito btwn. Magallanes and Olavarría

The Caminito (also the name of an evocative tango) is one of Buenos Aires's most emblematic streets. The cobbled Caminito was once the terminus of a short rail line and it's still an obligatory tourist stop. On weekends, especially, artists of variable talent hawk their paintings between rows of brightly painted houses with corrugated metal siding, but on weekdays it's no less picturesque.

### MUSEO DE BELLAS ARTES DE LA BOCA BENITO QUINQUELA MARTÍN

Pedro de Mendoza 1835, tel. 011/4301-1080

**HOURS:** Tues.-Sun. 10 A.M.-6 P.M.

**COST:** Free; donations welcome

Boca's very own artist-in-residence, Benito Quinquela Martín (1890–1977), was an orphan who became a son of his barrio, living and painting in the building that is now a homage to his life and work promoting the community. His well-lighted studio displays a collection of his oils of working-class life (Quinquela himself was a stevedore before devoting himself to painting). There's also a collection of brightly painted bowsprits that reflects the barrio's maritime orientation and a selection of works by other notable Argentine painters, including Antonio Berni, Raquel Forner, Eduardo Sívori, and Lino Spilimbergo.

The Museo de Bellas Artes shares a street-level entrance with the Escuela Pedro de Mendoza, an elementary school.

### MUSEO DE LA PASIÓN BOQUENSE

Brandsen 805, tel. 011/4362-1100,
www.museoboquense.com

**HOURS:** Daily 10 A.M.-6 P.M., hours may change on game days

**COST:** US$4.50, US$7 with guided stadium tour

In the catacombs of La Bombonera, Boca's newest museum is a thunderous interactive homage to the barrio's passion for soccer and its role in the community. Professionally organized, this state-of-the-art facility's 1,800 square meters include photographs of almost every individual who's ever stepped on the pitch, ranging from single-match nobodies to Roberto Morizo, who played in 426 matches. The museum also includes roster cards, trophies, and even

© WAYNE BERNHARDSON

Caminito

a photograph of Eva Perón in a blue-and-gold jersey. Boca's ultimate icon, though, remains retired striker Diego Maradona, whose adoring fans seem as oblivious to his drug problems and other erratic behavior as Barry Bonds's partisans are to his steroid use.

Interactive video timelines attempt to integrate local, national, and international events—even the Dirty War that the military dictatorship waged as Argentina hosted the 1978 World Cup—with those in the sporting world. In the end, though, non-soccer fans will find it dull except for its depiction of the barrio.

## MUSEO HISTÓRICO DE CERA

Del Valle Iberlucea 1261, tel. 011/4301-1497, www.museodecera.com.ar
**HOURS:** Daily 11 A.M.-6 P.M.
**COST:** US$5

The only one of its kind in the country, La Boca's historical wax museum, occupying a century-old Italian Renaissance residence, re-creates events, scenes, and significant figures in Argentine history. Among its themes are the founding of the city, the gaucho, the tango, and even the Afro-Argentine dance *candombe;* the latter serves as an open acknowledgement of the capital's once-substantial black community. In addition to historical and political figures, such as Pedro de Mendozá, Juan Manuel de Rosas, and Guillermo Brown, there are representations of indigenous leaders, including Calfucurá and Ceferino Namuncurá, and of cultural icons, like Carlos Gardel and Juan de Dios Filiberto (composer of the tango *Caminito*), and the artist Quinquela Martín.

# Balvanera Map 4

West of Avenida Callao, between Avenida Córdoba and Avenida Independencia, Balvanera's most obvious sights are major public buildings, like the **Congreso Nacional,** which faces the **Plaza del Congreso** from Avenida Entre Ríos, and architectural landmarks, like the sadly neglected **Confitería del Molino,** a national monument at Avenida Callao and Avenida Rivadavia. In contrast to this neglect is the magnificently preserved **Palacio de las Aguas Corrientes,** the former city waterworks, which fills an entire block at the barrio's north end.

The neighborhood of **Once,** roughly bounded by Avenida Córdoba, Junín, Avenida Rivadavia, and Avenida Pueyrredón, is the city's garment district; it takes its colloquial name from the **Estación 11 de Septiembre,** the westbound Ferrocarril Sarmiento station that has both commuter rail service and a few remaining long-distance trains. It is one of the most densely populated parts of town, with little green space, but its **Plaza Miserere,** alongside the station, and **Plaza 1° de Mayo** are undergoing renovation.

fountains on the Plaza del Congreso

Ethnically, Once is the capital's most conspicuously Jewish area, where men and boys in yarmulkes and Orthodox males in their plain suits and long beards are common sights, especially east of Pueyrredón between Córdoba and Corrientes. There are several Jewish schools, noteworthy for the heavy concrete security posts outside them: Once saw the notorious 1994 bombing of the **Asociación Mutualista Israelita Argentina** (AMIA, Pasteur 633, between Viamonte and Tucumán). Investigation of this terrorist act, which killed 87 people, has been a chaotic bungle, despite suspected links to Iran and the Buenos Aires provincial police.

## MERCADO DE ABASTO

Corrientes 3247, tel. 011/4959-3400,
www.abasto-shopping.com.ar
**HOURS:** Daily 10 A.M.–10 P.M.

Until 1893, the area bounded by Avenida Corrientes, Anchorena, Agüero, and Lavalle was a sprawling open-air market for wholesale fruits, vegetables, and meats. In that year, though, the Italian Devoto family's construction of the Mercado de Abasto made room for merchants displaced by Mayor Torcuato de Alvear's ambitious transformation of the city's civic axis along the newly created Avenida de Mayo.

Rebuilt in 1934 by Italian architect José Luis Delpini, under the auspices of the Bunge & Born conglomerate, the cavernous Abasto served its purpose until the 1970s, when the military dictatorship moved its functions to the new and far larger (if clearly misnamed) Mercado Central in La Matanza, beyond the city limits in Buenos Aires province.

In 1998, after nearly two decades of neglect, the Abasto reopened as a four-story shopping center with 120,000 square meters of display space, 186 shops, 12 cinemas, parking, and a food court (with a kosher McDonald's!). Part of a project for rejuvenating the neighborhood, sponsored by U.S.-Hungarian financier George Soros (who has since bowed out of Argentina), this adaptive reuse saved a magnificent building from demolition. Unfortunately, it's notoriously noisy and less appealing than competitors like the

Galerías Pacífico and Patio Bullrich; the restored exterior is all that's worth seeing.

One unique feature is its children's museum, the **Museo de Niños Abasto** (tel. 011/4861-2325, www.museoabasto.org.ar), which amuses and presumably educates the children when they tire of toy shopping. Hours are Tuesday–Sunday 1–8 P.M.; admission costs US$3 pp, but there are packages for families with children (comprising most of the museum's patrons).

## PALACIO DE LAS AGUAS CORRIENTES (OBRAS SANITARIAS)

Riobamba 750, tel. 011/6319-1104 (museum)
**HOURS:** Mon.-Fri. 9 A.M.-1 P.M. (museum)
**COST:** Free

Arguably the capital's most photogenic building, the former city waterworks (1894) glistens with 170,000 rust-colored tiles and 130,000 enameled bricks imported from Britain, crowned by a Parisian mansard. Filling an entire city block bounded by Avenida Córdoba, Riobamba, Viamonte, and Ayacucho, the extravagant exterior of the building popularly known as Obras Sanitarias (Water Works) disguises a utilitarian interior of 12 metallic tanks that held more than 60 million liters of the growing city's drinking water. There were similar, though less conspicuously lavish, structures in the barrios of Caballito and Villa Devoto.

Swedish architect Karl Nystromer conceived the building, whose tanks became superfluous as engineers developed a series of subterranean tunnels for shifting water through the city. Since its 1990s privatization as part of Aguas Argentinas, the building has housed offices and the small but interesting **Museo del Patrimonio Aguas Argentinas.**

The museum, which offers excellent guided tours in Spanish only, displays an astonishing assortment of antique plumbing fixtures ranging from taps, tubs, pipes, and sinks to bidets and urinals, many of them imported, all of them needing approval from what was then a state-run bureaucracy. The old storage tanks now hold the archives of city maps and plans that were created in conjunction with the waterworks.

Balvanera's Palacio del Congreso Nacional is home to Argentina's bicameral legislature.

© WAYNE BERNHARDSON

While the Palacio's street address is Riobamba 750, the museum entrance is on the Córdoba side; follow the arrows to the elevator, which takes you to the 1st floor.

## PALACIO DEL CONGRESO NACIONAL

Avs. Rivadavia and Callao, www.congreso.gov.ar

Balvanera's largest landmark, the neoclassical Congreso Nacional, is the Congreso neighborhood's centerpiece. One of the last major public works projects undertaken before Francophile architecture became the norm, the Italianate building faces the Plaza del Congreso and, in the distance, the Casa Rosada.

Argentines typically view their legislators with skeptical and even cynical eyes, and the Congreso gave them good reason from the start. The progressive but authoritarian mayor Torcuato de Alvear chose the site in 1888, after the city's designation as federal capital, but in 1895 the Italian Victór Meano won a controversial design competition (decades later, his rival Alejandro Christopherson wrote that Meano did not prepare the sketches submitted for the competition). The project went far over budget, launching a major congressional investigation, and Meano died mysteriously, shot in his maid in 1904. The building was functional by 1906, but not until 1946 were the final touches applied.

The building's 80-meter-high bronze cupola still shows scars from the 1930 military coup against Hipólito Yrigoyen. Presidents who have died in office, such as Perón, have lain in state here, as did Perón's wife Evita.

Phone at least an hour ahead for free guided tours of the upper-house **Senado** (Hipólito Yrigoyen 1849, tel. 011/4010-3000, ext. 3885, www.senado.gov.ar). Tours take place Monday–Friday at 11 A.M., 5 P.M., and 6 P.M. in Spanish; the 11 A.M. tour can accommodate English and French speakers. There's a separate 4 P.M. tour for English speakers.

Spanish-only visits to the lower **Cámara de Diputados** (Av. Rivadavia 1864, tel. 011/6310-7222, www.diputados.gov.ar) take place Monday, Tuesday, Thursday, and Friday at 10 A.M., noon, and 4 P.M. The congressional website has separate pages for each house.

# Retiro                                      Map 5

Well north of Juan de Garay's refounded Buenos Aires of 1580, Retiro (literally, a retreat) was home to an isolated monastery in the 17th century. The name Retiro, though, does not appear formally until 1691, when Spanish governor Agustín de Robles built a house on the *barranca* (terrace), where Plaza San Martín now sits, above the river. For a time, Retiro became a zone of *quintas* (country houses), but by 1862 the erection of General San Martín's equestrian statue marked its definitive urbanization. Beginning in the late 19th century, the surrounding streets became the city's most elite residential area.

## MUSEO DE LA SHOÁ

Montevideo 919, tel. 011/4811-3588, www.fmh.org.ar
**HOURS:** Mon.-Thurs. 11 A.M.-7 P.M., Fri. 11 A.M.-4:30 P.M.

**COST:** US$3

Opened in October 2001, Buenos Aires's Holocaust museum is a professional endeavor with both permanent collections and rotating exhibits on such topics as the Warsaw ghetto, the Danish resistance to deportation of the Jews, and the liberation of Auschwitz. Its bright explanatory panels, illustrated with photographs and documents, intertwine European events with those in Argentina; its Sala de la Memoria (Memorial Hall) evokes the memory of Argentine Jews who died in the European carnage.

Note that even when the museum is open, the sturdy metal door is closed for security purposes, and the friendly but muscular young men at the entrance are a further deterrent to potential malefactors.

© WAYNE BERNHARDSON

Retiro's Torre de los Ingleses

## MUSEO MUNICIPAL DE ARTE HISPANOAMERICANO ISAAC FERNÁNDEZ BLANCO

Suipacha 1422, tel. 011/4327-0272,
www.museos.buenosaires.gov.ar
**HOURS:** Tues.-Sun. 2-7 P.M.; guided tours
Sat.-Sun. 4 P.M.
**COST:** US$1; free Thurs.

Housing the extensive colonial and independence-era art collections of its namesake founder, the municipal art museum contains an impressive array of Spanish- and Portuguese-American religious painting and statuary, as well as exquisite silverwork and furniture. It occupies the Palacio Noel, an impressive neocolonial residence built for city mayor Carlos Noel by his brother Martín in 1921. With its nods to Andalucía, Arequipa (Perú), and especially Lima for its balconies, the building was an overdue antidote to the fashionable Francophile architecture of the time, especially in this neighborhood. The adjoining administrative offices were once the residence of poet Oliverio Girondo, a literary (and romantic) rival of Jorge Luis Borges.

The museum hosts occasional concerts and other cultural events. It sometimes closes during the summer months of January and February.

## PALACIO SAN MARTÍN

Arenales 761, tel. 011/4819-8092
**HOURS:** Tours Tues. and Thurs. 2:30 P.M.
**COST:** Free

Mercedes Castellano de Anchorena, matriarch of one of Argentina's most powerful families, ordered the construction of the three interconnected Beaux-Arts residences that constitute the Palacio San Martín. Designed by renowned architect Alejandro Christopherson and finished in 1912, the three houses share imposing gates and a common circular courtyard, but each has its own separate entrance, marble staircases and balustrades, elaborate stained-glass windows, immense dining rooms (still used for state functions), and other elements of Parisian-style opulence. The satellite plaza immediately south of the palace was, de facto at least, the Anchorena family's private garden.

Sold to the foreign ministry in 1936, the building has served diplomatic purposes ever since; however, since construction of the new high-rise *cancillería* (chancellery) immediately west across Esmeralda, it no longer houses permanent offices. Now open to the public, it provides an unmatched opportunity to grasp the Argentine oligarchy's lifestyle. It also holds a small museum of pre-Columbian antiquities from northwestern Argentina and works by famous Latin American artists, including the Argentine Antonio Berni, Uruguayan Pedro Figari, and Chilean Roberto Matta. One of its gardens holds a chunk of the Berlin Wall.

When not needed for official functions, the Palacio San Martín is open for free guided tours in both Spanish and English.

### PLAZA SAN MARTÍN AND AROUND

Bordered by Av. Leandro N. Alem, Florida, and Av. Ramos Mejía

The most extravagant of the mansions in this square is the 12,000-square-meter **Palacio Paz** (1909), at the west end of the plaza, now open for guided tours (US$5 in Spanish, US$10 in English) at 11 A.M. and 4 P.M. Tuesday–Saturday. In any other context than its proximity to the Palacio Paz, the neo-Gothic **Palacio Haedo** (home to Argentina's national park service) would seem truly lavish.

At the plaza's southeast edge, the **Edificio Kavanagh** (1935, Florida 1035) is a 33-story high-rise that was Buenos Aires's first skyscraper. Built in 14 months and inspired by the Chicago skyscrapers of the 1920s, this deco landmark was and is a symbol of the capital's modernization. Unfortunately, it literally overshadows the nearby **Basílica Santísimo Sacramento** (San Martín 1035), a 1916 construction based on its Parisian namesake and sponsored by Mercedes Castellano de Anchorena (who built and lived in the Palacio San Martín with her children and their families).

Plaza San Martín's most recent major addition is the **Monumento a los Caídos de Malvinas,** a marble monument that lists the names of those who died in the 1982 war over the Falkland (Malvinas) Islands. Across Avenida del Libertador to the northeast, the **Plaza Fuerza Aérea Argentina, Plaza del Carril,** and **Plaza Canadá** are extensions of Plaza San Martín. Plaza Fuerza Aérea Argentina, once known as Plaza Britania, was renamed after the Falklands War, in which Argentina's air force was the only branch of the services that performed credibly. Its centerpiece, though, is still architect Ambrose Poynter's **Torre de los Ingleses** (1916), a clock tower resembling London's Big Ben that was donated by the once-substantial, but now diminishing, Anglo-Argentine community.

Immediately across Avenida Ramos Mejía is the **Estación Retiro** (1915), a recently restored relic of the British-run railroad era, when trains once ran to Argentina's northern and northwestern provinces. Today, though, it receives mostly suburban commuter trains on the Mitre and San Martín lines.

To the northwest, foreign diplomatic missions acquired several impressive mansions that did not become state property, including the **Palacio Pereda** (Arroyo 1130), now occupied by the Brazilian Embassy. In March 2002, Israeli ambassadors from all over Latin America attended the dedication of the **Plaza Embajada de Israel** (Arroyo and Suipacha), where a 1992 car bomb destroyed the embassy that had occupied the site since 1950. The embassy's outlines are still visible on the wall of the building next door, while 22 freshly planted trees commemorate the diplomatic personnel and passersby who lost their lives.

South of Plaza San Martín are a handful of other landmarks, most notably the Beaux-Arts **Centro Naval** (Naval Center, 1914) at Avenida Córdoba and Florida; the nautical-theme doors were the work of architects Jacques Dunant and Luis Gastón Mallet. Literary great Jorge Luis Borges resided in the apartment building at **Maipú 994,** immediately south of the Museo de Armas. Across Avenida 9 de Julio, opposite Plaza Lavalle at the corner of Libertad, the sumptuous plateresque **Teatro Nacional Cervantes** (1921) is one of the capital's most important theater venues; state-run, it also houses the **Museo Nacional del Teatro** (National Theater Museum).

# Recoleta and Barrio Norte     Map 6

Once a bucolic outlier of the capital, Recoleta urbanized rapidly after the 1870s yellow fever outbreaks, when upper-class *porteños* concluded that low-lying San Telmo was too unhealthy for their families. Originally the site of a Franciscan convent (1716), the neighborhood is internationally known for the Cementerio de la Recoleta (Recoleta Cemetery, 1822), whose elaborate crypts and mausoleums cost more than many, if not most, *porteño* houses and apartments.

### BIBLIOTECA NACIONAL

Agüero 2502, tel. 011/4808-6000,
www.bibnal.edu.ar
**HOURS:** Mon.-Fri. 9 A.M.-8 P.M., Sat.-Sun. noon-7 P.M.

On the site of the former presidential residence (which moved to the northern suburb of Olivos in 1958), Italian architect Clorindo Testa's national library is a concrete monolith whose construction took more than three decades before its formal inauguration in 1992. Nearly two decades later, it's showing plenty of wear and tear, in part because its pathways and pyramids have proved a serendipitous godsend to skateboarders and stunt bikers.

Still, the library makes a major contribution to the capital's cultural life, hosting lectures by literary figures, exhibits by local artists, and major expositions like 2002's "Evita, una vida, una historia, un mito"—a remarkably thorough and thoroughly remarkable retrospective on Evita's life and influence, on the 50th anniversary of her death. On the other hand, its administration has been chaotic and priceless items have disappeared in recent years.

The library website has a regularly updated events calendar. There are free guided tours Monday–Friday at 3 P.M. through the Asociación Protectores de la Biblioteca Nacional (tel. 011/4806-9764, apbn@netizen.com.ar). There are no tours from mid-December to early March, however.

### BUENOS AIRES GRAFF

Charcas and Sánchez de Bustamante,
www.bagraff.com

For spontaneous and contemporary work, see the elaborate spray-can street art by Buenos Aires Graff covering the walls from the corner of Charcas and Sánchez de Bustamante; its own work has been vandalized, though.

According to legend, Evita Perón's ghost roams the stacks at Biblioteca Nacional, the national library built on the site of Juan Perón's demolished presidential palace.

SIGHTS

## CASA MUSEO RICARDO ROJAS

Charcas 2837, tel. 011/4824-4039
**HOURS:** Mon.-Fri. 10 A.M.-5 P.M., Sat. 1-5 P.M., Sun.
10 A.M.-2 P.M.
**COST:** US$0.35

Ricardo Rojas (1882–1957) was a poet, essayist, and playwright who, unlike many
Argentine intellectuals who saw their society as a struggle between civilization and
barbarism, tried to reconcile indigenous and
immigrant aspects of South American development. Perhaps because of his provincial origins in the Andean northwestern city
of Tucumán, he considered highland South
America's pre-Columbian civilizations equal
to those of Europe—an attitude rare among
Argentines.

Rojas's 1929 house, designed by architect
Angel Guido to the author's specifications,
incorporates elements from both traditions.
Its facade is a colonial-style replica of the
Tucumán house in which the country now
known as Argentina declared its independence
in 1815. Yet Rojas consciously incorporated
Incaic ornamentation into the building design,
according to his *doctrina euríndica* (Euro-
Indian doctrine), which posited a harmonious
fusion of indigenous, Hispanic, creole, and
cosmopolitan influences.

Donated to the state by Rojas's wife Julieta
Quinteros a year after the author's death, the
house features an impressively decorated vestibule, a patio embellished with bas-reliefs
of Incan and Spanish colonial origins, and a
Cuzco-style balcony. The colonial-style furniture is of dark polished wood.

Admission includes a guided tour conducted
by motivated, congenial personnel. As of press
time, it was undergoing a major restoration, so
hours and other information could change.

## ◖ CEMENTERIO DE LA RECOLETA

Junín 1790, tel. 011/4803-1594
**HOURS:** Daily 8 A.M.-6 P.M.
**COST:** Free

For the quick and the dead alike, Recoleta is
Buenos Aires's most prestigious address. The
roster of residents within its cemetery walls

Boxer Luis Angel Firpo, who nearly beat
Jack Dempsey in Madison Square Garden,
was buried in Cementerio de la Recoleta
thanks to influential benefactors in the
Martínez de Hoz family.

© WAYNE BERNHARDSON

represents wealth and power as surely as the
inhabitants of surrounding Francophile mansions and luxury apartment towers hoard their
assets in overseas bank accounts. Arguably,
the cemetery is even more exclusive than the
neighborhood—enough cash can buy an impressive residence, but not a surname like
Alvear, Anchorena, Mitre, Pueyrredón, or
Sarmiento.

Seen from the roof of the Centro Cultural
Recoleta immediately to the east, the cemetery
seems exactly what it is—an orderly necropolis
of narrow alleyways lined by ornate mausoleums and crypts that mimic the architectural
styles of Buenos Aires's early-20th-century
belle epoque. Crisscrossed by a few wide diagonals but with little greenery, it's a densely populated area that receives hordes of Argentine and
foreign tourists.

Many, if not most, go to pat the crypt of
Eva Perón, who overcame humble origins

with a relentless ambition that brought her to the pinnacle of political power with her husband, general and president Juan Perón, before her sudden and painful death from cancer in 1952. Even Juan Perón, who lived until 1974 but spent most of his post-Evita years in exile, failed to qualify for Recoleta and, after spending decades in the more democratic Cementerio de la Chacarita, now reposes in a custom crypt in the suburb of San Vicente.

There were other ways into Recoleta, though. One unlikely tomb is that of boxer Luis Angel Firpo (1894–1960), the "Wild Bull of the Pampas," who nearly defeated Jack Dempsey for the world heavyweight championship in New York in 1923. Firpo, though, had pull—one of his sponsors was Félix Bunge, a powerful landowner whose family owns some of the cemetery's most ornate constructions.

The economic crisis of recent years has had an impact on one of the world's grandest graveyards. Even casual visitors will notice that more than a few mausoleums have fallen into disrepair, as once-moneyed families can no longer afford their maintenance. Municipal authorities, recognizing the cemetery's importance to tourism, have intensified overdue repairs to sidewalks and the most significant sculptures, and improvements are noticeable.

Many private travel agencies offer guided tours on demand; the municipal tourist office sponsors occasional free weekend tours. Robert Wright, a U.S. citizen resident in Buenos Aires, has produced the best map of the cemetery, on sale for US$7 through his website (www.urbex.com.ar); if all goes well with the bureaucracy, they should also be on sale at the cemetery entrance.

Flanking the cemetery is the colonial **Iglesia de Nuestra Señora de Pilar** (1732), a Jesuit-built baroque church that's a national historical monument. Surrounding them are sizable green spaces, including **Plaza Intendente Alvear** and **Plaza Francia,** the latter home to a growing Sunday crafts fair that's steadily advancing toward the cemetery; there are also many street performers and a legion of *paseaperros* (professional dog

walkers), some with a dozen or more canines under their control.

Other landmarks and attractions scattered around the cemetery include the crumbling neo-Gothic **Facultad de Ingeniería,** which fills an entire block fronting on Avenida Las Heras between Azcuénaga and Cantilo.

## FUNDACIÓN INTERNACIONAL JORGE LUIS BORGES

Dr. T.M. de Anchorena 1660, tel. 011/4822-8340

Jorge Luis Borges's widow María Kodama established the Fundación Internacional Jorge Luis Borges, which offers a series of Borges-focused city tours. The innovative paintings of Borges's close friend Alejandro Schulz Solari are on display at the **Museo Xul Solar** (Laprida 1212, tel. 011/4824-3302).

## MUSEO NACIONAL DE BELLAS ARTES

Av. del Libertador 1473, tel. 011/4803-0802, www.mnba.org.ar

**HOURS:** Tues.-Fri. 12:30-8:30 P.M., Sat.-Sun. and holidays 9:30 A.M.-8:30 P.M.; guided tours Tues.-Sun. 5 and 6 P.M.

**COST:** Free

Argentina's traditional fine arts museum mixes works by well-known European artists, such as Degas, El Greco, Goya, Kandinsky, Klee, Monet, Picasso, Renoir, Rodin, Tintoretto, Toulouse-Lautrec, and Van Gogh, with their Argentine counterparts, including Antonio Berni, Ernesto de la Cárcova, León Ferrari, Raquel Forner, Cándido López, Benito Quinquela Martín, Prilidiano Pueyrredón, and Lino Spilimbergo.

In total, it houses about 11,000 oils, watercolors, sketches, engravings, tapestries, and sculptures. Among the most interesting are the works of López, an army officer who re-created scenes from the Paraguayan war (1864–1870) in a series of minutely detailed oils, despite losing his right arm to a grenade.

Oddly enough, architect Julio Dormald designed the building, in a prime location on the Avenida del Libertador's north side, as a pumphouse and filter plant for the city waterworks in the 1870s; the renowned architect Alejandro

© WAYNE BERNHARDSON

**Museo Nacional de Bellas Artes had an inauspicious beginning as a pumphouse and filter plant.**

Bustillo adapted it to its current purpose in the early 1930s. The collections are generally stronger on classic than contemporary art.

Immediately behind the museum, the **Asociación Amigos del Museo Nacional de Bellas Artes** (Av. Figueroa Alcorta 2280, tel. 011/4803-4062 or 011/4804-9290, www.aamnba.com.ar) regularly sponsors well-attended interviews with well-known Argentine artists, such as Guillermo Kuitca, Juan Carlos Distéfano, Aldo Sessa, and others. Check their Spanish-English website for the most current events, which are normally free of charge.

## PALACIO PIZZURNO
Pizzurno 935

Facing Plaza Rodríguez Peña, one of Barrio Norte's most striking buildings is the Palacio Pizzurno, now occupied by the Ministerio de Cultura y Educación (Culture and Education Ministry). Originally built as a girls' school, the building owes its blend of Spanish and German styles to architects Hans and Carlos Altgelt. Officially known as the Palacio Sarmiento after the education-oriented 19th-century president, it takes its popular name from three career teachers, all brothers, for whom the block-long street behind it was named.

# Palermo
Map 7

Buenos Aires's largest barrio, Palermo enjoys the city's widest open spaces, thanks to 19th-century dictator Juan Manuel de Rosas, whose private estate stretched almost from Recoleta all the way to Belgrano, between present-day Avenida del Libertador and the Río de la Plata. Beaten at the battle of Caseros by Entre Ríos caudillo Justo José de Urquiza, a onetime confederate, Rosas spent the rest of his life in British exile. The property passed into the public domain and, ironically enough, the sprawling **Parque Tres de Febrero** takes its name from the date of Rosas's defeat in 1852.

Once part of the capital's unsavory *arrabales* (margins), its street corners populated by stylish but capricious *malevos* (bullies) immortalized in the short stories of Jorge Luis Borges, Palermo hasn't entirely superseded that reputation—in some areas, poorly lighted streets can still make visitors uneasy. Yet it also has exclusive neighborhoods, such as **Barrio Parque,** also known as **Palermo Chico,** across Avenida del Libertador immediately north of Recoleta.

Across Avenida del Libertador from Barrio Parque, the **Botánico** is an upper-middle-class neighborhood that takes its name from the **Jardín Botánico Carlos Thays,** though it also abuts the **Jardín Zoológico** (zoo) and **Parque Las Heras** (the former site of a federal prison). For a glimpse of what the neighborhood used to look like, visit the **Edificio La Colorada** (1911; Cabello 3791), a 24-unit apartment building of imported British brick; created for officials on the British-run railways, it features a skylighted central patio that was unusual in its time.

South of Parque Las Heras and across Avenida Santa Fe (one of Palermo's main arterials), **Alto Palermo** is a densely built area that has given its name to one of the city's major shopping centers. The real center of action, though, is slightly northwest in **Palermo Viejo,** at **Plaza Serrano** (also known as **Plazoleta Cortázar**). Jorge Luis Borges set his

poem "La Fundación Mítica de Buenos Aires" (The Mythical Foundation of Buenos Aires) on the block bounded by Guatemala, Serrano, Paraguay, and Gurruchaga.

Palermo Viejo further subdivides into **Palermo SoHo,** a trendy term to describe the area south of Avenida Juan B. Justo, and the more northerly **Palermo Hollywood,** where many *porteño* TV and radio producers have located their studios. Shaded by sycamores, many of Palermo Viejo's streets still contain low-slung *casas chorizos* (sausage houses) on deep, narrow lots. Picturesque *pasajes* (alleyways), such as Russel, Santa Rosa, and Soria, with their squat houses, were cozy centerpieces of architect Antonio Buschiazzo's Villa Alvear *microbarrio* that now hosts hyperactive nightlife.

At the northern end of Palermo, overlapping with Belgrano, **Las Cañitas** is a gastronomic and nightlife area challenging Palermo Viejo among *porteño* partygoers.

## CENTRO CULTURAL ISLÁMICO REY FAHD

Av. Bullrich 55, tel. 011/4899-1144, www.ccislamicoreyfahd.org.ar

**HOURS:** Tours Tues. and Thurs. noon–1 P.M.

**COST:** Free

Built with Saudi funds on three hectares of land donated by former President Carlos Menem's scandal-ridden administration, Buenos Aires's Islamic cultural center is a pharaonic monument to megalomania. Holding up to 2,300 worshippers in a high-rent neighborhood, it rarely draws more than a few hundred to Friday prayers. Unless Buenos Aires becomes the Mecca of a South American hajj, it will remain a questionable project, utterly out of proportion with its surroundings.

According to its Saudi director, though, the mosque, its ancillary constructions, and its grounds are intended to become South America's major Muslim cultural center. Unfortunately, its tedious guided tours only

## THE *PORTEÑO* PSYCHE

When grad student Mariano Ben Plotkin returned from Berkeley to Buenos Aires on vacation, his aunt asked him about the cost of living in California, which she found astonishingly cheap. Asking him for an item-by-item accounting, the *porteña* psychoanalyst listened patiently and, when he finished, she commented, "Oh, now I understand – there you don't need to budget for psychoanalysis."

New Yorkers may chatter about their therapists, but *porteños* can more than match them – in Buenos Aires, psychoanalysis and other therapies are not for the upper and upper-middle classes alone. During registration at the Universidad de Buenos Aires medical school, a proliferation of flyers offers psychoanalysis and psychotherapy with UBA professionals – the first session free – for individuals, couples, and groups. Flyers in the Subte assert that "Asking for help is the start of solving the problem" and tempts commuters with "unlimited sessions." Nervous fliers at the international airport can talk to a shrink before boarding.

A few years back, the obsession with therapy may have been a function of economic crisis, and even the former *corralito* banking restrictions were interpreted in that context. According to an early 2002 interview by National Public Radio's Martin Kaste, a Freudian psychiatrist made the case that "Money has a certain symbolic equivalence to the penis. People put their money in the bank, but at the moment they want to withdraw it they lose their money, so this produces a castration anxiety."

Another commented that "sexual desire has also been caught in the *corralito* – men worry about lack of desire and premature ejaculation, and women are unable to have orgasms." The 2002 Festival de Tango even included a session on *Tango de Autoayuda* (Self-Help Tango).

In a different context, angry real-estate brokers picketed the residence of caretaker president Eduardo Duhalde, himself a former realtor, but not necessarily in the hope that they would get any relief for a frozen real-estate market. Rather, proclaimed one of the protestors, "This turned into our therapy, a place to set our anguish free."

Therapy, though, is not just a function of the times; it has a long history here, beginning with the 1930s arrival of Jewish refugees from Europe. Ben Plotkin himself has chronicled this

---

offer generalities about Islam, with little about Argentina's Muslim community and even less about this particular mosque's origins.

South America's largest Islamic center is open for guided tours only. Female visitors must put on tunics—some women have shown up in shorts and other clothing that would be considered truly offensive in the Muslim world—but need not cover their heads. Tours are suspended if it rains.

### FONDO NACIONAL DE ARTES
Plaza Grand Bourg

Across the street from Instituto Nacional Sanmartiniano, dating from 1929, the headquarters of the Fondo Nacional de Artes (National Arts Fund, Rufino Elizalde 2831) once belonged to writer Victoria Ocampo. Against architect Alejandro Bustillo's better instincts—he's famous for the Andean rusticism of San Carlos de Bariloche's civic center—Ocampo persuaded him to create this Le Corbusier–inspired rationalist residence for her. Le Corbusier (whose only Argentine building is in the city of La Plata) approved of it. The building is not open to the public for tours.

### INSTITUTO NACIONAL SANMARTINIANO
Plaza Grand Bourg

Barrio Parque boasts some of Buenos Aires's highest property values. One of its landmarks is the Instituto Nacional Sanmartiniano, housing the research institute on national hero José de San Martín's life. Built to mimic San Martín's home-in-exile in Boulogne sur Mer, France—but a third larger—it no longer serves as a museum, since its collections have moved to San Telmo's Museo Histórico Nacional.

tale in *Freud on the Pampas: the Emergence and Development of a Psychoanalytic Culture in Argentina* (Stanford University Press, 2001).

Many of Buenos Aires's thousands of shrinks practice in Palermo's so-called Villa Freud, an area bounded by Avenida Santa Fe, Avenida Las Heras, Avenida Scalabrini Ortiz, and Avenida Coronel Díaz. Many businesses play on this reputation – patients can top off their medications at, and even get home delivery from, **Farmacia Villa Freud** (Medrano 1773, 011/4825-2612). One online magazine specializes in listings for professional office rentals. Even acting classes are often exercises in therapy.

Several institutions contribute to the capital's therapeutic ambience. The **Asociación Psicoanalítica Argentina** (Rodríguez Peña 1674, 011/4812-3518, www.apa.org.ar) organized a month-long exhibition on *Psychoanalysis, Culture and Crisis* at the Microcentro's Centro Cultural Borges. Buenos Aires's **Museo de Psicología Horacio Piñeiro** (Av. Independencia 3063, 3rd fl., 011/4957-4110, Mon.-Fri. 1-3 P.M., plus Tues. and Thurs. 10 A.M.-noon) recounts the experimental efforts of an early-20th-century pioneer.

The locus of Villa Freud, though, is the bookstore **Librería Paidós** (Av. Las Heras 3741, 011/4801-2860, www.libreriapaidos.com.ar), the intellectual community center for shrinks, inconspicuously located in the Galería Las Heras. It now has a Barrio Norte branch (Av. Santa Fe 1685, 011/4812-6685) as well.

While *porteños* and other Argentines continued to feel the need for therapy, their Chilean neighbors seemed briefly to have had the last word. In the midst of the 2002 crisis, a satirical Santiago newspaper published a short note under the headline "New Foundation, Argentines Anonymous, Created." According to the article, "A group whose members hope to rehabilitate themselves from their nationality met yesterday for the first time. At the beginning, each one must announce his name and then continue, 'I am an Argentine.'"

Since then, though, matters have improved both economically and, apparently, psychologically. One measure of improvement may be the fact that Plaza Güemes's Bar Sigi, a favorite *confitería* with therapists and patients alike for its Freudian ambience, closed in early 2008. Its replacement is a standard Italian restaurant.

## JARDÍN BOTÁNICO CARLOS THAYS
Av. Santa Fe 3951, tel. 011/4831-4527
**HOURS:** Summer daily 9 A.M.-7 P.M.; winter daily 9 A.M.-6 P.M.
**COST:** Free

One of Buenos Aires's shadiest spots, this botanical garden boasts a wide variety of trees from around Argentina and the world. Originally part of Parque Tres de Febrero, it dates from 1892, when French landscape architect Carlos Thays requested its separation from the park to create a roughly eight-hectare space bounded by Avenida Santa Fe, República Árabe Siria, and Avenida Las Heras.

Thays was successful enough that when U.S. conservationist John Muir visited in 1911, he found the gardens "well laid out for future development. The park, by its tree life, shows the fertility of the soil in this country. The begum tree grows better in Palermo than in some parts of Australia, where it is native."

More than 30 sculptures dot the garden, including those of Thays and Patagonia explorer Francisco P. Moreno; near the Árabe Siria side stands one of the last of the hideous grottos placed around city parks by 1880s mayor Torcuato de Alvear.

The city's Dirección General de Espacios Verdes also operates a gardening school and a specialized library here. The main entrance to the fenced and gated triangular garden is at the Plaza Italia end of the property, but the mid-block entrances on Árabe Siria and Santa Fe are usually open as well. Guided tours take place weekends and holidays at 10:30 A.M. and 3:30 P.M. The Friday tour is available in English.

## JARDÍN JAPONÉS

Avs. Casares and Adolfo Berro, tel. 011/4804-4922, www.jardinjapones.com.ar
**HOURS:** Daily 10 A.M.–6 P.M.; free guided tours Sat.–Sun. and holidays 3 P.M.
**COST:** US$1.60 adult, US$0.35 child 6–10, free under 6

An oasis of calm in an often chaotic city, Buenos Aires's Japanese garden opened in 1967, when Crown Prince Akihito and Princess Michiko visited Argentina. Administratively part of the Jardín Botánico, it enjoys better maintenance and, because there's chicken wire between the exterior hedges and the interior fence, it's full of chirping birds rather than feral cats.

Like Japanese gardens elsewhere, it mimics nature in its large koi pond (cheap fish food is available), *taki* (waterfall), and *shinzen jima* (isle of the gods), but also culture in its *sambashi* (pier), *tourou* (lighthouse), *yatsuhashi* (bridge of fortune), *taiko bashi* (curved bridge), *tobi ishi* (path of stones), and *yusanju no to* (tower of thirteen eaves). There is also a *vivero kadan* (plant nursery) with bonsai trees for sale at reasonable prices.

In addition, the garden contains a **Monumento al Sudor del Inmigrante Japonés** (Monument to the Effort of the Japanese Immigrant), erected during the military regime of 1976–1983 (a plaque bearing the name of then dictator Jorge Rafael Videla as "president" has since been replaced). Argentina has a small but well-established Japanese community in the capital and in the suburban community of Escobar.

In addition to the garden features, there is a fine *confitería*/restaurant and an exhibition hall.

## JARDÍN ZOOLÓGICO EDUARDO LADISLAO HOLMBERG

Avs. Las Heras and Sarmiento, tel. 011/4011-9900, www.zoobuenosaires.com.ar
**HOURS:** Mon.–Fri. 10 A.M.–6 P.M., Sat.–Sun. 10 A.M.–6:30 P.M.
**COST:** US$2.25 adult, free child under 13, free retirees and people with disabilities Tues.–Fri.

When Palermo was his private preserve, dictator Juan Manuel de Rosas kept his own collection of exotic animals. When, according to one legend, his pet jaguar ran in fright from a group of female visitors, he sarcastically suggested that it was because the animal "had never seen so much ugliness in one place." In the not-too-distant past, because of political cronyism, one could have made a similar comment about the zoo; since the 1990s, though, the once-decrepit facility passed into private hands and, rejuvenated, became a facility that is once again a favorite with *porteño* families.

What is now the zoo, an 18-hectare area bounded by Avenida Sarmiento, Avenida Las Heras, República de India, and Avenida del Libertador, was separated from Parque Tres de Febrero in 1888. Its first director was Eduardo Ladislao Holmberg, who saw it primarily as a research facility, but by the early 20th century it was drawing more than 150,000 recreational visitors per year. From the early 1920s, authorities built decorative fountains and lakes, a monkey island, tanks for hippopotami and crocodiles, an aviary, and other large enclosures in lieu of cages and pits.

After the 1940s, there were various projects to shift the deteriorating facility to the outskirts of town, given the potential real estate value of such a large property in a prime neighborhood, but local objections in the 1980s kept the zoo in the present location. Today, it holds some 2,500 animals of about 350 different reptile, mammal, and bird species; it also includes sculptures of important figures in Argentine natural history, including Domingo F. Sarmiento, Florentino Ameghino, Clemente Onelli, and William Henry Hudson. For children, there are a *granja infanta* (petting zoo), a *calesita* (merry-go-round), a *trencito* (miniature train), and a *laberinto* (maze).

In addition to the standard enclosures, the zoo also features a reptile house, a tropical rainforest exhibit, and an aquarium that includes a sea lion pool (with deafeningly inappropriate hip-hop). The concessionaire has repaired historic structures within the park, but it could do more; and despite warnings, the public toss unsuitable food to the animals.

The Jardín Zoológico has entrances opposite

Plaza Italia and at the intersection of Avenidas Sarmiento and Libertador. A US$4.50 "passport" includes access to the aquarium, the reptile house, and the tropical rainforest exhibit.

### ◖ MUSEO DE ARTE LATINOAMERICANO DE BUENOS AIRES (MALBA)

Av. Figueroa Alcorta 3415, tel. 011/4808-6500, www.malba.org.ar

**HOURS:** Wed. noon-9 P.M., Thurs.-Mon. noon-8 P.M.

**COST:** US$4, US$2 senior; free Wed.

Buenos Aires's newest, most deluxe art museum is a striking steel-and-glass structure dedicated exclusively to Latin American art rather than the European-oriented collections of so many Argentine art museums. Designed by Córdoba architects Gastón Atelman, Martín Fourcade, and Alfredo Tapia, the building devotes one entire floor to the private collection of businessman Eduardo F. Constantini, the motivating force behind the museum's creation; the 2nd floor offers traveling exhibitions, often from foreign countries.

The most famous works are by the Mexican artists Frida Kahlo and Diego Rivera, but there are also works by Antonio Berni, Chilean Robert Matta, Uruguayan Pedro Figari, and others. Since the 2002 economic crisis, MALBA curator Marcelo Pacheco has focused primarily on contemporary Argentine art, both for the museum's own exhibitions and those it sends abroad, rather than importing megabucks exhibits from overseas.

### MUSEO DE MOTIVOS ARGENTINOS JOSÉ HERNÁNDEZ

Av. del Libertador 2373, tel. 011/4803-2384, www.mujose.org.ar

**HOURS:** Tues.-Fri. 1-7 P.M., Sat.-Sun. and holidays 10 A.M.-8 P.M.

**COST:** US$1; free Sun.

It's tempting to call this the "museum of irony," as Argentina's most self-consciously gaucho-oriented institution sits smack in the middle of what may be the country's single most urbane, affluent, and cosmopolitan neighborhood, also

© WAYNE BERNHARDSON

The Fundación Constantini's Museo de Arte Latinoamericano de Buenos Aires (MALBA) is the region's top modern art museum.

home to many international diplomatic missions. Named for the author of the epic *gauchesco* poem *Martín Fierro*, it specializes in rural Argentiniana, regional history, and occasional special exhibitions on similar themes.

Even more ironically, the land-rich oligarch Félix Bunge built the house, a derivative French-Italianate building with marble staircases and other extravagant features. Originally known as the Museo Familiar Gauchesco de Carlos Guillermo Daws after the family who donated its contents, it became the Museo de Motivos Populares Argentinos (Museum of Argentine Popular Motifs) José Hernández. The 1976–1983 military regime excised the inflammatory word "popular" (which in this context also means people's) from its official name. Thus, perhaps, it could justify depicting Argentine gentry like the Martínez de Hoz family—one of whose scions was the dictatorship's economy minister—as archetypes of a bucolic open-range lifestyle.

That said, the museum has worthwhile exhibits, ranging from magnificent silverwork and vicuña textiles created by contemporary artisans to pre-Columbian pottery, indigenous crafts, and even a typical *pulpería,* or rural store. Translations of Hernández's famous poem, some in Asian and Eastern European languages, occupy a prominent spot.

The museum is normally closed in February, and on New Year's, Good Friday, May 1, and Christmas.

## ◖ MUSEO EVA PERÓN

Lafinur 2988, tel. 011/4807-9433,
www.museoevita.org
**HOURS:** Tues.-Sun. 11 A.M.-7 P.M.
**COST:** US$3

At her most combative, to the shock and disgust of neighbors, Eva Perón chose the prosperous Botánico neighborhood for the **Hogar de Tránsito No. 2,** a shelter for single mothers from the provinces. Even more galling, her Fundación de Ayuda Social María Eva Duarte de Perón acquired architect Estanislao Pirovano's imposing three-story mansion, built for José María Carabassa in

---

## PALERMOS'S FAMOUS PRIVATE RESIDENCES

Borges himself lived at **José Luis Borges (formerly Serrano) 2135,** a street renamed for the literary great (though still marked by a plaque, the house here replaced Borges's original residence). Likewise, the nondescript modern apartment building at **Aráoz 2180** shares the onetime address of legendary revolutionary Ernesto Guevara, but is not the house in which "Che" lived. One of the most interesting private residences is the **Casa Jorge García** (Gorriti 5142), whose garage facade features Martiniano Arce's *filete* caricatures of the García family.

---

1923, to house the women in their transition to the capital.

Since Evita's death in 1952, the neighborhood has undergone steady if undramatic change, as middle- to upper-middle-class apartment blocks have replaced most of the elegant single-family houses and distinctive apartment buildings that once housed the *porteño* elite (many of whom have since moved to Zona Norte suburbs, such as Olivos and San Isidro). Fifty years later, on the July 26th anniversary of her death—supporting Tomás Eloy Martínez's contention that Argentines are "cadaver cultists," celebrating their heroes on the day of their death, rather than on the day of their birth—Evita's great niece María Carolina Rodríguez officially opened the Museo Eva Perón "to spread the life, work and ideology of María Eva Duarte de Perón."

Five years in the making, this is the first Argentine museum to focus specifically on a woman. The 2002 economic crisis and *corralito* banking restrictions placed much of the work on volunteer shoulders, but since then it has expanded coverage to include video footage from both her film and political careers.

What it still lacks, as yet, is a critical

perspective that would make it possible, again in Rodríguez's words, "to understand who this woman was in the 1940s and 1950s, who made such a difference in the lives of Argentines"—a goal not necessarily consistent with her other stated aims, which do more to promote Evita's iconic image. Rather than a balanced account of her life, the museum is an homage that divides Evita's life into phases: Eva Duarte (her childhood and adolescence, acting career, and first encounters with Juan Perón), Eva Perón (marriage to Perón, becoming Argentina's first lady, and the Spanish journey that brought her international attention), Evita (as her political influence grew through the Fundación Eva Perón), and her death and legacy.

All this material is professionally presented but, with a couple minor exceptions, it sidesteps the issue of personality cults that typified both Evita and her husband. One minor exception is the display of the Anglo-Argentine author Mary Main's *The Woman with the Whip,* published in Argentina as *La Mujer del Látigo* under the pseudonym María Flores.

While this hatchet-job biography at least suggests Evita's polarizing effect on Argentine society, the museum would do well to display excerpts and other similar materials to suggest how her opponents viewed her. As long as the curators refrain from presenting the opponents' case, the exhibits here tell barely half the Evita story.

The museum also contains a library, a graphic archive, and a film and video library, open Monday–Friday 2–8 P.M. The museum shop has a selection of Evita souvenirs, and there's a café/restaurant as well.

### ◖ PARQUE TRES DE FEBRERO
Avs. Sarmiento and Pte. Figueroa Alcorta

Argentine elites got their revenge on José Manuel de Rosas with the creation of Parque Tres de Febrero. Not only does the equestrian **Monumento a Urquiza** (Avs. Sarmiento and Figueroa Alcorta) commemorate Rosas's conqueror at the battle of Caseros, but Unitarist President Domingo F. Sarmiento's name graces one of the park's main avenues. Sarmiento,

Rosas's implacable enemy, oversaw the estate's transformation into a park during his presidency (1868–1874).

In the early 20th century, British diplomat James Bryce described what the area had become:

> On fine afternoons, there is a wonderful turnout of carriages drawn by handsome horses, and still more of costly motor cars, in the principal avenues of the Park; they press so thick that vehicles are often jammed together for fifteen or twenty minutes, unable to move on. Nowhere in the world does one get a stronger impression of exuberant wealth and extravagance. The Park itself, called Palermo, lies on the edge of the city towards the river, and is approached by a well-designed and well-planted avenue.

Today, by contrast, the park is a more democratic destination. There are no more carriages and the few automobiles go slower than elsewhere in the city. On weekends, in particular, it gets plenty of picnickers, walkers, joggers, in-line skaters, and bicyclists who enjoy its verdant serenity and other recreational and cultural attractions.

Among those attractions are the **Jardín Japonés** (Japanese Gardens, Avs. Casares and Adolfo Berro) opposite Plaza Alemania; the **Planetario Galileo Galilei** (Av. Sarmiento and Belisario Roldán); the **Rosedal** (Rose Garden, Avs. Iraola and Presidente Pedro Montt); the nearby **Museo de Artes Plásticas Eduardo Sívori** (Av. Infanta Isabel 555), a painting and sculpture museum; the **Hipódromo Argentino** (racetrack, Avs. del Libertador and Dorrego); and the **Campo Argentino de Polo** (polo grounds, directly across Av. del Libertador from the Hipódromo).

At the park's northeast corner, the **Nuevo Circuito KDT** is a velodrome where cyclists can work out without worrying about the pace of motor-vehicle traffic. To its north, beyond park boundaries, the landmark **Club de Pescadores** sits at the end of a long pier extending into the river. The park's greatest drawback is the

# EVITA ON TOUR

© WAYNE BERNHARDSON

A plaque on the side of the Duarte family crypt honors Evita's memory at Cementerio de la Recoleta.

Eva Perón became famous for her 1947 visit to Europe when, representing an Argentina that emerged from WWII as an economic powerhouse, she helped legitimize a shaky Franco regime in Spain and, despite missteps, impressed other war-ravaged European countries with Argentina's potential. But even her death five years later did not stop her touring.

Millions of *porteños* said "adiós" to Evita in a funeral cortege that took hours to make its way up Avenida de Mayo from the Casa Rosada to the Congreso Nacional, where her corpse

lay in state before finding temporary repose in the headquarters of the Confederación General del Trabajo (CGT), the Peronist trade union. There, the enigmatic Spanish physician Pedro Ara gave the body a mummification treatment worthy of Lenin, in preparation for a monument to honor her legacy.

Evita remained at the CGT until 1955, when the vociferously anti-Peronist General Pedro Aramburu overthrew her husband, ordered her removed, and eventually (after a series of whistle stops that included a visit to an officer who apparently became infatuated with

proximity of **Aeroparque Jorge Newbery,** the city's domestic airport; its relocation, proposed but apparently stalled, would open up an even larger area to public use.

## ROSEDAL
Parque Tres de Febrero
Reached by a gracefully arching bridge over a narrow neck of the **Lago del Rosedal,** an artificial

the mummy) exiled her to a pseudonymous grave near Milan, Italy. For Aramburu, even Evita's cadaver was a symbolic reminder of Peronism's durability.

Despite banning the Peronist party, Aramburu had reason to worry. For many years, Argentines dared not even speak Perón's name, while the former strongman lived in luxury near Madrid. In 1970, though, as Argentine politics came undone in an era of revolutionary ferment, the left-wing Peronist Montoneros guerrillas kidnapped Aramburu and demanded to know Evita's whereabouts.

When Aramburu refused to answer, they executed him and issued a public statement that they would hold the retired general's body hostage until Evita was returned to "the people." A common slogan of the time was "Si Evita viviera, sería Montonera" (If Evita were alive, she would be a Montonera), but Perón himself detested the leftists – even as he cynically encouraged their activism to ease his return to power.

The police found Aramburu's body before the proposed postmortem prisoner-swap could take place, but a notary in whom Aramburu had confided came forward with information as to Evita's whereabouts. In September 1971, Perón was stunned when a truck bearing Evita's casket and mutilated corpse arrived at his Madrid residence; remarried to dancer María Estela (Isabelita) Martínez, he neither expected nor wanted any such thing. His bizarre spiritualist adviser José López Rega, though, used the opportunity to try to transfer Evita's essence into Isabelita's body, as the mummy reposed in the attic.

Perón returned to popular acclaim in 1973 – leaving Evita in Madrid – and was soon elected president with Isabelita as his

vice president. Meanwhile, the Montoneros once again kidnapped Aramburu – this time from his crypt in Recoleta cemetery – until Evita's return.

Angry but increasingly ill and senile, Perón died the following year, but now-president Isabelita flew Evita on a charter from Madrid to Buenos Aires and then sent her to the presidential residence at Olivos, north of the capital. The cadaver stayed there until March of 1976, when General Jorge Rafael Videla's brutal military junta overthrew Perón's living legacy.

Evita, for her part, finally achieved the "respectability" that she so resented throughout her rise to power. Though she was an illegitimate child who went by her mother's Basque surname Ibarguren, she landed in the family crypt of her father Juan Duarte (a provincial landowner) – only a short stroll from Aramburu's tomb.

Even that may not be the end of Evita's wanderings. In mid-2002, there were rumors of yet another move – to the Franciscan convent at Defensa and Alsina in San Telmo. (Ironically, the convent was set afire by Peronist mobs in 1955, and is also the place where her confessor Pedro Errecart is buried.)

Another possibility is Juan Perón's *quinta* (country house) in the southern suburb of San Vicente, where a new mausoleum would reunite the two (Perón moved there from Chacarita cemetery in 2006). Astonishingly, in the midst of Argentina's ongoing economic crisis, in 2003, caretaker president Eduardo Duhalde made this a priority, but it's languished for lack of funds and family objections. The major obstacle to the move, it seems, is that Peronist politicians like the idea better than the Duarte heirs do.

lake, Parque Tres de Febrero's rose garden contains a diversity of both bush roses and climbers on pergolas. Its southeast corner contains the **Jardín de los Poetas,** a sculpture garden of famous literary figures—mostly Spanish speakers, such as Argentina's Jorge Luis Borges and Alfonsina Storni and Guatemala's Miguel Angel Asturias, but also global greats, such as Shakespeare.

# Outer Barrios Map 8

Beyond its most touristed barrios, Buenos Aires has a variety of sights that range from relatively mundane to the morbid. Most are less easily accessible by Subte, but have regular *colectivo* (city bus) service.

## BELGRANO

Readily linked to central Buenos Aires by Subte, bus, and train, Belgrano remains a barrio apart. In fact, before becoming a barrio of the capital, it was a separate city and then, briefly in the 1880s, served as the country's capital. After the Buenos Aires provincial capital moved to the new city of La Plata, Buenos Aires became the federal capital and, in 1887, it absorbed Belgrano into the city.

Its main thoroughfare, Avenida Cabildo, is a disorientingly noisy commercial boulevard with a cluster of cinemas and theaters; the tree-lined streets immediately to the east contain most points of interest.

### IGLESIA NUESTRA SEÑORA DE LA INMACULADA CONCEPCIÓN

Vuelta de Obligado 2042, tel. 011/4783-8008
**HOURS:** Mon.-Sat. 7:30 A.M.-noon and 4-8:30 P.M., Sun. 7:30 A.M.-1:30 P.M. and 4-9:15 P.M.

Opposite Plaza Manuel Belgrano, the church colloquially known as "La Redonda" plays a key role in Ernesto Sábato's psychological novel *On Heroes and Tombs.* Marble columns support the circular dome, which is capped by a small belfry, while elaborate paintings and icons cover its walls.

### MUSEO DE ARTE ESPAÑOL ENRIQUE LARRETA

Av. Juramento 2291, tel. 011/4783-2640,
www.museos.buenosaires.gov.ar/larreta.htm
**HOURS:** Mon. and Wed.-Fri. 2-8 P.M., Sat.-Sun. and holidays 3-8 P.M.; guided tours Sun. 4 and 6 P.M.
**COST:** US$1; free Thurs.

When many Argentine writers were forging

Belgrano's Iglesia Nuestra Señora de la Inmaculada Concepción figures prominently in Ernesto Sábato's novel *On Heroes and Tombs.*

© WAYNE BERNHARDSON

# LA FERIA DE MATADEROS

*Gauchesco* traditions thrive in the weekend Feria de Mataderos, where city-bound *paisanos* (countrymen) and would-be *paisanos* immerse themselves in the nostalgia of the *campo*, or countryside. In addition to a diverse crafts selection, this spirited street fair features open-air *parrilladas* (mixed grills) and regional delicacies such as tamales, plus live music and dancing in rural styles such as *chamamé*, gaucho horseback races, and even – during Carnaval – a neighborhood *murga* (troupe) to kick off the season in the style of northwestern Jujuy province.

Despite some exaggeratedly nationalistic overtones, the Feria generates genuine enthusiasm. It dates from the mid-1980s under the sponsorship of a Jewish *porteña*, Sara Vinocur, who still directs it as the link between city authorities and neighborhood residents.

In the southwesterly barrio of Mataderos, in the streets surrounding the arcades of the former Mercado de Hacienda at Lisandro de la Torre and Avenida de los Corrales, the *feria* (www.feriademataderos.com.ar) is about an hour from the Microcentro by *colectivo* No. 180 and *ramal* (branch) 155 from Tucumán, Talcahuano, or Lavalle. In summer, it takes place 6 P.M.-midnight on Saturday; the rest of the year, it starts at 11 A.M. on Sunday.

a national literature, Enrique Larreta's novels evoked nostalgia for the Spanish motherland, and his Belgrano house and art collection reflect that orientation. Most exhibits either come from Spain or reflect Spanish traditions: polychrome religious carvings and *retablos* (altarpieces), *bargueños* (gilt boxes), tapestries, carpets, braziers, ceramics, paintings, and furniture from the 13th to the 20th centuries. The 19th-century fans, painted with elaborate landscapes, are exceptional.

The museum's rooms are large enough to house an enormous number of artifacts without seeming cluttered. Look for special exhibitions, such as the display of regional costumes given to Evita Perón during her 1947 Spanish tour—which took place at a time when Francisco Franco's dictatorship was desperately seeking legitimacy after the defeat of Nazi Germany and Fascist Italy, which had supported his uprising against the Spanish Republic in the 1930s.

The grounds are no less impressive, with formal Andalusian gardens and an open-air theater that offers dramatic and musical performances, including tango, in the summer months. The theater entrance is on the Vuelta de Obligado side of the building.

Like many other museums, it usually closes the entire month of January.

## MUSEO HISTÓRICO SARMIENTO
Cuba 2079, tel. 011/4783-7555,
www.museosarmiento.gov.ar
**HOURS:** Mon.-Fri. and Sun. 1-5:30 P.M., Dec.-Mar. closed Sun.; guided tours Sun. 3 P.M.
**COST:** US$0.35; free Thurs.; tours US$1.50

When President Nicolás Avellaneda felt insecure in Buenos Aires in mid-1880, he briefly shifted the government's executive and legislative branches to Juan A. Buschiazzo's Italian Renaissance building (1874), originally designed for the Municipalidad de Belgrano. After the congress declared Buenos Aires the federal capital and conflict subsided, the building returned to municipal authorities until 1938, when it became a museum honoring Argentine educator and president (1868–1874) Domingo Faustino Sarmiento—on the 50th anniversary of his death.

Though Sarmiento never lived here, the exhibits contain many of his personal possessions and a model of his birthplace, in San Juan province. He detested provincial warlords like Rosas and Facundo Quiroga, after whom he titled his polemic *Facundo: Or, Civilization and Barbarism*, still used as a text in many Latin American studies courses in English-speaking countries.

In addition to Sarmiento's life, the museum includes displays on Avellaneda and the near civil war of the 1880s that resulted in Buenos

# THE OTHER SOUTH

According to Jorge Luis Borges, the south of Buenos Aires is the key to understanding the city, but few foreigners get to know its unassuming working-class neighborhoods. Such Barrios as Barracas, Nueva Pompeya, Parque Patricios, and Boedo may lack San Telmo's colonial romance, La Boca's garish colors, and Recoleta's haughty chic, but they tell much more about the way most *porteños* work and live – even if reaching their spread-out sights is more challenging than elsewhere in the city.

In **Barracas,** immediately south of San Telmo, the emblematic British biscuit factory **Bagley** (Av. Montes de Oca 169) was once a household word that, after its acquisition by a French multinational, now stands empty despite demonstrations against its closure at the end of 2004. Not so far away, the former chocolate-maker **Aguila** (Herrera 803) suffered the same fate before housing a failed Home Depot and then, more successfully, its Argentine counterpart Easy. Fortunately, despite the change in function, the recyclers preserved Aguila's classic facade.

With the neighborhood's working-class history, it's not surprising that left-of-center political movements would take root here. In 1904, Alfredo Palacios became the first Socialist deputy elected to the Argentine congress; the architecturally idiosyncratic party headquarters **Casa del Pueblo de Barracas** (Alvarado 1963) was his legacy to the barrio. Socialists here have been linked with Freemasonry, as in the headquarters of the **Hijos del Trabajo** (San Antonio 814), also known as the Casa Egipcia (Egypt House); dating from 1890, the *casa chorizo* (sausage house) was recently restored to its original form, intricate design, and wild colors. Twin sphinxes guard the doorway lintel of its outlandish facade.

British capital built the railways that connected Buenos Aires with its suburbs and the rest of the country, influencing life immeasurably. In some instances, this influence came in the form of landmark architecture: In a style known as Catalonian Modernist, **Estación Barracas** (Pasaje Darquier and Villarino), now known as Estación Hipólito Yrigoyen, differs greatly from most other stations on the Roca line south from Constitución.

In an effort to recast this area as a tourist zone, city government has promoted film production facilities on this picturesque cobbled passageway, and the **Casa del Polaco Goyeneche,** a *tanguería* named for the great singer, occupies a nearby corner. Its revival, though, still has far to go.

Many laborers crowded into *conventillos* like those of La Boca or San Telmo, but there were also progressive efforts to accommodate working families. Near the Estación Solá cargo facilities, the 300 cottage-style units of the **Barrio Ferroviario** (Australia 2700) are now 120 years old and crumbling, but in their time they were exemplary.

Between 1917 and 1925, the Acción Católica Popular (People's Catholic Action) created the **Barrio Monseñor Espinoza** (Alvarado and Perdriel), a classic *barrio obrero* (workers' barrio) that's resisted industrial decline. Originally financed by government credits, this park-like 60-house greenbelt has remained a model of its kind.

Barracas is not all work, though. Along the railroad embankment, **Pasaje Lanín** is a cobbled three-block-long diagonal where painter Marino Santamaría and his neighbors have covered some 40 houses with colorfully abstract schemes, turning the whole street into an *objet d'art*. Santamaría's own works are for sale in his home studio (Pasaje Lanín 33, tel. 15/5728-3364).

Immediately west of Barracas, the barrio of **Parque Patricios** has undergone a steady metamorphosis from when, at various times, it was the site of slaughterhouses, a cemetery for yellow-fever victims, and a garbage dump known as the Barrio de las Quemas (Barrio of

© WAYNE BERNHARDSON

**Recently restored, its facade repainted in bright colors, Barracas's Hijos del Trabajo (sausage house) has long been the headquarters of the capital's freemasons.**

the Incinerators) or Barrio de las Latas (Barrio of the Tin Cans). By the early 1900s, though, the intention was to create a "Palermo de los Pobres" (Palermo of the Poor) with broad open spaces – if only to brake the weekend invasion of working-class families into areas frequented by "*gente decente*" (decent people).

Authorities designated the renowned landscape architect Charles Thays to get to work in the barrio's namesake **Parque Patricios,** bounded by Uspallata, Monteagudo, Caseros, and Almafuerte. Thays's efforts, though, never achieved the enduring success here that they did elsewhere in the city and the country.

One challenge was to house the workers, and the prestigious Jockey Club went so far as to build a *barrio obrero* here to try to mitigate militant labor discontent. In January 1919, though, during a strike against the Fábrica Pedro Vasena steel factory, police strikebreakers incited street battles that culminated in the notorious *Semana Trágica:* Over several days, more than a thousand workers died. In an ominous precedent, spurred by paranoia over Russian Bolshevism, the police armed paramilitary forces who attacked Jewish immigrants in Once and Villa Crespo.

Southwest of Parque Patricios, in **Nueva Pompeya,** Avenida Sáenz leads to the Río Riachuelo and the ornately neocolonial **Puente Alsina,** a 1930s landmark that's easily the city's most picturesque bridge; it also gave its name to a tango and a movie. The barrio is also the site of a balconied water tower, in a *barrio obrero* bounded by Einstein, Traful, Gramajo Gutierrez, and Cachi, that figures prominently in Ernesto Sabato's remarkable novel *On Heroes and Tombs.*

North of Pompeya and west of Parque Patricios, **Boedo** was a transitional barrio whose leftist intellectualism had its roots in an upwardly mobile working class that moved here from Patricios. Among the Grupo de Boedo literary figures, many of whom lived elsewhere but met here, were Antonio Zamora, who translated Maxim Gorki into Spanish, and noirish novelist Roberto Arlt.

The barrio is probably best known, though, for tango lyricist Homero Manzi, who described it wistfully in the tango *Sur;* in fact, the intersection of Avenida Boedo and Avenida San Juan is known as the **Esquina Homero Manzi** and is home to a commercial *tanguería* of that name. These days, though, the barrio's freethinkers frequent locales such as **Café Margot** (Av. Boedo 857).

While Borges and others may have respected The South, that didn't mean they ventured too deeply into it; Borges, who spent much of his working life at San Telmo's Biblioteca Nacional, lived in comfortable Retiro, and few residents of the wealthy northern barrios go here. Travel agencies, though, do organize guided visits. That's not to say that it's not safe for visitors to go here during the day on their own, it's more that the sights are spread out, the street plan is more complex, and consequently the logistics are difficult. (For suggestions on visiting this area, see the *Organized Tours* section in the *Essentials* chapter.)

Aires's federalization. There is also an 11,000-volume library.

The museum may close on weekends in summer.

## CABALLITO AND VICINITY

Now precisely in the center of the federal capital, but still well off the tourist circuit, the middle-class barrio of Caballito once lay on the city's western fringes. It takes its name (little horse) from a weathervane design placed by Italian immigrant Nicolás Vila on the roof of his *pulpería* (general store) at Avenida Rivadavia and Cucha Cucha; Vila's establishment was a landmark in an area of country-style houses with large gardens.

Today, sculptor Luis Perlotti's replica of Vila's weathervane sits atop a flagpole at **Plazoleta Primera Junta,** now the terminus of the Subte's Línea A. Immigration and the Subte have transformed Caballito into a residential barrio for downtown workers, with notable open spaces. One of those open spaces, **Parque Rivadavia,** was formerly the *quinta* (country estate) of Ambrosio Lezica, cofounder of the influential *porteño* daily *La Nación*.

In the vicinity of Parque Rivadavia are several significant buildings, such as the **Liceo de Señoritas** (Av. Rivadavia 4950), immediately to the north. Across the street, the restored Romanesque **Parroquia Nuestra Señora de Caacupé** (Rivadavia 4879) was once part of a convent; it is particularly precious to Paraguayans, for whom the Virgin of Caacupé is their patron saint. Especially appealing in the late-afternoon light, it holds an image of the saint that, legend says, was carved by an indigenous man who pledged to do so if he escaped his enemies. Down the block, dating from 1910, the rococo **Club Italiano** (Rivadavia 4731) sports a mansard dome and an ornate ballroom with parquet floors.

Caballito is also the site of Buenos Aires's last operating tramway, the **Tranvía Histórica,** which operates weekends only from the corner of Avenida Rivadavia and Emilio Mitre (the car itself had to be imported from Portugal, since all other city tramlines have been torn up and the cars scrapped). North of the suburban Ferrocarril Sarmiento's railroad tracks, the **Museo de Esculturas Luis Perlotti** is a small but outstanding art museum that is due to re-open sometime in 2008.

On Caballito's northern edge, the nearly circular **Parque Centenario** is known for its exceptional natural sciences museum, **Museo Argentino de Ciencias Naturales Bernardino Rivadavia,** its **Observatorio Astronómico,** and its open spaces.

## ◖ MUSEO ARGENTINO DE CIENCIAS NATURALES BERNARDINO RIVADAVIA

Angel Gallardo 490, tel. 011/4982-1154,
www.macn.secyt.gov.ar
**HOURS:** Daily 2-7 P.M.
**COST:** US$1, free child under 7

Housing one of the country's largest and best-kept natural history collections, the Museo Argentino de Ciencias Naturales Bernardino Rivadavia veers between a traditional stuff-in-glass-cases approach and more sophisticated exhibits that provide ecological, historical, and cultural context. Its imposing quarters, dating from 1937, are only one-third the size of the original grandiose project, but they have some exquisite details: bas-relief spider webs around the main entrance and sculpted owls flanking the upper windows, for instance.

The main floor contains geological and paleontological exhibits, including a reconstruction of the massive Patagonian specimens *Giganotosaurus carolini* (the world largest carnivorous dinosaur) and the herbivore *Argentinosaurus huinculensis* (whose neck alone measures about 12 meters). Other prized items are meteorites from the Campo de Cielo field in Santiago del Estero province. There is also an aquarium, plus material on marine flora, mollusks, and deep-sea creatures, a diorama of seagoing megafauna such as sharks, rays, giant squid, and sailfish, and Antarctic fauna, plus a sperm whale cranium.

The 2nd floor stresses mostly South American mammals (including marine mammals), comparative anatomy, amphibians and reptiles, birds, arthropods, and botany, with an ecology exhibit still in preparation.

There is also a library, open Monday–Friday 11 A.M.–4 P.M.

## CHACARITA
### Ⓒ CEMENTERIO DE LA CHACARITA
Guzmán 680, tel. 011/4553-9338
**HOURS:** Daily 8 A.M.-6 P.M.

Buenos Aires's second cemetery may be a more affordable final destination than Recoleta, but eternity at the Chacarita can still mean notoriety. Many high-profile Argentines in fields ranging from entertainment to religion and politics (the lines separating these categories are often blurred) repose at Chacarita.

The most universally beloved is tango singer Carlos Gardel, who died in a 1935 plane crash in Medellín, Colombia. Hundreds of admirers from around the globe have left plaques on his tomb, many thanking him for miracles, and every June 26 they jam Chacarita's streets—gridded like a small city—to pay homage. As often as not, the right hand of his bronze statue holds a lighted cigarette and a red carnation adorns his lapel.

In terms of devotion, probably only Spanish-born faith-healer-to-the-aristocracy Madre María Salomé can match Gardel; on the second of every month—she died October 2, 1928—her tomb is covered in white carnations. She gained fame as the disciple of Pancho Sierra, the *curandero gaucho* (gaucho healer) of Salto, in Buenos Aires province.

Other famous figures entombed at Chacarita include pioneer aviator Jorge Newbery, for whom the city airport is named (he died in a 1914 plane crash); tango musicians Aníbal "Pichuco" Troilo (seated playing his *bandoneón*) and Osvaldo Pugliese; poet Alfonsina Storni; La Boca painter Benito Quinquela Martín; and theater and film comedian Luis Sandrini, whose bronze statue often holds a red carnation in its hand.

Certainly the most notorious, though, was Juan Domingo Perón, whose remains were recently relocated to suburban San Vicente. In June 1987, stealthy vandals entered the crypt, amputating and stealing the caudillo's hands in a crime that has never been resolved. People speculated, though there's no evidence, that the thieves sought Perón's fingerprints for access to supposed Swiss bank accounts.

Chacarita's role as the capital's most democratic cemetery dates from its origins, when it buried yellow-fever victims of the 1870s epidemic in then mosquito-ridden San Telmo and La Boca. The barrio, also known as Chacarita, takes its name from a Quechua term meaning a small farm; during the 17th century, it was a Jesuit agricultural property known as La Chacarita de los Colegiales, on the city's outskirts.

The Cementerio de la Chacarita covers 95 blocks with a total of 12,000 burial vaults, 100,000 gravesites, and 350,000 niches. It's only a short walk from Estación Federico Lacroze, on the Subte's Línea B.

In addition to Chacarita, there are two contiguous but formally separate cemeteries nearby: the **Cementerio Alemán** (German Cemetery, Av. Elcano 4530, tel. 011/4553-3206) and the **Cementerio Británico** (British Cemetery, Av.

© WAYNE BERNHARDSON

The tomb of Aníbal "Pichuco" Troilo, at the Cementerio de la Chacarita, is a memorial to his virtuosity with the *bandoneón*.

Elcano 4568, tel. 011/4554-0092). Both keep identical hours to Chacarita's.

The Británico is more diverse, with tombs belonging to Armenian, Greek, Irish, Jewish, and many other immigrant nationalities. The Anglo-Argentine Lucas Bridges, son of pioneer Anglican missionaries in Tierra del Fuego and author of the classic Fuegian memoir *The Uttermost Part of the Earth,* was buried here after dying at sea en route from Ushuaia. The Alemán features a large but politically neutral monument to Germany's World War II dead—no German or German-Argentine wants to be associated with the Third Reich.

## NÚÑEZ
### ESCUELA DE MECÁNICA DE LA ARMADA (ESMA)
Av. del Libertador 8200

Buildings often cause controversy, but none quite so much as the Escuela de Mecánica de la Armada (Naval Mechanics' School) in Núñez, beyond Belgrano near the Buenos Aires province border. It was not the architecture of this handsome neoclassical building that raised havoc, though—rather, it was the fact that during the 1976–1983 military dictatorship, more than 5,000 *desaparecidos* (disappeared persons)

passed through the country's most notorious clandestine torture center here.

Before his term expired in 1999, President Carlos Menem—himself a victim of the repression, though he later pardoned his jailers—relocated the institution to Puerto Belgrano, near the naval town of Bahía Blanca in southern Buenos Aires province. At the same time, he ordered the ESMA's demolition and its replacement by a dubious "monument to national unity." In the end, public outcry prevented the building's destruction.

Menem's decrees infuriated human rights groups and city officials, who saw the former ESMA as the most gruesomely suitable location for a Museo de la Memoria (Museum of Memory) that would preserve and present documentary records, oral histories, sound, film, and photographs of the military's brutal Guerra Sucia (Dirty War) against its own citizens. Authorized in 1996, the museum long lacked a physical facility, but in early 2005 President Néstor Kirchner and Buenos Aires mayor Aníbal Ibarra announced agreement to move remaining naval educational facilities elsewhere and open the ESMA grounds to visits. It will be years, though, before the proposed museum takes shape.

Escuela de Mecánica de la Armada (ESMA)

# RESTAURANTS

In creative gastronomy, Buenos Aires may well be the continent's top city, and many of its restaurants would be first-rate anywhere. Over the past decade-plus, the scene has become more cosmopolitan, adventurous, and nuanced. Brazilian, Japanese, Thai, Vietnamese, and other once-exotic cuisines—not to mention high-quality versions of Argentine regional dishes—have stepped out of the kitchen and onto the stage.

Many areas have fine restaurants, but the best barrios for dining out include the Microcentro, Palermo, Retiro, and Recoleta. Palermo, though, is ground zero—the Palermo Viejo, Palermo Hollywood, and Las Cañitas neighborhoods seem to have sprouted stylish, sophisticated, and creative new eateries on every corner and in between.

For most of the 1990s, dining out was financially challenging except for cheap cafeteria lunches and *tenedor libre* ("free fork") buffets. Though prices have recovered since the 2002 peso collapse, it's still possible to eat diverse and creative food for a fraction of the cost of North America or Europe.

Places to eat range from hole-in-the-wall *comedores* (eateries) or fast-food *bares* (unavoidably but misleadingly translated as bars) with no formal menu in bus and train stations, to cafés, *confiterías* (tea houses), and elegant *restaurantes* or even the *restó* (a trendy affectation for places that aspire to creative cookery).

A bar, of course, can also be a drinking establishment; this is usually obvious in context. And a café is both more and less than its English-language equivalent would suggest,

© WAYNE BERNHARDSON

**RESTAURANTS**

# HIGHLIGHTS

LOOK FOR ◖ TO FIND RECOMMENDED RESTAURANTS.

◖ **Best Pizza:** The deceptively simple *fugazzeta*, with mozzarella and sweet onions, is a favorite at **Pizzería Güerrín**'s standup counter, but the cheeseless *fugazza* may be even better (page 70).

◖ **Best Business Lunch:** Where else but **Sabot** do business leaders and politicians finish off their midday power lunch with tea from the forbidden coca leaf? The Italo-Argentine food and the good-humored service are the real stars, though (page 70).

◖ **Best Beef:** It's no contest – **Cabaña Las Lilas** raises its own beef and serves it succulent, with views of the Puerto Madero yacht harbor. Prices are higher than elsewhere, but it's worth every peso (page 72).

◖ **Best Buffet:** In high-rent Retiro, **Juana M.** produces standard Argentine dishes at a high quality-to-price ratio, with the best salad bar in town (page 78).

◖ **Best Empanadas:** You can eat cheaper, and you can eat better, but you can't eat cheaper *and* better than the tangy *salteñas* at Palermo Viejo's **La Cupertina** (page 82).

◖ **Best Genuinely Spicy Food:** Only a handful of *porteños* can handle the spiciest, most flavorful dishes that **Lotus Neo Thai** has to offer (page 83).

◖ **Best Dessert:** Brazil's diverse cuisine has made fairly few inroads here, but if more *porteños* sample the *maracuyá* (passion fruit) mousse from Palermo SoHo's **María Fuló,** their friends will come running to try it – and everything else on the menu (page 84).

◖ **Best Outdoor Dining:** Planting a sub-Arctic forest in muggy Buenos Aires goes against all global warming cautions, but Palermo Hollywood's **Olsen** is as audacious in its landscaping as it is in its Scandinavian–Patagonian cuisine (page 86).

◖ **Best Pasta:** It's hard to go wrong with *porteño* pasta, but Palermo's **Bella Italia Café Bar** gets the edge over its identically named restaurant because of its higher quality-to-price ratio (page 87).

◖ **Best Seafood:** The seafood tapas and fish dishes at Palermo's **Nemo** usually include at least one Paraná delta freshwater catch, which can be hard to find in the capital (page 91).

though it does serve food. Another interesting development is the appearance of restaurants with *puertas cerradas,* in private homes (see the sidebar *Behind Closed Doors* for details).

The Friday edition of the daily tabloid *Clarín* offers a variety of restaurant reviews. For English readers, Dereck Foster's Sunday *Buenos Aires Herald* column offers some of the latest suggestions; a separate column covers Argentine wines. The most thorough source in English, though, is Dan Perlman's SaltShaker (www .saltshaker.net), a blog by a transplanted New Yorker who, in addition to his knowledge of food in general and BA restaurants in particular, is also a talented writer. His *SaltShaker Spanish-English-Spanish Food & Wine Dictionary* (2007) is available directly from him in Buenos Aires or through online retailers such as Amazon.

It's worth emphasizing that the cost of eating out in Buenos Aires is rising faster than other sectors in the economy, so prices here could quickly become obsolete. Also, just because a restaurant does not appear in this book does not mean it's undeserving—limited space and time preclude including everything, and new places are opening constantly.

## PRICE KEY

**❸**     **Entrées less than US$10**
**❸❸**    **Entrées US$10-20**
**❸❸❸**   **Entrées more than US$20**

# Monserrat

Map 1

In general, restaurants in the area from Avenida de Mayo south toward San Telmo are less inventive than rejuvenated neighborhoods in the northern barrios, but there are some exceptions and several good lunchtime options, especially west of Avenida 9 de Julio.

## INTERNATIONAL
### CAFÉ MOLIÈRE $$

Chile 299, tel. 011/4343-2623, www.moliere-cafe.com

**HOURS:** Mon.-Sat. lunch and dinner

Relocated from Recoleta, in what was once a ceramic tile factory, the cavernous Molière offers an international menu with inexpensive fixed-price lunches; late on weekends, it becomes a DJ-dominated disco, while the basement theater has more intimate tango floor shows.

## ITALIAN
### PROSCIUTTO $$

Venezuela 1212, tel. 011/4383-8058, www.prosciuttoilvero.com.ar

**HOURS:** Daily lunch and dinner

Prosciutto's classic cantina style, with intricately carved century-old woodwork, hanging hams, and museum-quality restaurant gear for decoration, is a prelude to its extensive, elaborate bilingual menu—Italian first, Spanish second—and truly professional service. Most entrées cost less than US$10 but a few, such as garlic prawns, can challenge the budget. The fairly conventional Italo-Argentine menu is strongest on antipasti and pastas.

## PERUVIAN
### STATUS $

Virrey Cevallos 178, tel. 011/4382-8531

**HOURS:** Daily lunch and dinner

Though Peruvian food is becoming more common in Buenos Aires, plain-Jane Status may be the best of its kind. South of the Plaza del Congreso, it offers inexpensive home-style Central Andean dishes, such as *aji de gallina* (chicken in a walnut cream sauce over rice, with potatoes), *lomo saltado* (stir-fried beef with vegetables and fries), and *papa a la huancaína* (a spicy potato appetizer) in the US$3–5 range. In a city where the cost of dining out has risen rapidly, prices here are stable.

Some garnishes are far spicier than the *porteño*

**RESTAURANTS**

---

## DINING VOCABULARY AND ETIQUETTE

Restaurant vocabulary is mostly straightforward. The usual term for menu is *la carta; el menú* is almost equally common, but can also mean a fixed-price lunch or dinner. The bill is *la cuenta. Cubiertos* are silverware, a *plato* is a plate, and *vaso* is a glass. A *plato principal* is a main dish or entrée.

Note that one might ask for a *vaso de agua* (glass of water), but never for a *vaso de vino* (literally, but incorrectly, a glass of wine); rather, ask for a *copa de vino*. When speaking English, native Spanish speakers frequently make a similar error in requesting "a cup of wine."

Many but not all Argentine restaurants assess a small *cubierto* (cover charge, not silverware in this case) for dishes, silverware, and bread. This is not a *propina* (tip); a 10 percent tip is the norm, but Argentines themselves often ignore this norm, especially in times of economic crisis. A good rule of thumb is that anyone able to afford a restaurant meal can afford a tip.

A professional waiter, usually in uniform, is a *mozo;* this term, by the way, is totally innocuous in the River Plate countries but an insult in neighboring Chile (where it implies rural servitude). A waitress, regardless of age or marital status, is a *señorita.* When trying to attract a server's attention, it's also possible to use such terms as *señor* or even *jóven* (young man or woman, so long as the individual is not obviously elderly).

# RESTAURANT TERMINOLOGY

The term **restaurante** (occasionally *restorán*) usually refers to places with sit-down service, but within this definition there can be great diversity. Most often, the term refers to a place with a printed menu, but this can range from any place with a basic beef and pasta menu to truly formal places with complex cuisine, elaborate wine lists, and professional waiters. It's worth emphasizing that the occupation of waiter is traditionally professional and male in Argentina, rather than a short-term expedient for university students or aspiring actors. This is changing in the capital, though – in the new, stylish restaurants of Palermo Viejo and Las Cañitas, servers are just as likely to be young and female.

The usual international fast-food villains have Buenos Aires franchises, but the best cheap food comes from **rotiserías** (delicatessens), which serve excellent takeaway food and sometimes have basic seating. Likewise, supermarkets such as Coto and Disco have *cafeterías* that are excellent options for shoestring visitors.

**Bares** and **comedores** are generally no-frills eateries with indifferent service, offering **minutas** (short orders); the term **comedor** can also mean a hotel breakfast nook or dining room. A **café**, by contrast, is a place where *porteños* may dawdle over coffee and croissants, but its de facto purpose is social interaction in personal affairs, business deals, and other transactions; in addition to coffee and pastries, cafés serve snacks, *minutas*, and alcoholic drinks (beer, wine, and hard liquor).

**Confiterías** often serve breakfast, light meals (e.g., sandwiches), snacks (cakes and other desserts), and a variety of coffee drinks. Generally, they are more formal than cafés, are popular destinations for afternoon tea, and some are prestigious. A number have full-scale restaurant menus, often in a separate sector of the establishment.

palate can handle; tangy pisco sours, foamy with cinnamon, are on the drinks menu, but they seem a bit more watery than in the past.

## SPANISH AND BASQUE
### CENTRO VASCO FRANCÉS ●●
Moreno 1370, tel. 011/4381-6696,
www.rvascofrances.com.ar
**HOURS:** Mon.-Sat. lunch and dinner, Sun. lunch only
Distinguished by its capacious dining room, high ceilings, and waistcoated waiters, this very French Basque restaurant specializes in traditional fish dishes such as *abadejo al ajo arriero* (conger eel, with garlic, in a casserole form).

The Provençal-style fries are lighter and tastier than the average Argentine *papas fritas,* and the portions are abundant.

### LAURAK BAT ●●
Av. Belgrano 1144, tel. 011/4381-0682,
www.restaurantlaurakbat.com.ar
**HOURS:** Mon.-Sat. lunch and dinner
A longstanding author's favorite, Laurak Bat is a classic Basque family restaurant with a focus on fish and seafood, including bream, hake, and garlic shrimp as entrées, and the tasty custard *natillas* for dessert. In a building that dates from 1906, the ambience is strictly traditional.

# Microcentro                    Map 2

Many of the city's traditional favorites are right downtown and in nearby neighborhoods.

## ARGENTINE AND REGIONAL
### LA CANDELA $
Bartolomé Mitre 1682, tel. 011/4383-3225
**HOURS:** Mon.-Fri. lunch, Thurs.-Fri. dinner

A step above most of Congreso's neighborhood eateries, La Candela offers a fairly conventional Argentine menu but the preparation and presentation are more painstaking. Three-course lunch specials, comprising pastas like *sorrentinos* (oversized ravioli) and meat items like grilled chicken, cost around US$5–6 with a starter and dessert included. The service is notably attentive and the decor, while not elaborate, transcends the simply utilitarian.

### CLUB DEL PROGRESO $
Sarmiento 1334, tel. 011/4371-5053,
www.clubdelprogreso.com
**HOURS:** Mon.-Sat. lunch and dinner

For a 19th-century experience with contemporary flourishes, try the Club del Progreso, in the same site since 1852—with its lofty ceilings, classic library, and other period features, this elaborate mansion served as a film location for British director Christopher Hampton's *Imagining Argentina,* starring Antonio Banderas and Emma Thompson. For about US$6–8 per person, the fixed-price meals are a little bland, but the singing waiters, with their tangos and boleros, make dining here a unique experience.

### LA ESTANCIA $$
Lavalle 941, tel. 011/4326-0330,
www.asadorlaestancia.com.ar
**HOURS:** Daily lunch and dinner

The Microcentro and nearby neighborhoods have several picture-window *parrillas* that make a fetish out of staking their steaks over glowing coals in circular barbecue pits tended by bogus gauchos in full regalia; while they play for the cliché and serve far too many tourists to be able to give patrons individual attention,

the quality is good and their prices reasonable. Popular with individuals and tour groups, La Estancia is typical of its class; its nightly tango show (US$50 pp), oddly inappropriate given the gaucho-centric menu, is overpriced.

### EL PALACIO DE LA PAPA FRITA $
Av. Corrientes 1612, tel. 011/4374-8063,
www.elpalacio-papafrita.com.ar
**HOURS:** Daily lunch and dinner

Misleadingly named, this *porteño* classic offers an enormous Argentine and international menu—while you can get its namesake french fries here, it would be a mistake to focus on them. Portions are abundant; their saffron-flavored *arroz a la valenciana,* with chicken and a mixture of vegetables, can feed at least two hungry mouths. The three-course lunch or dinner (US$15) also includes beer, wine, or a soft drink. A good choice for families because it appeals to everyone from fussy children to discriminating adults, it has additional branches (Lavalle 735, tel. 011/4393-5849; Lavalle 954, tel. 011/4322-1599) on the pedestrian mall near Avenida 9 de Julio.

### LA POSADA DE 1820 $$
Tucumán 501, tel. 011/4314-4557,
www.laposadade1820.com.ar
**HOURS:** Daily noon-1 A.M.

On the edge of the financial district, this lunchtime favorite serves a standard but above-average Argentine menu of beef and pasta at reasonable prices in bright, cheerful surroundings accented with burnished wood. Because of its size, seating up to 200 diners, it often gets tour groups for relatively homogenized meals.

## AUSTRIAN AND HUNGARIAN
### ABC $$
Lavalle 545, tel. 011/4393-3992
**HOURS:** Mon.-Sat. lunch and dinner

In the same location since 1929, near the junction of the two pedestrian malls, ABC seems a relic of the Austro-Hungarian empire, with its continental atmosphere and sausage, schnitzel, and goulash

RESTAURANTS

menu. It's a popular lunch spot for businessmen and bankers from the La City financial district.

## ITALIAN
### BROCCOLINO ❸❸
Esmeralda 776, tel. 011/4322-9848,
www.broccolino.com
**HOURS:** Daily lunch and dinner
Broccolino is an unfailingly reliable Italian choice, with impeccable service (all the waiters speak at least two languages) and a diverse menu ranging from pizza and pasta to seafood and beef dishes. Perhaps the menu's a little too diverse, as it's hard to maintain quality over such a range of dishes. Portions are abundant.

It's also fair to say that Broccolino hasn't kept pace with some of the more innovative trends in *porteño* cuisine, but that's not necessarily bad. Because it draws foreign tourists, it's open as early as 7 P.M. for dinner.

### EL GATO NEGRO ❸❸
Av. Corrientes 1669, tel. 011/4374-1730
**HOURS:** Mon.-Fri. lunch, Fri. dinner
Hard to pigeonhole, El Gato Negro is a hybrid downtown institution whose unadorned upstairs bistro serves seafood-based Italian dishes, such as saffron risotto with fish, scallops, and shrimp, in the US$9–15 range. Most of its ground floor is a traditional *confitería* with coffee, tea, and a diversity of appetizing desserts. Few places in town, though, can match the ceiling-high cases stocked with bulk spices, teas, and dried fruits, as well as homemade jams, to take home.

### ◖ PIZZERÍA GÜERRÍN ❸
Av. Corrientes 1372, tel. 011/4371-8141
**HOURS:** Daily lunch and dinner
Güerrín remains a Corrientes classic, a one-of-a-kind survivor that sells pizza by the slice at the street-side standup counter—at giveaway prices, the onion-based *fugazza* and *fugazzeta* are simply exquisite (and exquisitely simple), and the baked chicken empanadas (avoid the fried ones) are exceptional.

There are many more options for toppings, though, if you choose table seating in its vast interior. The place can be mobbed at

dinnertime, but service is always quick and attentive, and the price is invariably right.

### ◖ SABOT ❸❸
25 de Mayo 756, tel. 011/4313-6587
**HOURS:** Mon.-Fri. 12:30-3 P.M.
Possibly downtown's best restaurant of any sort, the bankers' and powerbrokers' preference, Sabot serves Italo-Argentine dishes of the highest quality in a notably masculine environment (women are few but not unwelcome). With good-humored but professional service, less formal than its clientele might imply, it's moderately expensive by current standards; choice entrées include *matambre de cerdo* (rolled pork), *chivito* (roast goat), and fish dishes. For an unexpected post-meal infusion, try the *mate de coca* brewed from fresh coca leaves (for digestive purposes only!).

## MEXICAN
### CALIFORNIA BURRITO COMPANY ❸
Lavalle 441, tel. 011/4328-3057,
www.californiaburritoco.com
**HOURS:** Mon.-Fri. 8 A.M.-6 P.M.
Mexican and Tex-Mex are hard to find in Buenos Aires, and their quality is often ordinary at best. On the Lavalle pedestrian mall, taking its cues from U.S. chains like Chevy's, the CBC is affordable (around US$5–6 for most dishes) and palatable, though in California it would be only run-of-the-mill.

## ICE CREAM
### CADORE
Av. Corrientes 1693, tel. 011/4374-9797
**HOURS:** Daily 11 A.M.-2 A.M. or later
Many Buenos Aires ice creameries are outstanding, but Cadore is the only one to merit an extensive description in this book. With over half a century in the same location, recognizable by the outline map of Italy above the storefront, this one-of-a-kind place produces the richest *chocolate amargo* (bittersweet chocolate) and lemon mousse imaginable, and even the sorbets such as the *arándano* (blueberry) flavor taste deceptively creamy. If you only visit one ice creamery in the city, this should be it.

# COOLING DOWN WITH HELADOS

Though it stems from the Italian tradition, Argentine ice cream lacks the high international profile of gelato – when a pair of *porteños* opened an ice creamery in the author's hometown of Oakland, California, they chose the compromise name of Tango Gelato, stressing its Italian origins while acknowledging its Buenos Aires detour. Buenos Aires has a remarkable number of high-quality ice creameries, and a remarkable diversity of flavors, ranging from the standard vanilla and chocolate (with multiple variations, including white chocolate and bittersweet chocolate) to lemon mousse, *sambayón* (resembling eggnog), the Argentine staple *dulce de leche* (caramelized milk, its own major food group), and countless others.

Buenos Aires has two types of *heladerías*. The first is the chain that produces large industrial batches; some chain products are nevertheless very fine, others are truly awful, and most fall in between. The other is the neighborhood creamery that creates *helados artesanales* in smaller quantities.

Though the legendary Freddo has made something of a comeback, **Chungo** (tel. 0800/888-2486, www.chungo.com.ar) is probably the best industrial ice cream, and is good enough by any standard; the most convenient branch is in Recoleta (Av. Las Heras and Rodríguez Peña). **Bianca** (Av. Scalabrini Ortiz 2295, tel. 011/4832-3357) is the Palermo franchise of a medium-sized chain that offers a wide selection of flavors.

Founded by the former owners of Freddo, always-crowded **Persicco** (Salguero 2591, tel. 011/4801-5549) is putting up a challenge to the other chains. **Un Altra Volta** (Quintana and Ayacucho, Recoleta, tel. 0810/888-6582, www.unaltravolta.com.ar) is a more recent addition to the scene, with several branches around town.

Over the past couple decades, Congreso's **Cadore** (Av. Corrientes 1695, tel. 011/4374-3688) has been consistently one of the city's best ice creameries, but its small storefront (often obscured by construction) gives it a much lower profile than the chains. Their *chocolate amargo* (bittersweet chocolate),

At Congreso's Heladería Cadore, owner Gabriel Famá offers up a cone of bittersweet chocolate and lemon mousse.

*mousse de limon* (lemon mousse), and *pistacho* (pistachio) deserve special mention, and even the fruit-flavored sorbets taste remarkably creamy.

Only a few blocks south, **Sorrento** (Av. Rivadavia 2051) is both good and inexpensive; it has a second branch in La Boca (Olavarría 658).

The Microcentro is shorter on quality ice creameries than might be expected, but **Vía Flaminia** (Florida 121) is a more-than-respectable choice, as is **Abuela Goye** (Av. Córdoba and Florida), in the basement food court of Galerías Pacífico.

Across from Parque Lezama, the no-frills **Florencia** (Brasil and Defensa, tel. 011/4307-6407) has been San Telmo's best. The new **Nonna Bianca** (Estados Unidos 425, tel. 011/4362-0604) is at least its equal, with more style, but it's also more expensive.

Palermo's **Mento e Cannella** (Salguero and Seguí, tel. 011/4801-2346) is also worth a stop.

Belgrano's hole-in-the-wall **Gruta** (Sucre 2356, tel. 011/4784-8417), the barrio's finest, has added an exquisite mango mousse flavor.

# Puerto Madero Map 2

Over the past few years, redeveloped Puerto Madero has made a big impact on the restaurant scene, but more because of the area's overall appeal than because of its quality—there's only one truly memorable restaurant. Most places, though, have outdoor as well as indoor seating, and when the weather's fine it's a great option for people-watching along the yacht harbor. Because the area is popular with foreigners who stay at nearby luxury hotels, restaurants here are accustomed to dealing with dinnertimes as early as 7 P.M.

## ARGENTINE AND REGIONAL
### C CABAÑA LAS LILAS ❸❸❸
Alicia Moreau de Justo 516, tel. 011/4313-1336,
www.laslilas.com
**HOURS:** Daily lunch and dinner
Opposite the northerly Dique No. 4, arguably Buenos Aires's best *parrilla,* Cabaña Las Lilas serves only beef from its own *estancias* in Buenos Aires, Santa Fe, San Luis, and Chaco provinces; its *bife de chorizo* (US$10) may be the most succulent in town. As it's often

packed despite its size, reservations are advisable; if you have to wait, they provide complimentary champagne and snacks.

With its high quality and impeccable service, this is the one can't-miss for beef-eaters, well worth its relatively high prices (US$15 and up for entrées). In reality, it's Puerto Madero's only truly memorable restaurant, though many others are suitable for lunch.

## ASIAN
### ASIA DE CUBA ❸❸
Pierica Dealessi 750, tel. 011/4894-1328,
www.asiadecuba.com.ar
**HOURS:** Mon.-Sat. lunch and dinner
Across the Dique, Asia de Cuba has a promising menu of sushi, sashimi, tempuras, and curries that help give it its name (the Cuba part is a mystery, though). In practice, though, its prices exceed its quality except for weekday lunch specials, but its late-night DJs (nightly except Sun. and Mon.) make it popular with sectors of the fashion-conscious elite.

# San Telmo Map 3

Despite San Telmo's tourist allure, it lags behind other barrios in creative gastronomy. That's not to say there is nothing worth trying—there are some real classics and a few audacious experiments—but for the most part they're better lunchtime values than dinnertime indulgences.

## ARGENTINE AND REGIONAL
### BAR EL FEDERAL ❸
Carlos Calvo 399, tel. 011/4300-4313
**HOURS:** Daily lunch and dinner
Dating from 1864, El Federal looks its age—in a positive way, with its worn tiled floor and its indescribably intricate carved wooden bar, symmetrically embellished with stained glass and a central clock (which no longer ticks off

the minutes but reinforces the aura of timelessness). The menu is large but the house specialty is turkey ravioli (US$5), with any of a variety of sauces; there's refreshing hard cider on tap. So out of style that it's stylish again, this classic also contains a bookstore in the back of the restaurant. Note that in hot weather, the bathrooms become virtual ovens.

### DESNIVEL ❸
Defensa 855,
tel. 011/4300-9081
**HOURS:** Tues.-Sun. lunch, daily dinner
Sunday visitors to the Plaza Dorrego flea market queue up outside DesNivel, and many locals swear by it as well, for *parrillada* and pasta

© WAYNE BERNHARDSON

**Bar El Federal, San Telmo**

at bargain prices. It's not so intimate as Bar El Federal—multiple dining rooms stretch seemingly infinitely toward the back of the deep lot—but the service is good natured and, for the price, this casual restaurant is one of the barrio's best values for beef, in particular. At peak hours, the crowds can make it claustrophobic.

## 1880 🟢

Defensa 1665, tel. 011/4307-2746
**HOURS:** Tues.-Sat. lunch and dinner

If you're looking for a traditional parrilla that oozes barrio atmosphere without DesNivel's crowds, visit 1880, immediately opposite Parque Lezama. Festooned with *filete* by San Telmo artist Martiniano Arce, it draws almost exclusively local residents, with entrées (including pasta dishes like ñoquis) in the US$3–4 range.

## MÍTICO SUR 🟢

Pasaje San Lorenzo 389, tel. 011/4362-4750,
www.miticosurpatagonia.com.ar
**HOURS:** Mon.-Sat. lunch, Sun. all day

In a picturesque cobbled passageway, its round tables poised atop wine barrels, Mítico Sur is a casual wine bar that serves exclusively Patagonian vintages, from the provinces of Neuquén and Río Negro. Equally significant, its *tablas* of smoked meats (including wild game) and cheeses are large (the half *tabla* of "Quimey" easily feeds two) and reasonably priced. For visitors to Sunday's Plaza Dorrego flea market, this is *the* ideal stop.

## LA OVEJA NEGRA 🟢🟢

Bolívar 860, tel. 011/4300-1691,
www.laovejanegraresto.com.ar
**HOURS:** Tues.-Sat. lunch and dinner

New in 2008, La Oveja Negra has preserved a handsome brick interior to create an intimate dining experience that nevertheless is large enough to give diners a bit of breathing space. The menu is Argentine, but with uncommon touches such as bites of chicken and a mint sauce to give flavor to the gnocchi (US$9), and a crispy, slightly spicy covering for the lightly cooked salmon (US$13). The service is attentive and friendly, but not overbearing.

### TERRITORIO ⓢ
Estados Unidos 500, tel. 011/4300-9756
**HOURS:** Daily lunch and dinner

Territorio prepares uncommon items, such as Patagonian sandwiches of smoked venison, and other regionally based dishes, but also Peruvian-style stir-fried lamb with vegetables and *tablas* of smoked meats and cheeses. Fine homemade bread and free olives complement the main plates. Portions are substantial, but the desserts sound better than they really are.

Though it's small, Territorio has a good selection of brews on tap and in bottles. The music and noise level is moderate; the sidewalk seating can be too sunny at lunchtime.

## INTERNATIONAL
### PAPPA DEUS ⓢⓢ
Humberto Primo 496, tel. 011/4307-1571,
www.pappadeus.com.ar
**HOURS:** Daily lunch, Tues.-Sun. dinner

In new quarters half a block west of Plaza Dorrego, Pappa Deus has been more imaginative than most San Telmo eateries, serving items such as arugula and sun-dried tomatoes, with a variety of pastas in addition to standards such as *bife de chorizo*. Recently, though, the menu seems to have lost some of its former adventurousness.

## SPANISH AND CATALAN
### CASAL DE CATALUNYA ⓢⓢ
Chacabuco 863, tel. 011/4361-0191,
www.restaurantedelcasal.com
**HOURS:** Tues.-Sun. lunch and dinner

Reopened under its original name, with fresh young blood who trained in the kitchen of chef Juan Coll, Buenos Aires's Catalonian cultural center is well worth a visit for regional Iberian seafood, Spanish-style tapas, and the occasional special such as roast leg of goat (US$12). The service can be erratic, ranging from perfunctory to truly engaged and accommodating.

While it's formal looking, with dark mahogany woodwork in the bar, colorful Spanish tiles in the main dining room, and a magnificent ceremonial staircase in a building that dates from Argentina's

At San Telmo's Catalonian cultural center, its namesake Casal de Catalunya restaurant has a rejuvenated Mediterranean menu.

© WAYNE BERNHARDSON

early 20th-century boom, in reality it's more casual. In fact, it can be a little too casual—the rock music soundtrack isn't bad and it's not too loud, but it somehow seems inappropriate here.

## URUGUAYAN
### MEDIO Y MEDIO ⓢ
Chile 316, tel. 011/4300-7007
**HOURS:** Mon.-Sat. 9 A.M.-2 or 3 A.M.

Taking its name from the blend of sparkling and white wines popular with Uruguayans, Medio y Medio (literally, half and half) bursts with lunchgoers who themselves might burst while consuming Uruguay's caloric/cholesterol overdose known as the *chivito,* a steak sandwich garnished with lettuce, cheese, tomato, and bacon (note that, in the Argentine context, *chivito* normally means kid goat). A fried egg crowns the *chivito al plato,* a dinner plate that includes a larger cut of beef plus potato salad, green salad, and French fries.

# La Boca

Map 3

La Boca is no gourmet ghetto, but there's enough good food for lunch—most people visit the barrio during the daytime—and even an occasional dinnertime foray.

## ARGENTINE AND REGIONAL

### BANCHERO ⑤

Suárez 396, tel. 011/4301-1406, www.bancheropizzerias.com.ar

**HOURS:** Sun.-Thurs. 7:30 A.M.-1 A.M., Fri.-Sat. 7:30 A.M.-2 A.M.

This is the original locale of the pizzeria that claims to have invented the onion-and-mozzarella *fugazzetta*. Whether or not that's true, theirs is one of the best; even if it's not worth a cross-town trip to sample a slice, it's well worth a stop on a walking tour of the barrio. Banchero has a more central branch at Avenida Corrientes 1300 (tel. 011/4382-4669), but there it has to compete with nearby Güerrín.

### LA BARBERÍA ⑤

Pedro de Mendoza 1959, tel. 011/4303-8256, www.barberia.com.ar

**HOURS:** Daily 11 A.M.-8 P.M.

With umbrella-shaded sidewalk seating on the Vuelta de Rocha, its facade and interior adorned with dazzlingly colorful *filete,* La Barbería serves empanadas, tapas, pasta, pizza, sandwiches, and seafood, plus beer and cold hard cider straight from the tap. The food's not bad but it's fairly expensive for simple food, as you're paying as much or more for the daytime tango dancers on the sidewalk.

### EL OBRERO ⑤

Agustín Caffarena 64, tel. 011/4362-9912

**HOURS:** Mon.-Sat. lunch and dinner

In an area where taxis are obligatory at night and maybe even advisable in the daytime (though some cabbies have trouble finding it), El Obrero is where Argentine and foreign celebrities go slumming for steaks. Its walls are plastered with posters of soccer icon Diego Maradona and little else except photos of high-profile clientele on the order of Bono and Robert Duvall—it hasn't even taken down the image of disgraced ex-President Fernando De la Rúa. There is no printed menu—check the chalkboards scattered around the dining room. Prices are low.

### PATAGONIA SUR ⑤⑤⑤

Rocha 801, tel. 011/4303-5917, www.restaurantepatagoniasur.com

**HOURS:** Thurs.-Sat. lunch and dinner, Sun. lunch only

Seemingly slumming himself, celebrity restaurateur Francis Mallman has placed one of several gourmet restaurants in La Boca. The name is misleading, as the menu carries dishes from throughout the country, from the desert highlands of Salta through the fjords of Tierra del Fuego; the focus is on beef and other meats. Prices are high—a three-course dinner without wine costs nearly US$90 per person, and it's hard to imagine that it's more than twice as good as his 1884 restaurant in Mendoza's Escorihuela winery. The cheapest wine is about US$20 per bottle, but some vintages go in excess of US$1,000.

RESTAURANTS

# THE RITE OF *MATE*

It's rarely on the menu, but the single most social drink in Argentina and the rest of the River Plate region – including Uruguay, Paraguay, and southern Brazil – is *yerba mate,* the dried, shredded leaf of *Ilex paraguayensis.*

Espresso, in its many forms, may dominate café society, but the *mate* infusion transcends commercialism. Its production is a major industry, but its consumption belongs to home and hearth. Native to the forests of the upper Río Paraná, a relative of the everyday holly, *yerba mate* became a commercial crop on colonial Jesuit mission plantations.

Transplanted Europeans took to it – the Austrian Jesuit Martin Dobrizhoffer asserted that *mate* "speedily counteracts the languor arising from the burning climate, and assuages both hunger and thirst." Unlike coffee and tea, though, it never really established markets across the Atlantic or even elsewhere in the Americas, except in parts of Chile.

Production diminished with the Jesuits' 1767 expulsion from the Americas, but "Paraguayan tea" kept its place in humble households and privileged palaces alike. According to English sailor Emeric Essex Vidal, who visited Buenos Aires in the 1820s:

Mate is in every house all day long, and the compliment of the country is to hand the mate cup to every visitor, the same cup and tube serving for all, and an attendant being kept in waiting to replenish for each person. Throughout the provinces, the weary traveler, let him stop at what hovel soever he may, is sure to be presented with the hospitable mate cup, which, unless his prejudices are very strong indeed, will be found a great refreshment.

In fact, the purpose of *mate* is hospitality; preparing and serving it is a ritual. It is also an equalizer, as everyone sips in turn from the same *bombilla* (metallic tube or straw) placed in the same *yerba*-stuffed *mate* (a term which also means gourd), filled by the *cebador* (brewer) with slightly-below-boiling-temperature water. It's customary to sip the gourd dry, and then return it to the *cebador,* who will pass it clockwise around the group. Note that, in this context, saying *gracias* (thank you) means that you want no more.

Not all rituals are equal, though, and *mate*'s material culture differs according to social

# Balvanera                                    Map 4

Gastronomic points of interest are scattered around Balvanera and its bordering barrios.

## ARGENTINE
### LA CONTINENTAL ⑤
Av. Callao 202, tel. 011/4374-1444, www.lacontinental.com
**HOURS:** Daily 24 hours

Part of a city-wide chain, Congreso's **La Continental** has fine chicken empanadas and pizza slices, including a particularly choice *fugazzeta;* the fresh orange juice also deserves a mention. With several other branches around town, its delivery service reaches almost everywhere.

## BASQUE AND SPANISH
### MIRAMAR ⑤
Av. San Juan 1999, tel. 011/4304-4261
**HOURS:** Wed.-Mon. lunch and dinner

In the barrio of San Cristóbal, near Monserrat's

© WAYNE BERNHARDSON

**Mate gear can be works of art even for those who don't sip Argentina's traditional bitter herbal tea.**

class. Although having a servant whose sole job was to prepare and serve it is a thing of the past, upper-class households own far more elaborate paraphernalia than working-class families do – just as British nobility have more ornate tea sets than the untitled. Simple *mates* might be plain calabashes or from plastic, but others consist of elaborately carved wood set in silver or even gold; the *bombilla*, likewise, can range from utilitarian aluminum to ceremonial silver.

Most Argentines prefer *mate amargo* (bitter, i.e., without sugar), but northerners often take

it *dulce*, with sugar and fragrant herbs known as *yuyos* (literally, weeds). While it's a mostly homebound custom in Argentina, Uruguayans (who consume even more than Argentines) make it a public affair as they walk the streets with leather-encased gourds and enormous thermoses. In the open-air sauna that is the Paraguayan summer, street vendors sell ice-cold *yerba* in the form of *tereré*.

Supermarkets sell *yerba* in bulk packages with engaging designs that look half a century old. It's also available in tea bags as *mate cocido*, which is weaker, and may be more palatable to neophytes than the first bitter sips from the freshly prepared gourd. Do not confuse it, however, with *mate de coca*, another innocuous infusion made from the leaf of the notorious coca plant.

Fortunately for its Argentine aficionados, *mate* is inexpensive. No one really has to worry, as Dobrizhoffer did, that:

If many topers in Europe waste their substance by an immoderate use of wine and other intoxicating liquors, there are no fewer in America who drink away their fortunes in potations of the herb of Paraguay.

western edge, Miramar is a reliable *rotisería* (deli); it's also an unfashionable restaurant unsuitable for a formal meal or romantic night out, but great for unpretentious lunches or dinners with poised service. Unlike many recently gentrified—or plasticized—*porteño* cafés, this classic corner bar has applied nothing more than a fresh coat of paint to walls that sport black-and-white photos of traditional tango musicians (rather than glitzy contemporary dancers). That's the backdrop for flavorful entrées such as oxtail soup, *gambas al ajillo* (garlic prawns), and *lechón* (roast pork). Prices range US$5–8 for most items.

## JAPANESE
### ICHISOU ❸❸

Venezuela 2145, tel. 011/4942-5853

**HOURS:** Mon.-Fri. noon-2:30 P.M., Mon.-Sat. 7-11:30 P.M.

Notably Japanese in its minimalist decor and cuisine, Ichisou occupies an improbable Once location with no other restaurants and few other businesses of any kind. Relatively expensive by current standards, with lunch for US$15 and up, it may be a lesser value than some more recent additions to the Asian scene, but discriminating diners and longtime consumers vouch for its authenticity and quality.

RESTAURANTS

# BEHIND CLOSED DOORS

One of the most notable developments in Buenos Aires's dining scene over the past couple years is the appearance of private restaurants with *puertas cerradas* (closed doors). Unlike most restaurants, they occupy houses or apartments where the chef and his family live, though they've upgraded their (sometimes small) kitchens to professional standards.

Rather than large, diverse menus, they offer fixed multi-course tasting menus that change weekly; they can sometimes accommodate special needs (most notably allergies). In addition, they aim at a select public, often but not exclusively of foreign visitors or residents, by reservation only. Everyone sits at one or two tables, making it seem more like a dinner party, where strangers soon share their conversations. The chef himself may wait on tables and usually explains the idea behind each dish.

Reservations are essential, most often by Internet but occasionally by telephone. Since drop-ins are not possible, no addresses appear in the listings here, but they occasionally have last-minute cancellations and keep waiting lists for such instances. Starting time is usually around 9 or 9:30 P.M.

## CASA SALTSHAKER

Highly publicized (thanks to *The New York Times* and LAN's in-flight magazine *In*), Casa Salt-Shaker (www.casasaltshaker.com) surmounts the hype with Friday and Saturday dinners that normally focus on a theme or a region: for example, an "Aztec-Inka faceoff" comparing Mexi-can and Peruvian dishes. Chef Dan Perlman, a transplanted New Yorker who also writes an exceptional food blog (www.saltshaker.net), can accommodate only a dozen diners in his Barrio Norte garden apartment. If demand is high, he and his Peruvian partner Henry Tapia add Thursday and/or Sunday dinners.

Dinner costs US$25 per person. For another US$10 pp, guests can enjoy wines paired with each course, but other vintages are available by the bottle. Those bringing their own wine pay US$3 for corkage.

## CASA FÉLIX

In the barrio of Caballito, not far from Chacarita cemetery, Casa Félix (tel. 011/4555-1882, www.diegofelix.com) draws from varied Latin American traditions to produce predominantly vegetarian dishes, though fish often appears on the menu. Chef Diego Félix, who worked several years in San Francisco Bay Area restaurants, prepares unique appetizers such as hibiscus flowers stuffed with ricotta and zucchini, and main dishes such as *surubí* (Paraná catfish) with fresh tomato sauce, accompanied by fried manioc and arugula.

Félix and his American wife, Sandra, work out of a PH (horizontal house) that has an attractive patio for warm evenings. Twelve guests is the norm, but they can occasionally handle a couple more. It's open Thursday, Friday, and Saturday night; dinner costs US$28, plus US$12 for paired wines if desired. Wine is also available by the bottle, and there's a US$3 corkage fee.

# Retiro                                           Map 5

While Retiro isn't a gastronomic focus in the same way that Palermo is, it has a smattering of quality eateries.

## ARGENTINE AND REGIONAL
**( JUANA M. $$**
Carlos Pellegrini 1535,

tel. 011/4326-0462

**HOURS:** Daily lunch and dinner, closed Sat. lunch

In an inconspicuous location, close to Retiro and Recoleta luxury hotels, this cavernous basement restaurant serves *parrillada* and pasta dishes, including unlimited access to a spectacularly diverse salad bar (reason enough to eat here). Steel girders support the high ceilings and local artists' paintings decorate the walls, while the plain white wooden tables make a certain no-frills style statement.

Prices are rising here but it's still good for groups on a budget, with a quick kitchen and friendly service. Its main drawback is a high noise level, even when it's not all that full. It closes for vacation the first two weeks of January.

## ITALIAN
### FILO ⑤⑤

San Martín 975, tel. 011/4311-0312, www.filo-ristorante.com
**HOURS:** Daily noon-2 A.M.

In the sector newly known as the Nuevo Bajo, Filo is Buenos Aires's hippest and most adventurous pizzeria (along with *parrillada*, even when pizza is good, it stands obstinately among the capital's most conservative cuisines). In both food and decor, the basics are Mediterranean, but the details are avant-garde (such as its basement art space, which showcases contemporary painters and sculptors).

Filo occupies a long, deep lot where a stylish bar—tightly stretched cattle hides protect it from footmarks—leads to a split-level dining area. The pizzas, starting around US$7 and large enough for two adults with reasonable appetites, feature a light thin crust and uncommon toppings, such as artichoke hearts. Other Italian specialties, likewise embellished with contemporary touches, are also available in the US$10 and up range, and there's a large list of Argentine and foreign wines.

At lunchtime, Filo is popular with bankers and business people, but at night it becomes a fashion-conscious scene, and it can get distractingly noisy—and not just from bad techno. The food, though, remains the centerpiece, and the service is enthusiastic.

## SCANDINAVIAN
### CLUB DANÉS ⑤

Av. Leandro N. Alem 1074, 12th fl., tel. 011/4312-5442
**HOURS:** Mon.-Fri. lunch

For short-term visitors whose usual lunchtime question is "where's the beef?", authentic Danish *smørrebrød* (open-faced sandwiches) may seem an improbable alternative. Still, anyone spending an extended time in Buenos Aires might appreciate this unfashionable but still appetizing cuisine, which is also cheap—no more than US$4 per sandwich, and there are daily specials in the US$7 range.

On top of that, so to speak, it's one of the city's best view restaurants, with a condor's view of Avenida Alem and the nearby ferry port; other tall buildings, though, block Puerto Madero. The sparse Scandinavian decor and travel posters pay homage to Hans Christian Andersen and the Danish monarchy.

## SPANISH
### TANCAT ⑤⑤

Paraguay 645, tel. 011/4312-5442
**HOURS:** Mon.-Sat. noon-12:30 A.M.

Even in the midst of economic crisis, the *tasca*-style Tancat remained wildly popular for lunches (now around US$8–14 pp) and good-natured service; don't miss the *jamón serrano* (prosciutto) appetizer. Reservations are almost essential for tables, which are few, but individual lunchgoers can slide into a seat along the long wooden bar, which is backed by shelves of wines covered with business cards, posters, and photos. Its Spanish owner delivers a personal greeting to everyone who comes through the door.

## THAI
### EMPIRE BAR ⑤⑤

Tres Sargentos 427, tel. 011/4312-5706, www.empirethai.net
**HOURS:** Mon.-Fri. lunch and dinner, Sat. dinner only

Despite splitting from Las Cañitas's culinary landmark Lotus Neo Thai, the Empire Bar still offers a fine Thai menu with some spicy dishes (by *porteño* standards, at least). Midday specials go for around US$9, most entrées for US$9–17, and there's a 6–9 P.M. happy hour at the bar. While the menu remains the same as it was before, the decor is now more contemporary.

## CATTLE CULTURE ON THE PAMPAS

From his hotel room on Avenida de Mayo, U.S. poet Robert Lowell once wrote that he could hear "the bulky, beefy breathing of the herds." Ever since feral livestock transformed the Pampas in the 16th century, displacing the native guanaco and rhea, cattle have been a symbol of wealth and the foundation of the Argentine diet. Riding across the pampas, Charles Darwin found the reliance on beef remarkable:

I had now been several days without tasting any thing besides meat: I did not at all dislike this new regimen; but I felt as if it would only have agreed with me with hard exercise. I have heard that patients in England, when desired to confine themselves exclusively to an animal diet, even with the hope of life before their eyes, have scarce been able to endure it. Yet the Gaucho in the Pampas, for months together, touches nothing but beef.... It is, perhaps, from their meat regimen that

the Gauchos, like other carnivorous animals, can abstain long from food. I was told that at Tandeel, some troops voluntarily pursued a party of Indians for three days, without eating or drinking.

Recent research has suggested that this diet has not been quite so universal as once imagined – urban archaeologist Daniel Schávelzon has unearthed evidence that, for instance, fish consumption was greater in colonial Buenos Aires than people thought – but there's no doubt that the *porteño parrilla* is a culinary institution. Beef may not be healthy in the quantities that some Argentines enjoy, and many of them will even admit it. But few *porteños* can bypass the capital's traditional restaurants – or even the tourist-oriented grills where flamboyantly clad urban gauchos stir the glowing coals beneath a vertical spit – without craving that savory beef.

For most Argentines, *bien cocido* (well done) is the standard for steak, but *jugoso* (rare) and *a punto* (medium) are not uncommon.

# Recoleta and Barrio Norte    Map 6

Recoleta has some of Buenos Aires's swankiest restaurants, but also some of its best bargains.

## ARGENTINE
### LOS PINOS ⑤
Azcuénaga 1500, tel. 011/4822-8704
**HOURS:** Daily lunch and dinner
Occupying an old-style apothecary, its stained wooden cases still stocked with antique bottles and rising nearly to the ceiling, this Barrio Norte favorite offers fixed-price lunch and dinner specials, with a range of choices; the à la carte menu of beef, seafood, and pasta is not much more expensive, as the comparably priced entrées include a side order. The service is well-intentioned but inconsistent.

## SPANISH
### JOSÉ LUIS ⑤⑤⑤
Av. Quintana 456, tel. 011/4807-0606
**HOURS:** Daily lunch and dinner
A Recoleta stalwart, José Luis is an Asturian seafood restaurant that stresses fresher and lighter dishes than most of its counterparts, though the food falls short of truly elite. The menu is enormous, with some expensive imported Spanish items that reflect neighborhood standards; more affordable are starters like the refreshing gazpacho (US$6) and main dishes like the *lomo de merluza* (hake filet, garnished with prosciutto and clams, US$14).

Less formal than it looks from outside, José Luis's latticed walls and ceilings face a subtropical patio with a rushing waterfall, but when big groups dine here, the noise level inhibits quiet conversation. It has a big wine list and, while there's no wine by the glass, there are half-bottles of decent Argentine wines.

### OVIEDO $$$

Beruti 2602, tel. 011/4822-5415,
www.oviedoresto.com.ar

**HOURS:** Mon.-Sat. lunch and dinner

Internationally recognized Oviedo specializes in Spanish seafood but also serves Patagonian lamb and standards like steak, with most entrées in the US$13–18 range (though some reach US$30 or more). Fresh from Mar del Plata, the catch of the day is usually one of the better choices. Though it has a track record, Oviedo is arguably overpriced compared to more audacious restaurants in Palermo.

The extensive wine list reaches upwards of US$200 for some bottles, though others cost less than US$10. The decor is traditional, with dark wood paneling, and formal; the upstairs dining room has better light, but it's also a smoking area. At midday, the business-oriented clientele is overwhelmingly male, but at night it gets a blend of neighborhood residents and tourists. Service is commendable.

# Palermo                                    Map 7

Palermo is, without question, Argentine cuisine's creative center. The main geographical areas of interest are Palermo Viejo (subdivided into Palermo Soho near Plaza Serrano—also known as Plazoleta Cortázar—and Palermo Hollywood north of Avenida Juan B. Justo); the Botánico (between Avenida Las Heras and Avenida del Libertador); and Las Cañitas (the area between Avenida Luis María Campos and the Campo Argentino de Polo). That said, there are other options scattered around the city's largest barrio.

## AMERICAN
### MARK'S DELI AND COFFEE HOUSE $

El Salvador 4701, tel. 011/4832-6244

**HOURS:** Mon.-Sat. 8:30 A.M.-9:30 P.M., Sun. 10 A.M.-7 P.M.

In the heart of Palermo SoHo, Mark's is a U.S.-style deli, bright and cheerful with indoor and patio seating, outstanding sandwiches, and choice sweets, including cookies and brownies; there's a small selection of wines by the glass and large and refreshing glasses of lemonade for those hot afternoons.

## ARGENTINE AND REGIONAL
### CABERNET $$

Borges 1757, tel. 011/4831-3071,
www.cabernet-restaurant.com.ar

**HOURS:** Daily noon-2 A.M.

While its Palermo SoHo location places it in Argentine cuisine's new wave, this elegant restaurant and wine bar owes much to the handsomely traditional features of the defunct downtown Clark's. Dishes, such as glazed lamb accompanied by a spinach-based risotto, tweak conventional tastes without alienating them; the portions are substantial but not gluttonously large. The wine list *is* large.

Where Cabernet differs from most other Palermo restaurants is the preservation and restoration, rather than recycling, of the corner building it occupies. While the pastel-yellow exterior and large picture windows may not be quite traditional, the surviving *vitreaux*, along with its burnished interior woodwork and chandeliers, link the past with the present. It also has a large, attractive patio for outdoor dining.

### LA CABRERA $

Cabrera 5099, tel. 011/4831-7002

**HOURS:** Tues.-Sun. lunch, daily dinner

At the *parrilla* of the moment, the US$10 *bife de chorizo* should satisfy two hungry diners, as it also comes with a sampler of side dishes that includes pureed potatoes, pumpkin, and

RESTAURANTS

RESTAURANTS

© WAYNE BERNHARDSON

Palermo SoHo's Cabernet may be better than any other Buenos Aires restaurant at pairing food and wine.

applesauce, and several salads. The decor is informal, its exposed brick walls covered with art works for sale, while an electric train chugs above the bar.

Reservations are advisable at dinnertime, when it has a more formal branch a few doors north. There's a 10 percent discount for cash customers.

### ( LA CUPERTINA $

Cabrera 5300, tel. 011/4777-3711
**HOURS:** Tues.-Sat. 11:30 A.M.-3:30 P.M. and Tues.-Sun. 7:30-11 P.M.

For quality-to-price ratio, the hands-down best choice for empanadas and regional dishes is Palermo SoHo's La Cupertina, which also wins points for its invitingly rustic style, with sturdily handsome wooden chairs and tables. The chicken empanadas, *pizzetas, locro* (a spicy stew), and *humitas en chala* (similar to tamales, wrapped in corn stalks) are exquisite and so cheap that price is irrelevant, even with wine; try also the desserts, especially the Spanish custard *natillas* and *arroz con leche*.

The menu hasn't changed in years, and that's a good thing; the only drawback is inconsistent (if well-intentioned) service.

### LELÉ DE TROYA $$

Costa Rica 4901, tel. 011/4832-2726
**HOURS:** Daily lunch and dinner

Showcasing Palermo SoHo's informality, Lelé de Troya does the traditional but adds nouvelle touches that set it apart from run-of-the-mill Argentine food. The braised mixed vegetables that accompany the Patagonian lamb, for instance, come enclosed in a light, flaky phyllo dough. There's also a good dessert list.

Physically, Lelé is invitingly casual from its corner entrance, where an arbor of verdant climbing vines shades the sidewalk tables, to its rooftop terrace, where a canopy of sycamores overhangs the weekend barbecues. In between, there's a wine bar and three levels with at least a dozen different dining rooms, painted in bright primary colors. In the daytime, a central skylight illuminates the open kitchen and one of the dining areas.

## MIRANDA 💲💲
Costa Rica 5602, tel. 011/4771-4255
**HOURS:** Sun.-Thurs. 9 A.M.-1 A.M., Fri.-Sat. 9 A.M.-2 A.M.
In Palermo Hollywood, the spacious and stylish Miranda is more than a step above the conventional corner *parrilla,* and also diverse enough that beef need not be the centerpiece of a meal here. Lunchtime specials (US$10) that include a starter, main dish, dessert and drink are a phenomenal bargain. The chicken salad (US$5), with a mustard vinaigrette dressing and grilled pumpkin, is a meal in itself. The service can be a little too self-consciously hip.

## LA PAILA 💲
Costa Rica 4848, tel. 011/4833-3599,
www.lapaila-restaurante.com.ar
**HOURS:** Tues.-Sun. lunch and dinner
Even more specifically regional than most places of its sort, La Paila prepares a Catamarca-based cuisine of empanadas, *guiso* and *locro* (both stews), llama steaks, quinoa-based dishes, and tamales, plus sweets (*mate* with homemade bread and regional jams). In summer, it's closed at midday, but the rest of the year there are bargain lunches.

The regional emphasis extends to the wine list, with bottles from Catamarca, Salta, and La Rioja provinces. In addition, there's live folkloric music on Friday and Saturday nights, but occasionally Thursdays and Sundays as well; in part a cultural center, La Paila sells indigenous crafts and also has a library.

## STANDARD 💲💲
Fitz Roy 2203, tel. 011/4779-2774
**HOURS:** Daily lunch and dinner
Utterly unlike the owners' other restaurant, the Southeast Asian landmark on the opposite corner, this diner-style locale appeals to mid-1950s *porteño* nostalgia, but both the decor and the menu have adapted themselves to the 21st century. Sophisticated versions of home-cooked dishes such as fried chicken, *milanesa,* roast pork, and lamb, as well as nightly specials, fall in the US$10–13 range.

Portions are large, but the diet-conscious can ask for half-portions (which are cheaper,

as well). Given the conservative *porteño* palate, some dishes—the crab cake appetizer, in particular—are surprisingly spicy.

## ARMENIAN
### GARBIS 💲💲
Scalabrini Ortiz 3190, tel. 011/4511-6600,
www.garbis.com.ar
**HOURS:** Daily noon-3:30 P.M. and 8 P.M.-midnight
In the Botánico neighborhood, the Armenian-Arab Garbis prepares outstanding hummus and a variety of kebabs (stick with the lamb rather than chicken, which tends to dry out). Some more elaborate kebabs (around US$15) are large enough for two, so ask before ordering.

## ASIAN
### 🄲 LOTUS NEO THAI 💲💲
Ortega Y Gasset 1782, tel. 011/4771-4449,
www.restaurantelotus.com.ar
**HOURS:** Tues.-Sun. dinner
Reached by a narrow staircase that eventually reveals an expansive 1st-floor dining room with floor-hugging tables and cushions, Lotus was Argentina's Thai-food pioneer. A quiet locale with soothing music and striking lotus-themed decor, it's still one of few places in the country where it's possible to taste truly spicy Southeast Asian dishes, flavorful plates that challenge the palate even of those accustomed to it. Even after 2002's steep devaluation, Lotus remained, and still is, relatively expensive, but it's worth the splurge.

### SUDESTADA 💲💲
Guatemala 5602, tel. 011/4776-3777
**HOURS:** Daily lunch and dinner
Chopsticks are the default option at Sudestada, one of the city's first and finest Southeast Asian restaurants. Its punning name comes from its region of origin but also from the term for the South Atlantic storms that often drench Buenos Aires.

Just over the Palermo Hollywood line, this Vietnamese kitchen can be slow, but dishes such as fried rice with shrimp and pork, pot stickers (known here as "dumplings"), and

Thai noodles (for which chopsticks are inappropriate) are simple but tasty. On request, dishes can be genuinely spicy.

Under the same ownership as nearby Standard, Sudestada exudes simplicity, with plain white slatted walls, plain white tables, wooden chairs, and huge windows with street views. The kitchen is visible from the dining area.

## BRAZILIAN

### ☪ MARÍA FULÓ ❺❺
Cabrera 5065, tel. 011/4831-0103,
www.mariafuloresto.com.ar
**HOURS:** Tues.-Sat. from 8 P.M., Sat.-Sun. noon-4 P.M.

After a brief closure, Palermo SoHo's brilliant Brazilian restaurant has reopened as good as ever, in bright new quarters with a small interior patio for open-air dining. For US$8, the *ximxim de galinha* of chicken breast, shrimp, and cashews in coconut milk is exquisite enough, but the *maracuyá* (passion fruit) mousse may be the city's best dessert.

## CAFÉS

### MOTTA ❸
Humboldt 1855, tel. 011/4774-7671,
www.mottahelados.com.ar
**HOURS:** Daily 11 A.M.-11 P.M.

Palermo Hollywood's Motta is a hybrid café and creamery with lunch specials (US$7) that include a large salad or baguette sandwich, plus a drink and a sample of their own outstanding ice cream. Unlike several nearby restaurants, it's not worth a trip across town for a meal, but it's ideal for a light lunch or dessert.

### VOULEZ BAR ❸
Cerviño 3802, tel. 011/4802-4817
**HOURS:** Mon.-Sat. 8 A.M.-midnight (later on Fri. and Sat.)

"Paris of the South" may be an overused cliché, but this Francophile café's name makes a pun on the term boulevard, which Argentines use to describe a divided street with a heavily landscaped median (as Cerviño is here). There's sidewalk seating on its Botánico corner, to enjoy diverse lunch specials, ample sandwiches, and especially fine salads—try the *ensalada*

*blanc,* of chicken over diverse greens flavored with vinaigrette (US$5). The ceviche, though, depends too much on mussels.

## FUSION

### ACABAR ❸
Honduras 5733, tel. 011/4772-0845,
www.acabarnet.com.ar
**HOURS:** Daily 8 P.M.-2 A.M.

Young and hip, its very name a double entendre with sexual connotations, Acabar is a Palermo Hollywood bar/restaurant with a labyrinth of rooms and eclectic decor even down to the physical menu itself—which consists of piles of cue cards. Strong on pastas, such as ravioli and gnocchi, Acabar also is notable for its *entrada oriental* of hummus, tabouleh, pita bread, and the like (US$3.50), but the food on balance is slightly above pub-grub standards. There are good mixed drinks, but its wine list is limited. The service is attentive.

### AZEMA ❸❸
Carranza 1875, tel. 011/4774-4191
**HOURS:** Mon.-Sat. dinner

Its "exotic bistro" label sounds pretentious, but the French colonial menu at this Palermo Hollywood locale delivers a creative and flavorful blend of continental and Asian styles. Starters, for instance, might mean dim sum pot stickers (US$3) with a ginger/peanut dip, and the catch of the day could be *abadejo* (pollock) with a coconut curry sauce and baked banana slices (US$10). It's also comfortable, and the service is some of Buenos Aires's best and most knowledgeable—the staff knows the menu, and what to recommend, inside out. Even the breads are diverse and far tastier than the norm.

That said, it's worth getting the name of the person who takes your reservation, and reconfirming that reservation earlier in the day.

### BAR 6 ❸❸
Armenia 1676, tel. 011/4833-6807,
www.barseis.com
**HOURS:** Mon.-Sat. from 8 A.M.

With its high ceilings and mezzanine loft,

popular Bar 6 embodies the modishly recycled Palermo SoHo aesthetic. Quality entrées like *ojo de bife* (rib-eye steak), stir-fried vegetables, and polenta with goat cheese fall into the US$10 range, with a few pricier items, but the menu is less diverse than some others in the neighborhood. Even on weeknights, reservations are advisable for a table; otherwise, eat at the bar.

## BAR URIARTE 🟢🟢

Uriarte 1572, tel. 011/4834-6004,
www.baruriarte.com.ar
**HOURS:** Daily lunch and dinner

Exuding post-industrial chic, Bar Uriarte's kitchen is visible from the street and from the entryway aisle that leads to a long wooden bar. At the back, a spacious, sparsely decorated dining area draws natural light from a large picture window. Atop concrete floors, simple but handsome wooden furniture looks onto a patio where potted citrus trees and gardenias stand before a brick-wall background covered by ficus vines and ornamental conifers.

Uriarte's food is a tasty Mediterranean blend of starters, including *provoleta*, thin-crusted pizzas with unusual toppings (at least for Argentina) like asparagus, and heartier main dishes, such as *matambre de cerdo* (pork flank) with pumpkin puree. The weekend/holiday brunch is an excellent way to sample Uriarte's best, but weekday lunch specials cost only about US$8. The service is attentive and there's a happy hour 7–10:30 P.M.

On the downside, some tables are too close together, and the music is dreary elevator electronica (with an occasional tango touch). Staircases at each end of the building lead to a mezzanine with a few additional tables and an art space (www.espaciouriarte.com.ar).

## BOBO 🟢🟢

Guatemala 4882, tel. 011/4774-0505,
www.bobohotel.com
**HOURS:** Daily 8 A.M.–1 A.M.

On the ground floor of its namesake hotel, this comfortably stylish Palermo SoHo restaurant prepares very fine three-course lunches (US$10), plus entrées such as smoked-cheese ravioli (US$9), braised lamb with sautéed vegetables, hummus, and arugula pesto (US$12), and an intriguing dessert menu. Its creators have preserved the traditional woodwork of the recycled building, integrating it with clean interior lines and a contemporary color scheme. There's plenty of space between the metal-frame tables, topped with handsome dark wood, and comfortable armless easy chairs for seating.

## DIVINA PATAGONIA 🟢🟢

Honduras 5710, tel. 011/4771-6864,
www.divinapatagonia.com
**HOURS:** Daily from 8 P.M.

At Divina Patagonia, painted wildflowers adorn the walls of a recycled residence that fuses contemporary urban design with a sophisticated menu based on Argentina's southern lakes, seas, steppes, and woodlands. As a starter, the *tabla* of smoked meats and cheeses (US$12) is too big for two diners unless they're also sharing a single entrée such as wild boar with a mango sauce, embellished with a light pumpkin flan (US$13). If spending more than a certain amount, diners paying with cash instead of credit can take home a bottle of house wine.

## LOBBY 🟢🟢

Nicaragua 5944, tel. 011/4770-9335
**HOURS:** Daily 9 A.M.–midnight

Hard to categorize, this cozy and informal locale is a hybrid restaurant, wine bar, and wine shop whose breakfast and lunch menu is both inexpensive and outstanding. For US$8, the seafood salad, with shrimp, prawns, and mussels, is an exceptional value; in addition, there are sandwiches, vegetarian dishes, a large by-the-glass wine selection, and they'll sell a bottle off the wall for on-site consumption with only a token corkage fee. They also carry an ample selection of magazines and newspapers, but the good-natured waitresses sometimes seem to be suffering from ADD. There is limited sidewalk seating.

From January to mid-February, Lobby closes as early as 8 P.M.

### ⟨ OLSEN ❸❸
Gorriti 5870, tel. 011/4776-7677
**HOURS:** Tues.-Sat. from noon, Sun. from 10 A.M.

One of Buenos Aires's most creative restaurants, this Palermo Hollywood locale serves what might be called Scandinavian *criollo* cuisine, with dishes like ravioli with goat cheese and pork roast with raspberry sauce, for upwards of US$10. The bar serves the standard aperitifs but also a literally dizzying variety of vodka-based cocktails. The mashed potatoes that accompany some dishes finish with a hot radish flourish, while bread consists of bagels and pretzels, with light dips to accompany them. The flatware is distinguished for its irregularity, as if each piece were custom-made for this restaurant.

Olsen is as notable for its ambience as its food, having devoted at least part of what was once a PH (horizontal house) lot into a sculpture garden that replicates a Scandinavian boreal forest of birches, cypresses, and pines. There's a garden deck with limited seating, and a canvas-covered deck that permits al fresco dining even when it's drizzling; sliding-glass doors, open in fine weather, separate the deck and the interior, which has a soaring ceiling and mezzanine seating. A central woodstove rises to the roof.

Olsen's noise level is only moderate but, on the downside, the deck and garden have become a free-fire zone for smokers (not permitted indoors). The service is attentive, but a little short of the standards set by the food.

### SOCIAL PARAÍSO ❸❸
Honduras 5182, tel. 011/4831-4556,
www.socialparaiso.com.ar
**HOURS:** Tues.-Sat. lunch and dinner, Sun. lunch

At this casual decor-free nouvelle-cuisine bistro in Palermo SoHo, the US$5 lunch specials feature items such as *bondiola* (pork loin) with a tabouleh salad; creatively presented entrées such as stuffed chicken breast with mozzarella and bacon, *sorrentinos* with goat and gruyere cheese with toasted almond and herb butter, and Patagonian lamb with grilled vegetables, fall into the US$8–11 range.

Social Paraíso also has innovative desserts, and a diversity of wine by the glass, at reasonable prices. When it gets crowded, though, the service can be shaky.

### TE MATARÉ RAMÍREZ ❸❸
Gorriti 5054, tel. 011/4831-9156,
www.tematareramirez.com
**HOURS:** Tues.-Sun. dinner

In a category of its own, definitely not a place to bring the kids or even sup alone, this self-styled "aphrodisiac restaurant" is notorious for suggestive food and decor. Diners are slow to order as they ogle the salacious menu while contemplating entrées (around US$10) like *la vertiente inagotable de tu deseo* (the inexhaustible spring of your desire, beef in a merlot sauce with vegetable tempura) and *cierro los ojos y me abismo en el mar del placer* (I close my eyes and sink into a sea of pleasure, swordfish with a salad of fava beans, bacon, and carrots in tomato vinaigrette).

Desserts include *estímulo lurioso* (lustful stimulation, ice cream with a sauce of forest fruits), and *amantes que se comparten* (shared lovers, a chocolate fondue with fruit, brownie, coconut, and fig truffles).

In new spacious and upgraded Palermo SoHo quarters, Ramírez also hosts occasional live theater (humorously sexual but far from pornographic) and jazz, and showcases erotic art.

### EL VIEJO INDECENTE ❸
Thames 1907, tel. 011/4775-2666
**HOURS:** Daily lunch and dinner

Taking its name from a collection of stories by Charles Bukowski—something of a deity among Buenos Aires's bohemians—El Viejo Indecente mocks itself as an outpost for lowlifes (the name is an idiom that translates as "dirty old man"). In fact, it's a casual bar/restaurant that's less trendy than some other Palermo SoHo locales, though it has its artsy side—the colorful tile fragments artistically embedded in the sidewalk add to its ramshackle charm.

The food is good enough, especially at weekday lunchtime when main menu entrées go for half price; the *fajitas de pollo* aren't what you might expect from a Tex-Mex restaurant in the Northern Hemisphere, but they're not bad, and the cheap carpaccio starter deserves a taste. Several nights a week it has live music.

## INDIAN
### KATMANDU $$
Av. Córdoba 3547, tel. 011/4963-1122,
www.katmandu.restaurant.com.ar
**HOURS:** Mon.-Sat. dinner

On the barrio's western border, Katmandu gets high marks from the capital's small Indian community of about 150 people. It uses Argentine basics (Patagonian lamb, for instance) but seasons them with ginger, cardamom, and other spices according to the client (most Argentine palates can't handle anything too strong). Side dishes include naan bread and basmati rice.

## ITALIAN
### BELLA ITALIA $$
República Árabe Siria 3285, tel. 011/4802-4253,
www.bellaitalia-gourmet.com.ar
**HOURS:** Mon.-Sat. dinner only

Under the same ownership as the nearby café, Bella Italia is a more formal restaurant, in one of a handful of horizontal houses that have survived the high-rise boom in the densely populated, upper-middle-class sector of the Botánico between Avenida Las Heras and Avenida del Libertador. The most economical plates are pastas; among other dishes, the carpaccio (US$6) and shrimp risotto (US$12) merit special mention, and there's wine by the glass. Its menu and decor are more elaborate, and the service more professional, than the café, but its food is not demonstrably superior.

### BELLA ITALIA CAFÉ BAR $
República Árabe Siria 3330, tel. 011/4807-5120
**HOURS:** Daily 7 A.M.-1 A.M.

Worth a Botánico detour from elsewhere in town, this is the informal, moderately priced café version of a nearby restaurant whose other unlikely location is Fort Worth, Texas. For around US$6, it has outstanding squash

gnocchi with a subtle cream sauce, along with fine cannelloni, panini, and salads. The small wine list, some available by the glass, is almost exclusively from Bodega Norton.

Architecturally, the locale blends distinctively Argentine touches with a Mediterranean villa decor of Doric columns. Sofa-style benches and small tables line one wall; a central skylight illuminates the space with a diffuse glow. Other chairs are freestanding. It has friendly management, good service, some shady sidewalk tables, and is cash only.

### DIMAGGIO'S $
Ugarteche 3154, tel. 011/4804-3558,
www.dimaggios.com.ar
**HOURS:** Daily 8 A.M.-1 A.M.

Several predecessors, including a truly exceptional one, have failed in this well-placed Botánico location, but DiMaggio's seems to be making a go of it as a neighborhood-oriented alternative that falls somewhere between a casual trattoria and a more formal restaurant. The thin-crusted pizzas, available in half-portions for individual diners, include a diversity of toppings (the prosciutto is outstanding). There are also fine gnocchi, ravioli, and salads, but the service is inconsistent.

In addition to the spacious dining room, which gets fine natural light and has glistening hardwood floors, a secluded back patio is studded with bamboo and Japanese maples. Sidewalk seating is also available.

### ELISABETTA $$
Sinclair 3027, tel. 011/4773-8629
**HOURS:** Daily 8 A.M.-1 A.M.

Prices for pastas may be a little higher in this high-rent neighborhood than elsewhere in the city, but the oversized pumpkin ravioli with an almond and mushroom sauce are worth the extra few pesos. Elisabetta, which has a luminous mezzanine and shaded outdoor seating in a building whose redbrick walls are a reminder of earlier years, also specializes in fish and seafood, and its dark chocolate mousse (US$5) is rich but light. The service is outstanding.

RESTAURANTS

### GUIDO'S BAR $

República de la India 2843, tel. 011/4802-2391

**HOURS:** Mon.-Fri. 7 A.M.-1:30 A.M., Sat. 7 A.M.-5 P.M.

Facing the zoo, an elaborately *fileteado* facade distinguishes this tiny but personable neighborhood cantina. Standard Italian entrées are in the US$4–6 range, but the US$10 lunch (including dessert and drink, plus a digestive *limoncello*) is an excellent value. Its character also comes from the movie stills (Frank, Dino, and Sammy) and posters that clutter its walls, along with such *piropos* (aphorisms) as "I don't mind if you point out my failures, but I can't stand constructive criticism."

### LUCKY LUCIANO $$

Blvd. Cerviño 3943, tel. 011/4802-3943,

www.lucky-luciano.com.ar

**HOURS:** Mon.-Sat. dinner

Seeming to name your restaurant for a New York mobster, and decorating (partially, at least) with *Godfather* posters, falls dangerously close to Mafia kitsch. It happens, though, that

the owner/sommelier of this Botánico trattoria is Luciano Sosto, who offers a quality menu notable for a nightly risotto (US$10) and a separate three-course dinner (US$16), as well as inexpensive pizzas. The decor is cinematic, the service attentive, and most of their wines are available by the glass.

### SA GIARA $$

Gurruchaga 1806, tel. 011/4832-5062,

www.sagiara.com.ar

**HOURS:** Tues.-Sun. 9 A.M.-1 A.M.

New in late 2007, Sa Giara brings something new to Italo-Argentine cuisine with Sardininian *culurgionis,* resembling Chinese or Japanese pot stickers but stuffed with sweet potato (US$11) or three meats (beef, lamb, pork, US$13), or other items. An early success, it also has inexpensive sandwiches of prosciutto, artisanal cheeses, and the like. The building is an attractive neo-Mediterranean villa with two covered patios, as well as sidewalk seating; it's also a late-afternoon

Sa Giara's Sardinian menu adds a twist to the Italo-Argentine gastronomical scene in Palermo SoHo.

© WAYNE BERNHARDSON

teahouse. The service is fine and the management cheerful and obliging.

## EL ÚLTIMO BESO $$

Nicaragua 4880, tel. 011/4832-7711,
www.elultimobeso.com.ar

**HOURS:** Mon.-Tues. noon-8 P.M., Wed.-Sun. noon-2 A.M.

In fashion-conscious Palermo SoHo, "The Last Kiss" has transformed a traditional Palermo house into a low-key restaurant. The lunch menu (around US$5) features starters, such as the mushroom omelette, and entrées, such as stir-fried chicken and vegetables. Pasta and risotto entrées fall into the US$10 range, while beef and fish dishes are slightly more expensive.

To the sounds of standards like "Don't Get Around Much Anymore" (all the music is in English), lunchgoers and diners sit on elongated sofas beneath soft interior pastels, or at French-style chairs and tables. There's also garden seating beneath a rose arbor with fountains and ficus shrubs.

El Último Beso is also an afternoon teahouse with panini and cakes.

## JAPANESE
### DASHI $$

Fitz Roy 1613, tel. 011/4776-3500, www.dashi.com.ar

**HOURS:** Mon.-Sat. lunch and dinner

Appropriately enough for its Palermo Hollywood location, Dashi hosted Antonio Banderas, Melanie Griffith, and Emma Thompson for Banderas's birthday celebration, but the food is the enduring star here. Dashi's sushi and sashimi are visually stunning and gastronomically satisfying, and the desserts are surprisingly good—though their names (e.g., Monte Fuji) are more Japanese than the sweets themselves. The building itself has large picture windows, high ceilings, and contemporary furnishings, but the service can be a little absent-minded for a restaurant with its aspirations.

## JARDÍN JAPONÉS $

Av. Casares 2966, tel. 011/4800-1322,
www.jardinjapones.com

**HOURS:** Wed.-Mon. 10 A.M.-6 P.M. and 7:30 P.M.-midnight

No other city restaurant can match the soothing view from the dining room at the Jardín Japonés, with its curving paths, koi ponds, picturesque bridges and temples, and meticulously maintained gardens. Even better, after years of mediocrity, the food finally matches the view, with combined boards of succulent sushi and sashimi in the US$6–7 per person range, as well as dishes like pot stickers and *teppanyaki*. Lunchgoers must pay the US$1 admission fee to the park itself, but at night, when the rest of the park is closed, there is no extra charge.

## JEWISH
### MAMÁ EUROPA $$

Benjamín Matienzo 1599, tel. 011/4777-3835,
www.mamaeuropa.com.ar

**HOURS:** Daily 8 A.M.-1 P.M.

Most Las Cañitas restaurants are fairly conventional *parrillas,* but Mamá Europa offers some Eastern European/Mediterranean flair and a good-humored menu—who else offers a "Shylock's pastrami" containing a "pound of flesh?" The "barely Sefardi" moussaka (US$12), with grated cheese and milk, isn't kosher but it's "too tasty to think about religion." The service is attentive, and there's a good choice of wine by the glass.

## MEXICAN

Mexican food is often not too authentic here, as most *porteño* palates can't handle truly spicy food.

### XALAPA $

El Salvador 4800, tel. 011/4833-6102

**HOURS:** Tues.-Fri. dinner, Sat. lunch and dinner

The kitchen at Xalapa makes a pretty good guacamole, decent margaritas, and pretty good entrées starting around US$5, though most items are a little more expensive. Sidewalk seating snakes around the Palermo SoHo corner lot in good weather, but there's also appropriately attractive interior decor for rainy days or nights.

## PERUVIAN

Peruvian food is enjoying a minor boom in Palermo. Almost exclusively, though, they are "fusion-style" eateries rather than "authentic" neighborhood restaurants catering to the immigrant community here.

### CEVICHE $$
Costa Rica 5644, tel. 011/4776-7373
**HOURS:** Mon.-Fri. 12:30-3 P.M., Mon.-Sat. 8 P.M.-1 A.M.

Its namesake dish is the reliable choice at this neo-Peruvian restaurant, new in late 2007, which is unproven but worth watching. Its spare decor reflects Andean motifs, with museum-style archaeological replicas behind glass insets on walls that are otherwise painted in primary colors. The three-course fixed-price lunches (US$10) are abundant, and the service is good, but the kitchen can be a little slow; for fine weather, it has an attractive rear patio.

### LIBÉLULA $$
Lafinur 3268, tel. 011/4803-6047,
www.libelula.com.ar
**HOURS:** Mon.-Fri. 12:30-3:30 P.M., daily 8 P.M.-12:30 A.M.

Only a painted dragonfly on a hanging shingle marks the entrance to this intimate Japanese-Peruvian restaurant, which seats about 40 people maximum for ceviche, sushi, a quinoa-based prawn "risotto" (US$11), and comparable hybrid dishes. In a Botánico location where only a few low-rise houses survive in the shadow of high-rise luxury flats, it has traditional charm and a secluded garden for outdoor dining. A few dishes, such as the traditional Peruvian favorite *aji de gallina* (chicken breast with potatoes in a cream sauce, US$9) look better than they taste, but the pisco sours are primo. Part of the menu is available for delivery or takeout.

Libélula is open for weekday lunches, but there is no special lunch menu.

### MOSOQ $$
El Salvador 5800, tel. 011/4775-7974, www.mosoq.com
**HOURS:** Mon.-Sat. lunch and dinner

With self-described "Nouveau Andean" food with Peruvian roots, Mosoq goes out of its way to get ingredients for items such as blue-corn cannelloni (US$8), available only in Liniers and brought from Salta. Stuffed manioc with mozzarella makes a fine appetizer, while the *seco de cordero* with lima beans and rice (US$12) is an equally outstanding entrée. Mosoq is nicely backlit with multi-colored modern decor and is popular from Monday to Wednesday when its self-styled martini bar offers a two-for-one happy hour for martinis the entire night.

### ZADVARIE DOC $$
Uriarte 1423, tel. 011/4831-2719
**HOURS:** Tues.-Sat. lunch and dinner, Mon. dinner

An oddball option for Palermo SoHo, Zadvarie has a large menu of fusion-style dishes, but is more notable for its "Peruvian-inspired" specialties. The menu changes every three months, but includes sophisticated versions of llama steaks and fish dishes. Peruvian-style pisco sours, flavored with Angostura bitters, and desserts like the tropical fruit *lucuma* parfait are on the menu. The restaurant also offers authentic, high-quality ceviche and excellent wines by the glass.

Zadvarie falls short in its decor, which is starkly post-industrial except for the appealing rooftop terrace; though a bamboo roof provides some shade, it's best on warm nights.

## POLISH
### LA CASA POLACA $
Jorge Luis Borges 2076, tel. 011/4899-0514
**HOURS:** Tues.-Sat. 8 P.M.-12:30 A.M.

Though they don't have the high profile of Spaniards and Italians, Polish immigrants have been a noteworthy presence in Argentina. Distinctly unhip compared to its neighbors—unless you consider medieval Polish coats-of-arms really cool—the Casa Polaca (Polish House) has a huge and remarkably diverse menu based on quality versions of ethnic specialties like pierogi. Meals are inexpensive, the service is friendly, and its daytime classes also make it the place to brush up on your Polish.

## PORTUGUESE
### EL PORTUGUÉS $$
Báez 499, tel. 011/4771-8699
**HOURS:** Daily 11 A.M.-2 A.M.

One of Las Cañitas's signature restaurants, with interior and sidewalk seating, this *parrilla* serves a half-portion of *bife de chorizo* that some diners might consider a double—consider sharing and then order more if you're still hungry. Though it dominates the intersection of Báez and Ortega y Gasset with its restaurant, a separate pizzeria, and a small grocery, El Portugués unfortunately does not see fit to serve wine by the glass.

## SPANISH AND SEAFOOD

### JANGADA ⑤⑤
Bonpland 1670, tel. 011/4777-4193, www.restaurantejangada.com
**HOURS:** Tues.-Sat. dinner, Sun. lunch

Unique in the city, in new quarters, this Palermo Hollywood restaurant specializes in two-person platters (US$20) of *frutos del Paraná*, and river fish such as *boga, pacú,* and *surubí* (catfish). Starters include fish empanadas (US$1), though the desserts are more conventional. Reservations are advisable.

### MUNDANO ⑤
Malabia and Cabrera, tel. 011/4831-5667, www.mundano.restaurant.com.ar
**HOURS:** Tues.-Sun. 8:30 A.M.-midnight

On a shady corner lot, Mundano's entrance is really a portal to an inviting Mediterranean garden where, in fine weather, there's no need to walk a step farther to enjoy a menu of tapas and fish dishes, with the occasional beef and pasta diversion. The lunch or dinner special, about US$9 with dessert and wine included, is an outstanding value, and service is good as well. Those who venture a little farther can enjoy the airy interior or the sunny 1st-floor terrace. On Friday and Saturday, it may stay open an hour or so longer.

### ◖ NEMO ⑤⑤
Cabello 3672, tel. 011/4803-5878
**HOURS:** Daily lunch and dinner

Originally a branch of Palermo SoHo's Spirit, Nemo is a Botánico favorite that's established its own identity for light entrées, including seafood-based pastas (around US$7–11), and a diverse but steadily evolving fish menu (US$10–15), including at least one freshwater

catch. Its *cuarto tapeo mare*, suitable for two diners, makes an outstanding appetizer. What *Buenos Aires Herald* food writer Dereck Foster calls the capital's "consistently best seafood restaurant" has spare decor and limited sidewalk seating.

### PUNTA BRASAS ⑤
Honduras 5702, tel. 011/4776-2784
**HOURS:** Sun.-Thurs. 8 A.M.-2 A.M., Fri.-Sat. 9 A.M.-4 A.M.

On a corner where other restaurants have failed, Palermo Hollywood's Punta Brasas bills itself as a surf-and-turf *parrilla*, but it also prepares tasty chicken dishes with tangy sauces, and pastas that will satisfy vegetarians. In addition to limited sidewalk seating, it has an appealing rooftop terrace.

### SPIRIT ⑤⑤
Serrano 1550, tel. 011/4833-4360, www.spirit.com.ar
**HOURS:** Daily 9 A.M.-midnight or 1 A.M.

While the quality of Palermo SoHo restaurants surrounding Plazoleta Cortázar (Plaza Serrano) is generally lower than those just a short walk away, the tapas and oyster bar Spirit is a major exception. More often packed than not, it draws crowds for the quality of its seafood tapas (US$12), sufficient for two people, and other fairly priced Spanish dishes. The early opening hour makes it suitable for brunch.

## VEGETARIAN

### LA ESQUINA DE LAS FLORES ⑤
Gurruchaga 1632, tel. 011/4832-8528, www.esquinadelasflores.com.ar
**HOURS:** Mon.-Sat. 9 A.M.-9 P.M.

A pioneer in the organic sector, La Esquina de las Flores has become a *porteño* institution not just for its health-food market and restaurant, but also for its efforts at diversifying the Argentine diet through public workshops and radio and TV programs, and its judicious discrimination in terms of where it purchases what it sells. Both sit-down service and takeaway meals are available, and it's possible to buy many items, such as spices, that are difficult to find elsewhere in the city.

# Outer Barrios                    Map 8

## ALMAGRO
### Fusion
**MALEVO** $

Mario Bravo 908, tel. 011/4861-1008,
www.malevo-restaurant.com.ar
**HOURS:** Mon.-Fri. lunch and dinner, Sat. dinner
In Almagro, on the fringe of Palermo Viejo,
Malevo's menu is an eclectic mix of wok-fried
vegetables, meats, fish, tempura, and the like.
Painted in bright Mexican hues—the walls
around its 15 or so tables adorned with paintings
for sale—it continues to be a solid neighborhood
bistro. Excellent lunch specials (around US$6)
include items like stuffed calamari. Desserts include *mousse de maracuyá* (passion fruit), but it's
not the equal of Palermo's María Fuló's.

## BELGRANO

Perceived as remote—though it's only 20 minutes from downtown by Subte—Belgrano gets
few foreign visitors and even fewer casual diners. Its Chinatown, though, offers Buenos
Aires's best mainstream Asian food, and a
handful of other places deserve a visit.

### Chinese
**CANTINA CHINATOWN** $

Mendoza 1700, tel. 011/4783-4173
**HOURS:** Mon.-Fri. noon-3:30 P.M. and 7-11:30 P.M.,
Sat.-Sun. noon-11:30 P.M.
Belgrano's compact Chinatown is home to a
gaggle of moderately priced, mostly Cantonese,
restaurants. Drawing Chinese diners from
other parts of town, Cantina Chinatown serves
abundant portions and some spicy dishes, such
as kung pao beef, which may not seem quite so
spicy to an experienced palate, but extra hot
sauce is available.

### Italian
**CAPISCI** $

Vuelta de Obligado 2072, tel. 011/4788-4400
**HOURS:** Daily 7 A.M.-2 A.M. (24 hours on weekends)

Directly opposite Plaza Belgrano and alongside La Redonda, Capisci occupies a weathered brick building whose still detailed facade
is the backdrop for ample outdoor seating in
fine weather. Risottos and good pasta dishes,
with a variety of sauces, are good values, and
there's also good lemonade and other refreshing drinks ideal for a break from the Sunday
*feria*. On the downside, the barrio pigeons are
increasingly aggressive.

### Peruvian
**CONTIGO PERÚ** $

Echeverría 1627, tel. 011/4780-3960
**HOURS:** Tues.-Sun. 10 A.M.-midnight
In a cul-de-sac near the railroad tracks, Contigo
is a Peruvian spot that, from humble begin-
nings, has become a neighborhood success—the
decor is Inka kitsch, but its tangy pisco sours
and traditional specialties, such as *ají de gallina,*
are outstanding given the moderate, even cheap,
prices. Sometimes there aren't enough waiters
to handle the crowds, but the real downside is
dueling TVs—though one could argue that this
is authentically Peruvian.

## CHACARITA
### Vegetarian
**MASAMADRE ES CON M** $

Olleros 3891, tel. 011/4554-4555
**HOURS:** Mon.-Sat. 9 A.M.-midnight
It's barely on the periphery of Palermo's gourmet ghetto, but anyone visiting Chacarita
cemetery should make time for lunch at this
casual café, which earned its reputation for
exceptional breads (on sale separately) but also
has a diverse menu of vegetarian dishes and
light versions of fish, poultry, pasta, and even
a little beef. A typical dish is the *sorrentinos
de calabaza* (stuffed pumpkin pasta, US$7)
with a fresh mushroom sauce. The desserts
are outstanding, and the by-the-glass wines
varied and inexpensive.

# NIGHTLIFE

In terms of entertainment, Buenos Aires is a 24-hour city that has as much to offer as New York or London. Argentines in general and *porteños* in particular are night people—discos and dance clubs, for instance, may not even *open* until 1 A.M. or so, and they stay open until dawn. That said, not everything of interest takes place at those hours.

All the Buenos Aires dailies have thorough event listings, especially in their end-of-the-week supplements. These include *La Nación* on Thursday and *Ambito Financiero,* the *Buenos Aires Herald*'s "getOut!" section, and *Clarín* all on Friday. *Clarín*'s Friday edition includes "Sí!," a youth-oriented pullout. There are also listings in the German-language *Argentinisches Tageblatt* (Saturday) and *Página 12* (Sunday). In addition, there are listings in the monthly

*Viva Bue* (www.vivabue.com.ar), a freebie distributed by the national and municipal tourist offices; and in *Wipe* (www.wipe.com.ar), a privately distributed monthly brochure.

For tickets to events at major entertainment venues (Teatro Gran Rex, Paseo La Plaza, La Trastienda, Teatro Nacional Cervantes, Teatro Astral, Teatro Astros, Teatro Margarita Xirgú, Niceto Club, The Roxy, and Centro Cultural Borges) and to sporting events (for soccer teams, such as Boca Juniors, River Plate, and San Lorenzo), contact Ticketek (tel. 011/5237-7200, www.ticketek.com.ar). Ticketek, which adds a variable service charge to most tickets, has outlets in the Microcentro at the Galerías Pacífico (Viamonte 560, Local 6 and 8); in San Telmo at La Trastienda (Balcarce 460); in Barrio Norte at Lee-Chi (Rodríguez Peña

# HIGHLIGHTS

LOOK FOR 🅒 TO FIND RECOMMENDED NIGHTLIFE.

🅒 **Best Recent Restoration:** Balvanera's historic **Café de los Angelitos** probably looks better than it ever did in its lowlife heyday (page 95).

🅒 **Best Café:** Unlike *tanguerías* that reinvent themselves "for export," Monserrat's venerable **Café Tortoni** became a tourist attraction, and has remained one, by being itself (page 95).

🅒 **Best Brews:** For both dining and drinking, Recoleta's often overrated, but its **Buller Brewing Company** is more than credible for beer-lovers (page 97).

🅒 **Best Wine Bar:** Like the tango, the Argentine wine industry is booming. For those who can't visit the bodegas of Mendoza, Palermo Hollywood's **Lobby** replicates the informality of a boutique tasting, but there's also fine food to complement a representative selection of vintages from around the country (page 99).

🅒 **Best Recycled Mansion:** The bartenders and waitresses may not be your servants, but unwinding at Retiro's **Milión** will give you at least an inkling of how the *porteño* elite retreated from the capital's unruly streets (page 99).

🅒 **Best Rock Club:** Literally below the radar in its underground digs, Congreso's **Club Unione e Benevolenza** is the word-of-mouth place to see indie bands play surf, punk, and even rockabilly (page 101).

🅒 **Best Jazz:** It's no contest for big names in intimate surroundings at **Clásica y Moderna** (page 103).

🅒 **Best Tango Floor Show:** It's spectacle

© WAYNE BERNHARDSON

tango show at Esquina Carlos Gardel

instead of *milonga*, but the producers, musicians, singers, and dancers at **Esquina Carlos Gardel** are among the best in the business (page 104).

🅒 **Best Milonga:** Because *milongas* vary so greatly, ranging from no-frills social clubs to genuine landmarks designed for the purpose, with crowds that range from cordial to cliquish, it's particularly hard to choose the "best." Still, daily events at the **Confitería Ideal,** with its well-worn walls and floors, evoke tango's bittersweet nostalgia (page 108).

🅒 **Best Gay Venue:** Through numerous names and other changes, **Bulnes Class** has managed to hold its own in the gay nightlife scene (page 111).

1034); and in Recoleta at the Hard Rock Café (Pueyrredón 2501).

For discount tickets to certain events, including tango shows, cinemas, and live theater, try *carteleras,* agencies that offer last-minute specials. Among them are Cartelera Espectáculos (Lavalle 742, Local 2, tel. 011/4322-4331, www.123info.com.ar), on the downtown pedestrian mall; Cartelera Baires (Av. Corrientes 1382, Local 24, tel. 011/4372-5058, www.cartelerabaires.com); and Cartelera Vea Más (Av. Corrientes 1660, Local 2, tel. 011/6320-5319), in the Paseo La Plaza complex.

# Cafés

### LA BIELA

Av. Presidente Quintana 596/600, tel. 011/4804-0449,
www.labiela.com

**HOURS:** Sun.-Fri. 7 A.M.-3 A.M., Sat. 8 A.M.-4 A.M.

**Map 6**

Recoleta's La Biela is *the* classic breakfast and people-watching spot, though even post-devaluation it remains a relatively pricey place to eat. In good weather, try the patio, beneath the shade of the palms, bulbous *palo borracho* trees, and the giant *gomero* or *ombú* (which needs wooden beams to support its sprawling thick branches). It's slightly more expensive to eat outside,and the outdoor service can be inconsistent.

### ◖ CAFÉ DE LOS ANGELITOS

Av. Rivadavia 2100, tel. 011/4952-2320,
www.cafedelosangelitos.com

**HOURS:** Daily 10 A.M.-10 P.M.

**Map 4**

Just beyond the Microcentro and west of Congreso, Café de los Angelitos was once a lowlife hangout that got its name from a sarcastic police commissioner. Recently restored, it's a gentrified *porteño* classic, where a central chandelier illuminates the dark circular wooden tables, with marble insets, that cover the tiled floors. Tango and street scene *vitreaux* decorate the bar, while historic photographs and portraits line the walls. It now offers tango shows but, in a further concession to modernity, it also has WiFi.

### ◖ CAFÉ TORTONI

Av. de Mayo 825, tel. 011/4342-4328,
www.cafetortoni.com.ar

**HOURS:** Daily 7 A.M.-2 A.M.

**Map 1**

One of Buenos Aires's most fiercely if quietly traditional places, Tortoni's made no concessions to the 21st century and only a few to the 20th: Upholstered chairs and marble tables stand among sturdy columns beneath a ceiling punctuated by *vitreaux;* the wallpaper looks original between the dark-stained wooden

trim; and the walls are decorated with pictures, portraits, and *filete,* the traditional calligraphy of *porteño* sign-painters.

Among the patrons acknowledged on the walls are tango singer Carlos Gardel, La Boca painter Benito Quinquela Martín, dramatists Luigi Pirandello and Federico García Lorca, and pianist Arthur Rubinstein; more recently, the Tortoni has hosted King Juan Carlos I of Spain and Hillary Rodham Clinton. Almost everybody who visits the city should join them.

No single institution embodies *porteño* tradition better than Monserrat's Tortoni, founded in 1858. Originally facing Avenida Rivadavia, it acquired a new frontage on Avenida de Mayo as city mayor Torcuato de Alvear redeveloped the area in the 1880s. Though most tourists come for coffee and croissants, the bar serves good mixed drinks (US$8) that come accompanied by a sizable *tabla* (that easily feeds two

Café Tortoni and the Academia Nacional del Tango, Monserrat

people) of sliced salami, paté, cheese, olives, and other snacks; separately, drinks cost only about US$4 each.

The café also hosts live tango song-and-dance shows most nights at its Bodega and the Sala Alfonsina Storni, both separate from the main part of the café, for around US$13–17 per person plus drinks and food. Show times can vary slightly, as some nights there's a late program around 11 or 11:30 P.M.

### CONFITERÍA IDEAL

Suipacha 384, tel. 011/5265-8069, www.confiteriaideal.com
**HOURS:** Daily from 9 A.M.
Map 2

Superannuated but hanging on, the worn-around-the-edges Ideal is one of the Microcentro's most traditional settings for coffee and croissants, and for *milongas*. Huge pillars support oval ceilings with multiple chandeliers, but one still gets the notion that when a light bulb burns out it never gets replaced; the mahogany walls are in good shape, and the furniture's improved, but the floor tiles are cracked, stained, and worn from a century of shuffling shoes.

Then again, maybe this sort of slow corrosion is the essence of tango's bittersweet nostalgia. Ideal served as backdrop for director Alan Parker's cinematic Madonna-fest *Evita* and Sally Potter's even more appalling *The Tango Lesson*. There have been improvements, but it's hardly a full-scale renovation.

For information on the Ideal's afternoon *milongas*, see the *Milongas* section in this chapter.

### CONFITERÍA RICHMOND

Florida 468, tel. 011/4322-1341, www.restaurant.com.ar/richmond
**HOURS:** Mon.-Sat. 7 A.M.-10 P.M.
Map 2

In contrast with the Ideal, the elegant Richmond looks as good as the day it opened more than eight decades ago; one of Jorge Luis Borges's favorites, it draws the *porteño* elite for both breakfast and afternoon tea, and also serves as a bar and restaurant. Its woodwork, chandeliers, tables, and upholstery are all in primo condition. Prices are higher here than elsewhere, though, and the service can be inconsistent.

# Bars and Clubs

The distinction between cafés and bars is not always obvious—in fact, it's often more a continuum than a dichotomy. Some of the more stylish (or pretentious) bars often go by the English word pub, pronounced as in English, and many call themselves Irish. A number of these line Reconquista and other nearby streets in Retiro's so-called Nuevo Bajo area, where usually circumspect *porteño* drinkers become boozers on St. Patrick's Day.

### @LTERNATIVA

Sarmiento 777, www.alternaclub.com.ar
**HOURS:** Vary
Map 2

With a capacity of more than 500 people, @lternativa is a youthful dance club that plays

electronic music but also hosts punk and metal bands; Friday is the main night, after 1 A.M., but there's sometimes a Thursday matinee. The cover charge is about US$3 per person, but slightly less for women.

### BÁRBARO

Tres Sargentos 415, tel. 011/4311-6856
**HOURS:** Mon.-Fri. 7 A.M.-4 A.M., Sat. 10 A.M.-4 A.M.
Map 5

More casual than any other bar in its barrio, this pioneer pub takes its punning name from a *lunfardo* term roughly translatable as cool. And it is, but unpretentiously so, with slightly rickety wooden chairs and peanut shells scattered on both the main floor and the mezzanine. There's live music, in various styles, on weekends.

## BAR PLAZA DORREGO

Defensa 1098, tel. 011/4361-0141
**HOURS:** Daily 8 A.M.-2 A.M.
Map 3

At the corner of its namesake plaza, with large streetside windows that blend it with the scene outside during Sunday's landmark *feria*, this well-worn bar makes an ideal place to take a breather from flea marketing. In good weather, on non-market days, their plaza tables make it possible to enjoy a beer or snack in the open air.

## BAR SEDDON

Defensa 695, tel. 011/4342-3700
**HOURS:** Tues.-Sun. from 6 P.M.
Map 1

Relocated to the edge of San Telmo after the demolition of its classic 25 de Mayo locale in the Microcentro, Bar Seddon has made a successful transition to the capital's oldest neighborhood. It's never easy to recapture an earlier era but the current corner building, with its dark stained central bar, simple wooden tables, and casual ambience, has at least come close. There's live blues Friday and Saturday nights and tango Thursday and Sunday nights; at other times, the recorded music tends toward blues and Bob Marley. The food is simple but palatable pub grub.

## ◖ BULLER BREWING COMPANY

Presidente Ramón Ortiz 1827,
tel. 011/4808-9061,
www.bullerpub.com
**HOURS:** Daily from noon
Map 6

Opposite Recoleta's landmark cemetery, Buller's is a brew pub that produces up to seven varieties of beer: light lager, cream ale, honey beer, Oktoberfest, India pale ale, stout, and an occasional surprise. The kitchen, meanwhile, provides a credible menu of tapas, seafood, pizza, and other pub grub, with particularly good panini and the sandwich version of the Uruguayan *chivito*. There's shady garden seating, but increasingly aggressive pigeons can be a problem.

## CAFÉ BAR BANDERÍN

Guardia Vieja 3601, tel. 011/4862-7757,
www.elbanderin.com.ar
**HOURS:** Mon.-Fri. 8 A.M.-9:30 P.M., Sat. 10 A.M.-6 P.M.
Map 4

With their multiple giant TV screens, Recoleta's slick sports bars have glitz, but for traditionalists the Banderín is Buenos Aires's ultimate. Decorated with decades' worth of soccer pennants, from which it takes its name, it recalls the era when *porteños* argued about, rather than gawked at, soccer. There's TV now, but the mid-'50s atmosphere survives.

## LA CIGALE

25 de Mayo 722, tel. 011/4312-8275
**HOURS:** Mon.-Fri. 6 P.M.-3 or 4 A.M., Sat. 9 P.M.-3 or 4 A.M.
Map 2

In the Nuevo Bajo area on the Microcentro and Retiro border, La Cigale offers pub lunches in the daytime and, at night, electronica and occasional live music in a self-consciously hip atmosphere. There's live music on Monday, when it's rare to find much activity elsewhere in town.

## DOWNTOWN MATÍAS

Reconquista 701, tel. 011/4311-0327,
www.matiaspub.com.ar
**HOURS:** Mon.-Sat. from 9 A.M.
Map 2

At the Microcentro branch of Buenos Aires's oldest Irish-style pub, with a dark-stained wooden bar, booths, and free-standing tables, patrons consume a variety of beers on tap, including Guinness, Harp, and Kilkenny, along with a huge selection of whiskies and other hard liquor. At lunchtime, downtown workers pack the place for pub lunches in the US$7 range, while most drinks cost US$4-5. There's a 6-9 P.M. happy hour weeknights.

In addition to the usual bar offerings, depending on the night, Matías showcases live music (including Celtic). It also has branches in nearby Retiro (San Martín 979, tel. 011/4312-9844) and more distant Belgrano (Echeverría 3195, tel. 011/4545-1050).

NIGHTLIFE

# THE CROMAÑON LEGACY

In December 2004, Argentine *rock nacional* got a wake-up call when a fan of the suburban Buenos Aires group Los Callejeros set off a flare that started a fire in the Once nightspot República Cromañón; the venue's escape routes were either bolted or wired shut to prevent sneak entries, and nearly 200 of the group's fans died, mostly of smoke inhalation. It was the worst non-natural disaster in Argentine history.

In what was clearly an unnecessary tragedy, the aftermath was in many ways worse. Instead of deferring to the courts to identify and prosecute the culprit who set off the flare — the primary responsible party — opportunistic sectors of the public seemed most interested in scapegoating city mayor Aníbal Ibarra. While there were indications of shoddy inspections and even corruption in the city fire department, even Cromañón owner Omar Chabán, jailed for his responsibility in the matter, did not come in for the vituperative criticism that Ibarra did (the court case drags on interminably, and posters damning Ibarra and Chabán still appear around town).

Soon, it became obvious, there were problems with many entertainment venues, especially those used for rock shows. According to one estimate, 95 percent of performance spaces were not up to snuff. The official response was an immediate shutdown of many live-entertainment options, including some very innocuous *milongas* (tango aficionados are unlikely to set off fireworks), in a two-week orgy of inspections, but this was more symbolic than genuine. In such a short time, effective compliance was impossible, and many clubs remained closed more than two months later because of a shortage of inspectors.

Though a judge ordered the detention of band manager Diego Argañaraz (whose wife died in the fire) in addition to Chabán, there seemed to be little, if any, public interest in the band's responsibility (the crowd was, by some estimates, four times Cromañón's capacity of about 1,000 spectators). Nobody, for that matter, raised the issue of high-powered and dangerous fireworks, whose availability makes New Year's Eve so nerve-wracking in the capital.

In the short run, the Cromañón disaster brought Buenos Aires's nightlife nearly to a standstill, but tighter municipal supervision has eliminated at least the most precarious locales. Some rock events now take place at earlier hours rather than well after midnight, but that doesn't mean *porteños* won't still find a way to party all night. For all its ferocity, even Argentina's onerous 1976-1983 dictatorship felt unable to restrain Buenos Aires's night owls, even as Chile and other similar regimes enforced rigid curfews.

## DRUID IN
Reconquista 1040, tel. 011/4312-3688
**HOURS:** Mon.-Fri. noon-1 A.M. or later, Sat. from 8 P.M.
**Map 5**

At the Irish end of the spectrum, the Druid In is popular with the downtown crowd for its pub-grub lunches in the US$5 range, including staples like steak-and-kidney pie, but also Argentine *minutas,* such as *milanesas.* At night, drinkers crowd into the cozy booths for beer, wine, and whiskey, sometimes to the accompaniment of live Celtic music. The front section of the building is tobacco-free.

## FORO GANDHI
Av. Corrientes 1743, tel. 011/4374-7501, www.casonadelarte.com.ar
**HOURS:** Sun.-Thurs. 10 A.M.-10 P.M., Fri.-Sat. 10 A.M.-midnight
**Map 2**

In new quarters on theater row, the artsy Gandhi is a hybrid blend of bookstore, coffeehouse, and cultural center whose offerings include films, poetry readings, tango shows, and theater.

## GRAN BAR DANZÓN

Libertad 1161, tel. 011/4811-1108,
www.granbardanzon.com.ar
**HOURS:** Mon.-Fri. from 7 P.M., Sat.-Sun. from 8 P.M.
**Map 5**

On the edge of Recoleta, showcasing more than 200 Argentine labels, the Danzón is a sophisticated wine bar that doubles as a restaurant. Drinkers can lounge on comfy chairs and sofas or sit at the long bar; the dining area is separate. The music could be better—it tends toward *marcha,* as Argentines call techno—and softer. Conversation can be tough when the place fills, but the staff is cordial and the wine-by-the-glass selection is impressive. The sushi is outstanding. Danzón offers live jazz Wednesday and Friday evenings from 7–9 P.M.

## JOHN JOHN

Reconquista 924, tel. 011/4313-1428
**Map 5**

Typical of British/Irish–style pubs in Retiro's Nuevo Bajo, John John has good, reasonably priced drinks, nightly happy hours, live music on weekends, and spontaneous entertainment some other nights. It's one of the key destinations in the neighborhood's informal St. Patrick's Day pub crawl.

## THE KILKENNY

Marcelo T. de Alvear 399, tel. 011/4312-7291,
www.thekilkenny.com.ar
**HOURS:** Mon.-Fri. from 5:30 P.M., Sat.-Sun. from 8 P.M.
**Map 5**

Built in 1998 in consultation with Guinness, so that it looks and feels like a genuine Irish pub, the Kilkenny has Irish beers on tap, plenty of whiskey, a generous schedule of happy hours (posted on their website), and live bands on occasion. In addition, it has a pub-grub menu in its restaurant and, like its counterparts Downtown Matías, John John, and others, is particularly popular on St. Patrick's Day.

## LEVITAR AMBIENT BAR

Godoy Cruz 1715, tel. 011/4833-9030
**HOURS:** Wed.-Sun. from 11 P.M.
**Map 7**

In a recycled house with an ample patio and even an odd sort of wading pool, Ambient doesn't really get started until well after 1 A.M. and often goes well past daybreak with DJ-run electronica, techno, and/or R&B. Chilean management ensures inexpensive pisco sours, but the other drinks are reasonably priced and the modest bar menu is positively cheap.

## ◖ LOBBY

Nicaragua 5944, tel. 011/4770-9335
**HOURS:** Nightly 9 P.M.-midnight
**Map 7**

Hard to categorize, this cozy and informal locale is a hybrid restaurant, wine bar, and wine shop whose owners are happy to talk about the wines they stock and, if you decide to have lunch or dinner there, will sell you a bottle out of stock for on-the-spot enjoyment with only a small corkage charge.

From January to mid-February, Lobby closes as early as 8 P.M.

## ◖ MILIÓN

Paraná 1048, tel. 011/4815-9925, www.milion.com.ar
**HOURS:** Mon.-Fri. noon-2 A.M. or later,
Sat.-Sun. from 8 P.M.
**Map 5**

Bordering Barrio Norte, Milión is a tapas bar occupying three stories of an extraordinary 1913 French Academicist mansion; only minimally altered for its current use, it offers garden, patio, and interior seating, but get there early to be seated outside. The 2nd floor holds a gallery with rotating exhibits by local artists and photographers. The food menu is also outstanding, particularly the midday lunch specials; the à la carte menu, which is more diverse, is not much more expensive.

## MUNDO BIZARRO

Serrano 1222, tel. 011/4773-1967,
www.mundobizarrobar.com
**HOURS:** Daily 8:30 P.M.-4 or 5 A.M.
**Map 7**

In new quarters between Plaza Serrano and Avenida Córdoba, darkly lit in red and suggestively decorated with erotic kitsch, Palermo

In Palermo's Las Cañitas district, the Van Koning is a gathering place for Dutch expats.

SoHo's Mundo Bizarro attracts a youthful crowd and polarized responses from its patrons: Within a few minutes, you'll either love it or hate it.

### REMEMBER

Av. Corrientes 1983, tel. 011/4953-0638
**HOURS:** Daily 8:30 P.M.-3 or 4 A.M.
Map 4

Remember is a small (120-capacity) multipurpose venue that offers live theater—mostly one-person acts—but it's primarily a pub that also offers music (jazz and blues, but even metal and punk on occasion).

### SHAMROCK

Rodríguez Peña 1220, tel. 011/4812-3584,
www.theshamrockbar.com
**HOURS:** Mon.-Fri. from 6 P.M., Sat.-Sun. from 8 P.M.
Map 6

Sometimes derided as a pick-up bar, this Barrio Norte version of an Irish pub holds happy hour, for beer and a limited number of house drinks, until midnight. In the basement, there's DJ techno for dancing Thursday–Sunday, with no cover for women but US$4–5 for men (though, by some accounts, they waive the cover for foreign boozers as opposed to *porteños,* who nurse their drinks for hours on end).

### THE TEMPLE BAR

Marcelo T. de Alvear 945, tel. 011/4322-0474,
www.thetemplebar.com.ar
**HOURS:** Mon.-Tues. 9 A.M.-3 A.M., Wed.-Thurs.
9 A.M.-4 A.M., Fri. 9 A.M.-5 A.M., Sat. 6 P.M.-5 A.M.
Map 5

With dark wooden booths and tables, big-screen TVs, a pool tables, 30 varieties of beer (several of them on tap), and a slew of whiskies, The Temple Bar is an upscale stereotype of the Irish pub that, like its nearby counterparts, is a quotidian tribute to St. Patrick's Day. The food menu includes snacks, sandwiches, tapas, fish, and pastas, with sushi on Thursday.

## VAN KONING
Báez 325, tel. 011/4772-9909
**HOURS:** Nightly from 7 P.M.
Map 7

With its solid wooden beams and furniture, and appropriately dark interior, Van Koning is a Netherlands-style pub that capitalizes on the Argentine fixation with all things Dutch (the fascination may have begun with Holstein cattle, but became an obsession when the country acquired its own royalty with the 2002 marriage of Máxima Zorreguieta to Crown Prince William). Dutch expats hold a special gathering here the first Wednesday of every month.

# Live Music

After the República Cromañon disaster of December 2004, when nearly 200 rock fans died of fire and smoke inhalation in the Once district, many live music venues were shut down at least temporarily for safety inspections. Only a fraction have reopened, and some have moved to more suitable quarters. It's worth mentioning that nearly all entertainment venues were subject to this increased scrutiny, including some prestigious theaters and even modest *milongas*.

## BLUES SPECIAL CLUB
Almirante Brown 102, tel. 011/4854-2338,
www.bluesspecialrecords.com.ar
**HOURS:** Fri. and Sat. night
Map 3

In an appropriately down-in-the-mouth location opposite San Telmo's Parque Lezama, the Blues Special has traditionally flown in performers from Chicago and other blues hotbeds in the States, but the economic crisis has limited that practice. It does have its own house band, though, and other figures from the local blues scene play here on weekends only (late).

## ◖ CLUB UNIONE E BENEVOLENZA
Perón 1362
**HOURS:** Fri. and Sat. night
Map 2

It's usually word of mouth, but try Googling "Unione y Benevolenza" to find out what's happening in Buenos Aires's overlapping punk, rockabilly, and surf music scene (in this peripheral but dedicated sector, bands cannot afford to specialize). In this basement venue, events usually take place early Friday and/or Saturday evenings, but hours can vary. Playing with local legends The Tormentos and Los Kahunas, lead guitarist Danny Amis of the Nashville surf band Los Straitjackets drew a full house here.

## LA DAMA DE BOLLINI
Pasaje Bollini 2281, tel. 011/4805-6399,
www.ladama-debollini.com.ar
**HOURS:** Nightly
Map 6

Larger than it looks from outside, this casual but engagingly decorated bar enjoys a picturesque site on a secluded, cobbled alleyway behind Hospital Rivadavia. Jorge Luis Borges, who evoked images of 19th-century knife-fighters on the street in his poem *El Pasaje de los Cuchilleros* (The Cutthroats' Alleyway), participated in the 1984 founding of its weekly *café literario*.

Embellished with canvases by local artists, and boasting a small interior patio, the Bollini's brick walls and arches make it an outpost of San Telmo style in a Recoleta location. Its frequent live shows feature jazz, tango, and even Celtic music, but they are fewer in summer than in the rest of the year. Drinks are reasonably priced and there's a pub-grub menu, but food isn't why people come here—avoid the *picada* of bite-sized meats, cheeses, olives, and the like, which is far inferior to those elsewhere in the city.

## MITOS ARGENTINOS
Humberto Primo 489, tel. 011/4362-7810,
www.mitosargentinos.com.ar
**HOURS:** Thurs.-Sun. from 7 P.M.
Map 3

It once offered tango, but Mitos Argentinos

© WAYNE BERNHARDSON

The neoclassical facade of the Club Unione e Benevolenza masks a basement club where alt-rock bands play punk, rockabilly, and even surf music.

has jumped on the *rock nacional* bandwagon with live shows in recently remodeled facilities. Often these are cover bands or tribute bands to Argentine acts such as Charly García, Fito Páez, and Andres Calamaro. Some groups, though, also write and perform their own songs. Food and drink are moderately priced.

### NICETO CLUB
Niceto Vega 5510, tel. 011/4779-6396, www.nicetoclub.com
**HOURS:** Thurs.-Sat. from 9 P.M.
Map 7

Having become one of the area's top live music venues over the last several years, the Niceto Club is really a multi-space nightspot with three bars. The live music comprises a diversity of styles, from rock and jazz to reggae, salsa, and just about anything else. After the live music ends sometime around 1 A.M., it hosts all-night DJ dance parties.

### THE ROXY
Chacarita, Federico Lacroze and Alvarez Thomas,

tel. 011/4899-0314, www.theroxybsas.com.ar
**HOURS:** Showtimes vary
Map 8

In new Chacarita quarters, relocated from Palermo where it squatted beneath a railroad bridge, the Roxy no longer shakes when trains pass overhead or leaks in heavy rainstorms. It still rocks, though, thanks to performers of the caliber of Charly García and lesser-known Argentine acts. Programs usually take place weekends, after 10 P.M., but days and times are inconsistent.

### SALÓN PUEYRREDÓN
Av. Santa Fe 4560
**HOURS:** Vary
Map 7

For the alternative rock crowd, the best Palermo choice is Salón Pueyrredón, where indie bands play most weekends in a chaotic atmosphere—the Ramones are about as mainstream as it gets. Like Unione e Benevolenza, it relies on flyers and word-of-mouth for publicity—try Googling it for the latest information, as it has no phone contact or website.

## LA TRASTIENDA

Balcarce 460, tel. 011/4342-7650,
www.latrastienda.com

**HOURS:** Daily 4:30 P.M.-midnight, most shows start
at 9 P.M.

Map 1

Owned by former city mayor Jorge Telerman,
housed in a recycled warehouse that also serves
as a restaurant, La Trastienda books some of
the top Argentine and international live music
acts, as well as comedy, in a relatively intimate
environment. The restaurant serves mostly
standard Italo-Argentine dishes but, surprisingly, lacks stuffed pastas, such as ravioli.
Lunchtime specials cost around US$7–8, in-
dividual entrées US$5–10.

# Jazz

## C CLÁSICA Y MODERNA

Av. Callao 892, tel. 011/4812-8707,
www.clasicaymoderna.com

**HOURS:** Sun.-Thurs. 8 A.M.-2 A.M., Fri.-Sat. 8 A.M.-4 A.M.

Map 6

With a quirky clutter of antique barrels and
bicycles, this brick-walled hybrid of book-
store-café and live jazz venue has occupied the
same Barrio Norte location since 1938. Once
frequented by writers and intellectuals like
Alfonsina Storni and Leopoldo Lugones, it has
since seen performances by the likes of Susana
Rinaldi, Mercedes Sosa, and Liza Minelli. Pop,
rock, and tango singer Roberto Sánchez (popularly known as Sandro or to his true devotees
as El Maestro) donated the piano from his personal collection.

While it's a top live music venue, Clásica y
Moderna is also a fine choice for breakfast or
lunch, while reading the house's selection of
daily newspapers and magazines.

## ESPACIO ECLÉCTICO

Humberto Primo 730, tel. 011/4307-1966,
www.espacioeclectico.com.ar

**HOURS:** Tues.-Fri. noon–9 P.M., Sat.-Sun. 3–9 P.M.

Map 3

In a luminous locale that also serves as an art
space, Espacio Ecléctico has regular jazz events.
Meanwhile, it also presents live theater, dance,
film, and even an annual event for photographers to present their coffee-table books.

## NOTORIOUS

Av. Callao 966, tel. 011/4813-6888,
www.notorious.com.ar

**HOURS:** Mon.-Sat. 8 A.M.-midnight, Sun.
11 A.M.-midnight

Map 6

It's hard to pigeonhole Notorious, which is a
hybrid of jazz café, sophisticated but unpretentious restaurant, and CD store where patrons
can don headphones to preview music while
munching on a variety of gourmet sandwiches.
In addition to its dining room, the site for live
music performances at night, it has a large and
woodsy rear garden.

It's probably most notable, though, for live
music, primarily jazz, that takes place nearly
every night at 9 or 10 P.M.

NIGHTLIFE

# Tango and *Tanguerías*

Tango can be music alone; music and song; music, song, and dance; or a theatrical combination of all three. Many visitors mistake floor-show spectacles for the essence of tango, but these tourist-oriented events can be a deceptive introduction to tango as a widespread, even democratic cultural phenomenon. For spectators conscious of their limitations, they can be entertaining and, in their own way, satisfying.

*Tanguerías* with floor shows range from relatively modest and simple programs at low prices to extravagant productions at high (sometimes excessive) cost. Even the latter, though, can be a bargain when the peso sinks or discount tickets are available through *carteleras*.

Many, but by no means all, tango venues are in the southerly barrios of Monserrat, San Telmo, and Barracas, with a few elsewhere and in outlying barrios.

## BAR SUR
Estados Unidos 299, tel. 011/4362-6086,
www.bar-sur.com.ar
**HOURS:** Nightly 8 P.M.-3 A.M.
**COST:** dinner and show US$60, show only US$45
Map 3

Despite celebrity clientele, such as Antonio Banderas, Lucio Benetton, Robert Plant, and Mario Vargas Llosa, Bar Sur remains a relatively spontaneous and informal tango-show venue open late every night except Sunday. The show costs US$45, the dinner another US$15 per person including unlimited pizza and empanadas, but drinks are additional.

## EL CHINO
Nueva Pompeya, Beazley 3566, tel. 011/4911-0215,
www.barelchinofilm.com.ar
**HOURS:** Fri.-Sat. from 10 P.M.
Map 8

In an untouristed southern barrio, El Chino became a tourist hangout thanks to the rugged authenticity of its late owner Jorge Eduardo Garcés, whose nickname (the

Chinaman) was the source of the bar's name. Arrive well before midnight to get a table, though the live music—definitely not of the floor-show genre—may not start until later. The food is, for lack of a better description, working-class Argentine.

Cinema director Daniel Burak, who has made both a TV documentary and a feature film about the bar, is responsible for the website listed here, which is not official but does tell a great deal about El Chino.

## ESQUINA CARLOS GARDEL
Carlos Gardel 3200, tel. 011/4867-6363,
www.esquinacarlosgardel.com.ar
**HOURS:** Nightly dinner 8:30 P.M., nightly tango show 10:30 P.M.
Map 4

It's tempting to dismiss the Esquina Carlos Gardel, which veers dangerously close to a Vegas-style floor show, as time-warp tango that plays to the cliché. With a few exceptions, dancers clad in stereotypical early-20-th-century dress stress the most acrobatic moves possible at the expense of the more subtle movements that *milongueros* prefer. Nor is there any attempt to tell the story of tango, but for a brief introductory film (subtitled in English, with outstanding footage) to Gardel himself, the Abasto neighborhood, and the Mercado del Abasto's recent redevelopment.

Yet the quality of the musicians—two violinists, two *bandoneonistas*, a pianist, and a string bassist who play on an elevated stage above the dancers—is first-rate, lead dancer Carlos Copello is a near-legend, and vocalist Roberto Minondi is exceptional. While this show in its entirety may dismay purists, there is still much to appreciate.

On the site of the now-defunct restaurant Chanta Cuatro, literally in the shadow of the redeveloped Mercado del Abasto, the Esquina Carlos Gardel is part of a municipal project to sustain the legacy of the "Morocho del

# THE TANGO, THE *TANGUERÍA*, AND THE *MILONGA*

For foreigners visiting Buenos Aires, one of the city's legendary attractions is the tango, the dance that conquered European salons despite its dubious origins in the Argentine capital's *arrabales* (outskirts) and brothels. What they usually see, in high-priced dinner-show *tanguerías*, are pairs of lithe and sexy dancers executing acrobatically intricate steps to the sounds of a professional orchestra in an elaborate setting, often a recycled historical building. It's impressive and professional, but what locals often deride as "for export" (in English) is not the experience of most *porteños*.

For *porteños*, dance is a participatory pastime at *milongas*, informal gatherings that take place at modest neighborhood locales often lacking even a stage, normally with recorded music, and charging only a modest admission. *Milongueros*, those who frequent *milongas*, may dance tango, but that's not the only option – the term itself describes a common style of music and dance, in two-four time, traditional to the Río de la Plata region. A *milonga* can also mean a spontaneous outbreak of dancing at a party.

*Tanguerías*, whatever their appeal, are like spectator sports for tourists. *Milongas* belong to the barrio, but tourists are welcome if they want to see – and perhaps dance – the tango as a popular art form in which couples from their teens to their *tercera edad* (retirement age) take part. The *milonga* is more than just the tango; it's a part of the *porteño* experience that transcends the stereotype of youth and beauty.

Abasto" in his old neighborhood. One of the city's most ornate tango locales, seating up to 500 spectators, the Esquina offers nightly tango shows starting at US$57 per person (show only, starting at 10:30 P.M.) and US$83 per person (with dinner, starting at 8:30 P.M.). For more expensive VIP boxes, which offer the best views (especially from each side of the stage), the rates are US$113 per person and US$167 per person, respectively.

### ESQUINA HOMERO MANZI

Boedo, Av. San Juan 3601, tel. 011/4957-8488, www.esquinahomeromanzi.com.ar
**HOURS:** Nightly dinner 9 P.M., nightly show 10 P.M.
**Map 8**

Named for the great tango lyricist, a collaborator with composers such as Aníbal Troilo, this former corner bar was once part of the *arrabales* (outskirts) in the barrio of Boedo. Recycled to seat nearly 500 guests, and not quite so remote as it once was, it still holds a place as part of tango history. For three hours prior to dinner, there are tango lessons.

### MICHELANGELO

Balcarce 433, tel. 011/4342-7007, www.michelangelo.com.ar
**HOURS:** Nightly from 8:15 P.M.
**Map 1**

Michelangelo occupies a handsomely restored brick building in a historic neighborhood that is *not*, despite their assertions, in San Telmo (in reality, it's about one-block-plus to the north). Like most of its counterparts, it employs outstanding musicians and dancers, but never quite seems to overcome the stereotypes despite them. The floor show feels more abstract than heartfelt.

Michelangelo's charges patrons US$100 per person for dinner and show, which starts at 8:15 P.M.; without dinner, the show, which starts at 10:15 P.M., costs US$65 per person (including two drinks). The VIP version, which includes front-row seats, costs US$165 with dinner; the VIP show alone, with near-front-row seats, costs US$105 without dinner, but does include wine, beer, and/or champagne.

NIGHTLIFE

San Telmo's Torquato Tasso is one of the best venues for live tango music.

© WAYNE BERNHARDSON

### EL QUERANDÍ

Perú 302, tel. 011/5199-1770, www.querandi.com.ar
**HOURS:** Nightly from 8:30 P.M.
**Map 1**

Dating from 1920, the Querandí is another *porteño* classic; for US$80 per person, the nightly dinner (starting at 9 P.M.) and show (starting at 10:15 P.M.) tend toward the upper end of the price scale, but it's a truly elegant place. It's also small enough that everyone can easily see the faces of the musicians and actor/dancers, who are outstanding.

The show itself is theatrical—some might say excessively so. For the show alone, without dinner, admission costs US$57 per person including beer or house wine, plus a plate of snacks.

### SEÑOR TANGO

Barracas, Vieytes 1655, tel. 011/4303-0231,
www.senortango.com.ar
**HOURS:** Nightly from 8 P.M.
**Map 8**

Seating more than 1,500 spectators, Señor Tango is an over-the-top spectacle, with up to 40 dancers and musicians—nothing of the intimate *milonga* here. Visitors pay US$80 per person for dinner and show, which starts at 8:30 P.M.; without dinner, the show, which starts at 10 P.M., costs US$50 per person (including two drinks). All prices include transportation to and from its theater in Barracas, some parts of which are considered dodgy, especially at night.

### TORQUATO TASSO

Defensa 1575, tel. 011/4307-6506,
www.torquatotasso.com.ar
**HOURS:** Wed.-Sat. from 10 P.M.
**Map 3**

Opposite Parque Lezama, frayed around the edges but brimming with intensity, the Torquato Tasso provides more genuine barrio ambience than any other live-tango venue. Drawing performers of the caliber of Susana Rinaldi and La Chicana, it has notably authentic details—the tabletops, for instance, are all decorated with *filete* numbers, and wistful tangophile artwork lines the walls from the streetside stage to the bar at the back.

While its live music offerings have increased, the Tasso still offers its Sunday-night *milonga*, with recorded music, around 10 P.M.; admission is free. In addition, it holds tango classes (US$4–5 pp) throughout the week.

### EL VIEJO ALMACÉN
Balcarce and Av. Independencia, tel. 011/4307-6689, www.viejo-almacen.com.ar
**HOURS:** Nightly dinner 8 P.M., nightly show 10 P.M.
**COST:** dinner and show US$80, show only US$50
Map 3

One of the barrio's classic tango venues, occupying a late-18th-century building that's been turned into a truly charming small theater seating 240 spectators, El Viejo Almacén also does one of the city's most elaborate floor shows (sometimes exaggeratedly so). It costs US$80 per person with an 8 P.M. dinner at its restaurant, just paces away on the opposite corner of Balcarce; the show alone, which starts at 10 P.M., costs US$50 per person. The best vantage points are from the hanging balconies.

# Milongas

For those who want to dance or learn tango instead of watch, the best options are neighborhood *milongas,* many of which take place at cultural centers. Organized events charge in the US$3–5 range with live orchestra, less with recorded music.

According to recent estimates, more than 60 *milongas* operate in the city, some of them several nights per week. Of those, about 60 percent are less than five years old. For the most current information on dates and times, check Buenos Aires Milongas (www.buenosairesmilonga.com). At your first *milonga,* though, you're likely to be inundated with flyers announcing others.

Beginners, especially those without partners, often prefer afternoon events such as those at the Confitería Ideal. Many people don't feel at home immediately, but the sensation soon passes.

For classes, a good clearinghouse is Monserrat's **Academia Nacional del Tango** (Av. de Mayo 833, tel. 011/4345-6968, www.anacdeltango.org.ar), directly above Café Tortoni. For truly dedicated students, it even offers a three-year degree in tango as a cultural, social, and political phenomenon. It also has a tango museum which, while worthwhile, could be better.

### EL ARRANQUE (NUEVA SALÓN LA ARGENTINA)
Bartolomé Mitre 1759, tel. 011/4371-6767
**HOURS:** Mon., Tues., and Thurs. 3-10 P.M., Sat. 3-9 P.M.
**COST:** US$3 men, US$2 women
Map 2

One of few venues built with tango in mind, with its ample stage and mosaic floor, the urbane Nueva Salón La Argentina features live music at least once a month. At the same time, it has many regulars who know each other and may be skeptical of strangers; tango's unwritten codes are in full force, and for that reason, it's not so easy to fit in. Still, it's popular for its easy accessibility from all parts of the city, modest cover charge, and inexpensive drinks.

### CLUB ESPAÑOL
Bernardo de Irigoyen 172, tel. 011/4201-7199
**HOURS:** Thurs. 4-11 P.M.
Map 1

Possibly Buenos Aires's most elegant tango salon, the Club Español is an architectural classic with its burnished wood, gilt elevators, marble staircases, and red carpets—a place to see as much as dance. The afternoon schedule makes it suitable for visitors who don't care to pull an all-nighter, but serious *milongueros* can close up shop here, have dinner at its restaurant, and glide through the night at nearby Niño Bien.

NIGHTLIFE

The elegant entryway at Monserrat's Club Español is the portal to an equally elegant *milonga*.

### CLUB GRICEL

San Cristóbal, La Rioja 1180, tel. 011/4957-7157
**HOURS:** Fri. from 11 P.M., Sat. from 10:30 P.M., Sun.
from 9 P.M.

Map 4

Frequented mostly by couples, so that it's not the best place to find a partner, Gricel offers live orchestra *milongas* (admission US$2) Friday and Saturday; Sunday it has recorded music. With a fine parquet floor, it can hold up to 370 dancers. Lessons (US$3) are available prior to the *milonga*.

### C CONFITERÍA IDEAL

Suipacha 384, tel. 011/4729-6390,
www.confiteriaideal.com
**HOURS:** Daily afternoon and evening

Map 2

Several days a week, the upstairs ballroom at the well-worn Ideal offers some of Buenos Aires's least formal *milongas,* where amateurs can feel comfortable and strangers are readily accepted (though without any particular solicitousness), and there's occasional live music. Some dancers don't care for the hard tile floor, which doesn't have the give of parquet, but the frequent afternoon events make it a favorite with those who don't care to dance until daybreak.

Also frequented by teachers, it's a good place to make arrangements for lessons. Instructor Osvaldo Marrapodi also offers Tuesday lessons here, 3–11 P.M., and individual lessons by appointment, as do recommended Diego Alvaro and Zaraida Fontclara. The Ideal also offers nightly floor shows downstairs.

### ITALIA UNITA

Perón 2535, tel. 011/4953-8700,
www.saboratango.com.ar
**HOURS:** Sat. from 10:30 P.M.

Map 4

In the early evening it hosts a dinner and floor show for up to 500 spectators, but after midnight on Saturday the Italia Unita becomes a *milonga* that goes until 5 A.M. The US$5 admission fee includes lessons, which start around 10:30 P.M. in a separate room with

© WAYNE BERNHARDSON

a fine wooden floor. Fronted by Roberto Alvarez, a bandoneón player with tango legend Osvaldo Pugliese, the Orquesta Tango Color (www.colortango.com) often plays here. The sound system is excellent.

## LA NACIONAL

Adolfo Alsina 1465, tel. 011/4307-0146, www.la-nacional.com.ar
**HOURS:** Wed. 10:30 P.M.–4 A.M.
Map 1

Among the most intimate *milongas,* La Nacional has a fine wooden floor, occasional live music, and takes occasional breaks for a show with featured dancers—not a full-scale floor show, but a chance to appreciate some more skilled performers. Admission costs US$2, with lessons available for US$3 starting at 9 P.M.

## NIÑO BIEN

Constitución, Humberto Primo 1462, tel. 15/4147-8687
**HOURS:** Thurs. 10:30 P.M.–4 A.M.
**COST:** US$2
Map 8

While it's in a marginal neighborhood, Niño Bien occupies the spacious ballroom of the Centro Legión Leonesa, a fairly formal venue with parquet floors (among the city's best), cloth-covered tables, and dark wooden chairs. It attracts an older set of dancers who dress more elegantly than at some other venues.

After 11 P.M., it can be tough to get a table, at least until it thins out around 2 A.M.—or later. The sound system is good, but when it gets crowded the conversation level can make it difficult to hear the music.

# THE GAUCHO BALLET

In the Palermo fairgrounds of the Sociedad Rural Argentina (also known as La Rural), dancers from the prestigious Ballet Brandsen and acrobatic riders, chosen from thousands of male applicants from around the country, have given Buenos Aires its folkloric equivalent to the tango spectaculars that have long been a staple of the *porteño* tourist circuit. Staged several times weekly, the Opera Pampa is a stylized account of Argentine history from the Andean past and arrival of the Spaniards to the settlement of the pampas, through song, dance, and spectacular horsemanship.

Like elaborate tango floorshows, Opera Pampa is vulnerable to criticism for stereotyping historic episodes, such as the campaign against the Ranquel people and the civil wars of the 19th century. At the same time, the choreographers have done an extraordinary job of integrating more than 50 dancers and some 20 riders into a fluid spectacle on one of the world's biggest stages. The ballet showcases traditional rural dances, such as the male *malambo* (rather like gaucho tap dancing with riding boots) and the couples' *chacarera* (more typical of farm settlements).

**Opera Pampa** (Av. Sarmiento 2704, Palermo, tel. 011/4777-5557, www.operapampa.com.ar) takes place Thursday through Saturday, rain or shine; the doors open at 8 P.M. Even when it rains, its covered stands keep spectators dry. The show alone costs US$47 per person with empanadas and wine, while the combination show and *asado* (after the show) costs US$73 per person. There's a VIP version for US$113, with a more elaborate menu.

Spectators opting for the *asado* sit on the west side of the stands, reached by a red carpet across the sandy surface where *estancieros* traditionally show their finest livestock; show-only clients sit on the east side. Opera Pampa has transformed the adjacent western pavilion into a cavernous *parrilla* where guests enjoy empanadas and a glass of wine before the show, and browse the goods at a variety of gaucho-themed shops; after the show, they file into the *parrilla* for an all-you-can-eat buffet of roasted meats, plus salads, wine, and a sampling of traditional desserts.

NIGHTLIFE

### PARAKULTURAL
Scalabrini Ortiz 1331, tel. 011/4832-6753,
www.parakultural.com.ar
**HOURS:** Mon., Tues., and Fri. 11 P.M.–4 A.M.
**COST:** US$2
Map 7

In the Salón Canning, a classic no-frills *milonga* venue with perhaps the best floor in the city, Parakultural draws a younger, less traditional clientele who find mixing tango with electronica unremarkable; that young crowd, though, can be cliquish.

On other days, particularly Saturday, the Canning may host more conventional events with less adventurous but more agreeable participants. It has a good sound system.

### LA SHUSHETA
Piedras 936, tel. 011/4361-3537,
ww.mansiondandiroyal.com
**HOURS:** Wed. 10 P.M.–3 A.M.
Map 3

It's costly to stay at the tango-themed hotel next door, but anyone with the US$4 cover charge can show his or her steps at this weekly *milonga,* in a long, narrow ballroom on a century-old hardwood floor that can accommodate

up to 100 dancers (50 couples). Tables line the north wall, while there's a bar at the east end, and a food menu as well.

Novices appreciate that the staff make a special effort for everyone to feel welcome, but its relatively small size limits the space for errors. There's even less room when, once a month or so, a live trio takes the central stage which, like a Murphy bed, pulls out of the south wall to occupy part of the dancing area.

### TANGOCOOL
Villa Crespo, Av. Córdoba 5064, tel. 011/4383-7469,
www.tangocool.com
**HOURS:** Wed. 8 P.M.–1 A.M., Fri. 8 P.M.–3 A.M.
**COST:** US$1 Wed., US$2 Fri.
Map 7

In the Club Villa Malcolm, on the edge of Palermo SoHo, Tangocool avoids calling itself a *milonga*. Rather, all its sessions start with two-hour lessons, after which the students continue, and new participants arrive, for a *práctica* (translating roughly as "apprenticeship") for several hours more. Despite what sounds like a self-deprecating approach to their skills, the dancers here perform at a high level.

# Flamenco

As tango partisans, Argentines may feel ambivalent toward Spanish music and dance, but several venues offer flamenco shows and even lessons, almost always on weekends (as opposed to tango shows, which take place every night of the week).

### TIEMPO DE GITANOS
El Salvador 5575, tel. 011/4776-6143,
www.tiempodegitanos.com.ar
**HOURS:** Wed.–Sun. dinner and show
**COST:** US$20-27 per person (cash only)
Map 7

Run by a pair of documentary filmmakers—appropriately enough for its Palermo Hollywood location—Tiempo de Gitanos (Time of Gypsies) is a restaurant that specializes in flamenco dinner shows in an intimate locale adorned with souvenirs of the owners' own extensive travels. The menu is predominantly Spanish, tending toward tapas and paella, with beef and pasta options to keep the more conservative *porteño* diners contented.

Shows take place at 9 P.M. most nights but 10 P.M. on weekends, for US$20–27 per person (cash only).

# Gay and Lesbian

Buenos Aires has a vigorous gay scene, traditionally centered around Barrio Norte, where lots of gay men hang out on Avenida Santa Fe between Callao and Pueyrredón, especially Friday and Saturday night before going to clubs. Palermo Viejo is also popular; San Telmo is developing a higher profile; and there are other scattered gathering places and gay-oriented businesses throughout the city.

With only a few exceptions, gay and lesbian hangouts lack signage and, during daylight hours, they're virtually invisible. A series of widely available freebie publications keeps up with the local scene, including the monthly *La Otra Guía*, the quarterly *Gay Map Buenos Aires* (www.bleucards.net), and the quarterly *Circuitos Cortos BS As Gay* (www.circuitoscortos.com.ar), which has online map references.

Dance clubs and other venues are mostly tolerant and inclusive of heterosexuals; when non-Argentine heterosexual women tire of Argentine machismo, they sometimes prefer gay bars for dancing, but some *machistas* are catching on to this.

## ALSINA BUENOS AIRES

Alsina 940, tel. 011/4331-3231,
www.alsinabuenosaires.com.ar
**HOURS:** Fri.-Sat. from midnight, Sun. from 11 P.M.
Map 1

In a cavernous ballroom, a former Orthodox church that became a warehouse and has been recycled, the Alsina draws a mostly young crowd for twice-weekly electronica (the early Sunday program almost seems like a *milonga* schedule); other nights, it's more for general audiences. Halloween night can be a real experience here.

## AMERIKA

Almagro, Gascón 1040, tel. 011/4865-4416,
www.ameri-k.com.ar
**HOURS:** Thurs.-Sat. 1-8 A.M.
Map 8

It may claim to be in Palermo, but Amerika lies just over the Almagro line—not that it

makes much difference to the mixed crowd (mostly gay, but with more than a handful of heterosexuals) who flock here. There are three large but separate dance floors, one with electronica, another with Latin music, and yet another with 1980s pop. Saturdays and nights immediately before holidays, a US$12–13 cover includes all the beer you can drink.

## ANGEL'S

Viamonte 2168, www.discoangels.com.ar
**HOURS:** Thurs.-Sat. 1-7 A.M.
Map 4

One of Buenos Aires's most durable gay locales, Angel's is also one of few to flaunt its orientation with a conspicuous sign. Some members of Buenos Aires's gay and lesbian community consider it "unrefined," with large numbers of transvestites, but it has its public. The music is pulsing electronica. The cover is about US$6, but look for discount coupons on Santa Fe and Callao Avenues where flyers are often being passed out.

## BACH BAR

Cabrera 4390, www.bach-bar.com.ar
**HOURS:** Tues.-Sun. from 11 P.M.
Map 7

Bach's is a gay male and lesbian hangout that doesn't advertise the fact—there's no sign, the windows are blacked out, and there's a heavy security door—but there's usually a crowd as well. Some nights, there's live entertainment, which is often participatory, including karaoke and drag.

## ◖ BULNES CLASS

Bulnes 1250, tel. 011/4861-7492,
www.bulnesclass.com.ar
**HOURS:** Fri.-Sat. from 11 P.M.
Map 7

Having once again changed its name and the focus of its clientele, Bulnes Class is predominantly a gay male club, in a comfortable, spacious locale with contemporary style and lighting. The entertainment is primarily drag shows in the Liza Minnelli mold; women are welcome, and it often gets a mixed crowd.

## PRIDE CAFÉ

Balcarce 869, tel. 011/4300-6435

**HOURS:** Mon.-Fri. 9 A.M.-9 P.M., Sat. 11 A.M.-8 P.M., Sun. 10 A.M.-10 P.M.

Map 3

At the corner of Pasaje Giuffra, Pride Café is a cheerful corner café that serves specialty drinks, including Irish coffee, plus sandwiches and loads of sweets, including brownies, chocolate cake, cookies, muffins, and strudel. There are also mixed drinks, and happy hours 7–9 P.M. Sunday–Friday. While it gets a mixed audience of gay men and straight folks, it stays open later Thursday nights for gay-oriented live entertainment.

## SEARCH

Azcuénaga 1007, tel. 011/4824-0932, www.searchgaybar.com.ar

**HOURS:** Nightly from 11:30 P.M.

Map 6

Not far from the weekend hot spot of Santa Fe and Pueyrredón, Search is a small but long-lived Barrio Norte gay bar with drag shows and strippers. Having undergone several name and ownership changes, it remains a durable, reliable venue even if its inconspicuous basement facilities lack the glitz of other places.

## SITGES

Av. Córdoba 4119, tel. 011/4861-3763, www.sitgesonline.com.ar

**HOURS:** Wed.-Sun. from 10:30 P.M.

**COST:** US$3-5

Map 7

On the edge of Palermo and one of Buenos Aires's most popular gay and lesbian bars, Sitges packs them into three large but distinct spaces, including an ample patio, almost until daybreak. It's known for drag shows, but also gets some mainstream entertainment (such as the Joplinesque rock singer Patricia Sosa) and celebrity clientele (such as burlesque diva Moria Casán). The US$3–5 cover charge varies according to the night and includes at least one drink.

# ARTS AND LEISURE

Since independence, Argentina's impact on the arts has been remarkable for a geographically remote country with a relatively small population. Many Argentines have been eloquent writers and a much greater number are voracious readers. In the visual arts, particularly modern art, they have been innovative, and their architecture has often been grand even if derivative of Europe.

Classical music has always held a place in *porteño* society, but the city also exported the tango to Europe (where it became respectable) and around the world. It presently has one of the most vigorous rock-music scenes since 1960s London or San Francisco, creatively adapting polysyllabic Spanish to a frequently monosyllabic music. Likewise, Argentine cinema, theater, and dance have all been influential beyond the country's borders.

Even in the midst of Argentina's 2001–2002 financial crisis and loan default, one sector of Argentine society that showed resilience was arts and entertainment. After Tomás Eloy Martínez, a Tucumán native and professor of Spanish at Rutgers, the State University of New Jersey, won the Spanish Alfaguara literary prize (US$175,000) in 2002 for *El Vuelo de la Reina* (a novel about crime and corruption), he remarked, "One of Argentina's riches is forgotten but it is the quality, the leadership of our culture. [In that field] we can speak as equals to the U.S. or France."

Wild nightlife apart, Buenos Aires has plenty to do at almost all hours, with its critical mass of cinemas, concert halls, cultural centers, galleries, museums, theaters, and sports (for both spectators and participants). Still, for many

© WAYNE BERNHARDSON

# HIGHLIGHTS

LOOK FOR ( TO FIND RECOMMENDED ARTS AND ACTIVITIES.

( **Best Non-Urbanite Museum:** Buenos Aires is *not* Argentina, as the saying goes, and Monserrat's **Museo Etnográfico Juan B. Ambrosetti** suggests the ethnic and geographical diversity in the remote northwestern Andes, Patagonia, and Tierra del Fuego (page 120).

( **Best Tango Introduction:** The tango timeline at Monserrat's **Museo Mundial del Tango** summarizes the origins and development of Buenos Aires's iconic music and dance (page 121).

( **Most Extravagant Museum Quarters:** It's hard to believe the **Museo Nacional de Arte Decorativo** was once a single-family residence, even if the Errázuriz-Alvear family tried to unify the elites of both Chile and Argentina. Runner-up: Belgrano's Mudéjar-style Museo Yrurtia (page 121).

( **Best Gallery:** Since it opened in the 1950s, **Galería Rubbers** has been on the cutting-edge of Argentine and Latin American modern art, though its new Recoleta showroom is a recent development (page 124).

( **Best Community Theater:** Even native Spanish speakers from other countries may not understand everything that goes on in La Boca's **Teatro Catalinas Sur.** Somehow, though, this committed cast of non-professional actors, musicians, and singers communicate the epic of Argentine his-

Campeonato Abierto Argentino de Polo

tory even to spectators who don't know any Spanish (page 125).

( **Best Cultural Center:** Alongside the world-famous Cementerio de la Recoleta, the **Centro Cultural Ciudad de Buenos Aires** hosts some of Argentine art's most cutting-edge exhibitions, and its music, theater, and cinema programs also stand out in a neighborhood often derided for smug elitism (page 129).

( **Best Literary Event:** At Palermo's Sociedad Rural, April's **Feria del Libro** is South America's largest book fair, and the huge crowds it draws reflect the city's literary commitment (page 132).

( **Best Equestrian Event (Non-Gaucho Division):** November's **Campeonato Abierto Argentino de Polo** showcases some of the world's top polo riders in an elite spectacle (page 134).

© WAYNE BERNHARDSON

*porteños,* even sitting for hours in a café or *confitería* conversing and people-watching qualifies as a leisure pursuit. Sometimes, all these categories may overlap—the world-famous

Café Tortoni, for instance, is a traditional meeting place, but it's also a restaurant, a bar, and a venue for live music and dance, including tango floor shows and *milongas.*

# The Arts

Buenos Aires has a huge inventory of museums, which range from obscure to world-class. Several of them appear in the *Sights* chapter, as they are highlights that many visitors will want to see, but the ones that appear here have strong appeal among niche audiences. For art lovers, particularly those interested in modern Argentine art, the city's galleries serve much the same function. The quantity and diversity of theater offerings in Buenos Aires is also impressive.

## MUSEUMS

### BUQUE MUSEO *A.R.A. URUGUAY CORBETA*

Dique no. 4, tel. 011/4314-1090,
www.ara.mil.ar/hist_m_uruguay.asp
**HOURS:** Daily 10 A.M.-8 P.M.
**COST:** US$0.65
**Map 2**

Built in Birkenhead (one of England's biggest shipbuilding ports) in 1874, this motorized corvette served mostly as a coastal patrol vessel and a training ship until 1902, when it was up for decomission. The next year, though, the apparent loss of Otto Nordenskjöld's Swedish Antarctic expedition, on which the Argentine ensign José María Sobral was an officer, intervened. Under the command of Lt. (later Admiral) Julián Irízar, the reinforced and refitted *Uruguay* successfully rescued the expedition, marking the beginning of Argentina's Antarctic presence. (Julián Irízar's namesake icebreaker helped rescue the crew of the stranded German supply vessel *Magdalena Oldendorff* in the austral winter of 2002.)

The oldest Argentine vessel still afloat, the *Uruguay* experienced years of abandonment until its two-year restoration began in 1953, on the 50th anniversary of its Antarctic mission. Declared a national monument in 1967, it was anchored in La Boca until the mid-1990s, when it moved to Puerto Madero. In case of rain, it closes.

### BUQUE MUSEO *FRAGATA A.R.A. PRESIDENTE SARMIENTO*

Dique no. 3, tel. 011/4334-9386,
www.ara.mil.ar/hist_m_sarmiento.asp
**HOURS:** Daily 10 A.M.-8 P.M.
**COST:** US$0.65, free child under 5
**Map 2**

Built in Birkenhead in 1887, the frigate *Sarmiento* takes its name from Domingo F. Sarmiento, the Argentine president who founded the country's Escuela Naval (Naval School) in 1872. Its bowsprit, an effigy of the patriotic symbol La Libertad Argentina (analogous to the U.S. Statue of Liberty), crowns an iron-framed 85-meter vessel with wooden siding and copper veneer. The frigate undertook 37 international training voyages from 1899 to 1938 and served in Argentine waters in 1960. It also served a diplomatic function, having represented the country at the coronations of Edward VII in England and of Alfonso XIII in Spain, the centennial of Mexican independence, and the opening of the Panama Canal, among other occasions.

So famous as to be the subject of a feature film, the *Sarmiento* is now a museum that honors the ship's commanders and crew—including the stuffed cadaver of its canine mascot, Lampazo. (Embalming of human bodies is rare in Argentina; the most notorious case is Eva Perón's cadaver.)

In case of rain, it closes.

### FUNDACIÓN PROA

Pedro de Mendoza 1929, tel. 011/4104-1000,
www.proa.org
**HOURS:** Daily 11 A.M.-7 P.M.
**Map 3**

For the most part, La Boca trades on nostalgia, but the Vuelta de Rocha's cavernous Fundación Proa has become an ultra-modern display space. In a recycled three-story Italianate house, expanded to two adjacent houses, it hosts rotating exhibitions by both Argentine and international artists. In addition to painting and sculpture, there are also displays of

ARTS AND LEISURE

## BUENOS AIRES ON SCREEN

Foreign filmmakers have found Buenos Aires both visually appealing and thematically intriguing. Argentine-born but British-based, Martin Donovan made the cult thriller *Apartment Zero* (1989), which brilliantly and even humorously portrays *porteño* life – its depiction of busybody neighbors in a Buenos Aires apartment building is priceless – even as it deals with the Dirty War savagery. British actor Colin Firth plays the protagonist, an Anglo-Argentine cinema manager.

The worst of the worst is Alan Parker's kitschy version of the already kitschy musical *Evita* (1996). Filmed partly in Buenos Aires but also in Budapest, it's most notable for the controversy it caused with Peronist politicians obsessed with Evita's legacy and for the highly publicized meeting between Madonna and a flagrantly lecherous president Carlos Menem.

Nearly as bad, though, is British director Sally Potter's narcissistic *The Tango Lesson* (1997). For a better cinematic presentation of the tango, despite a weak story line, see Puerto Rican director Marcos Zurinaga's *Tango Bar* (1988); Zurinaga worked with his compatriot, the late Raúl Juliá, and an Argen-

tine cast and crew, including *bandoneón* player Rubén Juárez and singer Valeria Lynch.

It's only incidental, but the protagonist of Dutch director Paul Verhoeven's *Starship Troopers* (1997), a satirical adaptation of Robert Heinlein's sci-fi novel, is a *porteño*. Seen from space, Buenos Aires gets vaporized by alien bugs.

U.S. actor/director Robert Duvall, a frequent Buenos Aires visitor and fervent tango aficionado, filmed the so-so thriller *Assassination Tango* (2003) on location in Buenos Aires. British director Christopher Hampton filmed the adaptation of Lawrence Thornton's novel *Imagining Argentina*, starring Emma Thompson and Antonio Banderas, in the capital and the provinces.

More recently, Ernesto "Che" Guevara puttered off from Palermo's cobbled streets in Brazilian director Walter Salles's international hit *The Motorcycle Diaries* (2004). In a fitting footnote, Uruguayan singer-songwriter Jorge Drexler's *Al Otro Lado del Río* (To the Other Side of the River), from that movie's soundtrack, won a best original song Oscar – only days before Drexler flew home to participate in the inauguration of Tabaré Vásquez, Uruguay's first left-of-center president in history.

---

artisans' crafts and of photography. Occasional concerts and films also take place here.

As of press time, the Proa was closed for an expansion and was due to reopen in October 2008. Information on guided tours and admission prices was thus up in the air, though in the past general admission was US$1 for adults, US$0.35 for children and seniors. Children under age 12 accompanied by an adult did not pay.

### MUSEO CASA DE YRURTIA

Belgrano, O'Higgins 2390, tel. 011/4781-0385
**HOURS:** Tues.-Fri. 1-7 P.M., Sun. 3-7 P.M.; free guided tours Sun. 5 P.M.
**COST:** US$0.35
Map 8

Influenced by Auguste Rodin, sculptor Rogelio

Yrurtia (1879–1950) spent much of his career in Italy and France before returning to Buenos Aires in 1921. His signature work, *Canto al Trabajo* (Ode to Labor, 1923) on San Telmo's Plazoleta Olazábal, is a worthy antidote to the pompous equestrian statues that dominated decades of *porteño* public art.

Yrurtia designed, lived, and worked in this Mudéjar residence, which he intended as a museum for his sculptures and the paintings of his wife, Lía Correa Morales; on his death, he donated the house and his works to the state.

In addition to family creations, there are some works from other artists, most notably Picasso's painting *Rue Cortot, Paris.* The garden features Yrurtia's oversized *The Boxers,* which appeared at the 1904 St. Louis World's Fair.

© WAYNE BERNHARDSON

Rogelio Yrurtia's *The Boxers* stands in the gardens of his namesake Museo Casa de Yrurtia.

## MUSEO DE ARMAS DE LA NACIÓN
Av. Santa Fe 702,
tel. 011/4311-1079, ext. 179,
www.circulomilitar.org/web2/museo.htm
**HOURS:** Weekdays 1-7 P.M.
**COST:** US$1.60
**Map 5**

A field day for gun fetishists and other weapons zealots, the army's museum showcases arms and armor from medieval and colonial Europe, firearms from the 15th century on, antique artillery, and a few more events-oriented items: a diorama of the 1807 British landing at Ensenada de Barragán prior to the occupation of Buenos Aires, photographs of General Julio Argentino Roca's genocidal *Campaña del Desierto* (Desert Campaign) against the northern Patagonia Mapuche in the late 19th century, and a nod to the Falklands War, in which the Argentines seem to have produced an inordinate number of heroes for forces that lost so badly. There is also a roomful of antique Asian—mostly Japanese—weapons and armor.

The controversial General Roca himself founded the museum in 1904. All the exhibits are well presented and labeled, though like many Argentine museums this one is short on interpretation.

## MUSEO DE ARTE MODERNO
Av. San Juan 350, tel. 011/4361-1121,
www.aamamba.org.ar
**HOURS:** Tues.-Fri. 10 A.M.-8 P.M., Sat.-Sun. and holidays 11 A.M.-8 P.M.; guided tours Tues.-Sun. 5 P.M.; closed Jan.
**COST:** US$0.35; free Wed.
**Map 3**

San Telmo's modern art museum showcases contemporary Argentine artists in a converted warehouse with high ceilings; exhibits tend toward the abstract, with works from figures like Antonio Berni, León Ferrari, and Kenneth Kemble.

As of press time, the MAMBA was closed for remodeling and expansion, with no indication as to when it might reopen. Apparently it will be integrated with the around-the-corner Museo del Cine.

## MUSEO DE ARTES PLÁSTICAS EDUARDO SÍVORI

Av. Infanta Isabel 555, tel. 011/4772-5628,
www.museosivori.org.ar
**HOURS:** Tues.-Fri. noon-8 P.M., Sat.-Sun. and holidays
10 A.M.-8 P.M.
**COST:** US$0.35; free Wed.

**Map 7**

The Museo Sívori occupies a Bavarian-style house (1912) with a newer cement-block annex designed specifically for painting and sculpture, along with a separate sculpture garden. Argentine artists whose works are on display include Ernesto de la Cárcova, Lino Spilimbergo, and Luis Seoanes; there are also special exhibitions in other fields, such as photography.

## MUSEO DE ESCULTURAS LUIS PERLOTTI

Caballito, Pujol 644, tel. 011/4433-3396
**HOURS:** Tues.-Sun. 10 A.M.-6 P.M.
**COST:** US$0.35; free Wed.

**Map 8**

Luis Perlotti (1890-1969), an Italo-Argentine who traveled widely in the Andean highland countries of Peru and Bolivia, adapted the themes from those early American civilizations into exceptional *indigenista* sculptures, with strong social content but realist and naturalistic style. A friend and contemporary of La Boca painter Benito Quinquela Martín, Perlotti and his wife donated their Caballito house, along with about 1,000 pieces of his and others' works, to the city.

Hours at this municipally run museum, which has recently been rehabbed and reopened, are subject to change, but it's a worthwhile detour despite its out-of-the-way location.

## MUSEO DE LA POLICÍA FEDERAL

San Martín 353, 7th Fl., tel. 011/4394-6857
**HOURS:** Mon.-Fri. 2-6 P.M.
**COST:** Free

**Map 2**

It's faint but fair praise to say that Argentina's federal police are the country's most scrupulous police, if only because provincial forces seem beyond salvation. This museum tells only part of the story: It focuses on material items like uniforms, badges, and weapons over the centuries, as well as the force's role in monitoring and controlling gambling, robbery, drugs, counterfeiting, con artists, and faith healers. There is also a truly gruesome room dedicated to forensic medicine, which includes dismembered bodies and other unpleasant sights.

Still, the museum is as notable for what it excludes as for what it includes. There is only the briefest mention of its repressive role in events like the 1920s anarchist uprisings and the 1970s Dirty War. The museum gives no attention to the issue of police corruption—even if the feds are angels compared to the Buenos Aires provincial police, they still have plenty to answer for.

Children under age 16, as well as the very squeamish of any age, are not permitted in the goriest exhibits.

## MUSEO DEL CABILDO

Bolívar 65, tel. 011/4343-4387
**HOURS:** Wed.-Fri. 10:30 A.M.-5 P.M., Sat.-Sun.
8:30 A.M.-6 P.M.
**COST:** US$0.65

**Map 1**

The Plaza de Mayo's only remaining colonial structure, the Cabildo was a combination town council and prison, and the site where *criollo* patriots deposed Spanish viceroy Baltasar Hidalgo de Cisneros in 1810. The present structure preserves part of the *recova* (arcade) that once extended across the plaza.

Unfortunately, the museum itself is thin on content—a few maps, paintings, and photographs of the plaza and its surroundings, along with a portrait gallery of figures in the British invasions of 1806-1807, and the Revolution of May 1810. The real star is the building; part of it, at least, survived 19th-century mayor Torcuato de Alvear's wrecking ball, which created the Avenida de Mayo to connect the Casa Rosada with the Congreso Nacional.

The interior has a small *confitería* and occasionally hosts live music events.

© WAYNE BERNHARDSON

The Cabildo de Buenos Aires, which houses the Museo del Cabildo, is only a remnant of a larger colonial building partly demolished to create the Avenida de Mayo.

## MUSEO DEL CINE PABLO A. DUCRÓS HICKEN

Defensa 1220, tel. 011/4300-5967,
www.museodelcine.gov.ar
**HOURS:** Mon.-Fri. 10 A.M.-6 P.M., Sat.-Sun. noon-6 P.M.
**COST:** US$0.35; free Wed.
Map 3

In recent years, Argentina's movie museum has devoted space to special exhibits on topics such as 1974, a key year in cinema with the death of Perón and the chaos that led to military dictatorship; comedians and comedy in the country's movies over the last century; and movie posters. Permanent displays stress topics like film technology, including a collection of antique cameras, and there's a small cinema that shows Argentine classics for free (no subtitles, though, and on the oldest films, the soundtrack can be difficult even for those with a command of *porteño* Spanish).

The Museo del Cine also contains a library on Argentine cinema.

As of press time, it was closed for expansion and remodeling, with no suggestion as to when it might reopen. Apparently it may become integrated with the neighboring Museo de Arte Moderno.

## MUSEO DEL TRAJE

Chile 832, tel. 011/4343-8427,
www.funmuseodeltraje.com.ar
**HOURS:** Tues.-Fri. and Sun. 5-9 P.M.; Spanish guided tour Sun. 5 P.M.
**COST:** Free; donations welcome
Map 3

Buenos Aires's Museo del Traje (Museum of Dress) might more accurately be called the Museo de la Moda (Museum of Fashion), as it concentrates largely (though not exclusively) on women's clothing from colonial times to the present. In a middle-class *casa chorizo* (sausage house, so called because of its deep, narrow lot), the museum features three large patios typical of the mid-19th century; part of the building still awaits restoration.

ARTS AND LEISURE

## ◀ MUSEO ETNOGRÁFICO JUAN B. AMBROSETTI

Moreno 350, tel. 011/4345-8196,
www.museoetnografico.filo.uba.ar
**HOURS:** Wed.-Fri. 1-7 P.M., Sat.-Sun. 3-7 P.M.
**COST:** US$0.65, free retiree
Map 1

Affiliated with the Universidad de Buenos Aires, the city's ethnographic museum has first-rate archaeological, ethnographic, and ethnohistorical material on Argentina's Andean northwest (on the periphery of the great civilizations of highland Peru), northern Patagonia's Mapuche, and the Tierra del Fuego archipelago. Well organized, with good narration in Spanish only, it does a lot with what it has— and what it has is pretty good.

There are guided tours Saturday and Sunday at 4 P.M.; for English or French, it's necessary to make an advance request.

## MUSEO FORENSE DE LA MORGUE JUDICIAL DR. JUAN BAUTISTA BAFICO

Junín 760, tel. 011/4344-2035
**HOURS:** Mon.-Fri. 9 A.M.-2 P.M.; closed Jan., Feb., and Mar.
**COST:** Free
Map 4

Definitely not for the squeamish, the Forensic Morgue Museum is primarily a resource for students from the nearby medical school. It consists of a single large hall filled with glass cases displaying mutilated body parts from famous criminal cases or suicides (some of the remains are from tattooed prisoners).

Though it's not quite so grisly as that description might sound, the Museo de la Morgue has a serious purpose and is thus not open to casual drop-ins. It's for groups of 10 or more, but by phoning at least a day ahead between 10 A.M. and 3 P.M., it's possible to join an existing group.

Photography is prohibited.

## MUSEO HISTÓRICO BRIGADIER GENERAL CORNELIO DE SAAVEDRA

Saavedra, Crisólogo Larralde 6309, tel. 011/4572-0746
**HOURS:** Tues.-Fri. 10 A.M.-6 P.M., Sat.-Sun. and holidays 10 A.M.-6 P.M.; guided tours Sat.-Sun. and holidays 4 P.M.
**COST:** US$0.35; free Wed.

Focusing on 19th-century Argentina, this historical museum occupies the grounds of the onetime rural estate of Luis María Saavedra, nephew of independence hero Cornelio de Saavedra. Expropriated after 1929, the property came under municipal control as the Parque General Paz; the building, "modified for authenticity," became a museum in 1941.

Permanent museum exhibits include silverwork from the private collection of Ricardo Zemborain (1872–1912), who willed his possessions to the city; gems, coins, clothing, and furniture from the 18th and 19th centuries; and fashion accessories, such as *peinetones* (ornamental combs). Thematically, it covers events of the independence era and the early Argentine confederation.

The Museo Saavedra also functions as a cultural center, hosting concerts, films, and dance and theater events.

## MUSEO HOUSSAY DE CIENCIA Y TECNOLOGÍA

Paraguay 2155, 1st fl., tel. 011/5950-9500, ext. 2102, www.fmed.uba.ar
**HOURS:** Open on request
Map 6

This small but engaging museum at the UBA's Facultad de Medicina contains primarily educational and experimental equipment, instruments, and documents relating to Argentine medicine, but a long-overdue reorganization has barely progressed despite committed personnel. It takes its name from physiologist Bernardo Houssay, the son of French immigrants and winner of the 1947 Nobel Prize in medicine, and features some remarkable scientific curiosities, including an extraordinary German-built mechanical model of the eye dating from the late 19th century.

The Museo Houssay is normally open only when the university is in session, and until the reorganization is complete it's best to phone ahead. While it may not formally open, the staff are willing to show people around.

## MUSEO LIBERO BADII
Belgrano, 11 de Septiembre 1990, tel. 011/4783-3819
**HOURS:** Mon.-Fri. 9 A.M.-5 P.M.
**COST:** Free
Map 8

After the fall of Rosas, jurist Valentín Alsina acquired the property overlooking Barrancas de Belgrano for his *quinta* (country house), but it soon passed into the hands of the Atucha family, which built the 1870s Italian Renaissance house that survives, amid high-rises, to house this unique museum. The wildly imaginative Italian-born Badii, a naturalized Argentine, specialized in sculpture, engraving, design, collage, and illustration.

Operated under the auspices of the Fundación Banco Francés, the Museo Badii also offers special exhibits. Ring the bell for entry.

## ◖ MUSEO MUNDIAL DEL TANGO
Rivadavia 830, tel. 011/4345-6967,
www.anacdeltango.org.ar/museo.asp
**HOURS:** Mon.-Fri. 2:30-7:30 P.M.
**COST:** US$1.60
Map 1

On the 1st floor of the Academia Nacional de Tango, Buenos Aires's only dedicated tango museum falls into the good-but-could-be-better category. The approach is primarily chronological, from the music's 19th-century origins, and pays photographic homage to 20th-century giants such as Gardel, Troilo, Piazzolla, and the like. The representation of everyday household items, common in the barrios where tango was a passion, fleshes out its social history, but the lack of any English translation is inexcusable—especially since the Academia's personnel includes native and fluent English speakers.

Despite the official address, the museum has an additional entry at Avenida de Mayo 833, next door to the Café Tortoni. A museum store sells tango-related items.

## ◖ MUSEO NACIONAL DE ARTE DECORATIVO
Av. del Libertador 1902, tel. 011/4802-6606,
www.mnad.org.ar

**HOURS:** Tues.-Sun. 2-7 P.M.
**COST:** US$0.65; free Tues.
Map 7

Works ranging from Roman sculptures to contemporary silverwork, but mostly Asian and European pieces from the 17th to 19th centuries, fill the ornate four-story Beaux-Arts residence (1918) that now houses the national museum of decorative art. Many of its 4,000-plus items are anonymous; the best-known artists are Europeans like Manet and Rodin.

Both the building and the collections once belonged to Chilean diplomat Matías Errázuriz Ortúzar and his Argentine wife, Josefina de Alvear de Errázuriz, who lived less than 20 years in the house. After her death, the Errázuriz family sold both the building and the collections to the state.

The Museo de Arte Decorativo normally closes the last week of December and first week of January, and Sundays in January and February.

## MUSEO NACIONAL DEL GRABADO
Defensa 372, tel. 011/4345-5300
**HOURS:** Sun.-Fri. 2-6 P.M.
**COST:** Free
Map 1

Occupying the Casa de la Defensa, from which *porteños* routed British invaders in 1806–1807 by pouring boiling oil and water from the roof, Buenos Aires's museum of engraving owns 15,000 works by Argentine and foreign artists including Dalí, Picasso, and Siqueiros. Its mission, though, is to present rotating exhibits, often of very high quality, from Argentine artists in the medium.

## MUSEO NACIONAL DEL HOMBRE
3 de Febrero 1370, tel. 011/4784-9971,
www.inapl.gov.ar/museo.htm
**HOURS:** Mon.-Fri. 10 A.M.-6 P.M.
**COST:** US$0.35
Map 7

Small but well maintained and organized, the Museo Nacional del Hombre (National Museum of Man) is a modest but worthy

ARTS AND LEISURE

# THE REBIRTH OF *FILETE*

The flamboyant folk art called *filete* began with Sicilian immigrants whose horse carts were art on wheels. Their symmetrical ornamental lines, enriched by elaborate calligraphy, simulated the moldings and wrought-iron ornamentation on late-19th and early-20th-century buildings – the word *filete* derives from the Italian *filetto*, meaning a strip that separates moldings.

Gradually, the Argentine capital's *fileteadores* made their craft the standard for commercial sign painting, as it drew attention to fixed businesses like restaurants, cafés, and a variety of other services. It suffered, though, during the dark days of the Proceso dictatorship (1976–1983), when the generals banned it from public transportation for its alleged unreadability. Since the return to representative government, *filete* has made a comeback, and skilled *fileteadores* can now make a handsome living.

To see ready-made decorative plaques, visit Plaza Dorrego's Sunday Feria de San Pedro Telmo, where typical themes and subjects are tango (and tango legend Carlos Gardel), plus skillfully drawn dragons, flowers, and fruits. Many plaques display *piropos* (aphorisms or proverbs).

Perhaps typical of contemporary *fileteadores* is Martiniano Arce, whose San Telmo studio is literally a memorial to his craft – he has already chosen and painted his and his wife's coffins and keeps them on display in his house. He does not shy away from commercial work, saying that his art is incomplete until

© WAYNE BERNHARDSON

*Filete* painter Martiniano Arce of San Telmo has decorated his own casket – and his wife's.

someone owns it – in addition to the cover for rock band Los Fabulosos Cadillacs' *Fabulosos Calavera* CD, he has commemorated the 10th anniversary of McDonald's in Argentina with a custom design and even painted a symbolic bottle for Coca-Cola.

For information on purchasing *filete* from markets and directly from artisans such as Arce, see the *Shops* chapter.

---

complement to Monserrat's larger and more elaborate Museo Etnográfico. Providing information on the prehistory and contemporary status of Argentina's indigenous peoples, it could use more detailed maps of individual group territories, but its 5,000 pieces are a fine representative sample of indigenous material culture.

Part of the Instituto Nacional de Antropología y Pensamiento Latinoamericano, a research and training institute, the Museo

Nacional del Hombre has a museum shop with a small but excellent crafts selection.

## MUSEO PENITENCIARIO ARGENTINO ANTONIO BALLVÉ

Humberto Primo 378, tel. 011/4362-0099
**HOURS:** Wed.-Fri. 2-5 P.M., Sun. 1-7 P.M.
**COST:** US$0.35

Once poorly organized, Buenos Aires's improved penal museum features thematic

exhibits such as cell doors from various prisons throughout time and typically outfitted cells, including one from the women's prison this once was. From a historical perspective, the most intriguing items are photographs (including Anarchist Simón Radowitzky's release from the world's most southerly prison at Ushuaia, in Tierra del Fuego), and an elaborate wooden desk that Ushuaia inmates carved for Roberto M. Ortiz (no doubt to show their affection) during his 1938–1942 presidency. Note the large apothecary cabinet in the same room as Ortiz's desk.

Half a block east of Plaza Dorrego, the museum occupies the former convent wing of the Iglesia Nuestra Señora de Belén (1750), a colonial structure that has experienced several remodelings; taken over by Bethlemites after the Jesuit expulsion of 1767, it became a men's prison under secular President Bernardino Rivadavia and then a women's house of detention until 1978.

Still lacking interpretive text, the Museo Penitenciario is worth a stop if you're nearby during its limited hours.

## MUSEO XUL SOLAR

Laprida 1212, tel. 011/4824-3302,
www.xulsolar.org.ar
**HOURS:** Tues.-Fri. noon-7:30 P.M., Sat. noon-7 P.M., closed Jan. and Feb.
**COST:** US$2, US$0.65 retiree and child under 12
Map 6

Obsessed with architecture and the occult, Alejandro Schulz Solari (1897–1963) was an abstract painter who produced vivid oils and watercolors. During his lifetime, his work showed in Buenos Aires, Brazil, France, and Italy; after his death, it also appeared in Miami, New York, London, Madrid, Stockholm, and other European cities. Despite his own blindness, Jorge Luis Borges left vivid descriptions of the works of his friend and contemporary, better known as Xul Solar.

The Xul Solar museum displays a large assortment of his work, mostly smallish watercolors, in utilitarian surroundings with sheetrocked walls and relatively dim light

that contrast dramatically with the painter's intense colors. It also shows personal effects, such as postcards directed to famous writers like Nietzsche.

## MUSEO Y ARCHIVO HISTÓRICO DE LA DIRECCIÓN GENERAL IMPOSITIVA

Av. de Mayo 1317, 5th fl., tel. 011/4347-2396,
www.afip.gov.ar
**HOURS:** Mon.-Fri. 11 A.M.-5 P.M.
**COST:** Free
Map 2

Occupying part of the former Hotel Majestic, this museum, alternatively known as the Museo de la Administración Federal de Ingresos Públicos, focuses on the theme of taxation in a country infamous for money laundering and similar subterfuges.

## PLANETARIO GALILEO GALILEI

Av. Sarmiento and Belisario Roldán,
tel. 011/4771-6629, www.planetario.gov.ar
**HOURS:** Mon.-Fri. 9 A.M.-5 P.M., Sat.-Sun. 1-7:30 P.M.; guided tours Tues.-Fri. 1 and 5 P.M., Sat.-Sun. and holidays 4, 5, and 6 P.M.
**COST:** Free; guided tours US$1.35, free for child under 5 and retiree
Map 7

Since it opened in 1967, Buenos Aires's planetarium has introduced more than 10 million visitors, mostly school children, to the night skies projected on its interior dome in a 360-seat auditorium. It also has a telescope for viewing the stars directly, though the city's light pollution makes this problematical. There is a small artificial lake outside, the Lago del Planetario.

## GALLERIES

Buenos Aires has a thriving modern art scene, with the most innovative galleries in Retiro and Recoleta. Some dealers still focus on European-style works, but these will probably be of little interest to visitors, as they fail to indicate the vitality of contemporary Argentine art. The best dealers have outstanding websites that make it possible to preview their work.

ARTS AND LEISURE

### FLORIDA GARDEN

Florida 889, tel. 011/4312-7902
**HOURS:** Mon.-Fri. 6:30 A.M.-11:30 P.M., Sat. 7 A.M.-10:30 or 11 P.M., Sun. 8 A.M.-10:30 or 11 P.M.
**Map 5**

Although this venue is a café, the distinguishing feature here is the gallery of paintings that adorn its supporting columns. Tables are uneven, and the food—the *medialunas* (croissants) in particular—is mediocre, but it has a devoted clientele.

### GALERÍA FEDERICO KLEMM

Marcelo T. de Alvear 626, tel. 011/4312-4443, www.fundacionfjklemm.org
**HOURS:** Mon.-Fri. 11 A.M.-8 P.M.
**Map 5**

The legacy of the Czech-born Federico Klemm, a flamboyant figure who died in 2002, this gallery at the north end of the Florida pedestrian mall is particularly good at giving unconventional young artists a jump start through annual competitions. The gallery closes for two weeks in January.

### ◖ GALERÍA RUBBERS

Av. Alvear 1595, tel. 011/4816-1864, www.rubbers.com.ar
**HOURS:** Mon.-Fri. 11 A.M.-8 P.M., Sat. 10 A.M.-1:30 P.M.
**Map 6**

In a prime Recoleta location, Rubbers is a contemporary gallery that's worked with modern Argentine painters, such as Antonio Berni and Xul Solar, but also with photographers such as Aldo Sessa. They've also led the way with other Latin American artists, having been the first to exhibit Uruguay's Pedro Figari in Buenos Aires (shortly after opening in 1957), and gave the now-famous Colombian painter/sculptor Fernando Botero his first contract (in 1964).

### GALERÍA RUTH BENZACAR

Florida 1000, tel. 011/4313-8480, www.ruthbenzacar.com
**HOURS:** Mon.-Fri. 11:30 A.M.-8 P.M., Sat. 10:30 A.M.-1:30 P.M.
**Map 5**

Accessed by an inconspicuous staircase at the Florida pedestrian mall's north end, the Benzacar gallery is a bright, uncluttered subterranean space that showcases some of the capital's, and the country's, most avant-garde artists. Founded in 1965, it made an early-1990s list of the world's 200 best galleries, and has earned an international reputation in promoting the works of figures like Antonio Berni and León Ferrari. It also makes a point of selecting young, talented artists for their commercial debuts.

### GALERÍA VERMEER

Suipacha 1168, tel. 011/4393-5102, www.galeriavermeer.com.ar
**HOURS:** Mon.-Fri. 11:30 A.M.-7 P.M.
**Map 5**

In business since 1973, perhaps not so avant-garde as Galería Rubbers, Vermeer is still a quality gallery that has hosted exhibitions by contemporary artists such as Berni, Raquel Forner, Lino Spilimbergo, Xul Solar, and the Uruguayan Joaquín Torres García.

### GALERÍA ZURBARÁN

Cerrito 1522, tel. 011/4815-1556, www.zurbarangaleria.com.ar
**HOURS:** Mon.-Fri. 11 A.M.-9 P.M.
**Map 5**

Zurbarán may not be one of Buenos Aires's most adventurous galleries, but it's had an impressive roster of exhibitions and its website has abundant information on contemporary Argentine artists. It also has a separate showroom called Colección Alvear de Zurbarán (Av. Alvear 1658, Recoleta, tel. 011/4811-3004), which keeps slightly shorter hours.

## THEATER

Though the recent years of economic hardship took the luster off some of its venues, Buenos Aires remains the continent's theater capital. Avenida Corrientes is the traditional locus of live theater, and city authorities hope the widened sidewalks between Avenida 9 de Julio and Avenida Callao will draw pedestrians back to the area and help restore this tradition. Meanwhile, it's still worth seeking out less conventional alternatives.

Avenida de Mayo and myriad Microcentro side streets are also home to important theaters, several of them historic. At the same time, many smaller and less conventional "off-Corrientes" venues, some of them virtual micro-theaters, add diversity. For the latest information on those, check the website Alternativa Teatral (www.alternativateatral.com).

Ranging from vulgar burlesque with elaborate stage shows to Shakespearean and avant-garde drama, the theater scene is busiest June–August, but events take place all year. The difference between traditional theaters and shoestring venues is not so much skilled actors as the production budget; larger budgets allow much more elaborate sets at larger venues. The biggest productions can even move intact to the Atlantic beach resort of Mar del Plata for the summer.

For discount tickets, check *carteleras* or online ticket-purchasing services. All major *porteño* newspapers, including *Ámbito Financiero,* the *Buenos Aires Herald, Clarín, La Nación,* and *Página 12,* provide extensive listings and schedules.

## CENTRO LATINOAMERICANO DE CREACIÓN E INVESTIGACIÓN TEATRAL
Moreno 431, tel. 011/4342-1026, www.celcit.org.ar
**Map 1**

Known more conveniently by its acronym Celcit, this innovative theater and educational institution specializes in plays by modern and contemporary Latin American dramatists, such as Argentina's late Roberto Arlt and Chile's Marco Antonio de la Parra. As a company, they often take their show on the road to other Latin American locales, as far away as Mexico and Puerto Rico; in its quarters two blocks south of the Plaza de Mayo, the theater itself also hosts a variety of musical events.

## LIBERARTE
Av. Corrientes 1555, tel. 011/4375-2341, www.liberarteteatro.com.ar
**Map 2**

Liberarte is a politically and socially conscious

### OFF-CORRIENTES

Buenos Aires has big theater productions, but there are several smaller and less conventional "off-Corrientes" venues, some of which might be called micro-theaters – the three stages at **Teatro El Vitral** (Rodríguez Peña 344, tel. 011/4371-0948) seat 36-180 patrons.

Some companies lack regular venues in the strictest sense – they may appear spontaneously or rent theaters to put on their productions. Less conventional groups to watch for include **Teatreros Ambulantes Los Calandracas** (Centro Cultural Barracas, Av. Iriarte 2165, Barracas, tel. 011/4302-6825, www.ccbarracas.com.ar) and **Teatro Callejero La Runfla** (Centro Cultural Chacra de los Remedios, Av. Directorio and Lacarra, Parque Avellaneda, tel. 011/4672-3708, www.parqueavellaneda.org).

These groups often literally take it to the streets, performing in parks and other public venues, but the **Grupo Teatral Escena Subterránea** (Charlone 697, tel. 011/4553-8633) takes it beneath the streets, performing in Subte cars and stations, as well as other public spaces.

bookstore that also offers theater programs, mostly on weekends but occasionally on weeknights. In addition to stage plays, improv, and stand-up comedy, it also hosts dance (including tango) and even children's programs (at relatively early hours, around 5–6 P.M.).

### TEATRO CATALINAS SUR
Benito Pérez Galdós 93, tel. 011/4300-5707, www.catalinasur.com.ar
**Map 3**

To appreciate Catalinas Sur, a community theater group that illuminates the experience of working-class European immigrants, it's not necessary to understand a single word of Spanish. So visual is their approach (thanks largely to Omar Gasparini's psychedelically imaginative sets), and so expressive are the non-professional actors, singers, and musicians, the language is only secondary. Understanding *porteño* Spanish may enrich the experience of repertory works like *Venimos de Muy Lejos* (We Came from Far Away) and *El Fulgor Argentino* (a century of Argentine history through the experience of a neighborhood sports and social club), but it's not essential.

Catalinas Sur normally has Friday- and Saturday-night shows, but also appears in parks around the barrio and vicinity. Take a cab to the theater, a recycled warehouse in a dark and deserted part of La Boca (though plenty of people are around at showtime).

### TEATRO DE LA RIBERA
Pedro de Mendoza 1821, tel. 011/4302-9042,
www.teatrosanmartin.com.ar
Map 3

Before his death in 1977, La Boca artist and promoter Benito Quinquela Martín donated the building that serves as headquarters for the La Boca theater group Teatro de la Ribera. Since then, it's become part of the municipal Teatro San Martín complex, seating around 650 spectators. Its programs tend toward works by playwrights like the politically committed Italian Nobel Prize winner Dario Fo. It also has a gallery for art exhibits, including photography.

### TEATRO GENERAL SAN MARTÍN
Av. Corrientes 1530, tel. 011/4371-0111,
www.teatrosanmartin.com.ar
Map 2

Buenos Aires's single most notable theater facility, the San Martín is a multipurpose complex whose diversity of offerings helps compensate for its lack of architectural merit. Covering more than 30,000 square meters, this utilitarian building (1961) has three main auditoria, a cinema, exhibition halls, and other facilities that draw up to one million visitors per year. Students with international ID cards get 50 percent discounts for most shows, and there are many free events, as well.

### TEATRO NACIONAL CERVANTES
Libertad 815, tel. 011/4815-8883,
www.teatrocervantes.gov.ar
Map 5

Dating from 1921, the plateresque Cervantes was originally a private initiative but, when its Spanish owners fell into financial problems, the Argentine government took it over to create a national theater. After suffering an early-1960s fire, it underwent a major renovation/expansion and now holds three separate theaters, most notably the 860-seat Sala María Guerrero. The others hold 150 and 120 seats, respectively.

While the theater still pays homage to its famous Spanish namesake by presenting his classics, most offerings now lean toward 20th-century Argentine playwrights. The building is also home to the Museo Nacional del Teatro (National Theater Museum), open Monday–Friday 10 A.M.–6 P.M.

## CONCERT VENUES
The classical music and opera season lasts March–November but peaks in winter, June–August.

### LA SCALA DE SAN TELMO
Pasaje Giuffra 371, tel. 011/4362-1187,
www.lascala.com.ar
Map 3

High culture and popular culture, of a sort, meet at this intimate performing-arts locale, in an artfully restored colonial house. While its name suggests a classical orientation, La Scala actively seeks and encourages up-and-coming talent in folk, jazz, and tango music. Part of an institution that also trains aspiring performers, it even records and distributes their efforts through its website.

While it's not a casual venue—jeans, sandals, and T-shirts are not appropriate here—La Scala is not stiffly formal either. After each show, spectators and performers mix in its cozy bar, which serves empanadas, pizza, wine, soft drinks, and coffee. Program days and times vary, but most are around 8 or 9 P.M. from Thursday to Sunday. Cover charges fall in the US$3–5 range.

# CINEMA

Buenos Aires's traditional commercial cinema district is in the Microcentro along the Lavalle pedestrian mall west of Florida and along Avenida Corrientes and Avenida Santa Fe. In addition, there are multiplexes in the shopping malls of Puerto Madero, Retiro, Abasto, and Palermo, and clusters of cinemas in the outer barrios, such as Belgrano.

Imported films generally appear in the original language with Spanish subtitles, except for animated and children's movies, which are dubbed into the local language (Cine Los Angeles specializes in these). Translations of foreign-language titles are often misleading, but the *Buenos Aires Herald* prints the original English title and translations of other foreign-language titles.

Most tickets are in the US$4–6 range for first-run movies. Most cinemas offer substantial discounts Monday–Wednesday, and sometimes for the afternoon shows on other days. On Friday and Saturday nights, there is usually a *trasnoche* (midnight or later) showing, but even on weeknights there may be shows beginning as late as 11 P.M.

The following listings generally include cinemas that show Argentine and other foreign films, rather than multiplexes showing first-run Hollywood features; the latter are easy to locate in the *Buenos Aires Herald* and other daily newspapers. Independent films or reprises of commercial films generally show at cultural centers or smaller venues scattered around town.

## MICROCENTRO

The Instituto Nacional de Cine y Artes Visuales (www.incaa.gov.ar) operates two central cinemas that promote mostly Argentine films: the four-screen **Complejo Tita Merello** (Suipacha 442, tel. 011/4322-1195) and the three-screen **Cine Gaumont** (Rivadavia 1635, tel. 011/4371-3050).

At the Teatro San Martín's **Sala Leopoldo Lugones** (Av. Corrientes 1530, 10th fl., tel. 011/4371-0111, www.teatrosanmartin.org.ar), Werner Herzog is about as mainstream as it gets – most of its offerings and retrospectives tend toward obscure French, Italian, and even Korean films, but there are some real gems among these.

The two-screen **Complejo Cine Lorca** (Av. Corrientes 1428, tel. 011/4371-5017) shows mostly European films and the occasional off-center Hollywood flick (in the *Bad Santa* vein).

The three-screen **Cine Premier** (Av. Corrientes 1565, tel. 011/4374-2113) is more strictly commercial, but usually has at least one indie-type film on the docket.

The three-screen **Cine Los Angeles** (Av. Corrientes 1770, tel. 011/4372-2405) specializes in children's films, normally dubbed rather than subtitled.

## BALVANERA

The two-screen **Cine Cosmos** (Av. Corrientes 2046, tel. 011/4953-5405, www.cinecosmos. com) shows up to four different films, mostly European (Bergman is a favorite) and Latin American, on any given day.

## PALERMO

The **Cine Club Tea** (Aráoz 1460, tel. 011/4832-2646, cineclubtea@uol.com.ar) is an aficionados' club that operates out of a small Palermo Viejo locale.

The **Museo de Arte Latinomamericano de Buenos Aires** (MALBA, Av. Figueroa Alcorta 3415, tel. 011/4808-6500, www.malba.org. ar/web/cine.php) shows up to half a dozen classics, documentaries, and obscurities daily in its cinema, which is part of a much larger art facility that's one of the city's cultural highlights.

## TEATRO AVENIDA

Av. de Mayo 1222,
tel. 011/4381-3193
Map 1

Second only to the Colón as an opera venue,
the Teatro Avenida celebrated its centennial
in 2008, though this stunning Hispanophile
theater sat empty for 15 years after a 1979 fire
gutted its interior. When the famed Spanish
dramatist Federico García Lorca came to
Buenos Aires in 1933, his classic *Bodas de
Sangre* (Blood Wedding) played here.

While the theater owes its origins to a
taste for the Spanish light opera form *zarzu-
ela,* it also hosts flamenco programs and
even the occasional hybrid: Accompanied
by a 40-strong orchestra, former Soda Stereo
rock guitarist Gustavo Cerati debuted symphonic versions of 11 of the group's hits here
in 2003.

## TEATRO COLÓN

Libertad 621, tel. 011/4378-7344,
www.teatrocolon.org.ar
Map 2

Unquestionably, the capital's prime classical music locale remains the Colón, though
the recent economic crisis meant increasing
reliance on Argentines rather than high-profile foreigners (performers such as Luciano
Pavarotti and Plácido Domingo have often
graced the Colón's stage). At the same time,
internationally known figures with local links,
such as the Buenos Aires–born Israeli conductor Daniel Barenboim, have made special
efforts here.

Among other performers that play the Colón
are the Orquesta Filarmónica de Buenos Aires
(www.ofba.org.ar)—often with guest conductors from elsewhere in Latin America—and the
Mozarteum Argentino (www.mozarteumar-
gentino.org). Occasionally there is a surprise,
such as the rhythm-and-blues unit Memphis
La Blusera, the first of its sort to take the hal-
lowed stage, in conjunction with the Orquesta
Sinfónica Nacional.

For more information on the theater, see the
*Sights* chapter.

© WAYNE BERNHARDSON

As the Teatro Colón remains closed for
rehab, Monserrat's Teatro Avenida is keeping
opera alive in Buenos Aires.

## TEATRO MARGARITA XIRGÚ

Chacabuco 863/875, tel. 011/4300-2448,
www.margaritaxirgu.com
Map 3

In a magnificent neo-Gothic building that
was once the Spanish consulate, the Margarita
Xirgú is the performing-arts arm of the Casal
de Catalunya cultural center, with offerings
ranging from ballet to big bands, flamenco,
and even opera. The wildly comedic (but musically serious) band Les Luthiers made their
debut here, and the famous Catalan singer Joan
Manuel Serrat has also performed on its stage.

In addition to its cultural and entertainment
programs, the Xirgú complex has an outstanding restaurant.

## CULTURAL CENTERS

Buenos Aires has a multitude of municipal, national, and international cultural centers, all
of which offer live entertainment and events,
dance and language classes, films, and many
other activities.

## ASOCIACIÓN ARGENTINA DE CULTURA INGLESA

Suipacha 1333, tel. 011/4393-6941,
www.britishartscentre.org.ar
**HOURS:** Mon.-Fri. 3-9 P.M., Sat.-Sun. 11 A.M.-1:30 P.M.
Map 5

Also known as the British Arts Centre (BAC), one of the city's most active foreign cultural missions supplements its language instruction with a calendar of theater (including Shakespeare staged for kids), film cycles of British actors, directors, and even themes (such as adaptations of Agatha Christie), TV/video (would you believe Benny Hill?), and music (including Celtic). It also hosts exhibits by Argentine artists, and regular lectures and workshops.

The BAC shuts down in January, keeps limited hours in February, and resumes a full schedule in March.

## CENTRO CULTURAL BORGES

Viamonte and San Martín, tel. 011/5555-5359,
www.ccborges.org.ar
**HOURS:** Mon.-Sat. 10 A.M.-9 P.M., Sun. noon-9 P.M.
Map 2

Adjacent to the Galerías Pacífico and named for Argentina's most famous literary figure, this 10,000-square-meter cultural center has become one of the city's top cultural attractions. In addition to a diverse schedule of performing-arts events in its Auditorio Ástor Piazzolla, it holds film retrospectives in its *microcine* (small cinema), plus rotating fine-arts exhibitions and a variety of classes and seminars on topics ranging from Borges himself to Russian literature and the works of Woody Allen.

Admission costs US$3, though the ground and 1st-floor exhibit halls are open to the public without charge.

## ◖ CENTRO CULTURAL CIUDAD DE BUENOS AIRES

Junín 1930, tel. 011/4803-1040,
www.centroculturalrecoleta.org
**HOURS:** Tues.-Fri. 2-9 P.M., Sat.-Sun. and holidays 10 A.M.-9 P.M.
Map 6

In the 1980s, architects Clorindo Testa,

Jacques Bedel, and Luis Benedit turned the 18th-century Franciscan convent alongside the Iglesia Nuestra Señora del Pilar into one of Buenos Aires's major cultural centers; it now boasts exhibition halls, a cinema, and an auditorium that is one of the most important sites for Festival Buenos Aires Tango. In addition, outside the center proper, the architects added the Plaza del Pilar, a stylish arcade housing the upscale Buenos Aires Design shopping mall and a gaggle of sidewalk restaurants and cafés.

Immediately after Argentine independence, General Manuel Belgrano established an art school on the site. Thereafter, though, it served as a beggars' prison until reformist mayor Torcuato de Alvear cleaned up the site in the 1880s; Italian architect Juan Buschiazzo turned the chapel into an auditorium and gave adjacent walls and terraces an Italianate style. Until its 1980s remodel, it served as the Hogar de Ancianos General Viamonte, a retirement home.

The Centro's other facilities include the **Museo Participativo de Ciencias** (tel. 011/4807-3260, www.mpc.org.ar), a hands-on science museum for children, whose hours vary depending on whether school is in session; and a microcine with repertory film cycles.

Admission is free (but donations are encouraged) except for the Museo Participativo, which costs US$3 for those aged five and older. There are also charges for some film programs. For guided visits, make reservations (tel. 011/4807-6340).

## CENTRO CULTURAL DEL SUR

Barracas, Av. Caseros 1750,
tel. 011/4306-0301,
www.ccdelsur.blogspot.com
**HOURS:** Mon.-Sat. 10 A.M.-9 P.M.
Map 8

In a colonial-style house, this underappreciated cultural center hosts some of the Festival Buenos Aires Tango's biggest events on its open-air stage, alongside what was once the city's southern botanical garden. The building's enclosed patio is the site of an off-and-on crafts fair, and there are frequent children's and theater events on weekends. Admission is usually free, even for special events such as the tango festival, but it's necessary to pick up tickets at least a couple hours in advance.

### CENTRO CULTURAL RECTOR RICARDO ROJAS

Av. Corrientes 2038, tel. 011/4954-5521, www.rojas.uba.ar
**HOURS:** Mon.-Fri. 10 A.M.-7 P.M.
Map 4

One of Buenos Aires's most dynamic cultural centers, the Rojas sponsors events and exhibitions in the visual arts (specifically photography), cinema, dance (including tango), music, and theater. In addition, it hosts lectures on science and technology, and it has special interest in *porteño* circus and the participatory *murgas* (community performance groups) that are the grassroots of the city's late-summer *carnaval* off-site events. It also co-sponsors

Concerts, exhibitions, and lectures often take place outside the normal business hours listed here.

### INSTITUTO GOETHE

Av. Corrientes 319, tel. 011/4311-8964, www.goethe.de/hs/bue/spindex.htm
**HOURS:** Mon.-Fri. 9 A.M.-6 P.M.
Map 2

In addition to its library and German-language classes, the Goethe Institute hosts an ambitious schedule of films, lectures, theater, dance and music (including some very avant-garde electronica), and art and photography exhibits. Many events take place on-site, but others are co-sponsored in venues such as the Teatro Colón.

### PALACIO NACIONAL DE LAS ARTES (PALAIS DE GLACE)

Posadas 1725, tel. 011/4804-1163, www.palaisdeglace.org
**HOURS:** Tues.-Fri. noon-8 P.M., Sat.-Sun. and holidays 10 A.M.-8 P.M.
Map 6

A former skating rink—according to legend, Carlos Gardel was once shot in the vicinity—the Palais de Glace hosts a steady calendar of artistic and historical exhibitions, plus cultural and commercial events. The price of admission depends on the program.

# Holidays, Festivals, and Events

One Uruguayan called his country *"un país de feriados"* (a country of holidays), but Argentina might be called the same; it observes all the typical national holidays and quite a few special events on top of that. The summer months of January and February, when most *porteños* leave on vacation, are generally quiet; things pick up after school starts in early March.

## January

January 1 is **Año Nuevo** (New Year's Day), an official holiday. Although it resembles its counterpart in other parts of the world, it is important to note that there is an undisciplined use of illegal fireworks in many parts of the city.

## February and March
### CARNAVAL

Various neighborhoods

Dates for the pre-Lenten Carnaval (Carnival) vary from year to year but, in Buenos Aires, most celebrations take place on weekends rather than during the week. While unlikely ever to match the spectacle of Rio de Janeiro and other Brazilian locales, Carnaval is enjoying a revival, particularly with the performances of barrio *murgas* (street musicians and dancers) rather than elaborate downtown events. This festival takes place in many different neighborhoods. The daily newspapers contain a listing of parades and times closer to the event date.

# THE RESUSCITATION OF CARNAVAL

Carnaval is traditionally a far lesser celebration in Buenos Aires than in Brazil or even Uruguay, where Montevideo's Afro-Uruguayan communities uphold the tradition of syncopated *candombe* music. *Candombe* may still be more conspicuous on the San Telmo murals of its musicians than in the Argentine capital's pre-Lenten celebrations, but it is making a comeback.

*Candombe* nearly disappeared after the 1870s, as overwhelming European immigration overshadowed what remained of the Afro-Argentine heritage. Elements of it survived, though, thanks to *murgas*, bands of brightly costumed dancers accompanied by drums, who adopted the music of a nearly bygone way of life. Contemporary neighborhood *murgas*, with their subtext of political protest by an underclass betrayed by its owners, display a revived urgency.

Now, every summer, more than a hundred *murgas* of colorfully clad leaping dancers and pounding drummers participate in neighborhood *corsos* (parades). Bearing names like Los Amantes de La Boca (The Lovers of La Boca), Los Amos de Devoto (The Lords of Devoto), La Locura de Boedo (The Madness of Boedo), Los Mocosos de Liniers (The Snots of Liniers), Los Reyes del Movimiento (The Kings of Rhythm), and Los Quitapenas (The Sorrow Busters), they continue the revival of a tradition that nearly died with the 1976–1983 dictatorship.

Nevertheless, this protest music and dance has offered a colorful outlet in hard times. Popular commercial musicians, such as *rock nacional* icons Los Piojos, have also gravitated to this dynamic expression of disenfranchised voices.

## EXPOSICIÓN DE OTOÑO DE LA ASOCIACIÓN CRIADORES DE CABALLOS CRIOLLOS
Predio Ferial de la Sociedad Rural Argentina, Av. Sarmiento 2704
Map 7
In late March, this exposition is the best-of-breed showcase for the hardy horses of the sort that Aimé Tschiffely rode from Buenos Aires to Washington, D.C., in the 1920s. The event is sponsored by Balvanera's Asociación Criadores de Caballos Criollos (Creole Horse Breeders' Association, Larrea 670, 2nd fl., tel. 011/4961-3387, www.caballoscriollos.com).

## FESTIVAL BUENOS AIRES TANGO
Various venues, tel. 0800/333-7848 toll-free in Argentina, www.festivaldetango.gov.ar
Though it began in 1998 on Gardel's December 11 birthday, the increasingly popular Festival Buenos Aires Tango now follows Brazilian Carnaval in March (though it took place in August of 2008). Lasting several weeks, it includes dance competitions and numerous free music and dance events at venues like

the Centro Cultural San Martín, the Centro Cultural Recoleta, and the Centro Cultural del Sur, where calendars are available.

## SEMANA SANTA
Various venues
Semana Santa (Holy Week) is widely observed in Catholic Argentina, though only the days from **Viernes Santo** (Good Friday) through **Pascua** (Easter Sunday) are official holidays. Many Argentines, though, use the long weekend for a mini-vacation. This holiday is generally low-key in Buenos Aires. There are no elaborate processions of the sort found in some Latin American countries.

## ST. PATRICK'S DAY
Various venues
St. Patrick's Day (March 17) is not a formal holiday, but it has acquired a certain fashionability in Buenos Aires, but some *porteños* seem to see it as an excuse to get roaring drunk at any of several nominally Irish pubs (Buenos Aires did receive substantial Irish immigration in the 20th century). You can join

# FESTIVAL BUENOS AIRES TANGO

Despite its newness – the first event took place only in 1997 – the Festival Buenos Aires Tango (tel. 0800/3378-4825, www.festival-detango.com.ar) has become one of the city's signature special events. Lasting three weeks, normally from mid-February to early March, this festival of music, song, and dance ranges from the very traditional and conservative to the imaginative and even the daring.

Shortly after its creation, the festival moved from December to February and March to follow Brazilian Carnaval, but it is not strictly a tourist-oriented affair; it is also widely accepted and anticipated by a demanding *porteño* public. Unlike Brazilian Carnaval, it is not a mass spectacle, but rather a decentralized series of performances at relatively small, often intimate, venues around the capital. As such, it offers opportunities to see and hear not just established artists, but also developing performers.

Most of the funding for the city-sponsored festival goes to pay the artists, and admission is either free or inexpensive; however, tickets are usually available on a first-come, first-serve basis on the day of the performance. Among the locales hosting events are the Academia Nacional del Tango (Av. de Mayo 833, Monserrat); the Centro Cultural Plaza Defensa (Defensa 535, Monserrat); the Centro Cultural General San Martín (Av. Corrientes 1551, Congreso); the Teatro Presidente Alvear (Av. Corrientes 1659, Congreso); the Centro Cultural del Sur (Av. Caseros 1750, Barracas); the Centro Cultural Recoleta (Junín 1930, Recoleta); and the Anfiteatro Juan Bautista Alberdi (Juan Bautista Alberdi and Lisandro de la Torre, Mataderos).

In early 2008, however, the incoming mayoral administration of Mauricio Macris suspended the festival and then shifted it to August to precede the annual Mundial de Tango (World Tango Championships). As of press time, it was still uncertain whether the 2009 event would return to the usual schedule.

---

in the festivities at any pub in the city, such as Downtown Matías.

## April
### ( FERIA DEL LIBRO
Predio Ferial de la Sociedad Rural Argentina, Av. Sarmiento 2704, tel. 011/4777-5500
**COST:** US$1
Map 7

Buenos Aires's annual book fair, the Feria del Libro, has been a fixture on the *porteño* literary scene for nearly three decades. Dates vary, but it lasts three weeks and sometimes extends into May. Most but not all exhibitors are from Latin America; European and Asian countries also participate, and there are regular author appearances. It takes place in Palermo's Predio Ferial de la Sociedad Rural Argentina, but is sponsored by the Fundación El Libro (Hipólito Yrigoyen 1628, 5th fl., Monserrat, tel. 011/4370-0600, www.el-libro.org.ar).

## FESTIVAL INTERNACIONAL DE CINE INDEPENDIENTE
Various venues, www.bafici.gov.ar

Toward month's end, the Festival Internacional de Cine Independiente (International Independent Film Festival) features independent movies from every continent. It takes place at various cinemas around town but its center is the Mercado del Abasto. In 2007, it featured 97 Argentine films and another 371 from 47 different countries.

## May and June
May 1 is **Día del Trabajador** (International Labor Day), an official holiday. June 10 is **Día de las Malvinas** (Malvinas Day), an official holiday celebrating Argentina's claim to the British-governed Falkland (Malvinas) Islands. June 20, also an official holiday, is **Día de la Bandera** (Flag Day).

On May 25, Argentines observe the

© WAYNE BERNHARDSON

April's Feria del Libro is South America's biggest book fair.

**Revolución de Mayo** (May Revolution of 1810), when *porteños* made their first move toward independence by declaring the viceroy illegitimate. This is not, however, the major independence celebration, which takes place July 9.

### DÍA DE LA MUERTE DE CARLOS GARDEL
Chacarita, Cementerio de la Chacarita
**Map 8**

Though not an official holiday, June 24 commemorates the anniversary of the singer's death in a 1935 aviation accident in Medellín, Colombia. Pilgrims crowd the streets of the Cementerio de la Chacarita to pay tribute, and there are also tango events.

### FERIA DE GALERÍAS ARTE BA
Predio Ferial de la Sociedad Rural Argentina, Av. Sarmiento 2704, tel. 011/4777-5500, www.arteba.org
**Map 7**

For more than a decade now, mid-May's Feria de Galerías Arte BA has shown work from dozens of Buenos Aires art galleries.

Artists display works that use many different types of media, including painting and sculpture.

## July and August

July 9, **Día de la Independencia,** celebrates Argentina's formal declaration of independence in 1816 at the northwestern city of Tucumá. Later in the month, when school lets out, many Argentines take **Vacaciones de Invierno** (winter holidays), and flights and even buses out of the capital fill up fast.

August 17 is **Día de San Martín,** officially observing the death (not the birth) of Argentina's independence hero.

### EXPOSICIÓN INTERNACIONAL DE GANADERÍA, AGRICULTURA, Y INDUSTRIA INTERNACIONAL
Predio Ferial de la Sociedad Rural Argentina, Av. Sarmiento 2704, tel. 011/4777-5500
**Map 7**

During the winter holidays, the Sociedad Rural Argentina sponsors the Exposición

ARTS AND LEISURE

Internacional de Ganadería, Agricultura, y Industria Internacional, the annual agricultural exhibition at Palermo's Predio Ferial. For more than a century, this has been one of the capital's biggest events; for details, contact the Sociedad Rural Argentina (Florida 460, tel. 011/4324-4700, www.ruralarg.org.ar).

### CAMPEONATO MUNDIAL DE BAILE DE TANGO
Various venues, www.mundialdetango.gov.ar

For ten days from mid-August, the Campeonato Mundial de Baile de Tango, an international tango competition, takes place in various venues throughout the city. This is an invited event, with entries from cities around the world. Check out their website for venue information or if you're in Buenos Aires during mid-August look out for publicity about the event.

### September and October

October 12 is **Día de la Raza** (equivalent to U.S. Columbus Day, marking Columbus's arrival in the New World), an official holiday.

### SEMANA DEL LIBRO
Av. Corrientes at Av. Callao
Map 2

In early September, municipal authorities block off traffic from several blocks of Avenida Corrientes in San Nicolás and Balvanera, on either side of Avenida Callao, for the Semana del Libro (Book Week), where booksellers from around the city and the country maintain open-air stalls.

### November and December

**Día de los Muertos** (All Souls' Day) on November 2nd is the occasion for Argentines to visit their loved ones' graves, though this is not the colorful event it is in Mexico and Central America.

December 25 is **Navidad** (Christmas Day), an official holiday.

### CAMPEONATO ARGENTINO ABIERTO DE PATO
Campo de Mayo, Buenos Aires Province

In early November, the gaucho sport of *pato* holds its Argentine Open Pato Championship at the suburban Campo de Mayo in Gran Buenos Aires, outside of the city. For more information, contact the Federación Argentino de Pato (Av. Belgrano 530, 5th fl., Monserrat, tel. 011/4331-0222).

### ◖ CAMPEONATO ABIERTO ARGENTINO DE POLO
Campo Argentino de Polo, Av. del Libertador and Dorrego, tel. 011/4774-4517
Map 7

From mid-November to mid-December, one of the world's top polo events, the Campeonato Abierto Argentino de Polo (Argentine Open Polo Championship), takes place at Palermo's Campo Argentino de Polo. Some of the country's finest riders appear here. For details, contact the Asociación Argentina de Polo (Arévalo 3065, Palermo, tel. 011/4777-6444, www.aapolo.com).

### MILONGA DE CALLE CORRIENTES
Av. Corrientes (near Centro Cultural San Martín)
Map 2

Though the Festival Buenos Aires Tango has moved to March, the city still blocks off the street near the Centro Cultural San Martín for the Milonga de Calle Corrientes, in which partiers dance to live and recorded music on Gardel's December 11 birthday, when his grave at Chacarita also draws pilgrims.

# Sports and Recreation

Not just a city for sightseeing, Buenos Aires also offers options for activities, ranging from the quiet intensity of a chess match to the energy of a pickup soccer game.

In the densely built Microcentro and other close-in barrios, there's not much open space, but hotel health clubs and private gyms are good alternatives for those who can't get out to Puerto Madero's ecological reserve, Palermo's parks, and other open spaces for a bit of exercise. Parts of these areas are closed to automobiles all week or at least on weekends.

The main spectator sport is *fútbol* (soccer), an Argentine passion. Rugby, though, is also popular; the national team, Los Pumas, has a global reputation. *Basquetbol* or *básquet* (basket) is rapidly gaining popularity and boxing may be making a comeback.

Befitting a country that grew up on horseback, racing and polo also draw crowds, while the indigenous *pato* is a specialist interest.

## PARKS AND PROTECTED AREAS

The only unit of Argentina's national park system easily accessible from Buenos Aires is the **Reserva Natural Estricta Otamendi,** a 2,600-hectare riverside reserve on the right bank of the Río Paraná between Tigre and Zárate. Just east of Puerto Madero, though, the spontaneous colonization of a former landfill by native and introduced flora and fauna created the city's **Reserva Ecológifca Costanera Sur;** ironically enough, this former rubbish tip has become a favorite destination for jogging, cycling, and weekend outings by *porteños.* (For details, see the separate entry in the *Sights* chapter.)

Many other open spaces, such as Palermo's **Parque Tres de Febrero,** appear in detail in the *Sights* chapter.

### PARQUE CENTENARIO

Caballito, Av. Angel Gallardo and Av. Warnes
**Map 8**

Caballito's largest open space, Parque Centenario, is a heavily used park in a mostly residential neighborhood. Well-maintained, with a small artificial lake, the park attracts joggers, cyclists, sunbathers, and dogs. It includes the city's most important natural history museum (see the *Sights* chapter for details) and a separate **Observatorio Astronómico** (Av. Patricias Argentinas 550, tel. 011/4863-3366).

## *PILETAS*

For those who can't get to the beaches or afford five-star hotels, Buenos Aires has several *polideportivos* (sports clubs) with inexpensive *piletas* (public pools), but they get crowded. The most central is **Polideportivo Martín Fierro** (Oruro 1310, San Cristóbal, tel. 011/4941-2054, Subte: Urquiza, Línea E). Try also **Polideportivo Parque Chacabuco** (Av. Eva Perón 1410, Parque Chacabuco, tel. 011/4921-5776, Subte: Emilio Mitre, Línea E).

Many private pools are open to members only, with a membership fee and monthly dues, but others are open to the public at what, before devaluation, were high prices – as much as US$20 for day use. The weak peso, though, has made it worth looking at options like the indoor pool at Congreso's **Ateneo Cecchina** (Mitre 1625, tel. 011/4374-4958); Palermo's **Club de Amigos** (Av. Figueroa Alcorta 3885, tel. 011/4801-1213, www.clubdeamigos.org.ar); the outdoor pool at Palermo's **Punta Carrasco** (Av. Costanera Norte and Av. Sarmiento, tel. 011/4807-1010, www.puntacarrasco.com.ar); and the outdoor pool at Belgrano's **Balneario Parque Norte** (Av. Cantilo and Güiraldes, tel. 011/4787-1432, www.parquenorte.com).

ARTS AND LEISURE

The observatory's telescopes are open to the public 9–10 P.M. Friday and Saturday nights in clear weather. Admission costs US$1 for adults, slightly less for children.

## PARQUE RIVADAVIA

Caballito, Av. Rivadavia btwn. Doblas and Beauchef
Map 8

Today's Parque Rivadavia formed part of the Ambrosio Lezica estate but became municipal property in 1920; one reminder of its country origins is the remains of a *noria*, or well, from which a water wheel irrigated the grounds (according to legend, one of Lezica's washerwomen was murdered here, and her ghost can still be seen carrying her own head).

Parque Rivadavia has a handful of monuments, such as José César Avanti's Monumento a Bolívar, which won the competition for the 1934 centenary of Venezuelan independence; finished in 1942, it is unfortunately covered with graffiti. Sculptor Luis Perlotti, whose museum is a few blocks northwest of here, carved the *Escultura a la Madre*. There is a small shrine to the Virgin of Luján, the symbol of Argentine Catholicism.

Parque Rivadavia also has a large Sunday book fair, which began spontaneously but has since been formalized. In the 2002 economic crisis, unfortunately, it also became the site of the so-called Feria de los Desocupados (Jobless Fair), in which unemployed middle-class families from the barrio sold their personal belongings to pay their rents and mortgages.

## BIRD-WATCHING

### ASOCIACIÓN ORNITOLÓGICA DEL PLATA

San Cristóbal, Matheu 1246, tel. 011/4943-7216, www.avesargentinas.org.ar
Map 4

Argentina has about 3,000 dedicated birdwatchers, mostly affiliated with the Asociación Ornitológica del Plata in the barrio of San Cristóbal. The association also offers birdwatching classes and organized excursions in the vicinity of the capital.

### RESERVA ECOLÓGICA COSTANERA SUR

Av. Tristán Achával s/n
Map 2

Within city limits, the best bird-watching site is the Reserva Ecológica Costanera Sur, a former landfill where the spontaneous colonization of grasses, shrubs, and trees has mimicked the Paraná delta wetlands to create habitat for abundant bird life, not to mention aquatic mammals and reptiles. That said, it can't match the delta's more remote channels or the *estancias* of Buenos Aires province.

Palermo has the next-largest open green spaces, but most of its parks are poor for bird-watching because uncontrolled numbers of feral cats have decimated avian populations; the exception is the small but beautifully maintained Jardín Japonés, where chicken wire between the hedges helps keep the felines out.

## RUNNING

Many *porteños* have taken up running, but the congested downtown area often deters short-term visitors because the only open spaces are relatively small plazas, and the traffic (and consequent vehicle emissions) make street-running unpleasant and even dangerous.

Easily the biggest open space, with the least traffic (pedestrians and bicycles only), is the Reserva Ecológica Costanera Sur, the former rubbish tip recast as parkland near Puerto Madero. The next best are the parks of Palermo and Belgrano, which also have ample open space and little traffic.

## CYCLING

Buenos Aires's densely built city center, ferocious traffic, and lack of challenging terrain all make cycling at least superficially unappealing. Nevertheless, a surprising number of *porteños*—even including some policemen—get around on bicycles.

Though there's no really rugged terrain anywhere, mountain bikers commonly use the Reserva Ecológica Costanera Sur (where there's a 10-km-per-hour speed limit because bicycles share the trails with hikers). In addition, there's a small but growing network of paved bicycle trails and the car-free open spaces of Palermo's parks. The roads of suburban Buenos Aires province encourage some riders, though the vehicle traffic can be dangerously fast.

### NUEVO CIRCUITO KDT
Jerónimo Salguero 3450, tel. 011/4807-7700
**HOURS:** Tues.-Fri. 10 A.M.-7 P.M., Sat.-Sun. 10 A.M.-8 P.M.
**COST:** US$0.65
Map 7

Basic rental bikes are available along Avenida de Infanta Isabel in Palermo's Parque Tres de Febrero, on both sides of the Museo Sívori. Speed riders, meanwhile, can test themselves on the track at the park's Nuevo Circuito KDT, which has another entrance on Avenida Sarmiento.

## TENNIS
Argentine professional tennis has long enjoyed an international reputation, thanks to star players like Guillermo Vilas and Gabriela Sabatini. In 2002, David Nalbandian of Unquillo, in Córdoba province, became the first Argentine to reach the men's finals at Wimbledon before losing to Lleyton Hewitt of Australia.

As of late 2007, four Argentine men, including Guillermo Canas, Juan Ignacio Chela, Juan Monaco, and David Nalbandian, ranked with the world's top 22 players; in all a dozen Argentines occupied the top 100. Only two Argentines, though, ranked among the top 100 women.

### BUENOS AIRES LAWN TENNIS CLUB
Olleros 1510, tel. 011/4772-0983
Map 8

While it has a high professional profile, tennis is also a popular participant sport. Though most courts are private and some require substantial membership fees, when things are slow during the week they may open to nonmembers. Buenos Aires Lawn Tennis Club is a good place to swing a racket and it also hosts high-profile professional events. If there is an event going on there, try **Salguero Tennis/ Paddle/Squash** (Av. Salguero 3350, Palermo, tel. 011/4805-5144) instead.

## GOLF
*Porteño* golfers have one public 18-hole course, along with short courses, driving ranges, and putting greens, to test their skills. For information on facilities beyond the capital, contact the **Asociación Argentina de Golf** (Av. Corrientes 538, 11th fl., tel. 011/4325-1113, www.aag.com.ar).

### COSTA SALGUERO GOLF CENTER
Av. Costanera Rafael Obligado and Salguero, tel. 011/4805-4732, www.costasalguerogolf.com.ar
**HOURS:** Mon. noon-9:30 P.M., Tues.-Fri. 8:30 A.M.-9:30 P.M., Sat.-Sun. 8 A.M.-8:30 P.M.
Map 7

Along the riverfront near the city airport, Costa Salguero is a nine-hole pitch 'n' putt course (lighted at night), along with a driving range and putting green. Rental gear is available, and fees are low—the nine-hole course costs only US$3 per person, with a surcharge at night.

### GOLF CLUB LAGOS DE PALERMO
Av. Tornquist 1426, tel. 011/4772-7261
**HOURS:** Tues.-Sun. 7 A.M.-5 P.M.
Map 8

At Palermo's convenient 18-hole, par-72 public course, greens fees are absurdly cheap at US$7 weekdays, US$10 weekends (when reservations are advisable). Caddies, but not golf carts, are available.

## CHESS
### CLUB ARGENTINO DE AJEDREZ
Paraguay 1858, tel. 011/4811-9412, www.argentinodeajedrez.com.ar
Map 2

Like most megacities, Buenos Aires has a critical mass of serious chess players. For a chess match, tournament, or instruction, contact the Club Argentino de Ajedrez. Nonmembers are welcome to participate, but pay slightly more than members.

## WATER SPORTS
*Porteños* take readily to water, but the beaches along the capital's silt-laden Río de la Plata are nothing to speak of, and pollution makes

them even more questionable. There are better options in suburban Tigre, on the Paraná delta, and across the river in Uruguay. Boating, fishing, and even surfing are possible in some of those areas. Note that huge numbers of *porteños* spend their summers in and around Mar del Plata, on the southern coast of Buenos Aires province, but "Mardel" is five or six hours away except by plane.

### Boating and Fishing

Boating and fishing are best in and around the intricate channels of the Río Paraná, north and east of the suburb of Tigre. City-bound folks, though, choose the Reserva Ecológica Costanera Sur and the area around the Club de Pescadores, near the Aeroparque, for casting their lines. The denizens of La Boca even take their chances in the toxic sludge of the Riachuelo.

### Surfing

There's no surf to speak of anywhere in northern Buenos Aires province, but the beaches east of Punta del Este, Uruguay, get some legitimate South Atlantic waves—though not so good as those in Chile (Chile's Pacific Ocean currents, though, mean much colder water).

## SPECTATOR SPORTS
### Soccer

Argentina is a perpetual soccer power—having won the World Cup in 1978 and 1986—and the birthplace of Diego Armando Maradona, one of the sport's legends. What its English fans like to call "the beautiful game," though, often falls short of its billing; the *Buenos Aires Herald* may have said it best with the headline "Another Boring 0–0 Tie."

The *selección nacional* (national team) suffered an ignominious first-round exit from the 2002 World Cup, won the 2004 Olympic gold medal at Athens, but disappointed again in the 2006 World Cup by advancing no farther than the quarter-finals. By late 2007, it ranked second in the world behind Italy, but professional soccer still has many other problems.

One is the so-called *barras bravas,* the counterpart to British "football hooligans," who

Pickup soccer games, such as this one in Puerto Madero, take place all over the city.

© WAYNE BERNHARDSON

ARTS AND LEISURE

## SOCCER TICKETS

For schedules and tickets, contact the first-division clubs below. *Entradas populares* (standing-room tickets) are the cheapest, but *plateas* (fixed seats) have better security. Again, wear neutral colors to avoid clashes with partisans of either side.

**Argentinos Juniors** (Av. Punta Arenas 1271, Paternal, tel. 011/4551-6887, www.argentinosjuniors.com.ar)

**Boca Juniors** (Brandsen 805, La Boca, tel. 011/4309-4700, www.bocajuniors.com.ar)

**Huracán** (Av. Amancio Alcorta 2570, Parque Patricios, tel. 011/4911-0757, www.clubahuracan.com.ar)

**River Plate** (Av. Presidente Figueroa Alcorta 7597, Núñez, tel. 011/4788-1200)

**San Lorenzo de Almagro** (Av. Fernández de la Cruz 2403, Nueva Pompeya, tel. 011/4914-2470, www.sanlorenzo.com.ar)

**Vélez Sarsfield** (Av. Juan B. Justo 9200, Liniers, tel. 011/4641-5663, www.velez-sarsfield.com.ar)

make the cheap seats and the area outside the stadiums unsafe. Often provided tickets and transportation by the clubs themselves, soccer goons have caused injuries and even deaths; anyone attending a match should dress in neutral colors, such as brown or gray, to avoid showing an affiliation with either team.

Another problem is financial, as clubs often must sell their best players to wealthy European teams to stay solvent. Popularly known as the Millonarios, River Plate is one of the world's best-known teams, but being an Argentine millionaire isn't what it used to be—the club has had trouble meeting its payroll.

Still, Buenos Aires is a soccer-mad city, with six first-division teams in the city proper and another six in its Gran Buenos Aires suburbs. The season runs March–December; for the most current information, check the website

of the Asociación de Fútbol Argentina (www.afa.org.ar), which appears in English as well as Spanish.

For schedules and tickets, contact the first-division clubs below. *Entradas populares* (standing-room tickets) are the cheapest, but *plateas* (fixed seats) have better security. Again, wear neutral colors to avoid clashes with partisans of either side.

### BOCA JUNIORS

Brandsen 805, tel. 011/4309-4700, www.bocajuniors.com.ar

Map 3

Strongly identified with its working-class community, where the team is almost an obsession, Boca Juniors would be the soccer counterpart to baseball's 1950s Brooklyn Dodgers (as the on-site museum would suggest). Their stadium is the so-called "La Bombonera" ("Chocolate Box"), and on game days it's hard to move around the neighborhood except on foot.

### RIVER PLATE

Estadio Monumental, Av. Presidente Figueroa Alcorta 7597, tel. 011/4788-1200, www.cariverplate.com.ar

Map 8

In the more exclusive northern neighborhood of Núñez, River is Boca Juniors' arch-rival and, to continue the baseball analogy, is equivalent to the New York Yankees. Its Estadio Monumental, which seats more than 76,000 spectators, is a landmark but, despite its more auspicious location, River's been no more successful at controlling its hooligans than Boca Juniors has.

## Rugby
### UNIÓN DE RUGBY DE BUENOS AIRES

Pacheco de Melo 2120, tel. 011/4805-5858, www.urba.org.ar

Map 6

Argentine rugby is an amateur sport rather than a professional one, but the touring club Pumas has enjoyed great international success. In late 2007, the national team ranked seventh in the world, behind New Zealand, France, and South Africa. For up-to-date info on local competition, contact the Unión de Rugby de Buenos Aires.

ARTS AND LEISURE

## Boxing

Argentina has had international visibility in boxing since 1923, when Luis Angel Firpo (1894–1960), the "Wild Bull of the Pampas," nearly defeated Jack Dempsey for the world heavyweight championship in New York. More than 2,500 *porteños* paid 50 centavos each to hear the Firpo-Dempsey fight broadcast live from New York at Luna Park Stadium, which became the city's prime boxing venue.

Other notable boxers have come to untimely ends: heavyweight contender Oscar "Ringo" Bonavena (1942–1976) died from a gunshot in a Reno, Nevada, brothel, and former world middleweight titlist Carlos Monzón (1942–1995) died in an automobile accident while on furlough from prison (once shot by his first wife, he was convicted of murdering his second wife in 1988).

**LUNA PARK**
Bouchard 465, tel. 011/4311-5100
Map 2
For most of the past decade-plus, Luna Park has hosted rock concerts rather than fights, but boxing has returned in recent years. The organization that oversees Argentine boxing is the **Federación Argentina de Box** (Castro Barros 75, Almagro, tel. 011/4981-2965, www.fabox.com.ar), which maintains a smaller stadium at that address.

## Equestrian Sports

For a country raised on horseback, equestrian sports have great resonance even in the metropolis, though only the rarely played *pato* truly embraces the gaucho tradition.

In the capital's northern barrios, it's possible to take **horseback-riding lessons** (in the English rather than gaucho style) and even polo instruction. Tourist-oriented *estancias* in Buenos Aires province also provide riding opportunities. City venues include the Club Hípico Mediterráneo (Av. Figueroa Alcorta 4800, Palermo, tel. 011/4772-3828); the Club Alemán de Equitación (Av. Dorrego 4045, Palermo, tel. 011/4778-7060, www.cae-hipico.com.ar); and the Club Hípico Argentino (Av.

Palermo's Campo Argentino de Polo is the site of November's Campeonato Abierto Argentino de Polo, the national polo championships.

## DREAM TEAM

Argentine basketball's international profile has risen dramatically with victories over the so-called U.S. "Dream Team" in the 2002 World Basketball Championships and the 2004 Olympics. Many observers admired the Argentines' selfless team play and at least one National Basketball Association (NBA) coach cited them as an example his own team should follow.

Several Argentines have played in the NBA. One of the league's best players, 6-foot-6 (1.98-meter) guard Emanuel Ginóbili helped the San Antonio Spurs win championships (2002–2003 and 2004–2005) and made his first All-Star appearance in 2005. Rookies in 2004–2005, Chicago Bulls forward Andrés Nocioni, and Detroit Pistons guard Carlos Delfino have also be-come high-profile NBA players. Center Fabricio Oberto joined the Spurs in 2006, forward Walter Herrmann became a Piston in 2006, and center/forward Luis Scola became a starter for the Houston Rockets in 2007.

Buenos Aires has two teams in the first division of the Liga Nacional de Basquetbol: **Boca Juniors** (Arzobispo Espinoza 600, La Boca, tel. 011/4309-4748); and **Obras Sanitarias** (Av. del Libertador 7395, Núñez, tel. 011/4702-4655).

With arenas seating no more than about 3,000 spectators, basketball crowds are far smaller than those for soccer. The regular season runs early November to late March, with playoffs into mid-May.

Figueroa Alcorta 7285, Belgrano, tel. 011/4787-1003, www.clubhipicoargentino.org.ar).

### ASOCIACIÓN ARGENTINA DE POLO
Arévalo 3065, tel. 011/4576-5600, www.aapolo.com
`Map 7`

Argentine society has always been intricately involved with horseback riding; the British influence made them mount polo ponies. The gaucho tradition has left its mark, though, as the Argentine style is more rugged than its British antecedent.

First held at the suburban Hurlingham Club in 1893, the **Campeonato Abierto Argentino de la República** (Argentine Open Polo Championship) moved to Palermo's Campo Argentino de Polo, near the intersection of Avenida del Libertador and Avenida Dorrego, in 1928. It takes place beginning in mid-November, with several others throughout the year. Admission costs about US$3 per person.

### FEDERACIÓN ARGENTINA DE PATO
Salta 188, 3rd fl., tel. 011/4331-0222,
www.fedpato.com.ar
`Map 1`

For gauchos rather than gentlemen, *pato* is the anti-polo, a rural sport in which, originally, a live duck in a leather bag was flung into a goal from horseback. No longer so brutal, it uses a leather bag with handles, but the sport is clearly in decline even in the provinces.

Nevertheless, *pato* has not disappeared. For information on competitions, contact the Federación Argentina de Pato. Most matches take place at the **Campo Argentino de Pato** (Ruta Nacional 8 and Calle Avellaneda, Km 30, Campo de Mayo, tel. 011/4664-9211). The national championships, though, take place at Palermo's Campo Argentino de Polo.

### HIPÓDROMO ARGENTINO
Av. del Libertador 4101, tel. 011/4778-2800,
www.palermo.com.ar
`Map 7`

Seating around 8,000 racing fans in several different sections, Palermo's hippodrome is the country's landmark racetrack. Races may take place any day of the week, but mostly Friday–Monday. General admission is free; the minimum bet is one peso.

# SHOPS

Buenos Aires's main shopping areas are the Microcentro, along the Florida pedestrian mall toward Retiro; Retiro (especially around Plaza San Martín and along Avenida Santa Fe); Recoleta, in the vicinity of the cemetery; and the tree-lined streets of Palermo Viejo, where stylish shops sit between the newest restaurants and bars. The main street markets take place in San Telmo, Recoleta, and Belgrano.

San Telmo is the destination for antiques seekers, but some of the newer Palermo clothiers and other retailers have also set up shop there. Handicrafts, books (the city has some remarkable shops in this category), music, and wine dealers are scattered throughout the city.

After the 2001–2002 financial meltdown, fewer merchants accepted credit cards (though many still took debit cards), but the situation has returned to more or less normal—with one big caveat. While the practice of *recargos* (surcharges) for credit-card purchases had declined in recent years, some merchants have reinstituted the practice. Before handing over the plastic, shoppers should verify whether the business in question intends to collect a *recargo*. They should also be aware that some machines recognize foreign debit cards as credit cards, so that they may not be able to make purchases at shops that accept only debit cards.

Readers should note that the categories in this chapter are not always mutually exclusive. Both antiques and souvenir shops, for instance, might sell *mate* gourds, and clothiers and souvenir sellers might offer leather jackets.

# HIGHLIGHTS

LOOK FOR **(** TO FIND RECOMMENDED SHOPS.

**(** **Best Shopping Center:** For one-stop shopping, nothing beats **Galerías Pacífico.** Anti-consumers in the company of compulsive shoppers can pause to study its landmark murals or else seek refuge in the adjacent Centro Cultural Borges (page 144).

**(** **Best Street Market:** Like the Café Tortoni, Sunday's **Feria de San Pedro Telmo** is at least as popular with *porteños* as with foreign visitors. More than just a market, it's an event with street performers (page 145).

**(** **Best Antiques:** On San Telmo's antiques row, **Churrinche Antigüedades** has plenty for traditionalists whose standard is the "Paris of the South." At the same time, it's not so orthodox that it won't stock industrial artifacts that fit better in Palermo SoHo's hippest bars (page 146).

**(** **Best Bookstore:** Everyone mourned the closure of Barrio Norte's classic Grand Splendid cinema – in a worst-case scenario, it might have become yet another evangelical storefront – but **El Ateneo Grand Splendid** is now among the world's best bookstores. With bookshelves lining the curving balconies and a café on the elevated stage, both preservationists and Buenos Aires book buyers responded with enthusiasm (page 148).

**(** **Best Outlet Store:** For leather jackets, shoes, and other casual clothing with mostly insignificant defects, Palermo SoHo's **Cardón** is the place. Its only downside is the limited availability of sizes and styles (page 151).

**(** **Best Leather:** For more than half a century, **Guido Mocasines** has created fine handcrafted shoes and accessories more affordable than its Barrio Norte and Recoleta locations might imply (page 152).

**(** **Best Vernacular Art:** For ready-made *filete*, the traditional sign-painting art whose revival parallels the tango boom, check out the Feria de San Pedro Telmo. For custom work, consider a craftsman such as **Martiniano Arce** (page 155).

**(** **Best Music Store:** At the strategic corner of Corrientes and Callao, Congreso's **Zivals** is an independent store that specializes in tango but has a far wider selection of Argentine, Latin American, and world music. Its bargain bin may be the best in town (page 158).

**(** **Best Wine Shop:** Palermo's **Terroir** is selective in what it purchases and sells, featuring limited vintages of family reserve wines from some of the top bodegas in Buenos Aires (page 158).

# Shopping Centers

Over the past decade-plus, several older landmarks have been recycled into upscale shopping centers—known in Argentina as *shoppings* (in the plural). Several of them are ideal for one-stop mall-trawling.

## ABASTO DE BUENOS AIRES

Av. Corrientes and Anchorena, tel. 011/4959-3400, www.abasto-shopping.com.ar
**HOURS:** Daily 10 A.M.-10 P.M.
Map 4

Originally a project of U.S.-Hungarian financier George Soros, the recycled Abasto was once the city's main wholesale produce market and the centerpiece of Carlos Gardel's old neighborhood. As a massive shopping center, it's triggered an economic boomlet here, but its disorientingly noisy interior detracts from the magnificence of the building.

Among other features, the Abasto has a large food court that includes a kosher McDonald's in this heavily Jewish neighborhood. It also has a multi-screen cinema that hosts many events during the annual film festival.

## BUENOS AIRES DESIGN

Av. Pueyrredón 2501, tel. 011/5777-6000,
www.designrecoleta.com.ar
**HOURS:** Mon.-Sat. 10 A.M.-9 P.M., Sun. and holidays noon-9 P.M.

Map 6

Under the same management as Patio Bullrich, Buenos Aires Design is a 3,000-square-meter complex of shops and restaurants on two levels alongside the cultural center and the cemetery at Recoleta. As its name suggests, all the shops focus on design and interior decoration, including Oriental carpets, kitchen goods, and bedroom ware. Despite the street address, it's most easily accessible from its southeast corner, near Plaza Francia.

## ◖ GALERÍAS PACÍFICO

Florida and Av. Córdoba, tel. 011/5555-5110,
www.galeriaspacifico.com.ar
**HOURS:** Mon.-Sat. 10 A.M.-9 P.M., Sun. noon-9 P.M.

Map 2

Even compulsive anti-consumerists will appreciate this architectural landmark, which has preserved magnificent murals in its central cupola (for more details, see the separate entry in the *Sights* chapter). For a diagram of its three levels of more than 50 shops, many of which have separate but less conveniently concentrated locales elsewhere in town, check the street-level information booth at the Florida entrance. Shoppers making purchases of more than about US$300 receive a free lunch voucher for the basement-level Patio de Comidas.

## PATIO BULLRICH

Av. del Libertador 750, tel. 011/4814-7400,
www.shoppingbullrich.com.ar
**HOURS:** Daily 10 A.M.-9 P.M.

Map 5

Once a livestock auction house, Patio Bullrich has become a palatial 28,000-square-meter commercial space with nearly 90 shops, plus restaurants and cinemas, on four levels. While it's not the attraction that Galerías Pacífico is, it's packed with shoppers from nearby Recoleta and also has a food court.

Recoleta's Buenos Aires Design is one of the city's elite shopping malls.

## TAXES AND REFUNDS

Argentina imposes a 21 percent *Impuesto de Valor Agregado* (IVA or Value Added Tax) on all goods and services. Tourists, however, may request IVA refunds for purchases of Argentine products valued at more than 70 pesos from shops that display a "Global Refund" decal on their windows. Always double-check, though, that the decal is not out-of-date.

When making any such purchase, request an invoice and other appropriate forms. Then, upon leaving the country, present the forms to Argentine customs; customs will authorize payment to be cashed at Banco de la Nación branches at the main international airport at Ezeiza, at Aeroparque Jorge Newbery (for flights to some neighboring countries), or at Dársena Norte (for ferry trips to Uruguay). Refunds can also be assigned to your credit card.

At smaller border crossings, do not expect officials to be prepared to deal with tax refunds. Some crossings do not even have separate customs officials, but rather are staffed by the Gendarmería (Border Guards), a branch of the armed forces. For more information, in English, check the Global Refund website (www.globalrefund.com).

# Street Fairs

For sightseers and spontaneous shoppers alike, Buenos Aires's diverse *ferias* (street fairs) are one of the city's greatest pleasures.

### FERIA ARTESANAL PLAZA GENERAL MANUEL BELGRANO

Belgrano, Juramento and Cuba, www.belgrarte.com.ar
**HOURS:** Sat.-Sun. and holidays 10 A.M.-7 P.M.
`Map 8`

Crafts stalls cover most of Belgrano's main square at the easy-going Feria Artesanal Plaza General Manuel Belgrano, which gets better as the day goes on and sometimes stays open well beyond its ostensible closing hour. When it rains, the stalls are well-sheltered with tarps.

### ◖ FERIA DE SAN PEDRO TELMO

Defensa and Humberto Primo,
www.feriadesantelmo.com
**HOURS:** Sun. 10 A.M.-5 P.M.
`Map 3`

Easily the most prominent of all Buenos Aires's street fairs is Feria de San Pedro Telmo, which fills Plaza Dorrego and surrounding streets with booths of antiques, *filete* artwork, and other crafts; authorities close Defensa to vehicle traffic. There are professional tango musicians and dancers, and the dozens of other street performers range from the embarrassingly mundane to the amazingly innovative. The neighborhood is also home to many sidewalk cafés and upscale antique shops. (For more details, see the entry in the *Sights* chapter.)

### FERIA PARQUE LEZAMA

Defensa and Brasil, www.artezama.com.ar
**HOURS:** Sat.-Sun. and holidays 10 A.M.-5 P.M.
`Map 3`

So successful is the Feria de San Pedro Telmo that it has aided the increasingly thriving Feria Parque Lezama, a weekend crafts fair that's gradually spread north from its namesake park up Calle Defensa and under the freeway, beyond which only the broad Avenida San Juan has been able to stop it. Parque Lezama itself now gets street performers, though not so many as Plaza Dorrego.

### FERIA PLAZA INTENDENTE ALVEAR

Junín and Presidente Quintana, www.francarte.com.ar
**HOURS:** Sat.-Sun. and holidays 10 A.M.-7 P.M.
`Map 6`

After San Telmo, the most frequented tourist

*feria* is probably the Feria Plaza Intendente Alvear, a crafts-oriented event that's also strong on street performers. Immediately northeast of the Centro Cultural Recoleta, it's filled the space to Avenida Libertador and begun to stretch south along Junín.

# Antiques

For much of the 20th century, Argentina alternated between periods of prodigious prosperity and palpable penury. During the good times, Argentines both imported and produced items of great value, but during hard times they often had to dispose of them. Over time, of course, once-precious items have made their way through many owners and have ended up in the hands of antiques dealers.

In San Telmo in particular, antiques shops form an almost unbroken line along Calle Defensa, from Avenida San Juan in the south past Plaza Dorrego to Pasaje Giuffra on the north. The variety and quality of their goods are remarkable, but dealers know what they've got—so they're resolute bargainers. Whether you're seeking that French chess set or a YPF gasoline pump globe, expect prices to be quoted in U.S. dollars rather than pesos, and don't expect much give.

### ARTE ANTICA ANTIGÜEDADES
Defensa 1133, tel. 011/4362-0861,
www.arteantica.com.ar
**HOURS:** Daily 10:30 A.M.-7 P.M.
Map 3

At the Europhile end of the San Telmo spectrum, Arte Antica specializes in decorations and furnishings for traditional Recoleta sensibilities, with its inventory of intricate chandeliers, Louis XV furniture, and objets d'art of bronze, marble, porcelain, and terra-cotta. Their origins are Austrian, British, Czech, French, German, Venetian, and others.

### CÁNDIDO SILVA
Defensa 1066, Local 15, tel. 011/4361-5053,
www.candidosilva.com.ar
**HOURS:** Tues.-Sun. 10 A.M.-7 P.M.
Map 3

At the back of the Galería Solar de French,

Silva sells some dazzling colonial *platería* (silverwork), ranging from candelabras and *mates* to statuary and even Mapuche jewelry. In addition, it stocks traditional religious art and imagery, including canvases, crucifixes, triptychs, and wooden statuary, as well as elaborately carved wooden stirrups (seen more frequently in Chile than Argentina). Its adjacent crafts shop offers credible replicas of some of the originals on sale here.

### ◖ CHURRINCHE ANTIGÜEDADES
Defensa 1031, tel. 011/4362-7612,
www.churrinche.com.ar
**HOURS:** Tues.-Sun. 11 A.M.-6 P.M.
Map 3

One of San Telmo's classic antiques dealers, Churrinche carries a wild array of items, ranging from formal chandeliers and lamps to the glass globes that once topped the gas pumps of the then state-run YPF petroleum company. In addition, it carries life-size classical statues for formal gardens and Francophile furniture that would still fit in Recoleta's *fin de siecle* mansions. In at least one sense, it's very literally exclusive—for security reasons, Churrinche allows no more than four shoppers at a time.

### GALERÍA CECIL
Defensa 845, tel. 011/4307-0259
**HOURS:** Tues.-Fri. 10 A.M.-7 P.M., Sat. 10 A.M.-8 P.M.,
Sun. 10 A.M.-8:30 P.M.
Map 3

Beneath a luminous skylight, in what was once an enormous cinema—a statue of Jesus now fronts the original screen—the Galería Cecil holds dozens of small to medium-sized stalls stocking just about every trinket that made its way to Buenos Aires between the late 19th

© WAYNE BERNHARDSON

Most of Buenos Aires's antique shops are in San Telmo along Calle Defensa.

century and the mid-20th. A handful of items are older or younger than the rest, and there are some larger pieces, such as furniture. A café, situated where moviegoers once strode through the doors, makes a good spot for a breather.

### GALERÍA DE LA DEFENSA
Defensa 1179
**HOURS:** Daily 10 A.M.–8 P.M.
**Map 3**

Far less gentrified than the nearby Galería Solar de French, this worn but still distinctive gallery falls closer to the flea-market end of the continuum; a few places look as if the squatters just moved out and left everything *they* didn't want. Those with patience to sort through the dreck, though, may find the occasional gem in

its cluttered locales, many of which are closed early in the week. It's busiest, and best, on the Sunday market day.

### GALERÍA SOLAR DE FRENCH
Defensa 1066
**HOURS:** Daily 10 A.M.–8 P.M.
**Map 3**

Not exclusively an antiques gallery, the gentrified French is a two-story structure whose ground level resembles a picturesque urban alleyway, paved with handsome stones and shaded by an Araucaria tree and a bright red-blossomed bougainvillea. While it does have more than just a handful of antiques dealers, it also has some high-quality arts and crafts dealers, and design shops.

SHOPS

# Books

Once the center of South America's publishing industry, Buenos Aires has lost ground to other countries, but can still boast an impressive array of bookstores, from the antiquarian to the contemporary, along with specialist dealers. They are as much—or more—cultural as commercial institutions, and they take that role seriously.

In addition to bookstores proper, there are several *ferias* (outdoor stalls) scattered throughout the city. The most central of these takes place at the south end of **Plaza Lavalle,** between Talcahuano and Libertad, Mon.–Fri. 10 A.M.–6 P.M. There's also a big selection at **Plazoleta Santa Fe,** on the Avenida Santa Fe median strip (Subte: Palermo, Línea D). Caballito's **Parque Rivadavia** (Subte: Acoyte, Línea A) has a permanent weekend market with nearly a hundred stalls, and there are also stalls at the Línea A terminus at **Primera Junta.**

### ACME
Suipacha 245, tel. 011/4328-1662
**HOURS:** Mon.-Fri. 9 A.M.-7 P.M., Sat. 9 A.M.-1 P.M.
Map 2

In a sense, Acme is the anti-Ateneo, a utilitarian locale that's so decor-free it feels like an orderly but uninspired library in a provincial town. That's partly because Acme is also a wholesaler and importer, but it displays a selection of English-language literature that matches the Ateneo in both size and quality, even if it's no place to browse over a cappuccino.

### ANTIQUE BOOK SHOP
Libertad 1236, tel. 011/4815-0658,
www.servisur.com/antique/index.htm
**HOURS:** Mon.-Fri. 10 A.M.-8 P.M., Sat. 10 A.M.-1 P.M.
Map 5

Antique carries a good collector's selection, in many languages, on Buenos Aires, Patagonia, and travel, as well as on gauchos and Argentine art and literature. It charges premium prices: A first edition of U.S. engineer Bailey Willis's survey of Patagonia, undertaken for the Argentine

public works ministry, costs nearly US$700 in mint condition, with all maps.

### EL ATENEO
Florida 340, tel. 011/4325-6801,
www.tematika.com.ar
**HOURS:** Mon.-Fri. 9 A.M.-8 P.M., Sat. 9 A.M.-1 P.M.
Map 2

In a striking building in the heart of the pedestrian shopping district, Buenos Aires's signature bookstore is El Ateneo's Microcentro branch, now approaching its 2012 centennial. It carries a huge selection on Argentine history, literature, and coffee-table souvenir books, plus a good selection of domestic travel titles (it is also a publishing house), some of them bilingual; the basement travel section is strong on maps.

### ◖ EL ATENEO GRAND SPLENDID
Av. Santa Fe 1880, tel. 011/4813-6052,
www.tematika.com.ar
**HOURS:** Mon.-Thurs. 9 A.M.-10 P.M., Fri.-Sat. 9 A.M.-midnight, Sun. noon-10 P.M.
Map 6

Recently named the world's second-best in an admittedly subjective survey in Britain's *Guardian* newspaper, Buenos Aires's most elegant bookstore is El Ateneo's Barrio Norte branch, in a recycled and renovated cinema that deserves a visit simply to see its remarkable and apparently seamless transformation: The stage is a café, readers now recline in the opera-style boxes, and the curving walls of the upper stories are lined with bookshelves floor to ceiling. In addition to books, it stocks a diversity of quality CDs.

### DISTAL LIBROS
Florida 249, tel. 011/5218-4370,
www.distalnet.com
**HOURS:** Mon.-Fri. 9 A.M.-9 P.M., Sat.-Sun. 10 A.M.-9 P.M.
Map 2

Carrying this book and other travel guides published by Avalon Travel, including *Moon*

*Patagonia,* Distal is a chain with many other branches around town, including a convenient Retiro locale (Florida 914, Retiro, tel. 011/5218-4378) several blocks north.

## LIBRERÍA DE ÁVILA

Adolfo Alsina 500, tel. 011/4331-8989,
www.libreriadeavila.servisur.com
**HOURS:** Mon.-Fri. 8:30 A.M.-8 P.M., Sat. 9 A.M.-5:30 P.M.
**Map 1**

Occupying a notable Art Deco building, Ávila claims descent from the late-colonial Librería del Colegio—making it possibly the capital's most historic bookstore. Its classic inventory consists of titles on history, philosophy, ethnology, folklore, tango, travel literature, and the like. In addition to its well-stocked stacks, it also hosts author readings and even musical events (though it doesn't keep its website schedule up-to-date), and has a café.

## LIBRERÍA L'AMATEUR

Esmeralda 882, tel. 011/4312-7635
**HOURS:** Mon.-Fri. 10 A.M.-6 P.M.
**Map 5**

An antiquarian and rare-book dealer—its stacks look like a library from a Merchant Ivory movie—L'Amateur also holds a prodigious basement stock of maps, illustrations, and engravings from Argentina, South America, and around the world. Appealing to regional specialists and collectors, these are also works of art that are suitable for framing. While prices are high, the staff are knowledgeable, well-organized, and patient.

## LIBRERÍA PAIDÓS

Av. las Heras 3741, Local 31, tel. 011/4801-2860,
www.libreriapaidos.com
**HOURS:** Mon.-Fri. 9:30 A.M.-8 P.M., Sat. 10 A.M.-1:30 P.M.
**Map 7**

More than just a bookstore, for half a century the shrink's specialist Paidós has been a community institution for infinite numbers of inward-looking *porteños* preoccupied with psychology, psychoanalysis, philosophy, social theory, and (to a lesser degree) humanities. In an inconspicuous gallery location just

Monserrat's Librería de Ávila is the city's oldest bookstore.

© WAYNE BERNHARDSON

off Plaza Alférez Sobral, it also publishes a monthly bulletin and keeps a bulletin board full of listings for various therapies and related topics, such as office rentals "suitable for professionals."

Paidós also has a Barrio Norte branch (Av. Santa Fe 1685, tel. 011/4812-6685).

## LIBRERÍA PLATERO

Talcahuano 485, tel. 011/4382-2215,
www.libreriaplatero.com.ar
**HOURS:** Mon.-Fri. 8:30 A.M.-7 P.M., Sat. 8:30 A.M.-1 P.M.
**Map 2**

Near the Tribunales (law courts), Librería Platero specializes in books on history, law, politics, and tango. The shop's modest storefront is a deceptive facade for what may be Buenos Aires's best specialist bookstore, with an enormous stock of new and out-of-print books (the latter ensconced in the basement stacks). Experienced in filling overseas requests, it does a good trade with visiting academics, who can pass hours browsing its stacks and foreign libraries.

## LIBRERÍAS TURÍSTICAS

Paraguay 2457, tel. 011/4963-2866 or 011/4962-5547, www.libreriaturistica.com.ar

**HOURS:** Mon.-Fri. 9 A.M.-7 P.M.

Map 6

The first Buenos Aires bookstore to specialize in travel and tourism, Librerías Turísticas carries an outstanding selection of Argentine maps and guidebooks, including its own titles (some in English) on subjects that include the capital's cafés (three volumes!), neighborhoods, archaeology, and travelogues. In addition, it has a large stock of books for professionals in the travel and tourism sector.

## WALRUS BOOKS

Estados Unidos 617, tel. 011/4300-7135

**HOURS:** Tues.-Sun. 10 A.M.-8 P.M.

Map 3

In a cozy locale that invites browsing, Walrus carries a large selection of English-language books well beyond the usual Stephen King potboilers. Owner Geoffrey Hickman purchases used books or accepts them in exchange for store credit.

# Clothing and Accessories

*Porteños,* both male and female, are notorious fashion plates. The most elite clothiers line the Florida pedestrian mall and the avenues of Retiro, Recoleta, and Barrio Norte, while the edgiest inhabit Palermo Viejo. Many upmarket outlets have branches in the large *shoppings,* such as Galerías Pacífico and Patio Bullrich.

Leather goods, Argentina's traditional specialty, range from tightly woven *tiento* belts to shoes, jackets, coats, trousers, handbags, and many other items. In fact, there are two sorts of leather shops: A *marroquinería* is a place that makes leather wearables and accessories (such as belts, jackets, and shoes) while a *talabartería* produces riding boots, horse gear, and the like. This difference between the two is less obvious than it once was; a good shorthand distinction is that you can buy wearables in a *talabartería,* but not saddles in a *marroquinería.*

## ALBERTO VANNUCCI

Av. Callao 1773, tel. 011/4811-3112, www.avannuccisa.com.ar

**HOURS:** Mon.-Fri. 10 A.M.-1 P.M. and 3-7:30 P.M., Sat. 9:30 A.M.-12:30 P.M.

Map 6

In a prime Recoleta location, Vannucci is a clutter of the usual blankets, saddles, and other leather goods, but its specialty is polo gear for royalty, such as Prince Charles of Wales and the Prince of Dubai. The selection of mallets and saddles is particularly impressive.

## ALMACÉN DE BELLEZA

Nicaragua 4884, tel. 011/4778-0050, www.almacendebelleza.com

**HOURS:** Mon.-Sat. 11 A.M.-8 P.M.

Map 7

According to owner Gabriela Tomasini, the Almacén de Belleza carries "everything that a woman sees from when she gets up in the morning to when she goes to bed at night." The woman in mind, apparently, is also affluent and daring in her taste for clothing and accessories, which include vintage materials transformed into high fashion.

In fact, the Almacén is more than just a clothing store, as it includes household goods ranging from dishes and teacups to martini glasses and well beyond—all in very avant-garde style.

## BARBIE STORE

Scalabrini Ortiz 3170, tel. 0810/4444-2272, www.barbie-stores.com

**HOURS:** Mon.-Sat. 10 A.M.-8:30 P.M., Sun. 1-7 P.M.

Map 7

Argentine women may have reached the heights of politics—the prime example is president Cristina Fernández—but the country's cultural contradictions are apparent in an obsession with impossibly slender fashion models that starts early. There's

Palermo's Barbie Store is the first of its kind in the world.

no better place to observe the phenomenon than this first-of-its-kind, Mattel-approved Botánico locale that not only sells dolls, but also inspires pre-teens (and their mothers) to emulate their style. Where else can five-year-olds strut down the runway, in clothing designed with their favorite toy in mind, for their birthdays?

Franchises are available.

## BOKURA

Gurruchaga 1686, tel. 011/4833-4587,
www.bokura.com.ar
**HOURS:** Mon.-Sat. 11 A.M.-8:30 P.M., Sun. 3-8 P.M.
Map 7

No man older than about 25 will feel very comfortable with Bokura's sleeveless T-shirts, high-top rainbow sneakers, and calf-length denims, but for anyone younger it's the place to shop. The sweaters appeal to a more mature public.

Bokura's bright colors and diverse designs extend to the building itself, whose facade is a mosaic of brightly colored tiles surrounding a giant picture window.

## BOLIVIA

Gurruchaga 1581, tel. 011/4832-6284,
www.boliviaonline.com.ar
**HOURS:** Mon.-Sat. 11 A.M.-8 P.M., Sun. 3-8 P.M.
Map 7

Its name misleadingly implies ethnic affinities, but Bolivia specializes in aggressively hip clothing such as multi-colored sweaters and leather jackets, and rainbow-colored checkered or striped trousers (it's tempting to speculate whether their color and design consultants are golf pros and/or Florida retirees). The staff, though, are patient and enthusiastic, and more conservative dressers will find stylish jeans and shirts in more subdued colors and designs.

## ⬛ CARDÓN

Honduras 4755, tel. 011/4832-5925
**HOURS:** Mon.-Sat. 11:30 A.M.-8 P.M., Sun. noon-7 P.M.
Map 7

For males and females alike, the Cardón chain offers casual clothing, including leather jackets, shoes, and bags, as well as jeans and jean jackets, along with an ample range of accessories. This branch, though, stands out because it's an outlet for seconds and discontinued lines where it's possible to get top-quality items at a fraction of the usual prices. The selection, though, is smaller than at their regular stores.

## CASA LÓPEZ

Marcelo T. de Alvear 640/658, tel. 011/4311-3044,
www.casalopez.com.ar
**HOURS:** Mon.-Fri. 9 A.M.-8 P.M., Sat. 9:30 A.M.-7 P.M.,
Sun. 10 A.M.-6 P.M.
Map 5

López is one of the city's traditional clothiers and, as befits its location and clientele, charges premium prices. It has an additional installation at Galerías Pacífico for women's handbags and accessories in particular.

## DALLA FONTANA

Reconquista 735, tel. 011/4313-4354
**HOURS:** Mon.-Fri. 9 A.M.-8 P.M., Sat. 9 A.M.-5:30 P.M.
Map 2

Dalla Fontana is a longtime leather professional

that specializes in women's wear and accessories, primarily an over-the-top selection of handbags. For men, it does carry some jackets and shoes.

## FLABELLA

Suipacha 263, tel. 011/4322-6036,
www.flabella.com

**HOURS:** Mon.–Fri. 10 A.M.–8:30 P.M., Sat. 10 A.M.–6 P.M.

Map 2

Flabella works in the specialized field of shoes for tango dancers, both male and female. A small business, it produces only about 20 pairs per day in pure leather, patent leather, chamois, red lamé, and even some combinations thereof.

## FRENKEL'S LEATHER WORLD

Florida 1055/1075, tel. 011/4311-2300,
www.frenkelsleather.com.ar

**HOURS:** Mon.–Fri. 9 A.M.–7 P.M., Sat. 9 A.M.–5:30 P.M.

Map 5

Leather experts since 1943, occupying two nearly side-by-side locales in the historic Edificio Kavanagh, Frenkel's specializes in suede and leather jackets, but there are also shoes, handbags, belts, and similar items at prices that target foreign visitors and especially the Japanese (several Japanese-Argentines work the floor). Some items are made of spotted *carpincho* (capybara) hides.

Frenkel's also sells gaucho daggers, horse gear, and *mate* paraphernalia, as well as jewelry of rodocrosite (a sort of pinkish lapis lazuli). The ostensibly indigenous crafts, trite to the point of kitsch, barely deserve a glance.

## 🄲 GUIDO MOCASINES

Rodríguez Peña 1290, tel. 011/4813-4095,
www.guidomocasines.com.ar

**HOURS:** Mon.–Fri. 9:30 A.M.–8 P.M., Sat. 9:30 A.M.–1 P.M.

Map 6

Handcrafting shoes since 1952, Italian immigrant Luciano Bagnasco created one of the capital's most enduring leather stores in Guido, a Barrio Norte business that has since expanded to accessories like bags, belts, and billfolds. Some of its shoes, as inexpensive as

US$40, are very economical for what is top-quality footwear.

Guido's has a Microcentro branch at Florida 704 and a Recoleta branch at Avenida Quintana 333.

## HERMANOS ESTEBECORENA

El Salvador 5960, tel. 011/4772-2145,
www.hermanosestebecorena.com

**HOURS:** Mon.–Sat. 11 A.M.–1 P.M. and 1:30–9 P.M.

Map 7

Behind a modest Palermo Hollywood storefront, the Estebecorena brothers produce a diversity of casual menswear, for both summer and winter. Items range from socks and underwear to shirts, trousers, jackets, blazers, raingear, and even plaid Scottish-style vests. There's a second store in the Paseo Alcorta shopping center (Jerónimo Salguero 3172, 2nd fl., tel. 011/4836-0566).

## JORGE CÁNAVES

Belgrano, Av. del Libertador 6000,
tel. 011/4785-3982, www.jorgecanaves.com.ar

**HOURS:** Mon.–Sat. 9:30 A.M.–1 P.M. and Mon.–Fri. 4–8 P.M.

Map 8

Founded by a two-time Olympic rider and well-equipped with polo gear, Cánaves is particularly strong in saddles but also carries boots, blankets, mallets, and other accessories. There's a separate Retiro branch (Esmeralda 1062, tel. 011/4312-6093).

## LÓPEZ TAIBO

Av. Alvear 1902, tel. 011/4804-8585,
www.lopeztaibo.com

**HOURS:** Mon.–Fri. 10 A.M.–8 P.M., Sat. 10 A.M.–7 P.M.

Map 6

In business since 1897, leather specialist López Taibo focuses on men's shoes but also produces briefcases and handbags and a diversity of accessories. The really interesting items are goat-suede and sheepskin jackets, but their price tags will dismay the budget-conscious. In addition to its Recoleta flagship, it also has a Galerías Pacífico branch that's open Sundays.

## LA MARTINA

Paraguay 661, tel. 011/4576-7999,
www.lamartina.com
**HOURS:** Mon.-Fri. 10 A.M.-8 P.M., Sat. 10 A.M.-2 P.M.
Map 5

On its face, La Martina is a polo snobs' supply boutique, and there are plenty of bags, blankets, boots, mallets, saddles, spurs, and stirrups for those who don't need to work for a living. It also offers, however, a selection of its own brand-name clothing, such as 100-percent-cotton trousers, which are comfortably suitable for non-riders; prices are high by local standards, but still reasonable for overseas visitors.

La Martina also has a larger Belgrano branch, La Casona de la Martina (Arribeños 2632, tel. 011/4576-0010).

## PERUGIA

Av. Alvear 1862, tel. 011/4804-6340
**HOURS:** Mon.-Fri. 10 A.M.-8 P.M., Sat. 10 A.M.-2 P.M.
Map 6

Perpetually threatening liquidation of its stock (not an unusual business tactic in Buenos Aires), Perugia is a women's shoe specialist. Strategically located across from the Alvear Palace Hotel, its oozes patrician Recoleta style (with prices to match); footwear fetishists like Imelda Marcos would feel right at home here.

## RAPSODIA

El Salvador 4757, tel. 011/4832-5363,
www.rapsodia.com.ar
**HOURS:** Mon.-Sat. 10 A.M.-10 P.M., Sun. 10 A.M.-9 P.M.
Map 7

This women's "vintage" clothing specialist pushes gaudy, shimmering retro designs that, in their eyes, blend traditions from the Indian subcontinent with a 1970s rock 'n' roll aesthetic. In reality, it's closer to the 1960s fads that proliferated when the Beatles took up transcendental meditation with the Maharishi—though the designers do use post-Beatles imagery. In Rapsodia's case, though, the fad's enjoyed at least a little more staying power.

## ROSSI Y CARUSO

Av. Santa Fe 1377, tel. 011/4811-1965,
www.rossicaruso.com
**HOURS:** Mon.-Sat. 10 A.M.-8 P.M.
Map 6

Though it occupies newer quarters, Rossi y Caruso's leather business dates from the 1940s and, over that time, has catered to such celebrity clientele as Spain's King Juan Carlos, Britain's Prince Phillip, and Frank Sinatra—not to mention Argentina's own royalty, Princess Máxima Zorreguieta of the Netherlands. Its specialties include men's and women's clothing, billfolds, handbags, portfolios, purses, saddles, and silverwork.

Rossi y Caruso also has a Galerías Pacífico branch.

## TANGO MODA

Av. de Mayo 1370, tel. 011/4381-4049,
www.tangomoda.com
**HOURS:** Mon.-Fri. 1-8 P.M., Sat. 11 A.M.-2 P.M.
Map 1

Nobody wanders into Tango Moda by accident, as its fashion showroom occupies a luminous apartment on the 16th floor of the landmark Palacio Barolo. It's unusual in that it carries a wide selection of tango-oriented clothing, including shoes, for women *and* men; its extroverted owner Jorge Arias and his staff treat everyone like a dance partner who's returned to a treasured *milonga* after many years' absence. On top of that, it also offers some of the best views of the Plaza de Mayo and other parts of the city.

## UMA

Humboldt 1868, tel. 011/4771-1742,
www.umacuero.com
**HOURS:** Mon.-Sat. 11 A.M.-8 P.M.
Map 7

Tanned cowhide looks different when it's stitched to lycra in jackets, tops, and trousers at this fashionista favorite. This is Uma's outlet store, as its main stores are at Galerías Pacífico, Patio Bullrich, Paseo Alcorta, and Alto Palermo shopping centers.

### WELCOME MARROQUINERÍA

Marcelo T. de Alvear 500, tel. 011/4313-7847,
www.welcome-leather.com.ar

**HOURS:** Mon.-Fri. 10 A.M.-2 P.M. and 3-7 P.M., Sat.
10 A.M.-1:30 P.M.

Map 5

One of Buenos Aires's best-established leather-goods outlets, dating from 1930, Welcome specializes in briefcases, women's handbags, and travel bags and accessories. Within these broad categories, it has dozens of distinctive products ranging from simple purses to multi-pocketed attaches. Welcome takes two weeks' vacation in late January.

# Crafts and Souvenirs

Argentina's artisanal heritage is less immediately evident than, say, the indigenous textile traditions of the Peruvian or Guatemalan highlands, but both the city and the countryside have characteristic crafts.

The most solidly urban expression of folk art is *filete,* the elaborate rainbow signage that, in the hands of its most skilled practitioners, approaches the finest calligraphy. Embellishing the signs of so many businesses, it even used to cover city buses. While some of this is ready-made and can be trite, many *fileteadores* will produce custom pieces at a price.

For off-the-shelf *filete,* check Sunday's **Feria de San Pedro Telmo** on Plaza Dorrego; better yet, consider hiring a *fileteador* for custom work, which starts upwards of US$100 for a piece measuring about 20 by 30 centimeters (8 by 12 inches). If doing so, though, you'll have to give the artist at least a few days or more, depending on the size of the work.

Gaucho gear, such as the sharp silver *facón* (knife), wide coin-studded *rastra* (belt), silver *espuelas* (spurs), and *bombachas* (baggy trousers), makes worthwhile souvenirs. Before purchasing *bombachas,* though, be sure of what you're buying—in another context, the word can mean women's underwear.

In the 19th century, when wealthy households kept servants for the sole purpose of preparing *mate,* the paraphernalia, such as the *mate* (gourd) itself and the *bombilla* (straw), were works of art; many of them are now museum pieces. Small and lightweight but distinctive, they are popular with visitors. The *mate* is often a simple calabash but can be an elaborate carving of exotic wood; while the modern *bombilla* is often aluminum, it is traditionally silver with intricate markings and design. The *pie* (base or holder) for a formal *mate* may be made of leather.

To accompany the *mate* paraphernalia, check any supermarket for *yerba mate,* the dried leaf of *Ilex paraguayensis,* an infusion that Argentines sip in prodigious amounts. Some North American markets now stock *yerba,* especially in areas with large immigrant populations, though its consumption is most common among Argentines, Uruguayans, Paraguayans, and, to a lesser degree, Brazilians and Chileans.

There are also outlets for regional Argentine crafts, such as textiles from indigenous communities in the northwestern Andean provinces or in Patagonia. In some cases, *casas de provincia* (provincial government offices, all of which supply tourist information) display and sell products typical of the area.

For stamp collectors, Correo Argentino operates a **Servicio Filatélico** (Sarmiento 189, Oficina 51, tel. 011/5550-5176) in the main post office. The **Federación Argentina de Entidades Filatélicas** (Argentine Federation of Philatelic Entities, Perón 1479, 4th fl., Congreso, tel. 011/4373-0122, www.faef.8m. net) is open Tuesday 6–9 P.M.

Buenos Aires has many jewelers. The most typical materials, though, are not diamonds or gold but rather silver, transformed by skilled artisans into unique pieces often held together with *tiento* (finely braided leather). There is a concentration of prestigious silversmiths in the Buenos Aires province town of San Antonio de Areco, about 80 kilometers west of the capital. (For details, see the *Excursions from Buenos Aires* chapter.)

### ARTE ÉTNICO ARGENTINO
El Salvador 4656, tel. 011/4832-0516,
www.arteetnicoargentino.com
**HOURS:** Mon.-Fri. 11 A.M.-7 P.M., Sat. 10 A.M.-3 P.M.
**Map 7**

In new quarters remodeled to resemble an adobe from Argentina's Andean northwest, Arte Étnico acknowledges the country's indigenous heritage. Its specialty is textiles—specifically woolen rugs, with abstract designs, from the Mapuche of northern Patagonia, and clothing from the northwestern Andes. It also features rustically styled furniture, primarily chairs and the odd table. A few driftwood-style curios, carved into animal motifs, round out the offerings.

### ARTE INDÍGENA Y CRIOLLO
Balcarce 234, tel. 011/4343-1455,
www.arteyesperanza.com.ar
**HOURS:** Mon.-Fri. 9 A.M.-6 P.M.
**Map 1**

Nonprofit Arte Indígena contains a small but representative assortment of indigenous crafts from around the country. Items on display include Quechua tapestries from the northern highlands, carved Chané masks from Salta, Toba and Guaraní basketry from the humid northeastern lowlands, and Mapuche silverwork and weavings from the southerly Patagonian provinces.

### ARTESANÍAS ARGENTINAS
Montevideo 1386, tel. 011/4812-2650,
www.artesaniasargentinas.org
**HOURS:** Mon.-Fri. 10 A.M.-8 P.M., Sat. 10 A.M.-1:30 P.M.
**Map 6**

Artesanías Argentinas is a well-established nonprofit outlet for indigenous artisans, mostly from the northeastern Mesopotamian provinces and the northwestern Andean provinces. While the selection is small, the quality of its ceramics,

knives, tapestries, and hardwood boxes and carvings (with wildlife motifs) is high. Its website, in both Spanish and very good English, does a fine job of displaying the merchandise.

### ARTESANÍAS SALTEÑAS
Rodríguez Peña 1775, tel. 011/4814-7562
**HOURS:** Daily 10 A.M.-9 P.M.
**Map 6**

This small Recoleta shop deals exclusively with crafts from the northwestern province of Salta, where the indigenous Andean and colonial Spanish influences are among the country's strongest. Distinctive items include artwork with colonial-style religious motifs, blankets and other textiles, decorative boxes of *cardón* cactus, furniture crafted from native woods, and traditional silverwork.

### EL BOYERO
Florida 953, tel. 011/4312-3564,
www.elboyero.com
**HOURS:** Mon.-Sat. 9 A.M.-8:30 P.M.
**Map 5**

One of the city's most diverse souvenir shops, El Boyero showcases clothing and crafts from around the country. Items on the docket range from standard dress items, such as belts, boots, hats, and shoes—all with an artisanal touch—to silverwork, including gaucho knives and Mapuche jewelry, as well as *mates, bombillas,* and ceramics. In addition to the main shop, it has a Galerías Pacífico branch, which is open half an hour later daily and also open Sunday noon–9 P.M.

### ◖ MARTINIANO ARCE
Perú 1089, 1st Fl., tel. 011/4362-2739,
www.martinianoarce.com
**HOURS:** By appointment only
**Map 3**

One of San Telmo's most flamboyant *fileteadores*—his bright yellow house draws attention to itself—Arce is happy to undertake custom work. He has no fixed hours, though, and is not available for drop-ins, so be sure to phone ahead for an appointment.

### PAPELERA PALERMO
Honduras 4945, tel. 011/4833-3081,
www.papelerapalermo.com.ar
**HOURS:** Mon.-Sat. 10 A.M.-8 P.M., Sun. 2-8 P.M.
**Map 7**

Papelera is an art and art-supply store that stocks an eclectic mix of paper products, including albums, notebooks, pens, ink, origami, books on design, and even artwork itself, in comfortable surroundings.

For those who are going to be in town for longer than just a shopping trip, Papelera Palermo's Casa de Oficios (Cabrera 5227, tel. 011/4831-1080) offers art courses and workshops.

### RIGOLETTO CURIOSO
Av. Corrientes 1660, Local 10, tel. 011/6320-5310,
www.rigolettocurioso.com.ar
**HOURS:** Mon.-Fri. 10 A.M.-10:30 P.M., Sat. noon-2 A.M.,
Sun. 6-10:30 P.M.
**Map 2**

Rigoletto is a hard-to-categorize collectors' shop with books and magazines but most notably posters and still photos from vintage films, especially but not exclusively Argentine. The real classics, with cast members like Hugo del Carril, Mirtha Legrande, Niní Marshall, and Tita Merello, cost upwards of US$150, though few are truly immaculate (most are in pretty good condition, though).

# Household Goods and Furniture

Argentina's 1990s economic boom, while it may have had a shaky foundation, brought sophistication and style to design and furniture in particular. While many of these items, such as beds and tables, are large, the 2002 devaluation made them cheap enough to justify shipping them overseas. With a stronger peso, that's increasingly a judgment call, but their quality is undeniable.

Shopping centers like Recoleta's Buenos Aires Design may have set the tone, but smaller individual designers and shops in Palermo have been the most adventurous. Their cutting-edge influence is evident even in the standard furniture shops that line Balvanera's Avenida Belgrano, west of Avenida Entre Ríos, which do not produce such unique pieces.

### CALMA CHICHA
Honduras 4925, tel. 011/4831-1818,
www.calmachicha.com
**HOURS:** Mon.-Sat. 10 A.M.-8 P.M., Sun. 2-8 P.M.
**Map 7**

Defying easy categorization, Calma Chicha stocks a smartly designed, moderately priced diversity of household goods ranging from simple but well-made cups, penguin pitchers, and place mats to children's games, lambskin and tanned-leather rugs, and a sample of clothing. Bright, cheerful, and spacious, it's a place where even anti-shoppers can amuse themselves while their companions shop.

### CARPINTERÍA PAMPA
Dorrego 1669, tel. 011/4779-1421,
www.carpinteriapampa.com.ar
**HOURS:** Mon.-Sat. 10 A.M.-1 P.M. and Mon.-Fri. 4-8 P.M.
**Map 7**

For sturdy furniture of darkly rich subtropical hardwoods, such as *lapacho* and quebracho (axe-breaker), Pampa's rustically styled tables, chairs, benches, and the like are hard to surpass. Many of its woods and other materials are recycled, such as the leaf springs, salvaged pine, and forged iron used to create a garden bench resembling the passenger seat of a sulky (the single-horse cart that was once common on the pampas).

### LOS DÍAZ DE MARIO
Soler 5108, tel. 011/4774-7646
**HOURS:** Mon.-Fri. 10 A.M.-8 P.M., Sat. 10 A.M.-7 P.M.
**Map 7**

In materials, at least, no one can accuse D. Mario of a faux rusticism—almost everything in its showroom consists of weathered

© WAYNE BERNHARDSON

Calma Chicha has become an institution for imaginative but inexpensive household goods.

wood recycled into handsome furniture in its adjacent workshop or a larger factory in the provincial town of Pilar. Good examples include garden benches assembled from fence battens that once helped divide paddocks on provincial *estancias* and dining room tables of solid wooden planks rescued from rubbish tips.

## URANO
Honduras 4702, tel. 011/4833-0977,
www.uranodesign.com
**HOURS:** Mon.-Sat. 11 A.M.-7 P.M.
**Map 7**

Beds, benches, bookshelves, chairs, and tables at Urano all partake of a sleek, contemporary design that, on occasion, lapses into something dangerously close to retro 1950s fashion. Having outfitted several bars, restaurants, and other businesses around town, Urano also produces a large variety of accessories for bathrooms, dining rooms, and kitchens. Prices are at the high end.

# Music and Video

Compact discs and cassettes of locally produced music are readily available at bargain prices since the 2001–2002 devaluation—at US$8–10 per item, it's not so risky to try something unfamiliar. Even vinyl is available in used record stores.

## CASA PISCITELLI
San Martín 450, tel. 011/4394-1992,
www.piscitelli.com
**HOURS:** Mon.-Fri. 10 A.M.-7 P.M., Sat. 9 A.M.-1 P.M.
**Map 2**

In the same location since 1939, Casa Piscitelli is a throwback, a survivor that specializes in classical music, DVDs, videos, and books, with only the occasional detour into classic jazz. It stocks artists from around the world, but is probably most knowledgeable about Argentine performers such as pianist Martha Argerich

and conductor Daniel Barenboim (who, of course, have international reputations).

## DISQUERÍA OID MORTALES
Av. Corrientes 1145, Local 17, tel. 011/4382-8839,
www.oidmortalesdiscos.com.ar
**HOURS:** Mon.-Fri. 11 A.M.-8 P.M.
**Map 2**

A small shop in a large gallery, specializing in CDs, this ironically alternative music shop draws its name (Listen, Mortals!) from the opening lyrics of Argentina's pompous national anthem. Strongest in rock 'n' roll, it has some truly offbeat selections, including the obscure but legendary Thirteenth Floor Elevators, a 1960s Texas band whose lead singer Roky Erikson was once found innocent of marijuana possession—by reason of insanity.

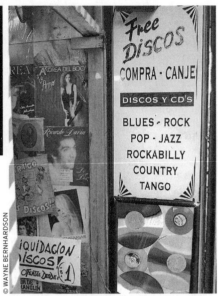
Free Blues stocks all sorts of music and spoken word, on CD and vinyl.

## FREE BLUES

Rodríguez Peña 438
**HOURS:** Mon.-Fri. 11 A.M.-8 P.M.
Map 2

Just off Avenida Corrientes, Free Blues is a collectors' shop that stuffs a lot of used CDs and vinyl in a small space. It's strong on blues and *rock nacional,* but also has a surprising amount of country music and even rockabilly. Prices are high for scarce items.

## ZIVALS

Av. Callao 395, tel. 011/5128-7500,
www.zivals.com
**HOURS:** Mon.-Sat. 9:30 A.M.-10 P.M.
Map 2

One of Buenos Aires's best music shops, the independent Zivals showcases a diversity of styles and artists at reasonable prices, including a larger and far better sale bin than its competitors; it is also a fine bookstore. Its specialized website, though, focuses exclusively on tango CDs, DVDs, VHS tapes, and sheet music.

# Wine

Argentine wine is underrated and was underpriced even before devaluation—in fact, it's one of few commodities that always seems reasonably priced, even in times of runaway inflation. Except for the cheapest vintages, they're rarely disappointing.

Two uniquely Argentine varietals are the red Malbec, usually from Mendoza province, and the fruity but dry white *torrontés* from Cafayate, in Salta province (*torrontés* produced elsewhere may not be bad, but it usually can't match that from Cafayate).

## LO DE JOAQUÍN ALBERDI

Jorge Luis Borges 1772, tel. 011/4832-5329,
www.lodejoaquinalberdi.com.ar
**HOURS:** Daily 11 A.M.-9:30 P.M.
Map 7

This is the retail wine outlet of the outstanding Cabernet restaurant across the street and, as might be expected, it carries a broad selection of fine Argentine wines in all price ranges. Strictly speaking, it's not a wine bar, but if you buy a bottle here and care to drink it on the spot there are tables, chairs, and glasses in a cozy bodega-like environment. You can also order a *tabla* of cheeses and cold cuts from the restaurant.

## TERROIR

Buschiazzo 3040, tel. 011/4778-3408,
www.terroir.com.ar
**HOURS:** Mon.-Fri. 11 A.M.-7 P.M., Sat. noon-6 P.M.
Map 7

Just a short distance from the U.S. Embassy, in a handsome mansard townhouse, Terroir is the city's elite wine shop, where patrons receive individual attention from owner Alejandro

© WAYNE BERNHARDSON

Alejandro Audisio inspects a premium red at Terroir.

Audisio, who speaks English with a native fluency, or his business partner Claudio Fontana. Audisio and Fontana even have access to limited vintages of family reserve wines from some of the country's top bodegas, as well as lesser-known brands that are just beginning to make a name for themselves, plus some more traditional and affordable choices. They ship orders overseas, and can also pack wines securely as airline baggage.

In addition to its wines, Terroir carries a selection of imported spirits and distilled beverages. It's also a small events center, with a covered rooftop terrace that's the site for business meetings and catered dinners with tastings.

### TONEL PRIVADO

Suipacha 299, tel. 011/4328-0953,
www.tonelprivado.com
**HOURS:** Mon.-Fri. 9 A.M.-8 P.M.
**Map 2**

Tonel Privado is an outstanding wine shop

with well-trained personnel and convenient branches at several other locations, including Galerías Pacífico, with even longer hours. Its website up-to-date.

### WINERY

Av. Libertador 500, tel. 011/4325-3400,
www.winery.com.ar
**HOURS:** Mon.-Sat. 10 A.M.-9 P.M.
**Map 5**

Tucked beneath the highway where Avenida 9 de Julio becomes the northbound Autopista Illia, Winery is a small chain that sells Argentine wines by the glass in its ground-level restaurant/wine bar (which serves excellent lunches at moderate prices, with sushi Wednesday and Thursday). On its upper level, it carries a representative stock of Argentine wines ranging from the economical to the truly premium, including some hard-to-find vintages.

Winery has several other outlets around town, but not all serve food.

# ACCOMMODATIONS

Buenos Aires has abundant accommodations in all categories, from hostel dorms to extravagant luxury suites and everything in between. While there's no camping in the city proper, many excursion destinations in Buenos Aires province and Uruguay do offer that option.

Traditionally, tourists stay in downtown hotels and in the elite barrios of Retiro and Recoleta. Many, though, are now opting for bed-and-breakfasts and more stylish boutique hotels in barrios such as San Telmo, Palermo, and even outlying Belgrano. Backpackers flock to hostels, several of which also have comfortable private rooms, in San Telmo, Monserrat, and Palermo. Another option, worth considering for those spending at least a week in town, is to rent a furnished apartment—as hotel prices rise with the tourism boom, the per-day price of an apartment can be a bargain.

Prices in the city often fall in the summer months of January and February, as business travel slows to a crawl, but then rise in March. For excursion destinations, though, they rise during this time as *porteños* flee town for sand, sun, and fun on the beach. Other peak seasons, when prices may rise, are Semana Santa (Holy Week) and July's winter school vacations, which coincide with patriotic holidays.

Note also that Argentine hotels levy 21 percent in Impuesto al Valor Agregado or IVA (Value Added Tax or VAT); there is also IVA in Uruguay—remember this if you take excursions there. Unless otherwise indicated, rates in this book include IVA, but if there's any question at the front desk, ask for clarification to avoid unpleasant surprises when paying the bill.

© WAYNE BERNHARDSON

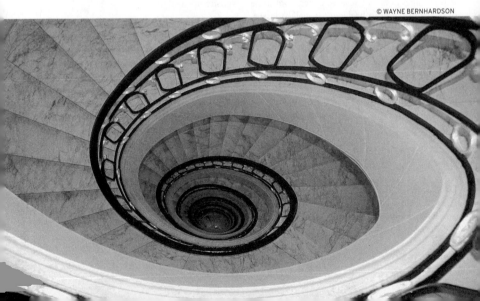

# HIGHLIGHTS

LOOK FOR 【 TO FIND RECOMMENDED ACCOMMODATIONS.

【 **Funkiest Decor:** At the pop-art **Hotel Boquitas Pintadas,** not far from San Telmo in the distinctly untouristed barrio of Constitución, every room reflects the work of the flamboyant novelist Manuel Puig. Even its restaurant's desserts, such as "Kiss of the Spider Woman," have Puigian names (page 165).

【 **Best Recycled Building:** French architect Philippe Starck has taken Puerto Madero's resurrection one step beyond in turning the crumbling El Porteño granary into the audaciously visionary **Faena Hotel & Universe** (page 171).

【 **Most Offbeat Decoration:** On occasion, usually during winter holidays, Puerto Madero's **Hilton Buenos Aires** has a Barbie-themed room, which is usually reserved for young daughters as part of a suite adjoining their parents' room (page 171).

【 **Best Thematic Hotel:** Guests at San Telmo's **Hotel Mansión Dandi Royal** don't just dance tango, they live it: Top instructors get them started or improve their technique, individualized service gets them to any *milonga* in town, and an à la carte breakfast is available at any hour (page 172).

【 **Best Hostels:** Competition's tough in this category, given how quality hostels have proliferated in recent years, but San Telmo's **Telmotango Hostel Suites** stands apart for

preserving magnificent period style while maintaining a casual manner (page 174). Runner-up: **Ostinatto Hostel,** for its imaginative interior design and ample activities calendar (page 173).

【 **Best Views:** From its north side, Retiro's **Sheraton Buenos Aires Hotel** provides panoramas from the Kavanagh building and Plaza San Martín past the monumental train stations that linked Buenos Aires to Argentina's northern and western provinces, and the current port that still connects the city to the world. To the south, there's the Hotel de Inmigrantes, where European arrivals first set foot on Argentine territory, and the recycled Puerto Madero waterfront (page 179).

【 **Best Service:** At Recoleta's elegant **Alvear Palace Hotel,** every floor has a butler and even the maids speak English (page 180).

【 **Best Value:** On a block-long street in Palermo SoHo, **Che Lulu Guest House** has stylishly designed private rooms at hostel-plus prices, within easy walking distance of the city's best restaurants, bars, and nightlife (page 185).

【 **Best Boutique Hotel:** Palermo Hollywood's secluded **Hotel Home Buenos Aires** may host the rich and famous, but it welcomes everyone equally and – who knows? – you might get to crash U2's garden party (page 185).

## CHOOSING AN ACCOMMODATION

When choosing a hotel, much also depends on personal needs and taste—by most standards, the Alvear Palace is one of the continent's and even the world's great hotels, but five-star French furnishings and a personal butler may seem excessive to someone looking for cheaper but charming boutique accommodations, such as Barrio Norte's Art Hotel. Likewise, Retiro's high-rise Sheraton might suit a business visitor for its location and meeting rooms, while

a backpacker might prefer a hostel near the nightlife of San Telmo or Palermo.

Visitors also should not take government-generated hotel ratings too literally: They often represent an ideal rather than a reality, and some one- or two-star places may be better values than others that rank higher on paper. National and municipal tourist officials offer accommodations lists and brochures, but these often exclude budget options and may even omit some mid-range and high-end places. Prices may be negotiable, especially if you pay

## PRICE KEY

| | |
|---|---|
| ❸ | **Under US$75** |
| ❸❸ | **US$75-150** |
| ❸❸❸ | **US$150-250** |
| ❸❸❸❸ | **Over US$250** |

cash; do not assume the *tarifa mostrador* (rack rate) is etched in stone.

## Camping

Camping is a traditional budget option for families and other groups, with or without their own vehicles, throughout Argentina and Uruguay. Visitors taking excursions into the countryside and even to provincial cities— some facilities are surprisingly central—may find them worth consideration. Prices rarely exceed a couple dollars per person.

Argentine and Uruguayan campgrounds are generally spacious affairs, with shade, clean toilets, and bathrooms with hot showers, and even groceries and restaurants. In summer and on weekends, though, the best sites can be crowded and noisy; remember that Argentines stay up late—very late—for their barbecues. It's often possible to find a quieter—but otherwise less desirable—site on the periphery.

## Hostels

Since devaluation, shoestring travelers have streamed into Buenos Aires and the local market has responded by adapting a variety of buildings in key barrios into hostels. While the bulk of their accommodations are inexpensive dorms, almost all of them have single or double rooms as well, and some of these are so comfortable and even stylish that non-backpackers can find some exceptional values.

Hostels, of course, offer an opportunity to socialize with a spectrum of like-minded travelers and some have restaurants, bars, and other entertainment facilities. While they may not be *youth* hostels per se, some do have rambunctious clientele who enjoy the city's nightlife, and potential guests should carefully consider whether a given hostel meets their peace-and-quiet standards.

Buenos Aires proper has several Hostelling International (HI) affiliates, where oversight ensures more than minimum standards; there are several more in the province and in Uruguay. That said, many independent hostels are at least as good and deserve consideration.

For up-to-the-minute information on official Argentine hostels, contact Hostelling

## HIGHER PRICES FOR FOREIGNERS?

In the aftermath of the 2002 peso devaluation, price levels fell for nearly everything in Argentina, including accommodations. As the year progressed, though, and the 2003 summer tourist season began, some hotels began to institute differential pricing for Argentine residents and foreign visitors. The practice is not universal, but it has continued.

Price increases have been particularly noticeable at the top of the accommodations scale, where foreigners may pay 40 percent or so more than Argentines, but much may depend on the individual traveler's language and negotiating skills. The trend is likely a steady move upward, but prices are nevertheless lower than they were in the years when the peso and the dollar were at par.

Everyone is vulnerable to Argentina's rising inflation. The government insists the rise in inflation is around 10 percent and independent economists estimate that it is at least 20 percent. Militant labor unions have gained major wage increases, the disgruntled farming sector's protests have contributed to rising food prices, and an undervalued peso has raised the cost of imports.

International Argentina (Florida 835, tel. 011/4511-8723, www.hostels.org.ar). The rather torpid Asociación Argentina de Albergues de la Juventud (AAAJ, Brasil 675, tel. 011/4300-9321, www.aaaj.org.ar) has a smaller affiliate network, though there is some overlap; oddly, its website appears in French but neither English nor Portuguese.

Uruguay's HI representative is Montevideo's Hostelling International Uruguay (Paraguay 1212, tel. 598/2-9005749, www.hosteluruguay.org).

## Other Budget Accommodations

Budget accommodations in Buenos Aires, the surrounding provinces, and Uruguay can cost as little as US$8–10 per person. Ranging from dingy fleabags with mattresses that sag like hammocks to simple but cheerful and tidy places with firm, new beds, they go by a variety of names that may be misleading as to their quality.

*Hospedajes* are generally family-run lodgings with a few spare rooms; *pensiones* and *casas de huéspedes* are comparable, nearly interchangeable terms. Some may have long-term residents as well as overnight guests. *Residenciales* (singular *residencial*) are generally buildings constructed with short-stay accommodations in mind, but may also have semi-permanent inhabitants. All these places may even go by the term *hotel,* though usually that belongs to a more formal category.

There are some exceptionally good values in all these categories. Many have shared bath and toilet (*baño general* or *baño compartido*) or offer a choice between shared and private bath (*baño privado*); bathtubs are uncommon. In some cases, they have ceiling fans and even cable TV, but there is often an extra charge for cable and almost always a surcharge for air-conditioning.

Travelers intending to stay at budget accommodations should bring their own towels. Likewise, as many budget hotels have thin walls and squeaky floors, earplugs are a good idea. Many but by no means all establishments include breakfast in their rates; ask to be certain.

## THERE'S NO PLACE LIKE HOME

Rather than just renting a hotel room, visitors spending at least a week in Buenos Aires should consider renting an apartment and living in a neighborhood. Shopping in the same place everyday, buying a newspaper from the corner kiosk, learning the bus lines and Subte system, and establishing a rapport with the *portero* (doorman) give a traveler the chance to feel like part of local society. It's especially good if you wish to stay in a neighborhood like Palermo, which still has relatively limited accommodations.

Daily newspapers, such as *Clarín, La Nación,* and the *Buenos Aires Herald,* all have rental listings. For short-term rentals, though, the best option may be an agency, such as **B y T Argentina Travel & Housing** (tel. 011/4876-5000, www.bytargentina.com); its online inventory of apartments and other housing is a good way to familiarize yourself with the options. Other possibilities include **BA House** (tel. 011/4815-7602, www.bahouse.com.ar), which has a smaller selection of housing in a more geographically restricted area, and **Alojargentina** (tel. 011/5219-0606, www.alojargentina.com.ar).

Perhaps the cheapest option, increasingly popular with backpackers, is "couch surfing," in which local residents offer impromptu accommodations via the Internet. This, of course, can provide great opportunities for interacting with locals; for options in and around Buenos Aires, explore The Couch Surfing Project (www.couchsurfing.com), which has a very active group in Buenos Aires.

## Mid-Range Accommodations

Mid-range hotels generally offer larger, more comfortable, and better-furnished rooms (almost always with private bath) than even the best budget places. Ceiling fans, cable TV, and even air-conditioning are common, but they may not have on-site parking. Some have restaurants. Rates can range anywhere from US$30 to US$100 d; some are better values than their high-end counterparts.

While star ratings can be misleading as to quality, it's worth mentioning the main distinction between two- and three-star accommodations: Generally, the former have showers, while the latter have bathtubs as well.

## High-End Accommodations

Upscale hotels with top-flight service, which can range well upwards of US$100 per night, are few outside the capital and major resort areas. In the capital, amenities often include restaurants and bars, swimming pools and gym facilities, business centers and conference rooms, and in-room broadband or WiFi Internet connections.

Some are traditionally elegant places in privileged neighborhoods like Recoleta; others are business-oriented downtown accommodations, while still others are cutting-edge options in pioneer neighborhoods like Puerto Madero. Invariably, they offer secure on-site parking.

Outside the capital, these are mostly resort hotels that lack the business facilities. Some of the best options in this category are country inn resorts on *estancias,* offering traditional hospitality and ambience with style unmatchable at other high-end places. Again, prices may be upwards of US$100—often substantially upwards.

# Monserrat                                     Map 1

Most budget accommodations in the vicinity of the Plaza de Mayo are now hostels whose cheapest options are dorms, but some of them have more expensive private rooms that are outstanding values. There are abundant mid-range options and a handful of fine upmarket options.

## AXEL HOTEL ⓢⓢⓢ
Venezuela 647, tel. 011/4136-9400,
www.axelhotels.com

For years, Buenos Aires has had a handful of gay-oriented or gay-friendly bed-and-breakfasts, but the "hetero-friendly" Axel is the city's first full-service hotel built and run with the homosexual community in mind. Architecturally, its creative use of transparent glass in the reception area, staircases, and even the rooftop health club pool—its shimmering waters visible from the ground level—metaphorically suggest that those who stay here have nothing to hide.

About 90 percent of Axel's clientele are gay males, with a much smaller percentage of lesbian couples and heterosexuals, but it's a cordial setting for anybody with an open mind. The decor of its 48 midsized guest rooms and common areas is modern and boutique-ish, with an iMac-equipped business center on each of its four floors. Rooms that face the street cost US$198 d, while those facing the ground-level pool go for US$220 d; prices do not include the 21 percent IVA. Suites go for US$335 plus IVA.

The semi-subterranean Chill Out Bar is also the site of weekend "pre-dance" parties starting at midnight, while non-guests are welcome at outdoor pool parties that take place Sunday afternoon from 5 P.M.; the rest of the time, the pool is for guests only. The Axel staff are particularly good at suggesting nightlife alternatives for their guests.

## CASTELAR HOTEL & SPA ⓢⓢⓢ
Av. de Mayo 1152, tel. 011/4383-5000,
www.castelarhotel.com.ar

One of the capital's most historic lodgings, dating from 1929, the four-star Castelar (US$129–183 s or d) oozes character out onto the Avenida de Mayo. In its time, it's hosted the likes of Spanish playwright Federico García Lorca (who lived in room 704 for six months), Chile's Nobel Prize–winning poet Pablo Neruda, Nobel Prize scientist Linus Pauling, and many Argentine politicians. Embellished with marble, it offers

© WAYNE BERNHARDSON

**Axel Hotel's secluded pool**

comfortable, well-equipped rooms (with entire nonsmoking floors), but a middling breakfast. With access to its own basement spa it's still a pretty good value.

### CHE LAGARTO YOUTH HOSTEL $

Venezuela 857, tel. 011/4343-4845,
www.chelagarto.com
This casual, spacious hostel charges from US$10 pp for dorm accommodations with breakfast, but also has private rooms from US$33 s or d (shared bath) to US$53 s or d (private bath) with breakfast, free 24-hour Internet and the like; most rooms have cooling fans but the private rooms have air-conditioning. The entire ground floor is devoted to the Madhouse Pub, open until 1 A.M., which extends into a large wooded patio rare in this part of town.

### CONCEPT HOTEL $

Santiago del Estero 186, tel. 011/4383-3473
In a rundown but rebounding area, the Concept Hotel is an anomaly in many ways: a high-tech budget hotel where every amenity

or utility, from room lights to cable TV, is computer-controlled. Recycled almost beyond recognition, the building itself retains a few original features, such as its verdant interior patio and exposed segments of the original brick walls, but the rest seems almost futuristic. Rates start at US$40/47 s/d, with larger rooms only slightly more expensive.

### ◖ HOTEL BOQUITAS PINTADAS $$

Estados Unidos 1393, tel. 011/4381-6064,
www.boquitas-pintadas.com.ar
Just outside Monserrat's boundaries, Constitución's Boquitas Pintadas takes it name from a novel by the late Manuel Puig. Popular with national and international show-biz and arts figures, despite the marginal neighborhood, it got a zany pop-art makeover from its German creators. Its bar Youkali, which pumps thumping techno at night, owes its moniker to a tango by German composer Kurt Weill.

All rooms come with private baths, but some are outside the rooms proper; rates range US$60–100 s or d.

### HOTEL CHILE $

Av. de Mayo 1297, tel. 011/4383-7877
Once a prestige hotel, now a reliable budget to mid-range option, French architect Louis Dubois's art nouveau monument now features modernized rooms for US$30/37 s/d with private bath and breakfast. On the upper floors, airy corner balcony rooms enjoy panoramas of the Plaza del Congreso and, by craning the neck a bit eastward, the Plaza de Mayo and Casa Rosada; the location, though, also means a high decibel count.

### HOTEL 562 NOGARÓ $$$

Diagonal Julio A. Roca 562, tel. 011/4331-0091,
www.562nogaro.com.ar
Dating from 1930 but renovated in 2006, this legitimately four-star, 145-room hotel has overcome its Francophile origins to become more of a design hotel. Rates run US$140/160 s/d with breakfast, and amenities include telephone, cable TV, air-conditioning, Internet connections, and in-room strongboxes.

ACCOMMODATIONS

## HOTEL IBIS 💲

Hipólito Yrigoyen 1592, tel. 011/5300-5555,
www.ibishotel.com

Reservations are almost essential for the enormously popular Ibis, part of the French Accor chain. Opposite the Plaza de los dos Congresos, the sleek 147-room high-rise has added minimalist style and comfort to an area that had been truly rundown and, in the aftermath of the 2002 meltdown, is still recovering. Rates of US$63 s or d, plus US$4 for the optional breakfast, are still a fine value.

## HOTEL INTERCONTINENTAL 💲💲💲

Moreno 809, tel. 011/4340-7100,
www.buenos-aires.intercontinental.com

According to magazines like *Travel + Leisure,* the swank Intercontinental consistently makes the list of Buenos Aires's best hotels. Affordable for what it offers, rates start around US$165–204 s or d for standard rooms, which are still spacious and comfortable, but Internet access costs an extra US$14 per day.

In addition to extensive personal and business services, two-thirds of the Intercontinental's 315 rooms are nonsmoking. It also has two restaurants, a gym and pool, and considerable open space in an adjacent public plaza maintained by hotel personnel.

## MILHOUSE YOUTH HOSTEL 💲

Hipólito Yrigoyen 959, tel. 011/4345-9604,
www.milhousehostel.com

Affiliated with Hostelling International, this refurbished period house is an immaculate, well-managed, well-located, and secure facility with spacious common areas that include a kitchen and a coffee shop. Close to popular San Telmo and to public transportation to all parts of the city, it charges from US$11 pp with breakfast in multi-bedded dorms to US$43 d for rooms with private bath. Many rooms have small balconies.

## NH CITY HOTEL 💲💲💲

Bolívar 160, tel. 011/4121-6464, www.nh-hoteles.com

Just south of Plaza de Mayo, the City Hotel is a spectacularly modernized 300-room building (dating from 1931) that had the misfortune to reopen at the nadir of Argentina's 2001–2002 meltdown; currently, with rates starting around US$150 s or d, it's making up for the business it lost then on its beautifully appointed rooms with all modern conveniences, plus luxuries like a rooftop pool, gym, and sauna.

## PORTAL DEL SUR YOUTH HOSTEL 💲

Hipólito Yrigoyen 855, tel. 011/4342-8788,
www.portaldelsurba.com.ar

Just south of Avenida de Mayo, Portal del Sur occupies a former *pension* (boarding house) with several floors of dorms (US$14–17 pp) and private rooms (US$51/57 s/d) surrounding a sunny atrium, plus a rooftop terrace (with *parrilla*) and bar for relaxing and partying away from the sleeping areas. Rates include breakfast, kitchen privileges, air-conditioning, WiFi, and similar amenities; there's also a travel desk for arranging excursions and other transportation.

# Microcentro

Map 2

Recent economic conditions have made some pretty good Microcentro hotels more affordable, but bargains are fewer as the economy stabilizes.

## ATLAS TOWER HOTEL 🟊🟊
Av. Corrientes 1778, tel. 011/5217-9371,
www.atlastower.com.ar

One of barely a handful of attractive new hotels in Congreso, the three-star Atlas Tower has midsized rooms with all modern conveniences, including telephone and broadband Internet, strongboxes, cable TV, and the like; the common areas are also inviting. Rates of US$70/80 s/d with breakfast are more than fair for what it offers, and there are discounts for Internet reservations.

## CLARIDGE HOTEL 🟊🟊🟊
Tucumán 535, tel. 011/4314-7700,
www.claridge-hotel.com.ar

One of the capital's classics, dating from 1946 but tastefully modernized, the Claridge charges US$198 s or d for rooms with the standard amenities in its range, including cable TV, telephone, and a work desk with Internet connection. Several floors are tobacco-free. While it's impeccable and efficient, some of its more contemporary competitors arguably offer better value for money.

## COLUMBIA PALACE HOTEL 🟊
Av. Corrientes 1533, tel. 011/4373-1906,
www.columbiapalacehotel.com.ar

Facing the Teatro General San Martín and close to other prestigious theater venues, the Columbia Palace is past its peak, but at least it's holding its own and is suitable for a night. Rates are US$51/65 s/d with breakfast.

## GOYA HOTEL 🟊
Suipacha 748, tel. 011/4322-9269,
www.goyahotel.com.ar

This is one of the Microcentro's best small hotels, with 40 cozy rooms and family-style

service. Rates start at US$36/50 s/d for decent quarters with private bath (shower only), while rooms with tubs go for US$48/60 s/d; there's a handful of slightly more expensive *presidente* rooms whose bathrooms havewhirlpool tubs. All rates include a continental breakfast, cable TV, and air-conditioning.

## GRAN HOTEL ARGENTINO 🟊🟊
Carlos Pellegrini 37, tel. 011/4334-4001,
www.hotel-argentino.com.ar

Housed in a striking art nouveau building a few blocks south of the Obelisco, the otherwise unremarkable Argentino (US$73 s or d) offers discounts for cash and for extended stays. Some will find the location on Buenos Aires's broadest avenue enthralling, but others may think it a little too fast-paced.

## GRAN HOTEL COLÓN 🟊🟊🟊
Carlos Pellegrini 507, tel. 011/4320-3500,
www.colon-hotel.com.ar

Only a block from the Obelisco, the business-oriented four-star Colón charges US$171/184 s/d, so it's still good value by international standards and convenient to almost everything in town. Rooms with better views go for US$200 s or d, and there are also more elaborate suites; stays of three days or more get significant discounts.

## HOTEL A&B INTERNACIONAL 🟊
Montevideo 248, tel. 011/4384-9616,
www.hotelayb.com

A real surprise in this part of town, the A&B has injected elements of style without going big budget, having created lofts with spiral staircases and balconies (US$53<#\208>58 s or d with private bath and breakfast) by combining small street-side rooms that were once on separate floors. At the same time, they've exposed sections of the original redbrick walls to give the hallways and other common areas a touch of distinction. The so-called "four-star" (US$62–72 s or d) and the whirlpool

ACCOMMODATIONS

tub–equipped suites (with a small patio and a large bathroom, US$87–102 s or d) fall a little short of their aspirations; still, on balance, this place offers superb value for money.

### HOTEL AMERICANO ⑤⑤
Rodríguez Peña 265, tel. 011/4382-4223, www.hotelamericano.com.ar

Though it's well located and friendly enough, the *común* rooms (US$45/53 s/d with breakfast) are claustrophobically small; if economics dictate a stay at the undistinguished Americano, the larger and comfier *especial* rooms (US$72/80 s/d) are worth the price difference.

### HOTEL DE LOS DOS CONGRESOS ⑤⑤
Rivadavia 1777, tel. 011/4372-0466, www.hoteldoscongresos.com

Arguably Congreso's best value, this rejuvenated gem boasts a stately exterior and refurbished interior. The spacious and comfortable rooms with cable TV, air-conditioning, telephone, and other standard amenities, as well as a buffet breakfast, run US$70/75 s/d. Reservations are advisable for one of the stylish lofts (US$90 s or d), which have spiral staircases and whirlpool tub–equipped bathrooms.

### HOTEL ESPLENDOR ⑤⑤⑤
San Martín 780, tel. 011/5256-8800, www.esplendorbuenosaires.com

Around the corner from Galerías Pacífico, in an earlier incarnation as Hotel Phoenix, this Microcentro hotel once hosted the Prince of Wales. Today, though, he'd only recognize the facade of what was once an antiques-strewn accommodations and is now an utterly transformed boutique hotel with all modern conveniences including designer furniture. In an uncommon touch, the doors reach all the way to the four-meter ceilings.

The relatively small "concept rooms" (US$174 plus 21 percent IVA) lack whirlpool tubs and some other amenities found in the larger "design suites" (US$209 plus IVA) and the "VIP Suites" (US$262 plus IVA). While a central atrium floods the common areas with natural light, those areas are surprisingly

few—just the reception area, the restaurant, and a small business center.

### HOTEL EUROPA ⑤
Bartolomé Mitre 1294, tel. 011/4381-9629, www.eurohotel.com.ar

Only the exterior retains its original art deco style, but the Europa is a spotless, rejuvenated budget hotel for US$35/44 s/d with breakfast; air-conditioning costs US$7 extra. A few interior rooms are relatively dark; the better rooms have exterior balconies.

### HOTEL FACÓN GRANDE ⑤
Reconquista 645, tel. 011/4312-6360, www.hotelfacongrande.com

The former Hotel Italia Romanelli, a very respectable hotel in its time, has undergone a *criollo* transformation into the gaucho-themed Facón Grande, suggesting a piece of Patagonian revolutionary history in the heart of Buenos Aires. Totally rehabbed, it offers 97 bright, cheerful midsize rooms, plus appealing common areas, on a reasonably quiet block. By current standards, rates of US$70 s or d are an excellent value.

### HOTEL HOSTERÍA POSTA CARRETAS ⑤⑤
Esmeralda 726, tel. 011/4322-8567, www.postacarretas.com.ar

The Posta Carretas has an older sector with smallish and dark but quiet rooms (US$70/75 s/d), and a newer addition with larger, comfier rooms but a noisier street exposure (US$130/145 s/d for two-room suites, US$155/165 s/d for a junior suite, and up to US$200 for the "Oriental Suite").

Amenities include cable TV, air-conditioning, pool, sauna and gym, bar, restaurant, and buffet breakfast. The staff is agreeable, and prices have risen more slowly here than at some other hotels.

### HOTEL LAFAYETTE ⑤⑤
Reconquista 546, tel. 011/4393-9081, www.lafayettehotel.com.ar

With large and modernized rooms for US$105 s

or d with a diverse buffet breakfast, the steadily improving Lafayette is better than several pricier hotels in the vicinity. Along with obliging personnel, it features such amenities as cable TV, telephone, air-conditioning, and WiFi.

### HOTEL MAIPÚ ⑤

Maipú 735, tel. 011/4322-5142

Catering to overseas backpackers and close to more prestigious Retiro, the Maipú occupies an attractive but aging building whose frills-free rooms cost US$17/23 s/d with shared bath, US$22/30 s/d with private bath. Breakfast is not included.

### HOTEL NH JOUSTEN ⑤⑤

Av. Corrientes 240, tel. 011/4321-6750,
www.nh-hoteles.com

Another affiliate of the Spanish chain, the Jousten has 85 rooms in an elegant, tastefully recycled French-style castle. Thanks to double-paned windows, it's quiet despite the busy avenue; each room has cable TV, stereo, telephone, air-conditioning, and Internet connections. Rates are US$135 s or d with buffet breakfast. The highly regarded basement restaurant serves Spanish cuisine.

### HOTEL O'REI ⑤

Lavalle 733, tel. 011/4394-7112, www.hotelorei.com.ar

Despite a record of notoriously cranky management, the O'Rei is a longstanding backpackers' choice because of its central pedestrian mall location and low prices—US$10/15 s/d for smallish rooms with shared bath, US$21/24 s/d with private bath. It's upgraded the rooms (not extravagantly, though) with cable TV and ceiling fans, as well as new furniture, and the kitchen is open to guests.

### HOTEL ORENSE ⑤

Bartolomé Mitre 1359, tel. 011/4372-4441,
www.hotelorense.com.ar

While it has no luxuries, the Orense is a meticulously spic-and-span budget hotel where most of the rooms front onto a luminous atrium; isolated from the street by the lobby, the rooms themselves are remarkably quiet for this part of town. Rates are US$36 s or d (cash only) with breakfast and private bath (showers only, no tubs), telephone, and ceiling fans; there's a surcharge for air-conditioning.

### HOTEL PLAZA ROMA ⑤⑤

Lavalle 110, tel. 011/4314-0666,
www.hotelplazaroma.com.ar

Opposite the historic Luna Park stadium, convenient to Puerto Madero's restaurants, cinemas, and open spaces, the Plaza Roma offers 65 rooms (US$83/100 s/d) with private bath, breakfast, air-conditioning, cable TV, and telephone. Some enjoy views of the Puerto Madero complex.

### HOTEL RECONQUISTA PLAZA ⑤⑤⑤

Reconquista 602, tel. 011/4311-4600,
www.hotelesreconquista.com.ar

Interesting in its design, the Reconquista Plaza has turned a corner lot into a hotel with a series of large trapezoidal rooms (even the elevators share this unusual form), all of which are at least 38 square meters. Unfortunately, though it's been open only a few years, there are signs of inconsistent maintenance (even if the staff are gracious and attentive). Skyrocketing rates, starting at US$207 s or d, are higher than those at nearby places that may be better values.

### HOTEL SHERATON LIBERTADOR ⑤⑤⑤

Av. Córdoba 680, tel. 011/4322-2095,
www.starwood.com

Sheraton's Microcentro hotel boasts a business center, restaurant, pool, gym, and other luxuries. The rooms themselves are showing signs of wear, with worn carpets and scuffed woodwork, even though they're still comfortable enough and the service is diligent. Rates start at US$156 s or d for a standard midsize room, with buffet breakfast included.

### HOTEL SPORTSMAN ⑤

Rivadavia 1425, tel. 011/4381-8021,
www.hotelsportsman.com.ar

In Congreso, the Sportsman has long been a musty backpackers' special whose main appeal was low prices, but it's upgraded its facilities—and raised its prices. Rates are still pretty modest at US$12/22 s/d with shared bath, US$22/37 s/d with private bath, but they rise about 20 percent during winter holidays; breakfast is extra. There are discounts for longer stays.

## NORMANDIE HOTEL ❸

Rodríguez Peña 320, tel. 011/4371-7001, www.hotelnormandie.com.ar

In the Congreso district, just off Avenida Corrientes, the Normandie is a respectable mid-range choice that charges US$57 s or d for carpeted rooms with private bath and breakfast. There are discounts for cash payments, though, and for stays longer than five consecutive nights; this is one of the best values in town. Check the website for occasional specials.

## PANAMERICANO BUENOS AIRES HOTEL & RESORT ❸❸❸

Carlos Pellegrini 525, tel. 011/4348-5000, www.panamericano.us

Near the Obelisco, the Panamericano consists of an older south tower, where rates start at US$145 s or d, and a newer north tower, beginning at US$185 s or d. Both are comfortable, but the north-tower rooms are technologically superior. All of its 400 rooms have access to amenities, including gym and rooftop pool; its restaurant, Tomo I, is widely considered one of the capital's best.

## SAVOY HOTEL ❸❸

Av. Callao 181, tel. 011/4370-8000, www.goldentulipsavoy.com

Congreso's prime upscale option is the Savoy, now part of the Dutch Golden Tulip chain, though it has a certain institutional impersonality. The distinguished neo-baroque building, though, has been undergoing restoration and improvements.

Rates start at US$115 s or d, with larger suites at higher prices; for stays longer than two weeks, there's a 10 percent discount. All windows are double-paned for silence, and rooms include phones (with voicemail), Internet connections and other business amenities, and a buffet breakfast.

## ST. NICHOLAS YOUTH HOSTEL ❸

Bartolomé Mitre 1691, tel. 011/4373-5920, www.snhostel.com

In the bustling Congreso area, this HI affiliate has dorm accommodations for US$12 pp (with breakfast and shared bath) and private rooms for US$37 s or d with shared bath, US$40 s or d with private bath; non-Hostelling members pay slightly more. Like several other Buenos Aires hostels, it's a handsome rehabbed period house with ample shared spaces (including a sunny rooftop terrace and even its own pub), but noise carries a little too well through the multistory atrium; consequently, it's not the best choice for the early-to-bed set.

## V&S HOSTEL CLUB ❸

Viamonte 887, tel. 011/4322-0944 or 011/4327-5131, www.hostelclub.com

In a recycled early-20th-century house, this well-located, independently operated hostel offers dorm beds for as little as US$11 pp with a buffet breakfast included; rooms with private bath cost US$50 s or d. The building itself has central heating, air-conditioning, and spacious and appealing common areas, including a kitchen, dining room, small gym, and a *parrilla* for barbecues.

# Puerto Madero Map 2

Buenos Aires's youngest barrio has only limited accommodations—all in the highest price ranges.

### ❰ FAENA HOTEL & UNIVERSE ⑤⑤⑤⑤

Marta Salotti 445, tel. 011/4010-9000,
www.faenahotelanduniverse.com

There's no faux modesty in the name of French architect Philippe Starck's latest project, which turned the landmark Edificio El Porteño, an early-20th-century granary, into a five-star-plus hotel. From outside, in fact, it's not evident that this redbrick structure on the edge of the Reserva Ecológica is a hotel, but its interior is an unexpected revelation of continental style.

In fact, the Faena is a 110-room hotel, but it's also home to permanent apartment residents and such amenities as a restaurant, a cabaret, a pool with a swim-up bar, and a library seemingly airlifted in from a 19th-century Parisian mansion. The rooms themselves—and their furnishings—look so Parisian as to be incongruous with the building, but there's no denying their quality and sophistication. In its "universe," the Faena also sells "experiences," such as polo with pros and workshops with famous photographer Aldo Sessa.

Rates at the Faena start around US$425 s or d, and rise into the US$750 range.

### ❰ HILTON BUENOS AIRES ⑤⑤⑤

Av. Macacha Güemes 351, tel. 011/4891-0000,
www.buenos.hilton.com

From the outside, it's a boxy, undistinguished, modern glass palace, but the Buenos Aires Hilton's lobby is an expansive seven-story atrium that warms the entire interior with spectacular natural light. Not reached by the narrow dark hallways of traditional hotels, its room entrances all face the atrium, while the

ACCOMMODATIONS

© WAYNE BERNHARDSON

Puerto Madero's Faena Hotel & Universe occupies a recycled granary.

accommodations themselves are large, comfortable, well designed, and immaculately maintained. On the upper floors, west-facing rooms have great views of the Puerto Madero yacht harbor and downtown.

While the Hilton is far from dark, it's had its noir side. In Fabián Bielinsky's con-man film *Nueve Reinas* (Nine Queens), its luminous lobby was one of few identifiable landmarks in a city otherwise depicted through its lowlifes and anonymously seedy bars.

Rates at the Hilton start around US$234 s or d and head upwards of US$500, but the lower rates compare favorably to some Recoleta hotels that aren't nearly so good. For a truly specialized market, room 538 is Barbie-themed (presumably for young daughters of parents in the adjoining room).

# San Telmo                                      Map 3

San Telmo's accommodations are limited and, historically, they've been mediocre at best. In recent years, though, the barrio's popularity with backpackers and other budget travelers has spawned a proliferation of quality hostel-style accommodations—some of *very* high quality.

### CARLOS GARDEL HOSTEL $
Carlos Calvo 579, tel. 011/4307-2606,
www.hostelcarlosgardel.com.ar
The great *tanguero* toting a backpack is the trademark of this inviting hostel barely two blocks from Plaza Dorrego. Options range from dorms (US$9 pp) to private rooms (from US$18–41 s or d, with either shared or private bath) in a quirky building with kitchen facilities, comfy common areas, and free Internet access. Rates also include breakfast.

### EL HOSTAL DE SAN TELMO $
Carlos Calvo 614,
tel. 011/4300-6899,
http://webs.satlink.com/usuarios/e/elhostal
A pioneer of contemporary hostel-style accommodations in Buenos Aires, this is a cozy—perhaps cramped would be closer to the truth—hostel in a prime location, but it's hard pressed to match the amenities of its more recent competitors. For US$8–9 pp (dorms only), though, rates are among the city's cheapest; shared amenities include kitchen facilities, a large terrace with a *parrilla*, cable TV, and Internet access.

### HOSTEL INN TANGO CITY $
Piedras 680, tel. 011/4300-5776,
www.hostel-inn.com
This engaging HI affiliate has dorms (US$11 pp) and doubles (US$42 d) with breakfast, kitchen facilities, free 24-hour Internet, tango and Spanish lessons, and plenty of other amenities (including free dinner Mon.–Thurs.). Members pay slightly lower rates. It's even dog-friendly, though owners must take responsibility for their pets.

### HOTEL MANSIÓN DANDI ROYAL $$
Piedras 922, tel. 011/4361-3537,
www.hotelmansiondandiroyal.com
Only slightly less distinctive than Boquitas Pintadas, but with a different style, the Dandi Royal is a boutique hotel whose primary clientele are foreigners who come not just to dance but to live tango 24 hours daily. The staff here arranges tango excursions, and directs their guests to the most appropriate locales. At the same time, it welcomes non-dancers who enjoy its peace, quiet, and individualized service, in a magnificently recycled mansion that, according to its managers, was originally a single-family residence and once a brothel.

All the original woodwork, once covered with paint, has been stripped and restored, the walls covered with tango-themed murals, and the common areas furnished with tables, chairs, and sofas from the Gardelian epoch. In three categories, the 15 rooms all have king-size beds and other modern amenities but also

© MANSIÓN DANDI ROYAL

**reception area of tango-themed Hotel Mansión Dandi Royal**

period touches, such as claw-foot tubs. Prices vary according to size: The "Dandi" costs US$105 s or d, the "Royal" US$161 s or d, and the "Suite Piazzolla" US$224 s or d. A "Royal Crown Suite" costs US$298.

An à la carte breakfast, included in the rates, is available at any hour (*milongueros* keep irregular schedules!); it also has a gym, a sunny terrace, a small rooftop pool, and a secluded patio.

For information on Dandi Royal's tango packages, see the *Special Interests* entry in the *Essentials* chapter.

### HOSTEL NÓMADE ⑤
Carlos Calvo 430, tel. 011/4300-7641,
www.hostelnomade.com

Barely a block from Plaza Dorrego, this cozy, friendly hostel in a traditional PH ("horizontal property," as opposed to multistory) has mostly dormitory accommodations (US$9 pp) but also a handful of private rooms (US$23 d); rates include breakfast. There's 24-hour Internet access, and common areas include a bar and a game room with a pool table.

### HOTEL VARELA ⑤
Estados Unidos 342, tel. 011/4362-1231,
hotelvarela@yahoo.com.ar

Non-hostel budget accommodations are few, but Hotel Varela (US$12–15 s or d) is a no-frills but spotless and reputable backpackers' choice, especially popular with French visitors. Rates depend on whether the room has shared or private bath.

### LUGAR GAY DE BUENOS AIRES ⑤
Defensa 1120, tel. 011/4300-4747,
www.lugargay.com.ar

With impeccable taste, the owners have recycled a century-old house into Buenos Aires's only bed-and-breakfast catering exclusively to gay men, without compromising the classic style of its steep marble staircases and other traditional features. Bordering Plaza Dorrego (one balcony looks diagonally onto the plaza), it has comfortable rooms with cable TV, strongboxes, and comfortable furnishings, though some lack view windows (but not natural light). There are two sunny but secluded rooftop terraces, one of which offers river views in the distance.

Lugar Gay has only eight rooms, so reservations are imperative; rates vary from US$35/50 s/d (with shared bath) to US$55/75 s/d (with private bath). Rates include breakfast, Internet access, a shared whirlpool tub, a weight room, and a kitchenette; the entire staff can handle English. Payment is by cash (pesos, dollars, or euros) or American Express travelers checks only.

### ◖ OSTINATTO HOSTEL ⑤
Chile 680, tel. 011/4362-9639,
www.ostinatto.com.ar

It's not quite the design hostel it aims to be, but Ostinatto has done some daring innovations while keeping prices modest, even low, with as many or more amenities than other hostels that are not nearly so well located. In a historic five-story building with strategic demolitions that have filled the interior with natural light, Ostinatto boasts a bar/restaurant, a scenic rooftop terrace that's the site of

© WAYNE BERNHARDSON

San Telmo's Lugar Gay de Buenos Aires is an intimate bed-and-breakfast in an attractively recycled century-old house.

Thursday-evening barbecues, a TV room, tango lessons, and even a mini-cinema. There's at least one free-of-charge activity per day, ranging from walking tours to pub crawls.

Dormitory accommodations start at US$10 pp, and even some of those enjoy privacy and even private baths that are uncommon in Ostinatto's competitors. Doubles range US$40–46 depending on whether they have shared bath, exterior private bath, or private bath within the room; some of these, though, have low ceilings and are relatively dark. There's one rooftop loft (US$80 s or d) and another under construction.

### ⟮⟯ TELMOTANGO HOSTEL SUITES $

Chacabuco 679, tel. 011/4361-5808, www.hostelmotango.com

This is the pick of San Telmo's hostel accommodations, in a magnificently preserved 19th-century house with stunning common areas, including a spectacular atrium and a sunny rooftop terrace. Some of its 33 rooms are a little small, but others are sizeable and the rates (US$33/37–47/50 s/d with breakfast) make it arguably the barrio's best value; the cheaper rooms have shared bath. It should be popular not just with backpackers, but also a broader spectrum of travelers seeking both style and value.

# Balvanera
Map 4

Most Balvanera budget hotels are on the borders of Monserrat and the Microcentro, within a few blocks of the Congreso Nacional.

## ABASTO PLAZA HOTEL $$

Av. Corrientes 3190,
tel. 011/6311-4466,
www.abastoplaza.com

Opposite the Mercado del Abasto, the former Holiday Inn has tried to reinvent itself as a five-star tango-theme hotel, and in truth it does have nearby tango landmarks: the market itself, the Esquina Carlos Gardel *tanguería,* and the Gardel museum. It also offers tango lessons, but they can't afford to ignore business clients (there's an ample business center); other amenities include a gym, a pool, and a solarium. There are several different kinds of rooms, ranging from standard to luxury suites, and dedicated tobacco-free floors. Rates fall into the US$121–200 s or d range, though a tango-themed suite goes for US$540.

## BAUEN SUITE HOTEL $$

Av. Corrientes 1856, tel. 011/4370-0400,
www.bauensuite.com

More business-oriented than its former affiliate around the corner on Callao, Congreso's other Bauen is a high-rise hotel with spacious, well-maintained suites (40 square meters with kitchenettes), incongruously decorated in a sort of Southeast Asian mode. Rates start at US$135 s or d, with breakfast and taxes included, but there's a 10 percent discount with Internet reservations.

## HOTEL BAUEN $

Av. Callao 360,
tel. 011/4373-9009,
www.bauencallao.com.ar

Following the 2002 peso collapse, the old Hotel Bauen closed, but in mid-2004 it reopened as a unique employee-run hotel cooperative—the first of its kind in the country, though some smokestack factories have seen similar experiments. With more labor than capital available, its unadorned rooms (US$60/73 s/d with breakfast) have improved, but no one will mistake this for a design hotel.

While constantly facing legal challenges to their proprietorship, the cooperative has so far fended them off. The new Bauen is perhaps most notable for the sense of purpose among its staff, who have rehabbed common areas like the bar, restaurant, and the basement club, which features live jazz, rock, and techno on weekends. It's unrelated to the Bauen Suites, around the corner on Corrientes.

## HOTEL GRAN SARMIENTO $

Sarmiento 1892, tel. 011/4374-8069,
www.hotelgransarmiento.com

Some exterior rooms in this 30-unit, French-style "petit hotel" have wrought-iron balconies; its original carved and stained banisters, as well as marble staircases, contribute to a genuine but faded gentility. At US$27/33 s/d without breakfast, the amiable Sarmiento remains a better value than some places that cost considerably more; its simple amenities include air-conditioning and ceiling fans.

## HOTEL LYON $$

Riobamba 251, tel. 011/4372-0100,
www.hotel-lyon.com.ar

For families or groups of friends, one of the capital's best options is the Lyon, which has spacious apartment-style rooms—ranging from 40 to 65 square meters—starting at US$60/80 s/d with breakfast. Even if its amenities haven't quite kept pace with newer hotels, it's one of the capital's best values for money.

## MOLINO HOTEL $

Av. Callao 164, tel. 011/4374-9112

Slightly worn but still tidy, the 60-room Molino is a perfectly decent choice in its price

ACCOMMODATIONS

range (US$37/50 s/d) with private bath, breakfast, telephone, and air-conditioning.

### NUEVO HOTEL CALLAO **$**
Av. Callao 292, tel. 011/4372-3861,
www.hotelcallao.com.ar

In a stylish building crowned by a corner cupola, near the theater district, the upgraded 45-room Callao has kept both its architectural and practical integrity while maintaining moderate prices. Rates are US$55/65 s/d with breakfast; make reservations for the more distinctive cupola rooms (US$70 s or d).

### SARMIENTO PALACE HOTEL **$**
Sarmiento 1953, tel. 011/4953-3404,
www.hotelsarmiento.com.ar

On a shady, leafy block that's unusual so close to the densely built Microcentro, the 120-room Sarmiento enjoys a reputation for personalized attention. For US$65/71 s/d with breakfast, the midsized rooms have dated decor and older units with air-conditioning but upgraded baths; a handful of larger, more expensive suites (US$87–104 s or d) include whirlpool tubs. Common areas include a bar, a small gym, and a sunny 3rd-floor deck.

# Retiro                                     Map 5

True budget accommodations are scarce in the northern barrios, but there are a few options. Many upscale Retiro hotels are close to extravagant Recoleta and often claim to be part of that barrio.

### AMÉRICAS TOWERS HOTEL **$$$**
Libertad 1070, tel. 011/4815-7900,
www.grupoamericas.com.ar

Almost next door to its sister Hotel de las Américas, listed later in this section, this is a 100-room business-oriented facility that has virtually identical services (plus a fitness center) and slightly higher rates (US$194/209 s/d).

### ARGENTA TOWER HOTEL & SUITES **$$**
Juncal 868, tel. 011/4325-0607,
www.argenta-tower.com.ar

For expansive rooms with all the modern conveniences, it's hard to top the 100 suites at the Argenta Tower. On a quiet block almost equidistant between the Microcentro and Recoleta, it's popular with business clients for its full-service facilities, including high-speed Internet connections in every room, but is also a fine tourist choice. Rates start at US$133 s or d for substantial studio suites; even larger rooms are not that much more expensive.

### BISONTE PALACE HOTEL
Marcelo T. de Alvear 910, tel. 011/4328-4751,
www.hotelesbisonte.com

Only a block off Santa Fe, the four-star Bisonte has fast-rising rates of US$148/172 s or d for soundproofed rooms with air-conditioning and buffet breakfast, with distinctive touches such as a newspaper of your choice in the morning.

### CAESAR PARK HOTEL **$$$$**
Posadas 1232, tel. 011/4819-1100, www.caesar-park.com

Operated by a Mexican chain, the extravagant Caesar Park seems to aspire to the Alvear Palace's traditional greatness, but it's closer to a nouveau riche pretender. An imposingly large lobby is the gateway to large and comfortable rooms—the smallest is 36 square meters—that enjoy access to a state-of-the-art business center, pool and spa, and lush gardens. Upper rooms have unobstructed river views.

Rates start at US$351 s or d, with buffet breakfast included. There are entirely tobacco-free floors, and the service is impeccable.

### CARLTON HOTEL **$$**
Libertad 1180, tel. 011/4812-0081, www.solans.com

The Carlton is a decent business hotel, with well-furnished midsize rooms and buffet breakfast but without luxuries. Its zooming rates of

US$132/144 s/d with breakfast have more to do with its location than with its presumptive four-star status.

## DAZZLER HOTEL 💲💲

Libertad 902, tel. 011/4816-5005,
www.dazzlerhotel.com

Overlooking Plaza Libertad, the Dazzler prides itself on "park view" rooms that overlook the plaza's dense wooded canopy. Rates start around US$102 s or d, reasonable enough in this part of town, but the hotel (which opened in the dark days of 2002) has shown early signs of corner-cutting or substandard workmanship. The facilities and amenities are still good enough, though, and the service is assiduous.

## FEIR'S PARK HOTEL 💲💲

Esmeralda 1366, tel. 011/4131-1900,
www.feirspark.com.ar

Barely two blocks from Plaza San Martín and only half a block from Avenida del Libertador, the 115 spacious suites at Feir's Park offer slightly lower prices than other nearby luxury facilities. Some of them, though, have awkward floor plans: The executive suites (US$254 s or d) are bright and cheerful where the sunlight penetrates from their outdoor terraces, but the light can't easily reach the recesses of their long, narrow interiors. The ambassador suites (US$285 s or d) have better floor plans but smaller terraces.

## FOUR SEASONS HOTEL BUENOS AIRES 💲💲💲💲

Posadas 1086, tel. 011/4321-1200,
www.fourseasons.com/buenosaires

Operated by an international chain, this luxury hotel consists of a 1990s tower with a contemporary sensibility, but also includes seven suites in an adjacent belle epoque mansion large and opulent enough to satisfy any Francophile visitor—the presidential suite covers 180 square meters. In aspirations and style, if not quite precisely in location, this hotel embodies the Recoleta sensibility. Rates start at US$450 s or d per night, plus 21 percent IVA (a lavish breakfast costs US$15 more), but there

La Mansión is the Four Seasons Hotel Buenos Aires's elegant older sector.

are occasional special packages. Not really in Recoleta, though it claims to be, it regularly makes the top ten lists of magazines such as *Travel + Leisure* and *Condé Nast Traveler*.

### GRAN HOTEL ORLY ❸❸
Paraguay 474, tel. 011/4312-5344,
www.orly.com.ar

The 180-room Orly is often full at rates of US$65/70 s/d, breakfast and taxes included, because it offers good value for money. Close to Plaza San Martín, Puerto Madero, and the Microcentro, its rooms are utilitarian but utterly reliable.

### HOTEL CONQUISTADOR ❸❸❸
Suipacha 948, tel. 011/4328-3012,
www.elconquistador.com.ar

Just off Avenida Santa Fe, the Conquistador is a modern multistory hotel appealing primarily to commercial travelers, with its business center, meeting rooms, workout facilities, and the like. Rates starting at US$169/177 s/d include a buffet breakfast.

### HOTEL DE LAS AMÉRICAS ❸❸❸
Libertad 1020, tel. 011/4129-4003,
www.grupoamericas.com.ar

Renovated in 2007, this 150-room hotel has king-size beds, telephones, dataports, voicemail, double-paned windows, bar and restaurant, and parking. The service is almost uniformly professional except for the front desk, which can show apparent indifference toward some requests; on the other hand, they'll open the breakfast salon at 5 A.M. for guests who have an early flight. Rates are US$161/172 s/d with an elaborate breakfast buffet.

### HOTEL NH CRILLÓN ❸❸
Av. Santa Fe 796, tel. 011/4310-2000,
www.nh-hoteles.com

The Crillón's Parisian style is not quite classic—it dates only from 1968, long after Buenos Aires's early-20th-century Francophile building boom—but its details and especially its staff project the feeling of a more venerable and far more exclusive place. Absorbed by the

Spanish NH chain, it hasn't needed as much upgrading as the Lancaster and others.

Near Plaza San Martín, its rooms offer all the contemporary comforts, including air-conditioning, cable TV, telephone, WiFi, voicemail, and even a cell phone; the corner rooms, though, are larger and have better views toward the Plaza. Rates start at US$125 s or d, with buffet breakfast.

### HOTEL PARK PLAZA KEMPINSKI ❸❸
Parera 183, tel. 011/6777-0200,
www.parkplazahotels.com

In a quiet location on the edge of fashionable Recoleta, the 54-room Park Plaza Kempinski has that Francophile style, but it's less appealing and slightly less well maintained than its nearby competitors. So-called "luxury" rooms (US$266 s or d) are really overpriced; the executive suites (US$339 s or d), with their sleeping lofts, are more interesting but there are better values in the vicinity.

### HOTEL PRESIDENTE ❸❸
Cerrito 850, tel. 011/4816-2222,
www.hotelpresidente.com.ar

Oriented toward business travelers, the well-located Presidente is a modern high-rise with 181 rooms, 28 suites, and 35 apartments. Rates start at US$127 s or d with breakfast, cable TV, Internet, gym and sauna, parking, room service, and other amenities. Its 24-hour business center appeals to the international crowd, as do its nonsmoking rooms.

### IMPALA HOTEL ❸❸
Libertad 1215, tel. 011/4816-0430,
www.hotelimpala.com.ar

Superbly located for a hotel in its category, the three-star Impala has smallish but modern, comfortable, and immaculate rooms for US$96/107 s/d with an ample buffet breakfast. Amenities include a business center; online reservations garner a 10 percent discount.

### MARRIOTT PLAZA HOTEL ❸❸❸❸
Florida 1005, tel. 011/4318-3000, www.marriott.com

Now under international-chain control, the

landmark (1909) Plaza Hotel overlooks Plaza San Martín at the north end of the Florida pedestrian mall. Though it's undergone a significant modernization, its German baroque charm survives and, with the Alvear Palace, this is one of the capital's truly elegant classics. Rates start at US$227–264 s or d and climb from there, but there are occasional discounts.

### NH HOTEL LANCASTER ❸❸

Av. Córdoba 405, tel. 011/4131-6464, www.nh-hoteles.com

Graham Greene, appropriately enough, once stayed at the British-styled Lancaster, which figures briefly in his novels *The Honorary Consul* and *Travels with My Aunt*. Really a hotel of another era, it still boasts marble staircases and burnished woodwork, but the Spanish NH chain has upgraded the rooms and all other facilities. Sadly enough, that also means the classic English-style pub on the ground floor has gone. Rates are US$135 s or d with breakfast.

### PARK TOWER HOTEL ❸❸❸❸

Av. Leandro N. Alem 1193, tel. 011/4318-9100, www.starwoodhotels.com

Dating from 1996, the Park Tower is the adjacent Sheraton's nouveau riche stepbrother—the two share a parent corporation, as well as gym and pool facilities, and even some doorways. The Park Tower, though, distinguishes itself from its elder, slightly aging sibling; in fact, it's distinguished itself enough to make the *Travel + Leisure* top-ten list of Latin American hotels. The hotel is newer and considerably more luxurious than the Sheraton and is often the choice of visiting dignitaries.

Famous figures who have enjoyed the 23rd-floor presidential suite include Brad Pitt, Bill and Hillary Clinton, and Luciano Pavarotti. In February 2005, populist president Hugo Chávez of Venezuela caused a commotion when Argentine *piquetero* (picketer) sympathizers—not usually seen on properties like these—gathered in hopes of meeting him. The Park Tower's rates start at US$296 s or d, but suites go for nearly US$600.

### RECOLETA YOUTH HOSTEL ❸

Libertad 1216, tel. 011/4812-4419, www.trhostel.com.ar

Boasting the most prestigious location in its category, this HI-affiliated hostel occupies an erstwhile mansion typical of Francophile Recoleta (though it lies geographically within Retiro, it's *close* to the Recoleta line). Bunks in multi-bedded rooms with shared bath and separate lockers cost US$11 pp; those with private bath cost US$13 pp. It also has private rooms for US$34–50 d, depending on shared or private bath; all rates include breakfast. There are ample shared spaces, including kitchen facilities.

### 🄲 SHERATON BUENOS AIRES HOTEL ❸❸❸

San Martín 1225, tel. 011/4318-9000, www.starwoodhotels.com

Near Puerto Madero, across from Plaza Fuerza Aérea Argentina, the mammoth 742-room high-rise Sheraton gets lots of international business trade but also plenty of tourists, especially in summer. Executive suites occupy most of the upper floors.

In addition to its accommodations, the Sheraton has tennis courts, an ample fitness center, a complex of indoor and outdoor swimming pools, two restaurants, and a gallery of high-class shopping options. The views from its 24th floor may be the city's best, with panoramas ranging from Plaza San Martín to the Retiro railroad stations and bus terminal, the current freight port, and the Buquebus passenger terminal, plus glimpses of Puerto Madero. Most of this floor, unfortunately, is closed to the public.

Rates start around US$232 s or d, but executive suites go for around US$290 s or d.

### SOFITEL BUENOS AIRES ❸❸❸❸

Arroyo 841, tel. 011/4131-0000, www.sofitel.com

If the Caesar Park is a failed effort to surpass the Alvear Palace's Parisian elegance, the Sofitel Buenos Aires comes closer to the mark: This modernization of the neoclassical Torre Mihanovich (1929) is a more credible effort at blending the Francophile tradition in *porteño* hotels with current design trends and modern functions. Rates for its 144 luminous rooms start at US$420 s or d, but ostensible "luxury" rooms (US$550 s or d) have larger bathrooms and slightly better views on one of the city's quietest blocks, known for its upscale art galleries. The lobby is an architectural masterpiece.

# Recoleta and Barrio Norte                    Map 6

Like Retiro, the Recoleta/Barrio Norte area has few budget accommodations, but among the ones it has, some are excellent. Some of the city's top upmarket hotels are also here.

## ALFA HOTEL ⑤

Riobamba 1064, tel. 011/4812-3719, www.alfahotel.com.ar
This is a small but well-kept and well-priced Barrio Norte choice with rates starting at US$47/58 s/d, but some slightly more expensive rooms have undergone substantial upgrades. All rooms have private bath, cable TV, telephone, and air-conditioning, with taxes and breakfast included; there's a 10 percent discount for cash payments.

## ⟨ ALVEAR PALACE HOTEL ⑤⑤⑤⑤

Av. Alvear 1891, tel. 011/4805-2100,
www.alvearpalace.com
Since 1928, the Alvear Palace Hotel has symbolized *porteño* elegance and luxury—not to mention wealth and privilege. Even during and after the 2002 crisis, it has maintained both its standards and its prices—rack rates start around US$660 s or d for the simplest suite and range up to US$5,445 for the royal suite; room amenities include Egyptian cotton sheets, Hermés toiletries, and three plasma TVs in every room—even at the foot of the whirlpool-equipped bathtub.

Francophobes may find the *ancien régime* decor cloying, but both *Travel + Leisure* and

the breakfast buffet at the Alvear Palace Hotel

© WAYNE BERNHARDSON

*Condé Nast Traveler* have consistently ranked it at or near the top of Latin America's hotel list and as one of the world's finest. All the suites undergo renovation on a rotating basis—rather like the Golden Gate Bridge, where the task of painting starts again as soon as it's finished.

In addition to its landmark restaurants La Bourgogne and L'Orangerie (with its stunning winter garden), the Alvear Palace has state-of-the art gym and spa facilities, plus high-end shopping in its adjacent gallery. Compulsive shoppers, though, will not lack for other options in this neighborhood.

Unlike many elite hotels, the Alvear Palace does not impose surcharges for services such as WiFi.

### ART HOTEL ⑤⑤
Azcuénaga 1268, tel. 011/4821-4744,
www.arthotel.com.ar

Behind the reception desk, shelves of bulky law books make a misleadingly formal entryway to this creatively rehabbed, 36-room boutique hotel and art space that was once a rooming house. Having stripped decades of paint to reveal its natural wood features, it has four kinds of rooms: "small and cozy" (US$85–105 s or d), queen (US$125 s or d), king (US$150 s or d), and king with balcony (US$190 s or d). Rates include taxes and breakfast; all rooms have high-speed Internet connections, and stylish but unpretentious furnishings disguise the cable TV and mini-bar.

Exhibits at the street-level art space, which change monthly, show well thanks to natural illumination from the 5th-floor skylight. All works are for sale, and this part of the hotel is open to the public during normal business hours.

### ART SUITES ⑤⑤
Azcuénaga 1465, tel. 011/4821-6800

Down the block from, but utterly unrelated to, its near namesake the Art Hotel, Art Suites is a sleekly modern "aparthotel" with light-filled suites, some with balconies, whose rates include a continental breakfast, though it's not a full-service hotel. Rates start at US$115 plus 21 percent IVA for an "executive" apartment, US$132

plus IVA for "penthouse" accommodations, and US$174 for "premium" rooms. As it gets business clientele as well as leisure travelers, in-room Internet access is universal at no extra cost.

### AYACUCHO PALACE HOTEL ⑤⑤
Ayacucho 1408, tel. 011/4806-1815,
www.ayacuchohotel.com.ar

It's less palatial than either its name or the elegant exterior suggests, but this is a solid, quiet mid-range hotel with friendly staff and 70 smallish but immaculate and well-furnished rooms. Rates of US$67/83 s/d include taxes and breakfast, and all the bathrooms have tubs. It's also on or near several key bus lines.

### DESIGN SUITES ⑤⑤⑤⑤
Marcelo T. de Alvear 1683, tel. 011/4814-8700,
www.designsuites.com

Though not quite new, the Design Suites is a still-sparkling boutique-style hotel with a striking ground-floor solarium and twin towers of 20 spacious suites each; amenities include cable TV, telephone, Internet and fax connections, kitchenette, minibar, air-conditioning, strongbox, and whirlpool tub. Rates start at US$260 s or d for standard rooms but rise to USD$315 s or d for two-room suites.

### ETOILE HOTEL ⑤⑤
Roberto M. Ortiz 1835, tel. 011/4805-2626,
www.etoile.com.ar

Facing Recoleta's famous cemetery, the high-rise Etoile is a modern place that lacks the character of older upscale *porteño* hotels but partly compensates with its location and services. Accommodations range from large bedrooms with interior light to sprawling suites with cemetery and plaza views; all have balconies, and many have been recently updated. Rates, starting around US$138 s or d, include breakfast and access to the 14th-floor spa, but Internet access costs US$10 extra.

### GUIDO PALACE HOTEL ⑤⑤
Guido 1780, tel. 011/4812-0674,
www.guidopalace.com.ar

Extraordinarily friendly, this modest hotel has

personality—the tiny antique elevator is a classic—but no frills other than its prime Recoleta location. The rooms are small but well-kept with decent natural light, but most bathrooms have showers rather than tubs. Rates (US$87/97 s/d) do *not* include breakfast, but its adjacent café will provide room service at no extra charge.

### HOTEL BEL AIR $$$
Arenales 1462, tel. 011/4021-4000,
www.hotelbelair.com.ar

In an ideal Barrio Norte location, only the elegant 1920s facade remains unchanged in this classy, modernized 77-room hotel, which has separate smoking and nonsmoking floors. One room has facilities for guests with disabilities.

On the ground level, the Bel Air has an inviting restaurant/wine bar called Bisabis, as well as a Business Corner with Internet access (also available in the rooms). Rates run from US$160/170 to US$176/186 s/d with breakfast.

### HOTEL DEL PRADO $
Paraguay 2385, tel. 011/4961-1192,
www.hoteldelprado-ba.com.ar

Near the Facultad de Medicina, the Prado is a simply but tastefully remodeled older building with a quiet interior, good beds, and friendly owner-operators. Rates start at US$22/25 s/d for rooms with private bath, a modest buffet breakfast, cable TV, telephone, and ceiling fans but no air-conditioning. Discounts are possible for stays of three days or more.

### HOTEL PLAZA FRANCIA $$
Eduardo Schiaffino 2189, tel. 011/4804-9631,
www.hotelplazafrancia.com

Close to Recoleta restaurants, entertainment, and open spaces, as well as the landmark cemetery, the Plaza Francia is a cozy multi-story hotel with rooms ranging from standard interior (US$113 s or d) to deluxe exterior (US$126 s or d) and junior suites (US$159 s or d), with buffet breakfast and amenities

like a business center. Some rooms face busy Avenida Libertador and the highest have river views, but effective sound insulation keeps things quiet

### HOTEL PRÍNCIPE $
Laprida 1454, tel. 011/4821-9818,
www.hotel-principe.com.ar

Rooms at the modest Príncipe are really mini-apartments with a refrigerator and sink (but no other kitchen facilities) for US$53/67 s/d with taxes and breakfast. While it's sound enough, its strongest point is its Barrio Norte location.

### JUNCAL PALACE HOTEL $
Juncal 2282, tel. 011/4821-2770,
www.juncalpalacehotel.com.ar

The 26-room Juncal Palace (US$40/50 s/d) remains one of the city's better values. Once a single-family home, this 1930s art deco building, embellished with glistening oak woodwork and Carrara marble staircases, inhabits a solid Barrio Norte location.

### LOI SUITES RECOLETA $$$$
Vicente López 1955, tel. 011/5777-8950,
www.loisuites.com.ar

Loi's neoclassical columns make a misleading approach to one of the city's most contemporary hotels. The hotel opened in 2001 and is a design pioneer for its open floor plan and use of natural light—with its retractable roof, the spectacular central pool house doubles as a breakfast solarium. Its 112 identically decorated rooms, for which rates range from US$300 to US$520 s or d, vary in size only.

### MELIÁ RECOLETA PLAZA $$$$
Posadas 1557, tel. 011/5353-4000, www.solmelia.com

Acquired in 2006 by the Spanish Meliá chain, this modern boutique-style hotel offers ample-sized suites (about 38–80 square meters) and affordable prices (from US$260 s or d) for the area. In a neighborhood where Francophilia runs rampant, and just down the block from Evita's old Recoleta haunts, its clean simplicity adds a welcome note of variety.

## PALACIO DUHAU-PARK HYATT
## BUENOS AIRES $$$$

Av. Alvear 1661, tel. 011/5171-1234,
www.buenosaires.park.hyatt.com

In 2006, the Hyatt chain rehabbed a crumbling mansion and, on the other side of its terraced gardens, erected a sparkling new tower that, nevertheless, fits into one of the city's elite historical neighborhoods. The former, the Palacio Duhau, retains its architectural integrity, but the rooms and suites showcase the latest in contemporary hotel design. The latter, the Posadas building (so called for its entrance on the parallel street), also enjoys an underground link that makes it easily accessible for the wheelchair-bound (in fact, the entire hotel is suitable for the handicapped). In all, there are 165 rooms and suites.

In addition to its rooms, the Duhau has a sophisticated modern wine bar with an adjacent cheese closet (showcasing Argentine-made varieties only). There are two fine restaurants (one with a decidedly Francophile orientation), a corridor art gallery that changes its offerings every 45 days, a 25-meter indoor swimming pool, and its Ahín Spa may be the city's best.

All this comes at Alvear Palace–level prices: The basic room rate is US$585 s or d plus 21 percent IVA, and the suites cost up to US$2,500 plus IVA.

## PRINCE HOTEL $

Arenales 1627, tel. 011/4811-8004,
www.princehotel.com.ar

In an almost ideal location on a shady but central street, the modest Prince Hotel offers cozy, quiet, and well-kept rooms, with attractive color schemes, in a building dating from 1917. Amenities include air-conditioning and cable TV; rates of US$57/70 s/d with breakfast are fair enough for a place with truly attentive, friendly personnel.

## SOUTHERN HOUSE BA $

Anchorena 1117, tel. 011/4961-6933,
www.southernhouseba.com

Utterly transformed from what was Barrio

© WAYNE BERNHARDSON

ACCOMMODATIONS

Recoleta's Palacio Duhau-Park Hyatt Buenos Aires has attracted attention even among the growing roster of elite hotels.

Norte's cheapest option, Southern House still has spacious dorms (US$12 pp) with four to six beds each, but they now have private baths instead of down-the-hall facilities. Doubles go for US$50, and there's also a lone single for US$25. In addition, it has WiFi and large common areas, including a kitchen, a bar, and a lushly landscaped interior patio.

## WILTON HOTEL $$

Av. Callao 1162,
tel. 011/4811-1818,
www.hotelwilton.com.ar

For US$99–148 s or d with breakfast, the Wilton is a solid mid-range hotel, but its formal four-star category seems an exaggeration. Its 120 rooms are simply decorated but spacious enough, and double-paned windows reduce the noise from the busy avenue. Rates include a buffet breakfast and access to its gym and business center.

# Palermo Map 7

Palermo's traditional budget accommodations, in the immediate vicinity of Plaza Italia, are generally not bad, but with a couple notable exceptions they're unremarkable. In recent years, though, Palermo Viejo has witnessed an influx of quality hostels, bed-and-breakfasts, and a growing number of intimate boutique hotels that are easy walking distance to restaurants and nightlife, but not so close that it's impossible to sleep at a reasonable hour. The neighborhood is well served by public transportation, both Subte and buses.

### ALPINO HOTEL ●
Cabello 3318, tel. 011/4802-5151,
www.hotel-alpino.com.ar
Located in the heart of the Palermo neighborhood, with quick access to many major sights and attractions, the Alpino Hotel (US$67/80 s/d) is a solid three-star hotel in a desirable, picturesque area that has few accommodations of any sort. The rooms are basic but comfortable and spacious.

### B&B BAYRES ●●
Av. Córdoba 5842, tel. 011/4772-3877,
www.bayresbnb.com
Strictly speaking, it's in Villa Crespo, but this spacious, sunny, and well-furnished bed-and-breakfast is literally just across the avenue from the abundant restaurants and bars of fashionable Palermo Hollywood. With only six guest rooms, its owners cater to gay men and lesbians; three rooms use shared baths while the other three have private baths, but all have access to the ample common spaces, including an enormous living room and a large, sunny terrace. Rates range from US$45/55 to US$65/75 s/d with buffet breakfast, depending on the facilities; the more expensive rooms have their own private terraces.

### BAUCIS BOUTIQUE HOTEL ●●
Carranza 1612, tel. 011/5235-5555,
www.baucishotel.com
New in late 2007, the Baucis has climbed aboard the boutique bandwagon as one of few hotels in Palermo Hollywood. A recycled single-family house, it retains a traditional facade, but some of the upper-floor exteriors are nondescript even though the rooms themselves are fine. In fact, the reception area is fairly drab compared to the spacious rooms, several of which have whirlpool tubs. Rates start at US$88/110 s/d, but the more luminous upstairs suites go for US$199 s or d, including taxes, a buffet breakfast, and a glass of Malbec on arrival.

### BOBO HOTEL ●●●
Guatemala 4882, tel. 011/4774-0505,
www.bobohotel.com
This self-deprecatingly style-conscious Palermo SoHo boutique hotel takes its name from U.S. author David Brooks, who coined the ironic term "bourgeois bohemians" to describe middle-class individuals with counter-cultural pretensions (in Spanish, for what it's worth, *bobo* is synonymous with stupid). Still, with its seven individually distinctive rooms and gourmet bar/restaurant, this quickly became one of the classiest options in a barrio that still has relatively few accommodations, and it's an ideal location for anyone who wants dozens of other gourmet dining options within easy walking distance. Rates range US$162–204 s or d, depending on the room.

### CASA ALFARO ●●
Gurruchaga 2155, tel. 011/4831-0517,
www.casaalfaro.com.ar
This is a charming house, dating from 1926, on a narrow but deep lot. Its 11 cozy rooms and one family suite feature high ceilings and share inviting common areas and several shady patios. Rates, ranging US$48–120 s or d with continental breakfast, depend on whether or not the room has a private bath. Casa Alfaro offers WiFi, English-speaking personnel, and air-conditioning.

## CASA JARDÍN ❸

Charcas 4422, tel. 011/4774-8783,
www.casajardinba.com.ar

Billing itself as a "creative hostel," the intimate Casa Jardín can accommodate only about 13 guests in an art-infused ambience with ample common spaces and gregarious management who act more like friends than business owners (though it's efficiently run). Dorm accommodations cost US$13 pp, while the only private room costs US$18 s or d; all baths are shared, however. Casa Jardín is tobacco-free except for the balconies and the enormous rooftop terrace.

## ◖ CHE LULU GUEST HOUSE ❸

Emilio Zolá 5185, tel. 011/4772-0289,
www.luluguesthouse.com

On a block-long street where the original cobbles still show through slabs of pavement, Che Lulu is an artist-inspired bed-and-breakfast where seven small but colorful rooms with rustically styled furniture go for bargain prices, ranging from US$20 pp in a double or quad to US$65 d with breakfast. Their main shortcoming is a lack of closet space, which can mean living out of a suitcase or backpack.

The large common areas, well-isolated from the bedrooms in this three-story house, make staying at the Lulu a sociable experience. While close to a busy avenue and a suburban railroad line, it's quiet and also easy walking distance to the restaurants and nightlife of both Palermo SoHo and Palermo Hollywood.

## FIVE COOL ROOMS BUENOS AIRES ❸❸

Honduras 4742, tel. 011/4774-8783,
www.fivebuenosaires.com

Built from scratch, rather than recycled, the deceptively named Five actually is a design hotel with a total of 17 rooms in three categories: small, medium, and large (the "five" derives from the number of brothers and sisters who own the place). The management deserves truth-in-labeling credit for the 11 "smalls," but in truth they're a bit bigger than the name implies: king-size beds, though, occupy most of the floor space. The baths are likewise compact but the showers spacious.

The capacious common areas, including a reading room, two large patios, and an even larger rooftop terrace with a whirlpool tub, help compensate for any small interior spaces. The entire hotel enjoys a quiet seclusion uncommon in this part of town, despite being surrounded by restaurants, bars, and shops.

Rates for the smalls are US$128 s or d, but the "mediums" that face the street, with stylish balconies and whirlpool tubs for US$170 s or d, may be better values. The "large" rooms go for US$170–194, depending on whether or not it has a whirlpool tub, but an "extra-large" with a separate private terrace costs US$242 s or d. There's WiFi throughout.

## HOTEL COSTA RICA ❸

Costa Rica 4137, tel. 011/4864-7390,
www.hotelcostarica.com.ar

In Palermo's "Villa Freud" neighborhood, this French-run property falls at the affordable end of the boutique hotel scale. Restored to their original configurations, with high ceilings in what was once a crowded family hotel, its 25 rooms are well-furnished but plain and frills-free (no TV, for instance).

A few rooms are unavoidably dark, but the hotel enjoys ample common spaces, including a bar, a patio, and two rooftop terraces suitable for barbecues. While less convenient than some barrio hotels, it's easy walking distance to the restaurants and bars of Palermo SoHo.

Rates, which include taxes, start at US$55 d for rooms with shared bath that, however, enjoy immediate access to the rooftop terrace. Rooms with private bath go for US$70–90 d. WiFi is available only in the lobby.

## ◖ HOTEL HOME BUENOS AIRES ❸❸❸

Honduras 5860, tel. 011/4779-1008,
www.homebuenosaires.com

Ever since the Bush twins partied in Palermo while their father's Republican party took a thumpin' in the 2006 U.S. midterm elections, every taxi driver in town knows where to find Hotel Home Buenos Aires. Even U2 stayed here (and welcomed other guests to their party) when they played Buenos Aires, but you

© WAYNE BERNHARDSON

Hotel Home Buenos Aires was the first design hotel in Palermo Hollywood.

needn't be a big name to enjoy its imaginative design, spacious rooms and suites, and ample common spaces, including a large garden with pool that's uncommon in this part of town. With neighboring properties, it forms a mini-greenbelt that's remarkably quiet for such a lively neighborhood.

Rates range US$120–155 s or d, plus taxes, with a few pricier suites and lofts; a secluded garden apartment goes for US$335. It also has a restaurant whose weekend brunch menu, in particular, is worth consideration; at the same time, it provides its own English-language pocket guide to nearby (and more distant) restaurants, entertainment, and shopping.

### HOTEL PALERMO ⑤
Godoy Cruz 2725, tel. 011/4774-7342,
www.hotel-palermo.com.ar
The barrio's oldest hotel, the Palermo began as accommodations for *estancieros* who came to the capital for livestock shows at the nearby Predio Ferial de la Sociedad Rural Argentina, but the cattle barons have since found more sumptuous

alternatives. Rates are US$43/50 s/d for small-ish but impeccable rooms that, post-renovation, lack the character they once had.

### LEGADO MÍTICO BUENOS AIRES ⑤⑤⑤
Gurruchaga 1848, tel. 011/4833-1300,
www.legadomitico.com
Every one of the 11 rooms at Legado Mítico takes its theme from a historic figure in Argentina's past and, if a couple of them had ever gotten together in the same room—most notably the 20th-century contemporaries Eva Perón and writer Victoria Ocampo—at least one would likely never have left alive. It might seem ironic that one of the largest and most luxurious is the "The Idealist" dedicated to Ernesto "Che" Guevara, but Guevara's family background placed him among the Argentine elite.

Legado Mítico's decor is a blend of classic and contemporary, with French-style furnishings often side by side with modern designs. Beyond the reception area, the entire ground floor is a single room that leads to a large patio where two rows of poplars will soon grow too large for the space and are likely to be removed. The room contains a small breakfast nook beneath a skylight and one side is a library where each historical figure has his or her own shelf. Oddly enough, for a hotel whose clientele is mostly foreign, nearly all the books are in Spanish, even though many works by and about Jorge Luis Borges, for instance, have appeared in English.

New in December 2007, Legado Mítico sits in the midst of Palermo's gourmet ghetto, with dozens of quality restaurants, not to mention shopping opportunities, within easy walking distance. Rates range from US$190 for "classic" rooms to US$250 for "luxury" rooms; the primary difference is size, though some of the classic rooms have tubs as well as showers. Rates do not include 21 percent IVA.

## MALABIA HOUSE $$$
Malabia 1555, tel. 011/4832-3345 or 011/4833-2410, www.malabiahouse.com.ar
Occupying a painstakingly remodeled 19th-century *casa chorizo*, Malabia House has become a stylish bed-and-breakfast with magnificent natural light, glistening wooden floors, handsome furnishings, and small but attractive patio gardens. Standard ground-floor rooms (US$145 s or d with breakfast) have external private baths; more expensive upstairs rooms (US$175–200 s or d) have air-conditioning and interior baths. There's a 10 percent discount for cash payment.

## TAILOR MADE HOTEL
Arce 385, tel. 011/4774-9620, www.tailormadehotels.com
Unlike Palermo Viejo, the fashionable Las Cañitas neighborhood near the Campo Argentino de Polo had failed to attract boutique hoteliers until the opening of the five-room Tailor Made Hotel in late 2007. The luminous rooms have almost total privacy, complete quiet, and clean modern furnishings, including Mac computers hooked up to 32-inch plasma screen TVs. The neighborhood offers good shopping and some bars, but the best restaurants are in Palermo Viejo, which is easy walking distance from the hotel.

Room rates (including taxes) at Tailor Made range from US$230 (rooms 1 and 3), US$305

(rooms 2 and 4), and US$430 (room 5, which is larger and has a rooftop terrace).

## TANGO BACKPACKER'S HOSTEL $
Thames 2212, tel. 011/4776-6871, www.tangobp.com
In Palermo SoHo's sleep-all-day, party-all-night sector, this HI affiliate occupies a grand old house that boasts a rooftop terrace with a *parrilla* for barbecues, a large kitchen, and free Internet access, plus dining and partying recommendations from the staff, who also lead inexpensive guided tours around town. Rates range from US$10 pp in dorms to US$35 s or d in private rooms.

## TORRE CRISTÓFORO COLOMBO $$
Santa María de Oro 2747, tel. 011/4778-4900, www.torrecc.com.ar
Rising well above everything else in this quiet, leafy neighborhood, the Colombo tower contains 160 fully equipped suites with kitchenettes and patios, accommodating 2–4 persons. Rates start around US$95 s or d with breakfast included, but larger units don't cost that much more. Until Palermo Hollywood's Home Buenos Aires opened, this was the only barrio hotel with a pool.

## VAIN BOUTIQUE HOTEL $$$
Thames 2226, tel. 011/4776-8246, www.vainuniverse.com.ar
In style-conscious Palermo SoHo, the Vain might be a hotel with attitude or, perhaps, one that doesn't take itself deadly seriously. Behind a traditional facade, the 15 nonsmoking rooms in the nearly totally recycled interior come in four categories: "V" (senior suites, US240 s or d); "A" (junior suites, US$224 s or d); "I" (superior, US$192 s or d), and "N" (US$150 s or d).

That said, there are anomalies in these categories. Some standard rooms, for instance, have whirlpool tubs, while superior rooms may have only showers (though they're state of the art, in honesty). The common areas are spectacular, particularly the luminous rooftop lounge and adjacent deck, and the design is clean, almost Scandinavian in concept. And how many hotels offer not just a welcome cocktail, but also a welcome facial?

# EXCURSIONS FROM BUENOS AIRES

When *porteños* tire of the city, there are plenty of nearby escapes both within and beyond Buenos Aires province. Truly unique are the intricate channels of the Río Paraná delta, easily reached by launch from the increasingly fashionable northern suburb of Tigre, itself easily reached by train. One of the highlights is the island of Martín García, a colonial fortress and onetime prison camp that offers nature trails and historic architecture.

Built on a grid resembling that of Washington, D.C., the streets of the provincial capital of La Plata, only an hour southeast, feature imposing architecture and cultural resources (including theaters and museums) that many national capitals cannot match. An hour west of Buenos Aires, the city of Luján, with its towering basilica, is a major pilgrimage destination and home to an impressive complex of historical museums. Another half-hour west, San Antonio de Areco is Argentina's symbolic gaucho capital.

For those wishing to go farther afield, daily ferries cross the Río de la Plata to the Uruguayan destinations of Carmelo (a quiet riverside resort), the town of Colonia (a UNESCO World Heritage Site for its 18th-century core), the capital city of Montevideo (a repository of colonial and art deco architecture), and the Atlantic beach resort of Punta del Este (traditionally overrun by Argentines in January and February).

In general, this chapter's excursions cover afternoon getaways, day trips, or weekend destinations that do not require air travel (that's an option for Uruguay, but not a particularly

# HIGHLIGHTS

LOOK FOR ◖ TO FIND RECOMMENDED SIGHTS, ACTIVITIES, DINING, AND LODGING.

◖ **Best Ex-Prison:** Just off the Uruguayan coast, its bedrock rising out of the River Plate's muddy waters, **Isla Martín García** has been a colonial fortress and even a political penal colony, but today it's an absorbing historical and natural getaway from Buenos Aires's bustle (page 195).

◖ **Best Pilgrimage:** The truly devout can walk 62 kilometers from Buenos Aires to the chamber of the Virgencita, Argentina's patron saint, in Luján's **Basílica Nacional Nuestral Señora de Luján** (page 198).

◖ **Best Time-Travel:** In the placid pampas west of Luján, Argentina's gaucho capital of San Antonio de Areco embodies a romantic vision of the countryside's past. Revel in that romantic idealization at **Parque Criollo y Museo Gauchesco Ricardo Güiraldes,** San Antonio's gaucho museum and 97-hectare park celebrating the *gauchesco* literature of Ricardo Güiraldes (page 204).

◖ **Most Ambitious Museum:** With all the aspirations of an international city, the Buenos Aires province's capital, La Plata, boasts an assemblage of century-old buildings and prestigious educational institutions, including its landmark natural sciences museum **Museo de La Plata.** It makes an ideal day trip from Buenos Aires (page 216).

◖ **Best Spontaneous Revival:** An endangered neighborhood not so long ago, Montevideo's colonial **Ciudad Vieja** has revived with an energy and style that resembles Buenos Aires's Palermo Viejo, with restaurants, bars, live music, theater, museums, and cultural centers (page 227).

◖ **Best Winery Excursion:** With its tasting room, new restaurant, and antique automobile museum, **Bodega Bouza** is best-prepared to receive visitors on a daily basis, but other Montevideo-area wineries are well worthwhile (page 240).

◖ **Best Colonial Complex:** It's not just

Palacio Salvo in Montevideo's Ciudad Vieja

another stamp in your passport – barely an hour from Buenos Aires, in the Uruguayan city of Colonia, the **Barrio Histórico** has the best-preserved colonial core in all the Southern Cone countries. It's a UNESCO World Heritage Site, and rightly so (page 245).

◖ **Best Country Inn:** It's benefited from traffic from the nearby Four Seasons Resort at Carmelo, but the restaurant, winery, and cheeses at the stylishly modernized **Finca y Granja Narbona** are making it an essential stopover in an otherwise out-of-the-way corner of the Uruguayan littoral. For those not at the Four Seasons, Narbona has its own upscale accommodations (page 256).

◖ **Culture in a Vacuum:** Punta del Este may be a monument to brainless hedonism, at least in summer, but painter Carlos Páez Vilaró's nearby hotel, restaurant, and museum, **Casapueblo,** is literally and figuratively a work of art (page 266).

© WAYNE BERNHARDSON

**EXCURSIONS**

EXCURSIONS

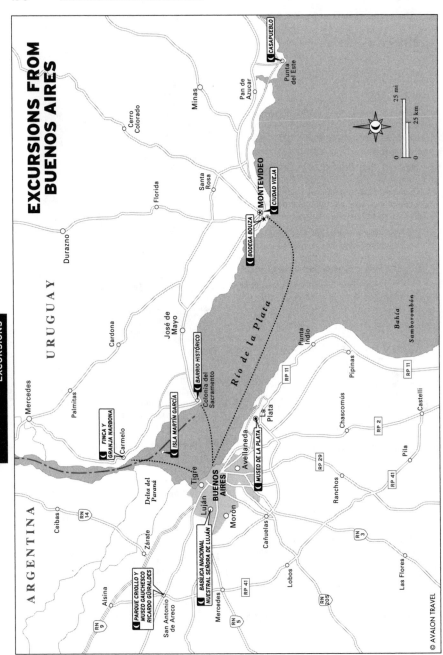

# EXCURSIONS FROM BUENOS AIRES

URUGUAY

ARGENTINA

CASAPUEBLO

Punta del Este

Pan de Azucar

Minas

Cerro Colorado

Florida

Santa Rosa

Durazno

MONTEVIDEO

CIUDAD VIEJA

BODEGA BOUZA

José de Mayo

Cardona

BARRIO HISTÓRICO

Colonia del Sacramento

Río de la Plata

Bahía Samborombón

Punta Indio

Mercedes

Palmitas

FINCA Y GRANJA NARBONA

Carmelo

ISLA MARTÍN GARCÍA

Delta del Paraná

Tigre

BUENOS AIRES

Avellaneda

La Plata

MUSEO DE LA PLATA

Pipinas

RP 11

RP 11

Castelli

Chascomús

RP 2

Pila

RP 41

Ceibas

RN 14

Zárate

Alsina

San Antonio de Areco

PARQUE CRIOLLO Y MUSEO GAUCHESCO RICARDO GÜIRALDES

Luján

Morón

BASÍLICA NACIONAL NUESTRAL SEÑORA DE LUJÁN

Mercedes

RP 41

Cañuelas

Ranchos

RP 29

Lobos

RN 5

RN 205

RN 3

Las Flores

25 mi

25 km

© AVALON TRAVEL

good one because ferries are faster); for this reason, popular but more distant sites, such as the southern Buenos Aires province beach resort of Mar del Plata and the thunderous Iguazú Falls, on the Brazilian border, do not appear here; they do appear in detail, though, in the author's *Moon Argentina.*

## PLANNING YOUR TIME

For the bulk of the excursions here, Buenos Aires is a hub for departures in all directions. For the most part, it's simplest to return to the capital before taking any other excursion.

The exception to this rule is Uruguay: Visitors can travel to Carmelo, Colonia, or Montevideo and return directly to Buenos Aires, but it's also possible to arrange convenient loops, of varying lengths, by public transportation. The simplest would be to take the ferry or catamaran to Colonia for at least an overnight stay or preferably longer, continuing overland to Montevideo and perhaps to Punta del Este for several days more. Instead of returning to Colonia, it's quicker (though more expensive) to take the high-speed catamaran from Montevideo back to Buenos Aires.

Likewise, it's possible to vary the trip by taking a catamaran from the riverside Buenos Aires suburb of Tigre to the placid Uruguayan port of Carmelo, then continue to Colonia and to Montevideo or vice versa, before recrossing the river to Buenos Aires. Punta del Este would be an easy extension from Montevideo.

# Tigre

After decades of decay, flood-prone Tigre is experiencing a renaissance. The train stations are completely renovated, the streets clean, the houses brightly painted (and many restored), and it remains the point of departure for delta retreats and historic Isla Martín García. In a decade-plus, the population has zoomed from a little more than 250,000 to over 300,000.

The number-one attraction near Buenos Aires, Tigre and its Paraná delta are barely half an hour by train from the capital. When the capital swelters in summer heat, the delta's maze of forested channels offers shady relief, just close enough for an afternoon off, but there's plenty to do for a day trip, a weekend, or even longer. The fewer than 4,000 people who inhabit the 950 square kilometers of "the islands" traditionally bring their produce to Tigre's Mercado de Frutos.

## HISTORY

Tigre began as a humble colonial port for Buenos Aires—destined charcoal from the delta, languishing until the railroad connected to the capital in 1865. From the late 19th century, it became a summer sanctuary for the *porteño* elite,

who built imposing mansions, many of which survive. Prestigious rowing clubs constructed extravagant headquarters and ran regattas on the river, but after the 1920s, Tigre settled into a subtropical torpor until its recent revival.

## ORIENTATION

Tigre is 27 kilometers north of Buenos Aires at the confluence of the north-flowing Río Tigre and the Río Luján, which drains southeast into the Río de la Plata. The delta's main channel, parallel to the Río Luján, is the Río Paraná de las Palmas.

East of the Río Tigre, the town is primarily but not exclusively commercial. West of the river, it's largely residential.

## SIGHTS

On the Río Tigre's right bank, along Avenida General Mitre, two classic rowing clubs are symbols of bygone elegance: dating from 1873, the Anglophile **Buenos Aires Rowing Club** (Mitre 226), and its 1910 Italian counterpart the **Club Canottierri Italiani** (Mitre 74). Both still function, but they're not the exclusive institutions they once were.

EXCURSIONS

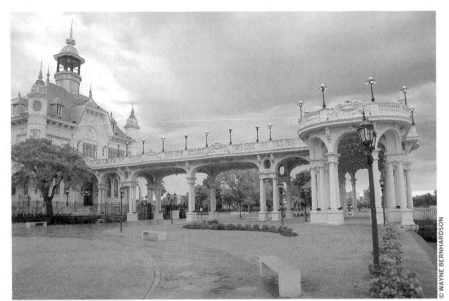

© WAYNE BERNHARDSON

Museo de Arte Tigre

Unfortunately, Tigre's revival has also brought fast-food franchises and the dreadful **Parque de la Costa** (Pereyra s/n, tel. 011/4732-6300, Wed.–Sun. 11 A.M.–midnight, shorter hours in winter, www.parquedelacosta.com.ar), a cheesy theme park. Open admission, valid for all rides and games, costs US$8–12 pp, but is free for children under three.

East of Parque de la Costa is the **Puerto de Frutos** (Sarmiento 160, tel. 011/4512-4493); though its docks no longer buzz with produce transported by launches from the deepest delta, it's home to a revitalized crafts fair that's open daily 11 A.M.–7 P.M. but is most active on weekends. Handcrafted wicker furniture and basketry, as well as flower arrangements, are unique to the area.

In the residential zone across the river, the **Museo de la Reconquista** (Liniers 818, tel. 011/4512-4496, Wed.–Sun. 10 A.M.–6 P.M., free) was the Spanish viceroy's command post while the British occupied Buenos Aires in 1806 and 1807. Not merely a military memorial, it also chronicles the delta, ecclesiastical history, and Tigre's golden age from the 1880s to the 1920s.

Several blocks north, fronting on the Río Luján, the **Museo Naval de la Nación** (Paseo Victorica 602, tel. 011/4749-0608, US$0.65) occupies the former **Talleres Nacionales de Marina** (1879), a cavernous naval repair station that closed as military vessels got too large for its facilities; it provides a narrative of Argentine naval history from its beginnings under Irishman Guillermo Brown to the present. Despite occasional jingoism, it houses a remarkable collection of model ships, along with maps and colonial portraits (including Spanish scientist Juan de Ulloa). An open-air sector includes naval aircraft and the bridge of a ship destroyed by the British during the 1982 Falklands war. Hours are Monday–Friday 8:30 A.M.–5:30 P.M., Saturday–Sunday 10 A.M.–6:30 P.M.

Tigre's newest landmark is the **Museo de Arte Tigre** (Paseo Victorica 972, tel. 011/4512-4528), which houses figurative works by Argentine artists from the late 19th to the

20th century. Housed in the spectacularly restored Tigre Club (1913), a belle epoque edifice that once housed a hotel and casino, it stresses but does not specialize in landscapes, portraits, and still lifes linked to Tigre. Artists represented include major figures such as Benito Quinquela Martín, Juan Carlos Castagnino, and Raúl Soldi. It's open Wednesday–Friday 9 A.M.–9 P.M., Saturday–Sunday and holidays noon–7 P.M.; admission costs US$1.60.

## RESTAURANTS AND ACCOMMODATIONS

Standard Argentine eateries are a dime a dozen at the Puerto de Frutos. One fine choice is **Lo de Negri** (Sarmiento 7, tel. 011/4749-6235, lunch only), a *parrilla* that does roaring weekend business but still manages to combine above-average food with quick and friendly service. Entrées, such as *lomo a la pimienta* (pepper steak) with creamed potatoes, run about US$8.

For a more sophisticated menu on a shady riverside terrace with good service, try 🄲 II **Novo María del Luján** (Paseo Victorica 611, tel. 011/4731-9613, www.ilnovomariadellujan. com, daily from 8:30 A.M.). Homemade pastas cost around US$6–8, more elaborate dishes around US$8–11.

In a classic Tudor-style mansion on the Río Tigre's west bank, the family-run 🄲 **Casona La Ruchi** (Lavalle 557, tel. 011/4749-2499, www.casonalaruchi.com.ar, US$53 d) has five spacious rooms that stay cool even on hot days, thanks to the building's stone-block exterior and high ceilings; there are three shared baths. With its sprawling and lushly landscaped gardens, and a sizeable pool, it's an exceptional value and just across the street from the port for launches to Carmelo, Uruguay.

## INFORMATION

In the Nueva Estación Fluvial, the **Ente Municipal de Turismo** (Mitre 305, tel. 011/4512-4497 or 0800/888-8447, www.tigre. gov.ar) is open daily 9 A.M.–5 P.M.

The private website **Tigre Tiene Todo** (www.tigretienetodo.com.ar) is also useful for services.

## TRANSPORTATION

Tigre is well-connected to Buenos Aires by bus and train, but heavy traffic on the Panamericana Norte makes the bus slow. Through the delta, there are numerous local launches and even international service to the Uruguayan river ports of Carmelo and Nueva Palmira.

### Boat

From Tigre's Nueva Estación Fluvial (Mitre 319), several companies offer *lanchas colectivas,* riverbound buses that drop off and pick up passengers at docks throughout the delta. Among them are **Interisleña** (tel. 011/4749-0900), **Líneas Delta Argentino** (tel. 011/4749-0537, www.lineasdelta .com.ar), and **Jilguero** (tel. 011/4749-0987). **Marsili** (tel. 011/15-4413-4123) and **Giacomotti** (tel. 011/4749-1896) use smaller *lanchas taxi.*

**Cacciola** (Lavalle 520, tel./fax 011/4749-0329, www.cacciolaviajes.com) has daily launches to Carmelo, Uruguay, at 8:30 A.M. and 4:30 and 11:55 P.M. (US$16, 2.5 hours), with bus connections to Montevideo (US$9 more). Fast, new catamarans make the trip quicker and more comfortable than it once was, but it also means they use broader, less scenic channels to get there.

Líneas Delta Argentino also operates launches to the Uruguayan town of Colonia (US$19, 3.5 hours) at 10:30 A.M. daily in summer but only Friday, Saturday, and Sunday the rest of the year. It also goes to Nueva Palmira, Uruguay (three hours; US$17), west of Carmelo, at 7:30 A.M. daily. Launches leave from Cacciola's international terminal, but sales take place at Delta Argentino's across the river.

International schedules may change seasonally.

### Bus

The No. 60 *colectivo* from downtown Buenos Aires runs 24 hours daily, but when traffic is heavy, reaching Tigre can take two hours.

### Train

Tigre has two train stations. From Retiro, Trenes de Buenos Aires (TBA, www.tbanet. com.ar) operates frequent commuter trains on the Ferrocarril Mitre from the capital to **Estación Tigre;** it's also possible to board these trains in Belgrano or suburban stations. The best-maintained and best-run of any rail line into Buenos Aires province, it charges less than US$0.40 each way.

Also from Retiro, a separate branch of the Mitre line runs to Estación Bartolomé Mitre, where passengers transfer at Estación Maipú to the **Tren de la Costa** (tel. 011/4002-6000, www.trendelacosta.com.ar), a tourist train that rumbles through several riverside communities and shopping centers to its terminus at Tigre's **Estación Delta**, at the entrance to the Parque de la Costa. This costs about US$2 including intermediate stops.

# Vicinity of Tigre

Tigre itself may have been revitalized, but many rusting hulks still line the Paraná's inner channels. Farther from Tigre, where colonial smugglers often hid from Spanish officials, summer houses stand on *palafitos* (pilings or stilts) to prevent—not always successfully—their being flooded.

Many operators at Tigre's Nueva Estación Fluvial and the Puerto de Frutos offer 40- to 90-minute excursions that are, not quite literally, enough to get your feet wet in the delta. It's also possible to use the *lanchas colectivas* to get where you want to go, including hotels and restaurants. A word of warning: powerboaters, especially on "personal watercraft," can be as reckless as motorists—don't jump in the water without looking around first.

## SIGHTS

A favorite excursion is the **Museo Histórico Sarmiento** (Río Sarmiento and Arroyo Los Reyes, tel. 011/4728-0570). Dating from 1855, built from fruit boxes and now encased by glass, president Domingo F. Sarmiento's onetime summer residence preserves some of his personal effects. Open Wednesday–Sunday 10 A.M.–6 P.M., it charges no admission; a one-kilometer footpath leads through a typical gallery forest.

For a quick sightseeing orientation, **Catamaranes Interisleñas** (Lavalle 499, tel. 011/4731-0261) has several spacious ships offering one- to two-hour excursions in the immediate vicinity of town (US$5–10 pp). These leave from Escalera 12, a riverside staircase at Mitre and Vivanco on the Río Tigre's right bank, and from the Muelle Municipal, in the 500 block of Lavalle on the left bank.

## RESTAURANTS AND ACCOMMODATIONS

Both accommodations and dining options are increasing in the delta and are accessible by launches from Tigre.

About 25 minutes from Tigre by Interisleña launch, **La Riviera** (Río Sarmiento 356, tel. 011/4728-0177, www.la-riviera.com.ar) offers outdoor dining in good weather, with a wide selection of beef, fish, and pasta dishes.

About 50 minutes from Tigre by Interisleña, **Hostería I'Marangatú** (Río San Antonio 181, tel. 011/4728-0752, www.i-marangatu.com.ar, US$37/60–53/73 s/d weekdays, US$53/70–67/83 s/d weekends and holidays) has 10 rooms; rates include breakfast and dinner.

About 80 minutes from Tigre by Delta Argentino launch, the **〖 Marco Polo Inn Náutico** (Paraná de las Palmas and Cruz Colorada, tel. 011/4728-0395, www.marco-poloinnnautico.com, US$63–73 s or d, US$95 t) is a Hostelling International affiliate with its own sandy beach on the Paraná de las Palmas, a separate pool, a restaurant, and expansive recreational areas including pool tables and a DVD room; it's working on adding a spa with whirlpool tub. The accommodations are simple and relatively small, but bright and cheerful; the rate difference depends on whether

© WAYNE BERNHARDSON

On the Paraná de las Palmas, the Marco Polo Inn Náutico provides inexpensive but stylish accommodations for a few days away from Buenos Aires.

or not the room has air-conditioning. There's WiFi throughout.

About 10 minutes from the Marco Polo by launch, the **Río Laura Hotel & Resort** (Río Paraná de las Palmas, tel. 011/4728-1019, www.riohotellaura.com.ar, US$100–167 s or d) has ample standard rooms and a handful of larger suites with whirlpool tubs, one of which faces the river and has a patio as well. It has spacious grounds and a large restaurant that sometimes offers river fish such as surubí. There are discounts for stays of two nights or longer but, even then, it's not so good a value as the Marco Polo.

Nearby the island of Martín García and the Uruguayan coast, the delta's most exclusive option is the new **La Becasina Delta Lodge** (Arroyo Las Cañas, tel. 011/4728-1253, www.becasina.com, US$147 pp with full board), which has 15 bungalow-suites and no neighbors within sight, for a truly placid getaway. Rates include kayaks, pedal boats, and other sporting gear, but not instruction or guides for them. From Tigre's Estación Fluvial, transportation out and back costs US$38 pp more on their own boat.

## ◖ ISLA MARTÍN GARCÍA

Rising out of the Río de la Plata, almost within swimming distance of the Uruguayan town of Carmelo, the island of Martín García boasts a lush forest habitat, a fascinating history, and an almost unmatchable serenity compared to the frenzied federal capital and even provincial suburbs.

### History

Spanish navigator Juan Díaz de Solís was the first European to see the island, naming it for a crewman who died there in 1516. In colonial times, it changed hands often before finally settling under Spanish control in 1777; in 1814, Guillermo Brown, the Argentine navy's Irish founder, captured it for the Provincias Unidas del Río de la Plata (United Provinces of the River Plate). For a time, mainlanders quarried its granite bedrock for building materials.

For a century, 1870–1970, the navy controlled the island and often used it as a political prison and a regular penal colony, though it was also a quarantine base for European immigrants. The famous Nicaraguan poet Rubén Darío (1867–1916) lived briefly on the island in the early 1900s, while serving as Colombian consul in Buenos Aires.

Political detainees have included presidents Marcelo T. de Alvear (in 1932, after his presidency), Hipólito Yrigoyen (twice in the 1930s), Juan Domingo Perón (1945, before being elected president), and Arturo Frondizi (1962–1963). In World War II's early months, Argentine authorities briefly incarcerated crewmen from the German battleship *Graf Spee,* scuttled off Montevideo in December 1939.

Although the island passed to the United Provinces at independence, it was not explicitly part of Argentina until a 1973 agreement with Uruguay (which was one of the United Provinces). After the navy departed, the Buenos Aires provincial Servicio Penitenciario (Penitentiary Service) used it as a halfway house for run-of-the-mill convicts, but it was also a detention and torture site during the 1976–1983 military dictatorship.

Reached by boat from Tigre, Isla Martín García's Cine-Teatro is the most distinctive of the island's many historic buildings.

## Orientation

Only 3.5 kilometers off the Uruguayan coast but 33.5 kilometers from Tigre, 168-hectare Martín García is not part of the sedimentary delta, but rather a pre-Cambrian bedrock island rising 27 meters above sea level. Its native vegetation is a dense gallery forest, and part of it is a *zona intangible,* a provincial forest reserve.

## Sights

Uphill from the island's *muelle pasajero* (passenger pier), opposite the meticulously landscaped **Plaza Guillermo Brown,** the **Oficina de Informes** was, until recently, the Servicio Penitenciario's headquarters; it now houses provincial park rangers. Along the south shore are several *baterías* (gun emplacements).

At the plaza's upper end stand the ruins of the onetime **cuartel** (military barracks that later became jail cells). Clustered together nearby are the **Cine-Teatro,** the former theater, with its gilt rococo details; the

**Museo de la Isla** (Island Museum); and the former Casa Médicos de Lazareto, the quarantine center now occupied by the **Centro de Interpretación Ecológica** (Environmental Interpretation Center). A bit farther inland, the *faro* (lighthouse, 1881) rises above the trees, but is no longer in use. To the north, the graves of conscripts who died in an early-20th-century epidemic dot the isolated *cementerio* (cemetery).

At the northwest end of the island, trees and vines grow among the crumbling structures of the so-called **Barrio Chino** (Chinatown), marking the approach to the **Puerto Viejo,** the sediment-clogged former port. Across the island, beyond the airstrip, much of the same vegetation grows in the *zona intangible,* which is closed to the public.

## Restaurants and Accommodations

Cacciola's own restaurant **Fragata Hércules** is decent enough, but **Comedor El Solís** is at

## CARICATURING THE GAUCHO

Few non-Argentines know Florencio Molina Campos by name, but many more have seen his paintings. These benign caricatures exaggerated the gaucho's physical features and showed his horses, with oversized heads and expressive eyes, as a physical extension – even an equal partner – of the pampas' legendary horseman.

Buenos Aires-born of a landowning family, Molina Campos (1891–1959) spent his summers on family *estancias* in Buenos Aires and Entre Ríos provinces. That experience taught him the gauchos' traditional virtues of courage, honor, hospitality, and sacrifice, and his art communicated those traits without patronizing his subjects. Following a 1926 exhibition of *motivos gauchos* (gaucho motifs) in Palermo's Predio Ferial de la Sociedad Rural Argentina, he taught drawing at the Colegio Nacional Nicolás Avellaneda for 18 years but continued to travel extensively around the country.

He became famous, though, after the Fábrica Argentina de Alpargatas, which made the linen slippers still common in today's Argentina, hired him to illustrate calendars that sold 18 million copies over 12 years. After traveling to the United States to study animation, he did similar work for the Minneapolis-Moline mills. He also worked on the Walt Disney cartoons *Goofy se Hace Gaucho* (Goofy Becomes a Gaucho), *El Volador Gaucho* (The Flying Gaucho), *El Gaucho Reidor* (The Laughing Gaucho), and *Saludos, Amigos* (Greetings, Friends), though he resigned when Disney's producers rejected his suggestions to make them more "authentic."

In addition to showing them in the United

*Carrera de Sortija*, the gaucho race in which they grab the ring

States, Molina Campos exhibited his paintings, as well as photographs and silverwork, in the United Kingdom, France, and Germany. Some of his gaucho-themed works appear as tiled murals in the Buenos Aires subway (Estación Constitución, Línea C).

Now a residential suburb of Gran Buenos Aires, the city of Moreno (with a population of almost 380,000) is only 36 kilometers west of the capital, but in Molina Campos's time, it was still *tierra de gauchos* (gaucho country). Built in the style of a mid-19th-century *estancia* house, the **Museo Florencio Molina Campos** (Florencio Molina Campos 348) keeps no regular hours, but large groups can arrange special guided visits through the **Fundación Molina Campos** (Ruggieri 2758, Buenos Aires, tel. 011/4804-9312, www.molinacampos.net).

Plans to move the museum collections to new facilities in Buenos Aires are on hold, but Molina Campos's heirs hope the new municipal administration will help find a more convenient site in the capital.

least as good and a bit cheaper; in winter, however, the Solís may be closed. **Panadería Rocío** is known for its fruitcakes.

Crowded in summer and on weekends, **Camping Martín García** (tel. 011/4728-1808, www.campingmartingarcia.com) charges US$3 pp for tent campers; reservations are advisable for hostel bunks with shared bath (US$4 pp) or with private bath (US$6 pp). Cacciola's

*Hostería Martín García* charges US$73 pp for overnight packages with full board that include transportation from Tigre. Each additional night costs US$35 pp.

### Recreation

Though the island offers fine walking and outstanding bird-watching, the river is unsuitable for swimming. The restaurant **Comedor El**

**Solís,** however, has a swimming pool open to the public.

## Transportation

On the Río Tigre's west bank, **Cacciola** (Lavalle 520, Tigre, tel. 011/4749-0329, www.cacciolaviajes.com) offers day trips Tuesday, Thursday, Saturday, and Sunday at 9 A.M., but get there half an hour before departure. Arriving at the island around noon, the tour includes an aperitif on arrival, a guided visit, and lunch at Cacciola's Fragata Hércules. The tour returns to Tigre around 5 P.M., but again get to the dock early. There is ample time for just roaming around.

Cacciola also has a Microcentro office (Florida 520, 1st fl., Oficina 113, tel. 011/4393-6100). Fares for a full-day excursion are US$32 for adults, US$23 for children ages 3–9, including port charges.

# Luján

History and legend blend in Luján, Argentina's single most important devotional center. Modern Luján, though, is an incongruous potpourri of piety and the profane, where pilgrims purchase shoddy souvenirs and, after making their obligatory visit to the landmark basilica, party until dawn.

Luján may merit a visit for the truly devout and those with an intellectual interest in orthodox Catholicism, but what really shines is its complex of historical museums in handsome colonial buildings—improvements have turned Luján from a mildly interesting side trip into a nearly obligatory one.

As a sacred symbol, Luján gets four million visitors per year, mostly on weekends and for religious holidays like Easter and May 8 (the Virgin's day). Also important are events like October's Peregrinación de la Juventud (Youth Pilgrimage), a 62-kilometer walk from Once that acquired a semi-political character during the Dirty War, but has since returned to its devotional origins. For most foreigners, it makes a better day trip, unless *estancia* accommodations are an option.

## HISTORY

Legend says that, in 1630, an oxcart carrying a terra-cotta image of the Virgin Mary stuck in the mud, unable to move until gauchos removed the statue. Its devout owner took this as a sign that the Virgin should remain at the spot and built a chapel for her. Apparently, though, Argentina's patron saint was not totally immovable—she has since shifted to more opulent quarters in the French Gothic basilica, five kilometers from her original abode.

## ORIENTATION

On the right bank of its eponymous river, Luján (pop. 78,005) is about 65 kilometers west of Buenos Aires via RN 7. Most points of interest are on and around Avenida Nuestra Señora de Luján, the broad avenue that enters town from the north, while most services are eastward toward the central Plaza Colón.

## SIGHTS

The basilica may be Luján's most imposing site, but its museums have undergone a professional transformation that transcends the standard stuff-in-glass-cases approach of so many provincial institutions.

### ◖ Basílica Nacional Nuestral Señora de Luján

Glazed in silver to protect her from deterioration, her robes painted in the blue and white of the Argentine flag, the ceramic Virgin is a diminutive 38-centimeter image baked in Brazil. In the 1880s, on a trip to Europe, the French Lazarist missionary Jorge Salvaire created her elaborate crown; apparently deciding that was not enough, he worked tirelessly to build the Gothic basilica whose pointed spires now soar 106 meters above the pampas. Not completed until 1937, its facade has been undergoing a restoration so slow that, once it ends, they may have to start again immediately. Pope John Paul II said Mass here in 1982, only a few days before Argentina's Falklands war surrender.

Twice removed from the world outside, the Virgencita (little virgin) inhabits a separate *camarín* (chamber) behind the main altar; begging her help, pilgrims proceed at a snail's pace past plaques left by their grateful predecessors.

The Basílica Nacional Nuestral Señora de Luján (San Martín 51, tel. 02323/412070, www. basilicadelujan.org.ar, daily 7 A.M.–8 P.M.) overlooks the renovated (but still barren) Plaza Belgrano.

## Complejo Museográfico Enrique Udaondo

On the west side of Avenida Nuestra Señora de Luján, immediately north of the basilica, the former *cabildo* (colonial town council, 1797) and the **Casa del Virrey** (House of the Viceroy, 1803) hold one of the country's finest museum assemblages. No viceroy every lived in Luján, by the way, but the Marqués de Sobremonte once spent a few hours here.

*Porteño* architect Martín S. Noel's 1918 restoration of the *cabildo* took some liberties with the original unadorned facade and a few other features. Still, the three hectares of buildings and well-kept grounds, bounded by Lezica y Torrezuri, Lavalle, San Martín, and Parque Ameghino, are distinguished for their contents as well.

Within the *cabildo* and the Casa del Virrey, the **Museo Histórico** has a thorough display on Argentine history, with a dazzling assortment of maps, portraits, and artifacts (such as caudillo Facundo Quiroga's blood-stained *vicuña* poncho) that bring history to life.

Immediately north, the **Museo de Transporte** houses an extraordinary collection of horse carriages in mint condition, including hearses, a carriage that belonged to General Mitre, and the stuffed carcasses of Gato and

Construction of the Basílica Nacional Nuestral Señor de Luján began in the 1880s.

© WAYNE BERNHARDSON

Mancha, the hardy *criollo* horses that 1930s adventurer A. F. Tschiffely rode from Buenos Aires to Washington, D.C. There is also a Dornier seaplane co-built by Spaniards and Argentines, and the country's first-ever locomotive, from the Ferrocarril Oeste. The main showroom's upper level contains an elaborate exhibit on *mate* and its ritual, from colonial times to the present.

The **Complejo Museográfico** (tel. 02323/420245, Wed.–Fri. 12:15–6 P.M., Sat.–Sun. and Holidays 10:15 A.M.–6:15 P.M., US$0.30) has a box office (Av. Nuestra Señora de Luján and Lavalle) with a salon for special exhibits; admission is valid for all museum facilities.

## RESTAURANTS

For breakfast and dessert, the best choice is **Berlín** (San Martín 135, tel. 02323/440780, daily breakfast, lunch, and dinner), half a block east of the basilica.

The exposed bricks in its 18th-century adobe exterior sag like a syncline and weeds may be sprouting on the roof, but that gives the **◖1800 Restaurant** (Rivadavia and Almirante Brown, tel. 02323/433080, daily noon–3:30 P.M. and 8 P.M.–late) part of its charm. That wouldn't mean much, though, if their moderately priced menu of meat, pasta, and fish and seafood were not so good, the service so agreeable, and the *pulpería* interior equally charming. Add fresh summer raspberries from El Bolsón for dessert and good wine by the glass, and there's no cause for complaint.

Befitting Luján's ecclesiastical importance, the traditional choice for a family lunch or dinner is the cross-town Carmelite-run **L'eau Vive** (Constitución 2112, tel. 02323/421774, Tues.–Sun. noon–2:15 P.M. and Tues.–Sat. 8:30–10 P.M.). Served by nuns, fixed-price lunches or dinners lean toward French specialties; they sometimes stop to observe a recorded version of *Ave Maria*. The main dining room is tobacco free.

## ENTERTAINMENT AND EVENTS

For most visitors, entertainment consists of spontaneous barbecues in Parque Ameghino or, when campgrounds are really crowded, on the median strip of Avenida Nuestra Señora de Luján. The biggest annual event has been February's **Encuentro de la Fe y la Historia** (Encounter of Faith and History), a four-day festival that traditionally blocks off Avenida Nuestra Señora de Luján for folkloric music by big-name acts. In 2008 it was scaled down, but there's a chance it'll return to its former glory.

## ACCOMMODATIONS

Across from the bus terminal, behind a drab facade, **Hotel Royal** (9 de Julio 696, tel. 02323/421295, US$20/27 s/d) has smallish but otherwise adequate rooms; it has a restaurant, but a buffet breakfast costs US$2 more. On the basilica's east side, the well-managed **Hotel de la Paz** (9 de Julio 1054, tel. 02323/428742, US$47 d with private bath) is a dignified inn that's been around nearly a century. Weekday rates fall about 15 percent.

The religious center of Luján is also a magnet for Argentine bikers.
© WAYNE BERNHARDSON

The 45-room **Hotel Hoxón** (9 de Julio 769, tel. 02323/429970, www.hotelhoxon.com.ar, US$27/45–32/50 s/d) is a major step up, and the only place in town with its own pool.

## INFORMATION AND SERVICES

At the west end of Lavalle, the municipal **Dirección de Turismo** (Parque Ameghino s/n, tel. 02323/420453, turismo@lujan.gov. ar, Mon.–Fri. 8 A.M.–5 P.M.) is located in the Edificio La Cúpula.

## TRANSPORTATION

Luján has road and rail connections with Buenos Aires. The bus station is within walking distance to everything, while the train station is across town. Cheap *remises* can carry up to four passengers for a minimal fare.

### Bus

The **Estación Terminal de Ómnibus** (Av. Nuestra Señora del Rosario betw. Almirante Brown and Dr. Reat, tel. 02323/420044) is three blocks north of the basilica. **Transportes Atlántida** (Línea 57, tel. 02323/420032, ext. 24) has express services to and from the capital's Estación Once, but also goes to and from Palermo's Plaza Italia (US$2.50, 1.5 hours).

## Train

TBA's **Línea Sarmiento** (Av. España and Belgrano, tel. 02323/421312, www.tbanet.com. ar) goes to and from Estación Once (Subte: Plaza Miserere, Línea A), but it's necessary to change trains in Moreno. The fare is negligible, but it takes at least two hours.

## VICINITY OF LUJÁN

Luján proper may draw the faithful, but some points of interest in the vicinity have little or nothing to do with faith. Even as folk musicians are charming listeners in the basilica's shadows, heavy-metal bands in nearby **Jáuregui** are driving February's annual **Motoencuentro As de Espadas,** an annual bikers' gathering. During the 2005 event, Argentine rock/blues guitarist Norberto Napolitano (better known as Pappo, he once shared the Madison Square Garden stage with B.B. King) literally made an impact here when he skidded his Harley under the wheels of an oncoming car; a monument with a guitar now marks the accident scene (RN 5, Km 71), which is becoming a pilgrimage site for his followers.

About 15 kilometers north of Luján, bypassed by time, the dying railroad, and relocated RN 7, the village of **Carlos Keen** has undergone a tourism revival thanks to its well-preserved 19th-century architecture, restaurants, and teahouses. Most of these are open weekends only, though a few work on Friday evenings.

*Estancias* still play an important role in the local economy and society: **Estancia Las Lilas** produces beef for its Buenos Aires restaurant nearby, and politician-crooner Ramón (Palito) Ortega (who once sought a government subsidy to bring Frank Sinatra to Buenos Aires!) owns **Estancia La Negrita.** The most interesting of them, though, is the historic **Estancia Los Talas,** which is open to day-trippers and overnight guests.

## Estancia Los Talas

In the same family for nearly two centuries—except for a time in the 1840s when tyrant José Manuel de Rosas confiscated it—the 890-hectare Estancia Los Talas raises dairy cattle and produces honey for the Argentine market. As an *estancia* open to guests, it's arguably the most authentic of the bunch: Its oldest adobe dates from 1824 and the main house, where most visitors stay in high-ceilinged, antique-filled, slightly musty rooms, from 1840.

Approached through a long avenue of mature eucalypti, Los Talas is also the unlikely home to the **Fundación Archivo y Biblioteca Jorge M. Furt,** guarding a 40,000-volume library of rare books and documents that belonged to the renowned philologist who resided here. In partnership with the Universidad Nacional San Martín, it includes valuable material, such as the archive of early Argentine intellectual, educator, and politician Juan Bautista Alberdi, whose ideas on immigration—"to populate is to govern"—became part of Argentine orthodoxy.

The library draws scholars from around Argentina and overseas; the building itself is a 1950s addition to the main house, but it so closely mimics the original style that it's nearly impossible to distinguish it. Los Talas's literary connections are even older, though: Poet Esteban Echeverría (1805–1851) lived and wrote here before Rosas's persecution drove him into Uruguayan exile.

The Furt family still operates Estancia Los Talas (RP 47 Km 19, tel. 02323/494995, biblioteca_furt@yahoo.com.ar, www.estanciasargentinas.com), which charges US$27 pp for its Día de Campo, which includes an *asado,* afternoon tea, and unlimited use of their horses and the swimming pool. Full-board accommodations cost around US$60 pp; three or four days' notice is advisable before a visit. A *remis* from downtown Luján costs around US$10 for up to four persons.

# San Antonio de Areco

Bidding for UNESCO World Heritage Site status, the 18th-century town of San Antonio de Areco is Argentina's unofficial gaucho capital, host to its biggest gaucho festivities, and home to a concentration of traditional craftsmen and artists unequalled in any other town its size. It's ironic, though, that many of those most closely associated with the gaucho traditions have Italian-immigrant surnames.

San Antonio was the home of *gauchesco* novelist Ricardo Güiraldes, who wrote *Don Segundo Sombra* (1927) here. It was also the location for director Manuel Antín's 1969 movie, which featured the author's late nephew Adolfo Güiraldes in the title role of a dignified rustic whose practical wisdom leaves a lasting imprint on a landowner's son.

While some small pampas towns have been struggling since 2002, San Antonio (pop. 17,820) emits an air of tidy prosperity, with many of its Italianiate houses and other buildings restored or recycled. The local real-estate market is booming with an influx of *porteño* refugees from big-city bustle.

San Antonio's biggest annual event is November's **Día de la Tradición,** celebrating the gaucho heritage, but weekends are busy all year. The pace is always relaxed, though, with greater deference to pedestrians and cyclists than anywhere else in the country. Many Arequeños, in fact, use bicycles to get around, and hotels often provide free *bicis* to their guests.

## ORIENTATION

San Antonio de Areco is 113 kilometers west of Buenos Aires via RN 8, which continues west toward San Luis, Mendoza, and the Chilean border. On the right bank of the Río Areco, it forms a mostly regular grid west of the highway; the commercial street of Alsina, leading south from the main Plaza Ruiz de Arellano, is the liveliest part of town.

## SIGHTS

In a country where motorists rarely even slow down for crosswalks, San Antonio is atypically pedestrian-friendly—so much so that townsfolk often stroll in the middle of the street. That's not really recommended, but its leisurely pace and compact core do make it attractive for walkers and cyclists.

Unlike most central plazas, San Antonio's **Plaza Ruiz de Arellano** is not the lively hub of local life, but it's an appealingly shady park surrounded by historic buildings and monuments: the **Casa de los Martínez,** site of the original *estancia* house, is at the northwest corner; the **Iglesia Parroquial San Antonio de Padua** (Parish Church, 1869) is on the south side; and the **Palacio Municipal** (1885), part of which has become the Draghi family's **Taller y Museo de Platería Criolla y Civil y Salón de Arte,** a combination museum, silversmith's workshop, and art gallery, is on the north side. In the plaza's center, the **Monumento a Vieytes** memorializes San Antonio's Juan Hipólito Vieytes (1762–1815), a participant in the 1810 revolution that eventually brought Argentine independence; he later became vice president.

Half a block north of the plaza, dating from 1901, the **Centro Cultural Usina Vieja** is an antique power plant recycled into a fine museum and cultural center. Three blocks northwest, the restored **Puente Viejo** (1857) over the Río Areco may have been the country's first toll bridge; originally designed for cart traffic, it lent its atmosphere to the movie version of *Don Segundo Sombra.* It's now a bike, horse, and pedestrian shortcut to the **Parque Criollo y Museo Gauchesco Ricardo Güiraldes,** a museum memorializing the author's *gauchesco* romanticism.

It's not the only *gauchesco* institution in town, though: Luis Gasparini, son of the late painter Osvaldo Gasparini, continues to paint and operate the **Museo Gauchesco del Pintor Gasparini.** At the intersection of RN 8 and

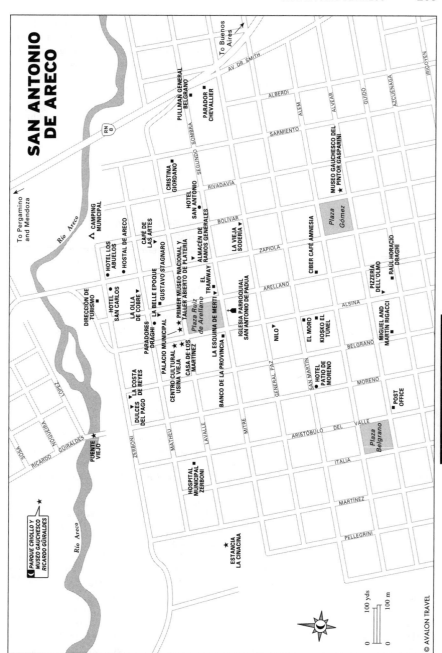

EXCURSIONS

# SAN ANTONIO DE ARECO

To Pergamino and Mendoza

To Buenos Aires

Río Areco

Río Areco

RN 8

PARQUE CRIOLLO Y
MUSEO GAUCHESCO
RICARDO GÜIRALDES

PUENTE VIEJO

DULCES DEL PAGO
LA COSTA DE REYES
CENTRO CULTURAL USINA VIEJA
CASA DE LOS MARTÍNEZ
PALACIO MUNICIPAL
PARADORES DRAGHI
BANCO DE LA PROVINCIA
LA ESQUINA DE MERTI
PRIMER MUSEO NACIONAL Y TALLER ABIERTO DE PLATERÍA
Plaza Ruiz de Arellano
IGLESIA PARROQUIAL SAN ANTONIO DE PADUA

DIRECCIÓN DE TURISMO
HOTEL SAN CARLOS
LA OLLA DE COBRE
LA BELLE EPOQUE
GUSTAVO STAGNARO
CAFÉ DE LAS ARTES
EL TRAMWAY
ALMACEN DE RAMOS GENERALES
LA VIEJA SODERÍA

CAMPING MUNICIPAL
HOTEL LOS ABUELOS
HOSTAL DE ARECO

CRISTINA GIORDANO
HOTEL SAN ANTONIO

PULLMAN GENERAL BELGRANO
PARADOR CHEVALLIER

AV. DR. SMITH
ALBERDI
SARMIENTO
RIVADAVIA
BOLÍVAR
ZAPIOLA
ARELLANO
ALSINA
BELGRANO
MORENO
ARISTÓBULO DEL VALLE
ITALIA
MARTÍNEZ
PELLEGRINI

ALEM
SOMBRA
SEGUNDO
GUIDO
ALVEAR
AZCUENAGA
IRIGOYEN

CIBER CAFÉ AMNESIA
PIZZERÍA DELL'OLMO
RAÚL HORACIO DRAGHI
MIGUEL AND MARTÍN RIGACCI
POST OFFICE

NILO
EL MORO
KIOSKO EL TÚNEL
SAN MARTÍN
HOTEL PATIO DE MORENO

Plaza Gómez

Plaza Belgrano

MUSEO GAUCHESCO DEL PINTOR GASPARINI

HOSPITAL MUNICIPAL ZERBONI

ESTANCIA LA CINACINA

GENERAL PAZ
MITRE
LAVALLE
MATHEU
ZERBONI
GÜIRALDES
NOGUEIRA
RICARDO
SOSA
LÓPEZ

0    100 yds
0    100 m

© AVALON TRAVEL

## THE PAMPA GAUCHA

The pampas west of Buenos Aires were transformed by the herds of cattle that proliferated on them after the Spanish invasion and by the horsemen who lived off those herds, making the pampas gaucho country. Eventually, and ironically, though, the free-ranging gauchos became the peons of the sprawling *estancias* (cattle ranches) that occupied almost every square centimeter of this prime agricultural land.

Unofficially, San Antonio de Areco is Argentina's gaucho capital, and the *estancias* that surround it are some of the country's most historic. The city of Luján, however, is equally if not more historic, with outstanding museums, and is also one of South America's major devotional centers.

Soldado Argentino, at the south end of town, the remains of both Ricardo Güiraldes and Segundo Ramírez (the author's model for the fictional Don Segundo Sombra) repose in the **Cementerio Municipal.**

### Centro Cultural Usina Vieja

Handsomely recycled as a museum and events center, San Antonio's century-old power plant holds permanent collections of odds and ends, such as an experimental biplane built here, and samples of work by local artisans. It's also managed impressive exhibits that re-create overlooked everyday institutions, like the simple barbershop and *botica* (apothecary), and the garden holds an array of antique farm machinery.

While it has plenty of good artifacts, the Centro Cultural Usina Vieja (Alsina 66, tel. 02326/452021, Tues.–Sun. and holidays 11:15 A.M.–4:45 P.M., US$0.50) presents little historical and cultural interpretation.

### Museo Gauchesco del Pintor Gasparini

Since his father's death, Luis Gasparini

continues to live in and operate this *gauchesco* art museum, with half a dozen rooms devoted to gaucho sculpture, silverwork, and painting (including works by Benito Quinquela Martín and Lino Spilimbergo, among others). There are also a chapel, an atelier with the family's own *gauchesco* works, and a library; appropriately enough, there's a hitching post outside for those who arrive on horseback.

The Museo Gauchesco (Alvear 521, tel. 02326/453930, gaspa@arecoonline.com.ar, daily 9 A.M.–8 P.M., free) is just off Plaza Gómez.

### Parque Criollo y Museo Gauchesco Ricardo Güiraldes

Set on 97 hectares of parkland, San Antonio's gaucho museum is a romantic idealization of the already romantic *gauchesco* literature of Ricardo Güiraldes, whose family lived on the nearby Estancia La Porteña. Created by the provincial government in the 1930s, the museum lacks the authenticity of the *estancia* (presently closed to visits), but it does offer ironic insights into the way Argentines —even *porteños*—have internalized the gaucho heritage.

The irony, of course, was that the landowning Güiraldes, however sincere, presumed to speak for the illiterate gaucho—a defiantly independent figure who became a humble, dependent laborer on the oligarchy's *estancias*. Nowhere is this clearer than in the principal **Casa del Museo,** a 20th-century replica of an 18th-century *casco* (big house): It devotes two rooms to Güiraldes himself; another to his wife Adelina del Carril; another to his painter cousin Alberto; a **Sala de los Escritores** to *gauchesco* literature, including Walter Owen's English-language translation of José Hernández's epic poem *Martín Fierro;* a **Sala Pieza de Estanciero** that includes the bed of the tyrant landowner Juan Manuel de Rosas (who exploited gauchos with a ruthless opportunism but counted them as enthusiastic allies); and, finally, a **Sala del Gaucho** that stresses horse gear and *gauchesco* art, but ignores the gaucho's marginal social and economic status.

The Casa del Museo gives only a partial account of the gaucho; the surrounding park contains the **Pulpería La Blanqueada,** a real 19th-century roadhouse with a life-size gaucho diorama. Nearby are three other aging structures, **La Ermita de San Antonio,** an adobe chapel with an image of its patron saint; the **La Tahona** flour mill (1848); and the **Galpón y Cuarto de Sogas,** a carriage house.

Reached by the Puente Viejo shortcut, the Museo Gauchesco (Camino Ricardo Güiraldes s/n, tel. 02326/455839, Wed.–Mon. 11 A.M.–5 P.M.) costs US$1 pp except for retired persons, who pay US$0.35, and children under age 12, who get in free. Free guided tours take place at 12:30 and 3:30 P.M. weekends and holidays.

## Primer Museo Nacional y Taller Abierto de Platería

Recycling a century-old residence that was in near ruin, the late silversmith Juan José

© WAYNE BERNHARDSON

Iglesia Parroquial San Antonio de Padua

Draghi enriched the moribund Plaza Ruiz de Arellano with his museum/shop and adjacent bed-and-breakfast. His death in early 2008 has deprived visitors of the opportunity to see a master craftsman at work, but the family and his protégés are continuing the tradition.

Thus, it still offers museum-quality displays of gaucho gear that reflect their regions of origin. *Facones* (gaucho knives) and spurs from the featureless pampas are unadorned, for instance, while their ornamented counterparts from Mesopotamian provinces, such as Entre Ríos and Corrientes, reflect the exuberant natural environment of riverside gallery forests.

Some items in the shop—such as ceremonial silver bridles that take a year to produce and cost up to US$20,000—are commissioned jobs awaiting shipment. Others, such as cutlery with intricately threaded leather handles and ritual silver *mates,* may be available for over-the-counter purchase.

The museum (Lavalle 387, tel. 02326/454219, www.draghiplaterosorfebres. com) is open Monday–Saturday 9 A.M.–1 P.M. and 4–8 P.M. It offers guided visits (US$1.65) from 10:30 A.M., on the half-hour, in Spanish or very good English.

## RESTAURANTS

In general, entrée prices are under US$10 throughout San Antonio. Most restaurants are open for lunch and dinner, although the ice creameries keep longer hours throughout the day.

**Pizzería Dell'Olmo** (Alsina 365, tel. 02326/452506) is a passable pizzeria. **La Costa de Reyes** (Belgrano and Zerboni, tel. 02326/452481) serves primarily *parrillada* but also pasta, with friendly service and moderate prices.

In a cozy bar environment with historic style, **La Vieja Sodería** (Bolívar 196) has fine cheap sandwiches and desserts. On Plaza Ruiz de Arellano, **La Esquina de Merti** (Arellano 149, tel. 02326/456705, www.esquinademerti.com.ar) serves a pretty good fixed-price lunch (US$8), in a stylish restoration

EXCURSIONS

# *ESTANCIAS* OF ARECO

In and around San Antonio, several historic *estancias* grow soybeans and raise livestock, but tourism pays the bills. All of them are quality establishments that take overnight guests and even offer "day in the country" excursions, including an *asado* and rural activities like horseback riding.

## ESTANCIA LA CINACINA

The most self-consciously tourist-oriented of all Areco estancias, the 50-hectare La Cinacina's "Fiesta Gaucha" mimics a day in the country without actually leaving town – the former dairy farm is only six blocks west of Plaza Ruiz de Arellano. It can accommodate up to 400 visitors for Tuesday, Friday, and Sunday visits (US$30 pp) that include snacks, a city tour, lunch, and folkloric music and dance; from Buenos Aires, with transportation, it costs about US$57 pp.

Effectively isolated from the day-trippers, a nearby cluster of recycled buildings at La Cinacina (Lavalle 1, tel. 02326/452045, www.lacinacina.com.ar, US$148-176 s or d with breakfast) now operates as a hotel. There are 16 rooms and two suites of "rustic luxury," so that travelers can spend the night. Bicycles are free, horseback rides extra.

## ESTANCIA EL OMBÚ DE ARECO

Named for Argentina's wide-crowned national tree, El Ombú de Areco belonged to General Pablo Ricchieri, who first forced military conscription onto Argentina's youth. Set among four hectares of formal gardens, with a pool, on a 300-hectare property, it's the area's most lavish *estancia* in terms of furnishings, facilities, and activities: satellite TV and video, telephone, horseback and bicycle riding, and games. There are six impeccable double rooms and three triples, with full board; vegetarians should verify the menu, which leans heavily toward beef.

Estancia El Ombú de Areco (tel. 02326/492080, tel. 011/4737-0436 in Buenos Aires, www.estanciaelombu.com, US$190/280 s/d) is about 11 kilometers northeast of San Antonio via RN 8, paved RP 41, and graveled RP 31. It also offers "day in the country" visits for US$60 pp and arranges transportation from the capital and its airports for guests.

## ESTANCIA LA BAMBA

Less accessible than La Cinacina, less luxurious than El Ombú, Estancia La Bamba is a little rougher around the edges, but its unique personality – it began as a *posta* (way station)

---

of a historic building, but high staff turnover means erratic service.

In a charmingly recycled house whose original brickwork peeks through the plaster, the ◖ **Almacén de Ramos Generales** (Zapiola 143, tel. 02326/456376, www.ramosgeneralesareco. com.ar) is primarily a *parrilla* but also has pastas and the occasional oddity, such as the Basque seafood casserole *txan gurro,* with king crab, tuna, red peppers, and tomatoes. Its walls festooned with bottles, ladles, padlocks, paintings, posters, and photographs, it also makes particularly good desserts and sells homemade salami and cheeses, but service can be spotty when it's busy.

Another good choice is **Café de las Artes** (Bolívar 70, tel. 02326/15-511684), very strong on pastas, including homemade gnocchi with a beet sauce. Likewise loaded with antiques and art works, it discourages smoking, but hasn't quite pulled the trigger on tobacco abusers. Not everyone will enjoy the oddball owner but, if you get past the prologue, it's an entertaining place.

**Nilo** (Alsina 234, tel. 02326/452341) serves fine ice cream, but **La Belle Epoque** (Arellano 82, tel. 02326/15-407038) prepares a wider variety of sophisticated chocolates and desserts in addition to ice cream.

## FIESTA DE LA TRADICIÓN

Since 1934, this November festival has feted San Antonio's gaucho heritage with guided visits to historic sites, lectures by top folklorists, crafts fairs, and folk music and dance—plus on the colonial Camino Real rather than as an *estancia* per se – gives it a unique ambience. It is perhaps the most relaxed of them all.

In addition to its accommodations, La Bamba has recently rebuilt its former carriage house into a country *pulpería* with Saturday-evening (7 P.M.) celebrations of gaucho *guitarreadas* and folkloric dances, along with traditional country food and wine. Open to both over-nighters and day-trippers, these are by advance arrangement only.

La Bamba, which served as a location for director María Luisa Bemberg's 19th-century drama *Camila*, can accommodate 11 persons in five rooms in the main house, another four in a cottage suitable for a family, and four more in an annex. Amenities include a swimming pool, game and video rooms, and activities, including horseback riding, bird-watching, fishing, and the like. High-season rates range from about US$260 to US$310 d with full board, depending on the room. IVA (21 percent) is extra.

Estancia La Bamba (tel. 02326/456293, tel. 011/4732-1269 in Buenos Aires, www.la-bamba.com.ar) is about 13 kilometers north-east of San Antonio via RN 8, RP 41, and RN 31. It also offers "day in the country" visits for about US$65 pp.

### ESTANCIA EL ROSARIO DE ARECO

Only six kilometers southwest of San Antonio, El Rosario raises polo ponies and offers a polo school, with two full playing fields on about 80 hectares of land. Non-players and even non-riders, though, will appreciate the design ingenuity that has turned its former stables into 16 comfortable, spacious, and tasteful suites.

In addition to the accommodations, part of a complex that includes a main house dating from the 1890s, owner Francisco Guevara has built a conical open-sided *quincho* (a covered shelter) for *asados*. There are also living and dining areas just far enough from the sleeping quarters to ensure peace and quiet, and a pool for guests.

Rates at El Rosario de Areco (tel. 02326/451000, tel. 914/220-7883 in the U.S., www.rosariodeareco.com.ar) are US$195/350 s/d with full board and activities included; an open bar costs another US$12 pp. "Day in the Country" visits cost US$66-72 pp, depending on the number of guests. Guevara tries not to mix overnight guests and day-trippers, nor unrelated groups, so reservations are essential – preferably as far in advance as possible. It also hosts business groups on retreat and has WiFi access and a dedicated conference room.

flamboyant displays of horsemanship on Plaza Ruiz de Arellano. While the principal Día de la Tradición is November 10, the festivities normally stretch over two weekends, climaxing on the final Sunday. Reservations are critical for anyone wanting to stay here rather than in the surrounding countryside or neighboring towns.

## SHOPS

San Antonio's silversmiths are the country's finest, so don't expect to find any giveaways—a silver mate can cost up to US$1,500, though there are, of course, cheaper versions. Other typical silver dress items include the long-bladed *facón* (gaucho knife), *rastra* (coin-studded belt), and *espuelas* (spurs).

In general, shops in San Antonio are open daily (except Tues.) from 10 A.M.–7 P.M. Some places are open Sunday by appointment only, but all of them may stay open on long weekends.

Juan José Draghi's magnificent museum/shop **Museo Draghi** and bed-and-breakfast are major contributions to San Antonio's appeal. Other silversmiths include **Raúl Horacio Draghi** (Guido 391, tel. 02326/454207), who also works in leather; **Gustavo Stagnaro** (Arellano 59, tel. 02326/454801, www.stagnaro.com.ar); and **Miguel and Martín Rigacci** (Belgrano 381, tel. 02326/456049). **Cristina Giordano** (Sarmiento 112, tel. 02326/452829, www.telarcriolloypampa.com.ar) is a weaver.

EXCURSIONS

**El Moro** (Alsina and San Martín, tel. 02326/455443) is a commercial dealer in leather, silver, ropes, and crafts, and good for an overview of what's available.

**El Tramway** (Segundo Sombra 411, tel. 02326/455561) is a spacious, entertainingly cluttered antiques dealer.

**La Olla de Cobre** (Matheu 433, tel. 02326/453105, www.laolladecobre.com.ar) produces artisanal chocolates and other sweets, while **Dulces del Pago** (Zerboni 136, tel. 02326/454751) specializes in fruit preserves.

## ACCOMMODATIONS

Until recently, San Antonio proper has had only limited (if good) accommodations, but they're improving in number and quality; some older hotels have expanded and services have improved, as even some moderately priced accommodations have added swimming pools and air-conditioning.

During November's Fiesta de la Tradición, when reservations are imperative, visitors lodge in communities for miles around. In general,

prices may rise on weekends, when reservations are advisable, but informal bed-and-breakfast accommodations may also be available—ask at the tourist office.

**Hotel San Antonio** (Segundo Sombra 515, tel. 02326/454940, US$13/20 s/d weekdays, US$20 s or d weekends) is a plain but perfectly decent budget choice.

The smallish rooms at modern **Hotel Los Abuelos** (Zapiola and Zerboni, tel. 02326/456390, www.sanantoniodeareco .com/losabuelos, US$20/33 s/d) are comfortable enough, but what might have been a secluded central garden has instead become a dreary driveway and parking lot (when tourists are few, it rents room by the hour). Rates include private bath, high ceilings with fans, telephone, cable TV, swimming pool, and breakfast.

Next-door **Hostal de Areco** (Zapiola 25, tel. 02326/456118, www.hostaldeareco.com.ar, US$35 s or d weekends) is not quite pristine, but it has large to huge rooms, ample and inviting common spaces in classic San Antonio

custom silverwork and horsegear at the Museo Draghi

style, and a spacious, woodsy, and pool-free garden that ensures quiet during the siesta hours. It's been up for sale, though, so things could change here.

In a less appealing location near the highway, **Hotel Fuaz** (Av. Dr. Smith 488, tel. 02326/452487, US$20/37 s/d) has air-conditioned rooms with breakfast. Rates at **La Posada del Ceibo** (Irigoyen between RN 8 and Av. Dr. Smith, tel. 02326/454614, www.laposadadelceibo.com.ar, US$42 s or d) include breakfast, private bath, cable TV, and pool access.

Across the street, expanding **Hotel San Carlos** (Zapiola and Zerboni, tel. 02326/453106, www.hotel-sancarlos.com.ar, US$40–60 s/d) provides cable TV, a pair of smallish pools (one with whirlpool tub), and other amenities, including bicycles. It can get noisy, though, when kids crowd around the pool. A few cozy rooms have what might be called micro-closets, but the more expensive rooms are really small apartments.

Until recently, Areco proper lacked stylish accommodations, but ( **Draghi Paradores** (Matheu 380, tel. 02326/454219, paradores@sanantoniodeareco.com, US$40/73 s/d) has filled that niche nicely. Entered from Matheu, immediately behind the Draghi museum on Plaza Ruiz de Arellano, this converted garage (combined with new construction) emulates traditional style on fountain-studded grounds that also have a pool. Furnished with antiques, the spacious rooms have high ceilings, and distinctive design flourishes suggesting a skilled silversmith's attention to detail; some but not all have whirlpool-equipped tubs. Museum admission and tours are free for guests, as are bicycles.

New in late 2007, ( **Patio de Moreno** (Moreno 251, tel. 02326/455197, www.patiodemoreno.com, US$145–180 s or d) is a former warehouse recycled into a six-room boutique "hotel with personality." That description might be self-serving, but the spacious bedrooms, some with whirlpool tubs, are accented with hand-woven blankets and cowhide rugs. A luminous, high-ceilinged wine bar is open

## ESTANCIA OPERATORS

Over the past decade-plus, weekending in the countryside of Buenos Aires province has become an increasingly popular option for those wishing to escape the capital. As *estancia* owners have struggled to diversify economically, some even make more income from hosting tourists than they do growing grain or raising livestock. Some *estancias* aim at day-trippers, but most of them prefer overnight guests. Some are reasonably priced places with limited services, but others are magnificent estates with castle-like *cascos* (big houses), elaborate services, including gourmet meals, and recreational activities such as horseback riding, tennis, and swimming.

Affiliated with the Sociedad Rural Argentina, the **Red Argentina de Turismo Rural** (Florida 460, 4th fl., tel. 011/4328-0499, www.raturestancias.com.ar) represents *estancias* in northern and southern Buenos Aires province, as well as in the northwestern Argentine provinces, Córdoba, and even some in Patagonia.

to the public, while the interior patio has an ample-sized swimming pool.

## INFORMATION

The municipal **Dirección de Turismo** (Zerboni and Ruiz de Arellano, tel. 02326/453165, www.pagosdeareco.com.ar, daily 8 a.m.–8 p.m.) distributes an excellent town map that includes a list of tourist-oriented services and local artisans.

## SERVICES

**Correo Argentino** (Alvear and Aristóbulo del Valle) is the post office. **Kiosko El Túnel** (Alsina 264) provides long-distance service, while **Ciber Café Amnesia** (Arellano 285-A) has reliable Internet access. Money is available through several ATMs, including **Banco de la Provincia** (Mitre and Alsina).

For medical emergencies, there's the **Hospital Municipal Zerboni** (Moreno and Lavalle, tel. 02326/452759).

## TRANSPORTATION

Just off the highway, on the east side of town, San Antonio's **Parador Chevallier** (Av. Dr. Smith and General Paz, tel. 02326/453904, tel. 011/4000-5255 in Retiro) has up to 12 buses daily to Retiro (US$7, 1.5–2 hours). Just to the north, **Pullman General Belgrano** (Av. Dr. Smith and Segundo Sombra, tel. 02326/454059) has four buses daily to and from Retiro.

# Lobos and Vicinity

South of Buenos Aires, RN 3 and its spur RN 205 might be called the "Ruta de Polo" for the scattered *estancias* that keep gigantic, closely cropped lawns in primo condition for a sport that's the dominion of the elite. At the same time, ironically enough, one of the area's largest towns is the birthplace of the caudillo and working-class hero Juan Domingo Perón.

## ORIENTATION

Lobos (pop. 26,801) is about 100 kilometers southwest of Buenos Aires via RN 3 and RN 205. Plaza 1810 is the center of its regular grid.

## SIGHTS
### Museo Juan Domingo Perón

For all his transformative impact on Argentine public life, and the persistence of a personality cult that allows hero-worshippers from extreme left to extreme right to claim his legacy, Juan Domingo Perón's hometown and birthplace museum is strangely understated. It's almost as if its curators decided that the story of the obscure army officer who became Latin America's stereotypical strongman is so well known that no commentary is necessary—a handful of his personal documents, family and political photos, and smiling portraits are sufficient.

The museum's own history is at least as interesting, dating from 1953 (when Perón was still president). Following his 1955 overthrow, it had to close until his 1973 return from exile; it stayed open only a few years until another coup closed it in 1976. Even after the 1983 return to constitutional government, it took six years more to reopen definitively.

Though it's seen substantial changes since its construction in 1894, a year before the caudillo's birth, the building itself is a national historical monument. Perón's former office desk, as well as furniture and other personal belongings from his Spanish home in exile, fill several rooms.

The museum's most offbeat exhibit—having no connection whatsoever to Perón—is the skull of the famous gaucho *bandido* Juan Moreira, shot dead by police only a few blocks

Juan Domingo Perón's boyhood home is a modest museum in Lobos.

© WAYNE BERNHARDSON

away in 1874. Moreira's life has been the subject of movies in 1936, 1948, and 1973, so he's probably overdue for a cinematic update.

The Museo Juan Domingo Perón (Presidente Perón 482, tel. 02227/424404, Wed.–Sun. 10 A.M.–noon and 3–6 P.M.), five blocks south of Plaza 1810, has recently undergone restoration and improvements.

## La Martina Polo Ranch

While the genteel sport of polo might seem antithetical to Argentina's gaucho tradition, the two come together at La Martina. Like many *estancias,* it's open to the general public, but its specialist public is polo riders from as far afield as the United States, the United Kingdom, and even Malaysia. It owes a good part of its reputation to its status as the home of international legend Adolfo Cambiaso, the Willie Mays of the sport, and its 88 hectares include two full-size fields.

At the same time, La Martina gets plenty of weekend visitors from the capital, as they enjoy its two finely furnished guesthouses, oak-shaded brick patio, broad lawns, tennis courts, and riding trails. If it gets crowded, the century-old *casco* (big house) is also available for accommodations. There are few visitors during the week, except for Buenos Aires companies who hold corporate retreats here.

"Day in the Country" excursions from Buenos Aires cost US$90 pp, including an arrival snack, a full lunch (including empanada appetizers, the traditional *asado,* a salad buffet, dessert, wine or soft drinks, and coffee or tea), and a late-afternoon tea with homemade cakes. In addition, day-trippers can use the pool, tennis courts, and the ranch's horses for riding (polo-playing day-trippers, though, pay at least twice as much).

Overnight accommodations at La Martina cost US$190/360 s/d with full board and activities; polo players, who tend to stay four or five days, usually purchase special packages. Rates above do not include IVA.

La Martina Polo Ranch (tel. 02226/430772, www.lamartinapolo.com) is about 50 kilometers southwest of Buenos Aires via the Ezeiza-Cañuelas freeway, and 50 kilometers northeast of Lobos; most of the staff speak good English. For visitors who don't care to drive, Lobos Bus drops passengers at the Puente Vicente Casares, an overpass barely a 10-minute walk from La Martina's gates.

## Estancia and Polo Club La Candelaria

For many Argentines, especially landowners, France was the ideal of elegance, but few took it so far as Manuel Fraga, who built an outlandish Norman-style *castillo* on the pampas in the early 1900s. Now, though, anyone who wants to feel like the guest of nobility can spend the night on this 400-hectare *estancia,* which doubles as a polo ranch.

With its painstakingly carved, stained, and burnished woodwork, meticulously detailed *vitraux,* and furniture that may indeed have come from French castles, "El Castillo" has an unquestionable air of upper-class privilege. Almost indescribably ornate, its interior includes an elaborate dining room (used only for special occasions, as visitors dine in a separate facility), a game room with a large pool table, and several high-ceilinged guestrooms that range from relatively modest doubles to sprawling suites.

Famed French landscape architect Charles Thays lined La Candelaria's roads with casuarinas and eucalyptus, studded its broad lawns with more than 240 species of trees, and punctuated them with classical statuary. Given its painstaking design, La Candelaria has the ambience of an exclusive planned village, rather than a ranch.

No longer in the Fraga family, **( Estancia Candelaria** (RN 205 Km 114.5, tel. 02227/424404, www.estanciacandelaria.com) is about 15 kilometers south of Lobos. Rates, with full board, range from US$67 pp in the Spanish colonial-style bungalows to US$133 pp in the castle's finest suite; weekend packages, from Saturday morning to Sunday afternoon, range US$120–233 pp. Included is unlimited access to recreational facilities: bicycles, swimming pool, tennis courts, and horses (but not polo ponies—polo packages are separate).

In addition, La Candelaria offers "Day in

© WAYNE BERNHARDSON

Near Lobos, Estancia Candelaria's Norman-style castle reflected the Francophile aspirations – or pretensions – of Argentina's landed elite.

the Country" excursions (US$55–67 pp); Saturday's more elaborate "Fiesta Gaucho" falls at the upper end of these. Transportation costs US$17 pp more.

## RESTAURANTS AND ACCOMMODATIONS

For day visitors, there's downtown's **La Marina** (Buenos Aires and Suipacha, tel. 02227/431097), which has good pastas and pizzas in the US$4 range. **Helados Florencia** (9 de Julio 365, tel. 02227/431105) has fine and very inexpensive ice cream.

Other than the surrounding *estancias,* the best option is the **Aquae Sulis Spa & Resort** (Independencia s/n, tel. 02227/424330 in Lobos, tel. 011/4658-1226 in Buenos Aires, www.aquaesulis.com.ar, US$67 pp with breakfast), a full-service spa that has 28 luxury rooms

and a restaurant. Multi-day packages permit use of all facilities until late afternoon on the day of departure.

## INFORMATION

Lobos's **Consejo Asesor de Turismo** (Salgado 40, tel. 02227/422275, Mon.–Fri. 8:30 A.M.– 2:30 P.M.) is opposite Plaza 1810. Even when it's closed, there's a large, detailed map that's helpful in finding the sights.

## TRANSPORTATION

La Martina (US$3.25, 45 minutes) and Lobos (US$6.50, 1.5 hours) are both easily reached by **Lobos Bus** (Mitre 1762, Congreso, tel. 011/4381-6000; Buenos Aires 579, Lobos, tel. 02227/431346; www.lobosbus.com.ar). Reservations are essential for this very efficient service.

# La Plata

In 1882, after barely avoiding civil war following the federalization of the city of Buenos Aires, indignant provincial authorities expropriated six square leagues in the former Municipio de la Ensenada to create their new capital of La Plata. Provincial governor Dardo Rocha chose Pedro Benoit's standard grid, superimposed with diagonals like those of Washington, D.C., to be embellished with pretentious neoclassical and Francophile buildings that have, nevertheless, achieved a remarkable harmony over time.

While government is its reason for existence, La Plata (pop. 553,002) has become one of the country's major cultural centers, with first-rate universities, theaters, concert halls, libraries, and museums. In January and February, though, when politicians go on vacation and university students return to their families, the cultural calendar thins out and many museums close.

## ORIENTATION

La Plata is 56 kilometers southeast of Buenos Aires via the Autopista Buenos Aires–La Plata. The city itself consists of a rectangular grid, with regularly distributed plazas, but the connecting diagonals (which run north–south and east–west) can make the layout disorienting to pedestrians—a slight wrong turn can send you far out of your way.

Most public buildings are on or around Plaza Moreno, La Plata's precise geographical center, but its commercial center is near Plaza San Martín, six blocks northeast. Unlike most Argentine cities, its streets and avenues are numbered rather than named; locations are most commonly described by their intersections and cross streets rather than building numeration.

## SIGHTS

In 1882, governor Dardo Rocha laid La Plata's **Piedra Fundacional** (Foundation Stone) in the center of sprawling **Plaza Moreno,** which fills four full blocks bounded by Calle 12, Calle 14,

Calle 50, and Calle 54. Along with architects Ernesto Meyer and Emilio Coutaret, Benoit designed the French neo-Gothic **Catedral de la Inmaculada Concepción de la Plata** at the plaza's southwest corner.

Rocha himself resided in what is now the **Museo y Archivo Dardo Rocha,** fronting on Calle 50 on the plaza's northwest side. Two blocks west, the French-style **Casa de Justicia** fills an entire block bounded by Avenida 13, Calle 47, Calle 48, and Calle 14.

On the northeast side of Plaza Moreno, fronting on Calle 12, Hannover architect Hubert Stiers built the elegant German Renaissance **Palacio Municipal** (1886), whose main **Salón Dorado** is adorned with marble staircases, imported oak floors, German stained-glass windows, and bronze chandeliers. Two blocks away, bounded by Calle 9, Calle 10, Avenida 51, and Avenida 53, the **Teatro Argentino** is a

The Casa Curutchet is architect Le Corbusier's only South American construction.

EXCURSIONS

# LA PLATA

© AVALON TRAVEL

## PARQUE ECOLÓGICO CULTURAL GUILLERMO E. HUDSON

Beyond La Boca, across the Riachuelo, the Zona Sur of Gran Buenos Aires is a low-profile, no-go zone for most tourists, but it's home to some offbeat sights. About midway to La Plata, at the Berazategui exit off the new freeway, the site where the late *cumbia* star Rodrigo Bueno rolled his car in 2000 has become a pilgrimage site for working-class fans convinced he was a saint. Near the slum suburb of Florencio Varela is Los 25 Ombúes, a onetime farm that was home to naturalist/novelist William Henry Hudson.

Known to Argentines as Guillermo Enrique, Hudson was the Argentine-born son of New Englanders Daniel Hudson and Carolina Kimble, who moved to Argentina in 1836. Born in 1841, Hudson passed his youth on the farm, which took its name from the *ombú* trees that once surrounded the humble house in what was then a wild and remote area. Today, the 18th-century adobe is a museum and the centerpiece of a 54-hectare forest and wetland preserve.

Hudson, who left Argentina for England in 1869, reminisced about his pampas days in *Long Ago and Far Away* (1918), but also left other memorable South American stories in *Idle Days in Patagonia* (1893) and *The Purple Land* (1885, republished in 1904). His passion, though, was natural history, particularly birds.

Alongside Hudson's birthplace, which holds his books and family documents, some of the original 25 trees still stand. The best time to see the park is after the spring rains, when the wetlands still teem with bird life – but also with mosquitoes.

The Parque Ecológico Cultural Guillermo E. Hudson (tel. 011/4901-9651) is about midway between Buenos Aires and La Plata; itÕs open Saturday-Sunday and holidays 10 A.M.-6 P.M. The simplest way there is to take the train from Constitución (Buenos Aires) to Estación Florencio Varela and bus No. 324, Ramal (Branch) 2. This will get you to within a few hundred meters of the entrance, which is up a dirt road.

performing-arts center that replaced a far more dignified building that burned to the ground in 1977.

Two blocks northeast, facing Plaza San Martín on Avenida 7, Hannoverian architects Gustav Heine and Georg Hagemann designed the provincial **Palacio de la Legislatura** in the Palacio Municipal's German Renaissance style. Across the plaza, fronting on Calle 6, Belgian architect Julio Doral designed the Flemish Renaissance **Casa de Gobierno,** home to the provincial executive branch and, seemingly, a challenge to the federal capital's nondescript Casa Rosada.

Across Avenida 51, the renovated **Museo de Bellas Artes Bonaerense** (Av. 51 No. 525, tel. 0221/4218619, www.ic.gba.gov.ar/dav, Tues.–Sat. 10 A.M.–1 P.M. and Tues.–Sun. 4–8 P.M., free admission) is a contemporary art museum.

To the northeast, the **Museo de Arte y Memoria** (Calle 54 No. 487, tel. 0221/4835590, www.comisionporlamemoria.org, free admission) occupies the former Dirección de Inteligencia de la Bonaerense, the provincial police force's "Dirty War" interrogation center. It's open Tuesday–Saturday 2–7 P.M.

At the northwest corner of Plaza San Martín, La Plata's first railroad station is now the **Pasaje Dardo Rocha** (1887), home to several museums and other cultural institutions. Two blocks farther on, the **Rectorado de la Universidad Nacional** (1905), on Avenida 7 between Calle 47 and 48, now houses university offices. About three blocks east of the plaza, topped by a view tower, the **Palacio Campodónico** (1892) fills a small triangular lot bounded by Diagonal 70, Calle 5, and Calle 56. Expropriated by the provincial government in 1976, it's now a cultural center with rotating exhibitions.

Several blocks northeast, facing Plaza Rivadavia, the **Casa Curutchet** (Calle 53 No. 320, tel. 0221/4822631, www.capba.org.ar, Mon.–Fri. 10 A.M.–2:30 P.M., US$8) was designed by the famed Swiss architect Le Corbusier as a private residence and office for Dr. Pedro Curutchet. One of just two Le Corbusier works in the Western Hemisphere (the other is Harvard University's Carpenter Center for the Visual Arts), the Casa Curutchet dates from 1948.

Across Avenida 1, the 60-hectare **Paseo del Bosque** is a forested park that contains recreational and educational facilities, including the **Anfiteatro Martín Fierro,** an outdoor theater; the exceptional natural sciences museum, **Museo de La Plata;** the **Observatorio Astronómico** (Astronomical Observatory); the **Jardín de la Paz** (Peace Garden), with small pavilions for each country with diplomatic representation in Argentina; and the **Jardín Zoológico** (Zoo).

## Catedral de la Inmaculada Concepción de la Plata

Construction of La Plata's cathedral is a story in itself, even by the standards of Argentine public-works projects. Begun in 1885, it did not open officially until 1932, and its three crowning towers went unfinished until 1999. So long, in fact, did the project take that the building underwent its first restoration (1997) even before its completion!

Overlooking Plaza Moreno, it contains a subterranean **Museo de la Catedral** (Calle 14 betw. 51 and 53, tel. 0221/4273504, www.catedraldelaplata.com, daily 8 A.M.–noon and 2–7 P.M.), which contains the tombs of provincial governor Dardo Rocha and his wife; a gallery also offers special exhibitions. An elevator goes to *miradores* (overlooks) at the 42-meter and 63-meter levels, but most of the rest will be of interest only to the truly devout.

## Jardín Zoológico

At the west end of the Paseo del Bosque, La Plata's 14-hectare Victorian-style zoo billets more than 180 native and exotic species, including giraffes, elephants, lions, monkeys, and rhinoceri. Admission to the Jardín Zoológico

© WAYNE BERNHARDSON

The neo-Gothic Catedral de la Inmaculada Concepción de la Plata soars above Plaza Moreno.

(Paseo del Bosque s/n, tel. 0221/4273925) costs US$0.70 pp; children under 12 get in free. Hours are daily 9 A.M.–7 P.M., but the gates close to incoming visitors at 6:15 P.M.

## ( Museo de La Plata

Patagonian explorer Francisco Pascasio Moreno donated his personal collections of anthropological, archaeological, and paleontological artifacts to Argentina's premier natural history museum, which opened in 1888 under his own lifetime directorship. Today, more than 400,000 visitors per annum view at least some of the 2.5 million items in its 21 exhibition halls, which also deal with botany, geology, zoology, and other fields.

The four-story building is a monument to its era, its exterior a hybrid of Greek regional styles with indigenous American—Aztec and Incaic—flourishes. Home to the Universidad Nacional de La Plata's natural sciences department, its interior also contains classrooms, libraries, offices, workshops, and storage space.

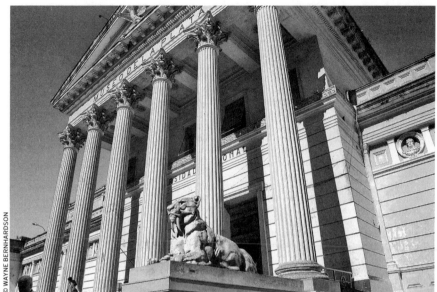

The Museo de La Plata is Argentina's top natural history museum.

The museum's public displays, though, have still not evolved far beyond taxonomy and its founder's 19th-century Darwinism.

The Museo de La Plata (Paseo del Bosque 1900, tel. 0221/4257744, www.fcnym.unlp.edu.ar/museo) is open Tuesday–Sunday 10 A.M.–6 P.M.; it's closed New Year's Day, May Day, and Christmas Day, but open other holidays when they fall on a Monday. Admission costs US$1.30 pp for those over 12 years of age; the official price for foreigners is US$4 pp, but enforcement is lax. There are guided tours at 2 and 4 P.M. weekdays except Monday, and hourly on weekends 10:30 A.M.–4:30 P.M.

### Museo y Archivo Dardo Rocha

Pedro Benoit also designed the residence of La Plata's founder, Dardo Rocha (1838–1921), whose varied career included stints as a journalist, soldier, diplomat, provincial legislator, national senator, and provincial governor. The museum, though, focuses on Rocha's personal effects, including furniture, art works, clothing, housewares, documents, and photographs, to the near exclusion of his role in the controversial shift of the provincial capital from Buenos Aires.

The Museo y Archivo Dardo Rocha (Calle 50 No. 933, tel. 0221/4251990, Mon.–Fri. 10 A.M.–10 P.M., Sat.–Sun. 2–6 P.M., free) is more an homage than an analytical or interpretive institution.

### Observatorio Astronómico de La Plata

Part of the Universidad Nacional de La Plata, the local observatory has both modern telescopes and historical instruments from the 19th century. It's open for nighttime tours, without reservations, Friday only at 8:30 P.M.

Otherwise, hours at the Observatorio Astronómico (Paseo del Bosque s/n, tel. 0221/4236953, www.fcaglp.unlp.edu.ar, US$1 pp) are 9 A.M.–noon and 1:30–4:30 P.M.

### Pasaje Dardo Rocha

Formerly the Estación 19 de Noviembre, La Plata's first major railroad station, the French classic–style Pasaje Dardo Rocha has

## REPÚBLICA DE LOS NIÑOS

Conceived by Evita Perón, executed by 1,600 laborers under Peronist governor Domingo Mercante, and officially opened by Juan Perón himself, República de los Niños was once a 53-hectare golf course built for the English meatpacker Swift. In the context of mid-century Peronism, what with its origins as an expropriated foreign property and a destination for working-class children, República de los Niños sent a political message that may not be obvious to non-Argentines.

The park displays a mélange of architectural miniatures from around the world, ranging from the medieval Europe of Grimm's fairy tales to Islamic mosques and the Taj Mahal. It also includes replicas of the Argentine presidential palace, legislature, and courts – with the obvious implication that its youthful public could aspire to office (and apparently to graft – there's also a jail).

According to some accounts, Walt Disney got the inspiration for Disneyland here. Disney, though, visited Argentina in 1941 – a decade before the Argentine park opened.

Admission to República de los Niños (Camino General Belgrano and 501, Manuel Gonnet, tel. 0221/4841409, www.republica.laplata.gov.ar, Tues.-Sun. 10 A.M.-7 P.M.) costs US$1 pp but is free for children under age seven and retirees; a miniature steam train makes the rounds of the park. Parking costs US$1.35.

From Avenida 7 in downtown La Plata, buses No. 518 and 273 go to República de los Niños, but not all No. 273s go all the way.

undergone an adaptive reuse that has turned it into a major cultural center with several museums, plus cinemas, auditoriums, conference rooms, cafés, and other features. The municipal tourist office is also here.

Opened in 1999, the **Museo de Arte Contemporáneo Latinoamericano** (Calle 50 betw. Calles 6 and 7, tel. 0221/4271843, www.macla.laplata.gov.ar, Tues.–Fri. 10 A.M.–8 P.M., Sat.–Sun. 4–10 P.M., free admission) features works by modern Latin American artists.

The **Museo Municipal de Bellas Artes** (tel. 0221/4271198, Tues.–Fri. 10 A.M.–7 P.M., Sat.–Sun. 4–9 P.M., free admission) is a painting and sculpture museum focusing primarily on local artists. Dedicated exclusively to photography, the **Museo y Galería Fotográfica** (MUGAFO, free admission) keeps the same hours.

### Teatro Argentino

Finally rebuilt after its destruction by fire in 1977, the hideous Teatro Argentino reopened in October 2000 with a presentation of *Tosca*. With all the elegance of a multistory parking lot, this 60,000-square-meter concrete structure looks like the product of the military dictatorship that approved it—a fortified bunker

that (had it been complete) might have bought the general and admirals a little more time in power after their 1982 Falklands debacle.

Still, the new Teatro Argentino looks and sounds better within than without and remains one of the country's major performing-arts venues, with its own orchestra, chorus, ballet, and children's chorus. Its principal theater is the Sala Alberto Ginastera, seating more than 2,000 spectators; smaller halls seat 300–700. Past performers include Arthur Rubenstein, Ana Pavlova, Andrés Segovia, and Richard Strauss.

The Teatro Argentino (Av. 51 betw. Calle 9 and Calle 10, tel. 0221/4291700, www.teatroargentino.ic.gba.gov.ar) offers guided tours Tuesday–Friday at 9 and 11 A.M. and 1:30 and 3:30 P.M., Saturday at 11:30 A.M. and 2:30 P.M., and Sunday at 11:30 A.M. (by reservation only). These cost US$1 pp except for bilingual English-Spanish tours, which cost US$1.50 pp. There are discounts for seniors and students.

### RESTAURANTS

For breakfast, coffee, or pastries, the best option is the tobacco-free **Confitería París** (Av. 7 and Calle 49, tel. 0221/4828840).

The **Colegio de Escribanos** (Av. 13, betw. Calles 47 and 48, lunch and dinner, under US$10) is a lunchtime favorite for lawyers and judges from the nearby Tribunales. Plaza Paso's **Don Quijote** (Avs. 13 and 44, tel. 0221/4833653, lunch and dinner, under US$10) specializes in seafood.

**La Trattoría** (Calle 47 and Diagonal 74, tel. 0221/4226135, lunch and dinner, under US$10) is a casual Italian restaurant with sidewalk seating, while **Abruzzese** (Calle 42 No. 457, tel. 0221/4219869, dinner only, US$10 and up) is more formal. Open for dinner only, **Gaucho Italiano** (Calle 50 No. 724, betw. 9 and 10, tel. 0221/4832817, lunch and dinner, under US$10) serves 50 varieties of pizzas, *tablas* of meats and cheeses, and pastas with a hybrid pampas touch. There's a tobacco-free area, but the background music can be dreadfully inappropriate.

The line between places to eat and places to drink is not always obvious in La Plata. The best blend of the two is the classic **〖** **Cervecería El Modelo** (Calle 5 and Calle 54, tel. 0221/4211321, lunch and dinner, under US$10), which prepares terrific sandwiches, plus draft beer and hard cider with free unshelled and unsalted peanuts. There's a fairly large tobacco-free area, and sidewalk seating in fine weather.

Another option is the **Wilkenny Irish Pub & Restaurant** (Calle 50 No. 797, tel. 0221/4831772, www.wilkenny.com.ar, lunch and dinner, under US$10), a legitimately Irish-style pub in the heart of La Plata. The food includes pub grub like lamb stew (though the bulk of the menu is Argentine and there are even a couple Chinese dishes), plus Irish beers (Guinness, Harp, and Kilkenny) on tap by the pint and half-pint. Lunch or dinner entrées cost around US$3–5; there's a larger selection of bottle brews, plus Irish and specialty coffees.

Beer also shares the bill with the food at **La Bartola** (Av. 44 No. 599, lunch and dinner, under US$10), which has inexpensive lunch specials and fine pastas.

For ice cream, try **La Sorbetière** (Calle 47 and Calle 10) or nearby **Thionis** (Diagonal 74 No. 1578, tel. 0221/4232030).

## CINEMA

La Plata has three downtown movie theaters: the six-screen **Cine Ocho** (Calle 8 No. 981, betw. Avs. 51 and 53, tel. 0221/4825554); the four-screen **Cine San Martín** (Calle 7 No. 923, betw. Avs. 50 and 51, tel. 0221/4839947); and the three-screen **Cinema City** (Calle 50 No. 723, betw. 9 and 10, tel. 0221/4235456). All share a common website (www.cinemalaplata.com).

## PERFORMING ARTS

La Plata is a major theater and live-music center, whose major venue is the **Centro de las Artes Teatro Argentino** (Av. 51 betw. Calles 9 and 10, tel. 0800/6665151 toll-free, www.teatroargentino.ic.gba.gov.ar). Its box office (tel. 0221/4291733) is open Tuesday–Sunday 10 A.M.–8 P.M. The Teatro Argentino provides free transportation from Buenos Aires for ticket holders.

Another major performing-arts locale is the **Teatro Coliseo Podestá** (Calle 10 No. 729, betw. Calles 46 and 47, tel. 0221/4248457). A landmark in the history of regional theater, it also has a museum open Monday–Friday 10 A.M.–noon.

For tickets, try **Ticketek** (Calle 50 No. 612, betw. Calle 7 and Calle 8, tel. 0221/4477200, www.ticketek.com.ar).

## ACCOMMODATIONS

Friendly but no-frills **Hotel Saint James** (Av. 60 No. 377, tel. 0221/4218089, www.hotelsj.com.ar, US$18/25 s/d) is the best choice for the truly budget-conscious, but it's often full. Rates include breakfast, private bath, and telephone, but cable TV costs extra.

On a quiet block near the Paseo del Bosque, **Hotel Roga** (Calle 54 No. 334, tel. 0221/4219553, www.hotelroga.com.ar, US$33/47 s/d) is modern, friendly, and comfortable; rates include private bath and parking, but breakfast costs another US$7 pp.

In a century-old building that once housed the provincial labor ministry, rooms at the restored **Hotel Benevento** (Calle 2 No. 645, at the corner of Diagonal 80, tel. 0221/4237721, www.hotelbenevento.com.ar, US$33/52 s/d) have high ceilings, traditional balconies, and modernized baths (showers only). It's worth mentioning that some singles are truly small (though still comfortable).

At the intersection of Avenidas 13 and 44, **Hotel del Rey** (Plaza Paso 180, tel. 0221/4270177, www.hoteldelrey.com.ar, US$36/52 s/d) is a 10-story tower with 40 well-kept midsize rooms and slightly more expensive suites with all the modern conveniences.

The utilitarian exterior at **Hotel San Marco** (Calle 54 No. 523, tel. 0221/4227202, www.sanmarcohotel.com.ar, US$40/58 s/d) disguises what is also a pretty good hotel. Despite a striking modern facade and handsome common areas, **Hotel del Sol** (Calle 10 No. 1061, tel. 0221/4272049, www.hoteldelsol-laplata.com.ar, US$40/58 s/d or US$70 s or d) is really a recycled older building, with midsized rooms and amenities such as WiFi.

Rates at centrally located 70-room **Hotel La Plata** (Av. 51 No. 783, tel./fax 0221/4229090, www.weblaplatahotel.com.ar, US$42/58 s/d) include breakfast *and* dinner, an outstanding value for what is a very good hotel with air-conditioning, cable TV, and similar conveniences.

The four-star 110-room high-rise **Hotel Corregidor** (Calle 6 No. 1026, tel. 0221/4256800, www.hotelcorregidor.com.ar, US$72/80 s/d) is a good upscale value.

## INFORMATION

In the Pasaje Dardo Rocha, the **Información Turística La Plata** (Calles 6 and 50, tel. 0221/4271535, www.laplata.gov.ar, daily 10 A.M.–6 P.M.) is the municipal tourist office. It distributes city maps, informational brochures, and bus schedules, and the staff is accommodating. It works under the **Dirección de Turismo** (Diagonal 79 at Calle 8, tel. 0221/4229764), open Monday–Friday 9 A.M.–6 P.M. in the historic Palacio Campodónico.

## SERVICES

As a provincial capital, La Plata has a full complement of services.

**Banco de la Provincia** has an ATM on Avenida 7 between Calles 46 and 47, while **Banco Nación** has one at the corner of Avenida 7 and Calle 49. There are many others.

For postal services, **Correo Argentino** is at the corner of Avenida 51 and Calle 4. **Locutorio Fono Cinco** (Av. 51 and Calle 5, tel. 0221/4895511) is open 24 hours for Internet access.

**Asatej** (Av. 5 No. 990, at the corner of Av. 53, tel. 0221/4838673, laplata@asatej.com.ar) is a branch of Argentina's student- and youth-oriented travel agency.

## TRANSPORTATION
### Air

La Plata has no airport, but **Manuel Tienda León** (tel. 0810/888-5366, US$22) provides door-to-door transportation to Buenos Aires's Ezeiza and Aeroparque.

### Bus

La Plata's **Terminal de Omnibus** (tel. 0221/4212182) is at Calles 42 and 4; **Costera Metropolitana** (tel. 0800/222-6798) and **Empresa Plaza** (tel. 0800/333-1970) have frequent buses to and from Retiro (US$2, one hour), but also pick up and drop off passengers along the capital's Avenida 9 de Julio.

### Train

The century-old **Estación Ferrocarril General Roca** is at Avenidas 1 and 44 (tel. 0221/4232575). **Transportes Metropolitana SA General Roca** (TMR, tel. 011/4304-0021) operates around 50 weekday trains from Constitución (Buenos Aires) to La Plata (1.5 hours, US$0.60); the number drops to around 35 or 40 trains on weekends and holidays. The last train returns to Constitución around 10:30 P.M., but they start up again around 3 A.M.

# Montevideo, Uruguay

Montevideo is a metropolis of 1.6 million people—almost half the country's inhabitants—but Uruguay's capital has somehow managed to maintain a small-town feel. Its revived colonial quarter, the Ciudad Vieja, is a pedestrian-friendly grid of narrow streets with distinctive plazas, dotted with restaurants, bars, antique shops, cultural centers, and galleries—though there are still *conventillos,* onetime mansions taken over by squatters.

Montevideo's port, superior to Buenos Aires in every aspect except access to the pampas, has given it an international flavor. Having begun to appreciate the Ciudad Vieja's potential, authorities plan to link the nightlife and restaurant zones along the streets of Bartolomé Mitre and Sarandí with the similarly picturesque port zone.

East of the Ciudad Vieja, a canopy of dense sycamores lines most streets on either side of Avenida 18 de Julio, and the avenue itself is home to a smattering of classical mansions and early-20th-century deco-style buildings. The southeastern suburban barrios toward Palermo and Pocitos enjoy access to sandy riverside beaches—something Buenos Aires's muddy shoreline cannot match.

Montevideo is also a bureaucratic city, home to Uruguay's major political institutions and the administrative headquarters for Mercosur, the shaky common market in which Argentina, Brazil, and Paraguay also participate. In between the two South American giants, Uruguay still plays the role of political buffer.

## HISTORY

The determined resistance of Uruguay's aboriginal Charrúa peoples discouraged permanent European settlement until the early 18th century; since then, the country's history has been that of a buffer—first between colonial Spain and Portugal, and then between republican Argentina and Brazil. Bruno Mauricio de Zabala's 1726 founding of fortified Montevideo was a direct response to Portuguese activity

along the river, but also to northern European smugglers and privateers. The first settlers arrived from Buenos Aires and the Canary Islands (rural Uruguayans are still known as *Canarios*).

At that time, though, it was a pretty primitive place. On the initial houses, according to one historian, "Leather made the protective roofs…. Nails being scarce, wire unheard of, rope and cord undreamed of…leather was used as cables, as chisels, in all manner of joining and riveting." By the late 18th century, though, Montevideo had acquired an air of permanence.

After several years under Brazilian rule in the 1820s, Montevideo spent most of the 1840s under siege from Buenos Aires strongman Juan Manuel de Rosas before finally achieving political and economic stability in the 1850s. Most surviving colonial buildings date from the early

Palacio Salvo is at the foot of Avenida 18 de Julio, east of the Ciudad Vieja.

EXCURSIONS

© WAYNE BERNHARDSON

EXCURSIONS

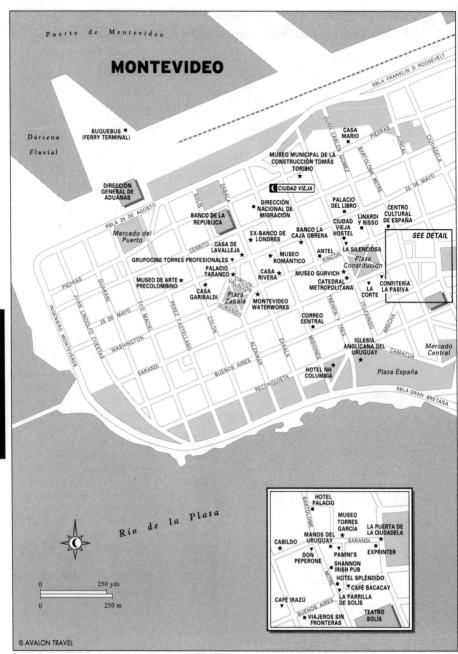

*Puerto de Montevideo*

# MONTEVIDEO

*Dársena Fluvial*

BUQUEBUS ■
(FERRY TERMINAL)

CASA MARIO

MUSEO MUNICIPAL DE LA CONSTRUCCIÓN TOMÁS TORIBIO ★

🌙 CIUDAD VIEJA

DIRECCIÓN GENERAL DE ADUANAS

DIRECCIÓN NACIONAL DE MIGRACIÓN ■

PALACIO DEL LIBRO

CENTRO CULTURAL DE ESPAÑA

BANCO DE LA REPÚBLICA ■

CIUDAD VIEJA HOSTEL

LINARDI Y RISSO

*Mercado del Puerto*

EX-BANCO DE LONDRES ★

BANCO LA CAJA OBRERA

LA SILENCIOSA

CASA DE LAVALLEJA ★

MUSEO ROMÁNTICO ▼

ANTEL

*Plaza Constitución*

GRUPOCINE TORRES PROFESIONALES ▼

CONFITERÍA LA PASIVA

PALACIO TARANCO ★

CASA RIVERA ★

MUSEO GURVICH ★

LA CORTE ▼

MUSEO DE ARTE PRECOLOMBINO ★

CATEDRAL METROPOLITANA ★

CASA GARIBALDI ★

*Plaza Zabala*

MONTEVIDEO WATERWORKS

CORREO CENTRAL ■

IGLESIA ANGLICANA DEL URUGUAY ★

*Mercado Central*

HOTEL NH COLUMBIA

*Plaza España*

*Río de la Plata*

0     250 yds

0     250 m

© AVALON TRAVEL

---

**Inset (SEE DETAIL):**

HOTEL PALACIO

MUSEO TORRES GARCÍA ★

LA PUERTA DE LA CIUDADELA

CABILDO

MANOS DEL URUGUAY ★

EXPRINTER

DON PEPERONE ▼

PANINI'S ▼

SHANNON IRISH PUB ▼

HOTEL SPLÉNDIDO

CAFÉ BACACAY ▼

LA PARRILLA DE SOLÍS ▼

CAFÉ IRAZÚ ▼

VIAJEROS SIN FRONTERAS ■

TEATRO SOLÍS

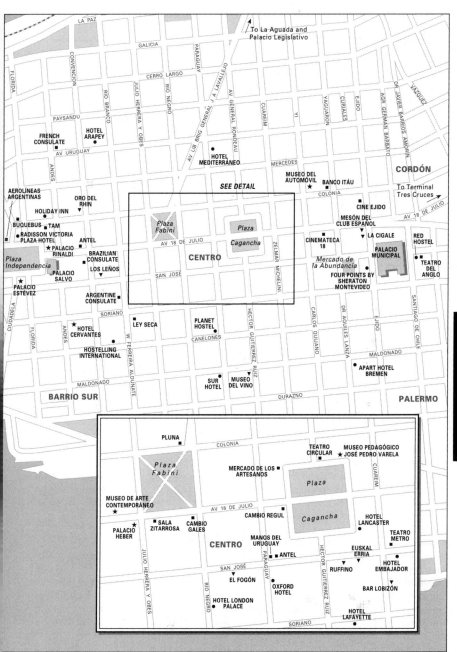

EXCURSIONS

# TRAVEL IN URUGUAY

Because so many travelers to the Argentine capital cross the Río de la Plata to Uruguay, Montevideo, Colonia, Carmelo, Punta del Este, and some other destinations are covered in this handbook. For the most part, conditions are similar to those in Argentina.

## VISAS AND OFFICIALDOM
Very few nationalities need advance visas for Uruguay, but requirements can change – if in doubt, contact Uruguay's Buenos Aires consulate. Ordinarily, border officials give foreign tourists an automatic 90-day entry permit.

## HEALTH
Uruguay requires no vaccinations for visitors entering from any country, and public health standards are among the continent's highest.

## MONEY AND PRICES
The Argentine political and economic meltdown of 2001-2002 had severe repercussions on the Uruguayan economy. With Argentines unable to travel because of their own weak peso, Uruguayan hotel occupancy fell, but the

Unlike most Latin American countries, Uruguay honors figures from the arts, such as painter Pedro Figari, on its banknotes.

Uruguayan peso slipped more slowly than the Argentine peso; because of the weak dollar, Uruguayan price levels have remained somewhat higher than in Argentina.

Traditionally, Uruguay has the continent's most liberal banking laws; exchange houses are numerous, and bureaucracy is minimal for U.S. cash and travelers checks. The U.S. dollar still operates as a parallel currency, at least in the tourist sector, where hotel and restaurant prices are often quoted in both; Argentine currency may be accepted, but sometimes at a

19th century, after which today's Centro, east of the entrance to the Ciudadela (walled city), gradually superseded the Ciudad Vieja.

From the 1850s, Montevideo followed Buenos Aires's economic example, as British investment, particularly in the railroads, fostered European immigration and the export of produce from countryside to capital and then overseas. For a time, this made Uruguay one of South America's most prosperous countries, with generous social welfare policies, but the economically active sector of the population proved unable to support a large pensioner class. Beginning in the 1960s, economic stagnation led to revolutionary political upheaval and, in reaction, a military dictatorship (1973–1985) from which the country and the capital slowly but steadily recovered until the economic setbacks of 2002. Things have steadily improved since.

Montevideo continues to dominate the countryside politically, economically, and culturally, even more than Buenos Aires does Argentina. Still, there has been a political tension between the countryside and the city, which has consistently voted the left-of-center Frente Amplio (Broad Front) into municipal power, but was unable to elect its candidates nationwide until former city mayor Tabaré Vásquez won the presidency in 2004.

## ORIENTATION
East of Buenos Aires, Montevideo occupies a hilly site on the left bank of the Río de la Plata. Passengers from Buenos Aires normally arrive at the Buquebus hydrofoil port on the Rambla 25 de Agosto, on the north side of the Ciudad Vieja, a gentrifying colonial grid of narrow streets west of Plaza Independencia. East of Plaza Independencia

poor rate. In areas away from the heavily tour-isted coast, acceptance of foreign currency is less common.

Banks keep limited hours – normally Monday-Friday 1-5 P.M. ATMs are common in Montevideo, Colonia, and Punta del Este, but in smaller towns they may not work with foreign plastic. Keep a close eye on exchange rates, and avoid buying too many pesos if the rate is unstable.

Interestingly, Uruguay has phased the faces of generals and politicians out of its banknotes, which now feature artists and writers like Joaquín Torres García (Ur$5), Eduardo Acevedo Vásquez (Ur$10), Juan Zorrilla de San Martín (Ur$20), José Pedro Varela (Ur$50), Eduardo Fabini (Ur$100), Pedro Figari (Ur$200), Alfredo Vásquez Acevedo (Ur$500), Juana de Ibarbourou (Ur$1,000), and Dámaso Antonio Larrañaga (Ur$2,000). The one-peso coin, though, remains the stronghold of independence hero General José Gervasio Artigas.

**COMMUNICATIONS**
Despite privatization pressures, Uruguayan

communications remain under the state monopoly Antel. Long-distance phone and Internet offices are fewer than in Argentina, but still numerous enough. Uruguay's country code is 598; each city or town has a separate area code, ranging from one to three or even four digits. Note that while most Montevideo telephone numbers have seven digits, a handful of informational and public-service numbers have only four digits, and a very few have eight. Rural and suburban numbers have between four and six digits.

**GETTING AROUND**
Distances in Uruguay are short and roads are good. Rental cars are readily available, but the cost of gasoline is high – around US$1.50 per liter.

Uruguayan buses resemble Argentine ones – modern, spacious, and fast – and service is frequent on most routes. Most, though not all, towns have a main bus terminal, usually on the outskirts of town; some bus lines have separate ticket offices in more central locations.

EXCURSIONS

lies the commercial Centro, split in half by the east–west thoroughfare Avenida 18 de Julio; businesses cluster around Plaza del Entrevero and Plaza Cagancha. South of the Centro, Barrio Sur is home to much of Montevideo's Afro-Uruguayan community; to the north, La Aguada is an improving area that's home to the national legislature and a new suburban train station. The riverside *rambla* (street or boulevard) leads southeast to suburban barrios with large wooded parks and sandy beaches.

## SIGHTS

Most of Montevideo's sights are concentrated in the compact Ciudad Vieja, but quite a few are also scattered around the Centro and neighboring barrios. The Ciudad Vieja's more north-westerly parts, around the port, have a history of petty crime after dark, but Montevideo's increased popularity with South Atlantic cruise

ships has spurred municipal authorities to improve security here.

Tourism authorities have produced an informative walking-tour map of the city, with details on many historic structures. It's widely available at tourist offices and hotels throughout the city.

## The Centro and Vicinity

About three blocks east of Plaza Independencia, construction of **Plaza Fabini** (1964), also known as **Plaza del Entrevero** for the monument by sculptor José Belloni, opened a view down the diagonal Avenida Libertador General Lavalleja toward the barrio of La Aguada, site of the Uruguayan congress. At the southeast corner of the plaza, dating from 1894, the ornate French-style **Palacio Heber** (Av. 18 de Julio 998) was built as a private residence but now holds the **Museo de la Moneda y del**

## SOUTH AMERICA'S SWITZERLAND

Uruguay shares many features with its larger neighbor, so much so that even some Uruguayans will reluctantly suggest that the country might as well be an Argentine province – and when Argentines pack the beaches of Punta del Este in summer, it can seem like one. Uruguayans themselves, while their appearance and accent differ little from that of their neighbors, do not have the reputation for arrogance that other Latin Americans often attribute to Argentines.

Nor do they bear the stigma of corruption – Uruguay ranks in the top 25 of Transparency International's clean government rankings according to perceived corruption levels. For that reason, and its traditional social welfare policies, Uruguay long held a reputation as the "Switzerland of South America," though its own 1971-1985 dictatorship subverted that assessment.

Uruguay has many attractions not easily found in the immediate vicinity of Buenos Aires – long, sandy beaches beneath rising headlands, extensive oceanside dunes, and verdant rolling hill country. It also has a lively capital city in Montevideo, one of the Southern Cone's cultural treasures in the UNESCO World Heritage Site town of Colonia, and the high-powered summer resort of Punta del Este.

Still, when Argentina sneezes, Uruguay catches cold, and the Argentine political and economic collapse of 2001-2002 hit the country hard. With their currency devalued and bank accounts frozen, Argentines could not even afford to travel across the river – except to fetch money from their Uruguayan accounts, which were also briefly frozen despite Uruguay's tradition of free-market banking. The Uruguayan peso also fell, though not so far as the Argentine currency, giving the Uruguayan tourist industry some breathing room by making it more competitive and attractive to Brazilians.

With an improving economy, Argentines have begun to return to Uruguay for their summer holidays, though they're spending less freely than they once did. Prices are, in general, about 15-20 percent higher than in Argentina, though much depends on individual indulgences and tastes.

Montevideo and Colonia are both easily accessible by ferry and catamaran from the port of Buenos Aires. Montevideo is the country's transport hub, with bus services west toward Colonia and east toward Punta del Este. There are also catamarans from the Argentine river port of Tigre through the Paraná delta to the Uruguayan riverside town of Carmelo.

**Gaucho,** on Uruguay's financial and rural history. The **Museo de Arte Contemporáneo** (Av. 18 de Julio 965, 2nd fl., tel. 02/900-6662, Tues.–Sun. 2–8 P.M., free admission) is across the street.

About two blocks south of the plaza, sadly closed after legal problems, the former **Hotel Cervantes** (Soriano 868) is a crumbling classic that dates from 1928. Designed with direct telephone connections to Buenos Aires—a novelty in those days—it was the favorite accommodations of figures such as tango singer Carlos Gardel, folksinger Atahualpa Yupanqui, and writers Jorge Luis Borges, Adolfo Bioy Casares, and Julio Cortázar.

Two blocks farther east, Avenida 18 de Julio splits **Plaza Cagancha** (dating from 1836, but handsomely remodeled in 1995) in two. At its northeast corner, the **Museo Pedagógico José Pedro Varela** (Plaza Cagancha 1175, tel. 02/902-0915, www.crnti.edu.uy/museo) deals with the evolution of Uruguayan public education. Hours are mid-March to mid-December Monday–Friday 9 A.M.–7 P.M.; the rest of the year, it's open Monday–Friday 8 A.M.–noon. Admission is free.

A short distance northeast, the Automóvil Club del Uruguay's **Museo del Automóvil** (Colonia 1251, 6th fl., tel. 02/902-4792, Tues.–Sun. 2–7 P.M., free) sports a collection of classic cars seen less frequently on Uruguay's streets and highways than they once were.

To the southeast, dating from 1904–1909, the art nouveau **Mercado de la Abundancia** (San José 1312) is a national historical monument that's been recycled as a crafts outlet and cultural center. Immediately east, but fronting on Avenida 18 de Julio, the ponderous **Palacio Municipal** (1929–1930) sits atop the site of the former British cemetery—appropriately enough for a monument to bureaucracy.

From Plaza Fabini, Avenida Libertador provides an unobstructed northeast view toward the neoclassical **Palacio Legislativo** (1908), the home of Uruguay's legislature and the work of Vittorio Meano. Meano, who also contributed to Buenos Aires's Teatro Colón and Argentina's Congreso Nacional, died in a mysterious gunshot incident before the Montevideo building's completion. Brightly illuminated after dark, at the north end of Avenida Libertador, the **Palacio Legislativo** (tel. 02/924-1783, Mon.–Fri. hourly 9 A.M.– noon and 2:30, 3:30, and 4 P.M.) offers free guided tours in both Spanish and English.

## C Ciudad Vieja

Dating from 1836 but remodeled completely in 1936, **Plaza Independencia** is a civic center marking the boundary between the colonial Ciudad Vieja to the west and the republican Centro to the east. The best starting point for an introduction to downtown Montevideo, its literal centerpiece is the massive equestrian statue atop the **Mausoleo de Artigas,** the subterranean crypt of independence hero José Gervasio Artigas. On the south side of the plaza, the **Palacio Estévez** (1873) served as the presidential palace for a century-plus; it is still home to the **Museo de la Casa de Gobierno** (Plaza Independencia 776, tel. 02/151-5902, Mon.–Fri. 10 A.M.–5 P.M., free admission), with guided tours available.

From the plaza, the late-afternoon sun illuminates architect Mario Palanti's photogenic **Palacio Salvo** (1922), a 26-story baroque hotel since converted into apartments, at the foot of Avenida 18 de Julio. Palanti designed the building to be visible from its Buenos

Aires doppelganger Palacio Barolo, which he also built. From the Salvo's upper floors, in December 1939, British agents observed the German battleship *Graf Spee* taking refuge in neutral Uruguay for a few days as permitted by international law, before its captain scuttled it in the river.

Montevideo has perhaps the finest assemblage of art deco architecture in the Southern Cone countries. Immediately across the avenue from the Palacio Salvo, dating from 1929, the **Palacio Rinaldi** (Plaza Independencia 1356) is one of the best specimens; note the decorative relief panels on the facade of this apartment building.

Upon its creation in 1836, Plaza Independencia symbolized a break with the colonial past; at its west end, **La Puerta de la Ciudadela** (1746) is one of the last remaining fragments of the citadel that surrounded what is now the Ciudad Vieja. Passing through the gate, the pedestrian mall Sarandí is a portion of

A monument to independence hero José Gervasio Artigas is the centerpiece of Plaza Independencia.

EXCURSIONS

© WAYNE BERNHARDSON

The facade of the Banco La Caja Obrera, with bas-reliefs by Edmundo Prati, recalls depression-era architecture in the United States.

© WAYNE BERNHARDSON

the partly rejuvenated colonial quarter; the first major point of interest is the **Museo Torres García,** dedicated to one of Uruguay's most notable 20th-century artists.

Opposite the museum, wall-to-wall with restaurants and bars, the narrow pedestrian mall Bacacay branches south to the 1837 **Teatro Solís,** a historic performing-arts venue.

Sarandí continues to **Plaza Constitución,** the colonial *plaza mayor* (1726) and predecessor to Plaza Independencia. Surrounded by colonial buildings, including the landmark **Catedral Metropolitana** (1790) and the neoclassical **Cabildo** (colonial council, 1804), the sycamore-shaded plaza also features Juan Ferrari's post-colonial central fountain. The **Cabildo** contains the **Museo y Archivo Histórico Municipal** (Juan Carlos Gómez 1362, tel. 02/915-9685, Tues.–Sun. 12:30–6 P.M., Sat. 11 A.M.–5 P.M.), the municipal historical museum.

Two blocks south of Plaza Constitución, Montevideo merchant Samuel Fischer Lafone (founder of the Falkland Islands Company) commissioned the 1845 **Iglesia Anglicana del Uruguay** (Anglican Church of Uruguay), which was dismantled in the 1930s to allow construction of the Rambla Francia and then rebuilt. Four blocks north of the church, dating from 1941, the facade of the **Banco La Caja Obrera** (25 de Mayo 500) displays extraordinary bas-reliefs by Edmundo Prati.

The rehabbed architectural **Museo Municipal de la Construcción Tomás Toribio** (Piedras 528, tel. 02/915-4087, Mon.–Fri. 12:30–5:30 P.M.) is two blocks farther north. Three blocks west, dating from 1926–1938, the monumental **Banco de la República** (Cerrito 351) fills an entire block bounded by Piedras, Solís, Zabala, and Cerrito.

Four blocks west of Plaza Constitución, French landscape architect Edouard André created **Plaza Zabala** (1880), named for the city's founder, on the site of the former Casa de Gobierno and an even earlier fortress. Occupying an irregular lot immediately to the north, the **Palacio Taranco** (25 de Mayo 376) houses the **Museo de Arte Decorativo.**

In the immediate vicinity of Plaza Zabala, several historic buildings are units of the **Museo Histórico Nacional** (National History Museum): the **Casa Rivera** (Rincón 437); the 1831 **Museo Romántico** (25 de Mayo 428); the **Casa de Lavalleja** (Zabala 1469); and the 1830 **Casa Garibaldi** (25 de Mayo 314). The museums are not the only points of interest. Dating from the late 19th century, the former **Montevideo Waterworks** (Rincón and Zabala) is now a bank. A little more than a block to the north, the neoclassical 1890 **Banco de Londres** (Zabala 1480) is due for rehab as the **Biblioteca Americanista** (Americanist Library), but progress has stalled.

Northwest of Plaza Zabala, the **Mercado del Puerto** (1868), on the Pérez Castellano pedestrian mall, is one of the capital's top tourist destinations for its seafood restaurants and casual atmosphere. The imposing building to its north, across the Rambla 25 de Agosto, is the deco-style **Dirección General de Aduanas** (1923), the customs headquarters.

## Museo Torres García

Pictured on Uruguay's five-peso banknote, Joaquín Torres García (1874–1949) was a Picasso contemporary who became widely known for both abstract and figurative work. Spending much of his career in Barcelona, Paris, and New York, he also produced historical portraits of *Hombres Célebres* (Famous Men), which in one instance he retitled *Hombres, Héroes y Monstruos* (Men, Heroes and Monsters), according to his interpretation of individuals such as Bach, Beethoven, Columbus, and Rabelais. The museum includes samples of the Torres García's legacy, but also works by contemporary artists.

The Museo Torres García (Sarandí 683, tel. 02/916-2663, www.torresgarcia.org.uy) is open Monday–Friday 9 A.M.–7 P.M., Saturday–Sunday 10 A.M.–6 P.M., except for January 1, May 1, July 18, August 25, November 2, and December 25. Admission is theoretically free, but donations are actively encouraged; guided visits in Spanish and English are available. There is a museum bookshop and gift shop.

## Teatro Solís

Montevideo's performing-arts counterpart to Buenos Aires's Teatro Colón, the neoclassical Teatro Solís (1856) has showcased performers of the caliber of Enrico Caruso, Arturo Toscanini, Vaslav Nijinsky, and Mstislav Rostropovich. Half a century older than the Colón—though Rosas's blockade delayed its completion—its facade features eight Ionic columns; the symmetrical lateral wings were a later addition. The horseshoe-shaped auditorium seats 1,600 spectators, far fewer than the Colón, but with outstanding acoustics.

Having completed a major renovation, the Teatro Solís (Buenos Aires 678, tel. 02/1950-3323 or 02/1950-3325, www.teatrosolis.org.uy) presents a full schedule of classical music, ballet, opera, and drama. Guided tours (US$2 in Spanish, US$4 in other languages) take place Tuesday–Sunday at 11 A.M., noon, and 5 P.M. There's an additional Saturday tour at 1 P.M.

## Palacio Taranco

Occupying an irregular lot opposite Plaza Zabala, the opulent Palacio Taranco (1907–1908) is the equal of Buenos Aires's French Renaissance palaces, with antique furniture, sparkling parquet floors, and marble fireplaces in almost every room. In 1979, it saw the signing of a papal mediation that avoided war between Argentina and Chile over a territorial dispute in the southern Beagle Channel.

The Palacio Taranco is also home to the **Museo de Arte Decorativo** (25 de Mayo 376, tel. 02/915-1101, www.mec.gub.uy/museo/taranco, Tues.–Sat. 12:15–6 P.M., Sun. 2–6 P.M., free) with a collection of European artwork on its upper floors and a basement gallery with brightly decorated classical Greek and Roman ceramics and bronzes, plus early Islamic ceramics from what is now Iranian territory.

Opposite Plaza Zabala, but entered around the corner, the museum offers guided tours at 4:30 P.M. every day the museum is open.

## Museo Histórico Nacional

Montevideo's national historical museum

EXCURSIONS

The restored Teatro Solís is Montevideo's prime performing arts venue.

consists of several Ciudad Vieja houses with distinct histories, contents, and perspectives. Admission to all of them is free of charge, but their hours differ.

The most broadly historical of them is the **Casa Rivera** (Rincón 437, tel. 02/915-3316, www.mec.gub.uy/museo/rivera, Mon.–Fri. 1–5 P.M., Sat. 11 A.M.–6 P.M.), a handsome late-colonial residence that was once the residence of General Fructuoso Rivera, the country's first president; the upper floor is a late-19th-century addition with wrought-iron balconies at every window and an octagonal watchtower. The display on pre-Hispanic Uruguay is more than just a token tribute to the country's aboriginal inhabitants (note the Charrúa sculpture by Juan Luis Blanes). It's most notable, though, for the massive canvases of Uruguayan political and military figures, and of independence-era battles.

Dating from 1782 but dramatically remodeled in the early 1830s, the **Casa Montero** houses the **Museo Romántico** (25 de Mayo 428, tel. 02/915-5361, www.mec.gub.uy/ museum/romantico). Also known as the Palacio de Mármol (Marble Palace) for its elaborate materials, its museum traces the tastes of upper-class Montevideo inhabitants from independence to the early 20th century through their household artifacts. Hours are identical to the Casa Rivera.

Dating from 1873, the **Casa de Lavalleja** (Zabala 1469, tel. 02/915-1028, www.mec. gub.uy/museo/lavalleja, Mon.–Fri. 1–6 P.M., free admission) was the residence of Juan de Lavalleja, who led the "33 Orientales" whose landing in 1825 began the liberation from Brazil. The two-story building (uncommon in colonial times) served as Montevideo's first theater; it's still an impressive building, but its contents are fairly ordinary and scantier than other historical museums.

Italian adventurer Giuseppe Garibaldi, who aided Uruguay's anti-Rosas resistance in the 1840s, lived in the 1830 Spanish neoclassical **Casa Garibaldi** (25 de Mayo 314, tel. 02/915-4257, www.mec.gub.uy/museum/garibaldi, open by appointment only).

## Mercado del Puerto

Originally intended as a Chilean train station, the British prefab port market—whose wrought-iron superstructure bears a strong resemblance to Santiago's historic Mercado Central—never made it out of Montevideo harbor. Erected just south of the port complex in 1868, its stalls and grills served stevedores and other laborers for nearly a century, but several decades ago the restaurants gradually grew more sophisticated, adding sidewalk seating and turning it into a tourist attraction.

Always packed for lunch into the late afternoon (when it closes for the day), the Mercado (Piedras 237, www.mercadodelpuerto.com.uy) is an informal venue whose surrounding streets teem with artisans, artists, and musicians. It's possible to eat well on stools at the grills, where you can pick your cut off the coals, but there is also table service (on cruise-ship days, it can be overwhelmingly crowded, however). The interior, which features a wooden "Big Ben" clock tower, would look more appealing if owners removed all the illuminated plastic signs surrounding it.

## Museo de la Moneda y del Gaucho

French architect Alfred Massüe designed the ornate French-style Palacio Heber (1896–1897) as a private residence for wealthy widow Margarita Uriarte de Heber, whose second marriage to politician Luis Alberto de Herrera took place here. Later sold to the Peirano family, then acquired by the Banco de la República, it was restored in 1985 to house two outstanding museums on Uruguayan economic history and the country's gaucho heritage: the Museo de la Moneda y del Gaucho (Av. 18 de Julio 998, tel. 02/900-8764, www.brounet.com.uy, Mon.–Fri. 10 A.M.–5 P.M., free).

Of the two museums, the 2nd-floor Museo del Gaucho is the better—in fact, even if the presentation romanticizes the past, its assortment of gaucho artifacts equals anything in Argentina. The items range from the usual saddles, spurs, stirrups, and belts to lances, *facones* (knives), and elaborate silver *mates* (gourds) and *chifles* (carved horns for drinking), plus paintings and sculptures by contemporary Uruguayan artists. It's the one Montevideo museum not be missed.

The Museo de la Moneda, on the 1st floor, is more pedestrian but does house an impressive collection of colonial coins and medals, not to mention Uruguayan public and private banknotes that offer insights into the country's economic history. Banknotes of 500,000 pesos, for instance, recall the disastrous hyperinflation of the 1980s.

## Museo de Arte Precolombino

It's still a work-in-progress, but Montevideo's pre-Columbian art museum, Museo de Arte Precolombino (MAPI, 25 de Mayo 279, www.museoprecolombino.org, Tues.–Fri. noon–6 P.M., Sat. 11–6 P.M., free), is impressive both for its collections and for a magnificent restoration of a historic building. Only the ground floor, with lithic artifacts from Uruguay and ceramics from the central Andes, really functions as a museum; renovations on the upper floor, where broad skylights let natural light flood into the building, have stalled.

Originally intended as a spa in the late 19th century, the building became Uruguay's defense ministry before the military abandoned it in the 1990s. The facade and some downstairs exhibit halls are complete, along with a stage now used for small live-music events (the tiled floor where spectators sit was originally a swimming pool).

## Museo Gurvich

New in 2007, this beautifully designed art museum displays the work of José Gurvich (1927–1974), a Lithuanian-born Jewish immigrant who became a disciple of Joaquín Torres García. His paintings, sculptures, and sketches, which touched frequently but not universally on the Jewish experience, show Torres García's influence in their colors and abstract shapes. Still, he was original enough to be widely exhibited throughout the Americas including New York, where he died unexpectedly of a heart attack.

Alongside the cathedral, the Museo Gurvich

(Ituzaingó 1377, tel. 02/915-7826, www.museogurvich.org) is open Monday–Friday 11 A.M.–6 P.M., Saturday 11 A.M.–5 P.M. Admission costs US$1.50.

## RESTAURANTS

Unless otherwise indicated, the following restaurants are open for lunch and dinner. Most of them offer main courses in the US$10 range.

It's hard to go wrong at the historic **Mercado del Puerto** (Pérez Castellano 1569). Some of its gaggle of *parrillas* (beef grills) and other restaurants are, according to *Buenos Aires Herald* restaurant critic Dereck Foster, "scruffy looking but they have wonderful food."

Best of the bunch, by consensus, the *tasca*-style **( El Palenque** (tel. 02/915-4704, www.elpalenque.com.uy) is a place where Galician owner Emilio Portela specializes in seafood (US$10–18 for most entrées), hams hang from the ceiling, and there's both indoor and patio seating. Particularly choice items include the *rabas* (squid rings) appetizer, swordfish steak, and the mixed seafood grill, generous enough to feed three hungry adults.

Lunchgoers meet on Plaza Constitución.

The innovation center for Uruguayan dining is the Ciudad Vieja, where imaginative new options seem to open on an almost daily basis. **Café Irazú** (Juan Carlos Gómez 1315, tel. 02/916-6419) has the area's best, most reasonably priced breakfasts, with Brazilian coffee in a bright, cheerful locale. Relatively expensive by neighborhood standards, **Café Bacacay** (Bacacay 1306, tel. 02/916-6074) gets the pre- and post-theater crowd, thanks to its proximity to the Teatro Solís. There's also the classic **Confitería La Pasiva** (Juan Carlos Gómez and Sarandí, tel. 02/915-8261), on Plaza Constitución.

**Panini's** (Bacacay 1339, tel. 02/916-8760, www.paninis.com.uy) is an upmarket sidewalk café with an excellent, diverse Italian menu that features entrées such as *ravioli neri* (black ravioli) in the US$10–18 range, plus fine desserts, Uruguayan wines, and ambience.

The name may sound like a chain cliché, but **Don Peperone** (Sarandí and Bartolomé Mitre, tel. 02/915-7493) deserves consideration for fine lasagna and *pizzetas,* as well as good desserts and good service. There's both inside and sidewalk seating.

**La Parrilla de Solís** (enter at Mitre 1308 or Bacacay 1309, tel. 02/916-9026) is the fashionable face of *parrillada,* with outstanding meats in the US$10–15 range, a fine selection of Uruguayan wines, and equally fine service in agreeable surroundings.

Upscale **La Corte** (Sarandí 586, tel. 02/915-7592, US$10–20) has a sophisticated international menu, but prices are not out of line for a place of its quality.

Montevideo's most atmospheric restaurant, in a colonial Jesuit seminary, **( La Silenciosa** (Ituzaingó 1426, tel. 02/915-9409, www.lasilenciosa.com) is ideal for a romantic dinner, but it's also where businessmen take their foreign clients to impress them at midday. Many locals consider it the city's top restaurant; the risotto is remarkable, the desserts are outstanding, and the service is exceptional. It's open weekdays for lunch, and Thursday–Saturday for dinner.

Downtown's **El Lobizón** (Zelmar Michelini 1264, tel. 02/901-1334) serves a fairly extensive pub-style menu of meat, pasta, chicken, and sandwiches with an accompaniment of rock music; it gets most of its business at night. For short orders, snacks, and coffee, there's the *confitería* **Oro del Rhin** (Convención 1403, tel. 02/902-2833).

Since Uruguayans are even more notorious carnivores than Argentines, traditional downtown *parrillas* like **Los Leños** (San José 909, tel. 02/900-2285) and **El Fogón** (San José 1080, tel. 02/900-0900) always draw crowds.

Other ethnic food is primarily European, at venues like the **Mesón del Club Español** (Av. 18 de Julio 1332, tel. 02/901-5145) and the Basque **Euskal Erria** (San José 1168, tel. 02/902-3519).

For seafood by the river, try **Che Montevideo** (Rambla Gandhi 630, tel. 02/710-6941), with ample outside seating. *Parrilla* costs in the US$8–10 pp range.

**La Cigale** (Ejido 1337) serves fine ice cream, though it's not at the level of Buenos Aires's best.

# NIGHTLIFE

Montevideo is not quite Buenos Aires for nightlife, but the Ciudad Vieja is gearing up along once moribund Bartolomé Mitre, nearly wall-to-wall with bars and restaurants. Most of these places are within staggering distance of each other but, as buses run less frequently than in Buenos Aires, it may be necessary to take a cab home.

## Bars and Pubs

Part of its namesake apart-hotel, the intimate bar at **Bremen** (Maldonado 1308, tel. 02/902-2094) occasionally hosts local tango singers (not dancers), backed by guitar, with spontaneous audience participation.

**Ley Seca** (Soriano 952, tel. 02/908-2481) has live music Thursday through Sunday.

In the Ciudad Vieja, the **Shannon Irish Pub** (Bartolomé Mitre 1381, tel. 02/916-9585) is a clone of its Buenos Aires counterparts. The

**Museo del Vino** (Maldonado 1150, tel. 02/908-3430) isn't really what the name suggests—this sophisticated wine bar serves some of the best of contemporary Uruguayan vintages in a contemporary ambience.

## Tango

Tango is almost as popular in Montevideo as in Buenos Aires. Within the Mercado Central, **Fun Fun** (Ciudadela 1229, tel. 02/915-8005) is the city's classic tango venue.

Though less youthful than its name implies, the Mercado de la Abundancia's **Joventango** (San José 1312, tel. 02/901-5561, joventango@hotmail.com) does host regular tango events, including classes and weekend *milongas.*

Newer on the scene, the Ciudad Vieja's **Tanguería El Farolito** (Juncal 1413, tel. 02/916-5411, tangueriaelfarolito@adinet.com. uy) is a beautifully restored ballroom with a handsome wooden floor. *Milongas,* sometimes with live music in a welcoming environment, take place Thursday through Sunday.

# THE ARTS
## Cinema

Downtown Montevideo has several movie theaters, including the repertory-style **Cinemateca 18** (Av. 18 de Julio 1286, tel. 02/900-9056); the **Grupocine Ejido** (Ejido 1377, tel. 02/901-4242); and **Grupocine Torres Profesionales** (Colonia 1297, tel. 02/901-4242).

The **Centro Cultural de España** (Rincón 629, tel. 02/915-2250) hosts art exhibits and free films.

## Theater

In addition to its cinemas, Montevideo has several live-theater venues, including the landmark **Teatro Solís.** Downtown locales include the **Teatro Circular** (Av. Rondeau 1388, tel. 02/901-5952) and the **Teatro del Anglo** (San José 1426, tel. 02/902-3773).

## Other Performing Arts

The **Sala Zitarrosa** (Av. 18 de Julio 1008, tel. 02/901-1756, www.salazitarrosa.com.uy) hosts

EXCURSIONS

# THE COUNTRY OF HOLIDAYS

Uruguay's devastating 1973-1985 dictatorship, followed by economic changes in which a relatively small working population could no longer support a large pensioner class, undercut the country's traditionally generous social welfare state. One feature still survives, though: Uruguay remains the País de los Feriados – the country of holidays.

Uruguay celebrates all the typical holidays that Argentines and most other South Americans do – **New Year's Day** (January 1), **Labor Day** (May 1), **Día de la Raza** (Columbus Day, October 12), and **Día de la Familia** (Christmas, December 25); Uruguayan workers get those days off. They also enjoy an official holiday on **Epifanía** (Epiphany, January 6).

April 19 marks the **Desembarco de los 33,** the 1825 date on which 33 returning exiles, with Argentine assistance, landed on the Banda Oriental to start the campaign for independence from Brazil. May 18's **Batalla de Las Piedras** (Battle of Las Piedras) commemorates a key independence battle.

June 19 is the **Natalicio de Artigas;** unlike the Argentines' celebration of José de San Martín, Uruguayans honor their great national hero on the date of his birth rather than his death. July 18 is **Jura de la Constitución** (Constitution Day), while August 25 is **Día de la Independencia** (Independence Day).

Oddly enough for a self-proclaimed secular country, Uruguay officially acknowledges November 2 as the **Día de los Muertos** (All Souls' Day). This is particularly peculiar as it does *not* acknowledge **Semana Santa** (Holy Week) in March or April as such – rather, this time is **Semana Criolla** (Creole Week) or even **Semana de Turismo** (Tourism Week). Though this week may occur only shortly after the end of the January and February summer vacations, many Uruguayans take the entire week off, rather than just Good Friday.

Uruguay's **Carnaval,** on the Monday and Tuesday before Ash Wednesday, is what Buenos Aires's must have been before the decimation of the Afro-Argentines; Montevideo's Barrio Sur still has a visible Afro-Uruguayan population that practices *candombe* (Afro-Uruguayan music and dance) ceremonies. Although these are not official holidays, they are popular ones.

As if all that were not enough, each Uruguayan is officially entitled to take the day off on his or her birthday.

events almost every night, ranging from evangelical and rock 'n' roll concerts to movies and live theater.

Upstairs at the Mercado Central, the **Complejo Cultural Mundo Afro** (Ciudadela 1229, tel. 02/915-0247, www.mundoafro.org) stresses Afro-Uruguayan theater and dance.

No longer a cinema, the **Teatro Metro** (San José 1211, tel. 02/902-2017) hosts live theater and musical events.

## SHOPS

The **Mercado de los Artesanos** (Plaza Cagancha 1365, tel. 02/901-0158) has a diversity of crafts. The recycled **Mercado de la Abundancia** (San José 1312, tel. 02/901-3438) has downstairs crafts stalls and upstairs *parrillas.*

For a broader crafts selection from around the country, try **Manos del Uruguay** (Sarandí 668, tel. 02/915-5345, www.manos.com.uy) in the Ciudad Vieja and downtown (San José 1111, tel. 02/900-4910).

The Ciudad Vieja is the place to look for antiques and artwork, at places like **Galería Latina** (Sarandí 671, tel. 02/916-3737). For leather, try the Ciudad Vieja's **Casa Mario** (Piedras 641, tel. 02/916-2356, www.casamarioleather.com), which sets the standard.

Also in the Ciudad Vieja, **Librería Linardi y Risso** (Juan Carlos Gómez 1435, tel. 02/915-7129, www.linardiyrisso.com) is a specialist bookstore dealing with Uruguayan literature and history, and Latin America in general. Once the studio of artist Joaquín Torres García, it has been frequented by literary figures ranging from Pablo Neruda to Mario Benedetti and Juan Carlos Onetti.

**Palacio del Libro** (25 de Mayo 577, tel. 02/915-7543) is another large antiquarian bookseller.

## ACCOMMODATIONS

Montevideo has abundant accommodations, with several excellent values in the budget and mid-range categories—especially since the recent devaluation. Choices are relatively few, however, in the Ciudad Vieja, the city's most interesting barrio.

### Under US$25

Many youthful international travelers enjoy the **Hostelling International** (Canelones 935, tel. 02/908-1234, www.montevideohostel.com.uy, US$9 pp) affiliate, in an early-20th-century house on a tree-lined block. Rates can vary depending on whether you're an HI member or not, Uruguayan or not, and your age; the dorm-style accommodations come with kitchen facilities, expansive common areas, information, and WiFi.

It has plenty of competition, though. The dorms-only **Planet Montevideo Hostel** (Canelones 1095, tel. 02/900-0733, www. planetmontevideohostel.com, US$10 pp) occupies a beautifully restored period house with two kitchens, a rooftop terrace, book exchange, and breakfast included. There's also friendly management.

The lively **Red Hostel** (San José 1406, tel. 02/908-8514, www.redhostel.com, US$12 pp in dorms, US$36 d) is a beautiful three-story home with a rooftop terrace surrounded by a canopy of sycamores. There are only a handful of private rooms; in addition to accommodations, it has kitchen and Internet facilities, and a small bar.

Likewise, the **C Ciudad Vieja Hostel** (Ituzaingó 1436, tel. 02/915-6192, www.ciudadviejahostel.com, US$12–18 pp) is a full-service hostel in the city's most historic section, also close to its nightlife and restaurants. It has a magnificent rooftop terrace, arranges excursions, and six nights a week offers inexpensive communal dinners—alternately, *asados, chivitos,* and pizza.

Classic in style, the no-frills **Hotel Palacio** (Bartolomé Mitre 1364, tel. 02/916-3612, www.hotelpalacio.com.uy, US$20–25 s or d) now lags behind better budget choices in the Ciudad Vieja, but it's worth consideration if you can get one of the two 6th-floor rooms with enormous terraces and expansive views of the old city.

### US$25-50

Under new ownership, with a new name, the nooks and crannies of the Ciudad Vieja's **Hotel Spléndido** (Bartolomé Mitre 1314, tel. 02/916-4900, www.splendidohotel.com.uy, US$19/25–24/35 s/d) still offer character on a budget. Rates for simple rooms with high ceilings and eclectic furnishings, in a two-story flatiron that Uruguayan president Baltasar Brum erected for his mistress in 1901, depend on whether the room has a shared or private bath, but all have balconies. There are also many good restaurants and bars in the vicinity and, while it's quieter than its density might suggest, the Spléndido is best for those who prefer to stay up late.

The **Oxford Hotel** (Paraguay 1286, tel. 02/902-0046, www.hoteloxford.com.uy, US$35/45 s/d) is a well-kept 1960s structure that's perfectly acceptable; rates include breakfast, a late-afternoon snack, parking, and WiFi in the lobby only. Some rooms, though, are a little small.

The best value in this category is the German-run **C Apart Hotel Bremen** (Maldonado 1308, tel./fax 02/903-2094, www.bremen-montevideo.com, US$38/43 s/d or US$65 s or d). This magnificently remodeled century-old building, with stained-glass skylights and windows, has been transformed into stylish one- and two-bedroom apartments with cable TV, fax, fast Internet connections, and kitchenettes. Rates depend on size; the offices are half a block north, at Aquiles Lanza 1168.

The highly recommended **Sur Hotel** (Maldonado 1098, tel. 02/908-2025, www.surhotel.com, US$35–43 d) is an attractively

EXCURSIONS

rehabbed hotel, on a quiet block, with gracious management; the more expensive rooms have whirlpool tubs. Breakfast costs US$2.50 extra.

Accommodations at the well-managed **Hotel Mediterráneo** (Paraguay 1486, tel. 02/900-5090, www.hotelmediterraneo.com. uy, US$32/35–41/48 s/d) range from utilitarian standard rooms to more spacious "superior" rooms with air-conditioning and free Internet connections; an abundant Brazilian-style buffet breakfast of croissants and fresh fruit costs US$4 more. Street-side rooms get a steady drone from passing vehicles on nearby Avenida Lavalleja.

The central **Hotel Lancaster** (Plaza Cagancha 1334, tel. 02/902-1054, www.lancasterhotel.com.uy, US$40/50 s/d) has very decent if unadorned rooms.

## US$50-100

Immaculate and cheerful rooms more than compensate for a bland exterior at the **Hotel London Palace** (Río Negro 1278, tel. 02/902-0024, www.lphotel.com, US$50/62–53/67 s/d). Amenities at this excellent mid-range hotel include a Brazilian-style buffet breakfast (plenty of fresh fruit), air-conditioning, and parking.

The high-rise **Hotel Embajador** (San José 1212, tel. 02/902-0012, www.hotelembajador.com, US$51/64 s/d) has 120 rooms with air-conditioning, cable TV, a Brazilian buffet breakfast, parking, swimming pool, and the like; the rooms, all of which enjoy WiFi, are spacious but not quite so good as those at the London Palace.

Overlooking the river, on the south side of the Ciudad Vieja, the Spanish NH chain has rehabbed the **Hotel NH Columbia** (Rambla Gran Bretaña 473, tel. 02/916-0001, www.nh-hotels.com, US$77 d), which offers 138 rooms including a dozen suites, with buffet breakfast and conveniences including Internet access and a fitness center.

**Hotel Lafayette** (Soriano 1170, tel. 02/902-4646, fax 02/902-1301, www.lafayette.com.uy, US$70/77–77/96 s/d) is a handsome contemporary hotel with spacious rooms and breakfast.

Tobacco-free rooms are available, and there are business facilities (including WiFi), a gym, and other amenities.

The 134-room **Holiday Inn** (Colonia 823, tel. 02/902-0001, www.holidayinn.com.uy, US$80–140 s or d), the local rep of the international chain, sits on a slightly shabby block, but has good facilities including a rooftop pool and terrace.

## Over US$100

Convenient to the city's financial district, the spacious **Four Points by Sheraton Montevideo** (Ejido 1275, tel. 02/901-7000, www.fourpoints.com/montevideo, US$90–120 s or d) fills with the business crowd during the week, but gets mostly tourists on weekends.

Under international-chain ownership after years as a Sun Myung Moonie outpost, the ◖ **Radisson Victoria Plaza Hotel** (Plaza Independencia 759, tel. 02/902-0111, U.S. toll-free tel. 800/333-3333, fax 02/902-1628, www.radisson.com, US$130–220 s or d) has expanded to include a state-of-the-art casino. It has a 24-hour business center, a full-service spa, and many other luxuries.

## INFORMATION

The **Ministerio de Turismo** (Rambla 25 de Agosto and Yacaré, tel. 02/188-5100, www.turismo.gub.uy, Mon.–Fri. 9 A.M.–5 P.M.) occupies spacious new port headquarters, opposite the Mercado del Puerto. Its Aeropuerto Carrasco branch (tel. 02/601-1757) is open daily 8 A.M.–8 P.M.

At Terminal Tres Cruces, the main bus station, the **Ministerio de Turismo** and the **Asociación de Hoteles y Restaurantes** (AHRU, Bulevar Artigas 1825, tel. 02/409-7399, www.ahru.com.uy, Mon.–Fri. 8 A.M.–10 P.M., Sat.–Sun. 9 A.M.–9 P.M.) maintain a particularly helpful information office. The latter helps find accommodations.

## SERVICES

As the capital and only real metropolis in a small country, Montevideo has a full range of services.

## Consulates

Several Latin American, North American, and European countries have diplomatic representation in Montevideo, including Argentina (W. F. Aldunate 1281, tel. 02/902-4929); Brazil (Convención 1343, 6th fl., tel. 02/901-2024); Canada (Plaza Independencia 749, Oficina 102, tel. 02/902-2030); Germany (La Cumparsita 1435, tel. 02/902-5222); the United Kingdom (Marco Bruto 1073, tel. 02/622-3630); and the United States (Lauro Muller 1776, tel. 02/418-7777).

## Immigration

For visa or tourist-card extensions, the Ciudad Vieja's **Dirección Nacional de Migración** (Misiones 1513, tel. 02/916-0471) is open Monday–Friday 8:15 A.M.–1:30 P.M. in summer; the rest of the year, hours are Monday–Friday 12:30–7 P.M.

## Money

ATMs, such as the Ciudad Vieja's **Banco Itaú** (25 de Mayo 391), are now abundant. On the west side of Plaza Independencia, **Exprinter** (Sarandí 700) changes travelers checks, as do exchange houses like **Cambio Gales** (Av. 18 de Julio 1048) and **Cambio Regul** (Av. 18 de Julio 1126).

## Postal Services

The **Correo Central** (main post office) is at Buenos Aires 451, in the Ciudad Vieja.

## Telephone, Fax, and Internet

Antel, the national telephone company, has long-distance Telecentros in the Ciudad Vieja (Rincón 501), the Centro (Av. 18 de Julio 891), and at the Tres Cruces bus terminal. All three have Internet access for fixed amounts of time—minimum 15 minutes.

Otherwise, for both phone service and Internet access, try **Cálculo** (Andes 1363, Centro).

## Travel Agencies

Partnering with Hostelling International, **Viajeros Sin Fronteras** (Buenos Aires 618, Oficina 001, tel. 02/916-5466, www.sinfronteras.com.uy) arranges excursions around Montevideo and the country.

# TRANSPORTATION
## Air

Montevideo's **Aeropuerto Internacional de Carrasco** (tel. 02/604-0330) is about 15 kilometers northeast of downtown, on the highway toward Punta del Este. A new terminal is going up a short distance from the existing building.

From December to April, **American Airlines** (Sarandí 699 bis, tel. 02/916-3979) offers three nonstops per week from Miami. Otherwise, it's only a short hop across the Río de la Plata from Buenos Aires with American and several other airlines.

**Aerolíneas Argentinas** (Plaza Independencia 749 bis, tel. 02/902-3691), which flies from Miami to Buenos Aires, has the most frequent connections across the river from Buenos Aires. At the airport only, **Sol Líneas Aéreas** (www.sol.com.ar) flies weekdays to and from Buenos Aires. Other options from North America are via São Paulo or Rio de Janeiro, Brazil, with **TAM** (Colonia 820, tel. 02/901-8451); via Santiago de Chile with **LAN** (Colonia 993, 4th fl., tel. 02/902-3881); or via El Salvador with TACA (Plaza Independencia 831, Oficina 807, tel. 000/405-1004). **Gol** (tel. 0004/055-126, www.voegol.com.br) flies to Brazilian destinations.

From Europe, the only direct connections are twice-weekly services from Madrid via Rio de Janeiro, with **Pluna** (Colonia 1021, tel. 02/900-9999, www.pluna.aero).

## Boat

Comfortable high-speed ferries from Buenos Aires take about three hours to cross the Río de la Plata. The rehabbed Puerto Fluvial, on the Rambla 25 de Agosto, is convenient to the Ciudad Vieja, Montevideo's colonial core.

**Buquebus** has its main office in the Edificio Santos (Rambla 25 de Agosto de 1825 and Yacaré, tel. 02/916-8801, www.buquebus.com), with a branch at the Hotel Radisson

(Colonia 751). Buquebus's *Silvia Ana* carries up to 1,000 passengers twice daily except Sunday, when there is only one departure, with bus connections to and from Punta del Este. Fares range US$72–104 pp depending on the class of service.

Buquebus also operates a bus-ferry combination via Colonia up to five times daily (US$38–67 pp), with prices again depending on the class.

At Terminal Tres Cruces, **Cacciola** (tel. 02/401-9350, www.cacciolaviajes.com) has bus-launch service to Tigre (US$27, 7.5 hours) via Carmelo. Departures are at 10:15 A.M. and 12:15 A.M. Monday–Friday, 12:15 A.M. and 1:15 P.M. Saturday, and 8:15 A.M. and 1:15 P.M. Sunday.

## Bus

About three kilometers northeast of Plaza Independencia, Montevideo's modern and orderly **Terminal Tres Cruces** (Bulevar Artigas and Av. Italia, tel. 02/401-8998, www.trescruces.com.uy) is a full-service bus terminal and shopping center with a helpful tourist information office, money exchange and ATM, baggage storage, toilets, restaurants, public telephones, and Internet access. The website has outstanding coverage of bus companies, schedules, and fares.

Although the ferry from Buenos Aires is faster and more convenient—especially as Argentine pickets have closed the Gualeguaychú border crossing—there is still nightly bus service from Montevideo to Retiro (US$27, 8.5–10 hours) with **Bus de la Carrera** (tel. 02/402-1313) and **General Belgrano** (tel. 02/401-4764). Although the closed Gualeguaychú border crossing is an ongoing issue, some buses can still get through at more northerly border crossings.

Domestically, Montevideo is the hub for Uruguayan bus services, eastbound toward Maldonado and Punta del Este, and westbound toward Colonia and Carmelo. **COT** (tel. 02/409-4949) and **Copsa** (tel. 02/408-6668) serve Maldonado and Punta del Este (US$8, two hours); companies serving Colonia (US$8, 2.5 hours) include **COT** (tel. 02/409-4949), **Chadre** (tel. 02/1717), and **Turil** (tel. 02/1990). For Carmelo (US$11, three hours), there's Chadre as well as **Sabelín** (tel. 02/1717) and **Intertur** (tel. 02/401-7729).

## Car Rental

Rental agencies include **Avis** (Uruguay 1417, tel. 02/903-0303); **Dollar** (Aeropuerto Carrasco, tel. 02/682-8350); **Europcar** (Bulevar Artigas 1875, tel. 02/401-0575); and **Multicar** (Colonia 1227, tel. 02/902-2555).

## Train

This is not a practical way to get around much of Uruguay, but dedicated trainspotters can catch the local to the suburbs of Canelones and 25 de Agosto (US$1.50, two hours) from the new **Estación Central** (Río Negro s/n, tel. 02/929-0125), just north of the handsome but rundown old station.

# The Montevideo Wine Country

In San Francisco's 2002 World Wine Market, the most impressive Latin American exhibitor turnout came not from traditional powerhouses Argentina and Chile, but rather from little-known Uruguay. Over the past decade-plus, 35 of the country's 272 wineries have begun to switch from traditional jug wines, for exclusively domestic consumption, to fine wines for more sophisticated Uruguayan palates and for export.

Uruguay produces many of the same varietals as Argentina, including the reds cabernet sauvignon, malbec, and merlot, and the whites chardonnay and sauvignon blanc, but its signature grape is the red tannat, of French Basque origin. Accounting for more than a third of Uruguayan production, this smooth, deep red varietal is uncommon elsewhere.

According to Daniel Pisano, who owns a small vineyard on Montevideo's outskirts, Uruguay's annual yield of 100 million bottles is roughly equivalent to Chile's giant Concha y Toro winery. Unlike Argentina and Chile, Uruguay does not need to irrigate its vineyards, and its lowland soils and rolling topography are distinct from the mostly alluvial soils in those countries.

If the Uruguayans cannot match their continental rivals in quantity, they're hoping to establish a niche market through quality. To this end, Pisano and other exporters have formed an alliance, the Asociación de Bodegas Exportadoras de Vinos Finos de Uruguay (www.winesofuruguay.com), to promote their wines overseas. More importantly for readers of this book, they've organized a fledgling Ruta del Vino (wine route) barely half an hour from the capital.

Most of the families here have Italian or Galician backgrounds, but the dominant wine-making tendency is French.

EXCURSIONS

© WAYNE BERNHARDSON

Dark blue tannat grapes on the outskirts of Montevideo.

Specifically, they adhere to their regional *terroir,* so that each bodega reflects the sum of its own soils, climate, grapes, and wine-making skills. The Montevideo area resembles Bordeaux in its mild, humid climate and clayey soils, but gets more sun than its French counterpart.

While Uruguay's wine route may be in its infancy, it's not hard to arrange a visit, though some smaller family-run vineyards need at least a day's advance notice and may not always be able to provide an English-speaker. All of them, though, treat visitors like family—there are no wine snobs here.

Though the wineries are close to Montevideo, some can be hard to find; it's simpler to hire a *remis* (car and driver) than to navigate the maze of rural roads or struggle with the multitude of public bus lines.

Alternatively, agencies such as **Cisplatina** (Bulevar España 2189, tel. 02/409-9107, www. cisplatinauruguay.com) can provide half-day English-speaking tours, visiting two bodegas, for US$61 pp.

## ◖ BODEGA BOUZA

The closest winery to Montevideo, Bouza may be the most ambitious of them all, a high-tech facility—all stainless steel tanks and state-of-the-art equipment—that's transformed a crumbling 1940s winery. It's rapidly renovated aging brick buildings, while preserving their facades, to create an outstanding restaurant and tasting facility, and may eventually add accommodations.

Bouza's vineyards include 12 hectares of well-established tannat, merlot, chardonnay, tempranillo, and the unusual dry white albariño at Las Violetas, about 40 kilometers away. Just outside the bodega, they have another five hectares of tannat, merlot, chardonnay, and albariño. Like all the other wineries described here, this is a family enterprise, where even fairly young children participate in the harvest, manual grape selection, and other tasks.

In addition to its wines, Bouza is also home to owner Juan Luis Bouza's growing collection of historic *cachilas* (antique automobiles,

Visitors sample a couple of wines before lunch at Bodega Bouza.

© WAYNE BERNHARDSON

now immaculately restored, plus a sample of classic motorcycles as well). The restaurant is open daily noon–4 P.M.; for the time being, the tasting room is here, and it's handsome enough, but it will eventually move to an antique rail car that's undergoing a painstaking restoration.

Actually part of Montevideo Rural (Greater Montevideo), Bodega Bouza (Camino de la Redención 7658 bis, tel. 02/323-3872, www.bodegabouza.com) is becoming one of the top destinations for wine-oriented visitors to Uruguay. Tours (US$17 with a sample of three wines and a *tabla* of cold cuts and cheeses) take place daily at 12:30 and 4 P.M.; for visitors who lunch at the restaurant, the tour is free of charge. It's worth phoning ahead to see if they can accommodate visitors at other hours, but in summer, when it gets a lot of cruise-ship trade, both tours and the restaurant can get crowded, and it's less likely that they will be able to accommodate independent visitors.

## BODEGAS CASTILLO VIEJO

Entered by a handsome corridor of deciduous ash trees, Castillo Viejo cultivates about 110 hectares of vineyards for both table wines and fine wines that include the signature tannat but also merlot and cabernet franc varietals, and blends of those and whites such as viognier, chardonnay, and sauvignon blanc. There's also sparkling wine.

Like tannat, the Etcheverry family has its roots in the French Basque country. Tours of the bodega, led by the family, end with a tasting in the handsomely appointed subterranean cellars, and include either a *tabla* of cured meats and cheeses (US$13) or an *asado* (US$25).

Castillo Viejo (Ruta 68 Km 24, Las Piedras, tel. 02/368-9606, www.castilloviejo.com) is open for guided tours Tuesday–Friday 4–6 P.M., and Saturday 10 A.M.–2:30 P.M. A day's advance notice is advisable.

## BODEGA DELUCCA

Educated as a plant pathologist in Pennsylvania and France, Reinaldo de Lucca views wine as a "living being" and takes a craftsman's approach, with constant visual monitoring of the vineyards and the wine-making process. About half his production consists of fine wines, with about 20 percent exported; the main reds are tannat, merlot, syrah, and cabernet sauvignon, with tannat/merlot and tannat/syrah blends. The whites are sauvignon blanc and the uncommon marsanne.

With about 50 hectares of vineyards scattered about 30 kilometers north of Montevideo, Delucca (Ruta 48, Km 13.1, El Colorado, Canelones, tel. 02/367-8076, delucccawines@adinet.com.uy) has a small tasting room, plus a pleasant outdoor seating area, and can also provide lunches. The basic visit costs US$5 with three wines and snacks, US$8 with five wines and snacks, but if you purchase more than US$27 worth of wine the tasting is free. De Lucca prefers 10 days' advance notice for a visit.

## VIÑEDOS Y BODEGA FILGUEIRA

While it's been in the Filgueira family for more than 80 years, only in the past decade has their bodega begun to produce fine wines, primarily tannat but also cabernet sauvignon, merlot, and sauvignon blanc, from freshly planted vines on only 12 hectares. All of them come in standard, oak, and premium lines, where the quality generally depends on yield (6,000–9,000 kg per hectare, with the lower yields corresponding to higher quality). The odd duck is the white sauvignon gris (sauvignon grigio, if you prefer).

Bodega Filgueira (Ruta 81, Km 7, Cuchilla Verde, Canelones, tel. 033/46438, www.bodegafilgueira.com) has an intimate tasting room in its modernized bodega; plans to build a larger facility are on hold. It needs 24 hours to arrange a visit; the staff handle English well, and the website also features excellent English text. Tours, with tasting and a light lunch, cost US$10–15 per person.

## ESTABLECIMIENTO JUANICÓ

Probably the country's closest thing to an industrial winery, Juanicó produces about a quarter of all Uruguayan wines, and half of that is still jug wines for domestic consumption. At the same time, it's one of the leaders in fine wines and its facilities, dating from the 1840s but modernized within, are the most historic and picturesque of any Montevideo winery (though Bouza, when finished, will be at least a close second).

On 600 hectares of rolling terrain, some 240 of them in vineyards and most of the rest in forest, Juanicó dates from colonial times. It takes its name from Francisco Juanicó, who built the current *cava* (wine cellar) around 1840, but the property passed through several hands, including the state oil company ANCAP, before being sold to the Deicas family in 1979. It employs 100 permanent laborers, plus another 100 during the March harvest, to produce a diversity of reds (tannat, merlot, cabernet sauvignon, cabernet franc, pinot noir, petit verdot, shiraz) and whites (chardonnay, gewürztraminer, sauvignon blanc, viognier). Some vintages from its Preludio line have become collectors' items.

Juanicó is well prepared to receive visitors, having converted the ground level of its historic *cava* into a restaurant and events center that can accommodate large groups for *asados* and tastings, but it also has an intimate subterranean dining room suitable for small groups. The latter is a de facto museum, filled with antique wine-making gear and a gallery of tannat-oriented artwork.

A basic tour, tasting four wines, costs US$7 pp. With a generous *picada* of cold cuts and cheese, plus empanadas, it costs US$19. With a full-scale lunch, the price is US$44 pp.

Juanicó (Estación Juanicó s/n, Juanicó, Canelones, tel. 033/59725, www.juanico.com) is actually the easiest of all the wineries to find—the property fronts directly on Ruta 5, about 37.5 kilometers northwest of Montevideo. While Uruguay has no "wine train" on the order of California's Napa Valley, it's conceivable to arrive on the slow suburban commuter train from downtown Montevideo—Juanicó station is easy walking distance from the property's entrance—but service is erratic.

## BODEGA CÉSAR PISANO

On 30 hectares, dating from the 1920s, the Pisano vineyards produce at least half a dozen premium varietals, including tannat, cabernet sauvignon, chardonnay, and sauvignon blanc, with others on the way. One interesting varietal is the dry white torrontés, normally grown on alluvial soils in high desert climates, such as in Argentina's Salta province, rather than on low-altitude clay in humid Uruguay.

Bodega Pisano (Camino de los Ingleses, Ruta 68, Km 29, tel. 02/368-9007, www.pisanowines.com) is a family business, with at least three generations directly involved in the process at all levels. The bodega's cook prepares an excellent *asado* that includes, unusually for this part of the world, lightly grilled vegetables (rather than the overdone style so common in lowest-common-denominator Southern Cone cookery).

In general, Pisano prefers providing tours for specialized appreciation groups, but if nothing else is going on they're happy to provide a free tour, with a modest tasting. Phone ahead, however.

## BODEGA CARLOS PIZZORNO

A fourth-generation family enterprise, Pizzorno started switching from jug wines to fine wines in the late 1980s to become a boutique winery on 15 hectares planted to tannat, cabernet sauvignon, merlot, sauvignon blanc, and chardonnay. Unusual for this area, it also produces sparkling wine from its chardonnay and sauvignon blanc.

Bodega Carlos Pizzorno (Ruta 32, Km 23, Canelón Chico, tel. 02/368-9601, www.pizzornowines.com) welcomes visits, but normally needs 72 hours' advance notice. There's a small tasting and sales room, a handsome new cellar, and a truly warm welcome for visitors. A three-wine tasting costs US$5 per person; with a *picada* of cold cuts and cheeses, the price is US$10.

## VIÑA VARELA ZARRANZ

About 30 kilometers north of Montevideo, the Varela Zarranz winery once belonged to the Italianate residence at family-run Viña Varela Zarranz

the influential Diego Pons, who hosted presidents and other prominent politicians in the colonnaded Italianate house where current owner Ricardo Varela now lives. When Varela's grandfather acquired the property, it produced mostly jug wines under the brand name Vudu which, though it still exists, has nothing to do with Caribbean witchcraft—rather, it was the acronym for a producers' cooperative.

Approached via an alameda flanked by aging olive trees, Varela Zarranz now focuses on fine varietals such as tannat, the fruity white petit grain muscat, and a rosé from cabernet sauvignon, along with blends of tannat-merlot and tannat-cabernet franc. Tastings take place in the atmospheric basement of the historic main house.

Varela Zarranz (Ruta 74 Km 29, Joaquín Suárez, Canelones, tel. 02/297-0049, www. varelazarranz.com) requires at least 24 hours' advance notice to arrange tours and tastings, which cost US$8 for three classic or sparkling wines, US$10 for four wines that include two premium tannats, and US$12 for five wines that include three premium tannats. A basic *tabla* of cheeses and cold cuts costs US$5 pp, a more elaborate one US$10 pp. An *asado,* which requires 48 hours' notice, costs US$20 pp with a 12-person minimum. Dessert costs US$5 extra.

# Colonia del Sacramento

Only a short sail across the river from Buenos Aires, Colonia del Sacramento's picturesque 18th-century architecture has made it a UNESCO World Heritage Site and tourist town, but it's still a neighborly place whose residents sip *mate* on the sidewalk and chat across cobbled sycamore-shaded streets. Its unhurried pace—local motorists even stop for pedestrians—could not contrast more with the Argentine capital's frenetic tempo.

Traditionally, Argentines descend upon Colonia in overwhelming numbers in summer and on weekends. The town suffered dramatically from the Argentine meltdown—a large majority of its annual visitors are *porteños*—but business has recovered quickly as the neighboring economy has risen from the depths of 2001–2002.

The economic crisis meant postponement of a dubious megaproject—a 42-kilometer series of five bridges from Punta Lara, near the Buenos Aires provincial capital of La Plata, across the river to a point seven kilometers east of Colonia. The Argentine-Uruguayan Comisión Binacional Puente Buenos Aires Colonia (Buenos Aires Colonia Binational Bridge Commission) has long promoted this environmentally dubious project to improve communications within the Mercosur common market, but it remains on hold. The recent international dispute over the Finnish-built pulp plant near the Uruguayan city of Fray Bentos and the Argentine city of Gualeguaychú (where demonstrators have blocked an existing bridge over the Río Uruguay) makes its completion even less likely.

Many foreign visitors cross the river on day trips from Buenos Aires. That's a good option for anyone short on time, but Colonia's worth at least an overnight stay and preferably more.

a Portuguese rancho on Calle de San Antonio in Colonia del Sacramento

© WAYNE BERNHARDSON

## HISTORY

Colonia do Sacramento (its original Portuguese name) dates to 1680, at a time when Buenos Aires was a backwater of Spain's mercantile empire and nearly all trade had to pass through the viceregal capital of Lima and then across the Andes and over the pampas. The Portuguese Manoel de Lobo established the settlement directly opposite Buenos Aires on the Río de la Plata's Banda Oriental (Eastern Shore), in order to exploit the Paraná delta's labyrinthine channels for contraband.

Colonia, then, became the focus of a continual tug-of-war between Spain and Portugal. A 1750 agreement to hand it over to the Spaniards failed when Jesuit missions, which operated with near-total autonomy until the Jesuits' 1767 expulsion from the Americas, refused to cede any of their upper Paraná territory. By the time the Spaniards finally established themselves in Colonia in 1777, the newly created Virreinato del Río de la Plata had made the contraband economy nearly superfluous, as foreign imports could use the port of Buenos Aires.

Beginning in the mid-19th century, Swiss, Italian, and German immigration gave the surrounding area a dairy- and farm-based prosperity, but Montevideo's rapid growth deflected infrastructural and industrial development toward the capital. Spared by the capital, Colonia's **Barrio Histórico,** its 18th-century core, remained largely intact for the evolution of the local tourist industry.

## ORIENTATION

Colonia is less than an hour by high-speed catamaran or two-plus hours by ferry from Buenos Aires. It is 180 kilometers west of Montevideo via Ruta 1, a smoothly paved two-lane highway that enters town from the east and turns southwest toward the ferry port.

The town itself consists of two distinct areas: a conventional grid west of Ruta 1, centered on Plaza 25 de Agosto, and the narrow irregular streets of the Barrio Histórico west of Ituzaingó, marking the limits of the peninsular *ciudadela,* the walled colonial city. The main commercial street is east–west Avenida General Flores, which runs the length of town on the south side of Plaza 25 de Agosto.

## ◖ BARRIO HISTÓRICO

Nearly all of Colonia's sights are in the Barrio Histórico, including its numerous museums, open daily 11:15 A.M.–4:45 P.M. in summer; they usually close Monday the rest of the year. Entrance tickets, which cost about US$2.50, may be purchased at the Museo Municipal and the Museo Portugués only, but are also valid for the Archivo Regional, the Museo Indígena, the Museo Español, and the Museo de los Azulejos. Individual museums charge US$1.25.

Early Colonia was a *ciudadela,* a walled fortress protected from sea and land by *bastiones* (bulwarks) like the southerly **Bastión de San Miguel,** the westerly **Bastión San Pedro** and **Bastión Santa Rita,** and the northerly **Bastión del Carmen.**

The entrance to the Barrio Histórico is the reconstructed **Portón de Campo** (1745), a gate approached by a drawbridge. To the west, several major landmarks surround the irregular quadrangle of **Plaza Mayor 25 de Mayo:** the **Museo Portugués** (Portuguese Museum, 1730), the **Casa de Lavalleja** (once the home of independence figure Juan Antonio Lavalleja), the **Museo Municipal Dr. Bautista Rebuffo** (Municipal Museum, also known as the **Casa del Almirante Brown,** though the founder of the Argentine navy never lived there), and the 17th-century ruins of the **Casa del Virrey** (also misleadingly named as no viceroy ever lived in Colonia).

At the plaza's southeast corner, low-slung colonial houses line both sides of the sloping, roughly cobbled **Calle de los Suspiros** (Street of Sighs); one of the city's most emblematic structures (though a private residence) is the pink stucco with red tiles at the corner of Calle San Pedro.

At the Plaza Mayor's southwest corner, ruins of the 18th-century **Convento de San Francisco** nearly surround the 19th-century **Faro de Colonia** (lighthouse; daily 11 A.M.–7 P.M., US$0.60), an almost pristine restoration. Climbing its 118 steps is the best

**EXCURSIONS**

EXCURSIONS

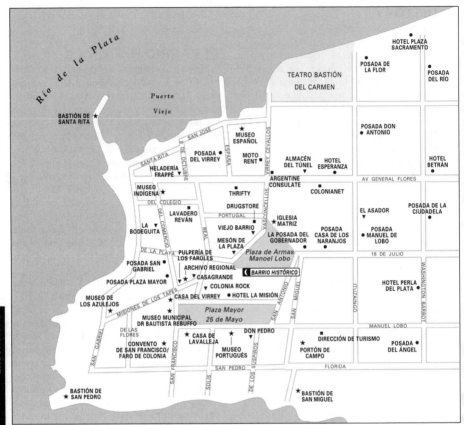

Río de la Plata

Puerto Viejo

HOTEL PLAZA SACRAMENTO

POSADA DE LA FLOR

POSADA DEL RÍO

BASTIÓN DE SANTA RITA ★

TEATRO BASTIÓN DEL CARMEN

POSADA DON ANTONIO

SANTA RITA

DE OCTUBRE

SAN JOSÉ

MUSEO ESPAÑOL ★

ESPAÑA

VIRREY CEVALLOS

POSADA DEL VIRREY ●

MOTO RENT ■

HELADERÍA FRAPPÉ ●

ALMACÉN DEL TÚNEL ■

HOTEL ESPERANZA ■

AV GENERAL FLORES

HOTEL BETRÁN ■

MUSEO INDÍGENA ★

DEL COLEGIO

THRIFTY ★

DRUGSTORE

ARGENTINE CONSULATE

COLONIANET ■

EL ASADOR ▼

POSADA DE LA CIUDADELA ●

LAVADERO REVÁN

PORTUGAL

VIEJO BARRIO ▼

IGLESIA MATRIZ ★

LA BODEGUITA ▼

REAL

DEL COMERCIO

MESÓN DE LA PLAZA ▼

VASCONCELLOS

LA POSADA DEL GOBERNADOR ▼

POSADA CASA DE LOS NARANJOS ■

POSADA MANUEL DE LOBO ●

18 DE JULIO

DE LA PLAYA

PULPERÍA DE LOS FAROLES ▼

Plaza de Armas Manoel Lobo

◀ BARRIO HISTÓRICO

POSADA SAN GABRIEL ●

ARCHIVO REGIONAL ★

CASAGRANDE ▼

POSADA PLAZA MAYOR ●

COLONIA ROCK ▼

MISIONES DE LOS TAPES

CASA DEL VIRREY ★

HOTEL LA MISIÓN ●

HOTEL PERLA DEL PLATA ●

SAN ANTONIO

SAN MIGUEL

ITUZAINGÓ

WASHINGTON BARBOT

MUSEO DE LOS AZULEJOS ★

MUSEO MUNICIPAL DR BAUTISTA REBUFFO ▼

Plaza Mayor 25 de Mayo

MANUEL LOBO

SAN GABRIEL

DE LAS FLORES

CASA DE LAVALLEJA ★

DON PEDRO ▼

DIRECCIÓN DE TURISMO ■

POSADA DEL ÁNGEL ●

CONVENTO DE SAN FRANCISCO/ FARO DE COLONIA ★

SAN FRANCISCO

MUSEO PORTUGUÉS ■

DE LOS SUSPIROS

PORTÓN DE CAMPO ★

FLORIDA

SAN PEDRO

SOLIS

BASTIÓN DE SAN PEDRO ★

BASTIÓN DE SAN MIGUEL ★

workout in town (and an enjoyable one when it's not humid); from the top, Buenos Aires, Quilmes, and even La Plata are visible in good weather. At some times of the year, the late closing hour makes it a fine place to see the sun set.

North of the plaza, dating from 1770, the **Archivo Regional** (Misiones de los Tapes 115) belongs to the simple architectural style known as *rancho portugués,* its adobe walls topped by a tile roof. The archive's contents are scanty, but the building is a relic of the era when, according to Jesuit priest Martin Dobrizhoffer, Colonia boomed with contraband wealth:

The houses are few and low, forming a village, rather than city, yet it is far from despicable; opulent merchants, wares of every kind, gold, silver, and diamonds are concealed beneath its miserable roofs.

To the west, on the riverfront, the **Museo de los Azulejos** traces local architectural history through its elaborate tilework. To the north, on Calle del Comercio, is the modest **Museo Indígena,** which displays indigenous tools, such as scrapers and *boleadoras,* plus some clippings on the pre-Columbian Charrúa and the romantic *indigenismo* of Uruguayan writer Juan Zorrilla de San Martín (1855–1931).

Northeast of the Plaza Mayor, the landmark **Iglesia Matriz** (1699) extends along the north side of the **Plaza de Armas Manoel Lobo,** but its twin-towered facade fronts on Calle Vasconcellos. Despite its early appearance, it has undergone major modifications due to combat damage, fire, and even an explosion of an arsenal during the Brazilian occupation of 1823.

On the north side of the peninsula, the two-story **Museo Español** (1725) was originally a private residence. Immediately north is the **Puerto Viejo,** the former port. The **Teatro Bastión del Carmen** (Virrey Ceballos and Rivadavia) integrates part of the colonial bulwarks and the Fábrica Caracciolo, a former soap factory, into the city's principal performing-arts center.

## Museo de los Azulejos

This collection (Misiones de los Tapes 104) of decorative tilework dates mostly from the mid-19th century—before then, beautification was a low priority in a city that was in an almost constant state of war. The stenciled artisanal tiles, many of them imported from France, vary slightly in size, shape, and design.

Sections of the floor and ceiling of the mid-18th-century building are original, others of subsequent brick. Some ceramic roof tiles

# THE VANISHING *CACHILAS*

Not so long ago, the finest assortment of antique automobiles south of Havana filled the streets of Colonia and Montevideo. In what was an open-air museum for vintage wheels, it wasn't unusual to see Model A Fords, Daimlers, Studebakers, and Willys parked at the curbs and rolling down Uruguay's roadways. Uruguay owed this abundance of *cachilas* (as they call classic cars) to its history of alternating good fortune and misfortune.

A prosperous country in the first half of the 20th century, Uruguay imported a wide variety of vehicles from Europe and the United States, but economic and political decline forced Uruguayans to maintain and operate what, in most other countries, would have been museum pieces. At times, it seemed, there were so many that the streets looked like sets for Mafia movies.

This began to change when, in the 1970s, foreign collectors began to discover the countless *cachilas*. As the country's fleet of motor vehicles modernized with the renewal of automobile imports from Argentina and Brazil during the 1990s boom, these stylish relics slowly but inexorably began disappearing.

Though less numerous than they once were, the *cachilas* have spawned their own niche within the automotive sector. Scouts still scour the garages of provincial towns and the backroads of the interior for hidden treasures worthy of restoration and sale to collectors. This, in turn, has created a job market for artisans (sometimes elderly) who can restore and reproduce irreplaceable items, such as wooden dashboards and leather upholstery. There's a market for parts as well as for entire vehicles.

© WAYNE BERNHARDSON

a classic Ford *cachila* outside the Argentine consulate

Uruguayans are aware of their automotive legacy, and the law defines historic vehicles as part of the national patrimony. Except in a few high-profile cases, though, this has not restricted their sale and export, for which there is a strong incentive – cars that cost a few thousand dollars when they were built can, in restored condition, fetch nearly US$100,000.

While the clock may be ticking for the *cachilas* that for so many decades lent their personalities to Uruguayan streets, roads, and highways, they haven't quite disappeared. Even now, along the highway from Montevideo to Punta del Este, there are roadside lots where the vehicles range from rusting wrecks to fairly well-conserved specimens awaiting a savior.

Even as its presence diminishes, the *cachila* keeps a high profile in the public consciousness. On being sworn into office in March 2005, newly elected Uruguayan president Tabaré Vásquez chose a family treasure, a Model T Ford that had belonged to his wife's father, for the traditional parade down Avenida del Libertador.

© WAYNE BERNHARDSON

The Museo de los Azulejos (Museum of Tiles) occupies a classic Portuguese rancho.

are *tejas musleras,* so called because they were formed on the thighs of mulatto women.

## Museo Español

The Spanish museum (San José 152) actually consists of two buildings, a mid-18th-century two-story Portuguese residence and a mid-19-th-century addition to the east. Its contents are mostly ordinary, though the narrative of events (in Spanish only) is thorough. What raises it above the routine are the historical portraits by contemporary Uruguayan artist and Colonia resident José Páez Vilaró, which complement the otherwise archaic materials.

## Museo Municipal Dr. Bautista Rebuffo

Unlike its Portuguese counterpart, Colonia's municipal museum displays more potential than accomplishment. Occupying the so-called **Casa de Almirante Brown** (1795, but rebuilt in the 1830s), it's a bit musty, both physically and in concept (or lack of it). While it's a little more informative than in past years, it's still

pretty much a stuff-in-glass-cases affair that could benefit from a professional curator to organize and interpret its documents and artifacts on aboriginal Uruguay, the struggle between Spain and Portugal, and Uruguay's early residents—plus fossils and a mass of deteriorating taxidermy specimens. One recent addition is material on the bullfights—long since outlawed—that brought Argentine tourists to nearby Real de San Carlos.

It would also be informative to add material on Colonia's transformation over the past 20 years, and its almost total dependency on the Argentine tourist trade. Its founder, from whom the museum takes its name, resisted all tampering with the exhibits; his death in 2005 may mean changes here.

## Museo Portugués

Built under Portuguese dominion beginning in 1730, the former **Casa de Ríos** underwent a late-18th-century reconstruction under the Spaniards. With help from the Portuguese government, its collections have improved dramatically—it has an excellent sample of maps on the Portuguese voyages of discovery (high-quality copies of the Lisbon originals), an extraordinary assortment of professionally displayed porcelain ceramics, and period clothing.

## BODEGA BERNARDI

Colonia can't match Montevideo's increasingly sophisticated wineries, but this unpretentious, low-tech bodega, dating from 1892, has begun to supplement its jug-wine production with an increasing variety of fine reds, mostly merlot and tannat, as well as their Isabella rosé, produced from the so-called "strawberry grape." They also make about 300 bottles per year of the deeply colored dry white moscato giallo, but the house specialty is several varieties of distilled grappa, once a state monopoly in Uruguay.

Founded by Italian-Swiss immigrants, Bernardi is open for free-of-charge, drop-in visits, but needs advance notice to be sure of accommodating English speakers. With 24 hours' notice, they can prepare a *tabla* of *fiambres* (cold cuts), cheeses, and empanadas to accompany a tasting of wine and grappa. Bodega Bernardi (Ruta 1, Km 171.5, tel. 052/24762, www.bodegabernardi.com, Mon.–Sat. 9 A.M.–noon and 2–5:30 P.M., Sun. 10 A.M.–2 P.M.) resides on undulating terrain about seven kilometers east of Colonia; it's ideal for a bike ride. In summer it stays open until 7 P.M., but closes on Sunday.

## RESTAURANTS

Until recently, Colonia's restaurants have displayed more colonial style than culinary imagination. The standard has been the *parrilla*, though this is changing as local cuisine diversifies.

For *parrillada*, **El Asador** (Ituzaingó 168, tel. 052/24204) is a no-frills choice that's maintained its popularity over the years, so it must be doing something right. **El Portón** (General Flores 333, tel. 052/25318) is a more upmarket alternative.

**Almacén del Túnel** (General Flores 229, tel. 052/24666) is a traditionally good restaurant with fixed-price lunches. Next-door **Lo de Renata** (General Flores 227, tel. 052/31061) serves mostly *parrillada* and pastas, but uniquely for Colonia it also serves a few Japanese dishes, such as tempura.

Facing the Plaza Mayor, **Suspiros** (Suspiros 99, tel. 052/22867) is a shady sidewalk café with excellent homemade pasta (around US$5), *chivitos*, and aggressive pigeons—watch your bread.

Having upgraded its menu, the Barrio Histórico's **Casagrande** (Misiones de los Tapes 143, tel. 052/28371) provides a more diversity of dishes, but the kitchen can be so quick as to raise suspicions of simple reheating. There's no wine by the glass.

**Pulpería de los Faroles** (Misiones de los Tapes 101, tel. 052/25399) has one of the Barrio Histórico's more diverse menus, but prices are moderate and the ambience is among Colonia's best. Like nearby Casagrande, it has ample outdoor seating.

**Viejo Barrio** (Vasconcellos 169, tel. 052/25399) may not have Colonia's best food, but it's decent enough, the portions are large, and the service easily the most attentive, entertaining, and extroverted in town. Pastas and seafood, in the US$6.50–9 range, are the best options.

**La Bodeguita** (Del Comercio 167, tel. 052/25329, www.labodeguita.net) has excellent beef dishes (around US$13) with varied sauces and a fine wine list, but it is most popular for its pizza. Its split-level wooden deck is a great place to watch the sun set and, after the sun goes down, the lights of Buenos Aires in the distance.

**Mesón de la Plaza** (Vasconcellos 153, tel. 052/24807) may be Colonia's most ambitious restaurant, with an adventurous menu that occasionally includes sturgeon, which is being farmed in northwestern Uruguay (caviar production is also beginning). The garden has a covered patio where it's possible to dine al fresco even when it rains; there's occasional live music, and the service is assiduous.

Rivalling La Bodeguita as Colonia's best view restaurant, **Restaurant del Yacht** (Escollera Santa Rita s/n, Puerto de Yates, tel.

052/31354) has a beautiful rooftop terrace and a smaller ground-level terrace with vistas across the river towards Buenos Aires. It serves a very fine *entrecot pantagruel* (grilled sirloin with a side of scalloped potatoes, US$12), a frothily light chocolate mousse, and a good but limited selection of wines by the glass. The by-the-bottle list is more diverse but mostly Uruguayan, with a few Argentine and Chilean vintages. The service can be uneven, and the background music odd: Would you believe jazz versions of Christmas standards in February?

On its visual merits, the rancho-style **Sacramento** (De La Playa 63, tel. 052/29245, www.sacramentorestaurante.com) should be among Colonia's best: The polished cement floors glisten, strategically placed wine bottles line the walls, and there's ample space between tables. A limited menu of fish, meats, and pastas in the US$13–20 range suggests the kitchen is focused, but the service can be indifferent. Oddly, with a similarly limited wine list, the house wine is Chilean rather than Uruguayan. Sacramento bears watching, but if you have only one dinner in Colonia, Meson de la Plaza and Restaurant del Yacht are better bets.

**Heladería Frappé** (General Flores and 8 de Octubre) has Colonia's best ice cream.

## ENTERTAINMENT

In a creatively recycled colonial building, **Colonia Rock** (Misiones de los Tapes 157, tel. 052/28189) serves mixed drinks and bar food. There is sidewalk seating and an interior patio, and there's live music Saturday nights.

The immensely popular, idiosyncratic **El Drugstore** (Vasconcellos 179, tel. 052/25241) has expanded its space, diversified its food menu, and also has live music some nights. One of its prime attractions is a parked *cachila* (antique car) with the front seat removed to allow for a comfy cushion seat and a table for candlelight dining.

New on the scene, **Blanco y Negro** (General Flores 248, tel. 052/22236, www.bynrestojazz.com.uy) is a restaurant that also offers live jazz, blues, and tango in a casual environment.

## SHOPS

The artisans' cooperative **Manos del Uruguay** (Av. General Flores 83, tel. 052/29616, www.manos.uy) has moved to spacious new quarters. Colonia's permanent **Feria Artesanal** (Crafts Fair, Suárez and Fosalba, two blocks north of Plaza 25 de Agosto) is open daily 9:30 A.M.–7:30 P.M.

## ACCOMMODATIONS

Colonia's accommodations, always pretty good, have improved—even modest places have air-conditioning and cable TV. Nothing that appears in the listings below is even close to marginal, but some are better than others.

In the same building as the municipal tourist office, the private **Cámara Hotelera** (General Flores 499, tel. 052/27302, www.hotelescolonia.com, daily 9 A.M.–5 P.M., and sometimes a bit later) provides information including current prices.

### Under US$25

The HI affiliate **Hostel Colonial** (General Flores 440, tel. 052/30347, hostelling_colonial@hotmail.com, US$7.50 pp in dorms, US$18 d) has five private rooms in addition to dorms. Rates also include loaner bicycles, but breakfast costs US$2.50 extra.

**Hotel Español** (Manoel Lobo 377, tel. 052/30759, elespaniol@adinet.com.uy, US$9–10 pp) has also reincarnated itself as a hostel; the higher prices correspond to rooms with private bath. Breakfast costs US$2 extra.

### US$25-50

Reinvented as an HI affliate, **⟨ El Viajero Hostel Suites** (Washington Barbot 164, tel. 052/22683, www.elviajerocolonia.com, US$10–16 pp in dorms, US$22/38 s/d) is the pick of local hostels, in a rambling colonial-style house with ample common spaces, including a bar, kitchen, two patios, and a rooftop terrace. Most of the rooms have air-conditioning and private bath. Towels cost extra, however.

Rates at **Posada del Río** (Washington

El Viajero Hostel Suites is a rejuvenated colonial-style house with both dorms and private rooms.

Barbot 258, tel. 052/23002, US$29/45 s/d) include start-of-the-art air-conditioning, attractive patios, and an ample breakfast served on the terrace, but it's fallen behind some more recent options. Service remains good and friendly, however.

In the heart of the historic district, **Posada San Gabriel** (Del Comercio 127, tel. 052/23283, psangabriel@adinet.com.uy, US$40–50 s or d) has cheaper rooms at ground level, while the more expensive upstairs rooms have river views. Both, though, have a colonial style remarkable for a place in this price range in this location.

## US$50-100

Some rooms at **Hotel Rivera** (Rivera 131, tel. 052/20807, www.hotelescolonia.com/rivera, US$39/58 s/d with breakfast) are small and slightly dark, but they're also perfectly maintained and it's exceptionally quiet. All rooms have air-conditioning, along with ceiling fans, plus cable TV.

Fittingly enough, all the cheerful, spacious rooms take their names from flowers at **Posada de la Flor** (Ituzaingó 268, tel. 052/30794, www.hotelescolonia.com/posadadelaflor, US$46–60 s or d). The cheapest rooms have ceiling fans rather than air-conditioning, but all rates include breakfast.

**Hotel Perla del Plata** (Washington Barbot 121, tel. 052/25848, www.hotelescolonia.com/perladelplata, US$50–60 s or d) has immaculate but styleless midsize rooms and a patio that's blindingly bright at midday. It's no desperation choice, though.

It has plenty of competition, but the beautifully furnished rooms at **Posada del Ángel** (Washington Barbot 59, tel. 052/24602, www.posadadelangel.net, US$60–70 s or d) offer some of the finest style for money in town, with (almost literally) heavenly murals in a luminous building. Though it lies outside the historic district, it's still quiet enough and has a gym and also a pool, alongside an ancient fig tree. The costlier rooms, some with river views, are upstairs, more spacious, and even brighter.

Like the Perla del Plata, **Hotel Leoncia** (Rivera 214, tel. 052/22369, www.hotelleoncia.com, US$70 s or d) may lack personality, but the rates are fair enough. It does have an indoor pool with, uniquely, a retractable roof.

Reopened under new management, the Barrio Histórico's traditional choice, **La Posada del Gobernador** (18 de Julio 205, tel. 052/22918, US$70 s or d), still fills rapidly, but its style is less colonial than its grounds. For an extra US$10–15, guests can postpone checkout until 6 P.M., when catching the boat back to Buenos Aires.

Just down the block from the more conspicuous Posada del Gobernador, **Posada Casa de los Naranjos** (18 de Julio 219, tel. 052/24630, www.posadalosnaranjos.com, US$50–75 s or d) is a handsome colonial house with friendly ownership, a large lush garden, and a pool, but has some minor drawbacks: Two street-side rooms lack air-conditioning because building codes prohibit altering its historic facade, and a couple others are slightly dark because their windows face an interior passageway.

One of Colonia's old reliables, **Hotel Beltrán** (General Flores 311, tel. 052/22955, www.colonianet.com/beltran, US$65–75 s or d) has pleasing rooms around a central courtyard. The handsome building dates from 1873.

The classic facade at **Posada Don Antonio** (Ituzaingó 232, tel. 052/25344, www.posadadonantonio.com, US$48/58–73/83 s/d) conceals a mostly modern but still appealing hotel with a large pool and landscaping that's helping to soften its once-rough edges. The cheaper rooms have fans but lack air-conditioning. There are also a few more expensive suites.

**Posada Manuel de Lobo** (Ituzaingó 160, tel. 052/22463, www.colonianet.com/posadamdelobo, US$70–90 s or d) has eight contemporary rooms and beautifully landscaped patios in an ideal location. The largest suite has an in-room whirlpool tub.

Cozy is no euphemism at the two-story **Hotel La Misión** (Misión de los Tapes 171, tel. 052/26767, tel. 011/4372-0892 in Buenos Aires, www.lamisionhotel.com, US$90 s or d with a buffet breakfast), whose 12 rooms surround a lushly landscaped central patio. Embodying the best in Colonia style, the common areas are no less engaging.

In a mid-19th-century building, **Posada del Virrey** (España 217, tel. 052/22223, www.posadadelvirrey.com, US$55/65–85/95 s or d) is one of many good, stylish Barrio Histórico hotels; note the elaborately carved Czechoslovakian doors. The staff can handle English and German; some more expensive rooms come with whirlpool tubs.

On a sycamore-shaded block, **Hotel Italiano** (Intendente Suárez 103, tel. 052/27878, www.hotelitaliano.com.uy, US$65–100 d) has undergone a dramatic expansion and modernization with every detail virtually perfect, including luminous and attractive common areas, a large outdoor pool, and a smaller indoor one; the facade, though, still fits into Colonia's historical style. The lower prices correspond to smaller but very decent rooms, but only a little more money brings more space and better amenities; the most expensive suites have whirlpools.

## Over US$100

**Posada Plaza Mayor** (Del Comercio 111, tel. 052/23193, www.posadaplazamayor.com, US$95–115 s or d) is a spectacularly restored mansion with shady patios, lush gardens, and 15 rooms with modern conveniences, including air-conditioning and private baths with whirlpool tubs. Still, the rooms retain colonial style—some beds nestle in arched alcoves—and furnishings. The upper dining room has excellent river views.

Substantially upgraded **Hotel Esperanza** (Avenida General Flores 237, tel. 052/22922, www.hotelesperanzaspa.com, US$90–150 s or d) now includes a pool, spa, and gym, but it's less stylish than most hotels in the historic district.

Stretching the limits of permissibility for construction in this part of town, the densely built **Radisson Colonia del Sacramento Hotel & Casino** (Washington Barbot 283, tel. 052/30460, www.radissoncolonia.com, US$120–145 s or d) overlooks the river with its pool and more expensive suites (US$220–245 s or d). It's the only luxury hotel within walking distance of the Barrio Histórico, though it lacks the personality of Colonia's boutique hotels.

On Colonia's outskirts, the **Sheraton Colonia Golf & Spa Resort** (Rambla de las Américas s/n, tel. 052/29000, www.sheraton.com/colonia, US$149–299 s or d, US$319–429 s or d for suites) is a luxury facility that incorporates elements of the town's historic architecture but also contains a soaring modern atrium and spacious rooms with all standard amenities and more. For some golfers and spa-goers, it's a destination in itself, despite its proximity to town.

## INFORMATION

The municipal **Dirección de Turismo** (General Flores 499, tel. 052/23700, www.colonia.gub.uy, daily 9 A.M.–7 P.M. or a little later) is well stocked with brochures and usually has an English-speaker in summer at least; there's another branch on the Plazoleta 1811, near the Puerta de Campo (tel. 052/28506).

There is a ferry port branch of the national **Ministerio de Turismo** (tel. 052/24897, daily 9 A.M.–3 P.M.).

## SERVICES
### Consulate

Argentina's consulate (General Flores 209, tel. 052/22093) is open Monday–Friday noon–5 P.M.

### Immigration

For visa matters, visit Migraciones (18 de Julio 428, tel. 052/22126).

### Laundry

Lavadero Reván (Calle del Colegio 92) can do the washing.

### Medical

Hospital Colonia is at 18 de Julio 462 (tel. 052/22579).

### Money

Visitors coming for the day needn't bother changing money, as Argentine pesos, U.S. dollars, euros, and Brazilian reais are all widely accepted. Downtown's **Cambio Colonia** (General Flores 401) or **Cambio Dromer** (General Flores 350) can change cash or travelers checks. **Banco Comercial** (General Flores 356) has an ATM, and there are many others.

### Postal Services

Correo Uruguayo is at Lavalleja 226.

### Telephone and Internet

**Antel** (Rivadavia 420) has long-distance telephone service and Internet access. **Colonianet** (General Flores 240) has Internet access as well.

## TRANSPORTATION
### Boat

Catamarans and ferries to Buenos Aires leave from the Puerto de Colonia, the ferry port at the foot of Avenida Roosevelt, which is undergoing an expansion and modernization that should finish by 2010.

In new quarters at the bus terminal, **Buquebus** (Av. Roosevelt and Manoel de Lobo, tel. 052/22975 in Colonia or 011/4316-6500 in Buenos Aires, www.buquebus.com) can sell tickets for its own fast catamarans (US$37, one hour to Buenos Aires) and its own slower, cheaper Ferrylíneas (US$17–23, about 2.5 hours). Both can carry automobiles.

Buquebus now has competition, though, from the passengers-only **Colonia Express** (tel. 052/29676 at the port, tel. 011/4313-5100 in Buenos Aires, www.coloniaexpress.com), which charges only US$25 (Tues.–Thurs.) or US$32 (the rest of the week). It has only two departures daily, though: at 10:45 A.M. and 9:30 P.M. daily except Sunday, when the earlier departure is at 5 P.M.

### Bus

Colonia's **Terminal de Buses** (fronting on Av. Roosevelt, also bounded by Vicente García and Manoel de Lobo, tel. 052/30288) occupies a triangular site. **Turil** (tel. 052/25246) and **COT** (tel. 052/23121) go frequently to Montevideo (US$8.50, two hours), while Berrutti (tel. 052/25301, www.berruttiturismo.com) goes to Carmelo (US$3.50, 1.5 hours) four times daily. Chadre has an early (5:40 A.M.) bus to Carmelo and another at 12:40 P.M.

### Rental Cars, Motorbikes, and Bicycles

**Thrifty** (General Flores 172, tel. 052/22939) rents bicycles, motor scooters, golf carts, and automobiles at reasonable prices. **Multicar** (Manoel Lobo 505, tel. 052/24893) also rents cars, while **Moto Rent** (Virrey Cevallos near Av. General Flores) has scooters and golf carts.

# Carmelo

Rediscovered by Argentine tourists in the years before the 2001–2002 crash, the town of Carmelo (pop. 24,000) is a secluded river port where the Río Uruguay and the Río Paraná Guazú unite to form the Río de la Plata. It's not fair to compare it with historic Colonia, but Carmelo does exude a certain century-old calm and charm, and visitor services are improving.

Yachting and water sports are the main activities; getting there used to be half the fun, but Cacciola's fast, new catamarans from Tigre now use broader river channels rather than the smaller (but less comfortable) launches that used to weave through the lush gallery forests of the Paraná delta islands en route to the Uruguayan side.

Founded in 1758 on a swampy site near the ominously named Arroyo de las Víboras (Arroyo of Vipers), Carmelo moved to the more promising Arroyo de las Vacas (Arroyo of Cattle) in 1816, after petitioning independence hero José Gervasio Artigas.

## ORIENTATION

In the department of Colonia, Carmelo is 75 kilometers northwest of Colonia del Sacramento via paved Ruta 21, and 235 kilometers from Montevideo via Ruta 1, Ruta 22 (which bypasses Colonia), and Ruta 21. Its recreational focus is the area around the arroyo, but most services line both sides of Calle 19 de Abril, to the north.

## SIGHTS

Running along the north bank of the arroyo, the **Rambla de los Constituyentes** is the starting point for riverside excursions. The human-powered **Puente Giratorio** (Revolving Bridge, 1912), the first of its kind in the country, crosses the arroyo to the **Yacht Club Carmelo.**

EXCURSIONS

the riverfront esplanade in Carmelo, Uruguay

© WAYNE BERNHARDSON

© WAYNE BERNHARDSON

The restaurant at Carmelo's Finca y Granja Narbona is also a wine tasting room.

In the town proper, dating from 1860, the **Casa de Ignacio Barrios** (19 de Abril 246) was the residence of a major Uruguayan independence figure and is now the **Casa de la Cultura,** also housing the city's tourist office.

Four blocks west, facing the placid Plaza Artigas, the **Templo Histórico del Carmen** (Barrios and J. P. Varela) dates from 1830; it's the focus of July 16's Festival de la Virgen del Carmen, honoring Carmelo's patron saint. The adjacent **Archivo y Museo del Carmen** (Mon.–Fri. 4–8 P.M., Sat.–Sun. 10 A.M.–noon, www.ciudadcarmelo.com/museodelcarmen, free), originally built in 1848 as a school, focuses on local and ecclesiastical history, with artifacts from the original settlement on the Arroyo de las Víboras, and an antique selection of carved religious statuary. It also has a gallery of paintings by local talent Gregorio Gil Martín and a small crafts shop that's mostly but not exclusively kitsch.

## La Estancia de Narbona
Near Carmelo's original site on the Arroyo de las Víboras (Km 263 of Ruta 21 toward Nueva Palmira, Mon., Wed.–Thurs., and Sat.–Sun. 9 A.M.–noon and 4–7 P.M.), this crumbling 18th-century *estancia* sits atop a prominent hillock just north of the highway. Uruguay still has many *estancias,* but few can match the antiquity of Narbona's *casco* (main house), chapel, and *campana* (bell tower), though it still needs urgent attention to arrest the decay.

## Finca y Granja Narbona
Carmelo has its own little Ruta del Vino, and Finca y Granja Narbona, about 13 kilometers north of town, may be the gem of the bunch. Eduardo Cantón, its Argentine owner, has preserved all the venerable vineyard buildings and recycled them into a stylish restaurant that also serves as a tasting room, as well as an upmarket bed-and-breakfast above the bodegas themselves. As if that weren't enough, there's a remarkable collection of antique wine-making equipment and an equally remarkable assortment of *cachilas,* the antique automobiles that are slowly disappearing from Uruguayan highways.

Finca y Granja Narbona (Ruta 21 Km 267, tel. 0540/4778, www.fincaygranjanarbona. com, US$180 d) is about 13 kilometers north of Carmelo. Two-night (US$150 d per night) and three-night (US$120 d per night) stays get discounts. Restaurant meals cost about US$25 pp; it also sells its own wine, primarily the red tannat and white viognier, as well as eight-kilogram rounds of its homemade parmesan cheese.

## Four Seasons Resort Carmelo

Eight kilometers north of town, attracting an international clientele for whom it's a destination in its own right rather than just a place to sleep, the luxury Four Seasons Resort Carmelo (Ruta 21, Km 262, tel. 0542/9000 in Carmelo, tel. 011/4321-1710 in Buenos Aires, www. fourseasons.com/carmelo, US$360–390 s or d) has made *Travel + Leisure*'s list of the world's 50 most romantic hotels, thanks to its dispersed rooms and elegant use of Asian decor.

On a former pine and eucaluptus plantation that includes a huge outdoor pool and its own riverside beach, its 44 rooms are equally divided between split-level apartments and sprawling bungalows. All feature handsomely crafted teakwood furniture, fireplaces, and considerable privacy and quiet. It has a spectacular spa, a somewhat smaller indoor pool, and arranges excursions, including horseback rides and winery visits for guests. Across the highway, golfers may play at the 18-hole course, and there are also bicycles and tennis courts.

The Four Seasons also flies in its own guests from Buenos Aires's Aeroparque, often as part of a package with its sister hotel in Retiro; few visitors come for fewer than two or three days. Its main drawback is that, because it's so self-contained, guests here have little contact with Uruguayans other than the English-speaking hotel staff, who are not necessarily typical.

## RESTAURANTS

In town proper, *minutas* such as the *chivito* are the standard at **Perrini** (19 de Abril 440, tel.

0542/2519), which faces Plaza Independencia. A recent addition, also facing the plaza, *Fay Fay* (18 de Julio and Uruguay, tel. 0542/4827) has a more diverse menu that includes both *parrillada* and pastas, and has soothing decoration. Ravioli (US$3.50) and cannelloni (US$4.50) are both worth consideration, along with more expensive meats.

The best around is certainly the Four Seasons Resort Carmelo's all-day restaurant **Pura** (Ruta 21, Km 262, tel. 0542/9000), which does a fine job with the seared freshwater *boga,* accompanied by grilled vegetables and pumpkin puree, or its nighttime-only Italian restaurant **Mandara.** On the grounds of its namesake winery, **Finca Narbona** (Ruta 21 Km 267, tel. 0542/9041) comes close in quality and is far more authentically Uruguayan in style (though its owner is an Argentine). Both are substantially better, and more expensive, than anything in town.

**Heladería Azul** (19 de Abril 483) has pretty good ice cream.

## THEATER AND CINEMA

For most Carmelitanos, entertainment is billiards or video games, but the town's **Cine Teatro Uamá** (Uruguay 220, tel. 0542/4830) is a 500-seat deco landmark that shows recent movies and occasionally hosts live theater. While basically in good condition, it's scheduled for a facelift.

## ACCOMMODATIONS

In recent years, rates have risen as the Uruguayan peso has strengthened against the dollar.

Alongside the arroyo, the **Camping Náutico Carmelo** (Embarcadero s/n, tel. 0542/2058) charges US$7.50 per tent. The site offers hot showers, electricity, fire pits, and a pool.

**Hotel Bertoletti** (Uruguay 171, tel. 0542/2030, US$15/25 s/d) lacks personality but is otherwise acceptable. **Hotel Centro** (Uruguay 370, tel. 0542/4488, www.ciudadcarmelo.com/hotelcentro, US$21/30 s/d) is tidy enough, but several of the rooms are dark, their small windows facing an already shady corridor.

Behind the well-preserved Italianate facade of **Hotel Timabe** (19 de Abril and Solís, tel. 0542/4525, www.ciudadcarmelo.com/timabe, US$25/40–42/62 s/d), there stands a modern, comfortable hotel with luminous midsized rooms that's probably the best choice in town proper. On the downside, the shower-only bathrooms are tiny, and the cheapest rooms lack air-conditioning.

Near the docks, **Hotel Rambla** (Uruguay 55, tel. 0542/2390, www.ciudadcarmelo.com/ramblahotel, US$27/42 s/d or US$65 d) resembles the Bertoletti in its lack of style; rooms on the upper floors are slightly cheaper, as there's no elevator and they lack air-conditioning.

Across the Arroyo de las Vacas, **Hotel Casino Carmelo** (Rodó s/n, 0542/2314, www.hotelcasinocarmelo.com, US$25–34 pp) has bed-and-breakfast accommodations but also packages with half board or full board.

## INFORMATION

The improving municipal **Oficina de Turismo** (19 de Abril 246, tel. 0542/2001, turiscar@adinet.com.uy), in the Casa de la Cultura, the town cultural center, is open daily 9 A.M.–7 P.M., at least in summer. Across the street and down the block, there's a reliable private office (19 de Abril 213, tel. 0542/5389, www.ciudadcarmelo.com/infoturismo).

## SERVICES

Directly on the central Plaza Independencia, **Banco Comercial** (Uruguay 401) has an ATM.

**Compuservice** (19 de Abril 462) offers both long-distance telephones and Internet access.

**Hospital Artigas** (Uruguay and Artigas, tel. 0542/2107) can handle medical problems.

## TRANSPORTATION

The Four Seasons Resort flies its guests to and from Buenos Aires via the airstrip at nearby Balneario Zagargazú. For others, though, bus and boat are the primary options.

**Berrutti** (Uruguay 337, tel. 0542/2504) has six buses each weekday to Colonia (US$3.50, 1.5 hours), beginning in Nueva Palmira; there are only five Saturday and three Sunday buses. To Montevideo (US$7, three hours), service is offered by several carriers on 18 de Julio between Uruguay and 19 de Abril (tel. 0542/2987), including Sabelín and Chadre, which also has two daily buses to Colonia (at inconvenient early-morning and late-evening hours).

On the waterfront, **Cacciola** (tel. 0542/3042) crosses to Tigre (US$11, 2.5 hours) at 4 A.M. and 2:30 P.M. daily except Saturday, when the afternoon departure is at 5 P.M., and Sunday, when the only departure is at 5:30 P.M.

**Budget** (19 de Abril 241, tel. 0542/7073) provides rental cars.

# Punta del Este and Maldonado

High-rise hotels soar behind sandy Atlantic beaches and elegant vessels crowd the sprawling yacht harbor at Uruguay's Punta del Este, one of South America's flashiest summer getaways. In January and February, the southern summer, Punta irrupts with flamboyant Argentine celebrities who make the covers and gossip columns of glossy Buenos Aires magazines.

Ironically enough, it was once a place where a colonial Jesuit priest remarked that "you see nothing here but a few cabins, the abodes of misery." In 1832, though, Charles Darwin spent 10 solitary weeks searching for natural-history specimens at a "quiet, forlorn town" that is now the jewel of the "Uruguayan Riviera."

It was in the late 1970s, as money from the corrupt Argentine military dictatorship flowed in, that Punta del Este began to grow up—literally so, as high-rise hotels and flats replaced single-family homes. On the peninsula, only

In otherwise hyperactive Punta del Este, the El Faro (lighthouse) neighborhood is a beacon of calm.

the southernmost sector of El Faro, whose landmark lighthouse limits other buildings to three stories, has been spared.

Truth be told, there's not that much to see in Punta del Este itself, but the compact peninsula that juts into the ocean is the place where wealthy Argentines come to play and be seen in a frenetic summer season—except when the Argentine currency collapses. Avenida Gorlero is the axis of its hyperactive nightlife, but the beaches along Rambla Artigas, which rings the peninsula, are the focus of sunny summer days. Under different names, the *rambla* connects the peninsula to the riverside beaches to the west and to the ocean beaches to the east.

Maldonado, by contrast, is a business and administrative center that's been largely eclipsed by Punta's rapid growth and glitter, but still retains vestiges of its colonial origins. Founded in 1755, the fortified city fell briefly under British control during the invasion of Buenos Aires in 1806.

Darwin may have disparaged Maldonado as a place whose few residents were mostly landowners and merchants "who do all the business for nearly 50 miles around," but modern Maldonado is far better than that. In recent years, however, quite a few businesses have closed, and the city's economy is moribund compared with Punta's.

## ORIENTATION

Punta del Este and Maldonado are about 130 kilometers east of Montevideo via Ruta I—a four-lane toll road—and Ruta 93.

Punta del Este proper occupies a compact peninsula that juts south into the Atlantic, separating the rugged surf of the Playa Brava (Wild Beach) to the east from the calmer Playa Mansa to the west. This is the point that divides the Atlantic Ocean from the Río de la Plata; in practice, Punta del Este is a much larger area that includes the departmental capital of Maldonado and a multitude of residential suburbs.

The peninsula itself divides into two separate grids: To the north, on both sides of Avenida Juan Gorlero and side streets, is the high-rise hotel area with its restaurants and shopping; to the south, named for its lighthouse, the El Faro neighborhood is quieter, more residential, less pretentious, and more economical.

Punta del Este streets are commonly known by their numbers, though they also have names. Addresses below include both except in the case of Avenida Juan Gorlero, known consistently as Gorlero.

Punta del Este and Maldonado have gradually grown together, but Maldonado's center is a regular colonial rectangular grid centered on Plaza San Fernando. Outside the city center, thoroughfares like Avenida Roosevelt and Bulevar Artigas connect the streets of irregular suburban neighborhoods. The Rambla Claudio Williman follows the riverside beaches to the west, while the Rambla Lorenzo Batlle Pacheco tracks along the ocean beaches. Buses along each *rambla* pick up and drop off passengers at numbered stops, known as *paradas*.

EXCURSIONS

## SIGHTS

Punta del Este is the place to go and to people-watch, but Maldonado has more historic sites. The *rambla* around the peninsula is a wide, pedestrian-friendly circuit that encourages walkers (Uruguayan drivers, by the way, respect pedestrians more than their Argentine counterparts, but there are plenty of Argentines here, so caution still applies).

### Maldonado

Remodeled in 1975 and planted with dawn redwoods, Maldonado's **Plaza San Fernando** features a statue of independence hero José Gervasio Artigas, a fountain, and an amphitheater for musical events.

On the west side of the plaza, the neoclassical **Catedral San Fernando de Maldonado** (1895) took nearly a century to complete; Antonio Veiga sculpted its altar, while the image of the Virgen de Santander came from the steamer *Ciudad del Santander,* which sank near Isla de Lobos in 1829.

At the plaza's southwest corner, the Spaniard Bartolomé Howel designed the **Cuartel de Dragones y de Blandengues,** masonry military barracks with impressive iron gates, whose grounds fill an entire block bounded by 25 de Mayo, 18 de Julio, Pérez del Puerto, and Dodera. Built between 1771 and 1797, it includes the **Museo Didáctico Artiguista** (tel. 042/225378, daily 10 A.M.–7 P.M., free admission), dedicated to Uruguay's independence hero. In addition, it holds the fine-arts **Museo Nicolás García Uriburu** (Tues.–Sun. 3–9 P.M., free).

Two blocks east, the **Museo San Fernando de Maldonado** (Sarandí and Pérez del Puerto, tel. 042/223781, Tues.–Sun. 3–11 P.M., free) served as the colonial customs house and prison; it now houses a fine-arts facility with rotating exhibitions, and a permanent collection of puppets from Uruguay and around the world.

Two blocks west of the Cuartel de Dragones y de Blandengues, the **Plaza Torre del Vigía** (1800) surrounds a colonial tower built high enough to allow sentries to sight passing boats on the river.

A block north of Plaza San Fernando, better organized than in the past, the eclectic **Museo Regional R. Francisco Mazzoni** (Ituzaingó 789, tel. 042/221107, Tues.–Sat. 11 A.M.–10 P.M., free) occupies an 18th-century house filled with colonial-style furnishings and natural-history items. It has also added a modern art gallery in a rehabbed outbuilding.

### Punta del Este

Avenida Juan Gorlero is Punta del Este's throbbing heart, open for business all night in summer and on weekends, but at other times it can seem positively sedate. Lively **Plaza Artigas,** fronting on Gorlero between Arrecifes (25) and El Corral (23) is the site of a perennial crafts fair, the **Feria de los Artesanos** (summer daily 5 P.M.–1 A.M., rest of year Sat.–Sun. 11 A.M.–5 P.M.).

It's almost always sedate near the **Faro de Punta del Este** (1860), a 43-meter lighthouse built by Tomás Libarena with a crystal prism brought from France. A spiral staircase of 150 steps, not open to the public, leads to the top.

On the Playa Mansa side of the peninsula, the sheltered **Puerto Nuestra Señora de la Candelaria** has 400 slips for visiting yachts, but it's also a good place for wildlife-watching. Southern sea lions often haul up in the vicinity, and the shorebirds include grebes, gulls, sandpipers, terns, and other species.

On the Atlantic side, **Playa El Emir** is Punta's most popular surfing beach; to the north, note the *Mano en la Playa* (Hand on the Beach) by Chilean sculptor Mario Irarrázabal, who built a similar but much larger piece in the Atacama Desert, and another smaller one in Puerto Natales.

Calmer riverside beaches stretch west along the Rambla Williman toward and beyond Punta Ballena. To the east, the Rambla Lorenzo Batlle Pacheco passes a series of beaches facing the open Atlantic. All of these have *paradores,* simple restaurants with beach service.

For those who can't make it to artist Carlos Páez Vilaró's Casapueblo, at Punta Ballena, there's a representative sample of his work at his **Galería Atelier Casapueblo** (Solís 720,

© WAYNE BERNHARDSON

Chilean sculptor Mario Irarrázabal, who created Punta del Este's *Mano en la Playa* (Hand on the Beach), has similar works in Chile.

tel. 042/446594, www.carlospaezvilaro.com), in the basement of Hotel Palace.

## RESTAURANTS

Punta del Este has a larger and more fashionable selection of restaurants than Maldonado, but Maldonado does have some excellent values.

### Maldonado

Try **El Grillo** (Ituzaingó and Sarandí, lunch and dinner, US$10–20) for *chivitos* and other short orders, but **Sumo Evolution** (Sarandí and Florida, tel. 042/223959, lunch and dinner, US$10–20) has raised the bar on Uruguay's iconic steak sandwich and some more elaborate dishes.

**Pizzería El Oasis** (Sarandí 1105, tel. 042/234794, lunch and dinner, US$10–20) is also popular for its *parrillada*. The **Círculo Policial de Maldonado** (Pérez del Puerto 780, tel. 042/225311, lunch and dinner, US$10–20) has inexpensive lunch and dinner specials.

Open weekends only, the relatively expensive **Mesón del Centro Español** (18 de Julio 708, tel. 042/224107, lunch and dinner, US$10–20) specializes in Spanish seafood.

### Punta del Este

**Sumo** (Gorlero between El Corral/23 and La Galerna/21, tel. 042/446729, under US$10) has Punta's finest cheap *chivitos*, as well as pizzas and other short orders. **La Pasiva** (Gorlero and Los Meros/28, tel. 042/441843, under US$10) is an inexpensive pizzeria.

**El Pobre Marino** (Solís/11 and Virazón/12, tel. 042/443306, lunch and dinner, US$10–20) is a relatively inexpensive seafood restaurant. Other seafood choices include the Basque-style **Gure Etxe** (Virazón/12 and La Salina/9, tel. 042/446858, lunch and dinner, US$10–20) and the pricier **El Viejo Marino** (Solís/11 and El Foque/14, tel. 042/443565, lunch and dinner, US$10–20).

New in 2007, **Capitán Cook** (Solís/11 No. 663 between 2 de Febrero/10 and Virazón/12, tel. 042/440254, lunch and dinner, US$10–20) is a friendly family restaurant run by a married couple who are also lawyers, of all things. The lime-green decor is a bit jarring, but the fish and seafood options include an ample three-course lunch or dinner (US$17, plus drinks), a fine value by current Punta standards.

It would take a long time to work your way through the extensive Italian menu at **( II Baretto** (La Salina/9 betw. El Trinquete/8 and 2 de Febrero/10, tel. 042/447243, lunch and dinner, US$10–20), where everything is casual except for quality dishes like swordfish steak, seafood risotto, and a lemon mousse so light that a breeze might blow it away. Packed at night, less so for lunch, it recreates the color scheme of an Italian villa, with brightly painted tables and rustically styled wooden chairs. It also has a large wine list and premium prices but, for the budget-conscious, there's a moderately priced lunch special (cash only).

Between the peninsula and Maldonado, **La Bourgogne** (Pedragosa Sierra and Avenida del Mar, tel. 042/482007, lunch and dinner, US$20 and up) is a highly regarded (and expensive) French restaurant that flavors its entrées with herbs from its own gardens (the herbs themselves are also for sale here).

**( Lo de Tere** (Rambla Artigas and La Galerna/21, tel. 042/440492, www.lodetere.com, lunch from noon, dinner from 8 P.M., US$15–20) is one of Punta's top international/Italian restaurants, famous for its *taglierini neri* (black pasta) with seafood. Don't miss the *maracuyá* (passion fruit) parfait. The budget-conscious should note that the first four parties that arrive for lunch before 1 P.M. or for dinner before 9 P.M. get a 40 percent discount; all others before those hours get a 20 percent discount. There is a good tobacco-free area and outdoor seating for sunny days and warm evenings.

Its chairs and tables painted in a riot of primary colors, with walls by Carlos Páez Vilaró, **La Tuttie** (La Salina/9 and El Trinquete/8, tel. 042/447236, lunch and dinner, US$6–8 with a 5 percent discount for cash) serves a wide variety of seafood, such as *corvina negra* and

swordfish. There's wine by the glass, but the desserts are not so good as the fish dishes.

The best ice creamery is **Arlecchino** (Gorlero betw. La Galerna/21 and Comodoro Gorlero/19, tel. 042/441953).

## ENTERTAINMENT
### Cinema
Punta del Este's cinemas are down to two: the Galería Libertador's **Cine Libertador** (Gorlero and Los Arrecifes/25, tel. 042/444437); and the five-screen **Cines Lido** (El Remanso/20 and Inzaurraga/31, tel. 042/440911).

### Bars
Near the yacht harbor, **Moby Dick** (on Rambla Artigas between Virazón/12 and 2 de Febrero/10) is open in summer only.

## SHOPS
**Manos del Uruguay** (tel. 042/441953) has a leather shop on Gorlero (22) between Inzaurraga (31) and Las Focas (30) in Punta del Este. Uruguayan artists display their work at **La Ciudadela,** at the corner of Mareantes (13) and Virazón (12).

## ACCOMMODATIONS
Accommodations are fewer but generally cheaper in Maldonado than in Punta del Este proper; unless otherwise indicated, the lodgings below are in Punta. Rates can swing violently; January and February are the peak months, and at that time it's hard to find singles—expect to pay for a double even if you're traveling solo. February prices often drop a bit from January; the rest of the year, and especially when times are hard, rates are negotiable.

The private **Centro de Hoteles** (Plaza Artigas s/n, tel. 042/440512, www.puntadelestehoteles.com, daily 10 A.M.–10 P.M.) is the best single information source for accommodations and particularly helpful to those in desperate need of a bed.

### Under US$25
On the peninsula, Hostelling International's former facility has closed, but hostellers have

newer and better alternatives. Near Plaza Artigas, the 36-bed **Punta del Este Hostel** (Los Arrecifes/25 No. 544, tel. 042/411632, www.puntadelestehostel.com, US$15–20 pp) is the most economical alternative.

The ❢ **1949 Hostel** (Calle 30 and Calle 18, tel. 042/440719, www.1949hostel.com, US$17–19 pp) has shared dorm rooms with either shared or private baths, private lockers, breakfast, and a bar with a sort of beach view. It's only a short walk from the bus terminal.

## US$25-50

On the north side of Maldonado's Plaza San Fernando, the upstairs **Hotel Le Petit** (Florida and Sarandí, tel. 042/223044, US$40) is under the same ownership as Punta del Este's Hotel Galicia. Rates fall slightly outside the summer season.

Facing Plaza San Fernando from the west side, **Hotel Colonial** (18 de Julio 841, tel. 042/223346, www.elhotelcolonial.com, US$35/50 s/d) has rooms with private bath and TV, and a separate bar with Internet service; off-season rates fall to US$20/36 s/d.

Maldonado's **Hotel Catedral** (Florida 823, tel. 042/242513, hotel_catedral@yahoo.com, hotelcatedral@adinet.com.uy, US$44/50 s/d) has rooms with private bath, plain furnishings, heat, and ceiling fans, but no air-conditioning. Breakfast costs US$5 pp.

## US$50-100

Near the lighthouse, rates at the architecturally utilitarian but very friendly **Atlántico Hotel** (Capitán/7 and Dos de Febrero/10, tel. 042/440229, hatlanti@adinet.com.uy, US$50/70 d) include cable TV, telephone, swimming pool, and a buffet breakfast. Multiday discounts are available, and off-season rates fall by half.

As quiet as Punta gets, **Hotel Galicia** (Sotileza 718, tel. 042/444992, www.hotel-galicia.com.uy, US$55/73 s/d) has small but immaculate rooms directly opposite the lighthouse. Off-season rates fall to US$35/50 s/d.

One of the peninsula's oldest hotels, dating

from 1911 but unrecognizably modernized in the 1980s, the **Gran Hotel España** (La Salina/9 No. 660, tel. 042/440228, www.granhotelespana.net, US$65/75 s/d) also enjoys a fine location near the lighthouse.

Near the lighthouse, the ❢ **Petit Hotel** (La Salina/9 No. 717, tel. 042/441412, www.petithotel-puntadeleste.com, US$65–80 d) is a minor gem—a small, cheerful family-run hotel with quiet, attractive gardens and other common areas; the higher rates correspond to garden rooms. It's an outstanding value with continental breakfast, cable TV, and telephone, and discounts for cash, though some may find the color scheme—pistachio and violet exterior, pink and blue interior—not to their taste.

**Hotel Marbella** (Inzaurraga/31 No. 615, tel. 042/441814, www.hotelmarbella.8m.com, US$53/76 s/d or US$83 s or d) is a respectable middle-class hotel with reasonable comforts except for the breakfast room, which can be uncomfortably crowded even when the hotel isn't all that full. Rates fall dramatically off-season.

At the **Palace Hotel** (Av. Gorlero and Solís/11, tel. 042/441919, palacepunta@hotmail.com, US$90/95 s/d), most rooms look onto the palm-studded grounds, which have a substantial pool. Far larger than it appears from its modest entrance, the hotel also has a restaurant and a quiet bar.

Amid all the action on the strip, **Hotel Península** (Av. Gorlero 761, tel. 042/441533, www.hotelpeninsulapuntadeleste.com, US$100 s or d) has quieter, terraced interior rooms that face the pool rather than the street. Credit card payments, though, mean a hefty 15 percent surcharge.

## US$100-200

**Hotel San Fernando** (Las Focas/30 No. 691, betw. Baupres/18 and El Remanso/20, tel. 042/440720, hotelsanfernando@hotmail.com, US$119 d) is a modern hotel with a rooftop terrace for panoramic views. Each of the 60 rooms has air-conditioning, a strongbox, and other standard conveniences.

Rooms at **Hotel Champagne** (Gorlero 828, tel. 042/445276, www.champagnehotel.com.uy, US$130 d) are simple but attractively furnished. Rates the first two weeks of January, though, rise about 40 percent.

## Over US$200

On the peninsula, the **Punta del Este Golden Beach Resort & Spa** (El Mesana/24 No. 34, tel. 042/441314, www.goldenbeach.com.uy, US$225 s or d) is a luxury spa facility that has some real off-season bargains—as low as US$60 d. The 800-pound gorilla of Punta del Este accommodations is the pharaonic **Hotel Conrad** (Rambla Williman and Av. Chiverta, tel. 042/491111, www.conrad.com.uy, US$350 s or d), a 302-room megahotel-casino (part of the Harrah's chain) just north of the peninsula. As an entertainment venue, though, it brings in big-time international acts such as the Beach Boys, Bob Dylan, and Julio Iglesias.

## INFORMATION

Widely available around town, the free weekly *Que Hacemos Hoy* is a guide to what's going on, at least among the self-anointed beautiful people who dominate Punta's social scene.

Within the Punta del Este bus terminal, the helpful municipal **Centro de Informaciones de la Intendencia** (tel. 042/494042, www.maldonado.gub.uy) is open daily 10 A.M.–6 P.M., sometimes later in summer. Nearby, the private **Liga de Fomento** (Rambla Williman, Parada 1, tel. 042/446519) keeps similar hours.

At the western approach to town, there's another municipal **Centro de Informes** (Rambla Williman, Parada 24/Las Delicias, tel. 042/230050), normally open daily 8 A.M.–7 P.M., though it often keeps later hours in January and February.

The national **Ministerio de Turismo** (Gorlero 942, tel. 042/441218) is open daily 10 A.M.–2:30 P.M. and 5:30–10 P.M.

© WAYNE BERNHARDSON

Punta del Este's most conspicuous accommodations, Hotel Conrad, also hosts major international performers.

EXCURSIONS

## SERVICES

Punta del Este and Maldonado have similar but not identical services.

### Consulate

Argentina operates a seasonal consulate on the peninsula, normally Monday–Friday 4–8 P.M., from mid-December to mid-March and July to early August. It's been a moving target, changing its abode from year to year, but seems to have finally settled in the Edificio Espigón (Gorlero and Comodoro Gorlero/19, tel. 042/446162).

### Immigration

For visa matters, Maldonado's **Dirección Nacional de Migraciones** (Ventura Alegre 727, tel. 042/237624) is open Monday–Friday 12:30–7 P.M.

### Laundry

In Punta del Este, **Mr. Lav** (El Mesana/24, betw. Las Focas/30 and Las Gaviotas/29) is open daily 10 A.M.–6 P.M.

In Maldonado, try **Espumas del Virrey** (Zelmar Michelini 1081, tel. 042/220582).

### Medical

The **Hospital de Maldonado** (Ventura Alegre s/n, tel. 042/225852) is about eight blocks northwest of Plaza San Fernando.

### Money

In Punta del Este, **Citibank** has an ATM at Gorlero and La Galerna (21), but there are several others. In Maldonado, **Banco República** (Florida 774) has an ATM on the north side of Plaza San Fernando.

Maldonado has several exchange houses in the vicinity of Plaza San Fernando, including **Cambio Dominus** (25 de Mayo and 18 de Julio).

### Postal Services

There's a Punta del Este Correo Uruguayo on Gorlero between Izaurraga (31) and La Angostura (32). In Maldonado, the address is 18 de Julio 965.

### Telephone and Internet

In Punta del Este, **Antel** is at Arrecifes (25) and El Mesana (24). **Spot Internet,** at Gorlero and Las Focas (30), has good Internet access; there are also many others.

In Maldonado, **Antel** is at the corner of Joaquín de Viana and Florida. **Hotel Colonial** (18 de Julio 841) has its own cybercafe.

## TRANSPORTATION

Punta del Este and Maldonado have air connections with Buenos Aires, land links with Montevideo, and bus-boat combinations as well.

### Air

**Aeropuerto Internacional Laguna del Sauce** (tel. 042/559777) is about 15 kilometers west of Maldonado. There are regular shuttles from Punta del Este's bus terminal.

On the ground level of the Edificio Santos Dumont, **Aerolíneas Argentinas** (Gorlero betw. Inzaurraga/31 and Las Focas/30, tel. 042/444343) shuttles frequently to Buenos Aires's Aeroparque. So does **Pluna** (Av. Roosevelt and Parada 9, tel. 042/490101), which serves several Brazilian cities in summer. At the airport only, **Sol Líneas Aéreas** (tel. 000/405-210053 toll-free) flies daily to and from Aeroparque in Buenos Aires.

### Boat

In the Punta del Este bus terminal, **Buquebus** (Local 9, tel. 042/484995, tel. 011/4316-6500 in Buenos Aires) makes bus-boat connections to Argentina via Piriápolis, Montevideo, and Colonia.

### Bus

Most services into the area stop over at **Terminal Maldonado** (Av. Roosevelt s/n, tel. 042/225701) and proceed to **Terminal Punta del Este** (Playa Brava, tel. 042/489467), near the isthmus. **Copsa** (tel. 042/489205) and **COT** (tel. 042/486810) have such frequent services to Montevideo that reservations are rarely necessary.

To get around town, **Maldonado Turismo,** in the Galería Mejillón (La Angostura/32 and

Gorlero, tel. 042/495504, www.maldonadoturismo.com) links Punta del Este with the easterly suburbs of La Barra and Manantiales. Its buses leave from immediately behind the bus terminal.

### Rental Cars

Rental agencies include **Avis** (Inzaurraga/31 betw. Gorlero and El Mesana/24, tel. 042/442020); **Europcar** (Gorlero and Las Focas/30, tel. 042/495017); **Hertz** (Inzaurraga/31 betw. Gorlero/22 and El Remanso/20, tel. 042/489775); **Dollar** (Gorlero 961, tel. 042/443444); and **Thrifty** (Gorlero and Las Focas/30, tel. 042/447462).

# Vicinity of Punta del Este and Maldonado

In addition to water sports and sunbathing in the day and partying at night, there are some worthwhile sights in the vicinity of Punta del Este and Maldonado.

## ISLA GORRITI

From the yacht harbor, frequent launches (US$17 r/t) cross to and from Isla Gorriti, immediately west of the peninsula. In addition to its beaches and *parador* restaurants, Gorriti holds the remains of the **Baterías de Santa Ana,** a colonial Spanish fortress.

## ISLA DE LOBOS

About eight kilometers southeast of the Playa Brava, in the open Atlantic but readily visible from the mainland, the otherwise barren 41-hectare Isla de Lobos is home to a breeding colony of about 200,000 southern sea lions (*Otaria byronia*). It was once home to the southern elephant seal (*Mirounga leonina*), but uncontrolled hunting for its blubber eliminated the species here.

Topped by a lighthouse (1906), the rocky islet has been a tourist draw since 1920, though landings are not permitted. Rising 43 meters above the ocean, the structure boasts South America's most powerful sea-level light, with a range of 22.5 nautical miles.

Isla de Lobos played a grim historic role during the British invasion of 1806, as the British marooned Spanish prisoners here without food or water. Many died attempting to swim to the mainland.

For visits to Isla de Lobos, contact **Calypso Charters y Excursiones** (Rambla Artigas and Calle 21, tel. 042/446152, www.calypso.com.uy). The two-hour excursion, which normally leaves daily at 11:30 A.M., costs US$60 pp, half that for kids up to 12 years old.

## ◖ CASAPUEBLO

Lacking right angles, so blindingly white that you need sunglasses to approach it, Uruguayan painter Carlos Páez Vilaró's whimsical Mediterranean-style villa resembles the rounded mud nest of the *rufous hornero* (ovenbird). On a sloping headland at Punta Ballena, 10 kilometers west of Punta del Este, the area's most unusual sight is a showcase for unconventional art—Páez Vilaró is clearly a Picasso admirer—and Casapueblo has grown over the years to include a hotel, a restaurant, and a bar.

Parts are open to the public for a small charge, others to time-share members only. Hours are daily 10 A.M.–6 P.M.; for those unable to make the excursion, Páez Vilaró now has a downtown gallery on the peninsula. Any Montevideo-bound bus will drop you at the turnoff, from which it's about a 20-minute walk to Casapueblo.

Accommodations at ◖**Club Hotel Casapueblo** (tel. 042/579386, www.clubhotel.com.ar) start around US$84 s or d and can reach US$400 or more, but are lower in the off-season and even higher between Christmas and the first week of January.

## LA BARRA DE MALDONADO

Until the 1940s, when the construction of summer houses began apace, La Barra de

Carlos Páez Vilaró's hotel-museum Casapueblo is a work of art in its own right.

EXCURSIONS

Maldonado was a modest fishing village. The undulating **Puente Leonel Viera** (1965), a bridge crossing the Arroyo de Maldonado, opened up the area east of Punta del Este to beachside development.

Conspicuous because of the kitschy great white shark at its entrance, just across the bridge in Barrio El Tesoro, Barra's **Museo del Mar** (Los Bucaneros s/n, tel. 042/771817, www.museodelmar.com.uy, summer daily 10:30 A.M.–8:30 P.M., rest of year Sat.–Sun. and holidays 10 A.M.–6 P.M., US$5 adult, US$2.50 child) houses an impressive collection of shells and corals. It also covers historical material on Punta del Este, including photography and information on individuals such as Juan Gorlero, the former Maldonado mayor and tourism promoter for whom Punta's main avenue is named.

La Barra is no budget destination, but there's budget accommodation at the **Manantiales Hostel** (Ruta 10 Km 164, tel. 042/774427, www.manantialeshostel.com, US$17–25 pp), which also offers surfing lessons and rents surfboards. Amenities include breakfast and WiFi; in winter, rates fall as low as US$10 pp.

The 28-room beachfront **La Posta del Cangrejo** (Ruta 10 Km 160.5, tel. 042/770021, www.lapostadelcangrejo.com, US$80/100 s/d or US$480 suite) has hosted the rich and powerful since the 1960s, when it housed Kennedy-administration officials for a legendary meeting of the Organization of American States and the Argentine-born Cuban delegate, Ernesto "Che" Guevara, tweaked their noses (figuratively speaking, at least). Former U.S. president George H. W. Bush also experienced the Mediterranean elegance of La Posta's suites in 1990. Its restaurant comes highly recommended.

## JOSÉ IGNACIO

Beyond La Barra, about 30 kilometers east of Punta del Este, the former fishing village of José Ignacio has become a magnet for those—like plutocrat Argentine cement heiress Amalia de Fortabat—who'd rather not advertise their presence on the Uruguayan

Riviera. Fishing boats still sell the day's catch on the beach, and the most conspicuous landmark is the 32.5-meter **Faro José Ignacio** (1877), a lighthouse with a visibility of 16.5 nautical miles and a light visible for nine nautical miles.

Since the lamentable demise of the old reliable Santa Teresita, the newest star on the gastronomic scene is ◖ **Parador La Huella** (tel. 0486/2279, www.paradorlahuella.com), a beachfront restaurant specializing in fish and seafood (including sushi), but also lamb. With a wine list of Argentine and Uruguayan vintages, it's convinced visitors including A-list celebrities such as Shakira (who has a nearby house), but it's open to everyone.

# BACKGROUND

## The Land

Buenos Aires sits atop the coastal margin of the almost unrelentingly flat, pampas grasslands, whose beef and grain exports made Argentina a wealthy country throughout much of the 19th and 20th centuries. The city has little relief—its highest elevation is only about 25 meters—except along the original *barrancas* (riverbanks), which now lie well inland because of landfill along the Río de la Plata's muddy estuary. The only other significant body of water is the heavily polluted Riachuelo, a tributary that forms part of the city's southern boundary; the densely built city has covered all the smaller arroyos.

The Río de la Plata, misleadingly glossed into English as the River Plate (it literally means the River of Silver), is one of the world's great river systems—in terms of length, width, and flow, it's in a class with the Amazon, Nile, and Mississippi. Originating in the heights of the Bolivian altiplano and draining an area of more than 3.1 million square kilometers, in reality it's an estuary at the confluence of the Río Paraná (length 3,945 km) and the Río Uruguay (length 1,650 km).

Its delta, northwest of Buenos Aires proper, is a series of islands in a maze of muddy channels whose sedimentary surface is largely covered by dense gallery forest. The combined flow of the Paraná and Uruguay carries sediments far out into the south Atlantic Ocean.

© WAYNE BERNHARDSON

## GEOGRAPHY

The Ciudad Autónoma de Buenos Aires is a compact, politically autonomous federal district surrounded by contiguous suburbs of Buenos Aires province. It occupies 192 square kilometers on the right bank of the Río de la Plata.

Together with the federal capital, the conurbation of Gran Buenos Aires (Greater Buenos Aires) includes 24 contiguous and surrounding *partidos* (roughly translatable as counties): Almirante Brown, Avellaneda, Berazategui, Estéban Echeverría, Ezeiza, Florencio Varela, General San Martín, Hurlingham, Ituzaingó, José C. Paz, La Matanza, Lanús, Lomas de Zamora, Malvinas Argentinas, Merlo, Moreno, Morón, Quilmes, San Fernando, San Isidro, San Miguel, Tigre, Tres de Febrero, and Vicente López.

## CLIMATE

In the Southern Hemisphere, Buenos Aires's seasons are reversed from those in the Northern Hemisphere: The summer solstice falls on December 21, the autumnal equinox on March 21, the winter solstice on June 21, and the vernal equinox on September 21. For most Argentines, the de facto summer months are January and February, when schools are out of session and families take their holidays.

Thanks to its mid-latitude setting (34° 37' S) and proximity to the Atlantic Ocean, Buenos Aires's climate is humid and temperate, with annual precipitation of about 1.2 meters distributed evenly throughout the year. It resembles southern parts of the United States' eastern seaboard except in winter, when temperatures remain mild and frosts are rare. Summer can be uncomfortably hot and humid, as temperatures frequently exceed 30°C and thunderstorms are common. *Pamperos* (southwesterly cold fronts) and *sudestadas* (southeasterly cool, high winds) are the most problematical climatic phenomena; snow is unheard-of.

# Flora and Fauna

As one of the world's largest cities, Buenos Aires has no truly untouched natural habitat, but many birds, fish, and other wildlife survive among the gallery forests, channels, and oxbow lakes of the Río Paraná delta. Many of these plants and animals are opportunistic species that have colonized the former landfill east of Puerto Madero.

Like many other cities, the capital is home to unfortunately large numbers of stray dogs and even larger numbers of feral cats that infest areas like Palermo's Jardín Botánico (botanical garden). Because of their presence, the pigeon sometimes seems to be the only bird species to survive in substantial numbers.

## CONSERVATION ORGANIZATIONS

For information on protected areas, a few of which are in the vicinity of Buenos Aires, contact the **Administración de Parques Nacionales** (Av. Santa Fe 690, Retiro, tel. 011/4314-9325, www.parquesnacionales.gov. ar, Mon.–Fri. 10 A.M.–5 P.M.). Although its selection of brochures on national parks and other protected areas is improving, the staff themselves are best informed on the country's most high-profile destinations, such as Parque Nacional Iguazú and Parque Nacional Los Glaciares; on lesser units, they don't know much.

The **Fundación Vida Silvestre Argentina** (Defensa 251, Monserrat, tel. 011/4331-4864, www.vidasilvestre.org.ar) is a pro-wildlife and habitat advocacy organization. Membership rates, including the newsletter *Otioso,* start around US$16 per annum; higher-priced memberships include the foundation's magazine, *Revista Vida Silvestre.*

Bird-watchers can get information from the

Dense reeds on the back channels of the Río Paraná delta often shelter fish and wildlife.

**Asociación Ornitológica del Plata** (25 de Mayo 749, 2nd fl., Microcentro, tel. 011/4312-1015, www.avesargentinas.org.ar); its library is open to the public Wednesday and Friday 3–9 P.M.

Argentina's branch of **Greenpeace** (Mansilla 3046, Barrio Norte, tel. 011/4962-0404, www. greenpeace.org.ar) is very active and outspoken on local, national, and international environmental issues; actor Ricardo Darín is one of its high-profile members.

## FLORA

The main trees of the Paraná delta gallery forest are medium-size species, such as the contorted *ceibo* (*Erythrina crytagalli*), whose blossom is Argentina's national flower; the *sauce criollo* (*Salix humboldtiana*), a native willow; and *canelón* (*Rapanea iaetevirens*).

Seasonally flooded areas along the river feature sizeable marshes of large herbaceous plants like rushes, totora reeds, cattails, and bunch grasses. There are also "floating islands" of aquatic vegetation in calm, protected areas of the delta.

## FAUNA
### Marine, Coastal, and Aquatic Fauna

In the La Plata estuary's murky, sediment-filled waters, it can be difficult to spot any kind of aquatic fauna, but ocean-going fish species like the yellow corvina (*Micropogonias furnieri*) and the black corvina (*Pogonias cromis*), as well as crustaceans, such as crabs, and shellfish, such as mussels, do hide in the water. The outstanding marine mammal is the La Plata river dolphin (*Pontoporia blainvillei*). The nutria, or La Plata river otter (*Lutra platensis*), is also present here and farther up the estuary.

### Terrestrial and Freshwater Fauna

In the upper reaches of the Plata estuary, as far as the confluence of the Paraná and the Uruguay, freshwater game fish like the *boga* (*Leporinus obtusidens*), dorado (*Salminus brasiliensis*), sábalo (*Prochilodus platensis*), surubí (*Pseudoplatystoma coruscans*), and tararirá (*Hoplias malabaricus*) mix with some oceanic species.

Marshes along the river provide habitat

for mammals like the *carpincho* or capybara (*Hydrochoerus capybara,* a Rottweiler-sized rodent) and the marsh deer (*Blastocerus dichotomus*). The amphibian *rana criolla* (Creole frog, *Leptodactylus ocellatus*) is large (up to 130 mm in length) and meaty enough that it's occasionally eaten.

### Birds

In the gallery forests along the Plata estuary, common birds include the *boyero negro* or black cacique, an oriole-like species that breeds in hanging nests; the rufous-capped antshrike (*Thamnophilus ruficapillus*); and *pava de monte* (black guan, *Penelope obscura*). Typical aquatic species include coots, ducks, and swans.

Marshland species include the *junquero* (marsh wren, *Phleocryptes melanops*), the polychromatic *sietecolores* (literally, seven colors; *Thraupis bonariensis*), and the striking *federal,* with black plumage crowned by a scarlet hood. There are also several species of rails and crakes.

### Invertebrates

In such a dense urban environment, of course, the most conspicuous invertebrates are usually cockroaches, flies, and mosquitoes, but Buenos Aires remains free of contagious insect-borne diseases like malaria and dengue. Nonetheless, in well watered rural areas like the Paraná delta, mosquitoes can be a real plague, so a good repellent is imperative.

# Agriculture and Settlement Landscapes

In immediate pre-Columbian times, bands of nomadic Querandí hunter-gatherers peopled what is now Buenos Aires and its surrounding pampas. Living in smallish bands with no permanent settlements, they relied on wild game like the guanaco (a relative of the domestic llama) and the flightless, ostrich-like *ñandú* (rhea), as well as fish, for subsistence. What remains of their material culture is primarily lithic (arrowheads, spearheads, and the rounded stone balls known as *boleadoras*) and ceramics.

## AGRICULTURE AND THE LANDSCAPE

The arrival of the Spaniards, of course, brought major transformations. Though their initial efforts at colonizing the pampas failed because of Querandí resistance and their own poor preparation, feral European livestock—cattle and horses—proliferated almost beyond belief on the nearly virgin grasslands. By the late 19th century, large rural estates known as *estancias* produced hides, beef, and then wool for export to Europe via Buenos Aires; in the 20th century, Argentine agriculture diversified with grain exports. The pattern of large rural landholdings persists in Buenos Aires province, but the capital has expanded onto lands that were only recently agricultural.

## SETTLEMENT LANDSCAPES

Cities, of course, differ greatly from the countryside. By royal decree, Spanish colonial cities were organized according to a rectangular grid surrounding a central plaza where all the major public institutions—*cabildo* (town council), cathedral, and market—were located. Buenos Aires was no exception to the rule; though the transformation from colonial city to modern metropolis obliterated many landmarks, the essential grid pattern remains.

Traditionally, in colonial barrios such as San Telmo, houses fronted directly on the street or sidewalk, with interior patios or gardens exclusively for family use; houses set back from the street were rare. This pattern has persisted to the present, though materials have changed from adobe to reinforced concrete and multistory apartment buildings have replaced traditionally low-slung structures.

Though it's unusual to find houses with large yards or gardens of the North American suburban model in the capital city, they're common enough in the northern suburbs and a few other areas—often surrounded by high fences and state-of-the-art security.

# Environmental Issues

Like other global megacities, the Capital Federal and its suburbs suffer from environmental degradation, though not all indicators are negative.

## AIR POLLUTION

Buenos Aires's aging diesel buses may be the primary culprit in the capital's declining air quality, but private vehicles (some of which still run on leaded gasoline) and taxis contribute more than their share. Superannuated factories, with their subsidized smokestacks, are another source.

One advantage that Buenos Aires has over some other cities is the frequency of rain and even thunderstorms that clear pollutants from the air. Storms, though, also ensure that airborne pollutants hit the ground and drain onto city streets and eventually into the waterways.

## WATER POLLUTION

Buenos Aires may have potable drinking water, but the success of the early hides and livestock industry, and then of heavy industry, has left a legacy of polluted waterways. The textbook example is the Riachuelo, in the working-class barrio of La Boca. Its water more closely resembles sludge than water; its bottom sediments, thanks to chemical runoff from factories in La Boca and in nearby Avellaneda, are an even greater toxic hazard. To give credit where it's due, there's been progress in removing rusting hulks from the Vuelta de Rocha, near the popular tourist area of Caminito, but that's the easy part.

## NOISE POLLUTION

Just as motor vehicles cause most of the city's air pollution, they produce most of its noise pollution, due partly to inadequate mufflers.

According to one study, vehicular noise accounts for 80 percent of levels that, at corners like Rivadavia and Callao, reach upwards of 80 decibels.

Aeroparque Jorge Newbery, the capital's domestic airport, rates highly for convenience and accessibility, but noisy jet takeoffs and landings are particularly bothersome to residents of Palermo and Belgrano. Interestingly enough, it's these middle- and upper-class barrios, and not working-class neighborhoods, that have to put up with these high decibel levels. Plans to close Aeroparque are on the table, but it's unlikely to happen before the next edition of this book.

## SOLID WASTE

Like other megacities, Buenos Aires produces prodigious amounts of trash—according to the municipal waste management agency Ceamse, garbage trucks collect 14,000 tons per day from city streets. This misleading statistic, though, overlooks the issue of what's not collected because opportunistic *cartoneros* or *cirujas* (the latter, an ironic *lunfardo*, or slang, term derived from the Spanish word for surgeon, but meaning street scavengers), who appeared in force during the 2001–2002 economic crisis, recycle items left for streetside pickup.

Recycling might seem a solution to the problem, but *cartoneros* break open sealed plastic garbage bags to extract recyclables; when garbage trucks collect the broken bags, much of the remaining materials fall into the street (augmenting the trash that thoughtless *porteños* have already tossed there). Municipal authorities have attempted, so far without success, to create a formal recycling program that would require city residents to separate recyclables in the bags they place on the streets nightly.

On the Avenida de Mayo, *cartoneros* (scavengers) demonstrate against restrictions on their recycling activities.

There's also a dark side to informal recycling. Some *cartoneros*—apparently in league with criminal elements—have absconded with valuable bronze and other precious metals that cover utility boxes and similar objects accessible from the street. Sold and melted into ingots, the stolen items are virtually untraceable.

Another sort of solid waste is even more problematic. Greenpeace Argentina has protested an agreement with Australia to import that country's nuclear waste for reprocessing near the suburb of Ezeiza. Argentina's constitution prohibits storage of nuclear waste, though Argentina has its own aging 357-megawatt Atucha I reactor near the town of Lima, northwest of the capital.

## URBAN FORESTRY

Buenos Aires has some 375,000 street trees of more than 500 species. The *fresno* (European ash, *Fraxinus excelsior*) comprises nearly half the total, and the sycamore is the next most common. The distribution of trees, however, is uneven—the northern barrios are

woodsier—but even there, many specimens are in poor condition. Thunderstorms often knock down branches and even entire trees.

Municipal authorities estimate that at least 110,000 additional trees would be desirable, but inadequate maintenance is working against the existing urban forests, and the economic crisis works against afforestation. A new law that permits private parties to plant their own street trees from a list of approved species could help close the gap.

## ENERGY

Argentina is self-sufficient in fossil fuels and has substantial hydroelectric resources in the subtropical north and along the Andean foothills, but Argentine governments have promoted nuclear power since the 1950s. Although the country has renounced any intention to build nuclear weapons, the 357-megawatt Atucha I reactor has powered the capital's electrical grid since 1974. For much of the time since then, it has operated at reduced capacity thanks partly to the availability of cheaper hydroelectricity, but also due to inadequate maintenance; the controling Comisión Nacional de Energía Atómica (CNEA,

National Atomic Energy Commission) is not known for its transparency. Atucha I is due to close in 2014.

# History

Buenos Aires's origins are, in some ways, as murky as the muddy Río de la Plata. Everyone agrees that bands of Querandí hunter-gatherers roamed the southern banks of the river, but their encampments of *toldos* (tents of animal skins) shifted with the availability of game, fish, and other resources. No Querandí settlement could reasonably be called a city, a town, or even a village.

## THE FIRST BUENOS AIRES

Buenos Aires proper dates from January 1536, when the Spaniard Pedro de Mendoza, commanding a fleet of at least a dozen ships and perhaps as many as 2,500 men plus nearly 100 horses, landed on its shores. Mendoza came to establish a colony, but his summer arrival was too late for planting and the colonists suffered from food shortages during the cool, wet winter. Spanish demands for food and supplies provoked violent and effective Querandí opposition; within five years, the insecure colonists abandoned their settlement.

Traditionally, Argentine histories place Mendoza's settlement on the *barrancas* (natural levees) of what is now Parque Lezama, in the barrio of San Telmo, and a monument to Mendoza is one of the park's highlights. Though it's now well inland, thanks to nearly five centuries of landfill, during Mendoza's time it directly fronted on the river.

*Porteño* author Federico Kirbus, though, has argued that Mendoza's expedition didn't land anywhere near Parque Lezama or even within the area that now comprises the Capital Federal. Instead, relying on historical accounts of the time complemented by field observations, he concludes that the first Buenos Aires may have been some distance up what is now the Paraná delta, closer to the provincial town

of Escobar, before several centuries of sedimentary deposition would have filled in the river and complicated navigation for such a large fleet as Mendoza's. Although the evidence is circumstantial rather than definitive, it's an intriguing hypothesis.

## BUENOS AIRES BECOMES PERMANENT

While Mendoza's initial settlement failed, some expedition members sailed up the Paraná to found Asunción, capital of present-day Paraguay. Almost four decades later, in 1580, Juan de Garay led an expedition in the opposite direction to found Santa Fe; he also refounded Buenos Aires, settling 60 colonists near what is now the Plaza de Mayo. Garay fell victim to the Querandí within three years, but the settlement he established—peopled by *mancebos de la tierra* (offspring of Spaniards and native Guaraní)—survived.

On the river's muddy banks, the location had little to recommend it as a port, but this was largely irrelevant—the new Buenos Aires was subordinate to Asunción, which was in turn subordinate to the Viceroyalty of Lima and the Spanish capital of Madrid via a long, indirect overland-and-maritime route. It took nearly two centuries for Buenos Aires, a backwater of Spain's American empire, to match Lima's viceregal status.

## COLONIAL BUENOS AIRES

Barred from direct contact with Europe by Spain's mercantile bureaucracy, early colonial Buenos Aires had to survive on the resources of the sprawling pampas. The Querandí and other indigenous groups had subsisted on guanacos, rheas, and other game, in addition to edible fruits and plants they gathered, but these resources were inadequate and culturally inconceivable for the Spaniards.

The Mendoza expedition, though, had left behind horses that thrived on the lush but thinly populated pastures of the pampas, and the proliferation of the Garay expedition's escaped cattle soon transformed the Buenos Aires backcountry into a fenceless feral cattle ranch. The presence of horses and cattle, nearly free for the taking, spawned the gaucho culture for which Argentina became famous. Durable hides were the primary product; perishable beef had little market value.

Buenos Aires had no easily accessible markets in which to sell their hides, though, because hides were too low-value a product to ship to Spain via Lima and Panama; consequently, there developed a vigorous contraband trade with British and Portuguese vessels in the Paraná delta's secluded channels. As this trade grew, Spain acknowledged Buenos Aires's growing significance by making it capital of the newly created Virreinato del Río de la Plata (Viceroyalty of the River Plate) in 1776. Reflecting its significance and the need to curb Portuguese influence, the viceroyalty even included the bonanza silver district of Potosí in present-day Bolivia, then known as Alto Perú (Upper Peru).

The city's population, only about 500 in the early 17th century, grew slowly at first. By 1655, it was barely 4,000, and it took nearly a century to reach 10,000 in 1744. By the time of the new viceroyalty, though, the population exceeded 24,000, and nearly doubled again by the early 19th century. Open to European commerce as Madrid loosened its reins, the livestock economy expanded with the development of *saladeros* (meat-salting plants), adding value to beef that was almost worthless before.

Unlike the densely populated central Andean area, where the Spaniards established themselves atop an already hierarchical society and exploited the native population through tribute and forced labor, Buenos Aires lacked an abundant labor force. The improving economy and growing population—which consisted of peninsular Spaniards, *criollos* (creoles, American-born Spaniards), *indígenas* (indigenous people), and mestizos (the offspring of Spaniards and *indígenas*)—soon included African slaves. Increasing political autonomy and economic success accelerated the end of Spanish rule.

## The Dissolution of Colonial Argentina

Appointed by the Spanish crown, all major viceregal officials governed from Buenos Aires, and economic power was also concentrated there. Outside the capital and isolated by geographic barriers, provincial bosses created their own power bases. When Napoleon invaded Spain in the early 19th century, the glue that held together Spain's colonial possessions began to dissolve, leading to independence in several steps.

Contributing to the move toward independence was a changing sense of identity among the people of what is now Argentina. In the early generations, the Spanish settlers of course identified themselves as Spaniards, but over time *criollos* began to differentiate themselves from *peninsulares* (European-born Spaniards). It bears mention that while the mestizos and even the remaining indigenous population may have identified more closely with Argentina than with Spain, it was the *criollo* intelligentsia who found the Spanish yoke most oppressive, and to whom the notion of independence had the greatest appeal.

The South American independence movements commenced on the periphery, led by figures like Argentina's José de San Martín, Venezuela's Simón Bolívar, and Chile's Bernardo O'Higgins, but their heroism was built on a broad support base. In Buenos Aires, this base developed as opportunistic and unauthorized British forces took advantage of Spain's perceived weakness and occupied the city in 1806 and 1807.

As the shocked Viceroy Rafael de Sobremonte fled Buenos Aires for Córdoba, city residents organized a covert resistance that, under the leadership of the Frenchman Santiago de Liniers, dislodged the invaders. Based on the belief that Spain's legitimate government had fallen and as reflection of their confidence, the *porteños* chose Liniers as viceroy in an open *cabildo*. The royalist Liniers, ironically enough, died at the hands of independence fighters during the 1810 Revolution.

Returning from Spain to Buenos Aires, San Martín led independence armies against royalist forces deployed from Peru, in what is now northwestern Argentina. In 1816, in the city of Tucumán, delegates of the Provincias Unidas del Río de la Plata (United Provinces of the River Plate) issued a formal declaration of independence. But this was only a loose confederation that glossed over differences between Federalist caudillos—provincial landholders and warlords intent on preserving their fiefdoms—and the cosmopolitan Unitarists of Buenos Aires.

The struggle between Federalists and Unitarists was slow to resolve itself; according to historian James Scobie, "It took 70 years for Argentina to coalesce as a political unit." Even today, tensions between the provinces and the central government have not disappeared, but it took a Federalist to ensure the primacy of Buenos Aires.

## REPUBLICAN ARGENTINA AND BUENOS AIRES

Having achieved independence, the Provincias Unidas were less successful in creating institutions. Several attempts at agreeing upon a constitution failed, resulting in a series of ministates that quarreled among themselves. In Buenos Aires, the largest province, Federalist caudillo Juan Manuel de Rosas took command and ruled from 1829 until his overthrow in 1852. The shrewd, ruthless Rosas did more than anyone else to ensure the primacy of the city, which, nevertheless, did not become the country's capital until 1880.

By the time Rosas took power, Buenos Aires's population had grown to nearly 60,000; in 1855, only a few years after he left, it reached 99,000. In 1833, Charles Darwin (who admired the loyalty of Rosas's followers even as he questioned the dictator's ruthlessness) was impressed with the city's size and orderliness:

Every street is at right angles to the one it crosses, and the parallel ones being equidistant, the houses are collected into solid squares of equal dimensions, which are called quadras. On the other hand the houses themselves are hollow squares; all the rooms opening into a neat little courtyard. They are generally only one story high, with flat roofs, which are fitted with seats, and are much frequented by the inhabitants in summer. In the centre of the town is the Plaza, where the public offices, fortress, cathedral, &c., stand. Here also, the old viceroys, before the revolution had their palaces. The general assemblage of buildings possesses considerable architectural beauty, although none individually can boast of any.

In the early independence years, Unitarist visionaries like Mariano Moreno and Bernardino Rivadavia had advocated an aggressive immigration policy to Europeanize the young republic, but Rosas's dictatorial rule, obstinate isolationism, and continual military adventures deterred immigration. His defeat at the battle of Caseros (1853) opened the country to immigration and accelerated the diversification of the economy from extensive *estancias* and *saladeros* to the more intensive production of wool and grains for export.

For the city, still a provincial rather than a national capital, this meant explosive growth—its population more than doubled to 230,000 by 1875. In 1880, when the other provinces forced the federalization of Buenos Aires, irate provincial authorities shifted their own capital to the new city of La Plata, but the newly designated federal capital continued to grow. By the early 20th century, it became the first Latin American city with more than a million inhabitants.

## THE *PORTEÑOS* GET A PORT

Unfortunately, for a fast-growing city of *porteños*, Buenos Aires was a poor natural port. Its muddy river banks and shallow waters made loading and unloading slow, laborious, expensive, and even hazardous, as freighters had to anchor in deep water and transfer their cargo to shallow-draft lighters. Before it could become a great commercial port, Buenos Aires would have to speed up a process that took months rather than weeks for the average steamship.

Everyone agreed port improvements were imperative, but there were different visions of how to accomplish them. Engineer Luis Huergo offered the simplest and most economical solution: to broaden, dredge, and straighten the Riachuelo to provide better access to existing port facilities at La Boca and Barracas, in the city's southern barrios. As so often happens in Argentina, though, political influence trumped practical expertise, as the congress approved wealthy downtown businessman Eduardo Madero's vague plan to transform the mudflats into a series of deep *diques* (basins) immediately east of the central Plaza de Mayo, even as work advanced on the Riachuelo option.

Approved in 1882, Puerto Madero took 16 years to complete, came in well over budget, caused a scandal because of shady land dealings, and finally even proved inadequate for the growing port traffic. Only improvements at La Boca and the 1926 opening of Retiro's Puerto Nuevo (New Port) finally resolved the problem, but port costs remained high.

## FROM GRAN ALDEA TO COSMOPOLITAN CAPITAL

Federalization gave the city a new mayor—Torcuato de Alvear, appointed by president Julio Argentino Roca—and Alvear immediately imposed his vision on the newly designated capital. Instead of the traditionally intimate *gran aldea*, Buenos Aires was to become a city of monuments, a cosmopolitan showpiece symbolizing Argentina's integration with the wider world. Where single-story houses once lined narrow colonial streets, broad boulevards like the Avenida de Mayo soon linked majestic public buildings, such as the Casa Rosada presidential palace and the Congreso Nacional (the federal legislature).

Newly landscaped spaces like the Plaza de Mayo, Plaza del Congreso, and Plaza San Martín, not to mention the conversion of Rosas's former Palermo estate into parklands, reflected the aspirations—or pretensions—of an ambitious country. Some, though, castigated Alvear for favoring upper-class barrios, such as Recoleta, Palermo, and Belgrano, over struggling immigrant neighborhoods, like San Telmo and La Boca.

As immigrants streamed into town from Spain, Italy, Britain, Russia, and other European countries, such differential treatment exacerbated growing social tensions. In 1913, Buenos Aires became the first South American city to open a subway system, beneath the Avenida de Mayo, but in poorer neighborhoods large families squeezed into *conventillos* (tenements) and struggled on subsistence wages. The gap between rich and poor frequently exploded into open conflict. In 1909, following police repression of a May Day demonstration, anarchist immigrant Simón Radowitzky killed police chief Ramón Falcón with a bomb. In 1919, president Hipólito Yrigoyen ordered the army to crush a metalworkers' strike during what is now recalled as La Semana Trágica (The Tragic Week).

Ironically, Yrigoyen pardoned Radowitzky a decade later, and his was the first administration to suffer one of repeated military coups that plagued the country for most of the 20th century. The dictatorship that followed him continued the policy of demolishing narrow colonial streets to create broad thoroughfares like Corrientes, Córdoba, and Santa Fe, all parallel to the Avenida de Mayo, and the crosstown boulevard Avenida 9 de Julio. The populist Perón regimes of the 1940s and 1950s, despite public deference to working-class interests, splurged on pharaonic works projects, heavy and heavily subsidized industry, and unsustainable social spending that squandered the country's post–World War II surpluses.

## THE DIRTY WAR AND ITS AFTERMATH

As Gran Buenos Aires grew, encompassing ever more distant suburbs, the capital and its vicinity became home to more than one-third of the country's population; by 1970, it had more than eight million inhabitants. Continued political instability, though, became almost open warfare until 1976, when the military ousted president Isabel Perón (widow of Juan Perón, who died shortly after returning from exile in 1973) in a bloodless coup that introduced the most systematic and bloodiest reign of terror in Argentine history.

Under its euphemistically named Proceso de Reorganización Nacional (Process of National Reorganization), the military's Guerra Sucia (Dirty War) may have claimed 30,000 Argentine lives, ranging from leftist urban and rural guerrillas to suspected sympathizers and large numbers of innocent bystanders whose links to armed opposition groups were tenuous at best. Many more were imprisoned and tortured, and more still were either sent or escaped into exile. Only a few courageous individuals and groups, such as Nobel Peace Prize winner Adolfo Pérez Esquivel and the even more famous Madres de la Plaza de Mayo, who marched around Buenos Aires's main plaza in quiet defiance, dared risk public opposition.

One rationale for the military coup was political corruption, but the military and their civilian collaborators were just as adept at diverting international loans to demolish vibrant but neglected neighborhoods and to create decadent monuments, such as freeways that went nowhere. Much of the money, of course, found its way into offshore bank accounts. The horror ended only after the military underestimated the response to their 1982 invasion of the British-ruled Falkland (Malvinas) Islands; after a decisive defeat, the military meekly ceded control to civilians. The main coup plotters and human-rights violators went to prison—an unprecedented occurrence in Latin America, even if they were later pardoned.

Following the 1983 return to constitutional government, Argentina underwent several years of hyperinflation in which President Raúl Alfonsín's Radical government squandered an enormous amount of good will. The succeeding Peronist government of Carlos Menem overcame hyperinflation by pegging

Argentine soldiers in full dress gear stand guard at the Monumento a los Caídos de Malvinas.

the Argentine peso at par with the U.S. dollar through a "currency basket" that ensured the country would print no more pesos than it had hard currency reserves to back them.

Menem's strategy, economy minister Domingo Cavallo's brainchild, brought a decade of economic stability during which foreign investment flowed into Argentina, and Buenos Aires was one of the main beneficiaries. Privatization of inefficient state-run monopolies, which had had thousands of so-called *ñoquis* (ghost employees) on the payroll, brought major improvements in telecommunications, transportation, and other sectors. The financial and service sectors flourished, and ambitious urban renewal projects, like the transformation of Puerto Madero into a fashionable riverfront of lofts and restaurants, gave *porteños* a sense of optimism through most of the 1990s.

There was a dark side to the boom, however: "crony capitalism," in which associates of the president enriched themselves through favorable contracts for privatization. Governmental reform did not touch the provinces, which maintained large public payrolls for patronage, and even printed their own *bonos* (bonds), "funny money" that further reduced the confidence of international investors.

After the resignation of Menem's hapless successor Fernando De la Rúa in December of that same year, the country had a series of three caretaker presidents in two weeks. Following a dubiously extra-constitutional congressional vote, Peronist Eduardo Duhalde (whom De la Rúa had defeated two years earlier) stepped into office, serving until 2003, when Néstor Kirchner was elected president. In a controversial move, Duhalde ended Cavallo's convertibility policy and devalued the peso, which lost nearly 75 percent of its value within a few months. At the same time, he continued the De la Rúa administration's *corralito* policy, which restricted bank withdrawals to maintain hard currency reserves but also strangled the economy of the city and the country.

As the economy stagnated and unemployment rose, homelessness also rose and scavengers became a common sight even in prosperous barrios like Palermo and Belgrano. Strikes, strident pickets blocking bridges and highways, and frustration with politicians and institutions like the International Monetary Fund (IMF) contributed to the feeling of *bronca* (aggravation). Yet somehow, the city, with its blend of neighborhood integrity, cosmopolitan sophistication, and rich cultural life, continued to function.

Touching bottom by late 2002, the country gradually rebounded as the devalued peso made agricultural exports competitive internationally, and consequent low wages made some traditional smokestack industries viable again. Devaluation also brought a tourism boom from neighboring countries and overseas, and the *corralito*'s end unleashed domestic demand. Unemployment fell as well, though it remained alarmingly high.

# Government and Politics

Argentine politics is often contentious and includes little consensus. Since the end of the military dictatorship of 1976–1983, though, it has been remarkably stable and peaceful, all things considered. The major exception, of course, was the storm of political and economic protest that led to five demonstrators' deaths in the Plaza de Mayo on December 20, 2001. The country had three provisional presidents in two weeks before senator Eduardo Duhalde of Buenos Aires province, who had lost the 1999 presidential election to De la Rúa, assumed the office in a dubiously extra-constitutional congressional vote.

Argentines' lack of faith in institutions, however, led to barrio activism through *asambleas populares* (popular assemblies) and less-constructive extra-constitutional practices, such as *escrache,* in which groups of citizens loudly and publicly demonstrate against politicians, judges, bankers, or representatives of other institutions at their homes or workplaces.

*Escraches,* which often deteriorate into shouting matches, originated as a tactic to identify and publicize the whereabouts of alleged torturers and murderers from the military dictatorship after a series of pardons and other measures limited their prosecution.

Unlike 1970s Argentina, though, early-21st-century Argentina was imploding rather than exploding, and the villains were not always as conspicuous as they were in previous years and decades. Many placed the blame on former president Carlos Menem and his "neoliberal" free market policies and corruption, as well as foreign banks and institutions, such as the International Monetary Fund (IMF).

Other Argentine politicians, though, could be singled out for blame. Duhalde's "pesification" policy benefited his own industrial clients by turning their dollar debts into devalued pesos and decimated individual Argentines' personal savings.

## ORGANIZATION

Buenos Aires is Argentina's capital and also its economic powerhouse and cultural cornerstone. Like Washington, D.C., it is a geographically and administratively separate federal district; the 24 *partidos* (counties) of Gran Buenos Aires belong to Buenos Aires province, the most populous and important of the country's 23 provinces.

Superficially, Argentina's constitution resembles that of the United States. The popularly elected president leads the executive branch; a bicameral legislature consists of an upper house, the Senado (Senate), and a lower Cámara de Diputados (Chamber of Deputies); the Corte Suprema (Supreme Court) is the independent judiciary.

In practice, institutions are often weak and dysfunctional. The president dominates the system, often ruling by decree when the legislature obstructs his agenda, and the Corte Suprema is notoriously vulnerable to political pressure.

Much depends on individuals, as institutions are weak. The charismatic president Carlos Menem (1989–1999), for instance, exercised unquestionable power despite (or perhaps because of) his ethical shortcomings, while successors like Fernando De la Rúa (1999–2001) and Eduardo Duhalde (appointed in 2001 to serve until 2003) have proved ineffectual even with legislators of their own parties.

Politically, the Capital Federal holds a special constitutional status as the Ciudad Autónoma de Buenos Aires (Autonomous City of Buenos Aires, which is similar to the District of Columbia in the United States), with its own elected mayor and legislature. (Until 1996 reforms, the president appointed the mayor and legislature.) Unlike the largely disenfranchised voters of Washington, D.C., though, the Buenos Aires voters enjoy voting representation in the Congreso Nacional (National Congress) as well.

## POLITICAL PARTIES

Although the Peronists, or justicialists, are the country's largest political party, the capital's most important political force has been Alianza, an alliance of the rather misnamed Radical party (a middle-class institution that seems to function better in opposition than in power) and the slightly left-of-center Frente del País Solidario (Frepaso, National Solidarity Front). The current mayor is Mauricio Macri.

Whereas nearly 20 parties are represented in the 63-member legislature, several have only a single seat. None is close to a majority, though they often form transitory *bloques,* usually to obstruct others.

The Peronists, Radicals, and similar entities, however, are barely parties in the European or North American sense—it might be more accurate to call them movements. Voters, for instance, cannot vote directly for candidates, but only for lists chosen by party bosses to reward loyalists.

More often than not, the major Argentine parties are patronage machines that, after mobilizing their most militant members for elections, reward them with well-paid public posts that may not actually involve working for their paychecks. Such "ghost employees" are called *ñoquis* after the inexpensive potato pasta traditionally served the 29th of each month in restaurants and cash-strapped households— the insinuation is that they start making their appearance in the office just in time to collect their first-of-the-month salary.

Historically, many officeholders have used their supporters for political intimidation instead of dialogue. Ever since the default of 2001, though, political affiliations mean even less than they did in the past. Many Argentines have assumed a "plague on all your houses" attitude toward politicians in general. In fact, ambitious individuals, ranging from populist Elisa Carrió (a left-wing member of the Cámara de Diputados) to mayor Mauricio Macri, have consciously distanced themselves from traditional parties. Macri, in fact, rode his independent image to the city's mayoralty in June 2007, despite an overwhelming Peronist victory in national elections later in the year.

## ELECTIONS

On a national level, Argentina operates under an 1853 constitution, amended in 1994 to permit the president's re-election while reducing his or her term from six to four years; no president may serve more than two consecutive terms. Each of the 23 provinces, as well as the Buenos Aires federal district, chooses three senators; in the 257-member Cámara de Diputados, each province has a delegation proportionate to its population. The population and corresponding number of delegates is subject to revision with each new census. Senators serve six-year terms, deputies four-year terms.

*Porteño* voters choose the city's 63-member Poder Legislativo by proportional representation for four-year terms; half the legislature is renewed every two years. Term limits prohibit both the mayor and legislators from serving more than two consecutive terms without a lapse of at least four years.

## BUREAUCRACY

The government institutions most travelers are likely to come into contact with are immigration, customs, and police. Immigration and customs generally treat foreigners fairly, but

Argentine police are notoriously corrupt. The capital's Policía Federal are not quite so bad as the Buenos Aires provincial police, a "mafia with badges" who are particularly infamous for shaking down motorists for bribes after stopping them for minor equipment violations.

Repeated attempts at reforming the police have invariably ended in failure, but the recent creation of community police forces in some municipalities and a tourist police in Buenos Aires have brought some optimism. Still, a poll of newly recruited Buenos Aires provincial police yielded the disturbing response that nearly half of them would not arrest a relative accused of a crime.

The politicized administrative bureaucracy remains one of Argentina's most intractable problems due to the continuing presence of *ñoquis* at the federal, provincial, and municipal levels. Abuses are not so extreme as they were in the past, when individuals often drew multiple paychecks without performing any work whatsoever, but bloated government payrolls are still cause for concern.

© WAYNE BERNHARDSON

Just in case, the Policía Federal stand by at a demonstration on the Avenida de Mayo.

While the privatizations of the 1990s reduced federal sector employment by nearly two-thirds, they had little impact on the provinces. Provincial payrolls still include nearly 1.4 million Argentines—many in what might be more accurately called positions rather than jobs. For the tourist, it may be gratifying to find a tiny, obscure museum open 60 hours per week and staffed by three people, but the cumulative economic impact of such practices has been catastrophic.

In practical terms, lack of a professional civil service means a lack of continuity, as officials lose their jobs with every change of administration; continuing political influence in the bureaucracy means an abundance of uninterested and often ill-qualified officials who take their time dealing with any but the most routine matters. It also means nepotism and corruption—Transparency International consistently ranks Argentina among the world's worst countries in its annual survey of perceived corruption. In 2007, of 179 countries surveyed, Argentina was 105th (tied with Albania, Bolivia, Burkina Faso, and Egypt); on the South American continent, only Guyana (123rd), Paraguay (138th), Ecuador (150th), and Venezuela (162nd) rated lower.

## THE MILITARY

Because of repeated 20th-century coups and the notably vicious 1976–1983 Dirty War dictatorship, the Argentine military earned a reputation as one of the worst ever on a continent infamous for armed repression. Its ignominious collapse in the 1982 Falkland (Malvinas) Islands War, followed by public revelations of state terrorism and the conviction of the top generals and admirals responsible for kidnapping, torture, and murder, helped civilian authorities overcome the tradition of military impunity.

Since the 1983 return to constitutional government, civilian governments have eliminated conscription, the military budget has declined to barely 1 percent of the GDP (less than half that of neighboring Chile), and Argentine forces have undertaken more strictly military operations, such as peacekeeping missions in the Balkans. Although periods of political disorder, such as 2001–2002, always bring coup rumors, the military appears to have little or no interest in taking the reins of government.

The size of the military services has also been reduced, with only about 100,000 soldiers, sailors, and other personnel in uniform, though these are heavily weighted toward noncommissioned officers. Defense minister José Pampuro has said, "We conceive Argentina as a defensive country," but in recent years, he has directed investment in updated equipment for the army, navy, and air force. He has also added that involving the military in domestic security "would be a mistake," given its recent history.

Nevertheless, there remains an ugly reminder of military fanaticism in Colonel Mohamed Alí Seineldín, who earned a life term in a military prison after mounting a rebellion against the constitutional government in 1989. Inexplicably, in 2003, outgoing president Duhalde granted him a gratuitous pardon.

A fundamentalist Catholic despite his name, Seineldín has taken to making bizarre public statements regarding oral and anal sex. He has also made the bewildering assertion that the CIA and the Fuerzas Armadas Revolucionarias de Colombia (FARC, the leftist Colombian guerrilla forces) are conspiring to destabilize Argentina (as if Argentines were incapable of doing so themselves).

Despite the country's reputation for dictatorial bellicosity, two Argentines have won Nobel Peace Prizes: foreign minister Carlos Saavedra Lamas (1936) for mediating a Chaco War settlement between Paraguay and Bolivia, and Adolfo Pérez Esquivel (1984) for publicizing the 1976–1983 military dictatorship's human-rights abuses.

# Economy

The urban economy is mostly administrative, financial, and service-oriented. The capital remains the country's major port, but most industrial jobs are in provincial suburbs like Avellaneda. Along with northern Argentina's Iguazú Falls and Patagonia's Moreno Glacier, the city is one of the country's top tourist attractions.

To most foreign observers, Argentina's economy is an enigma. Rich in natural resources and having a well-educated populace and modern infrastructure, for most of seven decades it has lurched from crisis to crisis, with the notable exception of the stable, prosperous 1990s. In late 2001, it stunned the world and even many Argentines by defaulting on part of its US$141 billion foreign debt, triggering a political and economic meltdown comparable to the 1930s Great Depression. In the first quarter of 2002, the economy shrank 16.3 percent, marking 14 consecutive quarters of contraction; while steady growth has resumed since early 2003, there have been bumps in the long road back, especially since Cristina Fernández assumed the presidency in late 2007.

Argentina emerged from World War II in an enviable position, but the government of the charismatic General Juan Domingo Perón and its successors squandered enormous budget surpluses from agricultural exports by funding bloated state enterprises. Those enterprises, in collusion with corrupt labor leaders, became industrial dinosaurs impossible to reform. Then, during the 1970s and 1980s, large loans destined for massive public works projects filled the pockets—or Swiss bank accounts—of the nefarious generals and their civilian collaborators who ruled the country.

Corruption and deficit spending resulted in hyperinflation that reached levels of 30 percent or more *per month*. Shortly after taking power in 1989, president Carlos Menem's administration became the first Argentine government in recent memory to tackle the inflation problem through economy minister Domingo Cavallo's

"convertibility" policy; Cavallo's "currency basket" fixed the Argentine peso at par with the U.S. dollar, and required the government to back every peso printed with a dollar or other hard currency.

Selling off unprofitable state enterprises, such as Aerolíneas Argentinas, the state telecommunications enterprise Entel, and most of the extensive railroad network, made convertibility possible. Inflation dropped to zero and, after an initial glitch, there was steady economic growth. But the 1995 Mexican "tequila" crisis, followed by a Brazilian devaluation that reduced Argentine competitiveness, led to increasing unemployment and recession. After a brief recovery, convertibility proved to be an economic straitjacket that, by the De la Rúa administration's second year, was unsustainable.

In a desperate move, De la Rúa reappointed Cavallo to the Economy Ministry, but a run on bank deposits brought severe restrictions on withdrawals, known collectively as the *corralito* (literally, little fence). The *corralito*'s unpopularity triggered Cavallo's resignation and De la Rúa's downfall. De la Rúa's successor, Eduardo Duhalde, made things even worse by eliminating convertibility, changing dollar-based savings accounts to peso-based accounts at a 1:1.4 rate, and floating the local currency so that those accounts soon lost most of their value. At the same time, in a classic case of Argentine "crony capitalism," the new president converted dollar debts to peso debts at a rate of 1:1, benefiting the large industrialists who were his political base.

With devaluation, according to the Economist Intelligence Unit, in less than a year Buenos Aires went from the world's 22nd most expensive city (of 131 surveyed) to the 120th. As the peso plummeted from 1:1 to 1:3.5 in only a few months, disciplined savers saw their frozen wealth evaporate, while those who had accumulated large debts saw their dollar burdens reduced. Devaluation also brought renewed inflation, which has become more serious as the economy has recovered.

In 2002, the Argentine economy contracted by about 11 percent, but since then it enjoyed uninterrupted growth of up to nine percent per annum. Inflation, however, has returned to worrying levels. While the official figures are around 10 percent most independent economists consider it to be at least double that. Political interference in the ostensibly autonomous state statistics agency INDEC appears to be responsible for this discrepancy.

## EMPLOYMENT, UNEMPLOYMENT, AND UNDEREMPLOYMENT

With the recovering economy, Argentine unemployment has diminished—estimates as of mid-2007 are around nine percent—but many people are underemployed. These figures may be better in Buenos Aires than in the provinces, but street, bus, and subway vendors are still numerous, and the number of people rummaging through garbage

for recyclables—including children barely of school age—remains shocking.

During the early-2002 economic crisis, many unemployed individuals spent the night in line to buy dollars at Banco de la Nación and private exchange houses, in hopes of selling their spots to those who did have sufficient pesos to purchase dollars. Similarly, individuals waited in lines outside the Italian consulate and other European missions to sell their places in line for passports and visas.

While unemployment figures can help gauge trends, observers and analysts should not take them too literally. Many Argentines work *en negro* (in black, i.e., off the books), avoid paying taxes, and do not show up in official statistics. This does not mean that unemployment figures are irrelevant, but interpreting them requires a critical eye.

## AGRICULTURE

Since the 19th century, the Argentine pampas have developed from the meat locker and woolshed of the world to one of its main

Dogwalkers are a common sight in Palermo and other barrios in northern Buenos Aires.

granaries, growing corn, wheat, oats, sorghum, and soybeans, among other crops. The country's agriculture has diversified, though, to include vegetables, such as potatoes, onions, carrots, squash, beans, and tomatoes, and fruit crops like apples, pears, and grapes. Its grape harvest has helped make Argentina the world's fifth-largest wine producer.

Other commercial crops include subtropical cultigens, such as sugar cane, olives, tea, yerba mate, and tobacco, mostly in provinces to the north and west of the capital. Agriculture accounts for roughly eight percent of GDP, but at roughly US$28 billion per year, it delivers at least half of all exports by value.

In early 2008, however, the agriculture economy experienced a crisis as the federal government raised export taxes to almost confiscatory levels of 94 percent. This raised the ire of the rural sector, which responded with roadblocks that briefly caused the interruption of urban food supplies, and resulted in confrontational meetings with the government that showed no interest in compromise.

## INDUSTRY

Argentina's industrial heyday was the immediate post–World War II period, when president Juan Domingo Perón invested vast sums in manufacturing products, such as steel, chemicals, and petrochemicals; the military controlled large parts of the economy, including its own weapons manufacture and support industries.

Despite the privatization of the 1990s, much of Argentine industry is still inefficient and unable to compete without state assistance—or cronyism. The 2002 exchange rate collapse revived ailing factories as production costs fell in real terms, but the superannuated sector continues to face problems due to a lack of investment and modernization.

Accounting for about 22 percent of GDP, the industrial sector also includes food processing, motor vehicles, consumer durables, textiles, printing, metallurgy, and steel. Much of this activity is concentrated in the southern suburbs of Avellaneda and Quilmes, across the Riachuelo.

## RICH AND POOR

Historically, the disparity between rich and poor in Argentina has been far less extreme than in other Latin American countries, but the meltdown of 2001–2002, with its devastating impact on the middle class, has resurrected the issue. In early 2002, more than half of all Argentines were considered to fall beneath the poverty line, and six million (one-sixth of the population) were considered indigent, though five years later the poverty figure had fallen by half.

Statistics can be misleading, though. Given the political manipulation of inflation data, it's also plausible that poverty rates are higher than official figures admit.

## EDUCATION

Literacy is formally high, nearly 97 percent, one of the highest in the Americas. Education is free through high school and compulsory to age 12, but the curriculum is rigid. Some public secondary schools, most notably the Colegio Nacional Buenos Aires, are even more prestigious than some of their private bilingual counterparts.

Public universities like the capital's Universidad de Buenos Aires and the Universidad Nacional de La Plata, in the provincial capital, are generally superior to private universities. Public university education is free of charge, but has generated a surplus of high-status degrees in fields like law, psychology, and sociology—and not enough in hands-on disciplines like engineering and computer science.

School teachers generally do not receive university degrees, but attend special teachers' colleges. Frequent teacher strikes have disrupted both primary and secondary instruction throughout the country. There is vocational and technical training as well, but these skills enjoy little respect, even when those jobs pay more than white-collar positions or office work.

Several Argentine scientists have won Nobel Prizes, including Bernardo Houssay (Medicine, 1946), Luis Federico Leloir (Chemistry, 1972), and César Milstein (Medicine, 1984). One continual concern is the "brain drain" of educated Argentines overseas; Milstein, for instance, spent his most productive years in England because Perón-era political pressures at Argentine universities made research impossible. Many talented individuals, though, have left simply because the economy has failed them.

## TOURISM

For many overseas visitors, Buenos Aires is the gateway to globally famous attractions like the subtropical Iguazú Falls in the northern province of Misiones and the Perito Moreno Glacier in Patagonia's Santa Cruz province. Still, Buenos Aires is an attraction its own right—on the entire continent, Rio de Janeiro is probably the only other city with

an international profile anywhere close to the Argentine capital.

Thanks partly to the tourist sector, Buenos Aires's economy remains relatively prosperous compared to that of the provinces. According to 2007 statistics, the city received about 2.3 million foreign visitors. If previous years are any indication, nearly 20 percent of these visitors were from North America and about 32 percent from Europe. Most of the remainder came from the neighboring countries of Uruguay, Brazil, Paraguay, Bolivia, and Chile.

Many other visitors to Buenos Aires, of course, come from the provinces, drawn by family and other personal links, the city's cultural attractions, and the fact that the weak peso has made foreign travel too expensive for many Argentines.

# People and Culture

According to the 2001 census, Argentina's population is 36,223,947. Of these, 2,768,772 reside in Buenos Aires, the Capital Federal; this is a decline of 8 percent from the 1991 census, when its population was 2,965,403. Another 8,684,953 reside in the 24 counties of Gran Buenos Aires, for a total of 11,453,725.

## POPULATION GEOGRAPHY

Nearly a third of all Argentines live in the Capital Federal and Gran Buenos Aires. Most of the rest are also city dwellers, in population centers such as Rosario, Córdoba, Mar del Plata, Mendoza, Salta, and other provincial capitals and cities. The southern Patagonian provinces of Chubut, Santa Cruz, and Tierra del Fuego are very thinly populated.

### Indigenous Peoples

Argentina has the smallest indigenous population of any South American country except Uruguay, but many Kollas (Quechuas) from northwestern Argentina and Mapuches from the southern Patagonian provinces reside in

the capital. There is also a handful of Tobas, Matacos, and others from Chaco and Santa Fe provinces, and Guaraní in the Mesopotamian provinces, especially Misiones.

Simple population statistics, though, may understate contemporary Argentina's indigenous legacy. According to a DNA study by Universidad de Buenos Aires geneticist Daniel Corach, 56 percent of all Argentines have some indigenous ancestry, though only 10 percent of those qualify as "purely" indigenous.

### Ethnic Minorities

Argentina is a country of immigrants, both recent and not-so-recent, and the capital reflects that history. Spaniards, of course, first colonized what is now Argentina, but a 19th-century influx of Italians, Basques, English, Irish, Welsh, Ukrainians, and other nationalities made Buenos Aires a mosaic of immigrants. Italo-Argentines even came to outnumber Argentines of Spanish origin.

Some immigrant groups retain a high visibility, most notably a Jewish community

# AFRO-ARGENTINES

In a country of immigrants, the heritage of many Argentines is often conspicuous. According to some accounts, there are even more Argentines with Italian surnames than *gallegos* of Spanish ancestry. Anglo-Argentines are prominent and have their own daily newspaper, and German-Argentines still support a weekly. Buenos Aires has numerous Jewish community landmarks, and so-called *turcos* of Middle Eastern descent, such as former president Carlos Menem, have made their mark in politics.

Yet an Afro-Argentine population that, by official statistics, once comprised nearly a third of the city's population has been nearly invisible. When the revolutionary government of 1810 tentatively banned the slave trade three years later, nearly 10,000 of more than 32,000 *porteños* were of African origin. As late as 1838, the figure was nearly 15,000 of almost 63,000. Yet in 1887, the number had dropped to only 8,000 among more than 430,000 city residents.

After the turn of the century, Afro-Argentines virtually fell off the city map. In the 1970s, newspaper and magazine articles even puzzled over the disappearance of a community that fought honorably in the 19th-century civil and regional wars, supported a variety of social and charitable organizations, sponsored a lively local press, and made substantial contributions to the arts. How and why this could have happened was, seemingly, an enigma.

Two plausible hypotheses were widely accepted. One was that Afro-Argentines were made into front-line cannon fodder, particularly in the war with Paraguay, where they suffered disproportionate casualties. Another was that the 19th-century yellow-fever epidemics in San Telmo, where many Afro-Argentines lived, decimated their numbers as wealthier *criollos* moved to higher, healthier ground in the northern suburbs.

Historian George Reid Andrews, though, challenged the orthodoxy by arguing that there was slim evidence for either hypothesis and, moreover, little for the disappearance of the community itself. What he did learn, through examination of archival materials and the capital's Afro-Argentine press, was that the community itself was unconcerned with demographic decline but clearly worried about its socioeconomic status.

As the slave trade ended by the mid-19th century and massive European immigration transformed the city soon afterward, Afro-Argentines were clearly a declining *percentage* of the population, but that does not explain their plunging absolute numbers. Andrews, though, found that Argentine authorities and opinion-makers consciously excised the Afro-Argentine presence in an attempt to promote the country as a European outpost in the Americas.

Some of this, certainly, owed its origins to a

bers at least 200,000 and is historically centrated in Balvanera's Once district. the onset of the 2001–2002 economic though, many have needed assistance ewish community organizations, and nt numbers of Argentine Jews have d or considered emigrating to Israel security there. It's worth mentionrill-unsolved terrorist incidents in res killed 29 people in the Israeli Retiro in 1992 and 87 people in iación Mutua Israelita Argentina ewish cultural center, in 1994;

most Jewish community landmarks are well fortified.

Middle Eastern immigrants are less numerous, but have occupied high-profile positions—the most notable example of this is former president Carlos Menem, of Syrian descent. Argentines misleadingly refer to anyone of Middle Eastern descent as *turcos* (Turks), a legacy of the initial immigration from the region.

Asian faces have become more common in recent years. There has long been a community of about 30,000 Japanese-Argentines, concentrated in the capital and the Gran Buenos Aires racism that was present from early independence times. The political opponents of Bernardino Rivadavia, a presumed mulatto who served as president in 1826–1827 before his forced resignation, stigmatized him with the epithet "Dr. Chocolate." Modern Argentine school children are taught proudly that the country was among the first to abolish slavery, in 1813, but these measures were so half-hearted that the institution lingered nearly another half-century.

More insidiously, though, census-takers systematically undercounted Afro-Argentines by equally half-hearted efforts that sometimes even avoided the neighborhoods in which they lived. When summarizing the data, they minimized the black presence by creating vague new racial categories, such as *trigueño* (wheat-colored), and incorporating individuals with African background into them. Eventually, in Andrews's words, the Afro-Argentines of Buenos Aires were "forgotten, but not gone."

Even as more and more European immigrants streamed into Argentina, Afro-Argentines kept alive such institutions as the Shimmy Club, a social organization that held regular dances just half a block off Avenida Corrientes, into the 1970s. Here, at regular intervals, rhythmic drum-based *malambo, milonga,* and *zamba* filled the hall and, on occasion, spilled out into the street.

Andrews thought that Argentine society was absorbing blacks and, indeed, defining them as whites in accordance with an unspoken ideology, even as their societal contributions survived. In recent years, though, there has been a small but complex revival of black culture in Buenos Aires that involves Afro-Argentines (now estimated at about 3,000) but also Afro-Uruguayans, Afro-Brazilians, Cape Verde Portuguese (perhaps 8,000), and Cubans and Africans. This has not always been convivial, as the remaining Afro-Argentines clearly distinguish themselves from the latecomers even as they share some cultural features.

More and more individuals with African origins may be visible on Buenos Aires streets, but Argentine society's continued refusal to acknowledge their presence and its own African heritage may be their greatest adversary. Created in 1996, the Fundación Africa Vive (Africa Lives Foundation) claims there are more than two million Argentines of African descent; according to director María Magdalena Lamadrid, "A single drop of blood is enough" to define an Afro-Argentine.

Yet in 2002, when Lamadrid herself attempted to fly to Panama to participate in a conference on the life of Dr. Martin Luther King Jr., immigration officials detained the fifth-generation Argentine on suspicion of carrying a false passport. One said, apparently, that "she can't be black and Argentine."

suburb of Escobar. Belgrano also has a modest Chinatown near the Barrancas. Many Koreans work in Once and live in the southern barrio of Nueva Pompeya.

Other South Americans, mostly Bolivians, Paraguayans, and Peruvians, flocked to Argentina during the early 1990s boom. They generally work at menial jobs, and many have returned home since the economic meltdown of 2001–2002. They are mostly concentrated in certain neighborhoods—Peruvians in Congreso, Paraguayans in Constitución, and Bolivians in Nueva Pompeya.

## LANGUAGE

Spanish is Argentina's official language, but English is widely spoken in the tourist and business sectors of the economy. Foreign-language use is also vigorous among ethnic communities, such as Italo-Argentines, Anglo-Argentines, and German-Argentines. The Anglo-Argentine and business communities even support a daily tabloid, *The Buenos Aires Herald,* while the German-Argentine community has the weekly *Argentinisches Tageblatt.*

Buenos Aires also has its own distinctive street slang, known as *lunfardo,* which owes its origins to working-class immigrant communities. Many *lunfardo* words have worked their way into everyday Argentine speech even though they may be unintelligible at first to those who have learned Spanish elsewhere. Some are fairly obvious in context, such as *laburar* instead of *trabajar* for work or labor, but others are obscure.

While many of its idioms are crude by standards of formal Spanish, *lunfardo* has acquired a certain legitimacy among Argentine scholars. There is even an academy for the study of *porteño* slang, the Academia Porteña del Lunfardo (Estados Unidos 1379, Monserrat, tel. 011/4383-2393).

# The Arts

## VISUAL ARTS

Because of its small, dispersed settlements, Argentina mostly lacked the great tradition of colonial religious art of the populous central Andean highlands, which developed their own styles of painting and sculpture in the churches of Peru and Bolivia. As a political and demographic entity, the Viceroyalty of the Río de la Plata did not even exist until the late 18th century and, according to *porteño* art critic Jorge Glusberg, "Buenos Aires was practically devoid of any cultural life." Glusberg has gone so far as to claim that the colonial period, "characterized by subordination to the European models currently in vogue," lasted until after World War II.

Glusberg may underrate the work of some early painters and sculptors, but there is no question that innovative Argentine artists have flourished artistically, if not always financially, since then—in both figurative and abstract modes. His English-language *Art in Argentina* (Milan: Giancarlo Politi Editore, 1986) is a readable and well-illustrated introduction to currents in contemporary Argentine art, though it needs an update. The same is true of Rafael Squirru's Spanish-only *Arte Argentino Hoy* (Ediciones de Arte Gaglianone, Buenos Aires, 1983), with color displays of 48 20th-century painters and sculptors.

Buenos Aires galleries range from prosaically traditional to truly daring. While gallery-hopping, watch for street art in the form of elaborate graffiti (see the website www.bagraff.com) and *filete,* the traditional line painting

that once decorated horse carts, trucks, and buses; experiencing something of a revival, it now graces many cafés and restaurants, and has even returned to some buses.

### Painting

One of Argentina's first notable artists, European-trained Prilidiano Pueyrredón (1823–1870) painted landscapes and people of rural Buenos Aires. Other early painters of

A San Telmo newsstand attracts attention with its elaborate *filete.*

note included Eduardo Sívori (1847–1918) and Ernesto de la Cárcova (1866–1927), both of whom manifested concern with social issues, such as poverty and hunger.

One of Argentine painting's extraordinary stories, though, is Cándido López (1840–1902), a junior army officer who lost his right forearm to gangrene after being struck by a grenade in battle against Paraguay. Remarkably, López painted more than 50 oils of war scenes with his left hand; even more remarkably, his paintings were not romanticized scenes of combat heroism, but vivid landscapes depicting routine activities—ordinary encampments and river crossings, for instance—in addition to the occasional battle.

Benito Quinquela Martín (1890–1977) chronicled the struggles of immigrant factory workers and stevedores in his vivid oils of La Boca, many of which reside in his namesake museum in the barrio. One of Argentina's modern art pioneers was Jorge Luis Borges's friend Xul Solar (1887–1963; real name Alejandro Schulz Solari), who dealt with esoteric and mystical themes in his watercolors. His works are displayed in a Barrio Norte museum in his honor.

One of Argentina's best-known modern artists is the versatile Antonio Berni (1905–1981), who worked in painting, drawing, engraving, collage, and sculpture. His socially conscious canvases, such as *Juanito Laguna Bañándose entre Latas* (Juanito Laguna Bathing in the Trash), have fetched astronomical prices in the international art market. His *Monstruos* (Monsters) is a series of three-dimensional works (1964–1971) that depicts the nightmares of Ramona Montiel, a prostitute who dreams of war, death, and destruction.

In conjunction with other artists, including Lino Spilimbergo (1896–1964), Juan Carlos Castagnino (1908–1972), Galician-born Manuel Colmeiro (1901–1999), and Demetrio Urruchúa (1902–1978), Berni was an adherent of the politically conscious Nuevo Realismo (New Realism) movement. The movement's greatest public legacy is the ceiling murals in the recycled Galerías Pacífico shopping center,

under the influence of the famed Mexican painter David Alfaro Siqueiros.

Spilimbergo, when not collaborating on such projects, specialized in geometric forms, still lifes, and lighted landscapes. Castagnino specialized in rural, even gauchesque, landscapes, and Colmeiro and Urruchúa were both socially oriented painters and muralists.

Influenced by pop art, self-taught Jorge de la Vega (1930–1971) alternated figurative and abstract geometrical work; in his series of *Monstruos* or *Bestiario,* he attached objects, such as coins, sticks, and especially mirrors, to his canvases, deforming both the subject and the viewer.

One of Argentina's rising modern painters is Guillermo Kuitca, born in 1960 to a Russian-Jewish immigrant family. Kuitca contrasts small figures with large environments and transforms everyday abstractions, such as floor plans and road maps (most effectively in his *Kristallnacht II,* an observation on the Nazi genocide against German Jews). He also creates abstract visual expressions of popular music themes like the anti-lynching classic "Strange Fruit" and the Rolling Stones's "Gimme Shelter."

Daniel Barreto (born 1966) adapts popular figures, like the folk saint Difunta Correa of San Juan province and the rural bandit Gaucho Antonio Gil of Corrientes province, into colorful paintings that transcend the kitsch often associated with those figures.

## Sculpture

Buenos Aires is a city of monuments; unfortunately, many if not most of them are pretentious busts of ostensible statesmen and colossal equestrian statues of military men like national icon José de San Martín, caudillo Justo José Urquiza, and Patagonian invader Julio Argentino Roca. The Rodin-influenced Rogelio Yrurtia (1879–1950), though he did create the mausoleum of President Bernardino Rivadavia, displayed his talents better in statues like the larger-than-life-size *The Boxers,* displayed at his house and museum in the barrio of Belgrano; even better is his working-class tribute *Canto al Trabajo* (Ode to Labor), on San Telmo's Plazoleta Olazábal.

# THE *PORTEÑO* BOOKSHELF

In the 19th century, even as the free-roaming gaucho was becoming a wage laborer on the *estancias* of the pampas, Argentine literature enshrined his most positive qualities in **José Hernández**'s epic poem *Martín Fierro* (1872 and 1879), available in many editions and in English translation. This *gauchesco* (gauchesque) tradition has never completely disappeared, and it is most memorable in **Ricardo Güiraldes**'s novel *Don Segundo Sombra* (1926). Güiraldes's romanticized fiction is also available in many editions and has been translated into English and many other languages.

Born of U.S.-immigrant parents in Buenos Aires province, **William Henry Hudson** (1841–1922) left for London at the age of 33, but his memoir *Long Ago and Far Away* (1922) has been a staple of Argentine public education. An accomplished amateur field naturalist, he also wrote *Idle Days in Patagonia* (1893) about his explorations in search of birds, plus short stories and even a novel, *Green Mansions* (1904), set in Venezuela's rain forests. Argentines, who often translate forenames into Spanish, know him as Guillermo Enrique Hudson.

A more critical assessment of Argentina and its rural heritage came from the educator and politician **Domingo F. Sarmiento** (1811–1888). His *Life in the Argentine Republic in the Days of the Tyrants* (1845), an eloquent tirade against rural caudillos that betrays his provincial background, has overcome its polemical origins to become a staple of Latin American history courses in English-speaking countries.

No Argentine author has ever won a Nobel Prize for Literature, but three have won the Premio Cervantes, the Spanish-speaking world's most important literary honor: essayist, poet, and short-story writer Jorge Luis Borges (1979), and novelists Ernesto Sábato (1984) and Adolfo Bioy Casares (1990). Other noteworthy Argentine writers include César Aira, Roberto Arlt, Julio Cortázar, Victoria Ocampo, Manuel Puig, and Osvaldo Soriano, much of whose work is available in English translation. (Publication dates here indicate the Spanish-language original unless otherwise noted.)

Globally, the most prominent is **Jorge Luis Borges** (1899–1986), often mentioned but never chosen for the Nobel. Ironically enough for a classically educated and urbane figure who loathed Perón and Peronism, his short stories, poetry, and essays often focus on urban lowlifes and rural themes, including gaucho violence. Borges never wrote a novel; his most frequently read works are collections, such as *Labyrinths* (1970, in English), many of whose stories can seem obscure and even surrealistic.

**Ernesto Sábato** (born 1911) acquired some renown in the English-speaking world as the coordinator of *Nunca Más*, an official account of the 1976–1983 military dictatorship's brutalities. Born in Buenos Aires province but long resident in the capital, his best work may be the engrossing psychological novel *On Heroes and Tombs* (1961; New York: Ballantine, 1991), which credibly depicts places and examines people in the city; its subsection "Report on the Blind," capable of standing alone, is truly extraordinary. Sábato's novella *The Tunnel* (1950; New York: Ballantine, 1988), about artistic obsession, is equally absorbing but less conspicuously *porteño* in its approach.

Borges's close friend **Bioy Casares** (1914–1999) collaborated with the older man on detective stories under the pseudonym Honorario Bustos Domecq, but his own fantastical novella *The Invention of Morel* (Austin: University of Texas Press, 1985) is a purposefully disorienting work that director Eliseo Subiela transformed into the award-winning film *Man Facing Southeast*. Bioy's *Diary of the War of the Pig* (New York: McGraw Hill, 1972) takes place in the barrio of Palermo, mostly within the area popularly referred to as "Villa Freud." His *The Dream of Heroes* (New York: Dutton, 1987) paints a surrealistic portrait of the late 1920s, a time when Carnaval flourished in Buenos Aires.

Though he died young and unsuccessful, **Robert Arlt** (1900-1942) had a lasting impact on Argentine and especially *porteño* literature in depicting corruption from the scammer's point of view, in such novels as *The Seven Madmen* (London and New York: Serpent's Tail Publishing, 1998).

Son of a diplomatic family, the Belgian-born **Julio Cortázar** (1914-1984) was a short story writer, experimental novelist, and committed leftist who chose Parisian exile after losing his university post in a Peronist purge. Michelangelo Antonioni turned one of Cortázar's short stories into the famous 1960s film *Blow-Up*, but the author is also known for his novels *Hopscotch* (1963; New York: Random House, 1966), the story of a failed Francophile poet in Buenos Aires, and *62: A Model Kit* (1968; New York: Random House, 1972).

**Manuel Puig** (1932-1990) authored a series of novels concerning popular culture, and specifically the cinema, including *Betrayed by Rita Hayworth* (1968), the detective novel *The Buenos Aires Affair* (New York: Dutton, 1968), and *Kiss of the Spider Woman* (New York: Vintage, 1991), which Brazilian director Héctor Babenco made into an award-winning English-language film with William Hurt, Raúl Juliá, and Sonia Braga. Puig wrote *Eternal Curse on the Reader of These Pages* (New York: Random House, 1982), about an amnesiac victim of the 1976-1983 dictatorship, in English and later translated into Spanish.

Journalist/novelist **Osvaldo Soriano** (1943-1997) wrote satirical novels, such as *A Funny Dirty Little War* (Columbia, Louisiana, and London: Readers International, 1989), depicting the consequences of national upheaval in a small community, and *Winter Quarters* (same publisher and year). His *Shadows* (New York: Knopf, 1993), which takes its Spanish title *Una Sombra Ya Pronto Serás* from a classic tango lyric, became a surrealistically disorienting road movie under director Héctor Olivera.

Essayist **Victoria Ocampo** (1891-1979), whose poetess sister Silvina (1909-1994) was Bioy Casares's wife, founded the literary magazine *Sur;* some of her essays appear in Doris Meyer's biography *Victoria Ocampo: Against the Wind and the Tide* (Austin: University of Texas Press, 1990). One of her collaborators at *Sur,* which also became a prestigious publishing house and brought figures like Aldous Huxley, D. H. Lawrence, and even Jack Kerouac to the attention of Spanish-speaking readers, was Borges.

**Tomás Eloy Martínez** (born 1934) is author of several novels dealing with the Argentine condition through fictionalized biography, most notably *The Perón Novel* (New York: Pantheon Books, 1988) – based partly on his own extensive interviews with the late caudillo. *Santa Evita* (New York: Knopf, 1996), by contrast, can only be called post-biographical, as it traces the odyssey of Evita's embalmed body to Italy, Spain, and back to Buenos Aires.

Novelist **Federico Andahazi** (born 1963), also a psychiatrist, outraged industrialist heiress Amalia Fortabat when an independent jury awarded him her self-anointed literary prize for *The Anatomist* (New York: Doubleday, 1998), a sexually explicit (but less than erotic) tale set in medieval Italy.

Sometimes called an heir to Borges, **César Aira** (born 1949) writes seemingly obscure novels, such as *The Hare* (Serpent's Tail Publishing, 1998), about an English naturalist's search for a rare rodent. Set on the indigenous frontier in the 19th century, it manages to tie together several apparently loose and disparate ends.

Those following Yrurtia have been far more daring. León Ferrari (born 1920) created the prescient *La Civilización Occidental y Cristiana* (Western and Christian Civilization, 1965), a sardonic Vietnam-era work that portrays Christ crucified on a diving F-105. His 2005 retrospective at the Centro Cultural Recoleta drew howls of protest and a lawsuit from the Catholic Church that briefly shut it down. Ironically enough, the controversy gave Ferrari front-page publicity that he could never have paid for: After the courts dismissed an injunction against the exhibition, more than a thousand art lovers and curiosity seekers per day queued for an hour or more to see it.

Like Ferrari, Juan Carlos Distéfano (born 1933) blends sculpture and painting in works like *El Rey y La Reina* (1977), a disturbingly life-like representation of a couple shot to death in an automobile. In the context of its time, it was a thinly disguised portrayal of extrajudicial executions carried out by military and paramilitary death squads after the 1976 coup. Remarkably, the work was shown publicly, on the Florida pedestrian mall, shortly thereafter.

Albert Heredia (born 1924) mocks the pomposity of monumental public art in works such as *El Caballero de la Máscara* (The Masked Horseman). The title is misleading, as this headless parody of an equestrian statue is a collage of materials that ridicules 19th-century strongmen and their modern counterparts. Heredia originally titled it *El Montonero,* a reference to the early Federalist cavalry, but could not exhibit the piece under its original name because the leftist guerrilla movement Montoneros was a hot-button issue at the time.

In contrast to politically committed sculptors like Ferrari and Heredia, Yoël Novoa creates cleverly entertaining caricatures of *porteños* and Buenos Aires street scenes in papier mâché.

## ARCHITECTURE

Because Buenos Aires languished as a backwater of the Spanish colonial empire until the creation of the Viceroyalty of the River Plate in the late 18th century, little remains of its precarious early architecture. (There are older,

more impressive early colonial constructions in the northwestern provinces of Jujuy, Salta, Tucumán, and Córdoba.)

Nevertheless, the barrios of Monserrat, San Telmo, and some others boast a selection of worthwhile colonial buildings, many but not all of them churches. Vernacular architecture styles include the distinctive *casa chorizo,* a long, narrow construction—sometimes barely wider than an adult's arm span—on deep lots. The wood-frame, metal-clad houses of La Boca derive their traditional bright primary colors from the fact that early residents scavenged their paint from ships on the Riachuelo.

For most of the 19th century, *porteño* architecture evolved from its Spanish colonial origins to an Italianate style. Beginning in the early 20th century, the reigning architectural fashion was a Beaux-Arts academicism, both for public buildings and the ornate *palacetes* (mansions) of the landowning oligarchy. Some of these Parisian-style residences became public buildings when the Great Depression bankrupted and impoverished—relatively speaking, of course—Argentina's first families. Many French professionals, including landscape architect Carlos Thays, worked on *porteño* projects in what has been called, with some exaggeration, "the Paris of the South."

From the 1930s onward, the capital developed greater residential and commercial density with buildings such as the Edificio Kavanagh, a handsome 33-story high-rise on Plaza San Martín. Barrios like Recoleta and Palermo that were once almost exclusively single-family residences or *propiedades horizontales* (horizontal properties, or *PHs*) are now filled with soaring apartment blocks. Some of these are handsome, others much less so.

The late 20th century saw some hideous developments, such as Italian-born Clorindo Testa's brutalist Biblioteca Nacional (National Library) in Palermo (in fairness, the building's interior is more attractive and practical than its hideous exterior would suggest). One positive development is the recycling of historical structures, such as the Galerías Pacífico and the Mercado del Abasto into contemporary

© WAYNE BERNHARDSON

Now military property, the Palacio Paz in Plaza San Martín was once a single family residence.

shopping centers, and the former brick warehouses at Puerto Madero into fashionable restaurants, hotels, and residential lofts.

The best general guide to Buenos Aires's architecture, the Spanish-language *Buenos Aires: Guía de Arquitectura* (1994), edited by Alberto Petrina, includes suggested walking tours, architectural drawings, and sharp black-and-white photographs. Readers who know even basic Spanish can benefit from it.

## MUSIC AND DANCE

Argentines are musical people, their interests ranging from folk, pop, rock, and blues to classical. The country's signature sound and dance is the tango, both as instrumental and with lyrics; in its plaintiveness and melancholy, it's a cultural counterpart to the blues.

In their musical interests, Argentine performers are versatile and unselfconscious about crossing boundaries—folksinger Mercedes Sosa, for instance, has sometimes performed with the talented but erratic rock musician

Charly García. Throughout most of the 1990s, major international artists in both classical and popular music toured the country, but the peso's collapse placed many of them beyond the public's means. (Some have recently begun to return.) Nevertheless, qualified local performers were able to take up much of the slack, even at locales like the Teatro Colón, which traditionally attracts big overseas names.

### Classical Music and Dance

Since its completion in 1908, the **Teatro Colón** has been the preeminent high-culture venue on the continent and perhaps in the entire Southern Hemisphere (the Sydney Opera House cannot boast the Colón's history). Thanks to the presence of the Colón, the **Teatro Avenida,** and other classical venues, early-20th-century Argentina produced an abundance of classical composers, particularly in the fields of opera and ballet.

Among the notable figures of the time were Héctor Panizza (1875–1967); Constantino Gaito (1878–1945), who produced *gauchesco* ballet, such as *La Flor del Irupé* (The Flower of Irupé); Felipe Boero (1884–1958), and Italian-born Pascual De Rogatis (1880–1980). Possibly the most distinguished, though, was Juan José Castro (1895–1968), whose career suffered because of his outspoken opposition to the 1943 military government and the subsequent Perón regime. Castro's ballets include *Mekhano* and *Offenbachiana.*

The Spanish composer Manuel de Falla (1876–1946) spent the last seven years of his life in Alta Gracia—a provincial Córdoba town that was also the boyhood home of Ernesto "Che" Guevara—following the victory of Perón's ally Francisco Franco in the Spanish Civil War. Franco's regime had executed Falla's friend, playwright Federico García Lorca.

One of the outstanding figures in Argentine ballet is Roberto García Morillo (1911–1996), whose works include *Usher* and *Harrild.* Arnaldo D'Espósito (1897–1945), Luis Gianneo (1897–1968), and Alberto Ginastera (1916–1983) were his contemporaries. A later generation of opera composers includes Valdo

Sciamarella (born 1924), Mario Perusso (born 1936), and Gerardo Gandini (born 1936).

Contemporary Argentine classical music boasts figures like Daniel Barenboim (born 1942), a pianist and conductor who has held posts at the Orchestre de Paris, the Chicago Symphony Orchestra, and the Deutsche Staatsoper Berlin, among others. Barenboim (also an Israeli citizen who has played in the West Bank in defiance of Israeli government objections) is a versatile figure who has, among other achievements, recorded tango and other popular music. He performed at the Colón during the economic crisis of 2002, when the theater could not afford to pay high-profile international acts.

Pianist Martha Argerich (born 1941), though she lives in Brussels, has sponsored competitions in Buenos Aires. She has drawn rave reviews from the *New York Times* for her Carnegie Hall concerts and has won a Grammy for Best Instrumental Soloist.

U.S.-based Osvaldo Golijov (born 1960) is responsible for classical works like *The St. Mark Passion,* but is flexible enough to work on movie soundtracks (for British director Sally Potter's widely panned *The Man Who Cried*) and even with rock bands like Mexico's Café Tacuba.

Rosario-born but Europe-based tenor José Cura (born 1962) has drawn attention as a credible successor to Luciano Pavarotti on the international opera scene. Among ballet performers, by far the most significant is Julio Bocca (born 1967), a prodigy who has performed in New York, Paris, and elsewhere. He has formed his own company, the Ballet Argentino, and continued to perform in Argentina even during the economic crisis.

## Popular Music

Argentine popular music takes many forms, from the Andean northwest's folk tradition to the accordion-based immigrant *chamamé* of the northeastern lowlands and Buenos Aires's hard-nosed *rock nacional*. Its centerpiece, though, remains the tango, which overlaps categories—many classical composers and performers (see the preceding *Classical Music and Dance* section) have incorporated tango into their repertoires.

## TANGO

Tango overlaps the categories of music and dance, and even within those categories there are distinctions. As music, the tango can be instrumental but it gained its initial popularity and international reputation through the *tango canción* (tango song) as projected by the legendary Carlos Gardel and others (though to a lesser degree). One *porteño* songwriter has described the tango as "a sad feeling that is danced," and there is no doubt that it appeals to nostalgia for things lost—an old flame or the old neighborhood, for instance.

The charismatic Gardel, whose birth date and birthplace are both topics of debate, attained immortality after dying young in an aviation accident in Medellín, Colombia, in 1935. According to his die-hard admirers, "Gardel sings better every day." Uruguayan-born Julio Sosa (1926–1964), who also died young in a car accident, was nearly as important; at a time when Peronism was outlawed, his subtle smile and on-stage gestures evoked the exiled caudillo.

Orchestral tango, as opposed to that of the *tango canción*, is the legacy of bandleaders and composers like Osvaldo Pugliese (1905–1995), Aníbal "Pichuco" Troilo (1914–1975), and especially Ástor Piazzolla (1921–1992), whose jazz influences are palpable. Important lyricists include Enrique Santos Discépolo (1901–1951), also a composer, and Homero Manzi (1907–1951).

Practiced by skilled and sexy dancers in San Telmo and Monserrat night clubs, the "tango for export" floor show is popular with tourists, but tells only part of the story. The tango is not exclusive to the young and lithe—in fact, one could easily argue that its nostalgia lends it to older individuals with longer memories—and a recent revival has made it just as popular with mixed-age audiences at *milongas* (informal dance clubs).

Tango remains a daily presence in the lives of *porteños,* with both a 24-hour FM radio station (FM 92.7) and a cable TV channel, Sólo Tango. Contemporary performers of note include several women, such as Eladia Blásquez (born 1931), Susana Rinaldi (born 1935), and Adriana Varela (born 1958). Pop singers, such as Sandro and Cacho Castaña (born 1942),

Fresh flowers adorn the tomb of tango legend Osvaldo Pugliese in Cementerio de la Chacarita.

have also sung tango, and the much younger Omar Giammarco produces tango-flavored music using accordion instead of *bandoneón* in his *quinteto*. La Chicana is a tango song group that adds a flute to the traditional instrumental mix and even works with rock musicians.

## FOLK

Tango is arguably an urban folk music, but Argentina's true folk tradition stems from *payadores,* gauchos who sang verses to guitar accompaniment; in dance, it sometimes takes the form of the *malambo,* a competitive male-only affair that, despite its identification with the pampas, contains echoes of flamenco. An older current derives from the northwestern Andean provinces and their link to the Bolivian and Peruvian highlands, featuring the *zampoña* (panpipes) and *charango,* a tiny stringed instrument that uses an armadillo shell as its sound box. Born in Buenos Aires province, the late Atahualpa Yupanqui (1908–1992) belongs to these purist traditions, as does the Salta-based group Los Chalchaleros, an institution

for more than half a century. Tucumán native Mercedes Sosa (born 1935) also comes from this tradition but is less of a purist. Her contemporary León Gieco (born 1951) crosses the line into folk-rock and even rap.

Tomás Lipán, an Aymará Indian from the northwestern village of Purmamarca in Jujuy province, embodies the region's Andean folk roots but adds urban touches like the *bandoneón* to create an Argentine hybrid. Soledad Pastorutti (born 1980), who goes by her first name only as a performer, is a self-conscious folkie who sings and dresses in an exaggerated *gauchesco* style.

Immigrant communities have left their mark in *chamamé,* an accordion-based music typical of the humid lowland provinces along the Río Paraná and the Río Uruguay, north of Buenos Aires to the Brazilian and Paraguayan borders. Among the notable performers are Antonio Tarragó Ros (born 1947) and Chango Spasiuk (born 1968); the latter comes from a Ukrainian immigrant community in the province of Misiones.

## ROCK AND POP

It's no exaggeration to say that Buenos Aires, like London or San Francisco in the mid- to late 1960s, has one of the most vigorous rock scenes ever. Despite the handicap of trying to fit a multisyllabic language into a monosyllabic musical idiom, the practitioners of *rock nacional* have had remarkable success.

In terms of live music, there seems to be something happening every night. One down side to this is that some top bands have a small but pugnacious hard core of fans who tend to crowd the stage; most visitors unaccustomed to the scene will probably prefer to stand back a bit. The other drawback, ostensibly being remedied, is the questionable safety conditions; a catastrophic Once fire, in which nearly 200 fans of Los Callejeros died in December 2004, has prompted overdue inspections of the locales in which many groups play.

Argentine rock music's pioneer is Roberto Sánchez (born 1945), better known by his stage name, Sandro. As an early rock star who became a movie idol with a dominating manager, Sandro draws obvious comparisons with Elvis Presley, but "El Maestro" has also been a credible tango singer and the first Argentine to appear at Madison Square Garden. A surprisingly modest individual but also a heavy smoker who now needs oxygen on stage, he is the honoree of *Tributo a Sandro: Un Disco de Rock,* an exceptional tribute album by Argentine, Chilean, Colombian, and Mexican rock bands.

Charly García (born 1951), a founder of the legendary Sui Generis, transcends generations—many of his fans are in their 20s and even younger. García, who sings and plays mostly keyboards, incorporates women into his backing bands even as lead guitarists and saxophonists; he displays a sense of history in performing classics like Eddie Cochran's "Summertime Blues," the Byrds' "I'll Feel a Whole Lot Better," Neil Young's "Don't Let It Bring You Down," and even the obscure Small Faces gem "Tin Soldier." Rather than strict cover versions, these are adaptations, often with García's own Spanish-language lyrics.

Nearly as revered as Charly is the Dylanesque León Gieco; his album *Bandidos Rurales* (2002) bears thematic resemblance to Dylan's *John Wesley Harding.* He does a brilliant cover of Sandro's "Si Yo Fuera Carpintero," itself a brilliant Spanish-language adaptation of Tim Hardin's "If I Were a Carpenter."

Fito Páez (born 1963) and García protégé Andrés Calamaro (born 1961) also have solo careers, but many acts in the *rock nacional* idiom have a stronger group identity than individual identity. Among them are Attaque 77, Babasónicos, Los Divididos (a branch of the earlier Sumo and famous for their versions of the Mexican folk song "Cielito Lindo" and the Doors' "Light My Fire"), Las Pelotas (the other branch of Sumo), Los Piojos, Los Ratones Paranóicos (strongly influenced by the Rolling Stones), and Patricio Rey y Sus Redonditos de Ricota. Almafuerte and the power trio A.N.I.M.A.L are the leading heavy-metal bands.

Grammy winners Los Fabulosos Cadillacs (best alternative Latin rock group in 1998) have toured North America, playing salsa- and reggae-influenced rock at venues like San Francisco's legendary Fillmore Auditorium. Others in this idiom include Los Auténticos Decadentes and Los Cafres, but the band of the moment is Bersuit Vergarabat.

In a category of their own are Les Luthiers, an eclectic bunch who make their own unique instruments (which defy description) and caricature the most bourgeois and authoritarian sectors of Argentine society. While musically sophisticated, their shows are as much theater as concert.

## JAZZ AND BLUES

Both traditional and free-form jazz play a part in Argentina's musical history. A fixture in the traditional jazz scene is the Fénix Jazz Band, whose vocalist Ernesto "Cachi" Carrizo says he can't sing blues in Spanish because "the blues in Spanish seems as absurd to me as tango in English."

Better known outside strictly Argentine circles is saxophonist Gato Barbieri (born 1932), who also wrote the soundtrack for *The Last Tango in Paris.* Hollywood regular Lalo Schifrin (born 1932), famous for TV and movie soundtracks like *Bullitt, Cool Hand Luke,* and *Mission*

*Impossible,* originally moved north to play piano with Dizzy Gillespie. Schifrin, who also writes classical music, makes a brief on-screen appearance as an orchestra conductor in the opening sequence of the Hannibal Lecter gore-fest *Red Dragon* (2002); his father, Luis, was concertmaster of the Teatro Colón's orchestra.

Buenos Aires has a robust blues scene, thanks to individuals like the late guitarist Pappo and groups like La Mississippi and Memphis La Blusera, who have even taken their act to the stage of the Teatro Colón (almost causing nausea from classical music critics). The female vocal trio Las Blacanblus treats blues standards in a distinctive style with minimal accompaniment—only guitar and piano. International blues figures such as B. B. King, and many less-famous but still credible foreign artists, have also played in Buenos Aires.

## CINEMA

Given the country's political and economic instability, it's surprising that Argentine cinema has been as productive and successful as it has. In the year 2000, for instance, Argentine directors managed to make 30 full-length features and four documentaries. In October 2002, the American Cinemateque showed a dozen new films in the three-day New Argentine Cinema 2002 in Hollywood's Egyptian Theater, with attendance by Argentine directors and actors.

Special effects are generally limited, and it's worth noting that Argentine films, like European ones, tend to be more character- than plot-driven. There are plenty of outstanding directors and actors, and quite a few films from the last 20 years, in particular, are available on video.

Not only have Argentines made good films, but foreign directors have found Buenos Aires an interesting locale for filming—all the more so now that the peso's collapse has made it inexpensive to shoot in the capital. Readers who know Spanish should look for film critic Diego Curubeto's *Babilonia Gaucha* (Buenos Aires: Editorial Planeta, 1993), on the relationship between Argentina and Hollywood; Curubeto also wrote *Cine Bizarro* (Buenos Aires: Editorial

Sudamericana, 1996), on idiosyncratic films from Argentina and elsewhere.

**Alquileres Lavalle** (Lavalle 1199, tel. 4476-1118) rents and sells Argentine videos in the original Spanish. Argentine videos, however, use European PAL technology, which is incompatible with the North American VHS system. For DVDs, you may need a region-free player to connect to Argentine televisions.

## Argentine Directors, Movies, and Actors

In its earliest years, Argentine cinema dealt almost exclusively with *porteño* topics, such as Carnaval; even given the capital's Afro-American traditions, it's startling to see Argentine actors in blackface. Later, tango legend Carlos Gardel worked extensively in Hollywood as well as Buenos Aires, starring in films such as *El Día Que Me Quieras* (The Day You Love Me, 1935).

Over the years, several Argentine films have made respectable showings at the Oscars. Director Sergio Renán's *La Tregua* (The Truce, 1975), based on a story by Uruguayan Mario Benedetti, was the first nominated for best foreign-language film; it lost to the tough competition of Federico Fellini's *Amarcord.*

María Luisa Bemberg (1922–1995), astonishingly enough, made her first feature at the age of 58, but made up for lost time with films like *Camila,* nominated in 1984; it was based on the true story of 19th-century heiress Camila O'Gorman, her Jesuit lover, and their persecution by the Rosas dictatorship. In 1985, director Luis Puenzo's *The Official Story* won the Oscar for his treatment of the controversial issue of military adoptions of infant children of "disappeared" parents during the 1976–1983 Dirty War; it stars Norma Aleandro, a highly respected theater actress and director. Puenzo drew scorn, though, for implying that some Argentines were unaware of extrajudicial tortures and murders.

Based partly on Adolfo Bioy Casares's novella *The Invention of Morel,* Eliseo Subiela's *Man Facing Southeast* won a nomination in 1986; the plot of the 2001 Hollywood production *K-Pax,* starring Kevin Spacey and Jeff Bridges, bears a remarkable resemblance to Subiela's work. Most recently, in 2002, Juan José Campanella's maudlin *Hijo de la Novia* (The Bride's Son) received a nomination; Ricardo Darín plays the title role, a type-A *porteño* restaurateur whose father (Héctor Alterio) wants to give Darín's Alzheimer's-stricken mother (Aleandro) a belated church wedding.

The Oscars, though, showcase only a small percentage of Argentine films and are not necessarily representative. Often subtly and sometimes overtly political, they are frequently eloquent and passionate but also introspective—partly due, perhaps, to the popularity of psychoanalysis in the capital.

Subiela's *The Dark Side of the Heart* (1992), an erotic love story with both humor and pathos, takes place in Buenos Aires and Montevideo; based loosely on the life of *porteño* poet (and Borges's romantic rival) Oliverio Girondo, it features a cameo by Uruguayan poet Mario Benedetti.

Bemberg also made the English-language *Miss Mary* (1986), with Julie Christie in the title role of an English governess on an Argentine *estancia*, and *I Don't Want to Talk About It* (1992), a truly peculiar romance starring the late Marcelo Mastroianni and set in a conservative provincial town (the filming took place in the Uruguayan city of Colonia, across the river from Buenos Aires).

Adolfo Aristarain (born 1943) directed the versatile Federico Luppi in the Spanish-language thriller *Time of Revenge* (1981), a labor drama available on video, and in *A Place in the World* (1992). The latter is a socially conscious film that was disqualified for an Oscar nomination because it was unclear whether it was a Uruguayan, Argentine, or Spanish production (most of the filming took place in Argentina's scenic San Luis province). Aristarain also directed the English-language film *The Stranger* (1986), a psychological thriller with Peter Riegert, Bonnie Bedelia, and cameos from a cast of Argentine stars, but its ingenious structure can't compensate for a plot full of holes.

Uruguayan director Diego Arsuaga (born 1966) directs an aging all-star Argentine trio of Luppi, Alterio, and Pepe Soriano in the dramatic comedy *Corazón de Fuego* (2002), also known as *El Último Tren* (The Last Train). The original Spanish title refers to a steam locomotive stolen by geriatric trainspotters after a young entrepreneur (sympathetically played by Gastón Pauls, also an Argentine) makes arrangements to sell it to Hollywood. What ensues is a cleverly written rail movie (as opposed to a road movie) that showcases the Uruguayan countryside at its best before barely avoiding a *Thelma and Louise* finale.

Other films have gotten less international recognition but are worth seeing, such as Bruno Stagnaro's and Adrián Caetano's low-budget *Pizza, Birra, Faso* (1997), an unsentimental story of *porteño* lowlifes trying to get by. Ricardo Darín shares the lead with Gastón Pauls in Fabián Bielinsky's *Nueve Reinas* (Nine Queens, 2001), the twist-filled noirish tale of *porteño* con men who strike up a partnership in crisis-racked Buenos Aires.

Politically committed director Fernando "Pino" Solanas (born 1936), a left-wing Peronist, dealt with the theme of expatriation in *The Exile of Gardel* (1985). Tango legend Ástor Piazzolla wrote the soundtrack and also appears in the film, which, appropriately enough for a film whose title figure may have been born in France, takes place in Paris.

The prolific Leopoldo Torre Nilsson (1924–1978), who shot nearly 30 features in his relatively short lifetime, adapted Manuel Puig's novel *Boquitas Pintadas* (Painted Lips), a story of hypocrisy and petty jealousies in a small provincial town, to the screen in 1974. Torre Nilsson also filmed *La Guerra del Cerdo* (War of the Pigs, 1975); set in Palermo, it's a discomforting adaptation of Adolfo Bioy Casares's story of generational conflict and political polarization in the immediate pre-coup years. Argentine jazz legend Gato Barbieri wrote the soundtrack.

Director Héctor Olivera (born 1931) has turned two of Osvaldo Soriano's satirical novels into movies: *A Funny Dirty Little War* (1983), which depicts the comic consequences of a military coup in a provincial town (but has nothing to do, directly at least, with the 1976–1983 dictatorship); and *Una Sombra Ya Pronto Serás* (Shadows, 1994), a road movie that encourages disorientation by making it impossible to tell where the movie takes place. Federico Luppi (born 1936) appeared in the former.

Starting with a bungled robbery in Buenos Aires, Marcelo Piñeyro's *Wild Horses* (1995) becomes a road romance that ends with a chase in the Patagonian province of Chubut. Héctor Alterio is a hostage who goes along for the ride.

Gustavo Mosquera directed the innovative *Moebius* (1996), really a collaborative film-school project set mostly in a Borgesian Buenos Aires subway; a disappearing train, audible but not visible, serves as a metaphor for Dirty War victims. Displaying great creativity and technical proficiency on a shoestring budget, its anachronisms—antique dial telephones alongside cell phones, for instance—imply that despite modernization and the return to representative government, remnants of the old Argentina remain.

In addition to his Argentine films, Luppi has appeared in two outstanding films by Mexican director Guillermo del Toro: the sci-fi thriller *Cronos* (1992) and the politically charged ghost story *The Devil's Backbone,* set during the Spanish Civil War. Luppi also played the lead role of a socially committed physician in U.S. director John Sayles's *Men with Guns* (1997), an eloquent parable on political violence in Latin America.

Norma Aleandro (born 1936), best known overseas for *The Official Story,* has won many international acting awards. She has also appeared opposite Anthony Hopkins in Sergio Toledo's *One Man's War,* a human-rights drama set in Paraguay.

Cecilia Roth (born 1958), who appeared with Luppi in *A Place in the World,* has worked frequently with maverick Spanish director Pedro Almodóvar, most recently in *All About My Mother* (1999).

## THEATER

*Porteños,* traditionally, are theatergoers. In the year 2000, for example, more than 300,000 attended programs at both the Teatro Colón and the Teatro General San Martín combined, and nearly 200,000 went to the Teatro Cervantes. Even in September 2002, at the nadir of the country's worst economic crisis ever, there were 110 plays showing at 70 theaters, and three new theaters opened their doors the first weekend of that month.

The theater tradition dates from late colonial times, when creation of the Virreinato del Río de la Plata gave the city a certain legitimacy and pretensions, at least, to high culture. Over the course of the 19th century, the area's theater culture developed through institutions like the *sainete,* a humorous performance dealing with immigrant issues.

Formal theater dates from the late 19th century, thanks to the patronage of the Montevideo-born Podestá family, who built theaters in Buenos Aires and La Plata. Influential early playwrights included Montevideo-born Florencio Sánchez (1875–1910), who wrote *sainetes* but drew much of his inspiration from Ibsen; Gregorio de Laferrere (1867–1913), who wrote comic plays; and Roberto Payró (1867–1928), also a novelist.

Twentieth-century European dramatists, such as Federico García Lorca and Jean Cocteau, found that the Buenos Aires theater scene justified the long trip across the Atlantic in the days before jets. Among Argentina's best-loved 20th-century performers are comedian Luis Sandrini (1905–1980) and Lola Membrives (1888–1969); the best-known contemporary playwright is Juan Carlos Gené. Norma Aleandro, while primarily known for her films, is active as a theater director.

# Religion

Roman Catholicism remains Argentina's official and dominant religion, but evangelical Protestantism, with its street preachers and storefront churches, is growing even in sophisticated Buenos Aires, mostly but not exclusively among the working-class population. Other religions have fewer adherents, though there's still a sizeable Jewish community and a small but growing Muslim presence.

Catholicism in particular has left the city with many of its greatest landmarks, ranging from the colonial churches of San Telmo and Recoleta to the dignified neoclassical Catedral. Immigrant Protestant communities are also responsible for ecclesiastical landmarks like the Danish and Swedish churches of San Telmo and the impressive Russian Orthodox dome opposite Parque Lezama, also in San Telmo.

## ROMAN CATHOLICISM

Starting with the famous Dominican Bartolomé de las Casas in Mexico, factions in the Church have wrestled with the contradictions between its official mission of recruiting and saving souls and its duty to alleviate the misery of those who have experienced secular injustice and persecution. Argentina is no exception—figures such as the late Cardinal Antonio Quarracino were outright apologists for the vicious military dictatorship of 1976–1983, but others lobbied against its excesses and for return to democracy. Some more militant clergy worked in the slums under the influence of "liberation theology," and some lost their lives in the aftermath of the 1976 coup.

Folk Catholicism, including spiritualist practices, often diverges from Church orthodoxy in the veneration of unofficial saints, like the Difunta Correa of San Juan province, and even historical figures like Juan and Evita Perón, tango legend Carlos Gardel, and healer Madre María, all of whose tombs are in Buenos Aires's landmark cemeteries at Recoleta and Chacarita. Novelist Tomás Eloy Martínez has sardonically labeled his countrymen as "cadaver cultists" for their devotion to those dead and gone.

## PROTESTANTISM

Anglicans were the original bearers of Protestantism in Argentina, but Scandinavian communities were numerous enough to justify construction of Danish and Swedish churches. More recent Protestant denominations are often shrill evangelicals; nearby Uruguay's capital city of Montevideo is one of the centers for Reverend Sun Myung Moon's cultish Unification Church.

## OTHER RELIGIONS

The Argentine constitution guarantees freedom of religion, and adherents of non-Christian faiths are not rare, if not exactly widespread or numerous. The largest and most conspicuous of these other religions is Judaism, as the capital's Jewish community is at least 200,000 strong (a planned community census may well reveal a larger number). The government of Saudi Arabia sponsored the construction of Palermo's Centro Islámico Rey Fahd, whose capacity is disproportionately large for the capital's relatively small community of observant Muslims.

# ESSENTIALS

## Getting There

Most overseas visitors arrive by air, though many also arrive overland from Chile, Bolivia, Uruguay, Paraguay, and Brazil. Almost all of the latter arrive by bus or private vehicle; there is no international rail service. There are ferry connections to Uruguay.

### BY AIR

Buenos Aires has regular air links with North America, Europe, and Australia/New Zealand, plus less-frequent routes from southern Africa across the Atlantic (usually via Brazil). It is, however, a relatively expensive destination during peak periods, such as Christmas/New Year's and Holy Week holidays; an Advance Purchase Excursion (APEX) fare can reduce the bite considerably, but may have minimum- and maximum-stay requirements, allow no stopovers, and impose financial penalties for any changes. Economy-class (Y) tickets, valid for 12 months, are more expensive but allow maximum flexibility. Travelers staying more than a year, though, have to cough up the difference for any interim price increase.

Discount ticket agents, known as consolidators in the United States and "bucket shops" in Britain, may offer the best deals but often have drawbacks—they may not, for instance, allow mileage credit for frequent-flyer programs. Courier flights, on which passengers

© WAYNE BERNHARDSON

# INTERNATIONAL AIRLINES IN BUENOS AIRES

Unless otherwise indicated, the airline offices below are in the Microcentro.

· **Aerolíneas Argentinas:** Perú 2, Monserrat, tel. 011/4320-2000

· **AeroMéxico:** Reconquista 737, 3rd fl., tel. 011/5238-1200

· **Air Canada:** Avenida Córdoba 656, tel. 011/4327-3640

· **Air Europa:** Avenida Corrientes 880, tel. 011/4322-4595

· **Air France:** San Martín 344, Oficina 23, tel. 011/4317-4711

· **Alitalia:** Avenida Santa Fe 887, Retiro, tel. 011/4310-9999

· **American Airlines:** Avenida Santa Fe 881, Retiro, tel. 011/4318-1111

· **Avianca:** Carlos Pellegrini 1163, 4th fl., Retiro, tel. 011/4394-5990

· **British Airways:** Avenida del Libertador 498, 13th fl., Retiro, tel. 0800/222-0075

· **Continental:** Carlos Pellegrini 527, 7th fl., tel. 0800/333-0425

· **Copa:** Emma de la Barra 353, 7th fl., Retiro, tel. 0810/222-2672

· **Cubana de Aviación:** Sarmiento 552, 11th fl., tel. 011/4326-5291

· **Delta:** Avenida Santa Fe 887, Retiro, tel. 0800/666-0133

· **Iberia:** Carlos Pellegrini 1163, 1st fl., Retiro, tel. 011/4131-1000

· **KLM:** San Martín 344, 23rd fl., tel. 011/4317-4711

· **LAN:** Cerrito 866, Retiro, tel. 011/4378-2200

· **Lufthansa:** Marcelo T. de Alvear 590, 6th fl., Retiro, tel. 011/4319-0600

· **Mexicana:** Avenida Córdoba 1131, 1st fl., Retiro, tel. 011/4136-4136

· **Pluna:** Florida 1, Microcentro, tel. 011/4342-4420

· **Qantas:** Avenida Madero 900, 27th fl., Puerto Madero, tel. 011/4114-5800

· **Swiss International:** Avenida Santa Fe 846, 1st fl., Retiro, tel. 011/4319-0000

· **Transportes Aéreos de Mercosur (TAM):** Cerrito 1026, Retiro, tel. 011/4819-4800

· **United Airlines:** Avenida Madero 900, 9th fl., Puerto Madero, tel. 011/4316-0777

# AIRPORT TRANSPORTATION

There's a variety of options to and from the airports, ranging from *colectivos* (city buses) to shuttles, taxis, and *remises* (meterless taxis that quote a fixed price for the trip).

## COLECTIVOS

*Colectivos* provide the cheapest transportation to and from the airports, but they are more practical for close-in Aeroparque than distant Ezeiza, as they take circuitous routes on surface streets. To Aeroparque (about US$0.30), the options are No. 33 from Plaza de Mayo, the Microcentro, and Retiro; No. 37-C ("Ciudad Universitaria") from Plaza del Congreso, Avenida Callao, Avenida las Heras, and Plaza Italia; No. 45 northbound from Constitución, Plaza San Martín, or Retiro; and No. 160-C or 160-D from Avenida Las Heras or Plaza Italia. Return buses leave from the Avenida Costanera Rafael Obligado, a short walk outside the terminal.

To Ezeiza (about US$1), the backpackers' choice is the No. 86-A ("Aeropuerto"), from La Boca to Plaza de Mayo, Plaza del Congreso, Plaza Once, and onward, but the roundabout route takes up to two hours. *Servicio Diferencial* buses cost more (about US$3) but have more comfortable reclining seats. In Ezeiza, both leave from a stop at the Aerolíneas Argentinas terminal, a short distance from the main international terminal.

## SHUTTLES

Manuel Tienda León (Av. Madero and San Martín, tel. 011/4315-5115 or 800/777-0078, www.tiendaleon.com.ar) runs 35 shuttle buses daily to and from Ezeiza (US$12 pp) between 4 A.M. and 11:30 P.M. There are 25 daily to Aeroparque (US$5) between 8:30 A.M. and 10:45 P.M.; most buses from Ezeiza make connections to Aeroparque for domestic flights.

## TAXIS AND REMISES

Taxis and *remises* offer similar services, but taxis are metered and *remises* (generally newer and more spacious vehicles) are not. Offering door-to-door service, they are no more expensive than shuttles for three or more persons. Manuel Tienda León and many other companies offer *remises* to Aeroparque (US$6-10) and Ezeiza (US$25-35). Both *remises* and taxis sometimes add the cost of the toll road to Ezeiza, which is around US$1.

give up some or all of their baggage allowance to a company sending equipment or documents to overseas affiliates or customers, may be even cheaper but are less common to Latin America than to other parts of the world. These are also available for short periods only and often leave on short notice.

Other options include Round the World (RTW) and Circle Pacific routes that permit numerous stopovers over the course of much longer multi-continental trips, but putting these itineraries together requires some effort. Two useful resources for researching airfares are Edward Hasbrouck's *The Practical Nomad* (Emeryville, CA: Avalon Travel Publishing, 2007) and the same author's *The Practical Nomad Guide to the Online Marketplace* (Emeryville, CA: Avalon Travel Publishing, 2001).

While airlines reduced their services to Buenos Aires after the economic collapse of 2001–2002, as far fewer Argentines could afford to travel overseas and business travel from overseas likewise declined, the recent recovery has meant increased air traffic. American Airlines, for instance, has reinstituted nonstops to and from Dallas.

## Airports

Buenos Aires has two airports, both operated by the private concessionaire Aeropuertos Argentinos 2000 (tel. 011/5480-6111, www.aa2000.com.ar). The main international facility is Aeropuerto Internacional Ministro Pistarini, 35 kilometers southwest of downtown, popularly called Ezeiza after its Buenos Aires province suburban location. The other

© WAYNE BERNHARDSON

Aeroparque Jorge Newbery is the Argentine capital's domestic airport.

is Aeroparque Jorge Newbery, within the capital's boundaries at Avenida Costanera Rafael Obligado s/n (*sin número,* or unnumbered), Palermo; Aeroparque is primarily domestic but has a handful of international flights from neighboring countries.

International passengers leaving from Ezeiza pay a US$30.50 departure tax, payable in local currency or U.S. dollars, but it's partially included in the ticket price. On flights of fewer than 300 kilometers to neighboring countries, such as Uruguay and Chile (from Mendoza), the tax is only US$16.50, and on domestic flights it's US$2. Again, these fees are normally included in the ticket price.

## From North America

Miami, Atlanta, Washington, D.C. (Dulles), New York, Dallas, and Los Angeles are the main gateways to Buenos Aires. Aerolíneas Argentinas is the traditional flagship carrier, but other options include American Airlines, Copa, Delta, LAN (Chile), Mexicana, Southern Winds, and TAM Mercosur. Aerolíneas Argentinas, American, Delta, and United have the only nonstop services; others require changing planes elsewhere in Central or South America.

Canadian passengers can avoid connections in the United States by taking Air Canada from Toronto, some days nonstop and others via Santiago de Chile.

## From Mexico, Central America, and the Caribbean

Mexicana flies six times weekly from Mexico City via Cancún, while LAN has regional connections via Santiago de Chile.

Copa flies daily from Panama, with connections throughout Central America.

Cubana flies twice weekly from Havana, while Avianca has connections to the Caribbean, Central America, and Mexico via Bogotá.

## From Europe

From Europe, there are direct services to Buenos Aires with Aerolíneas Argentinas (from Rome and Madrid, with connections from London and Paris); Air Europa (from Madrid); Air France (from Paris); Alitalia (from Milan and Rome); British Airways (from London); Iberia (from Barcelona and Madrid); KLM (from Amsterdam via São Paulo); Lufthansa (from Frankfurt); Southern Winds (from Madrid); Swiss International (from Zurich and Geneva); and TAM (from Paris via São Paulo).

## From Asia, Africa, and the Pacific

The most direct service from the Pacific is Aerolíneas Argentinas' transpolar flight from Sydney and Auckland, though Qantas also flies from Sydney and Auckland via Santiago de Chile, and also links up with LAN flights via Tahiti, Easter Island, and Santiago, or with LAN via Los Angeles. From Japan, it's easiest to make connections via Los Angeles.

South African Airways flies six times weekly from Johannesburg to São Paulo, where TAM and Varig offer connections to Buenos Aires. Malaysia Airlines flies twice weekly to Cape Town, Johannesburg, and Kuala Lumpur.

## Within South America

Buenos Aires has connections to the neighboring republics of Uruguay, Brazil, Paraguay, Bolivia, Chile, and elsewhere on the continent. There are no flights to the Guyanas, however.

Some international airlines fly to and from Ezeiza to Montevideo, **Uruguay,** but most flights to the Uruguayan capital leave from the closer Aeroparque. There are also flights from Aeroparque to Punta del Este, Uruguay's popular summer resort and weekend getaway. Aerolíneas Argentinas and Pluna are the main carriers.

To **Brazil,** the main destinations are São Paulo and Rio de Janiero, but there are also flights to Florianópolis, Porto Alegre, Curitiba, and other cities. The main carriers are Aerolíneas Argentinas, TAM, and Varig.

Flights to **Paraguay** go to the capital city of Asunción, with TAM and Varig; some TAM flights continue to São Paulo (Brazil).

Lloyd Aéreo Boliviano flies to the lowland Bolivian city of Santa Cruz de la Sierra and on to Cochabamba and the highland capital of La Paz, as does AeroSur. Aerolíneas also flies to Santa Cruz, and TAM has connections to Santa Cruz and Cochabamba via Asunción.

Discount fares are often available from travel agents but are less common in Latin America than elsewhere; the major exception is the highly competitive Buenos Aires–Santiago de Chile route: European carriers like Air France and Lufthansa try to fill empty seats between **Chile** and the Argentine capital, where most transatlantic passengers board or disembark. This has kept fares low on competitors like Aerolíneas Argentinas and LAN.

Flights to **Peru, Ecuador, Colombia,** and **Venezuela** are all via capital cities, though some carriers stop elsewhere en route. Aerolíneas Argentinas goes to Lima and Caracas; Aeroméxico goes to Lima en route to Mexico City; and Avianca flies to Bogotá.

## From Elsewhere in Argentina

In addition to international air service, there is a network of domestic airports and airlines centered in Buenos Aires; indeed, to fly between Argentine cities, changing planes in Buenos Aires is almost unavoidable. Since none of the excursions in this book requires flying, these destinations and airlines are covered only generally here. Unless otherwise indicated, all of them use Aeroparque, the city airport.

Please note that in early 2003 some Argentine domestic airlines began to charge differential rates for Argentine residents and foreigners in dollars; while fares are moderate by international standards, Argentines can pay substantially less.

Aerolíneas Argentinas has domestic as well as international flights. Their domestic branch Austral (Perú 2, Monserrat, tel. 011/4320-2345) flies to destinations ranging from Puerto Iguazú on the Brazilian border to Ushuaia in Tierra del Fuego.

Líneas Aéreas del Estado (LADE, Perú 714, San Telmo, tel. 011/4361-7071) is the Argentine air force's heavily subsidized commercial aviation branch. Miraculously surviving budget crises and privatizations, it flies to southern Buenos Aires province and Patagonia on a wing and a deficit.

## BY LAND
### Bus

Buenos Aires's main bus station is Retiro's Estación Terminal de Omnibus (Av. Ramos Mejía 1860, tel. 011/4310-0700, www.tebasa. com.ar). The sprawling three-story building is home to nearly 140 bus companies that cover the entire country and international destinations as well. It's walking distance from the northern terminus of Subte Línea C, at the Retiro train station.

The ground floor is primarily for freight; buses leave from 1st-floor *andenes* (platforms), but ticket offices are on the 2nd floor. On the 1st floor, the Centro de Informes y Reclamos (tel. 011/4310-0700) provides general bus information and also oversees taxis that serve the terminal; direct any complaints about taxi drivers to them. There is also a separate tourist office, open daily 7:30 A.M.–1 P.M. only.

For international buses, reservations are a good idea, especially during the summer (January and February) and winter (late July) holiday periods, but also on long weekends like Semana Santa (Holy Week). Prices vary according to the quality of service, ranging from ordinary reclining seats to more spacious *servicio diferencial* and nearly horizontal *coche cama*.

Domestic bus services to the provinces do not appear in detail here. (For transportation to areas beyond the federal capital, see the appropriate geographical entry in the *Excursions from Buenos Aires* chapter.)

Several companies take the roundabout 600-kilometer route to **Montevideo, Uruguay,** which takes longer (eight hours) than the ferry but costs (US$24) less than half: Bus de la Carrera (four nightly, tel. 011/4313-1700); Cauvi (one nightly, tel. 011/4314-6999); and General Belgrano (one nightly, tel. 011/4315-1226). All leave between 9:30 and 11:30 P.M.

To the Paraguayan capital of **Asunción** (US$27–37, 17 hours), the main carriers are Nuestra Señora de la Asunción (tel. 011/4313-

Travelers purchase their long-distance bus tickets in Retiro at Estación Terminal de Omnibus.

© WAYNE BERNHARDSON

2349) and Chevalier Paraguaya (tel. 011/4313-2325). For **Brazilian destinations,** such as Foz do Iguaçu (US$36, 18 hours), Porto Alegre (US$42, 20 hours), São Paulo (US$80, 38 hours), and Rio de Janeiro (US$90, 42 hours), try Pluma (tel. 011/4313-3893) or Crucero del Norte (tel. 011/4315-1652).

For the trans-Andean crossing to **Santiago, Chile** (US$45, 21 hours), carriers include Fénix Pullman Norte (tel. 011/4313-0134) and Transporte Automotores Cuyo (TAC, tel. 011/4313-7012). For the Peruvian capital of **Lima** (via Chile, US$110, a 68-hour marathon), the choices are El Rápido Internacional (tel. 011/4313-3757) and Ormeño Internacional (tel. 011/4313-2259).

## Car, Motorcycle, and Bicycle

Overland travel from North America or elsewhere is problematic because Panama's Darien Gap route to Colombia is impassable for motor vehicles, and time-consuming, very difficult, and potentially dangerous even for those on foot. The route passes through areas controlled by drug smugglers, guerrillas, and/or brutal Colombian paramilitaries.

For travelers whose primary interest is the city, a vehicle is unnecessary, as public transport is cheap and excellent (parking, meanwhile, is next to impossible). Those visiting other parts of the continent, though, might consider shipping a vehicle, which is recommended over renting a car for extended trips. While rental cars are easy to find in both Argentina and Uruguay, crossing borders with them can be complicated (though not impossible) and requires extra expense for insurance and notarial documents. To locate a shipper, check the Yellow Pages of your local phone directory under Automobile Transporters. These are normally freight consolidators rather than the companies that own the ships—the latter will charge higher container rates. Since many more people ship vehicles to Europe than to South America, it may take patience to find the right shipper; one recommended North American consolidator is McClary, Swift & Co. (360 Swift Ave., South San Francisco, CA

94080, tel. 650/872-2121, www.glomato.com/ swift), which has agents at many U.S. ports.

Argentine customs has improved in recent years, so shipping a vehicle into the country is easier than it used to be. Vehicles arrive at the Estación Marítima Buenos Aires (Dársena B, Av. Ramon Castillo and Av. Maipu, Retiro, tel. 011/4311-0692, 011/4317-0675, or 011/4312-8677); here it is necessary to present your passport, vehicle title, and the original *conocimiento de embarque* (bill of lading), and to fill out a customs application. You will then obtain an appointment with a customs inspector to retrieve the vehicle, which involves about US$300 for port costs and another US$200 for the shipper; if the vehicle has been in port longer than five days, there will be additional charges. The vehicle can remain legally in Argentina for eight months, with an eight-month extension possible; of course, any visit to a neighboring country restarts the clock. In the event of any difficulty, consult a private *despachante de aduana* (customs broker) such as José Angel Vidal Labra (tel. 011/4345-7887, vidla@sinectis.com.ar).

Another option is via Chile, whose ports are less bureaucratic and safer for the vehicle than those of Argentina. The recommended and most probable ports of entry are San Antonio (southwest of Santiago), and Valparaíso (northwest of the capital). It pays to be there within a couple days of the vehicle's arrival, or storage charges can mount up. Leave the gas tank as nearly empty as possible (for safety's sake) and leave no valuables—including tools—in the vehicle.

To arrange a shipment from San Antonio or Valparaíso, contact the Santiago consolidator Ultramar (Av. El Bosque Norte 500, 18th fl., Las Condes, tel. 02/6301000, www.ultramar.cl). For a trustworthy customs agent to handle the paperwork, contact the office of Juan Alarcón Rojas (Fidel Oteíza 1921, 12th fl., Providencia, Santiago, tel. 02/2252780, alrcon@entelchile.net); Chile's country code is 56.

Bicycles, of course, can be partially dismantled, packaged, and easily shipped aboard airplanes, sometimes for no additional charge. There is rarely any additional paperwork for bringing a bike into the country, but many of the same overland travel concerns apply, like bad road conditions and drivers.

## VEHICLE DOCUMENTS, DRIVER'S LICENSE, AND EQUIPMENT

Most South American countries, including Argentina, Chile, Uruguay, and Brazil, have dispensed with the cumbersome *Carnet de Passage en Douanes* that required depositing a large bond in order to import a motor vehicle. Officials at the port of arrival or border post will issue a 90-day permit on presentation of the vehicle title, registration, bill of lading (if the vehicle is being shipped), and your passport. For shipped vehicles, there are usually some small but relatively insignificant port charges (unless the vehicle has been stored more than a few days).

Before traveling to Argentina, obtain an International or Interamerican Driving Permit. (Travelers intending to visit Uruguay should note that that country officially recognizes only the latter, though in practice they appear more flexible.) These permits are available through the American Automobile Association (AAA), or its counterpart in your home country, and are normally valid one calendar year from date of issue. Strictly speaking, they are not valid without a state or national driver's license, but Argentine police usually ignore the latter. Another form of identification, such as a national ID card or passport, is also necessary.

The police pay close attention to vehicle documents—*tarjeta verde* (green card) registration for Argentine vehicles, customs permission for foreign ones, and liability insurance (though many Argentines drive without it, it is reasonably priced from many insurers, including the Automóvil Club Argentino, the national automobile club). Vehicles without registration may be impounded on the spot. Argentine vehicles should have proof of a *verificación técnica* (safety inspection).

At roadside checkpoints, the police are also rigid about obligatory equipment, such as headrests for the driver and each passenger, *valizas* (triangular emergency reflectors), and *matafuegos* (one-kg fire extinguishers). In any instance of document irregularity or minor equipment violation, provincial police in particular may threaten fines while really soliciting *coimas* (bribes). A firm but calm suggestion that you intend to call your consulate may help overcome any difficulty.

### ROAD HAZARDS

Buenos Aires traffic is so fast and ruthless that it's amazing that Jorge Luis Borges, or any other blind person, could survive it—it's tough enough on sighted people in prime physical condition. According to statistics, 60–70 percent of the city's traffic fatalities are pedestrians; most culprits, unsurprisingly, are male drivers between 19 and 35 years of age. According to government statistics, the national traffic fatality rate of 25 per 100,000 residents is nearly double that of the United States, and more than triple that of Germany; one journalist has referred to its 38 deaths per day as a "weekly Cromañon," after the disastrous fire that killed nearly 200 *porteño* rock music fans in December 2004.

*Porteño* drivers in the city and stray cattle in the countryside might seem trouble enough, but the recent economic crisis has created an intractable movement of *piqueteros* (picketers, demonstrators protesting unemployment and other issues) who mount *piquetes* (roadblocks) to disrupt traffic. While they focus on stopping commercial traffic, picketers slow down everything else as well; never try to run a roadblock, as doing so can raise their wrath. If necessary, feign solidarity and, in all likelihood, you'll pass without incident.

## Train

There are no international rail services to or from Buenos Aires and only a few long-distance domestic services, mostly to the Atlantic beach resorts of southern Buenos Aires province. (See the *Getting Around* section for information on suburban and long-distance trains.)

Puerto Madero's Buquebus terminal is the main departure point for trips to Uruguay.

## BY RIVER

From Buenos Aires, there are ferry connections across the river to the Uruguayan capital of Montevideo, but also to the resort town of Piriápolis (summer only) and to the charming 18th-century town of Colonia. From the suburban river port of Tigre, there are launches to the Uruguayan river ports of Carmelo and Nueva Palmira.

### Buenos Aires to and from Colonia and Montevideo

From Puerto Madero's Dársena Norte, at the foot of Avenida Córdoba, **Buquebus** (Av. Antártida Argentina 821, tel. 011/4316-6500, www.buquebus.com) sails to Colonia, Montevideo, and Piriápolis; it also has a ticket outlet at Avenida Córdoba 879, Retiro. Services and fares vary, depending on the vessel—the ferry *Eladia Isabel,* for instance, has the cheapest but slowest crossing to Colonia (three hours, US$17–23), while the high-speed ferries *Juan Patricio* and *Patricia Oliva III* cover the much longer distance to Montevideo (US$52–67) in about the same time.

Buquebus now has discount competition from the 228-passenger **Colonia Express** (Av. Córdoba 753, tel. 011/4313-5100, www.coloniaexpress.com). Colonia Express, however, has only two daily departures, at 9 A.M. and 7:45 P.M., from the Terminal Internacional de Cruceros Benito Quinquela Martín (Av. de los Inmigrantes and Av. Castillo), the new cruise ship port northeast of the Retiro bus terminal.

### Tigre to and from Carmelo and Nueva Palmira

**Cacciola Viajes** (Florida 520, tel. 011/4393-6100, www.cacciolaviajes.com) connects the northern Buenos Aires province suburb of Tigre with the Uruguayan riverside resort of Carmelo.

# Getting Around

Even as automobiles clog the streets of Buenos Aires and other cities, most Argentines still rely on public transportation to get around. Services in the capital and Gran Buenos Aires are frequent and reasonably well integrated, but not perfectly so.

A local miracle, at least for visitors who can understand Spanish, is the free service (tel. 131 from any public or private telephone) that tells you the best Subte or bus route between any two points in the city; simply tell the operator exactly where you are, and he or she will tell you the closest stop.

## COLECTIVOS (BUSES)

More than 200 separate bus routes serve the Capital Federal and Gran Buenos Aires, but most visitors and even residents need to know only a few of them to get around easily. It's useful, however, to have one of the annually updated city atlases, such as the *Guía Lumi* or the *Guía T,* which include detailed bus routes. There are also abbreviated pocket versions of the bus lines. All are readily available at newsstand kiosks and bookstores.

Route signs at fixed stops often but not always list the bus's itinerary. If you don't have a written guide, ask someone for help—*porteños* often know the system by heart and are generous with information. Fares depend on distance traveled, but within the capital most are US$0.30 or less; after you tell the driver your destination, he will enter the fare in the automatic ticket machine, which takes only coins but does give small change. Though the driver will often give warning of your stop, his politeness may cease when he hits the accelerator.

## TRAIN

Buenos Aires has two types of rail systems: the Subte (subway) that serves the Capital Federal, and a series of surface commuter trains, run by

Articulated buses are making their debut on the streets of Buenos Aires.

© WAYNE BERNHARDSON

## TRAVEL AGENCIES

North of Plaza San Martín, Retiro's **American Express** office (Arenales 707, tel. 011/4310-3535, amexbueemp@aexp.com) offers the usual services and cashes its own travelers checks without additional commission.

**Swan Turismo** (Cerrito 822, 9th fl., Retiro, tel./fax 011/4129-7926, www.swanturismo.com.ar) is a full-service travel agency that's earned a reputation for willingness and ability to deal with some of the Argentine travel system's eccentricities.

There are also several student-oriented agencies, such as Retiro's nonprofit **Asatej,** in the Galería Buenos Aires (Florida 835, 3rd fl., tel. 011/4311-6953, www.asatej.com.ar). Since the Argentine economic crisis has reduced overseas travel by young Argentines, Asatej has shifted its focus to incoming tourism and is good at searching out the best airfares for anyone, not just students.

**Startravel** (Av. Córdoba 679, 3° C, tel. 011/5199-4445, www.startravel.com.ar) is the local affiliate of STA Travel. **Say Hueque** (Viamonte 749, 6th fl., Oficina 1, tel. 011/5199-2517, www.sayhueque.com) is comparably helpful.

**Pride Travel** (Paraguay 524 2° E, tel. 011/5218-6556, www.pride-travel.com) caters to homosexual visitors not just in the capital, but throughout the country.

several private companies, that connect downtown with more distant suburbs.

## Subte

Popularly known as the Subte, the Buenos Aires subway opened in 1913. South America's first underground railway, the 13th in the world, it has modernized and expanded in recent years, but its antique cars, with their varnished but worn woodwork and elaborately tiled but chipped murals, recall the prosperity and optimism of early-20th-century Argentina. Privatized in 1994, the Subte is still the fastest way to get around the capital.

Metrovías (www.metrovias.com.ar), a private concessionaire, operates the five existing underground lines and is building a sixth transverse line from Retiro through Recoleta, Once, and the southern part of the city, which will shorten many trips by reducing the need to transfer in the Microcentro. At present, there are 67 stations for 39.5 kilometers of track within the capital; in 2003, the system carried more than 225 million passengers. While this figure was lower than in previous years, it probably reflected growing unemployment rather than riders abandoning the system.

Since taking over the system, Metrovías has also improved the rolling stock, extended existing lines, modernized many stations, and built new ones. Electronic tickets have replaced the traditional Subte *fichas* (tokens) but, while this is perhaps more efficient than in the past, it means lots of litter. Another negative development is the system of SUBTV monitors that show nonstop advertising. Though some of the newest cars are air-conditioned, ventilation remains poor in many stations. Improvement plans are in progress.

## Suburban Trains

With few exceptions, suburban trains are less useful to short-term visitors than they are to commuters from Buenos Aires province. They are very cheap and, while some may be improving, most lag well behind the Subte.

The most useful and best is the Ferrocarril Mitre, operated by Trenes de Buenos Aires (TBA, tel. 011/4317-4400, www.tbanet.com.ar), which connects the classic Estación Retiro (Av. Ramos Mejía 1302) with Belgrano and Zona Norte suburbs, including Vicente López, Olivos, Martínez, San Isidro, and Tigre. Another branch of the line goes to Villa Ballester, for connections to Reserva Natural Estricta Otamendi.

TBA also operates the Ferrocarril Sarmiento from Estación Once (Av. Pueyrredón y Bartolomé Mitre, Subte: Plaza Miserere), which

# RIDING THE SUBTE

Operated by the private concessionaire Metrovías, the state-owned Subterráneos de Buenos Aires comprises six alphabetically designated lines, four of which (A, B, D, and E) begin in Monserrat or the Microcentro and serve outlying northern and western barrios, with numerous stations in between. Línea C is a north-south connector between major railway stations at Retiro and Constitución, while Línea H is a new north-south line between Once (Plaza Miserere) in the north and Caseros (Nueva Pompeya) in the south. Three other lines have been proposed, but construction has not yet begun.

Subte hours are Monday-Saturday 5 A.M. to about 11 P.M., but the system opens later (around 8 A.M.) and closes earlier (about 10:30 P.M.) Sundays and holidays, when services are less frequent. Fares are 90 centavos; to save time, purchase magnetic tickets in quantities of 2, 5, 10, and 30 rides. Two or more people may use the same ticket (legally) by passing it back and forth across the turnstile; you do not need a ticket to exit the system.

Before going through the turnstiles, be sure of the direction you're headed; at some stations, trains in both directions use the same platform, but at others the platforms are on opposite sides. Some stations have one-way traffic only; in those cases, the next station down the line usually serves one-way traffic in the other direction.

For complaints or problems, contact Metrovías's Centro de Atención al Pasajero (tel. 0800/555-1616 toll-free, www.metrovias.com.ar).

## SUBTE ROUTES

- **Línea A** begins at Plaza de Mayo in Monserrat and runs beneath Avenida Rivadavia to Primera Junta, in the barrio of Chacarita.

- **Línea B** begins at Avenida Leandro N. Alem in the Microcentro and runs beneath Avenida Corrientes to Federico Lacroze in the barrio of Chacarita, where it connects with the suburban Ferrocarril Urquiza. A recent northwesterly extension continues to

Scalabrini Ortiz station, Línea D

Tronador and Avenida los Incas and is due to reach Villa Urquiza.

- **Línea C** connects Retiro (which has northern suburban commuter surface rail lines) with Constitución, the transfer point for southern suburban commuter surface lines; Línea C also has transfer stations for all other Subte lines.

- **Línea D** begins at Catedral on Plaza de Mayo and runs beneath Avenida Santa Fe and Avenida Cabildo through Palermo and Belgrano to Congreso de Tucumán, in the barrio of Núñez.

- **Línea E** begins at Bolívar on the Avenida de Mayo and goes to Plaza de los Virreyes, in the barrio of Flores. At Plaza de los Virreyes, there's a light-rail extension known as the Premetro.

- **Línea H** now runs from Once (a transfer station with Plaza Miserere, on Línea A) in the north to Avenida Caseros in the south, with an additional transfer at Humberto Primo (connecting with Jujuy, on Línea E). Eventually, the Línea H will run north from Once to Recoleta.

goes to western destinations like Moreno, with connections to Luján. Unlike the immaculate, state-of-the-art Mitre, this is a rundown line on which vendors even sell switchblades.

Transportes Metropolitano (tel. 0800/666-358736) operates the Ferrocarril Roca from Estación Constitución, at Avenida Brasil and Lima, to the Buenos Aires provincial capital of La Plata and intermediate points, but its service and maintenance are poor.

## TAXI AND *REMIS*

Buenos Aires has an abundant fleet of taxis, painted black with yellow roofs. Since a spate of robberies that began some years ago, nearly all of them are now so-called radio taxis (which means you may call in advance for a cab). Some people prefer the security of phoning for a cab, but many if not most *porteños* still flag them down in the street. If in doubt, lock the back doors so that no one can enter the cab by surprise.

All regular cabs have digital meters. It costs about US$0.55 to *bajar la bandera* (drop the flag, i.e., switch on the meter) and another US$0.05 per 100 meters. Verify that the meter is set at minimum fare.

Drivers do not expect tips and sometimes, to avoid having to make change, will even round the fare *down*. It's best to carry small bills rather than have to rely on the driver's making change, especially if he has just come on shift. Since there are some dishonest drivers, before handing over the bill you may want to ask if he can change a large note, stating the amount of the note you're handing over.

*Remises* are radio taxis that charge an agreed-upon rate based on distance; the dispatcher will let you know the fare when you call, based on the pickup and drop-off points.

Hotels, restaurants, and other businesses will gladly ring taxis and *remises* for customers and clients.

## CAR RENTAL

Aggressive drivers, traffic congestion, and lack of parking make driving in Buenos Aires inadvisable, but some visitors may consider this option for excursions beyond the capital. To rent a car, you must show a valid driver's license and a valid credit card and be at least 21 years old.

Both local and international agencies maintain offices in Buenos Aires, where rental costs are typically lower than elsewhere in the country but higher than in North America. Since the 2002 devaluation, prices are more volatile, but they usually involve a fixed daily amount plus a per-kilometer charge; unlimited mileage deals are normally for rentals of a week or longer. Insurance is additional.

Prior to devaluation, Argentina had some of the most expensive gasoline in the Americas except for Uruguay, but prices have fallen in dollar terms—at least temporarily, even as they rose in peso terms. Regular gasoline now goes for about US$0.59 per liter, premium for about US$0.65 per liter, and super for about US$0.69 per liter. *Gasoil* (diesel) is typically cheaper than gasoline, about US$0.50 per liter, but the differential is shrinking. Because gasoline prices are unregulated, they may rise quickly.

Anyone driving in Buenos Aires should know that the Microcentro, bounded by Avenida Leandro Alem, Avenida Córdoba, Avenida de Mayo, and Avenida 9 de Julio, is off-limits to private passenger vehicles Monday–Friday 7 A.M.–7 P.M.

---

## CAR RENTALS

The following rental agencies have Buenos Aires representatives:

- **Avis:** Cerrito 1527, Retiro, tel. 011/4326-5542

- **Dollar:** Marcelo T. de Alvear 449, Retiro, tel. 011/4315-8800

- **Hertz:** Paraguay 1138, Retiro, tel. 011/4816-8001

- **Localiza:** Rivadavia 1126, Microcentro, tel. 011/4813-3184

- **Thrifty:** Carlos Pellegrini 1576, Local 24, Retiro, tel. 011/4326-0418

Cycling is an ideal way to get around Buenos Aires.

## BICYCLE

Cycling may not be the safest way of getting around Buenos Aires's chaotic traffic, but the number of cyclists has risen with the economic crisis. According to city government statistics, the number of cyclists rose by more than 50 percent from 2000 to 2001. For trips shorter than five kilometers, according to their calculations, the bicycle is both cheaper and faster than public transportation.

If riding around Buenos Aires, side streets may be safer than fast-moving avenues, but they are also narrower, with less room for maneuvering. Traffic is not so wild on weekends as on weekdays, and parts of downtown are virtually deserted on Sunday.

There are still few dedicated bike paths, except for the *bicisenda* that runs from Palermo to Retiro parallel to Avenida Figueroa Alcorta and Avenida Libertador. Cyclists should exit west at the *fin bicisenda* sign to avoid the *villa miseria* (shantytown) behind the Retiro train and bus stations. New bike lanes have appeared on Avenida San Juan and Avenida

Independencia, to be shared with automobiles, which must observe a speed limit of 40 km per hour.

The capital's main bicycle advocacy organization is the Asociación de Ciclistas Urbanos (Avenida Díaz Vélez 5563, Caballito, tel. 011/4981-0578, www.geocities.com/acubicicleta).

## WALKING

Thanks partly to its gentle topography, Buenos Aires is a walker's city or, one might even say, a jaywalker's city. Jaywalking is endemic, perhaps because it's not much more dangerous than crossing at the crosswalk with the light—for an overwhelming majority of *porteño* drivers, crosswalks are nothing more than decorative. While making turns, drivers weave among pedestrians rather than slowing or stopping to let them pass.

That said, in congested areas, pedestrians can often move faster than automobiles. In addition, barrios like San Telmo, La Boca, and the northern barrios of Recoleta, Palermo, and

Belgrano (with their shady sidewalks and expansive parks) are particularly rewarding to pedestrian explorers; the summer heat and humidity, though, make it essential to consume plenty of fluids. Thundershowers make an umbrella advisable.

## ORGANIZED TOURS

Some of the city's best guided tours are available through the municipal tourist office on Saturday and Sunday, often but not always with English-speaking guides. The *Buenos Aires Herald*'s Friday "getOut!" section and *Clarín*'s event section both contain listings, but the complete schedule also appears in *Cultura BA,* a weekly giveaway tabloid from the city government; they are also posted on the city government's website (www.buenosaires.gov.ar). In case of rain, the tours are canceled.

For conventional tours of the capital and vicinity, including the Microcentro, Recoleta and Palermo, and San Telmo and La Boca, a frequent choice is **Buenos Aires Visión** (Esmeralda 356, 8th fl., tel. 011/4394-2986, www.buenosaires-vision.com.ar).

Jorge Luis Borges's widow, María Kodama, leads fortnightly Borgesian tours, free of charge, sponsored by municipal tourism authorities and her own **Fundación Internacional Jorge Luis Borges** (Anchorena 1660, tel. 011/4822-8340); phone for schedules.

Highly recommended **Eternautas** (Av. Roque Sáenz Peña 1124, 4° B, tel. 011/4384-7874 or 15/4173-1078, www.eternautas.com) is an organization of professional historians

who offer inexpensive walking tours (as little as US$2) and longer half-day excursions, such as "El Otro Sur," a fascinating three-hour bus tour (US$5 pp) through working-class southern barrios like Barracas, Nueva Pompeya, Parque Patricios, and Boedo. They also go farther afield to such places as La Plata and Luján (including the historic Estancia Los Talas) for US$27.

Run by a Rick Steves' Europe guide who spends most of the year in Buenos Aires, **In Depth Travel** (tel. 15/5174-4440, www.indepth.com.ar) offers a variety of walking tours, including a distinctive art nouveau circuit (US$20 pp, 3–4 hours). English, Spanish, and Portuguese are spoken.

By its very name, **Tangol** (Florida 971, 1st fl., Local 59, tel. 011/4312-7276, www.tangol.com) combines those two *porteño* passions, tango and soccer in its offerings. It also does excursions farther afield, in Buenos Aires province and elsewhere. For a commercial website, it's surprisingly informative as well. **Travel Line Argentina** (Esmeralda 770, 10th fl., Oficina 34, tel. 011/4393-9000, www.travelline.com.ar) conducts specialty excursions, such as its "Evita Tour" (US$30, six hours), which takes in the CGT labor headquarters, Luna Park Stadium, the Perón and Duarte residences, and other locales associated with Evita's meteoric career.

One unique option is **Cicerones de Buenos Aires** (tel. 011/4330-0800, www.cicerones.org.ar), a nonprofit that matches visitors with enthusiastic non-professional guides who can provide a resident's perspective on the city.

# Visas and Officialdom

Citizens of neighboring countries—Bolivians, Brazilians, Chileans, Uruguayans, and Paraguayans—need only national identity cards to enter Argentina. In the Western Hemisphere, most other nationalities need passports; only Cubans, Belizeans, and a few others need an advance visa. Likewise, citizens of the European Union and Scandinavian countries and Switzerland, Israel, Australia, and New Zealand need only passports. Citizens of nearly all African and Asian countries, except for South Africa and Japan, need advance visas.

Regulations change, though, so check the visa page of Argentina's Ministerio de Relaciones Exteriores (Foreign Relations Ministry, www.mrecic.gov.ar/consulares.html). (See also the sidebar *Argentine Consulates in Other Countries* in this chapter for addresses and telephone numbers of key Argentine embassies and consulates.)

Argentina routinely grants 90-day entry permits to foreign visitors in the form of tourist cards that, theoretically, must be surrendered on departure from the country; in practice, it's the passport stamp that counts. For 100 pesos (US$33), the entry is renewable for 90 days at the Dirección Nacional de Migraciones (Av. Argentina 1355, Retiro, tel. 011/4317-0237, Mon.–Fri. 8 A.M.–1 P.M.).

In the provinces, renewal can be done at any office of the Policía Federal (Federal Police), but in smaller towns the police may not be accustomed to conducting renewals. Buenos Aires visitors may find it cheaper and simpler to take a day trip on the ferry to Colonia, Uruguay, which will reset the 90-day period.

Formally, arriving visitors must have a return or onward ticket, but enforcement is inconsistent—if you have a Latin American, North American, or Western European passport, for instance, it is unlikely you will be asked to show the return ticket. The author has entered Argentina many dozens of times over many years, at Buenos Aires's international airport and some of the most remote border posts, without ever having been asked for the return or onward ticket.

Airlines, though, may feel differently and not permit a passenger without a round-trip ticket to board a flight to Argentina. Likewise, if the arriving passenger comes from an Eastern European, Asian, or African country, he or she may be asked for proof of return transport. Immigration officials have a great deal of discretion in these matters.

Always carry identification, since federal and provincial police can request it at any moment, though they rarely do so without reason. Passports are also necessary for routine transactions, like checking into hotels, cashing travelers checks, and even payment by credit card, though a photocopy will usually suffice.

Dependent children under age 14 traveling without both parents presumably need notarized parental consent, but the author's daughter has visited Argentina many times with only one parent, and has never been asked for such a document.

Argentine-born individuals, if their parents were not Argentines or if they have been naturalized elsewhere, sometimes experience obstacles from immigration officials. Generally, they may enter the country for no more than 60 days on a non-Argentine document. Argentine passports renewed outside the country expire on reentry, making it necessary to renew them with the Policía Federal, a bothersome and time-consuming process on a short trip.

## LOST OR STOLEN PASSPORTS

Visitors who suffer a lost or stolen passport must obtain a replacement at their own embassy or consulate. After obtaining a replacement passport, it's necessary to visit the Dirección Nacional de Migraciones to replace the tourist card.

# FOREIGN CONSULATES IN ARGENTINA

As a major world capital, Buenos Aires has a full complement of embassies and consulates that provide services to foreign visitors. A country's embassy and consulate often share an address, but when the addresses are separate the list below provides the address of the consulate, as they are primarily responsible for dealing with individuals traveling for either business or pleasure.

- **Australia:** Villanueva 1400, Palermo, tel. 011/4779-3500, www.argentina.embassy.gov.au

- **Belgium:** Defensa 113, 8th fl., Monserrat, tel. 011/4331-0066, www.diplobel.org/argentina

- **Bolivia:** Adolfo Alsina 1886, Monserrat, tel. 011/4381-0539

- **Brazil:** Carlos Pellegrini 1363, 5th fl., Retiro, tel. 011/4515-6500, www.brasil.org.ar

- **Canada:** Tagle 2828, Palermo, tel. 011/4808-1000, www.dfait-maeci.gc.ca/argentina

- **Chile:** San Martín 439, 9th fl., Microcentro, tel. 011/4394-6582, www.embajadadechile.com.ar

- **Denmark:** Leandro N. Alem 1074, 9th fl., Retiro, tel. 011/4312-6901

- **France:** Santa Fe 846, 3rd fl., Retiro, tel. 011/4312-2409, www.embafrancia-argentina.org

- **Germany:** Villanueva 1055, Palermo, tel. 011/4778-2500, www.buenos-aires.diplo.de

- **Ireland:** Avenida del Libertador 1064, 6th fl., Recoleta, tel. 011/5787-0801, www.irlanda.org.ar

- **Israel:** Avenida de Mayo 701, 10th fl., Monserrat, tel. 011/4338-2500, http://buenosaires.mfa.gov.il

- **Italy:** Reconquista 572, tel. 011/4114-4800, www.ambbuenosaires.esteri.it

- **Japan:** Bouchard 547, 17th fl., Microcentro, tel. 011/4318-8200, www.ar.emb-japan.go.jp

- **Mexico:** Arcos 1650, Belgrano, tel. 011/4118-8800, www.embamex.int.ar

- **Netherlands:** Olga Cossentini 831, 3rd fl., Edificio Porteño Plaza 2, Puerto Madero, tel. 011/4338-0050, www.embajadaholanda.int.ar

- **New Zealand:** Carlos Pellegrini 1427, 5th fl., Microcentro, tel. 011/4328-0747, www.nzembassy.com

- **Norway:** Esmeralda 909, 3° B, Retiro, tel. 011/4312-2204, www.noruega.org.ar

- **Paraguay:** Viamonte 1851, Balvanera, tel. 011/4814-4803

- **Peru:** Florida 165, 2nd fl., Microcentro, tel. 011/4334-0970

- **Spain:** Guido 1760, Recoleta, tel. 011/4811-0070, www.mae.es/consulados/buenosaires

- **Sweden:** Tacuarí 147, Monserrat, tel. 011/4342-1422, www.swedenabroad.com

- **Switzerland:** Santa Fe 846, 10th fl., Retiro, tel. 011/4311-6491

- **United Kingdom:** Dr. Luis Agote 2412, Recoleta, tel. 011/4808-2200, www.britain.org.ar

- **United States of America:** Colombia 4300, Palermo, tel. 011/5777-4533, http://buenosaires.usembassy.gov

- **Uruguay:** Avenida Las Heras 1915, 5th fl., Recoleta, tel. 011/4807-3032

# ARGENTINE CONSULATES IN OTHER COUNTRIES

- **Australia:** Embassy – John McEwen House, 7 National Circuit, 2nd fl., Barton ACT, tel. 02/6273-9111, www.argentina.org.au

  Consulate – 44 Market Street, 20th fl., Sydney NSW, tel. 02/9262-2933

- **Bolivia:** Azpiazu 497, Sopocachi, La Paz, tel. 02/241-7737

- **Brazil:** Praia Botafogo 228, Sobreloja 201, Edificio Argentina, Rio de Janeiro, tel. 21/2533-1646

  Avenida Paulista 2313, Sobreloja, São Paulo, tel. 11/3897-9522

- **Canada:** 81 Metcalfe St., Ste. 700, Ottawa, Ontario K1P 6K7, tel. 613/236-2351, www.argentina-canada.net

  5001 Yonge St., Ste. 201, Toronto, Ontario M2N 6P6, tel. 416/955-9075, www.consargtoro.ca

  2000 Peel St, Montréal, Québec H3A 2W5, tel. 514/842-6582, www.consargenmtl.com

- **Chile:** Vicuña Mackenna 41, Santiago, tel. 02/582-2606

  Pedro Montt 160, 7th fl., Puerto Montt, tel. 065/282878

  21 de Mayo 1878, Punta Arenas, tel. 056/261532

- **France:** 6 Rue Cimarosa, Paris, tel. 1/4405-2700

- **Germany:** Kleiststrasse 23-26, 4th fl., Berlin, tel. 30/226-6890, www.argentinische-botschaft.de

- **New Zealand:** 142 Lambton Quay, 14th fl., Wellington, tel. 04/472-8330, www.arg.org.nz

- **Paraguay:** Banco Nación, 1st fl., Palma 319, Asunción, tel. 021/442151

  Artigas 960, Encarnación, tel. 071/201066

- **Switzerland:** Jungfraustrasse 1, Bern, tel. 31/356-4343, www.embargentina-suiza.org/

- **United Kingdom:** 27 Three Kings Yard, London W1Y 1FL, tel. 20/7318-1340, www.argentine-embassy-uk.org

- **United States of America:** 1811 Q St. NW, Washington, D.C. 20009, tel. 202/238-6471, www.embassyofargentina.us/

  5550 Wilshire Blvd., Ste. 210, Los Angeles, CA 90036, tel. 323/954-9155, www.consuladoargentino-losangeles.org

  1101 Brickell Ave., 5th fl., Miami, FL 33131, tel. 305/373-1889, www.consuladoargentinoenmiami.org

  245 Peachtree Center Ave., Ste. 2101, Atlanta, GA 30303, tel. 404/880-0805, www.consuladoargentinoatlanta.org

  205 N. Michigan Ave., Ste. 4209, Chicago, IL 60601, tel. 312/819-2610

  12 W. 56th St., New York, NY 10019, tel. 212/603-0400, www.consuladoargentinoennuevayork.com

  3050 Post Oak Blvd., Ste. 1625, Houston, TX 77056, tel. 713/993-0315

- **Uruguay:** Wilson Ferreira Aldunate 1281, Montevideo, tel. 02/902-8623, www.consuladoargentino.com.uy

  Avenida General Flores 226, Colonia, tel. 052/22086

## CUSTOMS

Notorious for truly egregious corruption, Argentine customs has improved from the days of the so-called *aduana paralela* (parallel customs) and normally presents no obstacle to tourists. Short-term visitors may import personal effects, including clothing, jewelry, medicine, sporting gear, camping equipment and accessories, photographic and video equipment, personal computers, and the like, as well as 400 cigarettes, two liters of wine or alcoholic beverages (adults over 18 only), and up to US$300 of new merchandise.

Customs inspections are routine, but at Buenos Aires's international airports, river ports, and at some land borders, incoming checked baggage may have to pass through X-ray machines; do not put photographic film in checked baggage. Fresh food will be confiscated at any port of entry.

A recent development for border-crossers is the Economy Ministry's currency declaration, intended to prevent money laundering and tax evasion. No visitor entering or leaving Argentina may carry more than US$10,000 in cash or travelers checks, without formally declaring that amount. Anything undeclared over the limit is subject to confiscation.

At some remote border posts, the Gendarmería Nacional (Border Guard) handles all formalities, from immigration to customs to agricultural inspections. Visitors arriving from drug-producing countries like Colombia, Peru, and Bolivia may get special attention at border posts.

## POLICE AND MILITARY

Argentina is notorious for police corruption. For this reason, *porteños* and other Argentines scornfully call both federal and provincial police *la cana*—an insult that should never be used to their faces.

The Policía Federal (Federal Police) are marginally more professional than provincial forces like that of Buenos Aires province; the latter is almost universally detested for harassing motorists for minor equipment violations and, even worse, for their *gatillo fácil* (hairtrigger) response to minor criminal offenses. This behavior is not completely unwarranted, however—many police officers have died at the hands of well-armed criminals (who are themselves sometimes police officers).

Police officers often solicit *coimas* (bribes) at routine traffic stops. To avoid paying a bribe, either state your wish to consult your consulate, or use broken Spanish even if you understand the language well. Either one may frustrate a corrupt official sufficiently to give up the effort.

Since the end of the 1976–1983 dictatorship, the Argentine military has lost prestige and appears to have acknowledged its inability to run the country, despite the occasional fringe group clamor in favor of a coup. Still, security is heavy around military bases and photography and video are taboo—signs that say *No Fotografiar o Filmar* are common.

# Food

## MEALS AND MEALTIMES

By North American and European standards, Argentines are late eaters except for *desayuno* (breakfast). *Almuerzo* (lunch) usually starts between 1 and 2 P.M., *cena* (dinner) around 9 P.M. or later. *Porteños* often bide their time between lunch and dinner with a late afternoon *té* (tea) usually consisting of a sandwich or some sort of pastry or dessert; it can be very substantial.

Since *porteños* often eat *after* the theater or a movie, around 11 P.M. or even later on weekends, anyone entering a restaurant before 9 P.M. may well dine alone.

## Breakfast and Brunch

Most Argentines eat only a light breakfast of coffee or tea with *pan tostado* (toast, occasionally with ham and/or cheese), *medialunas* (croissants), or *facturas* (pastries, also eaten for afternoon tea); *medialunas* may be either *de manteca* (buttery and sweet) or *salada* (saltier, baked with oil). *Mermelada* (jam) usually accompanies plain *tostados*.

An occasional side dish, eggs may be *fritos* (fried), *revueltos* (scrambled), or sometimes *duros* (hard-boiled). In some fashionable neighborhoods, such as Palermo Viejo and Las Cañitas, a more elaborate Sunday brunch has become an option.

## Lunch

Lunch is often the day's main meal, usually including an *entrada* (appetizer), followed by a *plato principal* (entrée) accompanied by a *guarnición* (side dish) and a *bebida* (soft drink) or *agua mineral* (mineral water) and followed by *postre* (dessert).

Upscale Buenos Aires restaurants customarily offer a fixed-priced weekday lunch (*menu ejecutivo*) that makes it possible to eat well and stylishly without busting the budget, but this is less common in the provinces. It's also possible to find local fast-food items like *hamburguesas* (hamburgers), sandwiches, pizza, and pasta without resorting to international franchises.

## Té

*Té,* the third of four meals in the typical Argentine day, can range from a late-afternoon sandwich to the equivalent of afternoon tea, with elaborate cakes and cookies, and is often a social occasion as well. Presumably intended to tide people over until their late dinnertime, it often becomes larger and more elaborate than its name would imply.

## Dinner

Dinner resembles lunch, but in formal restaurants it may be substantially more elaborate (and more expensive), and it can be a major social occasion. Argentines dine late—9 P.M. is early, and anything before that may earn incredulous "What are you doing here?" stares from waiters. The exception to this rule is at tourist-oriented areas, such as the Puerto Madero complex, where restaurateurs have become accustomed to North Americans and northern Europeans lodged at nearby luxury hotels, who often won't wait any later than 7 P.M.

## "Fast Food" Snacks

Argentina has some of the continent's best snack food. The best of the best is the empanada, a flaky phyllo-dough turnover most frequently filled with ground beef, hard-boiled egg, and olive, but it may also come with ham and cheese, chicken, onion, and (rarely) with tuna or fish. Also available in Buenos Aires, the spicier ground beef *salteña* comes from northwestern Argentina; the tangy empanada *árabe* (lamb with a touch of lemon juice) is harder to find. Empanadas *al horno* (oven-baked) are lighter than empanadas *fritas* (fried, sometimes in heavy oil).

Argentine pizza is also exceptional, though usually less diverse in terms of toppings than North American pizza. For slices, try the cheeseless *fugazza* with Vidalia-sweet onions or its cousin *fugazzeta,* enhanced with ham and mozzarella. Many *porteños* embellish their slices with *fainá,* a baked garbanzo dough that fits neatly atop.

## WHAT TO EAT

Argentina is famous for beef—in abundance—and grains, but fresh fruit, vegetables, and an underrated wealth of seafood add diversity to the country's cuisine. The stereotypical beef diet has serious shortcomings, and visitors will have no difficulty finding alternatives, especially in Buenos Aires.

According to historian John C. Super, whatever the Spanish invasion's negative consequences, it improved a pre-Columbian diet that was, by some accounts, nutritionally deficient (often protein-poor). In Super's opinion:

> The combination of European and American foods created diversified, nutritionally rich diets. Crop yields were higher than those in Europe, and longer or staggered growing seasons made fresh food available during much of the year. The potential for one of the best diets in the history of the world was evident soon after discovery of the New World. For Europeans, the introduction of livestock and wheat was an essential step in creating that diet.

When Europeans first set foot in South America, in the densely populated Andean region the staple foods were beans, squash, and a variety of potatoes and other tubers. The diet was low in animal protein—only the llama, alpaca, guinea pig, and wild game were readily available, and these not in all areas.

The Spanish introductions blended with the indigenous base to create many edibles found on Argentine tables today. European grains such as wheat and barley, which yielded only a four-to-one harvest ratio in Europe, reached at least two to three times that in the Americas. Furthermore, the abundance of seafood, combined with the increase of European livestock and the high productivity of European fruits, like apples, apricots, grapes, pears, and many others, resulted in a diverse food production and consumption system which, however, is changing today.

The stereotype that the Argentine diet consists of beef and more beef is not entirely mistaken, but local cuisine has always had a

Spanish touch and, for more than a century, a marked Italian influence. Though red meat consumption may be diminishing among more affluent Argentines, it remains the entrée of choice among lower classes. Thanks to the Italian influence, though, a diversity of pastas is available almost everywhere.

### Buying Groceries

Abundant across the city, supermarkets such as Coto, Disco, and Norte carry an abundance of processed foods but usually a lesser variety (and quality) of fresh produce than may be available in corner markets. Many of them, though, have cheap *cafeterías* with surprisingly good food.

In areas where supermarkets are fewer, almost all neighborhoods have corner shops where basic groceries and fresh produce are available, usually within just a few minutes' walk from wherever you're staying. Butchers are numerous, fishmongers less so.

### Vegetarianism

While vegetarian restaurants are relatively few except in Buenos Aires proper, the ingredients for quality vegetarian meals are easy to obtain, and many eateries prepare dishes, such as pasta and salads, which are easily adapted into a vegetarian format. Before ordering pasta, verify whether it comes with a meat sauce; in the Southern Cone countries (Argentina, Chile, Paraguay, and Uruguay), *carne* means "beef," and waiters or waitresses may consider chicken, pork, and similar products as part of another category—sometimes called *carne blanca* (literally, white meat). Faced with a reticent cook, you can always claim *alergia* (allergy).

### Grains

*Trigo* (wheat), a Spanish introduction, is most commonly used for *pan* (bread), but it's also common as pasta. *Arroz* (rice) is a common *guarnición* (side order).

*Maíz* (maize or corn) is a main ingredient in many dishes, including the traditional Italian polenta. Maize leaves often serve as a wrapping for traditional dishes like *humitas,* the northwestern Argentine equivalent of Mexican tamales.

## Legumes, Vegetables, and Tubers

Salads are almost invariably safe to eat, and all but the most sensitive stomachs probably need not be concerned with catching bugs from greens washed in tap water. (Note that restaurant salads are usually too large for a single person and often sufficient for two.)

*Porotos* (beans of all sorts except green beans) are traditional in families of Spanish descent. Other common legumes include *chauchas* (green beans), *arvejas* (peas), *lentejas* (lentils), and *habas* (fava beans).

In many varieties, *zapallo* or *calabaza* (squash) remains part of the traditional diet, as does the *tomate* (tomato). Many Old World vegetables are also widely consumed, including *acelga* (chard), *berenjena* (eggplant), *coliflor* (cauliflower), *lechuga* (lettuce), and *repollo* (cabbage). *Chiles* (peppers) are relatively uncommon; Argentine cuisine is rarely *picante* (spicy), except for dishes from the Andean northwest, and even those rarely challenge palates accustomed to Mexican or Thai cuisine.

Native to the central Andes, *papas* (potatoes) grow in well-drained soils at higher elevations in northwestern Argentina; *papas fritas* (French fries) are universal, but spuds also appear as *purée* (mashed potatoes) and in Italian dishes as *ñoquis* (gnocchi). Other common tubers include *zanahorias* (carrots) and *rábanos* (radishes).

## Fruits

Temperate Argentina produces many of the same fruits as Northern Hemisphere farms do, often available as delicious fresh juices. Items like *manzana* (apple), *pera* (pear), *naranja* (orange), *ciruela* (plum), *sandía* (watermelon), *membrillo* (quince), *durazno* (peach), *frambuesa* (raspberry), and *frutilla* (strawberry) will be familiar to almost everyone. When requesting *jugo de naranja* (orange juice), be sure it comes *exprimido* (fresh-squeezed) rather than out of a can or box.

Also widely available, mostly through import, are tropical and subtropical fruits like banana and *ananá* (pineapple). Mango, *maracuyá* (passion fruit), and similar tropical fruits are uncommon but not unknown.

*bife de chorizo*

© WAYNE BERNHARDSON

The *palta* (avocado), a Central American domesticate known as *aguacate* in its area of origin, often appears in Argentine salads.

## Meats and Poultry

Prior to the Spanish invasion, South America's only domesticated animals were the *cuy* (guinea pig, rare in what is now Argentina), the llama, the alpaca, and the dog (sometimes used for food). The Spaniards enriched the American diet with their domestic animals, including cattle, sheep, pigs, and poultry, including chicken and ducks.

*Carne,* often modified as *carne de vacuno,* or *bife* (beef) is the most common menu item in a variety of cuts. Among them are *bife de chorizo* (sirloin or rump steak), *bife de lomo* (tenderloin), *asado de tira* (rib roast), and *matambre* (rolled flank steak). *Milanesa* is a breaded cutlet or chicken-fried steak that, at cheaper restaurants, can be intolerably greasy.

The widest selection is usually available in the *parrillada* or *asado,* a mixed grill that includes prime cuts but also *achuras,* a broad term that encompasses offal such as *chinchulines* (small intestines), *mollejas* (sweetbreads), *criadillas* (testicles), *morcilla* (blood sausage), and *riñones* (kidneys). *Asado* can also mean a simple roast. *Chimichurri* is a garlic-based marinade that often accompanies the *parrillada.*

Sausages, such as the slightly spicy *chorizo,* may also form part of the *asado;* in a hot-dog bun, it becomes *choripán. Panchos* are basic hot dogs, while *fiambres* are processed meats.

*Cordero* (lamb), often roasted on a spit over an open fire, is a fairly common item from Argentine Patagonia, while farmed *ciervo* (venison) and *ñandú* (rhea) are becoming more common. *Cerdo* (pork) appears in many forms, ranging from simple *jamón* (ham) to *chuletas* (chops) to *lomito* (loin) and *matambre de cerdo* (pork flank). *Chivo* (goat) or *chivito* (the diminutive) is a western Argentine specialty that sometimes appears on menus in the capital; note that the Uruguayan *chivito* means something very different—a steak sandwich or plate slathered with eggs, fries, and other high-calorie extras.

Stews and casseroles include *carbonada,* which consists of beef, rice, potatoes, sweet potatoes, corn, squash, and fruit like apples and peaches, and *puchero,* of beef, chicken, bacon, sausage, *morcilla,* cabbage, corn, garbanzos (chickpeas), peppers, tomatoes, onions, squash, and sweet potatoes. Broth-cooked rice serves as a garnish.

*Ave* (poultry) most often means *pollo* (chicken), which sometimes appears as *gallina* (literally, hen) in a casserole or stew; eggs are *huevos. Pavo* (turkey) is becoming more common.

## Fish and Seafood

Argentina's fish and seafood may not have the international reputation of its beef, but an elongated coastline, extensive territorial seas, and huge freshwater rivers and lakes provide abundant options. Buenos Aires has some fine seafood restaurants, but these are less common in provincial cities and towns.

Seafood, among the most abundant sources of pre-Columbian animal protein, includes both *pescado* (fish) and *mariscos* (shellfish and crustaceans). The most common fish are *congrio* (conger eel, covering a variety of species, sometimes called *abadejo*), *lenguado* (sole or flounder), *merluza* (hake), and *trucha* (trout). *Salmón* (salmon) normally comes from Patagonian and Chilean fish farms.

Note that the cheapest restaurants often spoil perfectly fine fish by preparing it *frito* (overpoweringly deep fried), but on request almost all will prepare it *a la plancha* (grilled, usually with a touch of butter) or *al vapor* (steamed). Higher-priced restaurants will add elaborate sauces, often including shellfish.

Among the shellfish, visitors will recognize the relatively commonplace *almejas* (clams), *calamares* (squid), *camarones* (shrimp), *cangrejo* (crab), *centolla* (king crab), *mejillones* (mussels), and *ostiones* or *callos* (scallops, but beware—in Spanish restaurants, the latter word can also mean tripe), *ostras* (oysters), and *pulpo* (octopus). Spanish restaurants normally serve the greatest variety of fish and shellfish.

## Desserts

Many Argentines have a sweet tooth. At home, the usual *postre* is fresh fruit, ranging from grapes (many single-family homes have their own arbors) to apples, pears, and oranges. In restaurants, this becomes *ensalada de frutas* (fruit salad) or, somewhat more elaborately, *macedonia*. *Postre vigilante,* consisting of cheese and *membrillo* (quince) or *batata* (sweet potato) preserves, is another fruit-based dessert; it also goes by the name *queso y dulce.*

*Arroz con leche* (rice pudding) and *flan* (egg custard, often topped with whipped cream) are also good choices, as is the Spanish custard known as *natillas.* An acquired taste is *dulce de leche,* which one international travel magazine referred to as "its own major food group." Argentines devour prodigious quantities of this sickly sweet caramelized milk, spread on just about anything; at home, they often spoon it straight out of the jar and into their mouths.

Thanks to their Italian tradition, Argentine *helados* (ice cream) are popular everywhere, and the quality can be extraordinary where *elaboración artesanal* (small-scale production) is the rule. *Almendrado,* vanilla ice cream rolled with crushed almonds, is a special treat.

## WHAT TO DRINK
### Coffee, Tea, and Chocolate

Caffeine addicts will feel at home in Argentina, where espresso is the norm even in small provincial towns. *Café chico* is a dark viscous brew in a miniature cup, accompanied by enough sugar packets to make it overflow onto the saucer. A *cortado* comes diluted with milk—for a larger portion request a *cortado doble*—and follows lunch or dinner. *Café con leche,* equivalent to a latte, is a breakfast drink; ordering it after lunch or dinner is a serious faux pas.

*Té negro* (black tea) usually comes in bags and is insipid by most standards. Those wanting tea with milk in the British manner should ask for tea first and milk later; otherwise, they may get a tea bag immersed in lukewarm milk. Herbal teas range from the nearly universal *té de manzanilla* (chamomile) and *rosa mosqueta* (rose hips) to *mate de coca* (coca leaf), but sipping *yerba mate,* the so-called "Paraguayan tea," is one of the country's most deeply embedded customs.

Chocolate lovers will enjoy the *submarino,*

a bar of semi-sweet chocolate that dissolves smoothly in steamed milk from the espresso machine. Powdered chocolate is also available, but less flavorful.

## Water, Juices, and Soft Drinks

Tap water is potable almost everywhere except in some of the northerly tropical deserts; ask for *agua de la canilla.* For ice, request your drink *con hielo.* Visitors with truly sensitive stomachs might consider bottled water, which is widely available. Ask for *agua pura* or *agua mineral.* For carbonated water, add *con gas* or ask for the even cheaper *soda,* which comes in large siphon bottles.

*Gaseosas* (in the plural) are sweetened, bottled soft drinks (including most of the major transnational brands but also local versions, such as the refreshing tonic water Paso de los Toros).

Fresh-squeezed *jugos* (fruit juices) are exceptionally good though limited in diversity. *Naranja* (orange) is the standard; to be sure it's fresh, ask for *jugo de naranja exprimido.*

## Alcoholic Drinks

Argentina is the world's fifth-largest wine producer; historically, most production has been for domestic consumption rather than export, but this is changing and superb wines are now available. Most vineyards are in the western and northwestern provinces of Mendoza, San Juan, and Salta, but the northern Patagonian province of Río Negro is also making progress.

*Tinto* is red wine; *blanco* is white. Good wine is almost always reasonably priced, even during times of an overvalued peso and high inflation. The best restaurants have a wide selection of full bottles; it's sometimes possible to get a *media botella* (half bottle) or wine by the glass. Argentines often mix their table wines—even reds—with carbonated water and/or ice.

An increasing number of wine bars also offer Spanish tapas, sushi, and other light meals. Keep an eye out for the red Malbec, an Argentine specialty, and the white *torrontés,* a unique varietal that's best from high altitude vineyards around Cafayate, in Salta province.

Since the main wine regions are in western and northwestern Argentina, nowhere close to

Buenos Aires, wine tourism is not an easy option from the capital. With production booming across the Río de la Plata in Uruguay, though, there is an accessible Ruta del Vino in the outskirts of Montevideo.

Although Argentine wines are more than worthwhile, Argentines themselves lean more toward beer, which tastes best as *cerveza tirada* (direct from the tap) rather than from bottles or cans. The most widely available beer is Quilmes, produced in its namesake suburb across the Riachuelo from La Boca. In addition to beer, *sidra* (hard cider) from apple-rich Río Negro province is widely available, sometimes on tap.

Hard liquor is not quite so popular, but whiskey, gin, and the like are available. *Ginebra bols* (different from gin) and *caña* (cane alcohol) are local specialties. The legal drinking age is 18.

# Conduct and Customs

*Porteños,* like New Yorkers, have a stereotyped reputation for brusqueness and some of them complain that, especially in times of crisis, "nobody respects anybody here any more." In many contexts, though, they are remarkably courteous people.

Politeness goes a long way with bus drivers, officials, shopkeepers, and others with whom you may have contact. It's always good form to offer the appropriate polite greeting *buenos días* (good morning), *buenas tardes* (good afternoon), or *buenas noches* (good evening or good night), depending on the time of day.

In terms of general conduct, both women and men should dress conservatively and inconspicuously when visiting churches, chapels, and sacred sites. This, again, is an issue of respect for local customs, even if *porteños* themselves don't always observe it.

## VIVEZA CRIOLLA

Argentines in general, and *porteños* in particular, are infamous for *viveza criolla,* an inadmirable trait (roughly translatable as cunning, or perhaps guile) that somehow draws grudging respect in a country where playing by the rules often means being left behind. To achieve this sort of respect, though, you need to be successful at "artful deception."

Such was not the case for José María González, a former colonel and director of the army's Museo de Armas, who, just before his retirement in July of 2002, was shocked, *shocked,* to find valuable items missing. Soon afterward, federal police arrested him for sneaking at least 28 antique pieces out of the museum and into his private collection. The police also found a substantial illegal arsenal of modern firearms on the properties of González's presumed civilian accomplice.

An even more colorful example was the con-victed counterfeiter who, in the early independence years, falsified his own release papers from jail but had the misfortune to be executed for it. These days, many motorcyclists flaunt the traffic code by wearing helmets on their elbows, as apparently there's no requirement to use them on their heads (putting aside the question of where their brains are).

Certainly the best cinematic exploration of *viveza criolla* is Fabián Bielinsky's *Nueve Reinas* (Nine Queens), in which the con-men partners Ricardo Darín and Gastón Pauls match wits in tricking their victims (and each other, perhaps). In real life, the most famous example is probably Diego Maradona, who notched the winning goal against England in the 1986 World Cup, then praised "the hand of God" for helping him (finally, in early 2008, Maradona admitted to an English newspaper that He Himself directed the ball into the net).

# Tips for Travelers

## WORK

While the Argentine economy is recovering from its 2002 implosion, unemployment is still high and remunerative work can be hard to come by even for legal residents, let alone visitors on tourist or student visas. Nevertheless, foreigners have found work teaching English or another foreign language, working in the tourist industry, or doing casual labor in bars or restaurants. The problem with such jobs is that they either require time to build up a clientele (in the case of teaching) and may be seasonal (in the case of tourism) or poorly paid (in the case of restaurants, except in a handful of places where tips are high). Language teachers may find that few *porteños* can afford the luxury of one-on-one lessons.

Ideally, obtaining a work permit from an Argentine consulate is better than attempting to obtain one in-country, as employment may not begin until the permit is actually granted. Either way, the process requires submitting documents and takes some time. Some visitors, such as freelancers who do not receive payment locally, work without papers.

## BUSINESS

There are few if any legal limitations on foreign businesses operating in Argentina, but because of the lingering debt default, the climate has not been conducive to investment. While by-country risk assessments may no longer be featured like sports scores on the front page of *porteño* newspapers, Argentina ranks among the world's highest investment risks—by early 2008, this key statistic had risen to 603 compared to about 306 from two years earlier.

Corruption remains an issue. Political officeholders have an unfortunate reputation for shaking down foreign companies for bribes, and customs procedures can be trying despite increasing professionalization of the service. Intellectual property rights for computer software, CD and cassette recordings, and DVDs and videotapes are problematic.

The business dailies mentioned in the *Media* section of this chapter are good background sources on business, at least for those who read Spanish, as are magazines like *Apertura* (www.apertura.com). Though it often lags behind on events, the most thorough English-

---

## USEFUL BUSINESS ORGANIZATIONS

One critically important and unavoidable contact is the **Administración Nacional de Aduanas** (Azopardo 350, Monserrat, tel. 011/4338-6400, www.afip.gov.ar). If importing equipment for permanent use, it's essential to deal with them through a *despachante de aduanas* (private customs broker).

The **Cámara de Comercio de los Estados Unidos en Argentina** (U.S. Chamber of Commerce in Argentina, Viamonte 1133, 8th fl., Microcentro, tel. 011/4371-4500, www.amchamar.com.ar) is an organization run by and for U.S. businesses.

The **Cámara Argentina de Comercio** (Argentine Chamber of Commerce, Av. Leandro N. Alem 36, Planta Baja (ground floor), Micro-

centro, tel. 011/5300-9000, www.cac.com.ar) is an alliance of Argentine businesses, while the **Cámara de Importadores de la República Argentina** (Argentine Chamber of Importers, Av. Belgrano 427, 7th fl., Monserrat, tel. 011/4342-1101/0523, www.cira.org.ar) deals primarily with exports.

The **Bolsa de Comercio de Buenos Aires** (Sarmiento 299, 1st fl., Microcentro, tel. 011/4316-7000, www.bcba.sba.com.ar) is the city's stock exchange.

The **Sociedad Rural Argentina** (Argentine Agricultural Association, Florida 460, Microcentro, tel. 011/4324-4700, www.ruralarg.org.ar) is the traditional landowners' organization.

language source is the U.S. State Department's Country Commercial Guide service (www. export.gov, but easier to access through the U.S. Embassy in Buenos Aires: http://buenosaires.usembassy.gov). Its best bets for investment include travel and tourism services, computer equipment and software, management consulting, medical equipment, energy technology, building materials and supplies, and biotechnology.

While overseas investors have been cautious in recent years, some believe that Argentina may offer high yields on investments because devaluation has depressed prices in dollar terms. Residential real estate, for instance, has been a bargain, though prices are rising from the depths of 2002. In any event, before signing any business deal, consult a local lawyer recommended by your embassy, your consulate, or a trusted friend.

Conducting business is as much a personal and social activity as an economic one; even though initial contacts may be formal, with appointments arranged well in advance, topics such as family and sports are often part of the conversation. Formality in dress and appearance is less rigid than it once was, but in sectors like banking it's still the rule.

An ability to speak Spanish well is a plus, even though many Argentine business figures speak English (more than a few have been educated in English-speaking countries). The best months for business travel are April–November; in January and February, when school lets out and *porteños* take their summer vacations, the city can seem deserted.

## LANGUAGE STUDY

Buenos Aires's cultural resources and low cost of living have made it popular with students seeking to acquire a quick competence in Spanish or improve their language skills.

The Universidad de Buenos Aires (UBA) offers limited instruction at its **Laboratorio de Idiomas** (25 de Mayo 221, tel. 011/4343-1196, www.idiomas.filo.uba.ar). It also offers more intensive programs (15 hours weekly for one month, US$400) at its Centro Universitario de Idiomas (Junín 224, Balvanera, tel. 011/5238-3000, ext. 24, www.cui.com.ar).

The **Centro de Estudio del Español** (Reconquista 715, 11th fl., tel./fax 11/4315-1156 or 11/4312-1016, www.cedic.com.ar) offers a variety of options. Group instruction, four hours daily, costs US$120 pp per week, while individual tutoring costs US$9 hourly. In addition, it arranges housing.

In its Microcentro facilities, **Coined** (Suipacha 90, 2nd fl., tel. 011/4331-2418, www. coined.com.ar) has 20-hour weekly intensive group courses, with supplementary individual lessons as well. Rates start in the US$250–305 range, including accommodations.

The **Instituto de Lengua Española para Extranjeros** (ILEE, Av. Callao 339, 3rd fl., tel. 011/4782-7173, www.ilee.com.ar) offers conversation-based courses at various levels for US$200 per week, plus private classes (US$16 per hour). It will also help arrange accommodations.

For individual private tutoring, contact English-speaking Dori Lieberman (tel. 011/4361-4843, dori@sinectis.com.ar).

## TANGO

Often (but not always) inspired by films like Sally Potter's execrable *The Tango Lesson* or the Al Pacino vehicle *Scent of a Woman,* an increasing number of visitors come to Buenos Aires specifically—sometimes exclusively—to dance tango. It's not always what they expect; it's often better. Tango is an everyday presence and, if not quite 24/7, *milongas* take place every day and lessons are easy to arrange.

For those who do want to *live* tango 24/7, the **Mansión Dandi Royal** (Piedras 922, San Telmo, tel. 011/4307-7623, www.mansiondandiroyal.com) offers multi-day to one-week packages that include accommodations in its own boutique hotel, lessons from top instructors in its private salon, and interaction with *porteño milongueros* during its own regular Wednesday event, in a separate salon open to the public. They're also on top of the *milonga* scene elsewhere in town.

For individualized tango tours, try

At Tango Moda, Jorge Arias and his partner demonstrate their dancing passion.

**Tangofocus** (Santiago del Estero 145 4° H, tel. 011/4381-9153 or 15/4095-3023, www.tango-focus.com). It also has a U.K. contact address: 8 Mayhill Rd., Ross on Wye, Herefordshire HR9 7EU, tel. 44/7837/609388. California-based **Infusions Travel** (tel. 916/442-7191 in Sacramento, tel. 15/6475-7456 in Buenos Aires, www.infusionstravel.com) also specializes in tango, as well as shopping and fashion.

## TRAVEL WITH CHILDREN

In most ways, Argentina is a child-friendly country and Buenos Aires is a child-friendly city. In fact, since many Argentines have large extended families, some may feel little in common with people in their late 20s and older who do *not* have children. Traveling with kids can open doors.

Many of the capital's parks and plazas have playground equipment, and it's easy to mix with Argentine families there. What foreign parents may find unusual is that even toddlers may be out on the swings and slides with their families at 11 P.M. or even later. Additionally,

*porteño* kids are playing across the street, around the neighborhood, and even traveling on the buses and Subte at ages when nervous North American parents are driving their kids three blocks to school.

On public transportation, strangers may spontaneously but gently touch small children and even set them on their laps. While this may be disconcerting to non-Argentines, it's not necessarily inappropriate in cultural context.

Many cultural activities are child-oriented, particularly during late July's winter school holidays. Oddly enough, the Friday edition of the financial daily *Ambito Financiero* has the most complete listing of family events.

The northern barrios of Recoleta, Palermo, and Belgrano, with their spacious parks and playgrounds, are particularly good for children. Palermo's zoo is a favorite.

## WOMEN TRAVELERS

Like other Latin American societies, Argentina has a strong *machista* (chauvinist) element. Argentine women are traditionally mothers, homemakers, and children's caregivers, while men are providers and decision-makers, but there are increasing numbers of professional and other working women.

Many Argentine men view women—both foreign and Argentine—as sexually available. Harassment often takes the form of *piropos,* sexist comments that are often innocuous, even poetic, but are just as likely to be vulgar. It is best to ignore the comments, which are obvious by tone of voice even if you don't understand them. If the offender is persistent, seek refuge in a café or *confitería.* Some women have suggested wearing a bogus wedding ring, but truly persistent suitors might see this as a challenge.

Despite problems, women have acquired political prominence. The most prominent and notorious, of course, was Evita Perón, but her rise was an unconventional one. The highest-profile females in current politics are President Cristina Fernández, the wife of former president Néstor Kirchner, and populist politician

Elisa Carrió, a vociferous anti-corruption campaigner and former presidential candidate who, unfortunately, seems better at identifying problems than at offering solutions.

## GAY AND LESBIAN TRAVELERS

Like other Latin American countries, Argentina is culturally Catholic, but Buenos Aires has an active, visible gay scene focused around San Telmo, Barrio Norte, Recoleta, and Palermo Viejo. There are, however, gay-friendly venues throughout the city and even in the Paraná delta.

Demonstrative contact, such as kissing between males (on the cheek, at least) and holding hands for females, does not have the same connotation as it might in North America or some European countries. This does not mean that gay men and lesbians can always behave as they wish in public—the police have beaten and jailed individuals who have offended their sense of propriety. If in doubt, be circumspect.

The capital's leading homosexual organization is La Boca's Comunidad Homosexual Argentina (CHA, Tomás Liberti 1080, tel. 011/4361-6352, www.cha.org.ar). Early November's Marcha de Orgullo Gay (Gay Pride Parade) goes from the Casa Rosada to Congreso.

## TRAVELERS WITH DISABILITIES

For people with disabilities, Buenos Aires can a problematic city. The capital's narrow, uneven sidewalks, not to mention the fast-moving traffic, are unkind to people with disabilities, especially those who need wheelchairs. On the other hand, the city is fast installing ramps at intersections.

Public transportation can rarely accommodate passengers with disabilities, though the capital's newer Subte stations have elevators and others are being retrofitted. Avis has introduced rental vehicles that feature hand controls.

Few older buildings are specifically equipped, but many of them are low and can often accommodate people who have disabilities. Newer hotels are often high-rises, and disabled access is obligatory.

# Health and Safety

Midlatitude Buenos Aires and vicinity offer no major health risks beyond those associated with any large city; public health standards are good and tap water is potable. In some parts of northernmost subtropical Argentina, though, there's a small risk of malaria or similar tropical diseases.

A good general source on foreign health matters is Dr. Richard Dawood's *Travelers' Health* (New York: Random House, 1994), a small encyclopedia on the topic. Dr. Stuart R. Rose's *International Travel Health Guide* (Northampton, MA: Travel Medicine Inc., 2001) is regionally focused. Try also Dirk G. Schroeder's *Staying Healthy in Asia, Africa and Latin America* (Emeryville, CA: Avalon Travel Publishing, 2000).

For up-to-date information on health issues in Argentina and elsewhere in the Southern Cone, see the U.S. Centers for Disease Control (CDC) Temperate South America regional page (www.cdc.gov/travel/temsam.htm), which covers Argentina, Chile, Uruguay, and the Falkland Islands. Another good source is the United Kingdom's Department of Health website (www.doh.gov.uk).

## BEFORE YOU GO

Theoretically, no vaccinations are obligatory for entry to Argentina, but if you are coming from a tropical country where yellow fever is endemic, authorities might ask for a vaccination certificate.

Traveling to Argentina or elsewhere without

adequate medical insurance is risky. Before leaving your home country, obtain medical insurance that includes evacuation in case of serious emergency. Foreign health insurance may not be accepted in Argentina, so you may be required to pay out of your own pocket for later reimbursement. Often, however, private providers accept international credit cards in return for services.

Numerous carriers provide medical and evacuation coverage; an extensive list, including Internet links, is available at the U.S. State Department's website (www.travel.state.gov/Publications/medical.html).

## GENERAL HEALTH MAINTENANCE

Common-sense precautions can reduce the possibility of illness considerably. Washing hands frequently with soap and water, and drinking only bottled, boiled, or carbonated water will all help diminish the likelihood of contagion for short-term visitors—though Argentine tap water is potable almost everywhere.

Where purified water is impossible to obtain, such as back-country streams where there may be livestock or problems with human waste, pass drinking water through a one-micron filter and further purify it with iodine drops or tablets (but avoid prolonged consumption of iodine-purified water). Non-pasteurized dairy products, such as goat cheese, can be problematic and are best avoided.

## FOOD- OR WATER-BORNE DISEASES

While relatively few visitors to Argentina run into problems of this sort, contaminated food and drink are not unheard of. In many cases, it's simply exposure to different sorts of bugs to which your body soon becomes accustomed, but if symptoms persist the problem may be more serious.

### Traveler's Diarrhea

Colloquially known as *turista* in Latin America, the classic traveler's diarrhea (TD) usually lasts only a few days and almost always less than a week. Besides "the runs," symptoms include nausea, vomiting, bloating, and general weakness. The usual cause is the notorious *Escherichia coli* (more commonly called *E. coli*) bacterium from contaminated food or water; in some cases *E. coli* infections can be fatal.

Fluids, including fruit juices, and small amounts of bland foods, such as freshly cooked rice or soda crackers, may help relieve symptoms and aid you in regaining your strength. Dehydration is a serious problem, especially for children, who may need to be treated with an oral rehydration solution (ORS) of carbohydrates and salt.

Over-the-counter remedies, like Pepto-Bismol, Lomotil, and Imodium, may relieve symptoms but can also cause problems. Prescription drugs, such as doxycyline and trimethoprim/sulfamethoxazole, can also shorten the cycle. These may not, however, be suitable for children, and it's better for everyone to avoid them if at all possible.

Continuing and worsening symptoms, including bloody stools, may mean dysentery, a much more serious ailment that requires a physician's attention.

### Dysentery

Bacterial dysentery, resembling an intense form of TD, responds well to antibiotics, but amoebic dysentery is far more serious, sometimes leading to intestinal perforation, peritonitis, and liver abscesses. Like diarrhea, its symptoms include soft and even bloody stools, but some people may be asymptomatic even as they pass on *Entamoeba hystolica* through unsanitary toilet and food preparation practices. Metronidazole, known by the brand names Flagyl or Protostat, is an effective treatment, but a physician's diagnosis is advisable.

### Cholera

Resulting from poor hygiene, inadequate sewage disposal, and contaminated food, contemporary cholera is less devastating than its historic antecedents, which produced rapid dehydration, watery diarrhea, and imminent death without almost equally rapid rehydration.

While today's cholera strains are highly infectious, most carriers do not even come down with symptoms. Existing vaccinations are ineffective, so international health authorities now recommend against them.

Treatment can only relieve symptoms. On average, about 5 percent of victims die, but those who recover are immune. While not a common problem in Argentina, it's not unheard-of either, especially in northern subtropical areas.

## Hepatitis A

Usually passed by fecal-oral contact under conditions of poor hygiene and overcrowding, hepatitis A is a virus. The traditional gamma globulin prophylaxis has limited efficacy and wears off in just a few months. New hepatitis A vaccines, though, are more effective and last longer.

## Typhoid

Typhoid is a serious disease common under unsanitary conditions, but the recommended vaccination is an effective prophylaxis.

## INSECT-BORNE DISEASES

Argentina is not quite malaria-free but there's no danger in or around Buenos Aires; a few other insect-borne diseases may be present if not exactly prevalent.

## Dengue Fever

Like malaria, dengue is a mosquito-borne disease of the lowland tropics, but it's less common than malaria and rarely fatal. Often debilitating in the short term, its symptoms include fever, headache, severe joint pain, and skin rashes. While most people recover fairly quickly, there is no treatment. Uncommon but often fatal, the more severe dengue hemorrhagic fever sometimes occurs in children, particularly those who have suffered from the disease previously.

Eradicated in Argentina in 1963, the mosquito vector *Aedes egypti* is once again present as far south as Buenos Aires. There were several hundred confirmed dengue cases in lowland subtropical areas of Salta province in 1997, and outbreaks occurred in the northern provinces of Misiones and Corrientes in 2006 and 2007. In Buenos Aires, however, the odds of contracting dengue are low. The best prophylaxis is to avoid mosquito bites by covering exposed parts of the body with insect repellent or appropriate clothing.

## Chagas' Disease

Also known as South American trypanosomiasis, Chagas' disease is most common in Brazil but affects about 18 million people between Mexico and Argentina; 50,000 people die from it every year. Not a tropical disease per se, it has a discontinuous distribution—Panama and Costa Rica, for instance, are Chagas'-free.

Since it is spread by the bite of the conenose or assassin bug, which lives in adobe structures and feeds at night, avoid such structures (these still exist in the countryside); if it's impossible to do so, sleep away from the walls. Insect repellents carrying deet offer some protection. Chickens, dogs, and opossums may carry the disease.

Chagas' initial form is a swollen bite, which may be accompanied by a fever that soon subsides. In the long run, though, it may cause heart damage leading to sudden death, intestinal constipation, and difficulty in swallowing; there is no cure. Charles Darwin may have been a chronic Chagas' sufferer.

## HANTAVIRUS

Hantavirus is an uncommon but deadly disease contracted by breathing, touching, or ingesting feces or urine of the long-tailed rat. Primarily a rural phenomenon and most prevalent in the southern Patagonian area, the virus thrives in enclosed areas; avoid places frequented by rodents (particularly abandoned buildings). The disease normally loses potency when exposed to sunlight or fresh air, but a few hikers and farm workers have apparently contracted the disease in open spaces.

It is not a serious problem in urban Buenos Aires, but in July 2002 a veterinarian contracted the disease near the provincial capital of La Plata and later died.

## RABIES

Rabies, a virus transmitted through bites or scratches by domestic animals (like dogs and cats) and wild mammals (like bats), is a concern; many domestic animals in Argentina go unvaccinated, especially in rural areas. Human prophylactic vaccination is possible, but may be incompatible with malaria medication.

Untreated rabies can cause an agonizingly painful death. In case of an animal bite or scratch, immediately clean the affected area with soap and running water, and then with antiseptic substances like iodine or 40 percent-plus alcohol. If possible, try to capture the animal for diagnosis, but not at the risk of further bites; in areas where rabies is endemic, painful post-exposure vaccination may be unavoidable.

## SNAKEBITES

The federal capital does not have poisonous snakes, but the aggressive and highly venomous *yarará* (*Bothrops neuwiedi*) is a pit viper found in parts of Buenos Aires province and elsewhere in the country. The timid but even more venomous coral snake (*Micrurus coralinus*) is found is humid areas, such as the Paraná delta.

The *yarará,* whose venom paralyzes the nervous system, is responsible for most Argentine snakebite incidents, but such cases are uncommon. Death is not instantaneous and antivenins are available, but the wisest tactic is to be alert and avoid confrontation. If bitten, get to medical facilities as quickly as possible, but avoid excessive movement, which helps the venom circulate.

## SEXUALLY TRANSMITTED DISEASES

While AIDS is by far the most hazardous of sexually transmitted diseases (STDs) and certainly gets the most press, other STDs are far more prevalent and also serious if left untreated. All are spread by unprotected sexual conduct; the use of latex condoms can greatly reduce the possibility of contracting sexually transmitted diseases, but not necessarily eliminate it.

Most STDs, including gonorrhea, chlamydia, and syphilis, are treatable with antibiotics, but some strains have developed immunity to penicillin and alternative treatments. If taking antibiotics, be sure to complete the prescribed course, since an interrupted treatment may not kill the infection and could even help it develop immunity.

The most common of STDs is **gonorrhea,** characterized by a burning sensation during urination and penile or vaginal discharge; it may cause infertility. **Chlamydia** has milder symptoms but similar complications. **Syphilis,** the only major disease that apparently spread to Europe from its American origins in the aftermath of the Spanish invasion, begins with ulcer and rash symptoms that soon disappear; long-term complications, however, can include cardiovascular problems and even mental derangement. **Herpes,** a virus that causes small but irritating ulcers in the genital area, has no effective treatment. It is likely to recur, easily spread when active, and can contribute to cervical cancer. **Hepatitis B,** though not exclusively a sexually transmitted disease, can spread through the mixing of bodily fluids, such as saliva, semen, and menstrual and vaginal secretions. It can also spread through insufficiently sanitary medical procedures, inadequately sterilized or shared syringes, unsterile body piercing, and similar circumstances. Like Hepatitis A, it can lead to liver damage but is more serious; vaccination is advisable for high-risk individuals but is expensive.

## HIV/AIDS

As in most countries, HIV/AIDS (AIDS is *SIDA* in Spanish) is an issue of increasing concern. According to Argentina's Health Ministry, there are around 32,000 full-blown AIDS cases and some 124,000 HIV-infected individuals, but concerns are that the figure may be substantially higher—many carriers are probably unaware that they are infected.

HIV/AIDS is not exclusively a sexually transmitted disease (intravenous drug users, who can get it by sharing needles, constitute about 40 percent of cases here), but unprotected sexual activity is a common means of transmission; the use of latex condoms can reduce the possibility of infection.

Buenos Aires has several AIDS support and information organizations, among them Cooperación, Información y Ayuda al Enfermo de SIDA (Coinsida, Finocchieto 74, Constitución, tel. 011/4304-6664) and Línea SIDA (Zuviría 64, Parque Chacabuco, tel. 011/4922-1617).

## SUNBURN

Buenos Aires and vicinity lie within temperate latitudes comparable to those in the Northern Hemisphere. Sunburn here is not quite the serious problem it is in subtropical northern Argentina, where nearly vertical solar rays are far more intense. In southernmost Patagonia and Tierra del Fuego, ozone-destroying aerosols have permitted the entry of ultraviolet radiation, causing skin problems for people and even for livestock, such as cattle and sheep.

Still, sun worshippers in Argentina put themselves at risk even when the sun fails to break through the clouds. If you dress for the beach, use a heavy sun block; on city streets, walk in the shade whenever possible.

## TOBACCO

According to a 2005 survey, a little more than one third of Argentines between the ages of 16 and 64 smoke; tobacco is the direct cause of 40,000 deaths per annum. According to one survey, 3 out of every 10 Argentine *cardiologists* smoke, and few of them make any recommendation against smoking to their own patients. Former federal government health minister Ginés González García, however, made smoking a public health priority, and the city of Buenos Aires has implemented a highly effective campaign against smoking in public areas, including restaurants and bars.

Enforcement, though, is another issue entirely, as police routinely ignore even traffic-law violations, such as failure to observe pedestrian right-of-way and obligatory helmets

Since late 2006, Buenos Aires's anti-tobacco ordinance has proved surprisingly effective in bars, restaurants, and other businesses.

for motorcyclists. If faced with second-hand smoke in one of the few places where it's now expressly prohibited, such as buses or taxis, appeal to courtesy with a white lie, such as *"Soy asmático"* (I'm asthmatic).

The Unión Antitabáquica Argentina (Moreno 431, tel. 011/4343-3553, www.uata.org.ar, Mon.–Fri. 9 A.M.–1 P.M.) lobbies for clean indoor air. Sin Pucho (Tucumán 3527, tel. 011/4862-6913, sinpucho@infovia.com.ar) is an ex-smokers' support group.

## LOCAL DOCTORS

At present, thanks to devaluation of the peso, quality medical care is so cheap that in some cases it could justify a trip to Buenos Aires. Many if not most doctors speak English, some very fluently.

Public hospitals include the Hospital Rivadavia (Av. Las Heras 2670, Recoleta, tel. 011/4809-2002), and the Hospital Municipal Juan Fernández (Cerviño 3356, tel. 011/4808-2600). Visitors considering elective medical care, though, should choose private hospitals and clinics, especially since the economic crisis has strained the resources of public institutions.

The Hospital Británico (Perdriel 74, Barracas, tel. 011/4304-1082) is a highly regarded private hospital.

One of the city's best private clinics is Belgrano's Clínica Fleni (Montañeses 2325, tel. 011/5777-3200, www.fleni.org.ar), whose focus is pediatrics and neurology. It also has outstanding specialists in orthopedics. (Soccer star Diego Maradona did his detox here, and Argentine presidents have had arthroscopies here.)

Another exceptional institution is the Fundación Favaloro (Av. Belgrano 1746, Monserrat, tel. 011/4378-1200, www.fundacionfavaloro.org), whose specialty is cardiology.

The Instituto Oftalmológico Stefani (Juncal 2345, tel. 011/4826-7028) specializes in Lasik eye surgery.

## PHARMACIES

Pharmacies serve an important public health role, but also carry certain risks. Pharmacists may provide drugs on the basis of symptoms that they may not completely comprehend, especially if there is a language barrier; while the cumulative societal impact may be positive, individual recommendations may be erroneous.

Note that many medications available only by prescription in North America or Europe may be sold over the counter in Argentine pharmacies. Travelers should be cautious about self-medication even when such drugs are available; check expiration dates, as many expired drugs are not cleared off the shelf.

In large cities and even some smaller towns, pharmacies remain open all night for emergency prescription service on a rotating basis. The *farmacia de turno* and its address will usually be posted in the window of other pharmacies, or advertised in the newspaper.

## CRIME

Even though many Argentines believe assaults, rapes, homicide, and crimes against property are increasing, by almost any international standard Buenos Aires is a safe city. Because *porteños* keep late hours, there are plenty of people on the street at most times—rarely will you find yourself walking alone down a dark alleyway.

Still, certain precautions almost go without saying—most crimes are crimes of opportunity. Never leave luggage unattended, store valuables in a hotel safe, keep a close watch on your belongings at sidewalk cafés, and keep a passport photocopy that shows your date of entry into the country. Do not carry large amounts of cash (money belts or leg pouches are good alternatives for hiding cash and documents), do leave valuable jewelry at home, and do keep conspicuous items, such as photographic equipment, out of sight when possible. Do not assume that any area is totally secure.

If you should be accosted by anyone with a firearm or other weapon, do not resist. Although guns are relatively uncommon—knives are the weapons of choice—and truly violent crime against tourists is unusual, the consequences of a misjudgment can be lethal.

Certain barrios are more crime-prone than others. Parts of La Boca are inadvisable even during daylight hours, so keep alert as to your surroundings. San Telmo is reasonably secure in daylight hours, but requires caution at night, even though there are many restaurants and clubs in the area.

One disturbing phenomenon is the so-called *secuestro exprés* (express kidnapping), in which criminals hold an individual for a small ransom or, alternatively, force someone to withdraw money from an ATM. Far more common in Buenos Aires province than in the capital, such crimes have *not* targeted tourists—rather, they appear to concentrate on individuals whose movements are familiar to the kidnapper.

More common are crimes of distraction, in which a crook bumps a victim and spills a substance like ice cream or mustard; while the *mostacero* (mustard scammer) apologizes profusely and "helps" clean up the mess, an accomplice surreptitiously lifts valuable items. Pickpocketing occurs on crowded public transportation; carry wallets and other items of value in a front trouser pocket or, even better, an interior jacket pocket.

# Money

While traveling in Argentina, it makes sense to have a variety of money alternatives. International credit cards are widely accepted, and foreign ATM cards work almost everywhere. Because ATMs are open 24 hours daily, many visitors prefer this alternative, but it makes sense to have a cash reserve in U.S. dollars (still preferable to euros despite the dollar's weakness). Travelers checks may be the safest way to carry money, since they're refundable in case of loss or theft, but changing them outside Buenos Aires is a nightmarish experience even when stability reigns.

Prices throughout this book are given in U.S. dollars because of the Argentine peso's instability, but normally travelers will be paying in pesos. Nevertheless, merchants and services will often accept dollars at the prevailing exchange rate or sometimes at an even better rate.

If carrying an emergency cash reserve, use an inconspicuous leg pouch or money belt (not the bulky kind that fits around the waist, which thieves or robbers easily recognize, but a zippered leather belt that looks like any other).

## CURRENCY

Throughout the 1990s, money was a simple matter. The Argentine peso was at par with the U.S. dollar, which circulated almost interchangeably alongside it, but the economic collapse of 2001–2002 has complicated matters. Many merchants still accept cash dollars, but exchange rates vary and any change will come in pesos.

Banknotes exist in denominations of 2, 5, 10, 20, 50, and 100 pesos. Coins exist in denominations of 1, 5, 10, 25, and 50 centavos (cents), but 1-centavo coins are rare and most businesses generally round off prices to the nearest 5 or 10 centavos.

Counterfeiting of both U.S. and foreign currency appears to be increasing. Merchants will often refuse any U.S. banknote with the smallest tear or writing on it, but they will accept any peso note that is not flagrantly *trucho* (bogus). On any banknote, look for the conspicuous watermark with the initials of the historical figure depicted on it—J.S.M for José de San Martín on the five-peso note, for instance.

## EXCHANGE RATES

Following the debt default of early 2002, caretaker president Eduardo Duhalde's government devalued the peso from 1 to 1.4 pesos per dollar but, when that proved unsustainable, it floated the currency. After falling to nearly four pesos to the dollar late that year, it recovered to less than three pesos per dollar by early 2005. Since then the dollar has

Visitors watch the exchange rates in Colonia del Sacramento (Uruguay).

held its own and has even recovered to around 3.10. There are so many uncertainties in the Argentine economy, though, that the exchange rate remains a wild card.

Travelers with euros or British pounds, which have gained strongly against the dollar, will find that their money goes much farther at present. For the most up-to-date exchange rates, consult the business section of your daily newspaper or an online currency converter, such as www.oanda.com.

In Buenos Aires, the best sources on exchange-rate trends are the financial dailies *Ambito Financiero* and *Buenos Aires Económico*.

## CHANGING MONEY

During the 1990s (when the peso was at par with the dollar) changing money was a non-issue, as the two were virtually interchangeable. The early-2002 peso float and subsequent banking restrictions made banks, *casas de cambio* (exchange houses), and surreptitious exchanges relevant again, but the situation has since stabilized. However, the situation has fortunately stabilized after more than a year of chaotic banking restrictions.

ATMs, abundant and becoming universal except in a few remote areas, match the best bank rates and are accessible 24 hours daily. Unfortunately, they generally dispense large banknotes, often of 100 pesos and rarely smaller than 50 pesos. One way around this problem is to punch in an odd amount, such as 290 pesos, in order to ensure getting some smaller notes.

## TRAVELERS CHECKS AND REFUNDS

Despite the safeguards they offer, travelers checks have many drawbacks in Argentina. In addition to the time-consuming bureaucracy of changing them at banks and exchange houses, they often carry a substantial penalty in terms of commission—up to 3 percent or even more in many cases. Businesses other than exchange houses rarely accept them under any circumstances and, in out-of-the-way places, nobody will. Travelers checks, unfortunately, should be a last-resort means of carrying and changing money here; cash (despite its shortcomings) and ATM cards are better options.

## BANK TRANSFERS

Many Argentine exchange houses, post offices, and other businesses are affiliated with Western Union, making it relatively straightforward to send money from overseas. For a list of Western Union affiliates in Argentina, see their website (www.westernunion.com).

The American Express Money Gram is another alternative. AmEx has a large office in Retiro and affiliates throughout the country.

In an emergency, it is possible to forward money to U.S. citizens via the U.S. embassy in Buenos Aires by establishing a Department of State trust account through its Overseas Citizens Services (Washington, D.C. 20520, tel. 202/647-5225); there is a US$20 service charge for setting up the account. It is possible to arrange this as a wire or overnight mail transfer through Western Union (tel. 800/325-6000 in the United States); for details, see the State Department's website (www.travel.state.gov).

## CREDIT AND DEBIT CARDS

Credit cards have been common currency for many years and, in the aftermath of the peso crisis, when Argentines could not withdraw their savings, their use became even more widespread. Visa and MasterCard are most widely accepted, but there are inconsistencies—a significant number of businesses prefer American Express, sometimes to the exclusion of the others, or even Diner's Club. Debit cards are also widely accepted, at least those with Visa or MasterCard affiliation.

There may be drawbacks to using credit cards, however. During the 1990s boom years, Argentine merchants generally refrained from the *recargo,* a surcharge on credit card purchases because of slow bank payments. Many have reinstituted the *recargo,* which can be up to 10 percent, to cut their losses due to the peso's loss of value between the customer's

payment and the bank's reimbursement. Note that hotels in particular may offer equivalent discounts for payments in cash.

Fluctuating exchange rates may also affect the charge that eventually appears on your overseas account. If the rate has changed in the interim between your payment in Buenos Aires and its posting to the home account, it may be either greater or smaller in terms of dollars (or other foreign currency), depending on the peso's strength.

In general, *propinas* (gratuities) are *not* added to charges for restaurant meals. Keep some cash, either dollars or pesos, for tips.

To deal with lost or stolen cards, the major international credit card companies have local representatives: American Express (Arenales 707, Retiro, tel. 011/4310-3000); Diner's Club (Av. Santa Fe 1148, Retiro, tel. 011/4814-5627); MasterCard (Perú 143, Monserrat, tel. 011/4331-2088 or 0800/555-0507); and Visa (Av. Corrientes 1437, 3rd fl., tel. 011/4379-3300).

## COSTS

For most of the 1990s, Argentina was South America's most expensive country, so much so that even North Americans and Europeans found it costly. Wealthy Argentines, for their part, partied in Miami, Madrid, Rome, and other inexpensive destinations.

This anomaly was a function of former economy minister Domingo Cavallo's fixed exchange rate, which reduced previous hyperinflation to near zero. Cavallo's "convertibility" policy, however, also froze prices at a relatively high but unsustainable level that eventually made Argentine exports noncompetitive and brought the 2002 default.

Since the February 2002 float, followed by banking restrictions that limited the amount of money in circulation, Argentina has been a bargain for visitors who bring dollars or other hard currency. According to the Economist Intelligence Unit, Buenos Aires fell from being the 22nd most expensive city in the world to the 120th (of 131 surveyed). While a strengthening peso and renewed inflation have made things more expensive, by European or North American standards it's still economical, if not truly cheap.

Much, though, depends on the traveler's expectations. There are suitable services for everyone from bare-bones budget backpackers to pampered international business travelers. Budget travelers will find hotel rooms for US$10 pp or even less and some excellent values for only a little more money. Even hotels and resorts of international stature, like the Hyatt, Four Seasons, and Sheraton chains, had to lower their rates during the crisis. With the recovery, though, strong demand has meant rising prices at the upper end of the spectrum.

Likewise, meals can go for a couple dollars or even less at the simplest *comedores,* but restaurants with sophisticated international cuisine can charge a lot more; even the latter, however, often serve moderately priced lunchtime specials. Still, it's possible to eat exceptional food for half or less of what comparable meals would cost in Europe or North America.

Even now, truly frugal shoestring travelers can get along on US$25 per day or so for accommodations and food. For US$50 pp per day, it's possible to live very comfortably and eat well, and a budget of US$100 can buy you a lot. It's worth adding, though, that the volatility of Argentina's economy—hyperinflation was a recurrent phenomenon in the last half of the 20th century—makes it impossible to guarantee that prices will not rise.

## TAXES

Argentina imposes a 21 percent *impuesto al valor agregado* (IVA, value added tax or VAT) on all goods and services, though this is normally included in the advertised price; if in doubt, ask for clarification (*"¿Incluye los impuestos?"*). Tax evasion is a national sport, however, and hotel owners will often ignore the tax for payments in cash.

Foreign visitors making purchases intended for export can often get a legal IVA rebate upon leaving the country.

## TIPPING

In restaurants with table service, a 10 percent gratuity is customary, but in smaller family-run eateries, the practice is rare. Taxi drivers are customarily not tipped, but rounding off the fare to the next-highest convenient number is appropriate. Where there is no meter, this is not an issue.

## BARGAINING

Bargaining is not the way of life in Argentina that it is in some other Latin American countries, but in flea markets or crafts markets the vendor may start at a higher price than he or she expects to receive—avoid insultingly low offers or such a high offer that the vendor will think you a fool. Depending on your language and bargaining skills, you should be able to achieve a compromise that satisfies everybody.

Even in some upscale Buenos Aires shops, prices for items like leather jackets may be open to negotiation.

## STUDENT DISCOUNTS

Student discounts are relatively few, and prices are so low for most services that it's rarely worth arguing the point. In the case of foreign travel, however, students may be eligible for discount international airfares; consult student-oriented travel agencies and see *Getting There* and *Getting Around* in this chapter for details.

# Tourist Information

## MAPS

The Automóvil Club Argentino (ACA, Argentine Automobile Club, Av. del Libertador 1850, Palermo, tel. 011/4808-4000, www.aca. org.ar) publishes the country's most comprehensive series of maps, including the city road map *Carta Vial de Buenos Aires y Alrededores*. It also publishes excellent highway maps, including major city plans, of all Argentine provinces. Members of overseas automobile clubs like the AAA in the United States and the AA in Britain can buy these maps at discount prices.

For getting around town, though, street atlases, such as the annually updated *Guía Lumi* and *Guía T,* are the most useful resources, as they also have detailed bus itineraries and other information.

For topographic maps, visit the Instituto Geográfico Militar (Av. Cabildo 301, Palermo, tel. 011/4576-5576, www.igm.gov.ar).

## TOURIST OFFICES

The Secretaría Nacional de Turismo (Av. Santa Fe 883, Retiro, tel. 011/4312-2232 or 0800/555-0016, www.turismo.gov.ar) is open Monday–Friday 9 A.M.–5 P.M.; there's a branch at Aeropuerto Internacional Ministro Pistarini (aka Ezeiza, tel. 011/4480-0224), and another at Aeroparque Jorge Newbery (tel. 011/4773-9891). Both airport branches are open daily 8 A.M.–8 P.M.

The municipal Ente Turismo de Buenos Aires maintains information kiosks, all of which distribute maps and brochures and usually have English-speaking staff, at several locations: in the Microcentro (Florida and Diagonal Roque Sáenz Peña, Mon.–Fri. 9 A.M.–6 P.M. and Sat.–Sun. 10 A.M.–3 P.M., except May–Sept. Mon.–Fri. only); at Puerto Madero's Dique 4 (tel. 011/4313-0187, daily 11 A.M.–7 P.M.); at the Retiro bus terminal (tel. 011/4311-0528, Mon.–Sat. 7:30 A.M.–1 P.M.); in Recoleta (Av. Quintana and Roberto M. Ortiz, Mon.–Fri. 10:30 A.M.–6:30 P.M. and

Sat.–Sun. 11 A.M.–7 P.M.); and in San Telmo (Defensa 1250, Mon.–Fri. noon–6 P.M., Sat.–Sun. 10 A.M.–7 P.M.).

In addition, to help tourists who are crime victims, the Policía Federal operates a Comisaría de Turismo (Av. Corrientes 436, tel. 0800/999-5000 or 011/4346-5748), whose staff can handle English, French, German, Italian, Japanese, Portuguese, and Ukrainian.

## South American Explorers Club

With affiliates in Quito, Lima, and Cuzco, South American Explorers (Estados Unidos 577, San Telmo, tel. 011/4307-9625, www.saexplorers.org) is a nonprofit that provides information and other useful services (including use of their San Telmo clubhouse and its facilities) to both members (by subscription) and nonmembers (on a fee basis). It's open Monday–Friday 1—7 P.M., Saturday 1—6 P.M.

## FILM AND PHOTOGRAPHY

Color print film is widely available, color slide film less so. In any event, it tends to be cheaper in North America and Europe than in Argentina, so it's best to bring as much as possible. If purchasing film in Argentina, check the expiration date to make sure it's current, especially in out-of-the-way places. In the capital and larger tourist centers, competent print-film processing is readily available and moderately priced. However, it's better to hold slide film until your return to your home country if possible (but store it under cool, dark, and dry conditions) or to visit a specialist, such as Kinefot (Talcahuano 250, tel. 011/4374-7445). For prints, try Le Lab (Viamonte 624, tel. 011/4322-2785).

Environmental conditions can affect the quality of your photographs and the type of film you should use. Bright sun can wash out photographs; in these circumstances, it's best to use a relatively slow film, around ASA 64 or 100, and a polarizing filter to reduce glare. A polarizing filter also improves

## PHOTOGRAPHIC ETIQUETTE – AND A WARNING

Most Argentines, especially *porteños*, are not exactly camera-shy, but do be cautious about photographing political protests – the police are notorious for cataloging dissidents, so protestors may be wary or even hostile toward unknowns with cameras. Likewise, avoid taking photographs in the vicinity of military installations, although "The Sentry Will Shoot" signs are a thing of past.

Generally, if a person's presence in a photograph is incidental, as in a townscape, it's unnecessary to ask permission, but avoid the in-your-face approach. If in doubt, ask;

if rejected, don't insist. If you're purchasing something from a market vendor, he or she will almost certainly agree to a photographic request.

There is one absolute no-no – without explicit permission, do not even think about photographing Israeli or Jewish community sites anywhere in the country. Since car-bomb attacks on Retiro's Israeli Embassy in 1992 and Once's Jewish cultural center in 1994, federal police are stationed outside all of these sites. They will politely or, if necessary, not so politely, discourage would-be photographers.

contrast, dramatizing the sky and the clouds, but can result in a dark foreground if you're not careful.

In the basement of Retiro's Galería Buenos Aires, Gerardo Föhse (Florida 835, Local 37, tel. 011/4311-1139) can do basic camera repairs. Dependable José Norres (Lavalle 1569, 4th fl., Oficina 403, tel. 011/4373-0963) can perform more complex repairs except on some of the latest electronic equipment, and service is quick.

# Communications and Media

Buenos Aires is a modern city, and as such the communications infrastructure is similar to what you'd expect in other large cities around the developed world.

## POSTAL SERVICES

The privatized Correo Argentino, the Argentine post office, has meant more reliable service than in the past, but recent disagreements have brought government intervention. Domestic services are generally cheap, international services more expensive. Major international couriers provide fast, reliable services at premium prices.

The landmark Correo Central (Sarmiento 189, Mon.–Fri. 9 A.M.–7:30 P.M.) is worth a visit in its own right, but there are many other branch offices. The main building occupies an entire block bounded by Sarmiento, Avenida L. N. Alem, Avenida Corrientes, and Bouchard. General delivery at Argentine post offices is

*lista de correos,* literally a list arranged in alphabetical order. There is a small charge for each item addressed to you.

Note that in Spanish-language street addresses the number follows, rather than precedes, the name; the U.S. address "1343 Washington Avenue," for example, would read, "Avenida Washington 1343" in Argentina. Argentines and other Spanish speakers normally omit the word *calle* (street) from addresses; whereas an English speaker might write, "499 Jones Street," an Argentine would simply use "Jones 499," for example. It is not unusual for street addresses to lack a number, as indicated by *s/n* (*sin número,* without a number), especially in small provincial towns.

International parcels that weigh in excess of one kilogram must leave from the Correo Internacional (Antártida Argentina, tel. 011/4316-7777, Mon.–Fri. 11 A.M.–5 P.M.), near the Retiro train station.

The Correo Central is Buenos Aires's main post office.

Private couriers include DHL International (Moreno 927, Monserrat, tel. 011/4630-1110) and the Microcentro's Federal Express (Maipú 753, tel. 011/4393-6054).

## TELEPHONE AND FAX

Argentina has two major telephone companies, Telecom (north of Av. Córdoba) and Telefónica (south of Av. Córdoba). The country code is 54; the *característica* (area code) for the Capital Federal and Gran Buenos Aires is 11, but there is a bewildering number of area codes for individual cities, smaller cities and towns, and rural areas. All telephone numbers in the Capital Federal and Gran Buenos Aires have eight digits, while those in other provincial cities and rural areas vary. When calling out of the area code, it's necessary to dial zero first.

Cellular phone numbers in Buenos Aires all have eight digits and the prefix 15. Certain toll-free and other specialty numbers have six or seven digits with a three-digit prefix.

Public telephones are abundant; some of them operate with coins only, but most also accept magnetic phone cards or rechargeable-account cards. The basic local phone rate is 25 centavos (about US$0.09) for five minutes or so; domestic long distance is considerably more expensive. Phone cards are convenient for in-country calls but less useful for more expensive overseas calls.

For long distance and overseas calls and fax services, it's simplest to use *locutorios* (call centers), which are abundant in both Buenos Aires and the provinces. Prices are increasingly competitive, and now tend to be much cheaper than placing *cobro revertido* (collect) or *tarjeta de crédito* (credit card) calls to the United States or any other country. Calls are more expensive during peak hours, Monday–Friday 8 A.M.–8 P.M. and Saturday 8 A.M.–1 P.M.

### Cellular Phone Rental

Opening a cell phone account without a permanent Argentine address is something of a nuisance, but rental phones are available from Nolitel (tel. 011/4311-3500, www.nolitelgroup.com). It's also getting easier to buy phones with pre-paid card service from most of the major providers, such as CTI. Many upscale hotels include cell phones in their rates, but guests are liable for the calls.

## INTERNET ACCESS

In the last few years, public Internet access has become so ubiquitous that no single locale really needs mentioning. Many *locutorios* offer access, but there are also numerous Internet cafés with broadband. Some Internet service providers, most notably AOL, Compuserve, and Earthlink, have local dial-up numbers in Argentina, but these often collect a surcharge for modem access.

Internet services are also so cheap that, if price trends continue, providers will be paying customers to use their services. Rarely does access cost more than US$1 per hour, and it's often even cheaper.

## MEDIA
### Newspapers and Magazines

Historically, freedom of the press has been tenuous, as Argentine governments have controlled the supply of newsprint and withheld official advertising from newspapers and magazines that have published items not to their liking. Nevertheless, since the end of the 1976–1983 dictatorship, the trend has been largely positive for liberty of expression. Many of the newspapers and periodicals below have websites listed in the *Internet Resources.*

Though it's the Spanish-speaking world's largest-circulation daily, the middle-of-the-road tabloid *Clarín* (www.clarin.com.ar) is more sensitive to hard economic times than papers with a steadier niche clientele. Part of a consortium that includes TV and radio outlets, it also publishes the sports daily *¡Olé!.*

According to Anglo-Argentine journalist Andrew Graham-Yooll, you're not really dead until your obituary appears in the center-right *La Nación* (www.lanacion.com.ar)—a remark that reflects the social standing of the capital's most venerable daily, dating from 1870. With a circulation of nearly 200,000—twice that on Sunday, when it has an exceptional cultural section—the paper was the creation of Bartolomé Mitre, who later became president.

The Buenos Aires daily *La Nación*'s local bureau reports on Argentine doings in Punta del Este.

*Página 12* (www.pagina12web.com.ar) is the tabloid voice of Argentina's intellectual left and, while its outspokenness is admirable, it would benefit from more rigorous editing—many articles are far too long and indulge in hyper-analysis. Political columnist Horacio Verbitsky is one of the country's most famous and capable journalists, however.

*Crónica,* with a weekday circulation of 400,000 but far fewer on weekends, is a crime-and-celebrities tabloid. *Diario Popular* is somewhat less sensationalist, but in the same vein.

The capital has three financial newspapers, which publish weekdays only: the morning *Ambito Financiero* (www.ambitoweb.com), which also publishes an outstanding arts and entertainment section, the afternoon *El Cronista Comercial* (www.cronista.com), and *Buenos Aires Económico* (www.infobae.com).

With a circulation of only about 15,000, *Buenos Aires Herald* is an English-language daily whose niche market correlates highly with hotel occupancy. It stresses commerce and finance but also produces intelligent analyses of political and economic developments; its Sunday edition includes material from the *The New York Times* and Britain's *Guardian Weekly.*

The German-language *Argentinisches Tageblatt* (www.tageblatt.com.ar) began as a daily in 1889, but is now a Saturday weekly with a circulation of about 10,000.

*Noticias* is the *porteño* counterpart to English-language weeklies like *Time* and *Newsweek. Trespuntos,* though, is more critical and innovative. *La Maga* (www.lamaga.com.ar) is an arts-oriented monthly.

## Radio and Television

What was once a state broadcast monopoly is now more diverse, thanks to privatization and the advent of cable, but conglomerates like the Clarín and El Cronista groups now control much of the content. Both radio and TV tend to stress entertainment at the expense of journalism. TV news coverage, however, can be surprisingly good, and there is even a 24-hour tango channel on cable.

Radio Rivadavia, Argentina's most popular station (AM 630), plays popular music and also hosts talk programs. Radio Mitre (AM 790) is the voice of the Clarín group. FM Tango 92.7 plays all tango all the time, and Radio Folclorísimo (AM 1410) plays folk music 24/7.

## LIBRARIES

The Biblioteca Nacional (National Library, Agüero 2502, Recoleta, tel. 011/4808-6000, www.bibnal.edu.ar, Mon.–Fri. 9 A.M.–9 P.M., Sat.–Sun. noon–7 P.M.) offers guided tours at 3 P.M. daily except Sunday, from March to mid-December only. It also holds frequent special exhibitions, lectures, literary events, and free concerts.

The United States Information Agency's Biblioteca Lincoln is at the Instituto Cultural Argentino-Norteamericano (Maipú 672, tel. 011/4322-3855 or 011/4322-4557).

## BOOKSTORES

Buenos Aires has countless general-interest bookstores, as well as specialist shops that deal with academic and rare books, and others with English-language materials. (For details, see the *Shops* chapter.)

# Weights and Measures

## TIME

Argentina is three hours behind GMT for most of the year and normally does not observe daylight savings time (summer time). Because of an energy crisis in the summer of 2008, though, the government introduced daylight savings as an emergency measure until mid-March. Whether it will continue and when it might restart is uncertain.

Because of a drought-induced energy shortage—almost all its power comes from hydroelectricity—Uruguay now observes daylight savings time all year.

## ELECTRICITY

Throughout the country, nearly all outlets are 220 volts and 50 cycles, so converters are necessary for North American appliances, such as computers and electric razors (unless they are dual voltage). Plugs have recently changed to a pair of flat diagonal prongs; appliances using two rounded prongs still exist, and adapters are easy to find. Adequately powered converters are harder to find, so it's better to bring one from overseas.

## MEASUREMENTS

The metric system is official, but Argentines use a variety of vernacular measures in everyday life. Rural folk often use the Spanish *legua* (league) of about five kilometers as a measure of distance, and the *quintal* of 46 kilos is also widely used, especially in wholesale markets and agricultural statistics.

# RESOURCES

## Glossary

**aduana** customs

**aduana paralela** parallel customs, corrupt customs officials

**albergue juvenil** youth hostel, though the English word "hostel" is now in common usage as well

**albergue transitorio** a by-the-hour-hotel, frequently used by young and not-so-young couples in search of privacy; also called a *telo*

**anexo** telephone extension

**arrabales** geographically and socially peripheral parts of the city, identified with immigrants and the rise of the tango

**asambleas populares** neighborhood assemblies of protestors and activists frustrated with Argentine institutions

**avenida** avenue

**balneario** bathing or beach resort

**barrancas** high ground on the original banks of the Río de Plata, now far inland in San Telmo, Belgrano, and other parts of Buenos Aires because of continual landfill

**barras bravas** soccer hooligans, violent gangs affiliated with soccer teams

**barrio** neighborhood

**boleadoras** rounded stones tied together with a leather thong and used for hunting by indigenous people of La Pampa

**bono** bond, a provincial letter of credit serving as a parallel currency equivalent to the peso

**bronca** a singularly *porteño* combination of aggravation and frustration; there is no precise English equivalent; the closest meaning is wrath or, in Britain, aggro (the latter according to former *Buenos Aires Herald* editor Andrew Graham-Yooll)

**cabildo** colonial governing council

**caipirinha** a popular drink made with *cachaça* (Brazilian liquor made from distilled sugarcane juice), lime, and sugar

**cajero automático** automatic teller machine (ATM)

**camioneta** pickup truck

**candombe** music and dance of Afro-Argentine *porteños*, of whom few remain

**característica** telephone area code

**carne** beef; other kinds of meat are *carne blanca* (literally, white meat)

**cartelera** discount ticket agency

**casa chorizo** sausage house, a narrow residence on a deep lot

**casa de cambio** money-exchange facility, often just *cambio*

**casco** big house of an *estancia*

**casilla** post office box

**caudillo** in early independence times, a provincial warlord, though the term is often used for any populist leader, such as Juan Domingo Perón

**cerro** hill

**chamamé** accordion-based folk music of the northeastern Argentine littoral

**chopp** draft beer

**ciruja** literally surgeon, a scavenger who picks recyclables from the garbage on Buenos Aires streets; synonymous with *cartonero*

**cobro revertido** collect or reverse-charge telephone call

**cocoliche** pidgin blend of Italian and Spanish spoken by Mediterranean European immigrants

**coima** bribe

**colectivo** a city bus

**comedor** simple eatery or dining room

**confitería** a restaurant/café with a menu of *minutas* (short orders)

**conventillo** tenement, often an abandoned mansion taken over by squatters

**corralito** unpopular banking restriction imposed by the Argentine government during the 2001-2002 debt default and devaluation

**costanera** any road along a seashore, lakeshore, or riverside

**criollo** in colonial times, an Argentine-born Spaniard; in the present, normally a descriptive term meaning traditionally Argentine

**desaparecido** disappeared one, victim of the 1976-1983 military dictatorship

**descamisados** shirtless ones, working-class followers of Juan and Evita Perón

**dique** deep-water basin dredged in Buenos Aires harbor

**doble tracción** four-wheel drive, also known as *cuatro por cuatro* (the latter written as 4X4)

**edificio** building

**escrache** public demonstration, originally identifying human-rights violators at their residences, but since extended to perceived corrupt officials and institutions

**estancia** cattle or sheep ranch controlling large expanses of land, often with an absentee owner, a dominant manager, and resident employees

**estatuas vivas** living statues, mimes in touristed areas of Buenos Aires

**estero** estuary

**farmacia de turno** pharmacy remaining open all night for emergencies, on a rotating basis

**feria** outdoor crafts or antiques fair; alternately, an outdoor bookstall

**fichas** tokens, formerly used on the Buenos Aires subway

**filete** traditional art of *porteño* sign painters, in a calligraphic style

**fileteador** *filete* artist

**gasoil** diesel fuel

**gauchesco** adjective describing romantic art or literature about (not by) gauchos

**golfo** gulf

**golpe de estado** coup d'etat

**hipódromo** horserace track

**hospedaje** family-run lodging

**indígena** indigenous person

**indigenista** adjective describing romantically pro-indigenous literature, music, and art

**infracción** traffic violation

**isla** island

**islote** islet

**istmo** isthmus

**IVA** *impuesto de valor agregado*, or value added tax (VAT)

**lago** lake

**laguna** lagoon

**latifundio** large landholding, usually an *estancia*

**local** numbered office or locale, at a given street address

**locutorio** telephone call center

**lunfardo** *porteño* street slang that developed in working-class immigrant barrios like La Boca but is now more widely used in Argentine Spanish, though not in formal situations

**machista** male chauvinist

**malevo** street bully

**media pensión** half board (rates include breakfast and either lunch or dinner) at a hotel or guesthouse

**menú** menu; also, a fixed-price meal

**mestizo** individual of mixed indigenous and Spanish ancestry

**milonga** informal neighborhood dance club, which often includes tango as a participatory rather than spectator activity

**minuta** a short-order meal, such as pasta

**mirador** overlook or viewpoint

**museo** museum

**ñoqui** ghost employee, collecting a state salary despite performing little or no work; literally, gnocchi

**palacete** mansion

**pampa** broad, flat expanse in and around Buenos Aires

**pampero** southwesterly cold front

**parada** bus stop

**parque nacional** national park

**partido** administrative subdivision of an Argentine province, equivalent to a county

**paseaperros** professional dog walker

*payador* spontaneous gaucho singer

*peaje* tollbooth

*peatonal* pedestrian mall

*pensión* family-run accommodation

*pensión completa* full board, at a hotel or guesthouse

*picante* spicy-hot; the Argentine tolerance for spicy food is very low, however, and most visitors may find foods labeled *picante* to be relatively bland

*piquete* protestors' roadblock

*piropo* sexist remark, ranging from humorous and innocuous to truly vulgar; also, on *filete*, an aphorism

*playa* beach

*polideportivo* sports club

*porteño* native or resident of Buenos Aires

*propina* tip, as at a restaurant

*puente* bridge

*puerto* port

Pullman first-class bus, with reclining seats and luggage storage underneath

*pulpería* general store, usually in a rural area

*quinta* country estate

radio taxi a taxi that is available by appointment rather than hailed on the street

*recargo* surcharge on credit-card purchases

*remis* meterless radiotaxi charging a fixed rate within a given zone

*residencial* permanent budget accommodations, often also called hotel

*restó* self-styled trendy restaurant, whose food may or may not match its aspirations

*río* river

*rotisería* delicatessen

*ruta* route or highway

*saladero* meat-salting plant of late colonial and early republican times

s/n *sin número*, a street address without a number

*sudestada* cold wind out of the southeast

*tango canción* tango song, with music and lyrics expressing nostalgia

*tanguero* tango dancer

*tarifa mostrador* hotel rack rate

*tenedor libre* all-you-can-eat restaurant (literally free fork)

*toldo* tent of animal skins, inhabited by mobile indigenous people of the pampas in pre-Columbian times

*trasnoche* late-night cinema showing

*trucho* bogus

*turco* Argentine of Middle Eastern descent (literally, Turk)

*villa miseria* urban shantytown

*viveza criolla* artful deception, ranging from small-scale cheating to audacious chutzpah

# Spanish Phrasebook

Spanish is Argentina's official language, but the stereotypical *porteño* intonation – equivalent to a Bronx accent in New York – is unmistakably different from any other variant. Argentine Spanish in general is distinctive, often Italian-inflected, most notable for pronouncing the "ll" diphthong and "y" as "zh." "Llegar" (to arrive), for example, is pronounced "zhe-gar," while "yo" (I) is pronounced "zho."

Another distinguishing feature is the use of the familiar pronoun "vos" instead of "tu." Verb forms of the *voseo* differ from those of the *tuteo*, although Argentines will always understand speakers who use "tu."

At tourist offices, airlines, travel agencies, and upscale hotels, English is often spoken. In the provinces, it's less common, though its use is spreading, especially in the travel and tourism sector.

Visitors spending any length of time in Buenos Aires, especially students and business people, might look for Tino Rodríguez's *Primer Diccionario de Sinónimos del Lunfardo* (Buenos Aires: Editorial Atlántida, 1987), which defines *porteño* street slang. Note that some usage requires *great* caution for those unaware of *every* slang meaning.

## PRONUNCIATION GUIDE

Spanish is a more phonetic language than English, but there are still occasional variations in pronunciation, especially in Argentina.

### Consonants

**c** as 'c' in "cat," before 'a,' 'o,' or 'u'; like 's' before 'e' or 'i'

**d** as 'd' in "dog," except between vowels; then, like 'th' in "that"

**g** before 'e' or 'i,' like the 'ch' in Scottish "loch"; elsewhere like 'g' in "get"

**h** always silent

**j** like the English 'h' in "hotel," but stronger

**ll** like the 'z' in "azure"

**ñ** like the 'ni' in "onion"

**r** always pronounced as strong 'r'

**rr** trilled 'r'

**v** similar to the 'b' in "boy" (not as English 'v')

**y** like 'll,' it sounds like the 'z' in azure. When standing alone, it's pronounced like the 'e' in "me."

**z** like 's' in "same"

**b, f, k, l, m, n, p, q, s, t, w, x** as in English

### Vowels

**a** as in "father," but shorter

**e** as in "hen"

**i** as in "machine"

**o** as in "phone"

**u** usually as in "rule"; when it follows a 'q,' the 'u' is silent; when it follows an 'h' or 'g,' it's pronounced like 'w,' except when it comes between 'g' and 'e' or 'i,' when it's also silent (unless it has an umlaut, when it is again pronounced as the English 'w')

### Stress

Native English speakers frequently make errors of pronunciation by ignoring stress. All Spanish vowels – a, e, i, o, and u – may carry accents that determine which syllable of a word gets emphasis. Often, stress seems unnatural to nonnative speakers – the surname Chávez, for instance, is stressed on the first syllable – but failure to observe this rule may mean that native speakers may not understand you.

## NUMBERS

**0** *cero*
**1** *uno* (masculine)
**1** *una* (feminine)
**2** *dos*
**3** *tres*
**4** *cuatro*
**5** *cinco*
**6** *seis*
**7** *siete*
**8** *ocho*
**9** *nueve*
**10** *diez*
**11** *once*

**12** *doce*
**13** *trece*
**14** *catorce*
**15** *quince*
**16** *diez y seis*
**17** *diez y siete*
**18** *diez y ocho*
**19** *diez y nueve*
**20** *veinte*
**21** *veinte y uno*
**30** *treinta*
**40** *cuarenta*
**50** *cincuenta*
**60** *sesenta*
**70** *setenta*
**80** *ochenta*
**90** *noventa*
**100** *cien*
**101** *ciento y uno*
**200** *doscientos*
**1,000** *mil*
**10,000** *diez mil*
**1,000,000** *un millón*

## DAYS OF THE WEEK
**Sunday** *domingo*
**Monday** *lunes*
**Tuesday** *martes*
**Wednesday** *miércoles*
**Thursday** *jueves*
**Friday** *viernes*
**Saturday** *sábado*

## TIME
While Argentines normally use the 12-hour clock (A.M. and P.M.), they sometimes use the 24-hour clock, usually associated with plane or bus schedules. Under the 24-hour clock, for example, *las diez de la noche* (10 P.M.) would be *las 22 horas* (2200 hours).

**What time is it?** *¿Qué hora es?*
**It's one o'clock** *Es la una.*
**It's two o'clock** *Son las dos.*
**At two o'clock** *A las dos.*
**It's ten to three** *Son tres menos diez.*
**It's ten past three** *Son tres y diez.*
**It's three fifteen** *Son las tres y cuarto.*

**It's two forty-five** *Son tres menos cuarto.*
**It's two thirty** *Son las dos y media.*
**It's six A.M.** *Son las seis de la mañana.*
**It's six P.M.** *Son las seis de la tarde.*
**It's ten P.M.** *Son las diez de la noche.*
**Today** *hoy*
**Tomorrow** *mañana*
**Morning** *la mañana*
**Tomorrow morning** *mañana por la mañana*
**Yesterday** *ayer*
**Week** *la semana*
**Month** *mes*
**Year** *año*
**Last night** *anoche*
**The next day** *el día siguiente*

## USEFUL WORDS AND PHRASES
Argentines and other Spanish-speaking people consider formalities important. Whenever approaching anyone for information or some other reason, do not forget the appropriate salutation – good morning, good evening, etc. Standing alone, the greeting *"hola"* (hello) can sound brusque.

Note that most of the words below are fairly standard, common to all Spanish-speaking countries. Many, however, have more idiomatic Argentine equivalents; refer to the glossary for these.

**Hello.** *Hola.*
**Good morning.** *Buenos días.*
**Good afternoon.** *Buenas tardes.*
**Good evening.** *Buenas noches.*
**How are you?** *¿Cómo está?*
**Fine.** *Muy bien.*
**And you?** *¿Y usted?*
**So-so.** *Más o menos.*
**Thank you.** *Gracias.*
**Thank you very much.** *Muchas gracias.*
**You're very kind.** *Muy amable.*
**You're welcome.** *De nada.* (Literally, It's nothing.)
**Yes** *sí*
**No** *no*
**I don't know.** *No sé.*
**It's fine; okay.** *Está bien.*

**Good; okay.** *Bueno.*
**Please** *por favor*
**Pleased to meet you.** *Mucho gusto.*
**Excuse me (physical).** *Perdóneme.*
**Excuse me (speech).** *Discúlpeme.*
**I'm sorry.** *Lo siento.*
**Goodbye.** *Adiós.*
**See you later.** *Hasta luego.* (Literally, Until later.)
**More** *más*
**Less** *menos*
**Better** *mejor*
**Much, a lot** *mucho*
**A little** *un poco*
**Large** *grande*
**Small** *pequeño, chico*
**Quick, fast** *rápido*
**Slowly** *despacio*
**Bad** *malo*
**Difficult** *difícil*
**Easy** *fácil*
**He/She/It is gone; as in "She left," "He's gone."** *Ya se fue.*
**I don't speak Spanish well.** *No hablo bien el español.*
**I don't understand.** *No entiendo.*
**How do you say...in Spanish?** *¿Cómo se dice...en español?*
**Do you understand English?** *¿Entiende el inglés?*
**Is English spoken here? (Does anyone here speak English?)** *¿Se habla inglés aquí?*

## TERMS OF ADDRESS

When in doubt, use the formal *usted* (you) as a form of address. If you wish to dispense with formality and feel that the desire is mutual, you can say *Me puedes tutear* (you can call me "tu") even though Argentines use the slightly different verb forms that correlate with the familiar pronoun "vos."

**I** *yo*
**You (formal)** *usted*
**You (familiar)** *vos*
**He/him** *él*
**She/her** *ella*
**We/us** *nosotros*

**You (plural)** *ustedes*
**They/them (all males or mixed gender)** *ellos*
**They/them (all females)** *ellas*
**Mr., sir** *señor*
**Mrs., madam** *señora*
**Miss, young lady** *señorita*
**Wife** *esposa*
**Husband** *marido* or *esposo*
**Friend** *amigo* (male), *amiga* (female)
**Sweetheart** *novio* (male), *novia* (female)
**Son, daughter** *hijo, hija*
**Brother, sister** *hermano, hermana*
**Father, mother** *padre, madre*
**Grandfather, grandmother** *abuelo, abuela*

## GETTING AROUND

**Where is...?** *¿Dónde está...?*
**How far is it to...?** *¿A cuanto está...?*
**from...to...** *de...a...*
**Highway** *la carretera*
**Road** *el camino*
**Street** *la calle*
**Block** *la cuadra*
**Kilometer** *kilómetro*
**North** *norte*
**South** *sur*
**West** *oeste; poniente*
**East** *este; oriente*
**Straight ahead** *al derecho; adelante*
**To the right** *a la derecha*
**To the left** *a la izquierda*

## ACCOMMODATIONS

**Is there a room?** *¿Hay habitación?*
**May I (we) see it?** *¿Puedo (podemos) verla?*
**What is the rate?** *¿Cuál es el precio?*
**Is that your best rate?** *¿Es su mejor precio?*
**Is there something cheaper?** *¿Hay algo más económico?*
**Single room** *un sencillo*
**Double room** *un doble*
**Room for a couple** *matrimonial*
**Key** *llave*
**With private bath** *con baño privado*
**With shared bath** *con baño general; con baño compartido*
**Hot water** *agua caliente*

**Cold water** *agua fría*
**Shower** *ducha*
**Electric shower** *ducha eléctrica*
**Towel** *toalla*
**Soap** *jabón*
**Toilet paper** *papel higiénico*
**Air conditioning** *aire acondicionado*
**Fan** *ventilador*
**Blanket** *frazada; manta*
**Sheets** *sábanas*

## PUBLIC TRANSPORT

**Bus stop** *la parada*
**Bus terminal** *terminal de buses*
**Airport** *el aeropuerto*
**Launch** *lancha*
**Dock** *muelle*
**I want a ticket to...** *Quiero un pasaje a . . .*
**I want to get off at...** *Quiero bajar en . . .*
**Here, please.** *Aquí, por favor.*
**Where is this bus going?** *¿Adónde va este autobús?*
**Roundtrip** *ida y vuelta*
**What do I owe?** *¿Cuánto le debo?*

## FOOD

**Menu** *la carta, el menú*
**Glass** *taza*
**Fork** *tenedor*
**Knife** *cuchillo*
**Spoon** *cuchara*
**Napkin** *servilleta*
**Soft drink** *gaseosa*
**Coffee** *café*
**Cream** *crema*
**Tea** *té*
**Sugar** *azúcar*
**Drinking water** *agua pura, agua potable*
**Bottled carbonated water** *agua mineral con gas*
**Bottled uncarbonated water** *agua sin gas*
**Beer** *cerveza*
**Wine** *vino*
**Milk** *leche*
**Juice** *jugo*
**Eggs** *huevos*
**Bread** *pan*
**Watermelon** *sandía*

**Banana** *banana*
**Apple** *manzana*
**Orange** *naranja*
**Peach** *durazno*
**Pineapple** *ananá*
**Meat (without)** *carne (sin)*
**Beef** *carne de res*
**Chicken** *pollo; gallina*
**Fish** *pescado*
**Shellfish** *mariscos*
**Shrimp** *camarones*
**Fried** *frito*
**Roasted** *asado*
**Barbecued** *a la parrilla*
**Breakfast** *desayuno*
**Lunch** *almuerzo*
**Dinner, or a late-night snack** *cena*
**The check, or bill** *la cuenta*

## MAKING PURCHASES

**I need...** *Necesito . . .*
**I want...** *Deseo . . . or Quiero . . .*
**I would like...(more polite)** *Quisiera . . .*
**How much does it cost?** *¿Cuánto cuesta?*
**What's the exchange rate?** *¿Cuál es el tipo de cambio?*
**May I see . . . ?** *¿Puedo ver . . . ?*
**This one** *ésta/ésto*
**Expensive** *caro*
**Cheap** *barato*
**Cheaper** *más barato*
**Too much** *demasiado*

## HEALTH

**Help me, please.** *Ayúdeme, por favor.*
**I am ill.** *Estoy enfermo.*
**It hurts.** *Me duele.*
**Pain** *dolor*
**Fever** *fiebre*
**Stomachache** *dolor de estómago*
**Vomiting** *vomitar*
**Diarrhea** *diarrea*
**Drugstore** *farmacia*
**Medicine** *medicina*
**Pill, tablet** *pastilla*
**Birth control pills** *pastillas anticonceptivas*
**Condom** *condón, preservativo*

# Suggested Reading

## ARCHAEOLOGY, ETHNOGRAPHY, AND ETHNOHISTORY

Schávelzon, Daniel. *Historia del Comer y del Beber en Buenos Aires*. Buenos Aires: Aguilar, 2000. Urban archaeologist Schávelzon chronicles the evolution of the *porteño* diet through salvage excavations in the city, finding among other surprises that beef consumption was not always so great as some have assumed.

## GUIDEBOOKS AND TRAVELOGUES

Darwin, Charles. *Voyage of the Beagle* (many editions). Perhaps the greatest travel book ever written, Darwin's narrative of his 19th-century journey brims with insights on the people, places, and even politics he observed while collecting the plants and animals that led to his revolutionary theories. The great scientist observed the city of Buenos Aires, the surrounding pampas, and parts of neighboring Uruguay, and met key figures in the country's history, including the dictator Rosas.

France, Miranda. *Bad Times in Buenos Aires.* Hopewell, NJ: Ecco Press, 1998. A timeless title, perhaps, but it refers to the author's sardonic analysis of her early 1990s experiences.

Green, Toby. *Saddled with Darwin.* London: Phoenix, 1999. An audacious if uneven account of a young, talented writer's attempt to retrace the hoofprints—not the footsteps—of Darwin's travels through Uruguay, Argentina, and Chile. Self-effacing but still serious, the author manages to compare his own experience with Darwin's, reflect on contemporary distortions of the great scientist's theories, and stay almost completely off the gringo trail.

Guevara, Ernesto. *The Motorcycle Diaries: A Journey Around South America.* New York and London: Verso, 1995. Translated by Ann Wright, recently brought to the big screen by Brazilian director Walter Salles, this travelogue follows an Argentine drifter's progress from Buenos Aires across the Andes and up the Chilean coast by motorcycle and, when it broke down, by any means necessary. The author is better known by his nickname "Che," a common Argentine interjection.

Head, Francis Bond. *Journeys Across the Pampas & Among the Andes.* Carbondale, IL: Southern Illinois University Press, 1967. Nearly a decade before Darwin, in the early years of Argentine independence, "Galloping Head" rode across the pampas and over the Andes into Chile. Originally published in 1826, some of Head's observations on the gaucho's abilities and adaptability resemble Darwin's, but Head detested Buenos Aires itself.

Naipaul, V. S. *The Return of Eva Perón.* New York: Knopf, 1980. The great but controversial British Nobel Prize–winning author's acerbic observations on Argentine society, in the context of his visit during the vicious 1976–1983 dictatorship.

Petrina, Alberto, ed. *Buenos Aires: Guía de Arquitectura.* Buenos Aires and Seville: Municipalidad de la Ciudad de Buenos Aires and Junta de Andalucía, 1994. An outstanding architectural guide, embellished with architectural sketches and photographs, with eight suggested walking tours.

Symmes, Patrick. *Chasing Che: A Motorcycle Journey in Search of the Guevara Legend.* New York: Vintage, 2000. In a brilliantly conceived trip, Symmes follows the tiremarks of Che's legendary trip from Buenos Aires through Argentina and Chile in the early 1950s. At the same time, he encounters a different series of misfortunes than the guerrilla icon.

# HISTORY

Andrews, George Reid. *The Afro-Argentines of Buenos Aires, 1800–1900*. Madison: University of Wisconsin Press, 1980. Groundbreaking research on the supposed disappearance of the capital's Afro-Argentine community, which once comprised nearly a third of its total population.

Crow, John A. *The Epic of Latin America*, 3rd ed. Berkeley: University of California Press, 1980. A comprehensive but immensely readable history of the region, told more through narrative than analysis. Several chapters deal with Argentina.

Cutolo, Vicente Osvaldo. *Buenos Aires: Historia de las Calles y Sus Nombres*. Buenos Aires: Editorial Elche, 1988. This weighty two-volume set details the history not just of nearly every city street, but also the stories behind the street names.

Dujovne Ortiz, Alicia. *Eva Perón*. New York: St. Martin's Press, 1996. Filled with controversial assertions, this nevertheless absorbing biography is most eloquent in describing a poor provincial girl's transformation into a powerful international figure through relentless and bitterly ruthless ambition, blended with genuine concern for the truly destitute. Shawn Fields's translation into English, unfortunately, is awkward.

Goñi, Uki. *The Real Odessa*. New York and London: Granta, 2002. Remarkable account of the controversial links between Juan Perón's government and the shadowy organization that spirited Nazi war criminals into Argentina. Employing a variety of archival sources on a topic that most often relies on rumor, Goñi implicates the Vatican and its Argentine branch as go-betweens in negotiations with the Nazi regime's remnants.

Guy, Donna J. *Sex and Danger in Buenos Aires*. Lincoln: University of Nebraska Press, 1991. An academic account of immigration's seamier side, relating it to sexual imbalance in the population, homosexuality, prostitution, the rise of the tango, and even Peronism.

Lynch, John. *Spanish-American Revolutions, 1808–1826*, 2nd ed. New York: W. W. Norton, 1986. Comprehensive account of the Spanish-American independence movements.

Moya, José C. *Cousins and Strangers: Spanish Immigrants in Buenos Aires, 1850–1930*. Berkeley: University of California Press, 1998. An account of the capital's (and the country's) ambivalent relationship with immigrants often disparaged as *Gallegos* (Galicians).

Parry, J. H. *The Discovery of South America*. London: Paul Elek, 1979. Well-illustrated history of early voyages to and overland explorations of the continent.

Rock, David. *Argentina 1516–1987: From Spanish Colonization to the Falklands War and Alfonsín*. London: I. B. Taurus, 1987. Comprehensive narrative and analysis of Argentine history prior to Carlos Menem's presidency.

Rock, David. *Authoritarian Argentina: The Nationalist Movement, Its History and Its Impact*. Berkeley: University of California Press, 1993. Building on his earlier work, the author examines the durability of right-wing nationalism that led to the 1976–1983 Dirty War, even as comparable nationalist regimes were failing in Spain, Portugal, Mexico, and other countries.

Scobie, James R. *Buenos Aires: From Plaza to Suburb, 1870–1910*. New York: Oxford University Press, 1974. Classic account of the city's explosive late-19th-century growth and the transition from "Gran Aldea" to "Paris of the South."

Shumway, Norman. *The Invention of Argentina*. Berkeley: University of California Press, 1991. An intellectual history of Argentina's founding myths, and the degree to which elitist debate excluded entire sectors of society from participation, leading to frequent ungovernability.

Slatta, Richard. *Cowboys of the Americas.* New Haven and London: Yale University Press, 1990. Spectacularly illustrated comparative account of New World horsemen, including both Argentine gauchos and Chilean *huasos.*

Vidal, Emeric Essex. *Buenos Aires and Montevideo in a Series of Picturesque Illustrations Taken on the Spot.* Buenos Aires: Mitchell's English Book-Store, 1944. Originally published in London in 1820, this British naval officer's remarkable travelogue literally paints a picture—with full-color illustrations to complement his text descriptions—of Buenos Aires in the early independence years.

## GOVERNMENT AND POLITICS

Castañeda, Jorge G. *Utopia Unarmed: The Latin American Left After the Cold War.* New York: Knopf, 1993. A former academic makes Argentina the starting point in his analysis of the democratization in Latin America's revolutionary left, with a particularly good analysis of the Montoneros urban guerrilla movement.

Caviedes, César. *The Southern Cone: Realities of the Authoritarian State.* Totowa, NJ: Rowman & Allanheld, 1984. Comparative study of the military dictatorships of Chile, Argentina, Uruguay, and Brazil of the 1970s and 1980s.

Verbitsky, Horacio. *The Flight: Confessions of an Argentine Dirty Warrior.* New York: The New Press, 1996. Based on interviews with Francisco Scilingo, a self-confessed torturer and murderer who shoved political prisoners out of airplanes over the South Atlantic, this tells of the worst excesses of the 1976–1983 military dictatorship. Convicted in 2005 in Spain, Scilingo was the first Argentine officer to break the silence over human-rights violations.

## LITERATURE AND LITERARY CRITICISM

Martínez, Tomás Eloy. *The Perón Novel.* New York: Pantheon Books, 1988. Based on the author's own lengthy interviews with the exiled caudillo, for which fiction seemed the appropriate outlet. According to Jorge Castañeda, "Whether Perón ever actually uttered these words is in the last analysis irrelevant: he could have, he would have, and he probably did."

Martínez, Tomás Eloy. *Santa Evita.* New York: Knopf, 1996. One of Argentina's leading contemporary writers tackles the Evita myth in a fictional version of her post-mortem odyssey from Argentina to Italy, Spain, and back to Buenos Aires.

Meyer, Doris. *Victoria Ocampo: Against the Wind and the Tide.* Austin: University of Texas Press, 1990. Biography of the woman who led the Argentine equivalent of Britain's Bloomsbury Group, through her literary magazine *Sur* and friendships with Jorge Luis Borges, Adolfo Bioy Casares (married to her sister Silvina, also a writer), and international figures such as Andre Malraux, José Ortega y Gasset, and Rabindranath Tagore. The volume includes 15 of Victoria's own essays.

Vásquez Montalbán, Manuel. *The Buenos Aires Quintet.* London: Serpent's Tail, 2005. Before his death in late 2003, the Spanish novelist sent his fictional Barcelona detective Pepe Carvalho south to sample the food and unravel a lingering mystery from the Dirty War dictatorship of 1976–1983.

Wilson, Jason. *Buenos Aires: A Cultural and Literary Companion.* New York: Interlink, 2000. Part of the Cities of the Imagination series, this is a breathlessly thorough summary of what *porteño* authors as well as other Argentine and foreign authors have written about the capital. It's particularly good at conveying what untranslated Argentine authors have written about the city.

Wilson, Jason. *Traveller's Literary Companion: South & Central America, Including Mexico.* Lincolnwood, IL: Passport Books, 1995. An edited collection of excerpts from literature—including fiction, poetry, and essays—that illuminates aspects of the countries from the Río Grande to the tip of Tierra del Fuego, including Argentina (Buenos Aires in particular) and Uruguay.

Woodall, James. *Borges: A Life.* New York: Basic Books, 1997. An analytical—in the Freudian sense—biography of Argentina's most promi-nent literary figure. Originally appeared in Britain under the title *The Man in the Mirror of the Book* (London: Hodder & Stoughton, 1996).

## ENVIRONMENT AND NATURAL HISTORY

Hudson, William Henry. *The Bird Biographies of W. H. Hudson.* Santa Barbara, CA: Capra Press, 1988. A partial reprint, with illustrations, of the romantic naturalist's detailed description of the birds he knew growing up in Buenos Aires province.

# Internet Resources

The following list of general-interest sites does not include private tour operators (which are covered in the *Essentials* chapter), museums (covered in detail in the *Sights* chapter), or services like hotels and restaurants (covered in the *Accommodations* and *Restaurants* chapters).

### Aerolíneas Argentinas
### www.aerolineas.com.ar
This is the homepage for Argentina's erratic flagship airline.

### Aeropuertos Argentinos 2000
### www.aa2000.com.ar
The site for the private concessionaire operating most of Argentina's international and domestic airports, including Buenos Aires's Ezeiza and Aeroparque. In English and Spanish.

### Ambitoweb
### www.ambitoweb.com
Online version of *porteño* financial daily *Ambito Financiero.*

### AmeriSpan
### www.amerispan.com
Information on language instruction throughout the Americas, including Argentina.

### Apertura
### www.apertura.com
Business-oriented Buenos Aires magazine.

### Argentina Travel Net
### www.argentinatravelnet.com
Portal for Argentine travel sites, though not nearly all of the links are closely related to travel. In Spanish and English.

### Asociación Argentina de Albergues de la Juventud (AAAJ)
### www.hostelling-aaaj.org.ar
Argentine hostelling organization, with a limited number of facilities throughout the country.

### Asociación de Alberguistas del Uruguay
### www.hosteluruguay.org
Uruguayan Hostelling International affiliate, with a wide network of hostels around the country.

### Asociación de Fútbol Argentina
### www.afa.org.ar
Argentina's professional soccer league. In English and Spanish.

### Asociación Ornitológica del Plata
### www.avesargentinas.org.ar

Buenos Aires–based bird-watching and conservation organization.

### Automóvil Club Argentino (ACA)
### www.aca.org.ar

Argentine automobile association, useful for information and up-to-date road maps. Offers discounts for members of affiliated clubs, such as AAA in the United States and the AA in Britain.

### *Buenos Aires Herald*
### www.buenosairesherald.com

Abbreviated version of the capital's venerable English-language daily.

### Buenos Aires Milonga
### www.buenosairesmilonga.com

The most up-to-date site for those who want to participate in, not just watch, tango.

### B y T Argentina
### www.bytargentina.com/ecentro.htm

Short-term apartment rentals and other information on Buenos Aires, in English and Spanish.

### Caballito
### www.caballitoenlinea.com.ar

Portal website to an interesting but little-touristed residential barrio.

### Centers for Disease Control
### www.cdc.gov

U.S. government page with travel health advisories.

### CIA Factbook
### www.odci.gov/cia/publications/factbook/geos/ar.html

The world's most notorious spooks offer a handy public service in their annual encyclopedia of the world's countries, which appears in its entirety online.

### Ciudad Autónoma de Buenos Aires
### www.buenosaires.gov.ar

Comprehensive city-government site, which includes tourist information, in Spanish only.

### *Clarín*
### www.clarin.com

Outstanding online version of the capital's tabloid daily, the Spanish-speaking world's largest circulation newspaper.

### Currency Converter
### www.oanda.com

Present and historic exchange-rate information.

### Department of State
### www.travel.state.gov

Travel information and advisories from the U.S. government; its warnings often err on the side of extreme caution.

### Dirección General de Patrimonio
### www.dgpatrimonio.buenosaires.gov.ar

Within the city-government site, this separate page is a comprehensive guide to historical resources, both archaeological and contemporary.

### Dirección Provincial de Turismo
### www.vivalaspampas.com

Buenos Aires provincial tourism office, based in the capital city of La Plata.

### Feria del Libro
### www.el-libro.com.ar

Buenos Aires's heavily attended annual book fair.

### Festival del Tango
### www.tangodata.com.ar

Information on the capital's increasingly popular series of autumn (March–April) tango events.

### Fondo Nacional de las Artes
### www.fnartes.gov.ar

Official federal government site with information on performing arts, architecture, cinema, and related fields.

### Gay in Buenos Aires
### www.gayinbuenosaires.com.ar

Portal to articles and services of interest to homosexual residents and visitors.

**Hostelling International Argentina**
**www.hostels.org.ar**
Argentine Hostelling International affiliate, with information on travel and activities throughout the country.

**Instituto Geográfico Militar**
**www.igm.gov.ar**
Military geographical institute, preparing and selling maps of the country.

**Instituto Nacional de Estadísticas y Censos (INDEC)**
**www.indec.mecon.ar**
Homepage for the Argentine federal government's statistical agency.

**La Maga**
**www.lamaga.com.ar**
Website of the arts- and literature-oriented magazine.

**La Nación**
**www.lanacion.com.ar**
Major *porteño* daily, with an excellent Sunday cultural section.

**La Plata**
**www.laplata.gov.ar/index.htm**
Portal website of the capital city of Buenos Aires province.

**Latin American Network Information Center (LANIC)**
**www.lanic.utexas.edu**
Organized by the University of Texas, this site has a huge collection of quality links to Argentina and other Latin American countries.

**Lujanet**
**www.lujanet.com.ar**
Portal for Luján, the historical and pilgrimage center of Buenos Aires province.

**Mercado**
**www.mercado.com.ar**
Business-oriented Buenos Aires weekly magazine.

**Mercopress News Agency**
**www.falkland-malvinas.com**
Montevideo-based Internet news agency covering politics and business in the Mercosur common-market countries of Argentina, Brazil, Uruguay, and Paraguay, as well as Chile and the Falkland/Malvinas Islands. In English and Spanish.

**Metrovías**
**www.metrovias.com.ar**
Details on Buenos Aires's subway system.

**Ministerio de Relaciones Exteriores**
**www.mrecic.gov.ar/consulares/pag-con.html**
Argentine Foreign Ministry, with information on visas and consulates, in English and Spanish.

**Páginas Amarillas**
**www.paginasamarillas.com.ar**
Yellow Pages for all of Argentina.

**Página 12**
**www.pagina12.com.ar**
Outspoken left-of-center daily, which has shifted away from reporting and toward opinion, but features some of the country's best writers.

**PalermOnline**
**www.palermonline.com.ar**
Portal to sights and services in one of the city's liveliest barrios, Palermo.

**Puerto de Tigre**
**www.puertodetigre.com**
The suburban gateway to the popular Paraná delta.

**San Antonio de Areco**
**www.arecoturismo.com.ar**
The country's symbolic gaucho capital, in Buenos Aires province.

**Secretaría Nacional de Turismo**
**www.turismo.gov.ar**
National tourism authority, with information in Spanish and English.

## South American Explorers Club
**www.saexplorers.org/clubhouses/
buenosaires**

The Buenos Aires branch of an organization
with affiliates around the continent.

## UkiNet
**www.ukinet.com**

Freelance writer Uki Goñi's human rights–oriented website, with an archive of his best work
from Britain's *Guardian* and other sources.

## What's Up Buenos Aires
**www.whatsupbuenosaires.com**

What's Up is a popular culture and nightlife
site.

## Usenet Discussion Groups

### Rec.travel.latin-america

Regional forum dealing with all Latin
American countries, with a steady number of
postings on Argentina.

### Soc.culture.argentina

No-holds-barred forum that touches on many
issues.

# Index

## A

accommodations: 160-187; Balvanera 175-176; Microcentro 167-170; Monserrat 164-166; Palermo 184-187; Puerto Madero 171-172; Recoleta and Barrio Norte 180-183; Retiro 176-180; San Telmo 172-174
Afro-Argentines: 288-289
air travel: general discussion 303-308; see also specific place
antique automobiles: 248
architecture: 294-295
Archivo y Museo Histórico del Banco de la Provincia de Buenos Aires Dr. Arturo Jauretche: 26
arts and leisure: general discussion 113-141, 290-291, 294-301; concert venues 126, 128; cultural centers 128-130; galleries 123-124; holidays, festivals, and events 130-134; museums 115-123; sports and recreation 135-141; theater 124-126
Asociación Argentina de Cultura Inglesa: 129
Asociación Argentina de Polo: 141
Asociación Ornitológica del Plata: 136

## B

Balvanera: 7, 39-42, 76-78, 175-176; map 4 391
bargaining: 340
Barra de Maldonado, La: 266
Barrio Histórico: 245
Barrio Norte: see Recoleta and Barrio Norte
Basílica Nacional Nuestral Señora de Luján: 198
basketball: 141
beef: 80
Belgrano: 58; map 8
Biblioteca Nacional: 45
bicycling: 136-137; general discussion 316
birds/bird-watching: 136, 272
boating: 138
Boca Juniors: 139
Boca, La: 7, 37-39, 75; map 3 390
Bodega Bernardi: 250
Bodega Bouza: 240
Bodega Carlos Pizzorno: 242
Bodega César Pisano: 242
Bodega Delucca: 241
Bodegas Castillo Viejo: 241
bookstores: general discussion 345; see also Shop Index; shops
boxing: 140

Buenos Aires Graff: 45
Buenos Aires Lawn Tennis Club: 137
Buque Museo A.R.A. Uruguay Corbeta: 115
Buque Museo Fragata A.R.A. Presidente Sarmiento: 115
business: 328-329
business organizations: 328
bus transportation: general discussion 308-309, 312; see also specific place

## C

Caballito: 62; map 8 398-399
cachilas: 248
Caminito: 38
Campeonato Abierto Argentino de Polo: 134
Campeonato Argentino Abierto de Pato: 134
Campeonato Mundial de Baile de Tango: 134
Campos, Molina: 197
Carmelo: 255-258
Carnaval: 130, 131
car rental: general discussion 315
car travel: general discussion 309-310; see also specific place
Casa Museo Ricardo Rojas: 46
Casapueblo: 266
Casa Rosada (Casa de Gobierno Nacional): 19
Catedral de la Immaculada Concepción de la Plata: 216
Catedral Metropolitana: 20
cellular phone rental: 343-344
Cementerio de la Chacarita: 63
Cementerio de la Recoleta: 46
Centro Cultural Borges: 129
Centro Cultural Ciudad de Buenos Aires: 129
Centro Cultural del Sur: 129
Centro Cultural Islámico Rey Fahd: 49
Centro Cultural Rector Ricardo Rojas: 130
Centro Cultural Usina Vieja: 204
Centro Latinoamericano de Creación e Investigación Teatral: 125
Centro, The (Montevideo): 225
Chacarita: 63; map 8
chess: 137
children, traveling with: 330
cinema: 127; general discussion 299-301; see also specific place
City, La: 27
Ciudad Vieja: 227
climate: 270
Club Argentino de Ajedrez: 137

Club Atlético: 34
Colonia del Sacramento: 244-247, 249-254
communications and media: 342-345
Complejo Museográfico Enrique Udaondo: 199
conservation organizations: 270-271
Correo Central: 28
Costa Salguero Golf Center: 137
costs: 339-340
credit and debit cards: 339
crime: 336-337
Cromañon disaster: 98
currency: 337-338

**DE**
Dansk Kirke: 34
Día de la Muerte de Carlos Gardel: 133
dining vocabulary and etiquette: 67
disabilities, travelers with: 331
economy: 284-287
electricity: 346
environmental issues: 273-275
equestrian sports: 140-141
Escuela de Mecánica de la Armada (ESMA): 64
Establecimiento Juanicó: 241
Estancia and Polo Club La Candelaria: 211
Estancia de Narbona, La: 256
Estancia Los Talas: 201
*estancias:* Areco 206-207, operators 209
ethnic minorities: 287-289
etiquette: 327
excursions: 188-268
Exposición de Otoño de la Asociación
    Criadores de Caballos Criollos: 131
Exposición Internacional de Ganadería,
    Agricultura, y Industria Internacional: 133

**F**
fauna: 271-272
faxes: 343-344
Federación Argentina de Pato: 141
Feria de Galerías Arte BA: 133
Feria del Libro: 132
Feria de Mataderos, La: 59
ferry transportation: 311
Festival Buenos Aires Tango: 131, 132
Festival Internacional de Cine Independiente: 132
Fiesta de la Tradición: 206
*filete:* 122
film and photography: 341-342
Finca y Granja Narbona: 256
fishing: 138
flora: 271
Florida Garden: 124

Fondo Nacional de Artes: 50
food: general discussion 322-327; *see also*
    Restaurant Index
Four Seasons Resort Carmelo: 257
Fundación Internacional Jorge Luis Borges: 47
Fundación Proa: 115

**G**
Galería Federico Klemm: 124
Galería Rubbers: 124
Galería Ruth Benzacar: 124
Galerías Pacífico: 28
Galería Vermeer: 124
Galería Zurbarán: 124
gay and lesbian travelers: 331
geography: 270
golf: 137
Golf Club Lagos de Palermo: 137
gratuities: 340

**HI**
health and safety: 331-337
*helados:* 71
Hipódromo Argentino: 141
horseback riding: 140-141
horse racing: 141
ice cream: 71
Iglesia Apostólica Ortodoxa Rusa: 34
Iglesia Nuestra Señora de la Inmaculada
    Concepción: 58
Iglesia y Convento de Santo Domingo: 20
indigenous peoples: 287
Instituto Goethe: 130
Instituto Nacional Sanmartiniano: 50
insurance: 9
internet access: 344
Isla de Lobos: 266
Isla Gorrita: 266
Isla Martín García: 195-198
itinerary suggestions: 10-16

**JKL**
Jardín Botánico Carlos Thays: 51
Jardín Japonés: 52
Jardín Zoológico: 216
Jardín Zoológico Eduardo Ladislao
    Holmberg: 52
José Ignacio: 267
land: 269-270
landscape: 272-273
language: 289-290
language study: 329

lesbian and gay travelers: 331
LiberArte: 125
libraries: 345
literature: 292-293
Lobos: 210-212
Luján: 198-201
Luna Park: 140

# M

magazines: 344-345
Maldonado: 260; see also Punta del Este and Maldonado
Manzana de las Luces: 21
maps: Balvanera 391; Barrio Norte 394-395; Boca, La 390; Colonia del Sacramento 246-247; excursions from Buenos Aires 190; Microcentro 388-389; Monserrat 386-387; Montevideo 222-233; outer barrios 398-399; Palermo 396-397; Plata, La 214; Puerto Madero 388-389; Recoleta 394-395; Retiro 392-393; San Antonio de Areco 203; San Telmo 390; Subte 400
Martina Polo Ranch, La: 211
mate: 76-77
measurements: 346
Mendoza, Pedro de: 275
Mercado de Abasto: 40
Mercado del Puerto: 231
Microcentro: 6, 26-31, 69-70, 167-170; historical landmarks 27; map 2 388-389
Milonga de Calle Corrientes: 134
milongas: 105, 107-110
money: 337-340
Monserrat: 6, 19-25, 67-68, 164-166; map 1 386-387
Montevideo: 221-238
Montevideo wine country: 239-243
movie settings: 116
Municipal Dr. Bautista Rebuffo: 249
Museo Argentino de Ciencias Naturales Bernardino Rivadavia: 62
Museo Casa de Yrurtia: 116
Museo de Armas de la Nación: 117
Museo de Arte Español Enrique Larreta: 58
Museo de Arte Latinoamericano de Buenos Aires (MALBA): 53
Museo de Arte Moderno: 117
Museo de Arte Precolombino: 231
Museo de Artes Plásticas Eduardo Sívori: 118
Museo de Bellas Artes de La Boca Benito Quinquela Martín: 38
Museo de Esculturas Luis Perlotti: 118
Museo de la Ciudad: 24

Museo de la Inmigración: 32
Museo de la Moneda y del Gaucho: 231
Museo de la Pasión Boquense: 38
Museo de la Plata: 216
Museo de la Policía Federal: 118
Museo de la Shoá: 42
Museo del Cabildo: 118
Museo del Cine Pablo A. Ducrós Hicken: 119
Museo de los Azulejos: 247
Museo del Traje: 119
Museo de Motivos Argentinos José Hernández: 53
Museo Español: 249
Museo Etnográfico Juan B. Ambrosetti: 120
Museo Eva Perón: 54
Museo Forense de la Morgue Judicial Dr. Juan Bautista Bafico: 120
Museo Gauchesco del Pintor Gasparini: 204
Museo Gurvich: 231
Museo Histórico Brigadier General Cornelio de Saavedra: 120
Museo Histórico de Cera: 39
Museo Histórico Nacional (Buenos Aires): 34
Museo Histórico Nacional (Montevideo): 229
Museo Histórico Sarmiento: 59
Museo Houssay de Ciencia y Tecnología: 120
Museo Juan Domingo Perón: 210
Museo Judío de Buenos Aires Dr. Salvador Kibrick: 29
Museo Libero Badii: 121
Museo Mitre: 29
Museo Mundial del Tango: 121
Museo Municipal de Arte Hispanoamericano Isaac Fernández Blanco: 43Museo
Museo Nacional de Arte Decorativo: 121
Museo Nacional de Bellas Artes: 47
Museo Nacional del Grabado: 121
Museo Nacional del Hombre: 121
Museo Numismático Dr. José E. Uriburu: 29
Museo Penitenciario Argentino Antonio Ballvé: 122
Museo Portugués: 249
Museo Torres García: 229
Museo Xul Solar: 123
Museo y Archivo Dardo Rocha: 217
Museo y Archivo Histórico de la Dirección General Impositiva: 123
music and dance: general discussion 295-299; see also Nightlife Index; specific place

# NOP

newspapers: 344-345
nightlife: 93-112; bars and clubs 96-101;

cafés 95-96; flamenco venues 110; gay and lesbian venues 111-112; jazz venues 103; live music venues 101-103; *milongas* 107-110; tango and *tanguerías* 104; *see also* Nightlife Index
Nuevo Circuito KDT: 137
Núñez: 64; map 8 398-399
Observatorio Astronómico de La Plata: 217
Opera Pampa: 109
outer barrios: 8, 58-59, 62-64, 92; map 8 398-399
painting: 290-291
Palacio Barolo: 24
Palacio de las Aguas Corrientes (Obras Sanitarias): 41
Palacio del Congreso Nacional: 42
Palacio Nacional de las Artes (Palais de Glace): 130
Palacio Pizzurno: 48
Palacio San Martín: 43
Palacio Taranco: 229
Palermo: 8, 49-57, 81-91, 184-187; famous private residences 54; map 7 396-397
pampa gaucha: 204
parks and protected areas: 135-136
Parque Centenario: 135
Parque Criollo y Museo Gauchesco Ricardo Güiraldes: 204
Parque Ecológico Cultural Guillermo E. Hudson: 215
Parque Lezama: 35
Parque Rivadavia: 136
Parque Tres de Febrero: 55
Pasaje Dardo Rocha: 217
passports: 8
Perón, Evita: 56-57
pharmacies: 336
photography: 341-342
*piletas:* 135
Planetario Galileo Galilei: 123
Plata, La: 213-220
Plaza Coronel Olazábal: 35
Plaza de Mayo: 25
Plaza Dorrego: 36
Plaza San Martín: 44
police and military: 321
politics: 280-283
postal services: 342-343
Primer Museo Nacional y Taller Abierto de Platería: 205
Puerto Madero: 6, 31-33, 72, 171-172; map 2 388-389
Punta del Este and Maldonado: 258-266

**R**
radio: 345
rail travel: general discussion 312-313, 314, 315; *see also specific place*
Recoleta and Barrio Norte: 7, 45-48, 80-81, 180-183; map 6 394-395
religion: 302
República de los Niños: 218
Reserva Ecológica Costanera Sur: 32, 136
restaurants: 65-92; Balvanera 76-78; Boca, La 75; Microcentro 69-70; Monserrat 67-68; outer barrios 92; Palermo 81-91; private 78; Puerto Madero 72; Recoleta and Barrio Norte 80-81; Retiro 78-79; San Telmo 72-74; terminology 68; *see also* Restaurants Index
Retiro: 7, 42-45, 78-79, 176-180; map 5 392-393
River Plate: 139
Rosas, Juan Manuel de: 277
Rosedal: 56
rugby: 139
running: 136

**S**
San Antonio de Areco: 202-210
San Telmo: 6, 33-37, 72-74, 172-174; map 3 390
Scala de San Telmo, La: 126
sculpture: 291, 294
Semana del Libro: 134
Semana Santa: 131
shops: 142-159; antiques 146-147; books 148-150; clothing and accessories 150-154; crafts and souvenirs 154-156; household goods and furniture 156-157; music and video 157; shopping centers 143-144; street fairs 145-146; wine 158-159; *see also* Shops Index
sights: 17-64; Balvanera 39-42; Boca, La 37-39; Mirocentro 26-31; Monserrat 19-21, 24-25; outer barrios 58-59, 62-64; Palermo 45-57; Puerto Madero 31-33; Recoleta and Barrio Norte 45-48; Retiro 42-45; San Telmo 33-37
soccer: 138-139
south barrios: 60-61
spectator sports: 138-141
St. Patrick's Day: 131
student discounts: 340
subway system: 22-23; map 9 400
surfing: 138

**T**
tango: 13, 105, 296-297, 329-330

*tanguerías:* 104-107
taxes: 145, 340
taxis: general discussion 315; *see also specific place*
Teatro Argentino: 218
Teatro Avenida: 128
Teatro Catalinas Sur: 125
Teatro Colón: 30, 128
Teatro de la Ribera: 126
Teatro General San Martín: 126
Teatro Margarita Xirgú: 128
Teatro Nacional Cervantes: 126
Teatro Solís: 229
telephone: 343-344
television: 345
tennis: 137
theater: general discussion 301
therapy: 50-51
Tigre: 191-194
time: 346
tipping: 340
tourist information: 341-342

tourist offices: 341
tours, organized: general discussion 317; *see also specific place*
transportation: *see specific mode of transportation; place*
travel agencies: 313
travel documentation: 318, 319, 320, 321

## UVWXYZ
Unión de Rugby de Buenos Aires: 139
Uruguay travel essentials: 224-225
Viña Varela Zarranz: 242
Viñedos y Bodega Filgueira: 241
visas and officialdom: 8, 318, 319, 320, 321
*viveza criolla:* 327
walking: 316-317
water sports: 137-138
weather: 270
weights and measures: 346
wildlife: 271-272
women travelers: 330
Zanjón de Granados, El: 36

# Restaurants Index

ABC: 69
Acabar: 84
Asia de Cuba: 72
Azema: 84
Banchero: 75
Barbería, La: 75
Bar El Federal: 72
Bar 6: 84
Bar Uriarte: 85
Bella Italia: 87
Bella Italia Café Bar: 87
Bobo: 85
Broccolino: 70
Cabaña Las Lilas: 72
Cabernet: 81
Cabrera, La: 81
Cadore: 70
Café Molière: 67
California Burrito Company: 70
Candela, La: 69
Cantina Chinatown: 92
Capisci: 92
Casal de Catalunya: 74
Casa Polaca, La: 90
Centro Vasco Francés: 68
Ceviche: 90

Club Danés: 79
Club del Progreso: 69
Contigo Perú: 92
Continental, La: 76
Cupertina, La: 82
Dashi: 89
DesNivel: 72
DiMaggio's: 87
Divina Patagonia: 85
1880: 73
Elisabetta: 87
Empire Bar: 79
Esquina de las Flores, La: 91
Estancia, La: 69
Filo: 79
Garbis: 83
Gato Negro, El: 70
Guido's Bar: 88
Ichisou: 77
Jangada: 91
Jardín Japonés: 89
José Luis: 80
Juana M.: 78
Katmandu: 87
Laurak Bat: 68
Lelé de Troya: 82

Libélula: 90
Lobby: 85
Lotus Neo Thai: 83
Lucky Luciano: 88
Malevo: 92
Mamá Europa: 89
María Fuló: 84
Mark's Deli and Coffee House: 81
Masamadre Es Con M: 92
Medio y Medio: 74
Miramar: 76
Miranda: 83
Mítico Sur: 73
Mosoq: 90
Motta: 84
Mundano: 91
Nemo: 91
Obrero, El: 75
Olsen: 86
Oveja Negra, La: 73
Oviedo: 81
Paila, La: 83
Palacio de la Papa Frita, El: 69

Pappa Deus: 74
Patagonia Sur: 75
Pinos, Los: 80
Pizzería Güerrín: 70
Portugués, El: 90
Posada de 1820, La: 69
Prosciutto: 67
Punta Brasas: 91
Sabot: 70
Sa Giara: 88
Social Paraíso: 86
Spirit: 91
Standard: 83
Status: 67
Sudestada: 83
Tancat: 79
Te Mataré Ramírez: 86
Territorio: 74
Último Beso, El: 89
Viejo Indecente, El: 86
Voulez Bar: 84
Xalapa: 89
Zadvarie Doc: 90

# Nightlife Index

Alsina Buenos Aires: 111
@lternativa: 96
Amerika: 111
Angel's: 111
Arranque at Nueva Salón, El: 107
Bach Bar: 111
Bárbaro: 96
Bar Plaza Dorrego: 97
Bar Seddon: 97
Bar Sur: 104
Biela, La: 95
Blues Special Club: 101
Buller Brewing Company: 97
Bulnes Class: 111
Café Bar Banderín: 97
Café de los Angelitos: 95
Café Tortoni: 95
Chino, El: 104
Cigale, La: 97
Clásica y Moderna: 103
Club Español: 107
Club Gricel: 108
Club Unione e Benevolenza: 101
Confitería Ideal: 96, 108
Confitería Richmond: 96

Dama de Bollini, La: 101
Downtown Matías: 97
Druid In: 98
Espacio Ecléctico: 103
Esquina Carlos Gardel: 104
Esquina Homero Manzi: 105
Foro Gandhi: 98
Gran Bar Danzón: 99
Italia Unita: 108
John John: 99
Kilkenny, The: 99
Levitar Ambient Bar: 99
Lobby: 99
Michelangelo: 105
Milión: 99
Mitos Argentinos: 101
Mundo Bizarro: 99
Nacional, La: 109
Niceto Club: 102
Niño Bien: 109
Notorious: 103
Parakultural: 110
Pride Café: 112
Querandí, El: 106
Remember: 100

Roxy, The: 102
Salón Pueyrredón: 102
Search: 112
Señor Tango: 106
Shamrock: 100
Shusheta, La: 110
Sitges: 112

Tangocool: 110
Temple Bar, The: 100
Tiempo de Gitanos: 110
Torquato Tasso: 106
Trastienda, La: 103
Van Koning: 101
Viejo Almacén, El: 107

# Shops Index

Abasto de Buenos Aires: 143
Acme: 148
Alberto Vannucci: 150
Almacén de Belleza: 150
Antique Book Shop: 148
Arte Antica Antigüedades: 146
Arte Étnico Argentino: 155
Arte Indígena y Criollo: 155
Artesanías Argentinas: 155
Artesanías Salteñas: 155
Ateneo, El: 148
Ateneo Grand Splendid, El: 148
Barbie Store: 150
Bokura: 151
Bolivia: 151
Boyero, El: 155
Buenos Aires Design: 144
Calma Chicha: 156
Cándido Silva: 146
Cardón: 151
Carpintería Pampa: 156
Casa López: 151
Casa Piscitelli: 157
Churrinche Antigüedades: 146
Dalla Fontana: 151
Díaz de Mario, Los: 156
Disquería Oid Mortales: 157
Distal Libros: 148
Feria Artesanal Plaza General Manuel
    Belgrano: 145
Feria de San Pedro Telmo: 145
Feria Parque Lezama: 145
Feria Plaza Intendente Alvear: 145
Flabella: 152

Free Blues: 158
Frenkel's Leather World: 152
Galería Cecil: 146
Galería de la Defensa: 147
Galería Solar de French: 147
Galerías Pacífico: 144
Guido Mocasines: 152
Hermanos Estebecorena: 152
Jorge Cánaves: 152
Librería de Ávila: 149
Librería L'Amateur: 149
Librería Paidós: 149
Librería Platero: 149
Librerías Turísticas: 150
Lo de Joaquín Alberdi: 158
López Taibo: 152
Martina, La: 153
Martiniano Arce: 155
Papelera Palermo: 156
Patio Bullrich: 144
Perugia: 153
Rapsodia: 153
Rigoletto Curioso: 156
Rossi y Caruso: 153
Tango Moda: 153
Terroir: 158
Tonel Privado: 159
Uma: 153
Urano: 157
Walrus Books: 150
Welcome Marroquinería: 154
Winery: 159
Zivals: 158

# Accommodations Index

Abasto Plaza Hotel: 175
Alfa Hotel: 180
Alpino Hotel: 184
Alvear Palace Hotel: 180
Américas Towers Hotel: 176
Argenta Tower Hotel & Suites: 176
Art Hotel: 181
Art Suites: 181
Atlas Tower Hotel: 167
Axel Hotel: 164
Ayacucho Palace Hotel: 181
B&B Bayres: 184
Baucis Boutique Hotel: 184
Bauen Suite Hotel: 175
Bisonte Palace Hotel: 176
Bobo Hotel: 184
Caesar Park Hotel: 176
Carlos Gardel Hostel: 172
Carlton Hotel: 176
Casa Alfaro: 184
Casa Jardín: 185
Castelar Hotel & Spa: 164
Che Lagarto Youth Hostel: 165
Che Lulu Guest House: 185
Claridge Hotel: 167
Columbia Palace Hotel: 167
Concept Hotel: 165
Dazzler Hotel: 177
Design Suites: 181
Etoile Hotel: 181
Faena Hotel & Universe: 171
Feir's Park Hotel: 177
Five Cool Rooms Buenos Aires: 185
Four Seasons Hotel Buenos Aires: 177
Goya Hotel: 167
Gran Hotel Argentino: 167
Gran Hotel Colón: 167
Gran Hotel Orly: 178
Guido Palace Hotel: 181
Hilton Buenos Aires: 171
Hostal de San Telmo, El: 172
Hostel Inn Tango City: 172
Hostel Nómade: 173
Hotel A&B Internacional: 167
Hotel Americano: 168
Hotel Bauen: 175
Hotel Bel Air: 182
Hotel Boquitas Pintadas: 165
Hotel Chile: 165
Hotel Conquistador: 178

Hotel Costa Rica: 185
Hotel de las Américas: 178
Hotel de Los Dos Congresos: 168
Hotel del Prado: 182
Hotel Esplendor: 168
Hotel Europa: 168
Hotel Facón Grande: 168
Hotel 562 Nogaró: 165
Hotel Gran Sarmiento: 175
Hotel Home Buenos Aires: 185
Hotel Hostería Posta Carretas: 168
Hotel Ibis: 166
Hotel Intercontinental: 166
Hotel Lafayette: 168
Hotel Lyon: 175
Hotel Maipú: 169
Hotel Mansión Dandi Royal: 172
Hotel NH Crillón: 178
Hotel NH Jousten: 169
Hotel O'Rei: 169
Hotel Orense: 169
Hotel Palermo: 186
Hotel Park Plaza Kempinski: 178
Hotel Plaza Francia: 182
Hotel Plaza Roma: 169
Hotel Presidente: 178
Hotel Príncipe: 182
Hotel Reconquista Plaza: 169
Hotel Sheraton Libertador: 169
Hotel Sportsman: 169
Hotel Varela: 173
Impala Hotel: 178
Juncal Palace Hotel: 182
Legado Mítico Buenos Aires: 186
Loi Suites Recoleta: 182
Lugar Gay de Buenos Aires: 173
Malabia House: 187
Marriott Plaza Hotel: 178
Meliá Recoleta Plaza: 182
Milhouse Youth Hostel: 166
Molino Hotel: 175
NH City Hotel: 166
NH Hotel Lancaster: 179
Normandie Hotel: 170
Nuevo Hotel Callao: 176
Ostinatto Hostel: 173
Palacio Duhau-Park Hyatt Buenos Aires: 183
Panamericano Buenos Aires Hotel & Resort: 170
Park Tower Hotel: 179

Portal del Sur Youth Hostel: 166
Prince Hotel: 183
Recoleta Youth Hostel: 179
Sarmiento Palace Hotel: 176
Savoy Hotel: 170
Sheraton Buenos Aires Hotel: 179
Sofitel Buenos Aires: 179
Southern House BA: 183

St. Nicholas Youth Hostel: 170
Tailor Made Hotel: 187
Tango Backpacker's Hostel: 187
Telmotango Hostel Suites: 174
Torre Cristóforo Colombo: 187
Vain Boutique Hotel: 187
V&S Hostel Club: 170
Wilton Hotel: 183

# Acknowledgments

Similar to my efforts in writing about Guatemala, Chile, Argentina, and Patagonia, this book owes its existence in its present form to numerous individuals in North America, Buenos Aires, Montevideo, and elsewhere. Once again, thanks to Bill Newlin and his Berkeley staff at Avalon Travel for their efforts into getting this into print.

After more than 25 years' experience in Argentina and Buenos Aires, more than half that as a guidebook writer, I owe enormous unpayable debts to friends, acquaintances, and officials throughout the country. My apologies to anyone I may have overlooked or perhaps deleted because of an errant keystroke.

In Buenos Aires and vicinity, thanks to Joaquín Allolio; Jorge Arias; Eduardo Biraben; Diego Curubeto; Harry Ingham; Nicolás Kugler; José Massolo; Juan Massolo; Manuel Massolo; Cecilia Nigro; Dan Perlman; Patricia Thaxter; Lucila Draghi of San Antonio de Areco; and Cristián Soler of Tigre.

In Montevideo, thanks to Manuel Pérez Bravo of Hotel Mediterráneo; Nicolás Bonino and Sarah Cowley of Establecimiento Juanicó; Ana Etcheverry of Castillo Viejo; Reinaldo de Lucca of De Lucca Wines; the entire family plus Fabiana Bracco at Pisano Wines; Carlos and Ana Pizzorno; Federico Lavagna of El Viajero Hostels; Ricardo Varela and Magdalena Américo of Viña Varela Zarranz; Andrés Linardi of Librería Linardi y Risso; and Mónica de Mello of Hostelling International. Special mention to Fernanda Nogués of the Asociación de Exportadores de Vino for helping arrange my visit to Uruguayan wineries.

Stateside, thanks to Verónica Mellado, Bertha Merikanskas, and Ursula Velarde of LAN Airlines in Miami.

And finally, thanks to my wife, María Laura Massolo; my daughter, Clio Bernhardson-Massolo; and my Alaskan Malamute, Malbec, who reminds me when I need to take a walk.

# South America?
# We're all over it.

**For 79 years, LAN has been perfecting a more encompassing Latin American flight experience.**

✈ Daily flights from over 40 North American cities* to more than 50 South American destinations

✈ Vast regional network between major South American cities

✈ Expanding domestic networks within Argentina, Chile and Peru

**The LAN Alliance.**
Your host to more destinations in South America.

For more information visit us at LAN.com,
call us at 1 866 I FLY LAN or contact your preferred travel agent.

lan.com

LANPASS AAdvantage

# www.moon.com

For helpful advice on planning a trip, visit www.moon.com for the **TRAVEL PLANNER** and get access to useful travel strategies and valuable information about great places to visit. When you travel with Moon, expect an experience that is uncommon and truly unique.

## MOON BUENOS AIRES

Avalon Travel
A member of the Perseus Books Group
1700 Fourth Street
Berkeley, CA 94710, USA
www.moon.com

Editor and Series Manager: Erin Raber
Copy Editor: Amy Scott
Graphics Coordinator: Nicole Schultz
Production Coordinator: Sean Bellows
Cover Designer: Nicole Schultz
Map Editor: Kevin Anglin
Cartographer: Kat Bennett
Indexer: Greg Jewett

ISBN-10: 1-56691-991-6
ISBN-13: 978-1-56691-991-3
ISSN: 1543-6500

Printing History
1st Edition – 2003
3rd Edition – October 2008
5 4 3 2 1

Some photos and illustrations are used by permission and are the property of the original copyright owners.

Front cover photo: © Wayne Bernhardson
Front color photos: © Wayne Bernhardson
Floralis Generica fountain, page 5, designed by Eduardo Catalano; Mural Escenografico, page 5, designed by Omar Gasparini

Printed in the United States by RR Donnelley

# KEEPING CURRENT

If you have a favorite gem you'd like to see included in the next edition, or see anything that needs updating, clarification, or correction, please drop us a line. Send your comments via email to feedback@moon.com, or use the address above.

# MAP SYMBOLS

| | | | |
|---|---|---|---|
| ▨▨▨ Expressway | ◖ Highlight | ✗ Airfield | ⚲ Golf Course |
| ━━━ Primary Road | ○ City/Town | ✈ Airport | ⊡ Parking Area |
| ▨▨ Secondary Road | ◉ State Capital | ▲ Mountain | ▲ Archaeological Site |
| - - - - Unpaved Road | ⊛ National Capital | ✛ Unique Natural Feature | ⛪ Church |
| - - - - - Trail | ★ Point of Interest | | ⛽ Gas Station |
| ·········· Ferry | ● Accommodation | ⚐ Waterfall | Glacier |
| ▬▬▬ Railroad | ▼ Restaurant/Bar | ⚑ Park | Mangrove |
| ▨▨▨ Pedestrian Walkway | ▪ Other Location | ⊟ Trailhead | Reef |
| ▥▥▥ Stairs | ⋏ Campground | ⛷ Skiing Area | Swamp |

# CONVERSION TABLES

°C = (°F - 32) / 1.8
°F = (°C x 1.8) + 32
1 inch = 2.54 centimeters (cm)
1 foot = 0.304 meters (m)
1 yard = 0.914 meters
1 mile = 1.6093 kilometers (km)
1 km = 0.6214 miles
1 fathom = 1.8288 m
1 chain = 20.1168 m
1 furlong = 201.168 m
1 acre = 0.4047 hectares
1 sq km = 100 hectares
1 sq mile = 2.59 square km
1 ounce = 28.35 grams
1 pound = 0.4536 kilograms
1 short ton = 0.90718 metric ton
1 short ton = 2,000 pounds
1 long ton = 1.016 metric tons
1 long ton = 2,240 pounds
1 metric ton = 1,000 kilograms
1 quart = 0.94635 liters
1 US gallon = 3.7854 liters
1 Imperial gallon = 4.5459 liters
1 nautical mile = 1.852 km

| MAP 1 | Monserrat | 386-387 |
| MAP 2 | Microcentro and Puerto Madero | 388-389 |
| MAP 3 | San Telmo and La Boca | 390 |
| MAP 4 | Balvanera | 391 |
| MAP 5 | Retiro | 392-393 |
| MAP 6 | Recoleta and Barrio Norte | 394-395 |
| MAP 7 | Palermo | 396-397 |
| MAP 8 | Outer Barrios | 398-399 |
| MAP 9 | Buenos Aires Subte | 400 |

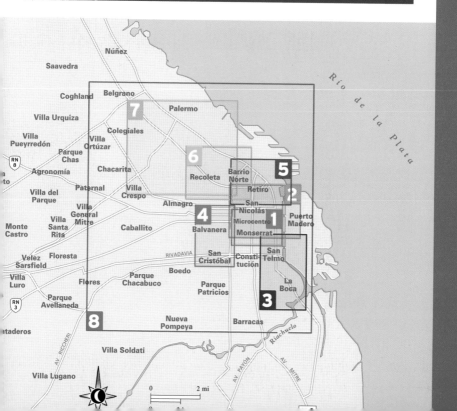

## ○ SIGHTS

1 CATEDRAL METROPOLITANA
2 **C** PLAZA DE MAYO
4 CASA ROSADA (CASA DE GOBIERNO NACIONAL)
6 PALACIO BAROLO
21 MANZANA DE LAS LUCES
25 MUSEO DE LA CIUDAD
37 IGLESIA Y CONVENTO DE SANTO DOMINGO

## ○ RESTAURANTS

15 STATUS
27 CENTRO VASCO FRANCÉS
33 LAURAK BAT
34 PROSCIUTTO
41 CAFÉ MOLIERE

## ○ NIGHTLIFE

12 **C** CAFÉ TORTONI
16 LA NACIONAL
19 CLUB ESPAÑOL
20 ALSINA BUENOS AIRES
29 EL QUERANDÍ
38 MICHELANGELO
39 LA TRASTIENDA
40 BAR SEDDON

## ○ SHOPS

5 TANGO MODA
24 LIBRERÍA DE ÁVILA
26 ARTE INDÍGENA Y CRIOLLO

## ○ ARTS AND LEISURE

3 MUSEO DEL CABILDO
8 TEATRO AVENIDA
13 MUSEO MUNDIAL DE TANGO
18 FEDERACIÓN ARGENTINA DE PATO
30 CENTRO LATINOAMERICANO DE CREACIÓN E INVESTIGACIÓN TEATRAL
31 **C** MUSEO ETNOGRÁFICO JUAN B. AMBROSETTI
32 MUSEO NACIONAL DEL GRABADO

## ○ ACCOMMODATIONS

7 HOTEL CHILE
9 CASTELAR HOTEL & SPA
10 MILHOUSE YOUTH HOSTEL
11 PORTAL DEL SUR YOUTH HOSTEL
14 HOTEL IBIS
17 CONCEPT HOTEL
22 HOTEL 562 NOGARÓ
23 NH CITY HOTEL
28 HOTEL INTERCONTINENTAL
35 CHE LAGARTO YOUTH HOSTEL
36 AXEL HOTEL
42 **C** HOTEL BOQUITAS PINTADAS

SEE MAP 4

MONSERRAT

0    200 yds
0    200 m

© AVALON TRAVEL

SEE MAP 1

MICROCENTRO

SARMIENTO

PERÓN

ROQUE SAENZ PEÑA

BARTOLOME MITRE

Plaza R
Arlt

SUIPACHA

ESMERALDA

MAIPU

FLORIDA

SAN MARTIN

RECONQUISTA

25 DE MAYO

AV LEANDRO N ALEM

AV ROSALES

1 ✪ Catedral
Metropolitana

Catedral ⚡

RIVADAVIA

2 ✪

Plaza de Mayo

Plaza de
Mayo

✪ 4
Casa
Rosada

Parque

Colón

L 13

N 12

Piedras

11 Ⓐ

L 3

Perú ⚡

Bolívar ⚡

HIPOLITO YRIGOYEN

⚡

⚡

Ⓐ 22

Ⓐ 23

Museo
de la
Ciudad

ADOLFO ALSINA

BALCARCE

Ⓢ 26

AV PASEO COLÓN

ESMERALDA

Ⓢ 24

25 ✪

✪ 21

Manzana de
las Luces

BOLIVAR

DEFENSA

L 30

MORENO

L 31

CHACABUCO

AV PTE J A ROCA

PERÚ

Ⓝ 29

28 Ⓐ

32
L

Plaza A P
Justo

TACUARI

Belgrano ⚡

AV BELGRANO

✪ 37

Iglesia y Convento
de Santo Domingo

38 Ⓝ

BALCARCE

Ⓝ 39

Ⓐ 35

36
Ⓐ

VENEZUELA

E DE JULIO

PIEDRAS

MÉXICO

PERÚ

BOLIVAR

DEFENSA

AV PASEO COLÓN

40
Ⓝ

R 41

CHILE

SAN
TELMO

SAN LORENZO

AV INDEPENDENCIA

Facultad de
Ingeniería

DR J M GIUFFRA

Plaza
Coronel
Olazábal

SEE MAP 3

MAP 2

MICROCENTRO AND PUERTO MADERO

388

## ⊕ SIGHTS

1 MUSEO DE LA INMIGRACIÓN
2 MUSEO JUDÍO DE BUENOS AIRES DR. SALVADOR KIBRICK
3 🅒 TEATRO COLÓN
11 GALERÍAS PACÍFICO
23 🅒 RESERVA ECOLÓGICA COSTANERA SUR
36 CORREO CENTRAL
64 MUSEO MITRE
66 LA CITY
67 MUSEO NUMISMÁTICO DR. JOSÉ E. URIBURU
68 ARCHIVO Y MUSEO HISTÓRICO DEL BANCO DE LA PROVINCIA DE BUENOS AIRES DR. ARTURO JAURETCHE

## 🍴 RESTAURANTS

7 BROCCOLINO
16 🅒 SABOT
19 LA POSADA DE 1820
27 LA ESTANCIA
30 ABC
31 CALIFORNIA BURRITO COMPANY
41 CADORE
42 EL GATO NEGRO
49 EL PALACIO DE LA PAPA FRITA
53 🅒 PIZZERÍA GÜERRÍN
54 CLUB DEL PROGRESO
69 🅒 CABAÑA LAS LILAS
72 ASIA DE CUBA
78 LA CANDELA

## 🌙 NIGHTLIFE

17 DOWNTOWN MATÍAS
22 LA CIGALE
29 CONFITERÍA RICHMOND
39 FORO GANDHI
57 🅒 CONFITERÍA IDEAL
61 @LTERNATIVA
75 EL ARRANQUE (NUEVA SALON LA ARGENTINA)
80 🅒 CLUB UNIONE E BENEVOLENZA

## 🎭 ARTS AND LEISURE

4 TEATRO COLÓN
14 CENTRO CULTURAL BORGES
24 RESERVA ECOLÓGICA COSTANERA SUR
34 INSTITUTO GOETHE
38 LUNA PARK
50 TEATRO GENERAL SAN MARTÍN
51 LIBERARTE
65 MUSEO DE LA POLICÍA FEDERAL
70 BUQUE MUSEO A.R.A. URUGUAY CORBETA
71 BUQUE MUSEO FRAGATA A.R.A. PRESIDENTE SARMIENTO
83 MUSEO Y ARCHIVO HISTÓRICO DE LA DIRECCIÓN GENERAL IMPOSITIVA

## 🛍 SHOPS

12 🅒 GALERÍAS PACÍFICO
15 DALLA FONTANA
33 CASA PISCITELLI
40 FREE BLUES
43 🅒 ZIVALS
48 RIGOLETTO CURIOSO
55 LIBRERÍA PLATERO
56 DISQUERÍA OID MORTALES
58 TONEL PRIVADO
59 FLABELLA
60 ACME
62 EL ATENEO
63 DISTAL LIBROS

## 🛏 ACCOMMODATIONS

5 GOYA HOTEL
6 V&S HOSTEL CLUB
8 HOTEL HOSTERÍA POSTA CARRETAS
9 HOTEL MAIPU
10 HOTEL SHERATON LIBERTADOR
13 HOTEL ESPLENDOR
18 CLARIDGE HOTEL
20 HOTEL RECONQUISTA PLAZA
21 HOTEL FACÓN GRANDE
25 PANAMERICANO BUENOS AIRES HOTEL & RESORT
26 GRAN HOTEL COLÓN
28 HOTEL O'REI
32 HOTEL LAFAYETTE
35 HOTEL NH JOUSTEN
37 HOTEL PLAZA ROMA
44 ATLAS TOWER HOTEL
45 NORMANDIE HOTEL
46 HOTEL AMERICANO
47 HOTEL A&B INTERNACIONAL
52 COLUMBIA PALACE HOTEL
73 🅒 HILTON BUENOS AIRES
74 SAVOY HOTEL
76 ST. NICHOLAS YOUTH HOSTEL
77 HOTEL DE LOS DOS CONGRESOS
79 HOTEL SPORTSMAN
81 HOTEL ORENSE
82 HOTEL EUROPA
85 🅒 FAENA HOTEL & UNIVERSE

© AVALON TRAVEL

RETIRO

Retiro
Plaza
Fuerza Aérea
Argentina

SEE MAP 5

1 Museo de la
Inmigración

Plaza
San Martín

San Martín

JUNCAL

PARAGUAY

AV CÓRDOBA

VIAMONTE

TUCUMÁN

LAVALLE

Florida

MICROCENTRO

Catedral

Perú

Bolívar

PUERTO
MADERO

Manzana
de las
Luces

Belgrano

SEE MAP 1

Darsena
Norte

Buquebus

Reserva Ecológica
Costanera Sur
23 24

BLVD CECILIA GRIERSON

MARIQUITA SÁNCHEZ DE THOMPSON

Galerías
Pacífico
11 12
13
14

15 16

17

21
22

18 19
20

32
30
31

33

34  Leandro
N. Alem

37

38
Luna
Park

Museo
Mitre
64

Museo
Numismático
Dr. José E.
Uriburu
65

35

Correo
36 Central

La City
63

62

67
66

68

Archivo y Museo
Histórico del Banco
de la Provincia

Plaza del
Correo

69

70

71

72

73

MACACHA GÜEMES

Dique
4

Rivadavia

Plaza de
Mayo

Plaza de Mayo

Hipólito Yrigoyen

Parque
Colón

Puente de
la Mujer

Edificio
Libertador

Customs

Plaza
A P
Justo

Dique
3

Dique
2

85

SEE MAP 3

28

29

9

10

61

## ✪ SIGHTS

| | |
|---|---|
| 5 | EL ZANJÓN DE GRANADOS |
| 18 | PLAZA CORONEL OLAZÁBAL |
| 25 | DANSK KIRKE |
| 31 | CLUB ATLÉTICO |
| 36 | PLAZA DORREGO |
| 45 | IGLESIA APOSTÓLICA ORTODOXA RUSA |
| 48 | PARQUE LEZAMA |
| 49 | MUSEO HISTÓRICO NACIONAL |
| 54 | MUSEO DE LA PASIÓN BOQUENSE |
| 57 | CAMINITO |
| 58 | MUSEO HISTÓRICO DE CERA |
| 59 | MUSEO DE BELLAS ARTES DE LA BOCA BENITO QUINQUELA MARTÍN |

## Ⓡ RESTAURANTS

| | | | |
|---|---|---|---|
| 6 | MEDIO Y MEDIO | 23 | TERRITORIO |
| 7 | MÍTICO SUR | 34 | PAPPA DEUS |
| 9 | CASAL DE CATALUNYA | 50 | 1880 |
| 13 | LA OVEJA NEGRA | 53 | EL OBRERO |
| 14 | DESNIVEL | 56 | BANCHERO |
| 21 | BAR EL FEDERAL | 62 | LA BARBERÍA |
| | | 63 | PATAGONIA SUR |

## Ⓝ NIGHTLIFE

| | | | |
|---|---|---|---|
| 8 | EL VIEJO ALMACÉN | 35 | MITOS ARGENTINOS |
| 16 | PRIDE CAFÉ | 40 | BAR PLAZA DORREGO |
| 17 | BAR SUR | 46 | TORQUATO TASSO |
| 20 | LA SHUSHETA | 51 | BLUES SPECIAL CLUB |
| 28 | ESPACIO ECLÉCTICO | | |

## Ⓛ ARTS AND LEISURE

| | | | |
|---|---|---|---|
| 1 | MUSEO DEL TRAJE | 41 | MUSEO PENITENCIARIO ARGENTINO ANTONIO BALLVÉ |
| 10 | TEATRO MARGARITA XIRGU | 52 | TEATRO CATALINAS SUR |
| 15 | LA SCALA DE SAN TELMO | 55 | BOCA JUNIORS |
| 29 | MUSEO DEL CINE PABLO A. DUCRÓS HICKEN | 60 | TEATRO DE LA RIBERA |
| 30 | MUSEO DE ARTE MODERNO | 61 | FUNDACIÓN PROA |

## Ⓢ SHOPS

| | | | |
|---|---|---|---|
| 11 | WALRUS BOOKS | 38 | CÁNDIDO SILVA |
| 12 | GALERÍA CECIL | 39 | GALERÍA SOLAR DE FRENCH |
| 27 | MARTINIANO ARCE | 43 | ARTE ANTICA ANTIGÜEDADES |
| 33 | CHURRINCHE ANTIGÜEDADES | 44 | GALERÍA DE LA DEFENSA |
| 37 | FERIA DE SAN PEDRO TELMO | 47 | FERIA PARQUE LEZAMA |

## Ⓐ ACCOMMODATIONS

| | | | |
|---|---|---|---|
| 2 | HOSTEL INN TANGO CITY | 24 | HOTEL VARELA |
| 3 | TELMOTANGO HOSTEL SUITES | 26 | EL HOSTAL DE SAN TELMO |
| 4 | OSTINATTO HOSTEL | 32 | HOSTEL NÓMADE |
| 19 | HOTEL MANSIÓN DANDI ROYAL | 42 | LUGAR GAY DE BUENOS AIRES |
| 22 | CARLOS GARDEL HOSTEL | | |

© AVALON TRAVE

SEE MAP 2

SEE MAP 1

**Facultad de Medicina**

Plaza Bernardo Houssay

**Facultad de Medicina**

Plaza Rodríguez Peña

**Callao (Línea D)**

**Palacio de las Aguas Corrientes**

**Mercado de Abasto**

**Carlos Gardel**

GARDEL

**Callao (Línea B)**

**Pueyrredón (Línea B)**

**Pasteur**

**BALVANERA**

Estación Once de Septiembre

**Once**

**Pasco**

**Congreso**

Plaza Miserere

**Plaza Miserere**

**Alberti**

**Palacio del Congreso Nacional**

Plaza 1° de Mayo

**Venezuela**

**San Cristóbal**

**SAN CRISTÓBAL**

**Entre Ríos**

**Pichincha**

**Jujuy**

200 yds

200 m

Plaza Martín Fierro

© AVALON TRAVEL

## ⬡ SIGHTS
- 2 MERCADO DE ABASTO
- 7 PALACIO DE LAS AGUAS CORRIENTES (OBRAS SANITARIAS)
- 21 PALACIO DEL CONGRESO NACIONAL

## ⓡ RESTAURANTS
- 17 LA CONTINENTAL
- 22 ICHISOU
- 25 MIRAMAR

## ⓝ NIGHTLIFE
- 1 CAFÉ BAR BANDERÍN
- 4 ESQUINA CARLOS GARDEL
- 8 ANGEL'S
- 9 REMEMBER
- 19 ITALIA UNITA
- 20 CAFÉ DE LOS ANGELITOS
- 23 CLUB GRICEL

## ⓛ ARTS AND LEISURE
- 6 MUSEO FORENSE DE LA MORGUE JUDICIAL DR. JUAN BAUTISTA BAFICO
- 10 CENTRO CULTURAL RECTOR RICARDO ROJAS
- 24 ASOCIACÓN ORNITOLÓGICA DEL PLATA

## ⓢ SHOPS
- 3 ABASTO DE BUENOS AIRES

## ⓐ ACCOMMODATIONS
- 5 ABASTO PLAZA HOTEL
- 11 SARMIENTO PALACE HOTEL
- 12 BAUEN SUITE HOTEL
- 13 HOTEL BAUEN
- 14 HOTEL GRAN SARMIENTO
- 15 NUEVO HOTEL CALLAO
- 16 HOTEL LYON
- 18 MOLINO HOTEL

SEE MAP 7

AV DEL LIBERTADOR

AV PRESIDENTE A. U. ILLA

AUTOPISTA PRESIDENTE A. U. ILLA

AVACUCHO

AV CALLAO

POSADAS

Patio
Bullrich
1 **S**

LIBERTAD

3 **L**

**S** 4

AV ALVEAR

RODRIGUEZ PEÑA

**A**
2

CERRITO

**R** 5

Museo Municipal de
Arte Hispanoamericano
Isaac Fernández Blanco

MONTEVIDEO

SEE MAP 6

**A**
7

8 ⚹

PRESIDENTE QUINTANA

PARERA

**A** 6

ARROYO

Plaza
Embajada
de Israel

9 **A**

10 **A**

GUIDO

VICENTE LÓPEZ

11 **L**

JUNCAL

Plaza

Vicente

López

PARANÁ

15 **S**

16 **A** **A** 17

**A**
12

**RETIRO**

21
Palacio
San Martín

ARENALES

18 **A** **N** 19

20 **L**

SARGENTO CABRAL

*San Martín*

TALCAHUANO

AV SANTA FE

22 **A**

26 **A**
LIBERTAD

AV 9 DE JULIO

AV 9 DE JULIO

31
**N**

32 **A**

SUIPACHA

URUGUAY

**N**
25

27 **A**

MARCELO T. DE ALVEAR

33 **A**

CARLOS PELLEGRINI

MONTEVIDEO

24
⚹ **Museo de la Shoá**

28 **A**

Plaza
Libertad

PARAGUAY

34 **S**

ESMERALDA

29 **L**

30 **A**

AV CÓRDOBA

Museo Judío de
Buenos Aires
Dr. Salvador Kibrick

Plaza
Lavalle

Teatro
Colón

0        200 yds

0        200 m

⚹ *Tribunales*

SEE MAP 1

*Lavalle*

© AVALON TRAVEL

Estación Terminal de Omnibus

Estación Retiro (Línea San Martín)

Estación Retiro (Línea Belgrano)

Estación Retiro (Línea Mitre)

Retiro

Plaza Canadá

Plaza del Carril

Plaza Fuerza Aérea Argentina

Plaza San Martín

Galerías Pacífico

MICROCENTRO

Plaza Roma

SEE MAP 2

AV DE LOS IMMIGRANTES

AV COMODORO PY

COMBATE DE LOS POZOS / COSTA BRAVA

CORBETA URUGUAY

AV INGENIERO JOSE N. QUARTINO

Antepuerto

AV ANTARIDA ARGENTINA

AV EDUARDO MADERO

AV RAMOS MEJIA

DR G M ZUVIRIA

GILARDO GILARDI

SAN MARTIN

FLORIDA

PARAGUAY

MAIPU

JUNCAL

BASAVILBASO

DR R ROJAS

MARCELO T DE ALVEAR

PAOLERA

RECONQUISTA

AV LEANDRO N ALEM

SARGENTOS

TRES

AV CORDOBA

AV CORDOBA

VIAMONTE

TUCUMAN

LAVALLE

## SIGHTS
8 MUSEO MUNICIPAL DE ARTE HISPANOAMERICANO ISAAC FERNÁNDEZ BLANCO
21 PALACIO SAN MARTÍN
23 PLAZA SAN MARTÍN
24 MUSEO DE LA SHOÁ

## RESTAURANTS
5 JUANA M.
37 CLUB DANÉS
45 FILO
47 TANCAT
52 EMPIRE BAR

## NIGHTLIFE
19 GRAN BAR DANZÓN
25 MILIÓN
31 THE TEMPLE BAR
38 DRUID IN
39 THE KILKENNY
49 JOHN JOHN
53 BÁRBARO

## ARTS AND LEISURE
3 GALERÍA ZURBARÁN
11 ASOCIACIÓN ARGENTINA DE CULTURA INGLESA
20 GALERÍA VERMEER
29 TEATRO NACIONAL CERVANTES
35 MUSEO DE ARMAS DE LA NACIÓN
42 GALERÍA FEDERICO KLEMM
43 GALERÍA RUTH BENZACAR
50 FLORIDA GARDEN

## SHOPS
1 PATIO BULLRICH
4 WINERY
15 ANTIQUE BOOK SHOP
34 LIBRERÍA L'AMATEUR
36 FRENKEL'S LEATHER WORLD
41 CASA LÓPEZ
44 WELCOME MARROQUINERÍA
46 LA MARTINA
48 EL BOYERO

## ACCOMMODATIONS
2 CAESAR PARK HOTEL
6 HOTEL PARK PLAZA KEMPINSKI
7 FOUR SEASONS HOTEL BUENOS AIRES
9 SOFITEL BUENOS AIRES
10 FEIR'S PARK HOTEL
12 ARGENTA TOWER HOTEL & SUITES
13 SHERATON BUENOS AIRES HOTEL
14 PARK TOWER HOTEL
16 RECOLETA YOUTH HOSTEL
17 IMPALA HOTEL
18 CARLTON HOTEL
22 HOTEL NH CRILLÓN
26 AMÉRICAS TOWERS HOTEL
27 HOTEL DE LAS AMÉRICAS
28 DAZZLER HOTEL
30 HOTEL PRESIDENTE
32 BISONTE PALACE HOTEL
33 HOTEL CONQUISTADOR
40 MARRIOTT PLAZA HOTEL
51 GRAN HOTEL ORLY
54 NH HOTEL LANCASTER

**○ SIGHTS**

| | | | |
|---|---|---|---|
| 2 | BIBLIOTECA NACIONAL | 33 | BUENOS AIRES GRAFF |
| 3 | MUSEO NACIONAL DE BELLAS ARTES | 35 | CASA MUSEO RICARDO ROJAS |
| 9 | CEMENTERIO DE LA RECOLETA | 52 | PALACIO PIZZURNO |
| 25 | FUNDACIÓN INTERNACIONAL JORGE LUIS BORGES | | |

**● RESTAURANTS**

| | | | |
|---|---|---|---|
| 18 | JOSÉ LUIS | 29 | LOS PINOS |
| 26 | OVIEDO | | |

**● NIGHTLIFE**

| | | | |
|---|---|---|---|
| 1 | LA DAMA DE BOLLINI | 39 | SEARCH |
| 10 | BULLER BREWING COMPANY | 43 | SHAMROCK |
| 12 | LA BIELA | 51 | NOTORIOUS |
| | | 53 | CLÁSICA Y MODERNA |

**● ARTS AND LEISURE**

| | | | |
|---|---|---|---|
| 6 | CENTRO CULTURAL CIUDAD DE BUENOS AIRES | 31 | UNIÓN DE RUGBY DE BUENOS AIRES |
| 7 | PALACIO NACIONAL DE LAS ARTES (PALAIS DE GLACE) | 34 | MUSEO XUL SOLAR |
| 21 | GALERÍA RUBBERS | 40 | MUSEO HOUSSAY DE CIENCIA Y TECNOLOGÍA |

**○ SHOPS**

| | | | |
|---|---|---|---|
| 4 | FERIA PLAZA INTENDENTE ALVEAR | 37 | LIBRERÍAS TURÍSTICAS |
| 5 | BUENOS AIRES DESIGN | 41 | ARTESANÍAS ARGENTINAS |
| 13 | LÓPEZ TAIBO | 42 | GUIDO MOCASINES |
| 14 | PERUGIA | 46 | ROSSI Y CARUSO |
| 19 | ALBERTO VANNUCCI | 49 | EL ATENEO GRAND SPLENDID |
| 23 | ARTESANÍAS SALTEÑAS | | |

**● ACCOMMODATIONS**

| | | | |
|---|---|---|---|
| 8 | HOTEL PLAZA FRANCIA | 28 | ART HOTEL |
| 11 | ETOILE HOTEL | 30 | ART SUITES |
| 15 | ALVEAR PALACE HOTEL | 32 | AYACUCHO PALACE HOTEL |
| 16 | MELIÁ RECOLETA PLAZA | 36 | SOUTHERN HOUSE BA |
| 17 | LOI SUITES RECOLETA | 38 | HOTEL DEL PRADO |
| 20 | PALACIO DUHAU-PARK HYATT BUENOS AIRES | 44 | PRINCE HOTEL |
| | | 45 | HOTEL BEL AIR |
| 22 | GUIDO PALACE HOTEL | 47 | WILTON HOTEL |
| 24 | HOTEL PRÍNCIPE | 48 | ALFA HOTEL |
| 27 | JUNCAL PALACE HOTEL | 50 | DESIGN SUITES |

SEE MAP 7

Plaza Alférez Sobral

Parque

Las   Heras

Hospital Rivadavia

AV GENERAL LAS HERAS

RECOLETA

AV SANTA FE

AV CÓRDOBA

Fundación Internacional Jorge Luis Borges
25

Deutsche Hospita

Agüero   24

26

Buenos Aires Graff   33

Casa Museo Ricardo Rojas   35

34

Pueyrredón

CHARCAS

36

Plaza Monseñor de Andrea

37

0        300 yds

0        300 m

© AVALON TRAVEL

Plaza
Naciones
Unidas

Plaza República
de Chile

Plaza
República
Oriental del
Uruguay

AV PRESIDENTE FIGUEROA ALCORTA

Plaza J J de
Urquiza

AV DEL LIBERTADOR

BRIG GENERAL JUAN FACUNDO QUIROGA

EDUARDO JUAN COUTURE

AUTOPISTA PRESIDENTE A U ILLIA

Museo Nacional
de Bellas Artes
★3

Plaza
Rubén
Darío

Plaza
Mitre

Biblioteca
Nacional
★2

ARJONILLA

AGÜERO    GUIDO    NEWTON

GALILEO

COPERNICO

Plaza
Francia

4 Ⓢ
Plaza
Intendente
Alvear

Ⓛ7

8

Parque
Carlos
Thays

5

6 Ⓛ

9 ★
Cementerio de
la Recoleta

16

13 Ⓢ   Ⓐ15

14

Ⓐ20

Plaza
Teniente
General E.
Mitre

Facultad de
Ingeniería

Ⓝ
Ⓝ 12
11
10

18 Ⓡ

Ⓐ17

19 Ⓢ

Ⓛ21

22

23 Ⓢ

SEE MAP 5

29Ⓡ
Ⓐ30

31
Ⓛ

32

JUNCAL

BARRIO NORTE

Ⓐ27

Ⓐ28

41 Ⓢ
Plaza
Vicente
López

42 Ⓢ

43 Ⓝ

44

ARENALES
Ⓐ45

46
Ⓢ

47

AV SANTA FE

48 Ⓐ   Ⓢ 49

50

Ⓝ39

51 Ⓛ
Facultad de
Medicina

Plaza
Rodríguez
Peña

52
★Palacio
Pizzurno

40 Ⓛ
Plaza
Bernardo
Houssay

53 Ⓝ

Facultad de
Medicina

Callao

AV CÓRDOBA

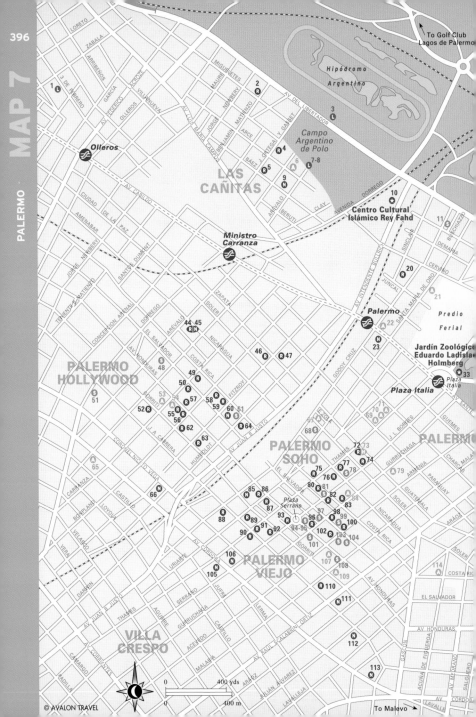

Olleros

LAS CAÑITAS

Ministro Carranza

Hipódromo Argentino

Campo Argentino de Polo

To Golf Club
Lagos de Palermo

Centro Cultural Islámico Rey Fahd

Palermo

Predio Ferial

Jardín Zoológico Eduardo Ladislao Holmberg

Plaza Italia

PALERMO HOLLYWOOD

PALERMO SOHO

PALERMO

Plaza Serrano

PALERMO VIEJO

VILLA CRESPO

To Malevo

© AVALON TRAVEL

0          400 yds
0          400 m

Aeroparque
Jorge Newbery

Parque Tres
de Febrero

Rosedal

Dársena F

Plaza
Seeber

Jardín
Japonés

Plaza
Alemania

Museo de Arte
Latinoamericano
de Buenos Aires
(MALBA)

Museo de Motivos
Argentinos José
Hernández

Fondo Nacional de Artes/
Instituto Nacional Sanmartiniano

Plaza
Grand Bourg

Plaza Naciones
Unidas

RECOLETA

Museo
Eva Perón

Plaza
Alférez
Sobral

Plaza
República
de Chile

Jardín Botánico
Carlos Thays

Scalabrini
Ortiz

Parque
Las Heras

Hospital
Rivadavia

## A ACCOMMODATIONS

| | | | |
|---|---|---|---|
| 6 | TAILOR MADE HOTEL | 69 | TANGO BACKPACKER'S HOSTEL |
| 21 | TORRE CRISTÓFORO COLOMBO | 70 | VAIN BOUTIQUE HOTEL |
| 22 | HOTEL PALERMO | 71 | CASA JARDÍN |
| 37 | ALPINO HOTEL | 73 | BOBO HOTEL |
| 53 | BAUCIS BOUTIQUE HOTEL | 79 | CASA ALFARO |
| 54 | HOTEL HOME BUENOS AIRES | 84 | LEGADO MÍTICO BUENOS AIRES |
| 65 | B&B BAYRES | 107 | FIVE COOL ROOMS BUENOS AIRES |
| 67 | CHE LULU GUEST HOUSE | 109 | MALABIA HOUSE |
| | | 114 | HOTEL COSTA RICA |

## O SIGHTS

| | | | | | |
|---|---|---|---|---|---|
| 10 | CENTRO CULTURAL ISLÁMICO REY FAHD | 33 | JARDÍN ZOOLÓGICO EDUARDO LADISLAO HOLMBERG | 40 | FONDO NACIONAL DE ARTES |
| 12 | ROSEDAL | 34 | MUSEO EVA PERÓN | 41 | INSTITUTO NACIONAL SANMARTINIANO |
| 14 | PARQUE TRES DE FEBRERO | 38 | MUSEO DE ARTE LATINOAMERICANO | 43 | JARDÍN BOTÁNICO CARLOS THAYS |
| 18 | JARDÍN JAPONÉS | 39 | MUSEO DE MOTIVOS ARGENTINOS JOSÉ HERNÁNDEZ | | |

## R RESTAURANTS

| | | | | | |
|---|---|---|---|---|---|
| 2 | MAMÁ EUROPA | 49 | AZEMA | 82 | CABERNET |
| 4 | LOTUS NEO THAI | 50 | MOSOQ | 83 | SA GIARA |
| 5 | EL PORTUGUÉS | 52 | OLSEN | 86 | BAR URIARTE |
| 19 | JARDÍN JAPONÉS | 55 | DIVINA PATAGONIA | 87 | SOCIAL PARAÍSO |
| 20 | ELISABETTA | 56 | PUNTA BRASAS | 88 | LA CUPERTINA |
| 24 | BELLA ITALIA CAFÉ BAR | 57 | ACABAR | 89 | ZADVARIE DOC |
| 25 | LUCKY LUCIANO | 58 | CEVICHE | 90 | MARIA FULÓ |
| 26 | LIBÉLULA | 59 | MIRANDA | 91 | LA CABRERA |
| 27 | BELLA ITALIA | 62 | JANGADA | 92 | TE MATARÉ RAMÍREZ |
| 28 | GUIDO'S BAR | 63 | DASHI | 93 | SPIRIT |
| 29 | VOULEZ BAR | 64 | MOTTA | 96 | LA ESQUINA DE LAS FLORES |
| 30 | DIMAGGIO'S | 72 | BOBO | 98 | XALAPA |
| 31 | GARBIS | 74 | LA CASA POLACA | 100 | MARK'S DELI AND COFFEE HOUSE |
| 35 | NEMO | 75 | LELÉ DE TROYA | 102 | BAR 6 |
| 44 | LOBBY | 76 | EL ÚLTIMO BESO | 110 | MUNDANO |
| 46 | SUDESTADA | 77 | EL VIEJO INDECENTE | 116 | KATMANDU |
| 47 | STANDARD | 80 | LA PAILA | | |

## N NIGHTLIFE

| | | | |
|---|---|---|---|
| 9 | VAN KONING | 105 | TANGOCOOL |
| 23 | SALÓN PUEYRREDÓN | 106 | MUNDO BIZARRO |
| 45 | LOBBY | 111 | PARAKULTURAL |
| 60 | TIEMPO DE GITANOS | 112 | BACH BAR |
| 66 | NICETO CLUB | 113 | SITGES |
| 85 | LEVITAR AMBIENT BAR | 115 | BULNES CLASS |

## O ARTS AND LEISURE

| | | | |
|---|---|---|---|
| 1 | MUSEO NACIONAL DEL HOMBRE | 13 | MUSEO DE ARTES PLÁSTICAS EDUARDO SÍVORI |
| 3 | HIPÓDROMO ARGENTINO | 15 | PLANETARIO GALILEO GALILEI |
| 7 | ASOCIACIÓN ARGENTINA DE POLO | 16 | NUEVO CIRCUITO KDT |
| 8 | CAMPEONATO ABIERTO ARGENTINO DE POLO | 17 | COSTA SALGUERO GOLF CENTER |
| | | 42 | MUSEO NACIONAL DE ARTE DECORATIVO |

## S SHOPS

| | | | |
|---|---|---|---|
| 11 | TERROIR | 81 | LO DE JOAQUÍN ALBERDI |
| 32 | BARBIE STORE | 94 | CALMA CHICHA |
| 36 | LIBRERÍA PAIDÓS | 95 | PAPELERA PALERMO |
| 48 | HERMANOS ESTABECORENA | 97 | BOKURA |
| 51 | CARPINTERÍA PAMPA | 99 | RAPSODIA |
| 61 | UMA | 101 | BOLIVIA |
| 68 | LOS DÍAZ DE MARIO | 103 | CARDÓN |
| 78 | ALMACÉN DE BELLEZA | 104 | ARTE ÉTNICO ARGENTINO |
| | | 108 | URANO |

SEE MAP 6

SEE MAP 5

Río de la Plata

Reserva
Ecológica
Costanera Sur

Puerto
Madero

Dársena
Norte

Dique 4

AV E MADERO

AV L N ALEM

ANTÁRTIDA ARGENTINA

Micro-
Centro

Retiro

San
Martín

L. N.
Alem

Florida

Lavalle

Tribunales

Uruguay

Carlos
Pellegrini

AV CORDOBA

Callao

San Nicolás

Callao

Callao

AUTOPISTA PRESIDENTE ARTURO UMBERTO ILLIA

Plaza Naciones
Unidas

AV DE LIBERTADOR

AV CALLAO

AV SANTA FE

Barrio
Norte

Retiro

Recoleta

Facultad de
Medicina

Pueyrredón

AV PUEYRREDÓN

AV CORRIENTES

AV SALGUERO

AV CORONEL DÍAZ

Aguero

GALLO

Once

AV CASARES

Parque 3 de
Febrero

AV LAS HERAS

Parque
Las Heras

Bulnes

Palermo

Jardín
Zoológico

Jardín
Botánico

Parque
C. Thays

Scalabrini
Ortiz

BULNES

MARIO BRAVO

R 18

AV SARMIENTO

Plaza
Italia

Palermo

Palermo
Viejo

AV HONDURAS

SALGUERO

MEDRANO

GASCON

Medrano

N 17

ESTADO DE ISRAEL

Aeroparque
Jorge Newbery

AV I LUGONES

AV INT BULLRICH

AV SCALABRINI ORTIZ

AV CORDOBA

Angel
Gallardo

AV CORRIENTES

Campo
Argentino
de Polo

AV JUAN B JUSTO

NICETO VEGA

Palermo
Hollywood

Ministro
Carranza

Villa
Crespo

Malabia

AV PRESIDENTE FIGUEROA ALCORTA

AV DEL LIBERTADOR

L M CAMPOS

OLLEROS

AV DORREGO

CORONEL

Golf Club
Lagos de
Palermo

2

3

Balneario
Parque Norte

INTENDENTE

CANTILO

AV COSTANERA R OBLIGADO

AV CABILDO

Barrancas
de
Belgrano

Belgrano

José
Hernández

AV F LACROZE

Colegiales

Frederico
Lacroze

Cementerio de
la Chacarita

Chacarita

AV WARNES

Museo Argentino de
Ciencias Naturales

AV ALVAREZ THOMAS

AV J NEWBERY

OLLEROS

AV DORREGO

FOREST

To Escuela de Mecánica
de la Armada (ESMA)

1

2

5

6

7

8

9

10

11

12

13

3

4

14

15

16

## SIGHTS

- 8  IGLESIA NUESTRA SEÑORA DE LA INMACULADA CONCEPCIÓN
- 9  MUSEO DE ARTE ESPAÑOL ENRIQUE LARRETA
- 10 MUSEO HISTÓRICO SARMIENTO
- 16 CEMENTERIO DE LA CHACARITA
- 19 MUSEO ARGENTINO DE CIENCIAS NATURALES BERNARDINO RIVADAVIA

## RESTAURANTS

- 5  CANTINA CHINATOWN
- 7  CONTIGO PERÚ
- 12 CAPISCI
- 15 MASAMADRE ES CON M
- 18 MALEVO

## NIGHTLIFE

- 14 THE ROXY
- 17 AMERIKA
- 23 ESQUINA HOMERO MANZI
- 24 NIÑO BIEN
- 26 EL CHINO
- 27 SEÑOR TANGO

## ARTS AND LEISURE

- 1  RIVER PLATE
- 2  GOLF CLUB LAGOS DE PALERMO
- 3  BUENOS AIRES LAWN TENNIS CLUB
- 4  MUSEO CASA DE YRURTIA
- 13 MUSEO LIBERO BADII
- 20 PARQUE CENTENARIO
- 21 MUSEO DE ESCULTURAS LUIS PERLOTTI
- 22 PARQUE RIVADAVIA
- 25 CENTRO CULTURAL DEL SUR

## SHOPS

- 6  JORGE CANAVES
- 11 FERIA ARTESANAL PLAZA GENERAL MANUEL BELGRANO

© AVALON TRAVEL